The Problem of Unbelief in the Sixteenth Century

The Problem of Unbelief in the Sixteenth Century ❧ The Religion of Rabelais BY LUCIEN FEBVRE

Translated by Beatrice Gottlieb

Harvard University Press
Cambridge, Massachusetts, and London, England
1982

This translation of *Le Problème de l'incroyance au XVIe*
siècle: la religion de Rabelais is published by arrangement with
Editions Albin Michel. (© Editions Albin Michel, 1942, 1968.)

The translation was made possible by a grant from the Translations
Program of the National Endowment for the Humanities, an independent
federal agency. Publication was aided by a grant from the Commission
d'Aide aux Traductions of the French government.

Library of Congress Cataloging in Publication Data

Febvre, Lucien Paul Victor, 1878–1956.
    The problem of unbelief in the sixteenth century:
the religion of Rabelais.

    Translation of: Le problème de l'incroyance au
XVIe siècle: la religion de Rabelais.
    Bibliography: p.
    Includes index.
    1. Rabelais, François, 1490 (ca.)–1553?—Religion
and ethics.   I. Title.
PQ1697.R4E3 1982   843'.3   82-1009
ISBN 0-674-70825-3   AACR2

To Fernand Braudel
with high hopes

Contents

Translator's Introduction

The Genesis of the Book

This book, the French title of which is *Le Problème de l'incroyance au XVIe siècle: la religion de Rabelais*, starts as an answer to a specific question and ends as something else. Lucien Febvre tells the story of the book's genesis in his General Introduction. In 1922 Abel Lefranc, one of the most prestigious literary scholars in France and the commanding general of an army of Rabelais experts, wrote that the secret message in his idol's rich, yeasty, ebullient outpouring of marvelous language was a thoroughgoing attack on Christianity. To a casual reader, in French or any other language, this sounds like a heavy burden to put on Rabelais; dedication to a serious mission of this kind seems inherently anticomic. There were other reasons why Febvre, who knew more about Rabelais and his period than a casual reader, was shocked by what Lefranc wrote. He knew perfectly well that there was a serious side to Rabelais—that, for instance, much of the learning of the period was reflected in his books—but Febvre had lived comfortably with the familiar notion that Rabelais was a man of his time, a genius who shared the life of his contemporaries even while towering above them. Of course Rabelais had made harsh comments on the religious life of his day, but did that constitute anything like the anti-Christian free thought of a much later time? Was Rabelais "ahead of his time"? Was he an atheist?

Febvre was pretty sure the answer was no. He could have responded to Lefranc in two different ways. He could have done what some other scholars did at the time, shown how Lefranc had misunderstood and misread the words of Rabelais and his contemporaries. Or he could have shown that Lefranc's approach was fundamentally wrong, that in dealing with the past he had not proceeded like a historian.

Febvre decided to do both. In Book One he takes up the specific points made by Lefranc. Part I deals with comments by contemporaries of Rabelais, Part II with what Rabelais himself wrote. In Book Two Febvre moves on to broader historical issues. Part III is a survey of some religious currents in the sixteenth century, showing Rabelais's relation to them. Part IV, the climax of the work, seems to have left Rabelais behind. It is a picture of the mental underpinnings of "a century that wanted to believe," and Febvre himself says it is possible to think of everything else as a scaffolding that could have been dismantled. Yet the last sentence of the whole work is about Rabelais, a Rabelais placed in the context of a broad sweep of time extending a century beyond himself.

The book has the tone of a debate. This gives it its pervasive tension and excitement. Febvre uses the imagery of the courtroom: Rabelais is on trial, witnesses are heard, and evidence is examined. For Americans of our time a better image might be a Congressional hearing. Experts and partisans of all kinds are called in. The examiner reacts to them and expresses opinions, not only on their testimony but also on the procedure being followed at the hearing. In a way, then, this is an informal book. It is not its subject matter alone that makes it, as Febvre says, the very antithesis of a textbook.

Yet for all its immediacy of tone, the book had an unusually long period of gestation. Lefranc published his introduction to *Pantagruel* in 1922, Febvre his response twenty years later. He says he worked on it for ten years. It reflects the whole range of things Febvre was thinking about during that period, and as a result transcends both the nominal subject and the immediate issue. It is one of the great books about sixteenth-century thought.

It is perhaps not very remarkable that a brilliant historian who had been thinking about Rabelais for twenty years should succeed in writing a great book about sixteenth-century thought. What is truly remarkable is the book's significance for historical scholarship in general. As the debate with Lefranc

unfolds we watch a certain kind of historian at work, we observe his method, we share his thoughts on the practice of history. The way he weaves a picture of the sixteenth century is a
model of how to do the same sort of thing for other times and
places. Specific and complex as the book is, it nevertheless
serves to express a general historical outlook. This makes it one
of the great history books of the twentieth century.

Distinctive as it is, this work is part of a series—a fact that
has as much to do with its genesis as the controversy with Lefranc. "L'Evolution de l'Humanité" was the brainchild of Henri
Berr, a man who was fifteen years older than Febvre and influenced him deeply. Berr had been trained as a philosopher.
He was passionately devoted to the idea of encompassing all
knowledge in a rational plan—reminiscent of the goal of some
Frenchmen of an earlier time, the eighteenth-century encyclo-
pedists. He had proclaimed his intention at the outset of his
career in his doctoral thesis: *The Future of Philosophy, an Outline of a Synthesis of Knowledge Based on History.* In 1900 he
founded the journal *Revue de Synthèse Historique,* later called
simply *Revue de Synthèse.* Febvre was a frequent contributor.
As part of the effort to construct a historical synthesis, Berr
published a series of studies of French regional history, among
them Febvre's *Franche-Comté* (1905). Berr believed in the use
by historians of various disciplines, in the comparative study of
times and places, and in the application of scientific methodology.

After World War I he started to work on a series of a hundred books that would embody the most advanced knowledge
to date of every aspect of world history, each book to be written
by a specialist and presented in a more or less uniform format.
He first listed all the books, with working titles and, whenever
possible, appropriate authors, and divided them chronologically
into four sections of approximately equal length. He made the
list in 1920, and even now all the slots have not yet been filled.
Lucien Febvre's name was prominent; he was down for six
books, two to be done in collaboration with others. One of the
first books to appear (in 1922) was *La Terre et l'évolution humaine,* an interdisciplinary collaboration by Febvre and Lionel
Bataillon, whose title clearly expresses its relationship to the series. It is among the few works by Febvre available in English

(as *A Geographical Introduction to History*). Berr expected
Febvre's main contribution to be in the third section of the series, the one on "the modern world" (modern, as the French
use the word, means up to the end of the eighteenth century),
where Febvre was scheduled for a book on Renaissance intellectual history, one on religion in the sixteenth century, one on
"kingdoms and empires" in the sixteenth century, and one, in
collaboration with "X," on economic history, tentatively entitled *Money and the Middle Class*. They were to be numbered
51 to 54.

The book on Rabelais's religion acquired the number 53 and
was the only one of this projected group to see the light of day.
That Berr's high hopes for Febvre's contributions were not ful-
filled may not mean very much. Berr's whole scheme was an act
of imaginative daring that could work out in practice only by
fits and starts. It is impressive to realize how nearly he succeeded. Febvre says in his introduction to no. 53 that there
seems to be something perverse about a book on *unbelief* doing
the job of telling the story of sixteenth-century religion. But
Berr was obviously perceptive enough to see what a valuable
contribution such a special and idiosyncratic work could be. In
a foreword to Febvre's book Berr wrote that so long as certain
conditions were met what mattered most to him was that each
contributor be free to reveal his own personality and style: "If I
could have had Michelet, I would have welcomed him with
joy." Berr realized that this book was, as Febvre put it, "in its
ambitious humility an essay on the meaning and spirit of the
sixteenth century." What Berr got was one book that in a way
combined two of his projected topics, Renaissance intellectual
history and religion in the sixteenth century. The slots for nos.
51 and 54, by the way, are still blank.

The other books in Berr's series may conform more docilely
to the prescribed format, but the Rabelais is in very good company. An American is tempted to say that only in the land of
d'Alembert and Diderot could a personal encyclopedic vision
have been so fruitful and inspired work of such high caliber.
Febvre's posthumous *L'Apparition du livre* (*The Coming of
the Book*) appeared in the series (no. 49), as did the two volumes of Marc Bloch's *Feudal Society* (no. 34). There were contributions by the medievalists Louis Halphen (*Charlemagne*

and the Carolingian Empire, no. 33) and Paul Alphandéry (*Le Chrétienté et l'idée de croisade*, no. 38). The slot for no. 52, originally assigned to Febvre, was filled by Robert Mandrou's *Introduction à la France moderne (1500–1640)*. Febvre in the present work makes reference to no. 31, Ferdinand Lot's *End of the Ancient World and the Beginnings of the Middle Ages*. Abel Rey's five-volume *Science dans l'antiquité*, which Febvre refers to a number of times, was part of a separate history-of-science division appended to "L'Evolution de l'Humanité."

The Author

Lucien Febvre was sixty-four years old when *Le Problème de l'incroyance* was published. He could look back on an extremely active scholarly career and a long engagement with the intellectual life of his times. Born in 1878, in the first decade of the Third Republic, he lived until 1956, not long before the Fourth Republic gave way to De Gaulle's Fifth Republic. From the perspective of historians outside France his most important achievement was the founding of the *Annales* together with Marc Bloch. The two men, both of whom followed classic academic careers, had first met in 1919 when they found themselves participating in the excitement of reconstituting the University of Strasbourg as a French university. Theirs was a wonderfully warm and fruitful collaboration. Bloch, a medievalist who blazed trails in the social history of the Middle Ages, is better known in the English-speaking world than Febvre. Febvre and he shared a vision of what history should be, and the journal they founded in 1929 was meant to promote that kind of history.

The war years were an important turning point. The two men were separated, Bloch joining the Resistance, Febvre spending most of his time in his country house in the Franche-Comté and occasionally visiting Paris in his capacity as member of the Collège de France. In that difficult time Bloch wrote two books that have moved many readers, *The Historian's Craft* and *Strange Defeat*, the first his reflections on being a historian, the second his reflections on being a Frenchman at a particular moment in history. Febvre meanwhile kept the *Annales* going, if in a considerably modified form, under the German occupation. Bloch never returned. He was captured by the Germans and shot to death in 1944. It would seem that Febvre's idea of the best way to resist fascism was to carry on the activities appropriate to an aging intellectual in a determined and, if necessary, ingenious fashion, thereby affirming the values of the cultural tradition he represented. He did not think military service was an appropriate use of the somewhat younger Bloch's talents, and he regarded Bloch's death as a terrible waste. The circumstances of the time—the interruption of his normal teaching, his isolation from colleagues, his near-exile in the country —provided Febvre with a curious opportunity to channel his energies into the writing of no less than three books. All were on "the religious heart of the sixteenth century" (*Au coeur religieux du XVIe siècle* was the title of a later collection of short pieces on the same subject). In addition to *Le Problème de l'incroyance* (1942), there were a book on Bonaventure Des Périers (*Origène et Des Périers ou l'énigme du Cymbalum Mundi*, 1942) and one on Margaret of Navarre (*Autour de l'Heptaméron, amour sacré, amour profane*, 1944). Febvre made little direct comment on the period of the occupation. At the end of the war he briefly reflected on those times in the introduction to a little book of selections written by Michelet a century earlier—one French historian talking about another French historian who had responded to events around him. In the work on Rabelais there is one oblique, if eloquent, sign of the times: a phrase in the General Introduction that calls the writing of the book "an act of faith in the future of intellectual freedom."

Apart from these three books on sixteenth-century religion, an earlier book on Luther, the books on printing and geography for "L'Evolution de l'Humanité," and three much earlier books on the Franche-Comté, Febvre's large output consisted almost entirely of articles, many of them general observations on historical questions, often in the form of book reviews. The flavor of his observations can be sampled in the present work, in footnotes like the one on p. 197 on possible future avenues of research. In a typical article, written midway in the gestation of this book, Febvre reviewed a new biography of Rabelais (Plattard's *La Vie de François Rabelais*), using the occasion to write an essay on the Rabelais legend as a problem in collective psychology. Much of it was later incorporated in the book, and can be seen on pp. 93–100. He loved to think about the potentials of historical scholarship, and when he was not writing and talking about them he was organizing institutional structures to help realize them: the *Annales,* the *Encyclopédie française,* the Sixth Section (social sciences) of the Ecole Pratique des Hautes Etudes. The legacy he and Bloch left has come to be called the *Annales* school of historians. However this school may be defined, it was certainly inspired by their ideas, especially those found in Febvre's wide-ranging observations.

Febvre was a quintessential product of French culture. That is why the book before you remains thoroughly French, even though the words are English and notes are supplied to fill in some of the gaps in an English-speaking reader's knowledge of things French. There is nothing mysterious about this Frenchness. Febvre had passed through an educational system that concentrated on certain subjects and disciplines. It was in the first place heavily literary, fostering an intimate knowledge of the French classics to the point of requiring the memorization of famous passages. When Febvre casually refers to parts of Rabelais without bothering to identify them or alludes to a character in Molière in order to elucidate a point, he is speaking like any educated Frenchman. In the second place, a course in philosophy was required in secondary school for everyone taking the preparatory program for university work. When Febvre says that he and his readers have attended classes in philosophy and thus know the meaning of certain concepts, he is obviously not addressing garden-variety American college graduates. The French have an awareness of Descartes in particular that may not go very deep but crops up on many occasions (as any reader of French newspapers can testify); hence Febvre's frequent references to Cartesianism as the most significant turning point in the development of modern thought. The emphasis on French literary classics and on Descartes has helped locate the time frame in which the French experience their culture. The seventeenth century, their Age of Gold, has an immediacy for them that it cannot have for us, whose living culture (with the exception of Shakespeare) barely extends back to the eighteenth century. The names Febvre drops so often (Molière, Pascal, Bossuet, Fénelon, Bayle) are the common coin of educated

French discourse, along with some representatives of the eighteenth-century Enlightenment (Voltaire, Rousseau) and nine-
teenth-century Romanticism (Lamartine, Hugo).

Of course, Febvre was no ordinary educated Frenchman. He
was a man of great learning. He had an especially deep and passionate intimacy with French literature, partly derived from his
father, a lycée teacher and, like himself, a graduate of the Ecole
Normale Supérieure. He read several languages with ease and
was conversant with German and Italian culture. Still, the non-
French reader of this book is sure to notice its ethnocentrism.
Although the book is about a French writer and about religion
in sixteenth-century France—which would seem to excuse a
purely French context—it also to some extent claims to be
about Europe as a whole, and, as befits an author who believed
in comparative history, is full of references to Luther, Erasmus,
Pomponazzi, Agrippa, and Pico della Mirandola. Even so, we
cannot help being struck by the French way in which this is
done. The brilliant discussion of language in the chapter on
philosophy ("Mental Tools") gives only French examples, although most of the same points could be made about other European languages. What this means is that we have to make an
adjustment as we read and keep in mind who and what the author was—an exercise in cultural relativism that probably
would have pleased him.

A strong personality comes through these pages. Febvre
knows what he thinks and does not hesitate to say it firmly and
in his own voice. The structure of the book is perfect for a man
who clearly revels in discourse and debate. The exigencies of
the quarrel with Lefranc give particular force to what Febvre
says about history in general, and his triumphant disposal of
point after point is a marvelously lively way of presenting a
mass of erudition. When the urge to pontificate came over Lucien Febvre it was always in the throes of combat, not in moments of detachment. Not for nothing is a collection of his theoretical writing, chiefly book reviews and occasional pieces,
entitled *Combats pour l'histoire*. It is not hard to find echoes of
these combats throughout the book on Rabelais, even in the
bibliography, where Febvre felt impelled to include his reviews
of some of the books listed. Here was a man of supreme self-
assurance, it would seem, accustomed to having attention paid

to him. He speaks like the adored only son and nephew he was —a person who knew he would always be at the center of whatever world mattered most to him.

What could have been insufferable arrogance was, however, tempered by his genuine love of discussion, by his voracious appetite for learning, by his infinite curiosity about everything, and by his accessibility to students. With his self-confidence he had little to fear from free-wheeling discussion. We get the impression that he cared less about scoring points for himself than "pour l'histoire." His book reviews show that nothing human was alien to him, as do many of the peripheral observations in this book—for example, the remarks on architecture on p. 399. He believed in collegiality and collective scholarship, and generously acknowledged what he learned from others, including Abel Lefranc.

Perhaps he regretted that he could not himself undertake all the studies and investigations he thought were such good ideas. He almost always sounds as though he were capable of doing them, but he could not possibly have done everything he was interested in. It was only in the war years, deprived of fellowship and his usual forums, that he sat down to write some of the books he dreamed of.

His writing style is conversational. A living voice can be heard, even through the more restrained medium of English. The man was a famous talker, who held court at an almost continuous gabfest. His style is not, however, totally idiosyncratic. As might be suspected, he was following a French tradition. The style of history writing in France is unlike most such writing in English and totally unlike history writing in German. A French historian is as much a literary artist as anything else and—following the example of Jules Michelet, the "Father of History"—an artist in the Romantic style. Although Febvre was very much a man of the twentieth century, like Michelet he was given to effusions, to crying out, to whispering, to building up suspense and springing surprises. He was not inclined by temperament to write in an impersonal manner, and his tradition encouraged him to clothe his persona in bright colors. Berr called him "a second Michelet." Febvre felt he was. He knew perfectly well he was not doing the same kind of history, but he too was a Frenchman responding to France's glories and defeats and sometimes speaking in France's voice—he came closest to this when comparing the Michelet of 1846 with Frenchmen (himself?) in 1946. In a Michelet-like effusion he called Rabelais's Friar John "the true, the exemplary Frenchman." This Romantic style has undoubted charms and graces, but it always hovers on the brink of excess. It is for each reader to decide whether Febvre ever falls over. I feel that by some miracle he always just avoids it. His success along these lines may be one of the less happy legacies he left the *Annales* school, however. The writers of that school tend to use the same devices: constantly asking questions, making casual allusions to things far afield and in other languages, trailing off suggestively into ellipses ... The epigones run the danger not so much of Romantic excess as of empty mannerisms.

In Febvre lushness is tempered by wit. He seems to have been endowed with some of the qualities of his ancient namesake, the Lucian of Samosata whom he mentions so often in this book. For all its erudition and serious purpose there is a lot of fun in it. There is, for example, the Molière-like comedy in which the main characters are the pretentious, cantankerous Julius Caesar Scaliger and a scholar named de Santi who has trouble with spelling. There is the spectacle of everyone calling everyone else an atheist. The wit sometimes comes in rapier thrusts, sometimes in response to what is ludicrous (for instance, an intendant ordering church bells to be flogged). Febvre delights in all this at the same time that he delights in winning his arguments.

The dogged adversary is not always lighthearted. Sometimes he sounds like a tough, hard-hitting district attorney, especially when he is considering not some error of fact or a simple contradiction but a matter of principle. It is no joke to commit what he regards as crimes against history, against logic—against humanity, when you come right down to it. Febvre is capable of a certain amount of dry, high-minded scorn, and even the tone of a solemn schoolboy debater.

The Historian and His Craft

Le Problème de l'incroyance is, and was meant to be, a demonstration of the kind of history Febvre spent his life promoting.

He tells us in the General Introduction that he did not discard the scaffolding because he wished to show quite openly "the workings of a mind," even though the historical conclusions are concentrated in the last part of the book. It is not easy to define Febvre's kind of history. One way of categorizing *Annales* history in general is to say it is all-inclusive—which is true but not very informative. Some notion of what that inclusiveness entails can be found in an article in English, written by Febvre and Henri Berr in 1932, under "History" in the *Encyclopedia of the Social Sciences* (New York, 1930–1934). It states the principles that Febvre and Berr agreed on, and is illuminating on the important but sticky point that history should be practiced as a science. The journal Bloch and Febvre founded has a somewhat ironic name, *Annales*, ironic because annals are histories of the most primitive and uncritical sort. The name is, however, not inappropriate, since the founders were committed to universal history, which they often called "global" or "total." Possibly the only way to grasp what they were after is to examine the issues of the *Annales* over the years and see the lines of inquiry that have been pursued and the subjects of its special issues, efforts at "synthesis" based on a comparative approach, inspired by Berr and yet different. The difference is in the focus suggested by the journal's present subtitle, *Economies, Sociétés, Civilisations.* The original title was more focused yet: *Annales d'Histoire Economique et Sociale.* The need to study economic questions and the social questions related to them was something the two men felt strongly about, and they regarded this not at all as a narrowing of history's scope but, on the contrary, as a way of broadening it.

Most historians nowadays have some notion of *Annales* history's wide ambitions, but it will do no harm to remind nonhistorians that there are many things that history, in the *Annales* view, is not. It is not great events, the phenomena most people (and newspapers) reserve the adjective "historical" for. The subject matter of history is not any special area of experience. History is not limited to national politics, international relations, and war. History is not some abstract, inexorable process. And it is not the job of historians to glorify or promote individuals or causes or nations.

A favorite metaphor of *Annales* theorists is that history is a sea: a moving, wide expanse that goes much deeper than what can be seen on the surface. There is a nice appropriateness in the fact that Fernand Braudel, the man to whom Febvre dedicated the present book and who became his successor as chief editor of the *Annales*, took a sea as his subject in his magisterial work, *The Mediterranean and the Mediterranean World in the Age of Philip II*. But Braudel's picture of the sixteenth century is not the one we get from Febvre. It is strong in the first element in the *Annales* subtitle, *économie*, and weak in the last, *civilisation* ("culture" in all its senses). Rabelais, for example, is hardly mentioned, except as the person who introduced romaine lettuce into France! And that perhaps tells the tale. Infinite are the questions that can be asked of the past, which encompasses all of human experience.

To get at human experience in the past—and, better yet, to get underneath its surface manifestations—both Braudel and Febvre welcomed the help of other disciplines. This openness to other disciplines, and particularly the conscious use of social science theory and method, is a mark of *Annales* history. It has strongly emphasized economics and econometrics, indeed "quantitative" history of all kinds, such as historical demography. Of this there is very little in the Febvre we have before us. He encouraged and approved of economic studies and inventive applications of quantitative methods, but his own predilections were for those studies—*sciences humaines* he called them, "human sciences"—that had influenced him from his earliest beginnings as a historian: geography, sociology, social psychology, and linguistics. He always made free use of these. There is not much geography in the book on Rabelais, but it is impossible to imagine what the culminating section would be like without Febvre's heavy reliance on the concepts and discoveries of anthropologists, archaeologists, and sociologists.

Related to this is another characteristic of *Annales* history that can be glimpsed in Febvre's book: the study of ordinary life, what has been called "history from the bottom" or the "history of the inarticulate." Febvre was painfully aware of standing on the threshold of this subject, and he devoted a brief but memorable part of his book to it. The section (in chapter 9) can be read not only as a picture of how religion fit into ordinary life in the sixteenth century but also as a series of suggestions about the kinds of sources to use. "There is a great gap in our knowledge of the men and things of that time," he writes, offering to "provide a quick sketch" and "suggest some topics for research." It is the only place in the book where he quotes directly from French departmental archives, which have since proved to be such a treasure house for social historians.

But what this book exemplifies most of all is the characteristic concern of the *Annales* school with *mentalité*. This word is often left untranslated—an odd tribute to what is seen as its origins. In some degree this concern touches the work of every *Annales* historian, even someone like Braudel, who is primarily an economic historian. It was Febvre's favorite subject. The aim of *Le Problème de l'incroyance* is to get at the mental life of the age in which Rabelais lived. Febvre says this over and over. Proceeding from the assumption that how people think and feel changes over time, the historian must try to understand the thoughts and feelings of the past. In every age people come in a variety of emotional and intellectual shapes, as Febvre demonstrates by talking about men as diverse as Postel, Luther, and Erasmus, but the possibilities for diversity are not endless. As Febvre puts it, some thoughts and feelings were not possible in the sixteenth century. The content of men's minds was affected by the material conditions under which they lived, the ideas they inherited, and the ways in which they organized their thoughts. Berr, in his foreword, praised Febvre for having produced a model of psychological analysis. He was of course referring not to the psychoanalysis of individuals but rather to a way of dealing with the psychological aspects of life in the past—actually, the entire subject matter of social psychology (including what is called the sociology of knowledge): ideas, information, beliefs, attitudes, and values shared by social groups.

Febvre's study of *mentalité* in this book has been much praised, but his achievement has been more monument than model. It stands practically alone. It is quite accurate to call this a work of intellectual history. The carefully organized bibliography, for one thing, is a guide to much of the high culture of the sixteenth century. What Febvre accomplished was a sort of tour de force. Most subsequent discussions of *mentalité* have dealt with lower intellectual levels, using court records, letters and diaries of nonintellectuals, reflections of life in drama and fiction. This is what one finds in Mandrou's *Introduction à la France moderne,* and it is fascinating. But, after Febvre, historians with an interest in *mentalité* have not done studies of great writers and thinkers. It is really too bad. To place an author firmly in his historical context without trivializing his work is a wonderful contribution to understanding. There are probably too few people with the intellectual equipment to accomplish what Febvre did.

As Febvre juggles Gargantua, Brother Francis, Professor Lefranc, scholasticism, olfactory sensation, and all the rest with his characteristic gusto, he keeps telling us that the unforgivable sin is anachronism. His preaching on this theme tells us what he thinks being a historian means. Abel Lefranc's colossal misreading of Rabelais resulted from his willingness to obliterate the differences between Rabelais's time and his own. Febvre's whole effort is to achieve the opposite by honoring the differences and spelling them out. Behaving like a historian may be less a matter of knowing a lot than having a certain attitude. What Febvre is saying is, "Watch out. Be a skeptic. Be cautious. If it looks simple and familiar it is probably not." Anachronism—making mistakes about where things belong—comes from not respecting the past, seeing false analogies with the present, and jumping to conclusions. "We never have absolute convictions when it comes to historical facts," adds Febvre. In other words, the historian should maintain a critical, scientific attitude toward his subject matter, the past.

For Febvre this is not flabby piety. He demands that we deal fairly with the past—approaching it with questions and hypotheses but without the urge to distribute praise and blame. He always sounds so irritated with the judgments he finds in other writers! The real antidote to anachronism is to recognize the complexity of the past. Febvre says the goal of history is not knowledge but understanding, and he as much as says the search is endless. To immerse oneself in the context of an age requires something that can be called historical imagination, but it is not mere intuition. It follows from the accumulation of facts. This sounds straightforward, even easy. The beauty of this book is that it gives us an idea of what is really involved. And while it may not be easy or straightforward, it is not mysterious. Febvre keeps asking how a statement would have been perceived by sixteenth-century eyes and ears. Does he know? Not really, but he works hard to find out, consciously resisting the temptation to commit anachronism, to substitute his own twentieth-century eyes and ears. He relies on all the lore he picked up over the years, making good use of the early research he did on the Franche-Comté (the odd little books about comets, mentioned on pp. 407 and 408, all have to do with the area in which his own house was situated). The accumulation of concrete details is consonant with Berr's notion that universal history is grounded in local history. Febvre cautions against substituting abstractions for those concrete details. He reads a widely used medical textbook of the period to learn what it says about the soul before he comes to any conclusions about Rabelais's originality on the subject. Vague generalizations about "soul"—*our* generalizations—will not do. As for the grand generalizations "medieval man" and "Renaissance man," they are meaningless: "those poor 'people of the Middle Ages'—what a sad picture of them has been painted for generations. Luckily for them, they never existed."

By precept and demonstration, then, Febvre tells us how he thinks history should be done. Whether this is a full-blown universally applicable methodology is another question. The precepts are mostly negative, and what is demonstrated is the mental processes of a man of unusual sensitivity, great intelligence, and much, much learning. Not that negative precepts are not extremely valuable. There is probably no better advice to give a historian than to avoid anachronism like the plague. If, as Febvre always said, the subject matter of history has no bounds except those of time, the challenge to the historian is how to deal with what once was (and may or may not still be, in whole or in part). The message that Febvre proclaims at the outset resounds through the whole book: the historian needs to be as aware of his own time as he is of the past, and the service he provides is to interpret the past in the light of the present, a present that will be different for another generation of historians ("history is the daughter of time"). It can be said that in the end Febvre does rely on intuition, both in assembling documentation and making choices and judgments. His documentation is extraordinarily varied, his choices are conditioned by his wide learning and a willing exposure to insights from the

"human sciences"—but Febvre's method is not quite methodi-
cal in a way that is transferable to other scholars. It is striking
that the "methodology" section of the bibliography includes
only Febvre's own ruminations, with the exception of one book
by his methodological mentor, Henri Berr.

What is transferable is something more like a code of conduct
than a methodology. The past is interesting to the present because it is full of unsolved problems. A good historian is excited
by problems that seem important to him or her and his or her
contemporaries, as Febvre was by the problem of Rabelais's religion. He believed that was the right approach to history. The
problem should be recognized, defined, and then honestly dealt
with, using all the resources at our command. We have to care
about what those people cared about. It is a challenging code of
conduct.

The Sixteenth Century and Rabelais

As a study of a specific subject Le Problème de l'incroyance is,
after so many decades, still indispensable. For one thing, it is a
thorough treatment of one side of Rabelais. Whatever a reader
may previously have thought about Rabelais's religious ideas,
he goes back to Rabelais with sharpened perceptions after sharing Febvre's close reading of him. Even if one prefers to read
Rabelais in something of a timeless vacuum, to enjoy him as an
artist rather than study him as a historical specimen, Febvre's
commentary is sympathetic and revealing. It reminds us of
what is actually in Rabelais, like the religious passages brought
together in chapter 6, "The Giants' Creed." In spite of his argumentative manner, Febvre's assessment of Rabelais's sentiments
is rather cautious and complex, because of his sensitivity to the
nuances found in a creative artist. Lefranc's label of "atheist"
lacked this complexity.

However sensitive a reader he was, Febvre had no intention,
as he tells us, of writing a literary monograph. This is a book
about a specific historical problem. To carp at it because it does
not go into all aspects of Rabelais's art would be foolish. The
problem raised by Lefranc was about Rabelais's relationship to
the time in which he lived and to our time—a historical problem. Febvre felt called on to weave a rich and plausible context

into which certain aspects of François Rabelais fit comfortably. For Febvre the historian, Rabelais was a convenient pretext for talking about the sixteenth century.

How Febvre locates that century in a larger time frame raises questions of deep concern to historians. To answer Lefranc, he stresses the continuities between the Middle Ages and the sixteenth century. For him there was nothing like the dramatic entry into the modern world that the Renaissance used to represent—a notion that stubbornly persists, even if most serious scholars today reject it. In relation to the present, however, the sixteenth century seems to be a totally remote time, in which every aspect of life was different from our own, sometimes in ways that most readers have never suspected. He seems to take it for granted that we in the twentieth century are firmly planted on the other side of a great divide, since the development of modern science brought about a revolutionary transformation in *mentalité* ("ways of thinking," "mental tools," "the sense of the impossible").

His certainty about the rationality of the twentieth century will surely strike many readers as exaggerated. Perhaps it reflects French pride in "clarity," that quality the French educational system is supposed to inculcate. It is unlikely that anyone writing in English today would say, as he does, "We have become used to clarity ever since Descartes established its conditions." But even Henri Berr in his foreword remarked that "primitivism" had survived into the present era.

Febvre's apparent denial of continuity between the sixteenth century and the present is puzzling. It makes us wonder what his general view of historical continuity and change is, since the situation before and the situation after the sixteenth century are presented as so different. Does he really mean that nothing of the sixteenth century survives? Would he deny continuity at some points in history? By what sort of process did the great transformation take place? When did the transformation start? When was it completed?

The answers are not to be found in this book. The period in which modern science developed lies outside its scope. Yet what can easily strike one as an inconsistent—or at least unexplained—view of historical processes may be clarified by hints scattered through the book. It was not to his purpose in his ar-

gument with Lefranc, after all, to stress the continuities between the sixteenth century and the present, and if there was
one thing Febvre was a master of, it was concentrating on one
problem at a time. When Descartes and Newton are mentioned,
Febvre connects them with sixteenth-century attitudes to religion—a hint that the transformation did not come suddenly.
Nor was there a total lack of movement within the sixteenth
century, even if Febvre tends to make many generalizations
about it as a whole. Indeed, one of his main points is that there
was a difference between the religious situation in France in
1532 and that in the 1550s. He seems to be saying that there is
always movement and change, but at different rates, and that no
period can be understood without its baggage from the past. In
a somewhat obscure passage on p. 422, he apparently complains
that history writing in the Renaissance had no concept of continuing change, of evolution, and hence no notion of the connection between present and past. This certainly suggests he
was fully aware of the complexities of the issue.

Rabelais's religion is the secondary subject of the book, as the
title indicates. Its primary subject is "unbelief." What Febvre
wanted to demonstrate was that the mental equipment available
in the sixteenth century made it as good as impossible for anyone to be an atheist, and, perhaps more important, that an atheist could only have been a solitary figure to whom nobody
would have paid any significant attention. It is a common notion that figures of the past are to be congratulated for being
ahead of their times, as Lefranc congratulated Rabelais. Febvre
thought that no one was ever really ahead of his times. Such a
notion could only derive from inadequacies in historical understanding. Things evolve, some people cling to old ways, some
people embrace newer ways, but it all happens in a context; isolated individuals cannot see into a future that has not yet taken
shape. This is another illustration of how Febvre's theory of
history wants to have nothing to do with mysterious processes.
Every bold and original idea that Rabelais has been credited
with Febvre attempts to reduce to human scale—not to deni-
grate it but to avoid recourse to superhuman explanations,
which he felt were never necessary. He makes it clear that
others in the sixteenth century were thinking the same way as
Rabelais, and that there was apparently room for a great variety

of opinions, a much greater variety than was available to practicing French Catholics of 1922, when Lefranc wrote.

Febvre recognized, of course, that new ways of thinking did eventually come into being. The change had to start sometime. Henri Berr was uncomfortable that Febvre overstated the impossibility of its having started in the sixteenth century. "Let us admit," he wrote in his foreword, "that what Rabelais might have said against religion would have been 'without social significance,' above all 'without any compelling force'; but to say that that 'did not matter, historically speaking,' seems debatable . . . There is a genealogy of ideas, a long and necessary genealogy in which Rabelais has a place." It is not likely that this difference can be resolved. It is much easier to find the source of the Nile than the source of an idea, especially an idea as complex as "unbelief." Febvre was not looking for its source. He was simply showing that the conditions of Rabelais's time were overwhelmingly against its emerging. But he could not lay the problem to rest. The problem is important but intractable.

The book is really about *croyance*. That is its main contribution to scholarship and what makes it valuable to anyone interested in the sixteenth century. "A Century That Wanted to Believe" is the title of the last chapter, but it could have been the title of the book. Belief is lavishly detailed in its almost infinite variety, from Erasmus to the peasant at the baptismal font, from Guillaume Postel's visions of a universal religion to the Sire de Gouberville's visions of hunters in the sky. As in everything Febvre did—and recommended—a wealth of concrete details make up a rich texture. Part of Febvre's originality was to reveal the presence of belief in less than obvious places, where a modern person might expect either its opposite (philosophy and science) or neutral ground (eating, making a living). Febvre says there was no room for unbelief in that world. Whether he is right or not, a reader must be impressed with how overwhelmingly crowded with belief it was.

The book contains a number of special insights into this complex sixteenth-century world. For example, there is the remarkable opening chapter on the neo-Latin poets, the longest chapter in the book. It is based on old-fashioned dogged library research into books that are about as dead as old books can be. Never mind that Febvre got to know more about them than the scholars who used them to build up a case about Rabelais's atheism. What Febvre does is convince us that the men who wrote them were once alive, and that they lived in a world we understand better for knowing about them. To start a work of intellectual history with a hundred pages on a group of second-raters is a bold move, but what an effective way of making a point about collective psychology! It avoids an error not infrequently made by intellectual historians when they generalize about periods in the past on the basis of what only the finest minds were thinking.

Some individuals are highlighted in a particularly dramatic way. There is something haunting about the constantly reappearing doomed figure of Etienne Dolet. The crabbed idiosyncratic notions of Guillaume Postel enrich the picture of the period's religious life, preparing us for the variety of ideas swirling about in the early days of the Reformation that Febvre takes up in the chapters on Luther and Erasmus. Time spent with Postel under Febvre's guidance should surely make a thoughtful reader resistant to the idea that "Reformation" and "tradition" are monolithic terms.

A high point of the book is the verbal round dance in which every participant eventually manages to call every other one an atheist. There are obviously period styles in name-calling, a subject well worth studying (as Febvre would have said). It is instructive to see the different occasions when the word "atheist" was so furiously brandished. It is one more display of Febvre's intelligent sensitivity to the language of the past. Of course, he did not lose the opportunity to preach a sermon on anachronism here, but the dramatic effect is so unforgettable he did not really have to.

The attention to less than obvious subjects, such as death and magic; the recognition of overlooked relationships, such as that between Rabelais and Luther; and the use of unusual historical evidence, such as diocesan archives, music, and architecture—all this still has the power to startle and to charm. Later scholarship has pursued in greater detail some of the subjects touched on by Febvre, but he has rarely been contradicted. That is because even at his most argumentative he never lost his historical sensitivity and critical intelligence. For the reader about to experience him for the first time, Febvre's passionate interest in all the things human beings have been capable of doing over the centuries may indeed provide an introduction to "a new kind of history."

About the Translation

Febvre's style is difficult to convey in English. It is hard to decide which would be worse—to let it run wild in all its Gallic colors or to tame it into drabness. I have tried to do neither. One problem with Febvre's writing is not so much a matter of color as of allusiveness. He has a way of casually referring to quite obscure things. Whenever possible I have tried to pin him down. I have also put references into a form currently in American use. I found a number of errors—wrong titles, misspellings, wrong volume and page numbers. These I have corrected to the best of my ability. The errors seem to have come from haste in the original editing, from the conditions of wartime publishing, and perhaps from the use of handwritten notes.

I have done most of the translations from Latin, except where Febvre gives a French paraphrase, in which case I translated that. All the verse translations are mine, except where indicated. Rabelais quotations are from the seventeenth-century English translation by Sir Thomas Urquhart (*Gargantua, Pantagruel,* and *Book Three*) and Peter Le Motteux (*Book Four* and *Book Five*). It is the most easily available translation and comes in many editions, including the Everyman Library. Quotations from his other writings are given in the version found in the English edition of Rabelais's works by Albert Jay Nock and Catherine Rose Wilson. Biblical quotations are from the King James version.

Febvre would have been surprised at the resources of American libraries. He speaks of how hard it was to get hold of some of the rare volumes he used, of having to track down single copies in provincial libraries. When I had to consult some of them I was able to find almost all in American collections: the New York Public Library, Columbia University, Harvard University, the New York Academy of Medicine, the Newberry Library, the University of Michigan, and the University of Wisconsin.

I am grateful to the reference librarians at Columbia University's Butler Library for many things, and particularly to Rita Keckeissen for her help with Catholic liturgy. I also received valuable help from the reference librarians at the Alliance Française in New York, from Denis Vatinel of the Société de l'Histoire du Protestantisme Français in Paris, from the Bibliothèque Nationale, and from the British Library.

The following people—some of them friends in need, some of them old friends—helped with various pieces of this project: Peter Bietenholz, André Burguière, Donald M. Frame, Harvey Gross, Kay Jaffee, John H. Mundy, Eugene F. Rice, J. W. Smit, Hilah F. Thomas, and Julius Wile. I am grateful to all of them.

The Problem of Unbelief in the Sixteenth Century

General Introduction

OOD TEXTBOOKS are fine things. But "L'Evolution de l'Humanité" is no collection of textbooks, however excellent they may be. Their partisans should therefore not hold it against me if, in assuming the weighty task of examining as part of this great project the religious problems that occupied such a large place in men's lives in the time of the Renaissance, I have taken the unusual step of devoting a thick volume entirely to what may be called the reverse of belief: unbelief.

The reader should not be misled by the title of the book. I like Rabelais, but this work is no act of homage paid by a curious reader to an author who gives him pleasure. It is not, in other words, a monograph on Rabelais. It is meant to be, in its ambitious humility, an essay on the meaning and spirit of the sixteenth century.

Another one? As if everything had not been said in all these years that we have had interpreters of the Renaissance, each copying the other. The one thing I have no wish to do is copy my predecessors—not out of a gratuitous love for the paradoxical and new, but because I am, simply, a historian, and a historian is not one who knows, he is one who seeks. And therefore calls into question answers that have been given and retires old cases when he has to.

When he has to. Doesn't that mean always? Let us not pretend that the conclusions of historians are not of necessity marked by contingency. Of all stupid sayings, the one about the book that "will never have to be rewritten" runs the risk of being the stupidest. Rather, that book will never have to be rewritten, not because it has achieved an absolute state of perfection, but because it is a product of its time. History is the daughter of time. I say this not, surely, to disparage her. Philosophy is the daughter of time. Even physics is the daughter of her own time; the physics of Langevin was not that of Galileo, and Galileo's was no longer that of Aristotle. Was there progress from one to the other? I hope so. But, as historians, let us speak of adaptation to the times. Every period mentally constructs its own universe. It constructs it not only out of all the materials at its disposal, all the facts (true or false) that it has inherited or acquired, but out of its own gifts, its particular cleverness, its qualities, its talents, and its interests—everything that distinguishes it from preceding periods.

Similarly, every period mentally constructs its own image of the historical past, its Rome and its Athens, its Middle Ages and its Renaissance. How? Out of the materials at its disposal. And that is how an element of progress can slip into historical work. We have more facts, and they are of greater variety and reliability—the gain is not negligible. Though he applies the same talents, a good architect does not build the same kind of house out of rubble and two or three old beams that he does out of a plentiful supply of excellent cut stone and fine finished timber. But not only materials are involved. There are also gifts (which can vary), qualities of mind, and intellectual methods. Above all, there are also interests and areas of concern, which are so quick to change and which direct the attention of men of a certain period to aspects of the past that were long hidden in obscurity and will soon recede into the shadows again. Let us not say that this is human but rather that it is the law of human knowledge.

Our fathers constructed their own Renaissance; it was unlike the Renaissance of their fathers. We have inherited something of that Renaissance. At fifteen my friends and I were reading Taine's *Voyage to Italy* and *The Philosophy of Art;* at eighteen we were feasting on Burckhardt. And for a long time my Rabelais was the Rabelais of Gebhart. But what tragedies and cataclysms have occurred between 1900 and 1941! If I had not been aware of this myself (I am not being facetious—men have such a great need for stability, stability is so sweet, that even those who are perceptive by nature and by training often instinctively refuse to be so and, shutting their eyes to reality, see only what they were accustomed to seeing)—if I had not been somewhat aware of this personally, it would have come to my attention in 1922 as a result of reading the long introduction that Abel Lefranc put at the beginning of *Pantagruel* in the critical edition of the *Oeuvres*. It shocked me. Hence this book, which by way of a response seeks to deal with the difficult problems of unbelief.

⋖§ Before us are some of the great minds of the sixteenth century. First of all, Rabelais. In his heart of hearts, what was this man? A mocking son of Touraine, simply an heir to the anti-clerical and ribald spirit of Jean de Meung of Orléans? Or a profound philosopher who, moving ahead of his contemporaries, so outdistanced them in criticism and unbelief that none of them could follow him? Was he the skeptic of Anatole France, propounding to his age "the faith most necessary to man, the one most consistent with his nature and most apt to make him happy: doubt"? Or, on the contrary, the fanatic of Abel Lefranc, determined to lead men to the secular certitudes of untrammeled science? Will we, somewhat calmer than that headstrong interpreter of Pantagruel, see Rabelais as one of those lukewarm Christians who set up on the altar of a god of Goodness a Christ totally bereft of a halo? Or as inspired with a passion for reform that was quickly held in check by fear of torture? We are like Panurge: what to accept, what to reject? As for authorities, there are at least ten—all highly respected—to be found lurking behind every one of these contrary opinions.

Rabelais, yes—but there is also Des Périers, the unknown Des Périers. A humanist infatuated with Platonic thought; servant of the *Marguerite des Marguerites*, now in her favor, now out; militant member of the courageous team that gave the French Reformation its first Bible "in the vulgar tongue"; collaborator with Etienne Dolet, prince of libertines, on the *Commentaries on the Latin Language;* undisputed author of pessimistic poems, probable author of lively, ribald tales, mysterious author of *Cymbalum mundi,* whose inspiration and origin have remained enigmas for four centuries. How can we choose among all these aspects of one man? What face is appropriate for a man whose critics point him in turn in the direction of the Reformation, free thought, mysticism, or ribaldry?

Des Périers, yes—but what of his patroness, Margaret of Na-

varre? The Christian of *Le Miroir de l'âme pêcheresse;* the
woman of the world of the tales in the *Heptameron;* the mystic
of the letters to Briçonnet; the Lutheran who translated Martin
Luther's *Commentary on the Lord's Prayer* into French verse;
the Calvinist who supported the future author of the *Institutes*
at the beginning of his career; the Spiritualist who protected
Poquet and Quintin from the fury of the man from Picardy
after he became a Genevan; the soul thirsting for divine love

> O doux amour au doux regard
> Qui me transperce de ton dard
> Hélas, j'ai peur
> De n'aimer point d'assez bon coeur.

> O sweetest love with sweetest glance,
> Transfixing me with your sweet lance,
> Alas, I fear
> That my own love is faint of heart.

With so many disparate traits (it would be pointless to try to
classify them according to historical periods), how can we delineate a living, coherent countenance?

Des Périers, yes—but what of his employer, Dolet? A martyr
of the Renaissance (see Christie). A champion of libertinism
(look at Boulmier, who refurbished Bayle). A believer in the
Gospel for all (if you listen to Nathanael Weiss, heir of Desmaizeaux). Authorities, assertions, doubts. Still, all the witnesses are there, friends and enemies alike. All the texts are
there, and, first of all, Dolet's own works, his moving outcries—
Second Enfer and the sorrowful *Cantique* of 1546. The distance
from Dolet the atheist to Dolet the Reformer is great; but no
agreement is possible among experts.

We could give many more examples, but these will do. they
allow us to say that when we confront a man of the sixteenth
century and question him and his contemporaries in an effort to
define his faith we will never be really sure about him—or
about ourselves. This states the methodological problem, and it
is what concerns us.

&§ Let us not say, "If only the texts were richer, the witnesses more loquacious, the confessions more detailed!" Don't

we seem today to have everything we need in order to know our contemporaries: their revelations on recordings, their facial expressions in photographs? And yet . . . A rascal, say some; a saint, say others, speaking of the same man.

The fact is that a monograph which is no more than a portrait bust, without background or setting, is misleading. No religious thought—no thought of any kind—however pure and disinterested, is unaffected by the climate of a period. Or, if you prefer, by the hidden operation of the conditions of life that a particular period creates for all the conventions and all the manifestations that meet on its common ground—and on which it leaves the imprint of a style never seen before, and never to be seen again.

At this point the problem becomes clearer and at the same time narrower. The problem is not (for the historian, at any rate) to catch hold of a man, a writer of the sixteenth century, in isolation from his contemporaries, and, just because a certain passage in his work fits in with the direction of one of our own modes of feeling, to decide that he fits under one of the rubrics we use today for classifying those who do or do not think like us in matters of religion. When dealing with sixteenth-century men and ideas, when dealing with modes of wishing, feeling, thinking, and believing that bear sixteenth-century arms, the problem is to determine what set of precautions to take and what rules to follow in order to avoid the worst of all sins, the sin that cannot be forgiven—anachronism.

How do books written between 1530 and 1550 by Rabelais, Dolet, and Margaret of Navarre sound today, to us as men of the twentieth century? That is not where the problem is. The problem is in knowing how men in 1532 heard *Pantagruel* and *Cymbalum mundi*, how they were capable of hearing and comprehending them. Let us turn the sentence around. It is, even more, in knowing how those men were absolutely incapable of hearing or comprehending them. We instinctively bring to bear on these texts our ideas, our feelings, the fruit of our scientific inquiries, our political experiences, and our social achievements. But those who leafed through them when they were brand-new, under a bookseller's awning on Rue Mercière in Lyon or Rue Saint-Jacques in Paris—what did they read between the carefully printed lines? Just because the sequence of ideas in these texts confers on them a kind of eternal verity, to our eyes at least, can we conclude that all intellectual attitudes are possible in all periods? Equally possible? A great problem for the history of the human mind. It compounds the methodological problem and gives it extraordinary scope.

❧§ "Like the other elements in its history, the moral beliefs of mankind at every moment in the past have been everything they were capable of being. In consequence, the moral truths of today, even if they had been anticipated earlier, would have been devoid of any practical value at the time—and anyone who maintained them would not have convinced his contemporaries." Thus did Frédéric Rauh in 1906 state in terms of the moral realm the great problem of the precursor, the man who cannot be proved right because he looks into the future. And Rauh added, speaking of what is the "moral truth" for us today, that man could not have grasped it in the past, he would not even have needed to—"he could only have dreamt it." An excellent indication, by the way, of this moral philosopher's historic sense.

The first of our aims at present is to transfer these formulas from the moral plane to the plane of beliefs—an aim in harmony with some of our period's deepest propensities. A while ago our teacher Lucien Lévy-Bruhl investigated how and why primitives reason differently from civilized men. Yet a good part of the latter remained primitives for a long time. They did not use exactly the same modes of reasoning in all periods to form their systems of ideas and beliefs. This is not a very precise formulation, and yet why, instead of refining it in applying it to their own field, are historians so willing to let philosophers be the only ones who bother to express it? Is it true there would be so little to gain?

When we try to reconstruct the frame of mind of our ancestors with regard to matters of religion, we tend to place reason on one side and revelation on the other—a choice has to be made. But what meaning do reason and revelation—the whole debate of abstractions, in fact—have for a real man, a man of flesh and blood? Renan stated in *The Future of Science* that among the most sincere believers are often found men "who have rendered the most eminent services to science," and he concluded that human nature, "in reality stronger than all the

religious systems, hits upon some secret modes of taking its revenge." He added, not at all unaware of what can be hidden in
the recesses of a mind yearning for faith, that "Kepler, Newton,
Descartes, and the majority of the founders of modern science
were believers."[1] The founders, yes, but what of the precursors? Descartes, yes, but what about Rabelais before him?

☬ It is an important question. Isn't it amazing how, on the
pretext of vindicating the great men whom they associate, quite
rightly, with the genesis of the modern world, our contemporaries insist on disparaging them? They are not satisfied unless they have made them into cowards, the only cowards in a
century peopled by heroes who cheerfully paid with their lives
for their devotion to highly contradictory truths. Some take a
barely concealed delight in setting forth this supposed cowardice and satisfying their instinctive hatred of the intellect and its
magnificence. They need a Lefèvre who is held back on his
headlong slide into heresy only by an old man's timorous caution. They need an Erasmus who refuses to associate himself
with a man and with doctrines totally opposed, as we know, to
everything in his nature, simply—so they say—out of his love
of tranquillity and his desire to avoid violent persecution. With
a lofty air many men who seem to have little familiarity with
intellectual daring reproach Margaret's protégé and Thomas
More's friend with what in their kinder moments they conde-
scend to characterize as "timidity." At the other end of the century they need a pusillanimous Montaigne, fleeing the plague
and the dangers of public life. In the middle, a Rabelais modeled on his Panurge—a wily jester, a cynical parasite, a complete unbeliever, but dissembling in order to pay the Church
the respect that was required. Or else (this is the new version)
a fanatical Rabelais, in violent rebellion not only against the
Catholic Church but also against Christian belief itself—disguised, however, out of fear. As if fear were the natural (and
laudable) companion of intelligence and reason in this world!

Thus they are summarily dismissed. But those men were
pursued by mystery. From the beginning of their lives to the
end they did battle with the unknown and thought of the uni-

1. Ernest Renan, *The Future of Science* (Boston, 1891), pp. 33–35.

verse, not (like their offspring of the seventeenth century) as a machine, a system of motions clicking away according to a known plan, but as a living organism, controlled by secret forces and by mysterious and profound influences.

For these fantasies of second-rate history, too often inspired by the personal concerns of men bogged down in endless detail, let us substitute a more truly human conception of a heroic century's spiritual conceptions. (Fear is human, but even more so is triumph over fear.) That is what this book aspires to. Is it a monograph on a man, Rabelais? As great as he was, I would not have bothered to write that. It is, rather, a search for a method, or, to be more precise, a critical examination of a complex of problems—historical, psychological, and methodological. That seemed to be worth a ten-year effort.

⋍§ And now, have I done the right thing by allowing the traces of my steps to show in the pages that follow? Perhaps I should have discarded my initial Rabelais scaffolding, forgone the discussion of works by my predecessors, and left only the second part—perhaps the third part, all by itself. But wouldn't that have made it quite arbitrary, isolated, and unreal? This book, with unequal parts arranged in order of decreasing mass (the part with most matter at the bottom, full of critical gravity; the second, somewhat lighter, in the center; the third capping the other two), whose very structure reveals the workings of a mind—I am glad it makes clear to the reader's eyes that it did not originate in a theoretical outlook, one of those a priori convictions that do scholarship so much harm. I would be very sorry if people saw in it an essayist's flash of insight, a brilliant sketch, an improvisation. It was my constant companion from the day at Strasbourg long ago when, in the company of Henri Pirenne, I first wrestled with Abel Lefranc's eloquent theory down to the day when I yielded to Henri Berr's entreaties and decided to publish it as it was, as an act of faith in the future of intellectual freedom, an affirmation of the will to understand and make others understand—which is how I like to define the function of history and the historian's creativity.

Was Rabelais an Atheist?

The Problem and the Method

HERE IS, then, a problem of method. It is of course always very difficult to know a man, a man's true visage. But in dealing with the sixteenth century, its writers and its religious views, the difficulty is really exaggerated. They are too casually assumed to have swung at will from aggressive unbelief to the most traditional kind of belief. Can it be that the problems about their views that we have declared to be insoluble have been brought into being by ourselves, and by us alone? Do we not substitute our thought for theirs, and give the words they used meanings that were not in their minds? Thus the problem that was formulated poorly can become a better formulated one. But it is the whole conception of the sixteenth century as humanist that is being called into question. In short, an entire century must be rethought.

Should it be done in a didactic manner? In dealing with man's inner being, the struggles of conscience with revealed truths as well as with growing doubts, such a procedure would be a betrayal. The approach we are going to use seems obvious: focus the inquiry on one man, chosen not only because he is still well known but also because the state of the documentation that enables us to reconstruct his thought, the statements contained in his work, and the meaning of the work itself seem to qualify him specially for such a study. That man is François Rabelais.

First of all, Rabelais has left us in his writings whole pages devoted to the problems that most divided his contemporaries—

problems of the soul and its immortality, of resurrection and the next life, of miracles, of the Creator's omnipotence, of the natural order's resistance to the deity's free will.

These are the principal concerns. Around them cluster hundreds of allusions to other, no less interesting, controversies, all of it presented by a born writer, the greatest prose artist of his time.

In the second place, even though the number of directly personal documents that we possess about Rabelais is far from enough to satisfy all our curiosity, nevertheless it is as considerable as the most considerable personal records the sixteenth century has left us of any of its great writers. The tremendously powerful personality of the first great modern novelist aroused violent reactions in his lifetime which resulted in numerous pieces in Latin and French, straightforward and in code (the codebook has been lost), that we take up, naturally, with lively curiosity. This is a dangerous business—and misleading. For one thing, we have a great tendency to multiply the number of these documents and so to add to the Rabelais record a lot of pieces that do not belong there. For another, what can we get out of these documents and how should we handle them? Should we take them literally or interpret them? It is a matter of common sense—that's what is always said, and of course it is necessary to be careful and make allowances for friendships and enmities, predilections and grudges. But to reread the texts with eyes of 1530 or 1540—texts that were written by men of 1530 and 1540 who did not write like us, texts conceived by brains of 1530 and 1540 that did not think like us—that is the difficult thing and, for the historian, the important thing. In a word, why Rabelais? Because any careful study of Rabelais's fiction and thought involves, beyond the works themselves, the entire evolution of the century that saw their birth—that, indeed, gave them birth.

◄§ For a long time we were told, "If you want to reconstruct the spiritual development of Gargantua's creator without getting too far off the track, first sketch the main outlines of his era. Reread the fine article by Henri Hauser published in 1897 in the *Revue Historique,* in which he described with a sure hand the parallel development of humanism and the Reformation."

There were three stages. First, an intimate connection between the innovative forces that were opposed to the survivals of the Middle Ages. The men whose thought had been regenerated by contact with ancient thought naively assumed that the first Reformers shared their desires and followed the same paths. A delusion of short duration: from about 1534 or 1535 many of the "Renaissants" wavered. In France, before their very eyes, there were the shifting policies of King Francis, the first serious persecutions, the hostile attitude of the upper nobility, the violence of a militant clergy stirred up by the magistrates. Outside France there were bitter theological disputes, violent condemnations of free inquiry and of learning. When the stake was lit for Servetus and for Dolet these disappointed optimists retreated from a contest in which the prize had become something totally foreign to them. A deep split seemed to have taken place between humanism and the Reformation. As it was for Rabelais's century, so it was for him. Each of his books highlights one of the stages of a development that he recorded—and precipitated. *Pantagruel* (1532) and *Gargantua* (1534) are two manifestations of the first phase of humanism, the humanism that believed it was being served by the first phase of the Reformation and served it in turn. In *Book Three* everything had changed. The Rabelais of 1546 was a philosopher who was irritated by the conflict of catechisms but had no further interest in it. As for the Rabelais of 1552, he was a Gallican nationalist. His *Book Four* served the cause of the king of France against Rome; it stands for no creed. On one side was "enraigé" Putherbeus, on the other side "demoniacal" Calvin. Equally revolted by the fanaticism of both—opposed to each other but sometimes sounding the same note—Rabelais turned away from their rabid fury and, like a true Platonist, lost himself in the contemplation of beauty and harmony.

◄§ For a long time this is what we were told. Then suddenly, in 1923, a ringing introduction to *Pantagruel* disturbed the harmony.

Rabelais was a reflection of his age? Certainly not. He was exceptional, the precursor of the atheists and freethinkers of the eighteenth century, and quite different from the Rabelais of Gebhart, who prefigured that of Anatole France. This Rabelais was a believer in incredulity. His work was a call to arms. He was one of those bold spirits who everywhere in the world from that time forward dreamed of complete religious emancipation.

In answering the very natural question "What was Rabelais's real purpose in writing *Pantagruel*—to make his contemporaries laugh or to pursue some mysterious design?" Abel Lefranc struck us to the very marrow by declaring, "The author of this book, at the beginning of his literary career, belonged to the rationalist faith." More than that, he harbored within himself a "secret thought." To see in Master Alcofribas a good Christian who (like so many others) was for a while won over by the first manifestations of a Reformation that offered its hand to humanism is a serious mistake. It is a mistake that has robbed critics of all curiosity; not one of them has wondered "whether Rabelais, in the last analysis, had not ceased to be a Christian." For Abel Lefranc, at any rate, there was no uncertainty. From 1532 on, the spiritual father of Panurge was an enemy of Christ, a militant atheist. Rabelais an adherent, more or less timid, of the Reformation? Hardly! He emulated Lucian and Lucretius, indeed "he went further than all contemporary writers along the path of philosophical and religious opposition." And since "the slightest change would have constituted an avowal that might have betrayed him," he retained his Promethean allusions with an imperturbable tranquillity and never touched them. "What power of latent and contained irony! This unknown aspect of the writer's genius holds many more surprises for the diligent, beyond the ideas that were called into question and their historical significance."[1]

Rabelais, Gebhart concluded in 1877, was a pure skeptic. Different doctrines took possession of his soul by turns and asked to be examined by his reason. "What is the real meaning of the external allegiance he later gave to the Catholic religion? It is a great Perhaps that cannot be fathomed." No, says Abel Lefranc, not a great Perhaps. Rabelais never was a skeptic. He was a believer, a believer in incredulity, and his creed was that of the scoffers, those in radical rebellion against revelation. And wherein consisted his originality? In his attempt to gather about him all the initiates, all those whose thinking was already inclined to ideas of liberty, "all who everywhere in the world dreamed of total religious emancipation." Besides, wasn't there

1. Abel Lefranc, "Etude sur *Pantagruel*," in Rabelais, *Oeuvres*, III (Paris, 1922), xli, li, liii.

someone in his own time who understood him and said so as clearly as he could: the enigmatic author of the enigmatic *Cymbalum mundi* of 1537? In the fourth of the dialogues that make up this work of Des Périers, the dog Hylactor, who has been granted the gift of speech but cannot be understood by his own species, until one day he runs into his old friend, the dog Pamphagus—isn't Hylactor Des Périers himself, calling in vain on Rabelais-Pamphagus to show his hand at last, so full of critical and devastating truths? "Behind the great satirist's enormous burst of laughter are concealed the most audacious intentions. The mask of lunacy is only a device used by Rabelais to hurl into the world the truths and denials that were impossible to be heard in any other way."[2]

This is about Rabelais, but by the same token it is about his century. To say that in Lyon in 1532 there appeared an atheist manifesto written in French and aimed not at the Latinist elite but at the great mass of readers for whom presses like those of Nourry and Arnoullet were printing chivalric romances in bourgeoisified prose or almanacs and bawdy tales is to turn the intellectual and religious history of the sixteenth century as we know it upside down, the one established by generations of historians and scholars. Just open the extensive account of the sources and the development of rationalism in French literature that came from the pen of Henri Busson the same year that Abel Lefranc published his introduction to *Pantagruel.* In the period defined on the title page the first date is not 1532, the year of *Pantagruel,* but 1533, the year of Dolet's first speech at Toulouse. Busson is very precise, saying that the idea of constructing a metaphysical or moral system outside of religion had never occurred to any author before 1533. And 1533 was only a beginning. It was only slowly, cautiously—underhandedly, if you will—in the course of the following decade that the disciples of the Paduans introduced their suspect doctrines into France, doctrines that "neither Rabelais in his first two books nor Des Périers in the *Cymbalum* seems to know." Thus Busson.[3] But for Abel Lefranc *Pantagruel* in 1532 was the first clarion call of the libertine attack. There you have the question formulated.

2. Ibid., p. lxviii.
3. *Les Sources et le développement du rationalisme dans la littérature française de la Renaissance (1533–1601)* (Paris, 1922), p. xiv.

◄§ Is it true that Rabelais, in the rebellious silence of his conscience, had since 1532 harbored the conscious—and perilous—
design of waging all-out war on Christianity as a revealed religion? Is it true that before the savage confessional conflict
thrust so many moderates into a skepticism teeming with
strange new notions, long before the Affair of the Placards, in
the France of 1530 to 1535, peopled entirely by Evangelicals,
Erasmians, and the "faithful," the historian might discover a
section called "Free Thought," which included, in addition to a
slyly resolute Rabelais, a whole company of men possessed by
the same feeling: hatred of Christ—fierce, implacable, but rational?

"Is it true that . . . ?" The wording sounds prosecutory. It is
indeed a matter of investigating a case, of weighing testimony—
that of Rabelais's friends and enemies, that of Rabelais himself
from the evidence of his life and his works. This is the case we
are about to reopen. But when the investigation is over, shall
we give a yes or no verdict? May not our critical examination of
the facts lead us to substitute for the prosecuting attorney's "Is
it true?" the historian's "How can we explain it?" Humane
wording, that—the wording of someone who knows that at
every point in its development humanity has had the beliefs it
has been capable of having. And so the problem is not in asking
whether, when we read certain passages in Rabelais, we find
ourselves tempted to exclaim, "Now *this* Rabelais was surely a
freethinker!" Rather, whether Rabelais's contemporaries (I
mean the most perceptive of them), when *they* read the same
passages, did or did not experience a temptation of this sort.
And finally, whether Rabelais himself—and, beyond Rabelais,
any man with a similar background—was or was not capable at
the time of harboring the design of "revealing" a doctrine
whose negative aspect has been clearly pointed out to us but
whose actual content is concealed, and for good reason.

In short, won't the method of "Is it true?" when applied to
religious history lead to a dead end, and won't that of "Was it
possible?" on the contrary guide the historian to the final goal
of all history, not knowledge but—in spite of the words that are
usually used—understanding? It is in this spirit that we reopen
the question. First, we examine testimony and witnesses.

PART I

The Testimony of Contemporaries

1. The Boon Companions

 C A S E has been brought against Rabelais. He has been accused of atheism and anti-Christian thought. His acts are said to date from 1532 and the appearance of *Pantagruel.* Witnesses have been called. A great deal of testimony has been entered into the record. But we are not greedy—we will be satisfied with a single, decisive text. Is there one?

Yes, was the answer given forty years ago by Louis Thuasne, a peerless digger. Yes, was the answer repeated twenty years ago by Abel Lefranc, the prince of Rabelais scholarship. Look at this text of 1533, earlier than *Gargantua* and contemporary with *Pantagruel.* It is a condemnation of Rabelais's first book on the grounds of atheism. And the judge is a competent one— would you take exception to John Calvin? What is more, read these Latin verses. Their authors were acquainted with Rabelais, were in contact with him, spent time with him. They were the audience for his libertine remarks. They too, somewhat later, like Calvin, accused him of being anti-Christian. How can we have any doubt?

Let us take the record again and look at it carefully. And for the moment let us put to one side the key piece, the Calvin document, the only one contemporary with *Pantagruel.* We will examine it later, with other texts by controversialists and theologians. Let us lend an ear to the companions, the "poets" whose testimony the two renowned scholars have joined in commending to us.

1. Academic Apollos

Let us take a look at them. But how? Here we must remain
faithful to our intention of refusing to have anything to do with
documents in isolation, without analyzing in general some
habits of mind, some ways of living, believing, and thinking
that were peculiar to the odd little world—at once appealing
and unattractive—of knights in the service of couplet and iamb.

⇜§ It is a little-known microcosm, one that has not yet found
its historian.[1] Perhaps it does not deserve one. The tedium of
reading so much labored prosody, and of reading it under difficult circumstances (the collections are extremely rare, so that
one has to go from library to library to track them down),
seems greatly to exceed any profit that might be derived. No
neglected chapter in the history of the human mind is to be
found there. But there are a few pieces of evidence of historical
psychology.

So let us conjure up the members of "Gallia Poetica" between 1530 and 1540, all vying in zeal if not in talent: Saumon
Meigret of Loudun, whom we shall call by the Latinized form
of his name, Salmonius Macrinus; Nicholas Bourbon the Elder,
the Horace of Champagne; Etienne Dolet, who composed verses
in his spare time; Gilbert Ducher, the Apollo of Aigueperse;
Vulteius, who borrowed a name from Horace, but whose real
name was Jean Visagier. There they are, the leaders, so to
speak, the *maiores,* accompanied by the *minores:* Germain de
Brie; Dampierre; Du Maine; Rosselet; Guillaume Scève of
Lyon; Antonio de Gouvea of Portugal; Julius Caesar Scaliger,
supposed scion of the Della Scala family of Verona; Jean de
Boysonné, a Toulouse lawyer; we nearly left out that aggressive
pedagogue, Hubert Sussanneau or Sussannet of Soissons. There
they all are, "Brixi, Dampetre, Borbone, Dolete—Vulteique
operis recentis author," as they are evoked in the refrain of a
hymn by Macrinus, with their traits in common, their professional defects, and, above all, their enormous, astounding, ingenuous vanity.

No flattery was too lavish for them. They bestowed it gen-

---

1. D. Murarasu, *La Poésie néo-latine et la Renaissance des lettres antiques en
France (1500–1549)* (Paris, 1928), is only an outline.

erously on their colleagues, but of course they expected to be repaid.[2] Listen to one of them—Ducher, not the most contemptible of the lot. Who is his example, his model? Great Macrinus, the Horace of his age, a Horace beside whom his ancestor Quintus Flaccus pales. Who is his friend, his supporter? Guillaume Scève of Lyon—oh, how far his poetic genius exceeds that of Catullus himself! How far? Ducher knows, and Ducher tells: exactly as far as a Bucephalus at full gallop can outdistance a tortoise ("Ut testiduneos incessus Pegasus, atque / Bucephalus, domini clarus amore sui").[3] As for Nicholas Bérault, he enjoys the company of Pallas and the Nine Sisters—anyone who ventures to doubt that is a madman. Charles de Sainte-Marthe is the equal of Phoebus himself. To vie with him is to seek the fate of Marsyas ("Phoebus es, et Phoebo tibi si me confero, fiam / protinus extracta Marsya pelle tuus").[4] Concluding his survey of lyricists with himself, the poet treats himself generously. He has the grace to excuse himself for this, and it is a jocular excuse: "You know well," he confides to his audience, resigned to carrying on its part of the dialogue in language provided by the poet, "you know well that poets live only for fame." ("Nosti, famam tantum peti a poetis.")[5] But Nicholas Bourbon does even better. To encourage a young follower, he says, "Go, apply yourself to your work. No rest or respite till you have gained your place in the sun. Thus you will show yourself to be a man. Thus you will become another me!" ("Sic vir, sic eris alter ego.")[6] A magnificent utterance, like that of

2. One finds, however, an outburst of sincerity in Macrinus, the most accomplished of the lot. He says to his young emulator, Vulteius, "Nec minimus, nec es poeta / summus, sed medium tenes, poetas / inter temporis huius." (You are neither the least nor the greatest of the poets of this age but are in the middle.) Having said this, he consoles him: "Brevi futurus / maior, si pede quo soles eodem / pergas ludere." (You will soon be greater if you go on composing in the same way.) *Jo. Vultei Rhemensis hendecasyllaborum libri quatuor* (Paris: S. Colinaeus, 1538), fol. 60r. [These verses addressed to Vulteius are actually indicated as being by Germain de Brie.—Translator.]

3. "As Pegasus the steps of the tortoise, and Bucephalus, too, renowned for his master's love." *Gilberti Ducherii Vultonis Aquapersani epigrammaton libri duo* (Lyon: S. Gryphius, 1538), p. 89.

4. "Thou art Phoebus, and if I compare myself to thee, Phoebus, I shall at once become thy Marsyas, bereft of my skin." Ibid., p. 117.

5. Ibid., p. 89.

6. *Nicolai Borbonii Vandoperani Lingonensis nugarum libri octo* (Lyon: S. Gryphius, 1538), p. 311.

Gustave Courbet three centuries later as he stepped back to look at one of his canvases: "Yes, it is very beautiful. And you know what? Titian, Veronese, Raphael, *I myself*—we've never done anything more beautiful!"[7] Yes, but Courbet was Courbet, and what he was looking at with such satisfaction was indeed "very beautiful."

≈§ Naturally, these turgid Olympians kept a suspicious eye on each other. Woe to him who injured their vanity! There were horrible insults and outcries of hatred, followed without pause by the most insane panegyrics and unrestrained dithyrambs.

We naively assume that the poetic quarrel was an actual quarrel. No doubt at the start there was some offense and some dispute, but the conflict served, most of all, as a convenient theme for a flood of compositions. A disagreement was a godsend to people who had nothing to say. First, there were the facts, recited in the tragic mode. Then the diatribes: first, second, third, then repeated. Following these came the mournful couplet on lost friendship; the high-minded justification; the peripeteia ("it's X's fault")—and, finally, the reconciliation.

Anyone who makes use of the biographical documentation provided by these "poets," with their too-perfect powers of recollection, must never lose sight of this. There is evidence here, no doubt, but, more than that, professional dexterity. There is sincerity, perhaps—but only what fits into couplets. There is true indignation, but it is governed by the opportunity to employ half a line from Catullus here or an epigram from Martial there. The reproaches may have been genuine, but they never prevented the injured party from borrowing, even at the cost of some distortion, the structure of a poem by Horace or Tibullus. He had to show that he was learned and, as Ausonius said of the cento, could work twenty allusions into ten lines. It was a tour de force. His competitors, even the objects of his invective, would appreciate it as connoisseurs when they saw it.

As for never throwing out anything they wrote—Oriental pearls like these were not to be destroyed! Sometimes the name of the original subject was removed (dedicated at first to Nicho-

7. Ludovic Halévy, "Trois dîners avec Gambetta; récit public par M. Daniel Halévy," *Revue des Deux Mondes*, 52 (July 1, 1929), 88.

las Bourbon, an epigram became an offering to Marot). Sometimes everything was printed just as it was, indiscriminately: exclamations of admiration, cries of hatred, protestations of tenderness, explosions of fury—nothing got lost. And if perchance Sebastian Gryphius offered the use of his press to the overwrought poet before the anticipated reconciliation that would permit him to compose the three requisite pieces—oh well! On page three of the collection the reader would see a dithyrambic eulogy of a man whom he found treated on page thirty as a sodomite, a murderer, or at the very least an atheist. In the next collection—if it ever saw the light of day—things would be set right and the account settled.

This points to a cardinal rule of criticism for historians to follow: never take these ornate diatribes as tragic. Indeed, it was not just the two adversaries who profited from a quarrel; friends and enemies got involved, every man for himself. And there is another rule: never read just one poet in order to form an opinion about an accusation made against him or by him. Take a turn around Parnassus and have a look at those who returned the favor or came to his support.

⁓§ One day one of these sons of the faded Muses, one of the most famous in his day, Nicholas Bourbon, chanced on the right word. He christened two collections in a row "Nothings," *Nugae*—248 pages of nothings in 1533, 504 in 1538 (they had proliferated). All the same, the title disturbed one of his colleagues: what if readers decided to take it literally?[8] It was a groundless fear. There was no dishonor in writing nothings. It was only the turn of phrase that mattered, and the prosody.

A poet would chance to find a "matter," and with the patience of a watchmaker would turn it over and over, twice, ten times, saying the same thing in the same words. Only the order would change. Look at the titles: "De eodem," "De eadem," "Ad eumdem," "Ad eamdem." Vulteius was the friend of a certain Junius Rabirius who in 1534 perpetrated in Paris a little

---

8. Gouvea made fun of the title: "Ad nugivendulum," *Antonii Goveani Lusitani epigrammaton libri duo* (Lyon: S. Gryphius, 1539), p. 18; "Ad Borbonium," p. 23; p. 30; and other pages. Dolet defined *nugae* as "sermones levium rerum, ac nullius ponderis, et plerumque scurriles joculatoriique" (discourses on light subjects, with no gravity and often scurrilous and witty). *Commentariorum linguae latinae tomus secundus* (Lyon: S. Gryphius, 1538), col. 1276.

work called *De generibus vestium* (*On the Types of Clothing*).
He had a marvelous idea: "Rabirius, my friend, who discourse
so learnedly on clothing, you don't even have a suit to put on
your back."[9] The idea looked like a good one. Again: "Qui
vestes, telas, aulaea, colores / intus habet, nudus stat sine veste
liber." (This book that has suits, cloth, embroidery, and colors
inside it stands naked, without a suit.) Now start all over, *de
eodem:* "Vestimentorum rationem nosse laboras." (You labor to
know the science of clothing.) But hadn't someone important,
Lazare de Baïf, published a *De re vestiaria* in Basel in 1526 that
had been reprinted several times? Quick, take up the theme
again with regard to him, making the alterations appropriate to
a former ambassador: "Romanas vestes docuit qui serica
fila / vestitus liber est pellibus exigius." (The book that describes Roman garments made of silk is dressed in ordinary
leather.)[10]

And how fiercely they stood guard over their paltry treasures! Though they had nothing to call their own but a certain
dexterity, they spent their entire existences crying, "Stop,
thief!" All those tiresome quarrels on which their poverty
thrived originated from this. A colleague robbed them, a colleague stole, took their ideas—oh monstrous!—and shamelessly
made off with their dactyls and spondees. There is a wonderful
line that one of them, Vulteius, put at the beginning of one of
the pieces in his *Hendecasyllables.* He had a Delia whom he
called Clinia. She died, or he had her die. Among the many
themes her death furnished him with, we find the following
marvelously unexpected one: "Alas, alas, her death has deprived
me of a subject matter!"[11]

Subject matter was such a rarity. Then, too, of the insulting
names they hurled at each other, Zoilus was by far the most
common. No sooner was it sent on its way than it was returned
to the sender in a feverish rage—the poor souls were aware of
the swift passage of time. To their ears a success like that of

9. "Veste cares, intrat penetrabile frigus in artus; / villosam cur non dat liber endro-
midem?" (You don't have a suit, the penetrating cold goes into your joints. Why
doesn't your book give you a woolen cloak?) *Joannis Vultei Remensis epigrammatum
libri II* (Lyon: S. Gryphius, 1536), I, 35.

10. Ibid., 45.

11. "Scribendi materiam sibi morte Cliniae ablatam." *Jo. Vultei Rhemensis hendecasyllaborum,* fol. 52v.

Marot, who disseminated his "vulgar French" from the peaks of Pindus with irresistible glee, tolled the end of hexameters. They became even more diligent in monitoring their craft. It would not have taken much for them to invent a new category of crime: the illegal practice of sapphics and iambics.[12]

⊷§ All of these descendants of medieval minstrels lived under the scrutiny of their customers, or rather, their patrons. (We should note in passing what a struggle it is for our minds to accept this curious reversal—for us the master is the author, while for them it was the reader.) We should realize that it was hard for them to make a living. While they sang of wonderful love affairs with golden princesses they had glimpsed in some castle where they happened to be the beneficiaries of the simple hospitality of the day, a fat wife with faded looks, surrounded by a brood of children clinging to her skirts, was struggling to feed the occupants of a wretched house in Touraine or Anjou—fat and shrewish, sometimes unfaithful, to whom Tibullus or Horace meant nothing. Such was the fate of Hans Holbein, who fled to London to escape the domestic ugliness and anxieties of Basel.

This is what made them nervous, irritable, and bad-tempered—the heavy care of earning their daily bread, the almost obligatory mendicity, the compromises occasioned by necessity. A revealing sign is the fact that no collection was without ten, twelve, twenty epigrams on parasites: "De parasito," "In parasitum." These express a repressed wish and an obsessive dream of having enough to eat for the rest of their lives without asking anybody for anything or needing to ingratiate themselves from morning to night. To be rich in their own right was another obsessive dream. It is revealed in the persistent claim they all made that although their rivals were always making fun of their poverty, they were really scions of rich families who had fallen victim to bad fortune. And one can detect from a thousand unmistakable signs their secret hatred of the bloated burghers who scornfully tossed them a bone under the table as payment for

---

12. "Cuivis libere poetari licere." (Anyone is allowed to practice poetry freely.) *Gilberti Ducherii*, p. 40. This was the development of an obvious theme: a person who had not studied sculpture did not understand how to carve marble, "attamen indocti doctique poemata parient" (yet learned and unlearned alike make poems).

their dithyrambs.[13] What contempt there was in the souls of the beholden:

> Quand j'ai pensé, je treuve bien estrange
> Vouloir juger des couleurs sans y voir—
> Celui qui a tousjours manié fange
> Veuille de l'or le jugement avoir.[14]

> To me the thought seems strange beyond compare
> That one might judge of colors never seen;
> And yet to judge of gold does this man dare
> Who mired in foulest filth has always been.

These well-fed illiterates were given fulsome tributes, as was required, but they were being observed with savage clarity. To cite Jean de Boysonné again, here philosophizing about the rich men of Toulouse:

> Si tu veux avoir un ami qui soit riche,
> Cherchez Nolet, Lancefoc, ou Bernuy,
> Et si tu veux un ami qui soit chiche,
> Prends ceux-là mesme . . .[15]

> You seek a wealthy friend? Then here's a list
> Which mentions Nolet, Lancefoc, and Bernuy.
> Or do you wish a friend with tight-closed fist?
> The list's the same . . .

Then, too, the richer they were the more enthusiastic the praise. If an epigram happened to be directed to someone else

13. *De miseria poetarum* (the poverty of poets) is a common theme. See *Nicolai Borbonii . . . nugarum* (1538), p. 394: "Ad Paulum Ant. Gadagnum" (Quoties quisque est hodie hominum praedivitum / qui non bonum coquum aut equum aut tibicinem, aut / malum scortum bono poetae praeferet?) (How often does one find a rich man today who does not prefer a good cook or horse or piper, even a bad woman, to a good poet?) See also *Les Trois Centuries de Maistre Jehan de Boyssoné*, ed. Henri Jacoubet (Toulouse, 1923), no. 45: "Si le sçavant est pauvre et indigent / de quoy sert-il tant se rompre la teste / si l'on n'estime à présent que l'argent?" (If the scholar is poor and penniless, what is the point of his making such an effort when the only thing that is valued now is money?) No. 3: "Les dons recuz par ton avare dextre / despriser font ton excellent sçavoir." (The gifts received by your greedy hand make your excellent learning contemptible.)

14. *Les Trois Centuries*, I, no. 26, p. 105.

15. Ibid., II, no. 50, p. 143.

in a second edition, the first recipient had nothing to complain of. For his money he had received precisely the length of time it took to get the new edition ready. Ducher's somewhat more refined touch was to solicit two patrons at the same time for each book in his collection—an epistle was written to one, a dedication to the other. With *two* epistles, four patrons of the arts were guaranteed immortality—if they were generous, needless to say.

On the other hand, these anxious, thin-skinned, touchy creatures, perpetually exposed to injury, showed themselves at times to be good friends ready to help each other out. Fee splitting goes back a long way, as can be seen from Ducher: "It was Nicholas Bourbon," he informs a rich man of Lyon loaded with coin of the realm, "who told me about you. If not for him, your name would not appear in this collection. In all fairness, you owe him something!"[16] When they were threatened they joined forces against the enemy, forgot their differences, and made common cause. In the front line were those who had arrived and who had regular incomes—the fat ones. In the rear were those who envied them, eyed their positions longingly, and for the time being used them as shields—the lean ones. The poor wretches formed a living Bruegel print. Its inscription could have been these verses by Antoine Du Saix, poet of Savoy and one of Rabelais's "master beggars":

> Fut-il cousin germain de Jupiter,
> Si n'aura-t-il que d'ung levrier les gages—
> Et bien souvent, vêtu comme les pages,
> Plus deffroqué que harnois d'étalons,
> Prêtre aux genoux et Argus aux talons,
> Voila l'estat des pauvres pédagogues.[17]

> No matter that he's kin to Zeus—
> A dog might live on such a wage:
> He's decked out like his master's page,
> Though horses wear far finer rags.
> Knees like a priest's and heels like Argus:
> Behold the needy scholar's sad estate!

16. *Gilberti Ducherii*, p. 150.

17. Joseph Texte, *De Antonio Saxano* (Thèse de doctorat ès lettres, Paris, 1895), p. 72.

◄§ There were virtues that went along with all of this. First of all, they believed in what they did, and even in what they said. Theirs was the sincerity of the actor who throws himself into his part. They were the first to believe the praise they bestowed on themselves. One needs to feed on pride when one's miseries are the constant butt of churlish jokes. The exalted notion these poor fellows had of their mission was what sustained them. It gave them the strength to write in their unheated garrets in the dead of winter, when the ink froze in their inkwells; they told about it with a wry smile.

And what of their naive faith in beauty, such as they conceived of it, and in the sovereign efficacy of literature? It was, no doubt, not disinterested—they lived off the very altar they themselves placed in such a high position—but it was not mere self-interest. They worshipped with real enthusiasm. They were prepared to suffer for their faith as humanists. This is their attractive side and what, in spite of their glaring faults, makes them worth studying.

All of them, contemporaries of *Gargantua* and *Pantagruel*, had a god on earth whom they venerated—the god of humanism, Erasmus.[18] To the cult of Erasmus, which was observed everywhere in Europe, the French added that of a national saint, Jacques Lefèvre d'Etaples, *le bonhomme Fabri*.[19] They did not repudiate Lefèvre even when he came under suspicion and was hounded by the Sorbonne (which defended itself by attacking). Most of them loudly proclaimed their reformist—we cannot say Reformed—convictions without worrying about the touch of illogicality involved in serving in the priesthood of Latin poets in Lyon or Paris around 1530 and also calling for a French Bible for all men, for psalms in French, and for services in French. They were not bothered. They defended their ideas. They invoked the name of Christ so loudly that sometimes the Sorbonne heard them, or Parlement. They had their minor martyrs. One day they would have a major one, Etienne

18. See, for example, Ducher's anger at Erasmus's enemies: "Musarum regem quicunque negarent Erasmum / Hoc saltem norint, se in solem meiere!" (Those who deny that Erasmus is king of the Muses do not even know they are pissing on the sun!) "Ad Godefredum Beringium," *Gilberti Ducherii*, p. 104.

19. It is as difficult to choose an example for Lefèvre as for Erasmus. See Salmonius Macrinus, "De obitu Fabri Stap.," in *Hymnorum libri sex ad Jo. Bellaium . . .* (Paris: R. Stephanus, 1537), p. 119.

Dolet— a martyr whom many of them had already repudiated and who later in the century paid for something that most of them had managed to wipe from their accounts. He was nonetheless *their* martyr, the author of *carmina* and *commentarii*. His faults were their own, in an exaggerated form. But his virtues were their own, too.

This has been a quick sketch, one that does not claim to be a substitute for the complete picture we do not have. It serves its purpose in this book at this point. It will enable us to place in their proper context, as they come up, the men whose testimony we are about to consider. They were Rabelais's friends and enemies, but—following the pattern we have found—they were friends who turned into enemies, enemies who became friends again.

2. Thuasne's Witness: Jean Visagier

We can now go back to Thuasne's discoveries, taken up and completed by Abel Lefranc. They cluster around the years 1536–1538, which saw a huge efflorescence of poetry collections in Lyon and Paris. It was in one of these, written in 1537, in Latin according to the fashion, that Thuasne first came upon proof that in the eyes of Rabelais's contemporaries the author of *Pantagruel* and *Gargantua* appeared without the slightest doubt to be a complete atheist.

Vulteius—Thuasne gallicized the name, taken from Horace, as Voulté; some overly ingenious souls have seen fit to call him Faciot; the poet, who should have known, called himself simply Visagier[20]—was one of those second-rate poets whose life duplicated in every detail the lives of a hundred other literary contemporaries. He was born in Vandy-sur-Aisne near Vouziers and described himself in his books as being from Reims (*Remensis*). He seems to have gotten a master's degree in Paris and taught for a living. When the municipal government of Bordeaux decided to found a great college in that city, one that would be the equal of the Brethren of the Common Life's School of Saint Jerome in Liège or Melanchthon's Wittenberg

20. An acrostic epigram, "Ad Maecenatum," yields JEHAN VISAGIER DE VANDÉ. M.B., "Quel est le véritable nom du poète remois . . . ?" *Revue d'Histoire Littéraire de la France*, I (1894), 530.

University, and a whole colony of Paris schoolmasters was settling on the banks of the Garonne, the first principal of the new
establishment, Jean de Tartas, hired Visagier as a member of
his staff. We have the contract, which granted the beneficiary a
much higher salary—forty livres a year—than that of the other
masters. (Was this a bonus for Greek?) After this the chronology is uncertain for three years, and there are any number of
riddles that need to be solved. All we know is that Visagier
would eventually publish some hostile verses directed at
Tartas.[21] We have no proof that he was at the Collège de
Guyenne under André de Gouvea (the greatest principal in
France, according to Montaigne) when the nephew of old
Diogo de Gouvea—the Portuguese Beda, the reactionary principal of the Collège Sainte-Barbe—took Tartas's place in April
1534 and brought a new team with him (the two Buchanans,
Juan Gelida, Elie Vinet, Antonio de Gouvea). In the first period of the school, at any rate, there was already an atmosphere
of innovative piety, and Visagier would have been able to become acquainted with interesting men. One such was Robert
Breton, a melancholy, uneasy, unstable man, whose answer to
everything was the constant "Homo sum miser, et peccator
inanis; sum quod sum, grato munere caelicolum." (I am a
wretched man and a worthless sinner; I am what I am by the
gracious gift of the gods.)[22] Another was the bearded Zébédée,
whom nobody could get to use a razor—vain, quarrelsome, and
headstrong. When he became a pastor in Switzerland, he was a
trial to Calvin.[23] Yet another was that prince of pedagogues,

21. On Tartas, see Paul Courteault, "Le premier principal du Collège de Guienne,"
in *Mélanges offerts à M. Abel Lefranc* (Paris, 1936), pp. 234-245. Visagier holds
against him, first of all, some difficulties over money. See *Joannis Vultei . . . epigrammatum* (1536), I, 39: "Quod cunctos spoliet nummis Tartesius, illud miraris?" (Does
it surprise you that Tartas robs everyone of his coins?) But there was something else
(ibid., p. 51): "Tu mihi qui imperitas, aliisque vicarius ipse es si me vis servum, sis
herus ipse prius." (You give me orders, but you are just a deputy for others; if you
want me to be your slave, become a master yourself first.) See also Ernest Gaullieur,
Histoire du Collège de Guyenne (Paris, 1874), pp. 60-61.

22. *Joannis Vultei . . . epigrammatum* (1536), I, 22. We have several letters, unfor-
tunately undated, by Breton, who was an unstable man, incapable of settling down.
See *Roberti Britanni epistulae . . .* (Toulouse, 1536), pp. 11, 19, 35, 81; *Rob. Britanni
Atrebatensis epistol. libri II* (Paris: G. Bossozelius, 1540), p. 138.

23. See *Antonii Goveani . . . epigrammaton*, no. 49, p. 23: "Nec voces hominum,
ne te decreta Senatus / Ut barbam ponas, ulla movere queunt." (Nothing men say, not
even senatorial decrees can move you to give up your beard.)

Mathurin Cordier, with his old schoolmaster's plodding manner—original and opinionated, very much like an autodidact.[24]

What is certain is that Visagier wanted to study law and went to Toulouse to enter the school of Jean de Boysonné. There, together with that liberal jurist, he got to know the Toulouse scene, which was then in turmoil, what with its persecutions of the *mal sentans de la foi,* the conflicts between "nations" at the university, and severe repression in the wake of student revolts. Was it then, or later in Lyon, that he met Dolet? At any rate, in the summer of 1536 Visagier saw his first collection of poems through the press: *Epigrammatum libri II,* published in Lyon by Gryphius, the prince of printers—"Castigat Stephanus, sculpit Colinaeus, utrumque Gryphius edocta manu menteque facit." (Estienne edits, Colines designs type, Gryphius with a learned hand and mind does both.)[25] The dedication to the Most Illustrious Cardinal of Lorraine contains a dithyrambic eulogy of Etienne Dolet, that prodigy, that youth who served the cause of the Latin tongue better than anyone else ("juvenis de lingua latina optime meritus") and was preparing to present to France his admirable *Commentaries,* written for the universal benefit of all who loved the Latin tongue ("ad publicam omnium linguae latinae amantium utilitatem").

◄§ Visagier was in touch, then, with the fascinating Lyon scene and was being initiated into the mysteries of that great city of merchants and bankers from all over who came flocking to the four fairs—Florentines and Lucchese, Venetians and Genoans, Swabians and Swiss, agents of the Medici and the Fuggers, Gadaigne who was proverbial for his wealth and Kleberger who was proverbial for his generosity—the city of manufacturers and of inventors, who founded the silk industry in Lyon (this was done in 1535, to be exact, by two Piedmontese from Cheraso, Turquetti and Nariz, in association with a

---

24. *Joannis Vultei ... epigrammatum* (1536), I, 47: "Cordatus linguae, morum vitaeque magister / Corderius censor crimina cuncta notat." (Prudent in speech, Cordier, master of morals and living, observes all crimes like a censor.) Again, in a frequently quoted passage: "Te docuit Christus spernere divitias ... ") (Christ taught you to spurn riches.) Ibid., p. 48.

25. Ibid., p. 54.

Frenchman, Vauzelles), established crafts, and attracted work-
ers. Lyon was a royal city, where the court was in residence for
weeks at a time—a picturesque army, a traveling circus of
courtiers on horseback, great ladies in carriages, servants and
jesters, beasts for riding and beasts of burden. The court in-
vaded the peninsula between the Saône and the Rhone in January of 1535 and set up its noisy camp:

> Lyon c'est ville entre toutes cités
> Pleine de gens, de richesse et d'avoir . . . ,
> Car l'on y peut des grandes choses voir,
> Le Roi, la Reine, Evêques, Cardinaux
> Les trois Enfants, les Seigneurs principaux,
> Ayant crédit envers ce puissant Roi.[26]

> Lyon is greater than all other towns,
> Full of folk and wealth and richest enterprise.
> We feast our eager eyes on many things:
> The king, the queen, the bishops, cardinals,
> The king's three children, all the mighty lords
> Who earned the trust of that powerful king.

This troop made outings from Crémieu to Saint-Chef and
Montbrison in the spring and from Valence to Avignon in the
fall. The Council, however, stayed in Lyon to be with its men
of letters—Lyon, the city of books, where a hundred presses
were in operation, where printers worked under the close scrutiny of the rich men who financed them. From their shops a
stream of paper poured out, paper in wholesale quantities,
printed in French: books of piety and devotion, books for the
popular taste, chivalric romances put into middle-class prose,
old wives' remedies and treasuries of drugs, displays of plants
in wonderful engravings. All of this sustained a small printers'
world that was receptive to innovation, strongly cosmopolitan,
dynamic, original, and turbulent. It was a magnet for men of
letters, attracted from great distances by the bright and warm-
ing Lyon flame. They all sought each other out, found each
other, came to love or detest each other, in shops like that of the
Württemberg printer Gryphius. Sebastian Greif of Reutlingen,

26. *Les Trois Centuries,* II, no. 20, p. 133.

VIRTVTE DVCE   COMITE FORTVNA.

A P V D   G R Y P H I V M
L V G D V N I
ANNO

The printer's mark of Sebastian Gryphius, the main feature of
which is a griffin.

near Tübingen, who used the device of a griffin, had settled in
Lyon at the end of 1522 and had been in business for himself
since 1528. He published classical editions like those of Aldus
and was a tireless promoter of the writings of Erasmus.[27] His
house was the resort of a score of well-known contributors and
proofreaders, from Alciati and Sadoleto to Rabelais and Dolet,
not to mention Sussanneau, Baduel, Hotman, Baudouin,
Guilland, Ducher, and others. It was the meeting place for a

27. See Henri and Julien Baudrier, *Bibliographie lyonnaise*, 12 vols. (Lyon,
1895–1921; photographic reprint, Paris, 1964), VIII, 11–286.

hundred literati of the region and elsewhere: from Marot to Macrinus, from the two Scèves (Maurice and his cousin Guillaume) to Jean de Boysonné, Nicholas Bourbon, Barthélemy Aneau, and who can say how many others from France or the Empire.[28] To visit Gryphius; to have entrée into the circles that were always forming and re-forming around the Lyon publishing houses; what is more, to be able to know in an instant, by leafing through the latest works, the newest and liveliest things that were being thought and written about in France, the Low Countries, Germany, and Italy—what a dream that was for neophytes buried in their native provinces, what a torrent of confused longings for the Athens of, not the Rhone as we would say today, but at that date still the Saône, longings for the allegorical "Lion" of which Clément Marot sang:

> On dira ce que l'on voudra
> Du Lyon, et sa cruaulté;
> J'ai trouvé plus d'honnesteté
> Et de noblesse en ce Lyon
> Que n'ai pour avoir fréquenté
> D'aultres bestes ung million.

> Say what you will of the lion,
> That he is the cruelest of beasts.
> Yet I have found in this Lion
> More honor, more noble features
> Than in a score of other creatures.

It was there, following in the footsteps of so many others, that in the course of 1536 Jean Visagier was initiated into the secrets of the turbulent literary world. He did not stay long. After the publication of his collection in August, he returned to Toulouse and Boysonné in September. Four months later, however, there was a tragic turn of events. In Lyon on December 31, 1536, Dolet stabbed the painter Compaing to death.

28. Letter of Boysonné to Breton, "Lettres inédites de Jean de Boysonné et de ses amis," ed. Joseph Buche, *Revue des Langues Romanes* (1896), p. 361; Boysonné to Mopha, ibid., p. 365; Vulteius to Boysonné, ibid., *Revue des Langues Romanes* (1897), p. 181. Dedicatory letter of Vulteius to Jean de Pins, *Joannis Vultei Remensis epigrammaton libri III. Ejusdem Xenia* (Lyon: M. Parmanterius, 1537), pp. 184–188.

Whether or not it was done in self-defense, as he claimed, it was a nasty business. As the murderer made his escape in great haste over the mountains and headed for Paris in order to plead his case, Visagier, heeding only the dictates of friendship, left for Lyon. When he found that Dolet had fled, he immediately left for Paris. He arrived just in time—on the eve of that memorable day on which Dolet, who had been pardoned by the king on February 9, was honored at a banquet given by his teachers and friends to celebrate his deliverance. In the account he left of this festival of friendship, the author of the *Commentaries* had a kind word ("Vulteius non parvam / De se spem praebens doctis")[29] for the neophyte he put at the same table as the great Budé, Nicholas Bérault, Danès, Salmonius Macrinus, Toussain, Nicholas Bourbon, Dampierre, Clément Marot—and François Rabelais, honor and glory of the art of medicine ("Franciscus Rabelaesus, honos et gloria certa / artis Paeoniae, qui vel de lumine Ditis / exstinctos revocare potest et reddere luci").[30] But Visagier already knew that famous man, certainly since his stay in Lyon. In the *Epigrams* of 1536 can be found a piece addressed to "Rabelaesus," which was reprinted in the 1537 edition. It is a warm defense of Rabelais against a detractor. "The man who said that your heart, Rabelais, was infected with rage when your Muse added spice to the truth lied in saying your writing expresses rage. Tell us, Rabelais, do you sing of rage? No, it was he, that Zoilus, who was armed with rabid iambs. Your writing does not express rage. It expresses merriment."[31] One of the more obvious translations of Rabelais's name provides the pun *rabie laesus* (afflicted by rage). Academic pleasantries like this were the fashion, a fashion that did not disappear quickly. We have only to recall the tag that followed the future Eagle of Meaux throughout his youth: *bos suetus ara-*

---

29. "Vulteius, who gives the learned considerable cause for hope about his future."

30. "François Rabelais, honor and true glory of the physician's art, who can summon the dead back from the shadow of the nether world and restore them to the light of day." The poem, "Ad Cardinalem Tournonium," is printed in Michael Maittaire, *Annales typographici*, III, part I (Amsterdam, 1726), 43-45. [Translator's note.]

31. "Ad Rabelaesum: Qui rabie asseruit laesum, Rabelaese, tuum cor / adjunxit vero cum tua Musa sales, / Hunc puto mentitum, rabiem tua scripta sonare / qui dixit: rabiem, dic, Rabelaese, canis? / Zoilus ille fuit, rabidis armatus iambis; / non spirant rabidem sed tua scripta jocos." *Joannis Vultei ... epigrammatum* (1536), I, 59; *Joannis Vultei ... epigrammatum* (1537), I, 61.

tro.[32] In 1536 Visagier got worked up over an anti-Rabelais play on words, and he took the side of the writer who was accused of being rabid. Who was the assailant? Julius Caesar Scaliger, it has been said. (We will come back to him.) In any case, there is not a word of disapproval or distrust of Rabelais in this 1536 book of verse written by a man who had had plenty of time since 1532 to read *Pantagruel.* The book was certainly known in the circles in which he moved. Yet, far from regarding Jean Du Bellay's physician as a buffoon with suspect ideas, Visagier honored him as a leading light not only of medicine but of Roman law: "Civili de jure rogas quid sentio, Scaeva? / Hoc verum noster quod Rabelaesus ait."[33]

◄§ Yet Visagier was a pious Christian. Like all the poets he emulated—some time ago Ferdinand Buisson devoted several pages to them that struck exactly the right note—he kept invoking CHRIST in his verse (frequently printed in capital letters), so that the name stood out on page after page in the poetry collections of the time "like a sort of homage to Christianity eternal and universal."[34] In the 1536 *Epigrams* there is a long sequence of couplets like so many litanies: "Christus promissus . . . , conceptus . . . , natus . . . , passus . . . , crucifixus," a way to Calvary in dactyls and spondees.[35] One lovely piece sings of Lefèvre d'Etaples, Christ's herald, and of Christ himself, "Christ, the delight of this humble old man; Christ, the refuge of this trembling old man":

> Christus, perfugium senis trementis . . .
> Quod fert pectore fert in ore Christum.[36]

Another piece gives Lefèvre's last will and testament in two lines:

32. "The ox broken to the plow," said of Bossuet (1627–1704). [Translator's note.]

33. "You ask me what I know about civil law? That whatever our friend Rabelais says is true." *Joannis Vultei . . . epigrammatum* (1536), II, 167.

34. Ferdinand Buisson, *Sébastien Castellion, sa vie et son oeuvre, 1515–1563,* 2 vols. (Paris, 1892), I, 52–58. See also Henri Hauser, *Etudes sur la Réforme française* (Paris, 1909), p. 32.

35. *Joannis Vultei . . . epigrammatum* (1536), I, 72.

36. "Christ, the refuge of this tremulous old man . . . What he keeps in his heart he keeps in his speech: Christ." Ibid., p. 73.

Corpus humo, mentemque Deo, bona cuncta relinquo
Pauperibus: Faber haec, cum moreretur, ait.[37]

Then suddenly, after another handsome offering of eulogies,
this time to Gérard Roussel, the compromiser compromised,[38]
comes a piece honoring King Francis and his sound opportunism: you renew the sanctuary, but you do not demolish the edifice of our fathers ("tu nova sacra facies; servas, Francisce,
priora"). This piece, curious evidence of a rather remarkable
state of mind, appeared in Lyon in August or September of
1536. It is pure irenicism. "Everything our fathers did you refuse to abolish; you do not allow the common people to despise
the ancestral rites—that, you tell them, would be a crime. And
you are engaged in destroying with sacred fire the leaders of the
Sects, in purifying Gaul of their damned breed." In August and
September 1536 there could still be heard the last echoes of the
Affair of the Placards (October 1534) and what came afterward.[39]

Nec pateris patrum facta priora mori,
Nec priscos veterum ritus contemnere vulgus
Permittis, tetrum sed scelus esse doces.

These are the sentiments of a moderate. In the same spirit, he
celebrates the accession of Paul III, here elevated to the dignity
of being Saint Paul's interpreter ("interpres Pauli Paulus sensu
abdita monstrat");[40] or the construction of the Collège Royal,
noble *gymnasium* built of living stone ("stant vivi lapides
operis").[41] If he attacks monks, he is quick to distinguish the
bad from the good: "More odious than monks there is nothing
in the entire universe; in the entire universe more holy than
monks there is nothing."[42] Even when confronting the ferocious
Beda, sworn enemy of the humanist race, the poet is careful to

37. "My body I leave to the earth, my mind to God, my goods to the poor: this is
what Lefèvre would say when dying." Ibid., II, 129.
38. Ibid., I, 13; II, 113, 168.
39. Ibid., I, 11.
40. "Paul, the interpreter of Paul, points out hidden meanings with understanding."
Ibid., p. 75.
41. Ibid., p. 65.
42. Ibid., II, 151.

use moderation: "The judgment that you casually render, Beda, disturbs the just, but more than the just it is you yourself who are harmed by your decisions."[43]

Visagier had no intention of compromising with iniquity. He attacked it frequently, as personified by unknowns whom he unhesitatingly consigned to the flames: "Nonne times flammam, carnificisque manus?"[44] At the same time, he confirmed that he was a good friend of Briand Vallée of the Bordeaux Parlement, who was supposed to be an atheist, and he dedicated a sensitive and fitting epitaph to the memory of another famous atheist— poor Agrippa, that ruined man tossed about on so many raging seas:

> Post tempestates, dubiae post somnia vitae,
> Agrippam parta mors requiete rapit;
> Et cui nulla fuit misero per regna vaganti
> Patria, cum superis gaudet habere domum.[45]

Two years after the *Epigrams* of 1536 this restrained liberal who based his judgments on a somewhat fluid set of beliefs published four books of *Hendecasyllables* in an elegant octavo (in Paris this time, at the shop of Colines). It was here that Thuasne, in 1904, discovered irrefutable proof of Rabelais's atheism. Abel Lefranc, taking up Thuasne's thesis, tells us that three poems leave "no doubt about the real religious views" of Rabelais. They constitute "a terrible indictment" drawn up "by the avenging pen of the Christian Visagier." The poet depicts the author of *Pantagruel* as "accusing the entire body of the Christian faith of 'stupid credulity.' Rarely have Rabelais's impiety and atheism [note the pair of postulates] been denounced more energetically." No doubt about it—between 1536 and 1538 Rabelais's break with Visagier had come about solely "for religious reasons."[46]

43. "Dum tua, Beda, levis vexat sententia justos / Plus tibi quam justis haec lingua nocet." Ibid., p. 149.

44. "Don't you fear the flames and the hands of the executioner?" Ibid., I, 46.

45. "After the storms, after the dreams of an uncertain life, death has seized Agrippa and he has found rest; and this poor man, who wandered from realm to realm but had no country of his own, rejoices in having a home among the beings on high." *Joannis Vultei ... epigrammatum* (1537), IV, 257.

46. Louis Thuasne, *Etudes sur Rabelais* (Paris, 1904); Abel Lefranc, "Etude sur *Pantagruel*," in Rabelais, *Oeuvres*, III (Paris, 1922), lvii.

Having read this, we can hardly wait to look at the avenging *Hendecasyllables* of 1538. With excitement we open up the rare collection that contains the Proof. What a disappointment! Rabelais's name does not appear once in the entire volume.

◆§ No matter. Rabelais is not called Rabelais. We are told, however, to look at this long diatribe against an irreligious votary of Lucian, "In quemdam irreligiosum Luciani sectatorem" (p. 10). Look at this fiery piece, no less extensive, directed against an ape of Lucian (p. 30). Finally, look at this imprecation "in Luciani sectatorem," with its carefully chosen insults (p. 71). No doubt about it. The zealous disciple of Lucian, the ape of Lucian, is Rabelais. It is as certain as if his name were printed as big as life on publisher Colines's royal paper. "Yea, but . . . ," said Panurge.

First of all, let us take care of some minor matters. Thuasne did not say a word about the piece "In Luciani sectatorem"; he said two epigrams were involved. Abel Lefranc, for his part, said there were three. I myself find five, adding to the list a diatribe "in quendam poetam" and a curious poem to Guillaume Scève; they are found, respectively, on folios 28 and 42 of the 1538 collection. Two, three, five—let us pray to heaven that someone does not take into his head tomorrow to make it seven! In any case, I have read and reread poor Visagier's boring "poems."

◆§ How is it that the poem to Guillaume Scève has been overlooked until now? It contains the key to everything. "Who is the ape of Lucian?" asks Visagier. "Who is the poet Tortonius? Who is the most ungrateful of comrades? Who, then, is the Zoilus mentioned in my *Hendecasyllables?* You may well ask me, Scève. I shall not tell you. For they will soon betray themselves in their own verses, the very persons whose misdeeds have first been denounced in my verses. And have no doubts: they will be harder on themselves than I am. I spare them. I keep their names secret. I simply attack their faults. They will take it upon themselves to tell you the name along with the fault."[47]

47. "Ad G. Scaevam": "Quis sit simius ille Luciani, / quis Tortonius ille sit poeta, / ingratissimus ille quis sodalis, / quis sit Zoïlus in meis libellis / undeno pede syllabaque factis / undena, licet usque me roges, id / non dicam tibi, Scaeve: nam brevi

Since we are better informed than Scève was said to be in 1538, we know what Visagier was pretending to hide from him. If the poet Tortonius and Zoilus were one and the same, and if that one was the poet Borbonius—Nicholas Bourbon—there is every likelihood that the most ungrateful of comrades and the ape of Lucian were similarly one and the same, and that he was Etienne Dolet.

3. Visagier, Bourbon, Dolet

Bourbon and Dolet. Visagier's 1536 *Epigrams* are full of these two names, and of their praises. From the preface written to the Cardinal of Lorraine, in which the young Dolet's prodigious work, *Commentaries on the Latin Language*, is extolled in dithyrambic terms ("at quod opus? quam minime a juvene exspectandum? quantae diligentiae? quanti laboris? quam exacti judicii?"),[48] to the end of the second book, a score or so of pieces, short and long, bear witness at once to Visagier's admiration, affection, and fondness for the young humanist. Corresponding to the almost amorous wording at the beginning ("Oh, to have won him over! *huic uni placuisse, prima laus*")[49] is the absurd prayer on page 11: "Oh, God, to be like him! *O Deus, o similem me daret esse Deus!*" Not to speak of the balanced epithets ("si quisquam orator sitque poeta bonus, / utraque viventi est laus concedenda Doleto")[50] or, finally, this ecstatic utterance: "Oh, how beautiful your body is! How beautiful your soul is! It is impossible not to say: this is a perfectly beautiful man!" (Tam pulchrum est corpus, mens est tam pulchra Doleti / Totus ut hoc possim dicere: pulcher homo est!)[51]

---

se / prodent, carmine seque vindicabunt. / Quorum crimina carmine ante risi. / In se, nec dubites, severiores / fient, quam fuero hactenus, peperci / horum nominibus, scelus notavi. / Nomen crimine cum suo, docebunt." *Jo. Vulteii Rhemensis hendecasylla- borum*, fol. 42.

48. "What a work it is! How little to be expected of a young man! How much care, how much work, what perfect judgment!"

49. "To have won his approval alone is the highest praise." *Joannis Vultei ... epi- grammatum* (1536), I, 8.

50. "If ever there was an orator and a poet of distinction, praise for both should go to Dolet now." Ibid., II, 102.

51. Ibid., p. 152. Other pieces in the same vein are: I, 12, 13, 16, 25, 29, 51, 53, 73; II, 100, 106, 110, 134, 158, 161, 173.

As for Bourbon, if he had a smaller share he still had nothing to complain about. Born in 1503 in Vendeuvre in Champagne, the son of an ironmaster, Bourbon was several years older than Visagier. He soon acquired a reputation for facile versifying and taught in Amiens, Troyes, and Langres. In 1529 he was received by Margaret of Navarre. In 1533 Vascosan in Paris and Cratander in Basel published his collection entitled *Nugae*, which immediately got him into considerable trouble.

◄§ His proselytizing tendencies were unmistakably revealed, starting with the preface, dated Troyes, April 1, 1533. He took the person he was addressing, Louis de l'Estoile (Lucius Stella) of Orléans, to task for his fear of death. "What do I hear?" he exclaimed with passion. "So, is your faith in Christ so feeble that the mere thought of death overwhelms you with terror? Was it for nothing then that you gave so much of your time and energy to Holy Writ?"[52] He went on to develop at great length various orthodox and Pauline themes—how the Son of God through his own death put an end to the death of men, how by the same death He reconciled the creation with the Creator, and so on. All of this had not the slightest taint of heresy. Similarly, who could reproach him for putting these grandiloquent words into Christ's mouth:

Aer, terra, fretum sylvae, mons, ignis, Olympus
Omnia transibunt, set mea verba manent.[53]

Or even for saying of a priest that he mumbled like a monkey ("non aliter turpis simia labra movet")—which, after all, did not require any great originality. It was less acceptable for him to castigate monks for their pride: "Without number at the present time, the wearers of cowls declare themselves to be worthy of heaven and judge themselves to be gods." Eyebrows at the Sorbonne were raised because of eulogies inspired by, and actually addressed to, the great Erasmus, the pious Gérard Roussel, and the suspect Michel d'Arande—suspect even

---

52. *Nicolai Borbonii Vandoperani nugae. Eiusdem Ferraria* (Basel: A. Cratander, 1533), fol. A3.

53. "Air, earth, sea, forest, mountain, fire, Olympus itself—all will pass away, but my words shall remain." Ibid., fol. B4.

though he was the consecrated bishop of Saint-Paul-Trois-Châteaux through the grace of Margaret: "Oh, prelate, subdue the world, the flesh, and the devil! Teach that justification is born of a living faith [*vivae justitiam fidei*]! And show the people what the celestial realms are, what is the way of death and what the way of salvation!" The exhortation and eulogy were perhaps not entirely disinterested: "O mihi concedant una isthic tecum" (May the gods give me leave to live there, in your diocese, with you),[54] he exclaimed a little further on. He could, however, in any case be reproached for hurling savage invectives, in an "Ode in Praise of the All High," not only at scholastic logic ("nil tenebamus, nisi syllogismos arte / contortos variosque nodos")[55] but even, in the manner of Luther, at the Roman she-wolf, the she-wolf clad in purple ("lupa purpurata, lerna malorum"),[56] and, perhaps even worse, at monkhood, which he flogged with the accustomed epithets: "greedy race, dissolute, lovers of your stomachs, abandoned to luxury" (gens rapax, vecors et amica ventris / perdita luxu). Everything was subjected to this treatment—the worship of images and the veneration of the saints, those false gods ("saxeis stabant simulacra templis / sacra diis falsis et item deabus / unde diversis variisque festis / cuncta fremebant / in statis poni pietas diebus").[57] And, according to him, the celibacy of priests abandoned them to desire: "nuptiis mire vetitis libido / foeda revixit."[58] All of this was duly concluded with praise of the king, of the Collège des Trois Langues, and of faith in Christ: "Laus Deo Patri Dominoque Christo / spiritu cuius bona cuncta fiunt!"[59] Of the Virgin Mary, however, not a word.

It would have been hard for such audacity not to provoke a reaction, especially since there was a piece at the end addressed to the crucified Christ, the first part of which developed the Lu-

54. Ibid., fols. C3, E3, I6, M4.

55. "We had nothing, only artfully twisted syllogisms and knots of various kinds."

56. "She-wolf in purple, procuress of evil men."

57. "In the stone temples stood the images sacred to false gods and goddesses, and they all demanded to be taken out and displayed on various fixed holidays as an act of piety."

58. "When marriage, strange to say, was forbidden, filthy lust was revived."

59. "Praise to God the Father and to Our Lord Christ, by whose spirit all is made good." Ibid., fol. L6 ff.; *Nicolai Borbonii Vandoperani nugae* (Paris: M. Vascosanus, 1533), fol. 18 ff.

Nicholas Borbonius Poeta.

Drawing of Nicholas Bourbon by Hans Holbein the Younger.
[He wears a simple cap, not a laurel wreath. In his description of
the drawing Febvre may have been relying on a mistaken memory.—Translator.]

Reproduced by gracious permission of Her Majesty Queen Elizabeth II.

theran theme of the Christian who is powerless to do good and
despairs as he contemplates his God suffering for him: "For it is
I, oh pious Jesus, who am the cause of thy great pain. I am full
of shame and heavy with impiety, I am to myself an abomina-
tion, to live is loathsome to me, but your voice restores my

courage, saying: Come to me, all who sin! With my wounds I shall heal your wounds."[60] It is not to be wondered at that Bourbon spent some time in the king's prisons. In spite of Margaret's intercession, it required some time, as well as the surety of the Cardinal of Lorraine, before the Parlement of Paris, under express orders from the king, released the culprit in May 1534. He thereupon thought it prudent to spend some time in England (do not forget that fateful date, October 17–18, 1534, the Day of the Placards). He was taken into the entourage of Anne Boleyn (he apparently had a high opinion of Cromwell and Cranmer). There he became the tutor of a series of well-known young aristocrats. To these favorable associations, on top of his unusual experiences, he owed the good fortune—rather irritating to us, because we would have liked Rabelais to have had such good fortune!—of meeting Holbein and having him do a marvelous drawing of him, one that captures all his absurdity to the life. He is shown crowned with a laurel wreath.

◄§ Nicholas Bourbon, Germain de Brie, Salmonius Macrinus—Visagier chose these as the three poets of the age, all learned and all pious. In the case of Bourbon the choice was all the more justified since, alone of the three, he was in exile: "Borbonium expulsum Gallia tota dolet"; and again: "Anglia me lacerum retinet, vestitque poetam; plus peregrina favet, quam mea terra mihi."[61] Ten more pieces bear witness to the devotion the Martial of Vandy felt for the Horace of Vendeuvre. Everything, it seemed, bound the two natives of Champagne closely together—their tastes, their talents, and their friends. So it seemed, and yet there was something else.

Anyone who has a mind to go carefully through the *Nugae* of 1533 in the Paris edition, the one put out by Vascosan, will find a short piece there, "Ad Visagerium remensem," which hints at feelings that are somewhat ambiguous: "What do you mean by weighing me down, crushing me by unrestrainedly praising my *Nugae* to the skies? Believe me, you are better at

---

60. *Nicolai Borbonii ... nugae* (Basel, 1533), fol. L8v; *Nicolai Borbonii ... nugae* (Paris, 1533), fol. m2.

61. "All of Gaul grieves for Bourbon in exile" (*Joannis Vultei ... epigrammatum* [1536], I, 68); "England has taken me in all tattered and clothes the poet; a foreign land is kinder to me than my own" (ibid., p. 58).

making nothings than I am; you must be, since you publish them on your own account and read mine at the same time."[62] Is this a not quite precisely stated fear of plagiarism? It seems likely. Besides, this 1533 collection is pervaded by an obsession with plagiarism. Bourbon keeps careful watch over his hemistichs. Woe to him who would come upon him in the night and try to steal them from him: "Cum mihi surripias noctu mea carmina, Rufe . . ."[63]

At any rate, Bourbon came back from England and immediately brought to Lyon a "short, youthful work on morals for young people."[64] Its preface, dated Troyes, September 1, 1536, speaks of the pious sentiments of the poet as well as of a recent discovery. He had just met something rare, a superior soul. In the very same ink with which he was to write a letter dated Lyon, the fifth of the Kalends of October, in which he categorically condemned atheists and infidels, Bourbon expressed his rapture at having seen face to face the noble, the pure, the beautiful Dolet. It was as unforgettable a moment as the earlier occasion of his first visit to the great Budé, father of both kinds of eloquence. Undoubtedly, Bourbon was repaying a debt. Dolet must have introduced him to Lyon's literary circles.[65] It must be said, however, that he paid generously.

After that, one day at the shop of Gryphius—but let Bourbon tell the story himself, as he did, not the very next day but two years later, in 1538, in the greatly expanded edition of his *Nothings:* "On my return from England I went to Lyon. I went to the shop of Gryphius, the famous printer. 'Well, what's new?' He handed me a book entitled *Epigrams.* I read it, avidly turning the pages. Why waste words? I found innumerable poems there that had been snatched from my *Nugae,* misappro-

62. *Nicolai Borbonii . . . nugae* (Paris, 1533), fol. O5v.

63. "Since you steal away my poems by night, Rufus . . ." *Nicolai Borbonii . . . nugae* (Basel, 1533), fol. B4v.

64. *Nicolai Borbonii Vandoperani opusculum puerile ad pueros de moribus, sive paidagogeion* (Lyon: S. Gryphius, 1536).

65. He said it in so many words in "De amicis lugdunensibus, ad Steph. Doletum" (On My Friends in Lyon, to Etienne Dolet): "Quos mihi Lugduni tua conciliavit amicos / fides, Dolete, et gratia / efficiam ut chartis mandata fidelibus olim / aeterna vivant nomina." (For the friends your steadfastness has procured for me in Lyon I shall repay you by putting their names one day in steadfast books, where they will live forever.) Ibid., p. 40.

Woodcut, probably based on Holbein's drawing, that appeared in some of Bourbon's books. It was the occasion of mocking verses by Jean Visagier.

priated sentences, stolen themes—all patched together with the ineptness of a man with no talent. I do not name him for the moment, but I shall expose him if he continues, and he will be seen in his true colors, that robber, that brazen thief."[66] It was

66. "Peregre agebam Lugduni, a Britannia / reversus nuper, et officinam Gry- phii, / typographi inclyti, ingressus, hominem rogo, / statim, novorum ecquid librorum excuderet? / Libellum tum profert, titulo Epigrammaton. / Lego, percurro avidissime: quid pluribus / verbis opus? Invenio illic e nugis meis / surrepta carmina innumera, et sententias / alio tortas et argumenta pleraque / adsuta ineptiis nebulonis illius! / Nunc

nice of Bourbon not to put Visagier's name in black and white
after giving the title and publisher of his 1536 collection! A
flood of diatribes and epigrams followed the first piece—"In
eundem," "In versificatorem furacem":[67] "Well, here I am. You
thought I died at sea, while I was over there among the English.
I've come to take back those goods of mine that you've stolen!"
Unrelenting, Bourbon said it over and over again. We feel like
shouting, along with Visagier, as we look at the ridiculously os-
tentatious crowned portrait, "Tu loqueris semper, semper at illa
tacet!" (You are always talking; at least it keeps quiet!)

❧ Visagier responded, starting in 1537. First, in a second
edition of his *Epigrams*, put out by Parmentier in Lyon—in
four books this time—he began by eliminating from the first
two books, in which the 1536 pieces were reprinted in the same
order, all the flattering dedications and compliments addressed
to Bourbon. "Grata bonis sunt, grata malis tua carmina"[68]—that
compliment was "ad Borbonium poetam" in 1536, but "ad
Marotum poetam" in 1537. Much patient effort was expended.
"Ut nunquam tulerit Campania Belgica vates,"[69] said Visagier
in 1536, speaking of Bourbon, who was a native of Champagne.
"Ut nunquam tulerit praeclara Gallia vates,"[70] said Visagier in
1537, speaking of Marot, who belonged to the nation. There
were no fewer than eight pieces that were thus transferred from
Bourbon to Marot between 1536 and 1537. Others were transferred from Bourbon to Etienne Dolet, a bit of bad luck that
Gilbert Ducher found amusing, since the following year Visagier broke with Dolet.[71] Visagier was undoubtedly sorry he

---

homini parco, olim nominabitur / si pergit; et suis pictum coloribus / videbit se, impro-
bum os, lavernio impudens!" *Nicolaii Borbonii . . . nugarum* (1538), p. 250, no. 77.
Other pieces referred to are: p. 251, nos. 78 and 79; p. 252, no. 85; p. 288, no. 33; p.
289, no. 36; p. 460, no. 62; and others.

67. "To the Same"; "To the Thieving Versifier."

68. "Your poems are pleasing to good and evil men alike."

69. "A Celtic bard such as Champagne had never before produced."

70. "A magnificent bard, such as France had never before produced."

71. "Dum laudare duos ille poeta poetas / Vulteius voluit, messuit antheria-
cum. / Illorum alter eum plagii condemnat, et alter / Scripta ejus gerrhas qualiacunque
vocat . . . / I nunc, pasce lupas immites mitis." (When the poet Vulteius wished to
praise two poets, he reaped a harvest of ashes. One of them accused him of plagiarism,
and the other said his writings were trivia . . . What can you expect when you use
kindness on cruel wolves?) *Gilberti Ducherii*, p. 101.

changed the inscription of the 1536 piece, "Gallia tres habuit doctosque piosque poetas,"[72] which had originally referred to Bourbon, de Brie, and Macrinus. He dedicated it to Dolet, de Brie, and Macrinus in 1537 and changed two of the verses. In 1536 Visagier was grieving over Bourbon's exile in England: "Lingonis ora gemit, Charitesque novemque sorores / Borbonium expulsum Gallia tota dolet."[73] In 1537 he was grieving over Dolet's flight after Compaing's murder: "Hunc Genabum, Charitesque novemque sorores / et Stephanum expulsum Gallia tota dolet."[74] A flood of diatribes followed. They are spread throughout Books III and IV of the new collection, and their titles are very clear: "In nugatorem poetam," "In quemdam poetam malum," "In quemdam ridiculum poetam," "De eodem et suo imagine," "In eundem furacem qui alium furti accusabat," "In eundem qui, simulachrorum osor, se sculpi jussit."[75] This was open war. Other epigrams were called simply, "Against Gorgonius." It was a veritable tidal wave of ridicule.

In 1538, in the *Hendecasyllables*, there was another change of tone. Visagier pretended to admit his plagiarism: "I took some verses from your famous collection? Well, so I did. I admit it. I was simply helping to circulate verses that were already well known." The irony became even more pointed: "Did I have the power to eclipse an author known throughout the universe?" After this came the direct assault: "Your verses have been stolen, you say? Don't you mean others' verses? *Tuas, inepte? Rides? Pelisso negat, et negat Perellus, negant scrinia nuda Pradiani, compilata tua rapacitate!*"[76] That was the final shot. Things began to cool down, and when we move from Book III to Book IV we suddenly find ourselves in the presence of pure idyll: "I beg you, oh poet Bourbon, tell me: who told you I

72. "France has had three learned and pious poets." *Joannis Vulteii . . . epigrammatum* (1536), I, 67.

73. "The region of Langres laments, and not only the Graces and the Nine Sisters, but all Gaul bemoans Bourbon in exile." Ibid., p. 68.

74. "Not only Orléans and the Graces and the Nine Sisters, but all Gaul bemoans this Etienne in exile."

75. "Against a Trifling Poet," "Against a Certain Bad Poet," "Against a Certain Ridiculous Poet," "On the Same and His Picture," "On the Same, a Thief Who Accuses Another of Theft," "On the Same, Who Hates Images But Ordered a Likeness To Be Made of Himself."

76. "Your own, you incompetent? Are you joking? Pelisso says they aren't, Perellus says they aren't, Pradianus' empty desk, rapaciously raided by you, says they aren't!" *Jo. Vulteii Rhemensis hendecasyllaborum*, fol. 44v.

wanted to do you harm? Who started this quarrel?"[77] The
question is comical, and Visagier was not without a sense of
humor. Still, it was necessary to find a scapegoat. Those were
the rules of the game. *Quis auctor dissidii fuit?* It was a fine excuse to reel off anathemas:

> Vae illi qui male vult tibi, Poeta;
> Vae illi qui male velle te mihi optat; . . .
> Communem, rogo te, putemus hostem![78]

What is amusing is that at this very moment Visagier was
writing to a friend, in his *Inscriptiones*, "You swear to me that
Bourbon feels as well disposed to Visagier as he does to himself? I find it hard to believe . . . Still, I would like to believe it.
But do you know the only reason I would? Because there is
really no reason for him to feel well disposed to me!"[79] Meanwhile, in his *Nugae* Bourbon was providing the same spectacle
as Visagier in his *Hendecasyllables*. Having cursed, he blessed.
Or, rather, he blessed and cursed in turn, with no apparent discomfort. In Book V two pieces "in Poetam furacem" repeat the
old accusations. Then, an amazing thing: there is a reconciliation ("Jo. Vulteio amico").[80] It is the same in Book VIII. There
is a final piece entitled "In quendam alienorum carminum sup-
pilatorem et corruptorem."[81] After that, two more pieces contain the name Visagier of Reims.[82] "Let all be forgotten. Some
evil person wanted to cause trouble between us. Let us frustrate
the knave with our loyal friendship." (At sceleratum hominem,
stabili fallamus amore.) "There is no better device with which
to frustrate him." (Ille potest falli non meliore dolo.) Using the
adjective *sceleratus*, concluding with the word *dolo*—didn't that
make one think of a familiar name? The second piece, however,
does not speak of only one evil person. There were impious

---

77. "Quaeso, dic mihi, Borboni poeta, / quis dixit male velle me tibi? / quis auctor
dissidii fuit?" Ibid., fol. 89v.

78. "Woe to those who wish you ill, O Poet. Woe to those who want me to wish
you ill; I call upon you to join me in finding our common enemy!" Ibid., fol. 90r.

79. *Joan. Vulteii Rhemi inscriptionum libri duo. Xeniorum libellus* (Paris: S. Colinaeus, 1538), fol. 29v.

80. *Nicolai Borbonii . . . nugarum* (1538), pp. 288, 289, 314.

81. "Against a Certain Raider and Corrupter of Other People's Poems." Ibid., p.
460.

82. Ibid., pp. 451, 474.

little men, *impii homunculi*, who wanted to destroy the friendship of the two poets: "Vides, amice Vultei, quibus illi
artibus / nituntur impii homunculi cavellere / amicitiam
nostram?"[83] Here impiety was directed against friendship, that
sacred sentiment, rather than religion. The heroicomic drama
came to an end with a reconciliation at someone else's expense.
The ingenuousness of the protagonists and their concern that
none of their lucubrations be lost permit us to follow the drama
all the way from Gryphius's shop to—shall we say the house of
Dolet? In any case, if there is some doubt about that, there is
none about something else. The *ingratissimus sodalis* of whom
Visagier spoke to Guillaume Scève was Dolet. But wasn't
Dolet—Dolet, not Rabelais—also the *simius Luciani* that
got Thuasne and (a more serious matter) Abel Lefranc so
worked up?

4. Etienne Dolet, Ape of Lucian

At the beginning of his career, Visagier had pursued Dolet with
a veritable frenzy of friendship. We know this from his own
words, and from the way he flew to his friend's aid when Dolet
was in danger. He was not alone. All of Dolet's other companions, already famous or competitors on the way to fame, had
with one mind applied themselves to finding favor with that
violent man. They had been successful. They congratulated and
embraced each other after their triumph. But someone disturbed the harmony, with his own hands dissipating the enormous capital of admiration and devotion that asked only to be
of service to him. Someone had zealously laid the groundwork
for the astonishing explosion of hatred in the abnormally large
number of poetry collections that came out in the year 1538,
hatred directed against that selfsame Dolet in which all the
Latin poets, now incensed, joined—from the Catholic, Sussanneau, doing battle with someone he called Three Bushels (Medimnus),[84] to the wag, Gouvea, who sneered: "I shall not praise

83. "Do you see, Vulteius, my friend, with what wiles impious little men try to ridicule our friendship?"

84. No one, I believe, has called attention to these 1538 pieces called "In Medim-
num" (*medimnus* = a measure equivalent to three bushels). They are savage. *Huberti
Sussannei, legum et medicinae doctoris, ludorum libri nunc recens conditi atque aediti*
(Paris: S. Colinaeus, 1538), fols. 16r, 16v, 34.

Dolet. Why should I? He does the job so well himself."[85] Even Gilbert Ducher, who attacked Dolet, under the name of Cloacus the mad Ciceronian, as the detractor of Erasmus.[86] Even Nicholas Bourbon, who in 1536, in his *Opusculum puerile*, had decked with garlands a person he no longer even cared to mention in his *Nugae* of 1538. They give us a curious gallery of portraits of Etienne Dolet that Christie did not know about and was not able to take into account. All of them agree and are in harmony, whether we are speaking of Sussanneau's Three Bushels, with his wooden face, horrible skinniness, madman's eyes, and stammer, wearing a short Spanish coat that his visitors found so remarkable, or Gouvea's Dolet, also with a wooden face, a sinister look that cut off merriment, smiles, and graces, and a monstrous body that could have been inhabited by the transmigrated soul of Roman Cicero, except that the soul had been diluted, having lost all its virtue and efficacy in that

85. "Quis te non laudem, credo, Dolete, requiris? / Id me tu melius facias." *Antonii Goveani . . . epigrammaton*, p. 16.

86. Nor has anyone, I believe, called attention to this piece by Ducher, "De Cloaco et Duro." Conforming to the rule of repetition stated above, it is related to a whole slew of short pieces on the same theme (Pythagoras, metempsychosis, and the reincarnation of Cicero and Simon de Neufville as Dolet). They are undoubtedly connected with no. 29, "Ad Villanovam defunctum," in Dolet's *Carmina* (*Stephani Doleti orationes duae in Tholosam. Ejusdem epistolarum libri II. Ejusdem carminum libri II. Ad eundem epistolarum amicorum liber* [undated, probably Lyon: S. Gryphius, 1534]). Ducher's piece of 1538 is followed by other pieces called "In Durum" (*Gilberti Ducherii*, pp. 12, 104, 105). These are followed by two pieces by Gouvea that appear in both his collections of 1539 and 1540 (*Antonii Goveani . . . epigrammaton*, pp. 22, 31; *Antonii Goveani epigrammata. Ejusdem epistolae quatuor* [Lyon: S. Gryphius, 1540], I, lv; II, xxiii). Marot himself participated in the debate by means of an epigram first published in 1538: "Le noble esprit de Ciceron romain / laissa le Ciel, en terre se vint rendre / au corps entra de Dolet." (Cicero the Roman's noble spirit / Has left its home in heaven, come to earth, / And entered into Dolet's body.) Finally, Rabelais—or, rather, Rabelais's publisher—in 1542: "Dont l'esperit de Villanovanus se indigna d'estre de ses labeurs frustré." (Thus the spirit of Villanovanus is indignant at being deprived of the fruit of his labors.) See Richard Copley Christie, *Etienne Dolet, the Martyr of the Renaissance* (London, 1899; reprint, Nieuwkoop, 1964), pp. 383–385.

That Durus is Dolet there can be no doubt. Apart from textual analysis, we should recall that his printer's colophon, adopted in 1538, read, "Durior est spectatae virtutis . . ." It is fascinating to read Dolet's definition of *durus* in his *Commentaries* of 1536: "asper, vel agrestis, vel crudelis, ferreus, inhumanus" (harsh, rude, cruel, fierce, inhuman). *Commentariorum . . . tomus secundus*, col. 529.

On the use of "transmigration" in the sixteenth century, see below, "Gargantua's Letter and the Immortality of the Soul" (chapter 4).

D O L E T V S,

Durior eſt ſpectatæ uirtutis,
quàm incognitæ,
conditio.

Etienne Dolet's mark shows a hatchetlike instrument (*doloire*)
cutting wood. The Latin motto means, "It is harder when
virtue is recognized than when it is unknown."

great blob of flesh.[87] It is a series of lifelike snapshots. They go with the one a young anti-Ciceronian addressed in October 1535 to Gilbert Cousin, the humanist from the Franche-Comté who was secretary to Erasmus in his old age. It sketched a Dolet barely thirty years old who looked forty because of his premature baldness, his high, wrinkle-furrowed forehead, his bilious pallor, his shaggy eyebrows, and his short coat that stopped above the hips.[88] He was fascinating for all that, coarse and sensitive, drunk with pride and crazy about music, a remarkable swimmer, quick to cross swords—he was a force of nature, one that was out of control and unsettling. This was the man Christie called the Martyr of the Renaissance and Boulmier the Martyr of Free Thought. First and foremost he was, unquestionably, a martyr to Etienne Dolet himself.

What was he thinking about in his prime, which for him was so close to the end of his life (he died at thirty-seven)? If we are to believe his Latin orations against Toulouse and its inhabitants—*Orationes duae in Tholosam,* published in Lyon by Gryphius in the spring of 1534—he belonged to no party. He was satisfied with the religion of his fathers and hallowed tradition. He avoided all "novelty." Yet his liberated intelligence was able to pass lofty judgments on men and their actions. There is a very fine passage in the *Orationes* in which he took

87. "Quem buxeus vultus, macerque, et oculi truces / et proferentis tertiata voca-bula / flagrare felle livido satis indicant." "In Medimnum" *Huberti Sussannei . . . ludorum,* fol. 16r. Again: "Extabet atra macie, et exili toga / tegitur Medimnus." Ibid., fol. 16v.

"Tuum os hic rigidum, minax, severum, / os dirum, os tetricum, os catonianum / romani fugiunt sales, jocique." *Antonii Goveani . . . epigrammaton,* p. 27; *Epigrammata* (1540), II, x. See also a short piece that for once is not without wit: "Pythagorae, Dolete, placet si dogma renati / non merum est animam si Ciceronis habes. / At tantam molem et tantos diffusa per artus, / virtutem certe perdidit ille suam." (If we believe the doctrine of Pythagoras, Dolet, it is no miracle if you contain the soul of Cicero reborn. But spread through such a mass and such huge limbs he has surely lost his power.) *Antonii Goveani . . . epigrammaton,* p. 31.

88. "Togulam gestabat hispanicam, vix nates contingentem, eamque crassam et attritam. Vultus adeo funesto quodam atroque pallore ac squalore . . . ut dicas ultricem Furiam pectori adfixam." And, predicting that he would be executed, "Nam et hoc accidere solet atheis." (For it often happens to these atheists.) *Gilberti Cognati Nozereni opera multifarii argumenti* (Basel: H. Pierre, 1562), I, 313; translated in Christie, pp. 224–228. What Odonus wrote here that Ortensio Landi said should not be attributed to Dolet: "As for other masters, I recognize only Christ and Cicero. Christ and Cicero are enough for me." The confusion has been made a number of times.

his text from the punishment inflicted on the regent Jean de Caturce, who was burned alive in Toulouse in June 1532. He
loudly proclaimed his hatred of persecution, which was inhuman and, moreover, totally useless: "I beg all to believe," he
began,

> that I am not in any way a follower of that impious and ob-
> stinate sect [of Lutherans], that nothing is more distasteful to
> me than their desire of new doctrines and systems, that there
> is nothing I more strongly condemn. I am one who honours
> and reveres only that faith, only those religious rites, which
> have the sanction of antiquity, which have been handed
> down to us by a succession of pious and holy men, which
> have been hallowed by the adhesion of our ancestors ... But
> what is the reason (it must be a bad one) that cruelty is the
> delight of Toulouse? ... You have lately seen one, whose
> name I forbear to mention, burned to death in this city ...
> He may have spoken at times rashly and presumptuously, at
> other times intemperately; he may even have acted at one
> time in such a manner as to deserve the punishment due to
> heresy. Yet when he inclined to repent, ought the way of sal-
> vation for both body and soul to have been closed against
> him? Do we not all know that any man may err? ... Why,
> when he was striving to emerge from the depths and whirl-
> pools in which he had been overwhelmed, and to reach some
> good and safe haven, did not all with one consent help to
> throw out a cable, so as to afford the possibility of reaching a
> safe anchorage?[89]

This is a passage of genuine and rare freedom of spirit, a passage that places in opposition to the persecutory Christianity of
Toulouse's inquisitors and judges the Christ of justice and charity, meekness and peace that a humanist would want to reconcile with the great teachings of antiquity. It is a passage that
also, while putting its author above the fray, nevertheless betrays Christian feeling. Can the same be said of another letter,
dated November 9, 1534, in Paris, the day before three heretics
were delivered to the flames on the very Place Maubert where

89. Christie, pp. 107–108.

twelve years later . . . ? In it we find a harsh condemnation of the Reformers, "a foolish sect, led away by a pernicious passion for notoriety," that by its absurd conduct had provoked a resurgence of hatred and persecution. "At these tragedies," Dolet then concluded, "I play the part of a spectator. I grieve over the situation, and pity the misfortunes of some of the accused, while I laugh at the folly of others in putting their lives in danger by their ridiculous self-will and unbearable obstinacy."[90] This is putting a low value on Christian convictions and dismissing them with alacrity. And can we speak of Christian feeling in connection with a piece, quite a remarkable one, in his *Carmina?* It is included in the book printed by Gryphius in 1534 that contains his *Orationes duae in Tholosam.* It deals with the theme of death, which is not to be feared but desired, or at least awaited with serenity: "Exspetandam esse mortem." Who would be so mad, so foolish, Dolet asks, not to want to exchange his life for death? Who would refuse to be freed of the body, that terrible prison? There is nothing unusual about all of this, but here is the conclusion: "Death? Let us not fear its blows. It will either grant us to be without feeling or it will allow us to enter a better world and a happy state—unless our hope of Elysium is entirely groundless."[91]

We should no doubt resist registering too strong a protest against the unbeliever. The dubitative remark introduced by *nisi* is a stylistic device found in the writing of far more authentic Christians than Etienne Dolet. All of them got it out of their notebooks of Latin expressions. As for the alternative "either . . . or," it could, after all, with a little good will, be taken as a rough approximation, a clumsy prefiguration, of Pascal's wager.

---

90. Christie, pp. 206–207. For Dolet's real thought, see *Stephani Doleti Galli Aurelii liber de imitatione ciceroniana adversus Floridum Sabinum. Confutatio maledictorum, et varia epigrammata* (Lyon: E. Dolet, 1540), p. 37. It is a remarkable passage: "Do not discuss doctrine! When you try to define it, it disappears. (*Dum religionem vellunt, elimant, perpoliunt.*) That is the outcome of Lutheran inquiry." An ambiguous position.

91. "Ne mortis horre spicula, quae dabit / sensu carere, vel melioribus / locis tegi, et statu esse laeto / Elysii est nisi spes inanis." *Stephani Doleti orationes duae,* p. 225. Busson observes that the piece summarizes the argument of Book I of the *Tusculan Disputations.* Henri Busson, *Les Sources et le développement du rationalisme dans la littérature française de la Renaissance (1533–1601)* (Paris, 1922), p. 130, n. 4; cf. later a different line of reasoning by Scaliger, which does not treat the body as a ragged garment or a prison but takes into account the beauty of its structure.

It is nonetheless true that the piece does not sound particularly
Christian. In addition, it must be noted that of the forty poems
contained in Book I of the *Carmina* of 1534 and the nineteen
poems in Book II there is no piece with a religious or Christian
inspiration—except for two, both dedicated to the Virgin Mary:
"De laudibus Virginis Mariae." They are next to the last ones
in the collection, as if by accident. The last piece, however, is
addressed "Ad Musam" (To the Muse), and so the Renaissance
has the last word.

⋙ Such was the position held by the author of the *Commentaries*—subtle, original, and for most educated men of the time
no doubt quite difficult to grasp. It was a position that was sure
to make him the object of attacks from all sides. To hold on to
it he would have had to be sure of passionate support and devotion, but with his unhappy turn of mind he undertook to tax
everyone's patience. All those who had devoted themselves
wholeheartedly to the task of freeing him from prison after
Compaing's murder were horrified to read in the dedication to
Budé in Book II the astonishing assertion that, since the universe had abandoned Dolet, Dolet had never received help from
anyone but Dolet.

We learn Visagier's reaction as soon as we open the *Hendecasyllables* of 1538. In the first few pages there is a piece addressed "to a certain ingrate" (In quemdam ingratum) that proclaims his indignation. Dolet is not named, but who could have
made a mistake? "Do you, who owe your life to your friends,
dare to say that none of them in the days of your misfortune
were to you what a friend should be? Do you dare to complain
to anyone who will listen that you were abandoned? Is that
how you mean to respond to everyone's affection, you scoundrel? When you took flight, full of anxiety and not knowing
where to turn—if no one had helped you, tell me, you miserable wretch, where would you be now?" This is followed
by an evocation that is tragic if one thinks of that stake on
Place Maubert. Poor Dolet always inspired such prophecies:
"Wouldn't dogs and wolves have devoured your limbs? And if
you had any relatives left to be present at the terrible scene
when the judgments rendered against you were carried out—

judgments so like the ones your father was familiar with—wouldn't your shameless eyes have beheld them standing in a circle around you?"[92]

This is the first. Others follow. In Book II, Visagier speaks of Guillaume Scève. Did Dolet swear that he really loved him? Come now, Dolet loves only Dolet. And he doesn't love himself as a reasonable person, a normal person, would ("Quibusque / Mens est integra, sana, pura, simplex"), but as the impulsive unfortunate he is: "hunc, cui nemo placet, placetque nulli" (nobody pleases him and he is pleasing to nobody).[93]

Again in Book III Visagier makes up a transparent anagram to denote Dolet, *Ledotus*. "You proclaimed that I was your greatest, your best friend . . . Now you say the opposite. Suddenly you reject our friendship. But you cannot give any reason for the change, except that I am different from you and that I will not approve of you when you do not deserve it . . . I want friends I can approve of!"[94] In Book IV several pieces marked "In Ledotum" resume the familiar themes: Dolet is the most evil of men—is that surprising? When one has a scoundrel for a father one is not likely to be an honest man.[95] And there is always the stinging reminder: "If you are still alive, it is because of those whom you abuse."

To summarize: What made the *Hendecasyllables* intriguing to readers in the know were Visagier's two quarrels, with Bourbon and Dolet. There is no mention at all of other well-known persons. There is not a thing that could possibly refer to Rabelais—nothing except the pieces entitled "In Luciani simium" and "In Luciani sectatorem" that engaged the attention of Louis Thuasne and Abel Lefranc. The time has come to look at them.

92. "Tibi nemo si vaganti / incerto pede et anxio adfuisset / dic, o dic ubi nunc miser jaceres? . . . / Canibus lupisque praeda / essent non tua membra? / Et superstites si / parentes tibi forte qui adfuissent / dum spectacula talia exhiberes / et jussas lueres, misere, poenas / exemplo miseri tui parentis / nonne illos oculi tui impudici / vidissent tibi proximos?" *Jo. Vulteii Rhemensis hendecasyllaborum*, fol. 9v.

93. Ibid., fols. 47v, 48r.

94. Ibid., fol. 84.

95. "Nam tuo parenti es / natus ipse simillimus; sed esset / certe res nova si mali parentis / esses filius optimus virorum." (For you were born in the exact image of your father, and it would surely be something unheard of if you, the son of an evil father, were the best of men.) Ibid., fol. 91v. Does this explain Dolet's silence about his family? Other pieces against Ledotus are: fols. 92r, 96r, 96v.

◄§ How many are there? Two? Or three? Three, says Abel Lefranc. Thuasne omitted one diatribe entitled "In Luciani sectatorem" in Book III of the *Hendecasyllables;* it is a declamatory, virulent imprecation, full of coarse obscenity, directed against a scoundrel: "Unclean spirit, criminal, cultivator of vices, storehouse of iniquity, enemy of God! Listen to the punishments to which I consign you!" There follows an enumeration of the repulsive labors to which Visagier condemns the votary of Lucian's infernal tongue.[96] But there is nothing, no characteristic detail, that allows us to apply this piece to Rabelais. It ends with a wish that the villain's immortal soul should really be destroyed, just as he claimed it would be, to serve as an example to those whom he had misled. The other two pieces have more interest.

One, "In quendam irreligiosum Luciani sectatorem," appears in Book I of the *Hendecasyllables* in the wake of two pieces marked "In quendam ingratum" that are directed against Dolet and that we have commented on above. (This is a physical detail of some significance.) In this piece one specific characteristic is mentioned: the accused Lucianist sneers every time he comes across the word CHRISTUS in Visagier's verse: "This is fine Latin! This is pure Latin! As if any Roman ever had a name like Christus on his lips!" Visagier was indignant: "Sneer away, you ape of Lucian. You won't win me over to your doctrines. To deny the existence of a God in Heaven who wished his son to die for the salvation of men; to deny the transgression of Adam who delivered the human race into the cruel jaws of death, to deny the Last Judgment and the punishments of Hell—this is madness. Take care. Take care and repent while there is still time." And once again there was the sinister prophecy that constantly trailed Dolet: "If you do not repent, you will soon die. It's all over, you wretch. It's all over. You're dead, *ah miser peristi!*"[97]

I'm sorry, but Dolet's name came out quite naturally. Can

96. Ibid., fol. 71v.

97. "In libris quoties meis loquor de / Christo, hoc sit quasi nomen haud receptum / rides ... / Dicis nec latio fuisse in ore / nomen ... / Nec te, bellua caeca, poenitabat / in caelo esse deum optimum negasse / qui natum voluit suum mori, ne / humanum misere genus periret? / Ad Christum igitur miser recurri. / Hoc si non facias brevi peristi. / Actum est, heu miser! ah miser, peristi!" Ibid., fols. 10–11.

Thuasne claim it is Rabelais—and Abel Lefranc along with him? Really? Do that ultra-Ciceronian Latin purism and that lunatic humanist affectation of proscribing Christ's name because it is not classical sound like Master Francis? Do they sound—wonder of wonders—like the pious Erasmian who wrote the so-called letter to Salignac in 1532, a gesture of affection and gratitude to the Ciceronians' bête noire, Erasmus himself? They do sound like Dolet—like the impassioned author of *De imitatione ciceroniana.* Many years ago Maittaire, in his lengthy account of the printer at the sign of the adze (*doloire*),[98] observed that in no Latin poem by Dolet is Christ mentioned. There are references to Deus, Jupiter, the Divi, the Superi—never Christus. There is a good reason why "In quendam irreligiosum Luciani sectatorem" comes right after the two pieces directed at the *ingratum* in Visagier's collection. Ingrate and Lucianist—Dolet was both. Dolet was ultra-Ciceronian, and it was Dolet who was destined to fall into the hands of the public executioner.

But what of the piece "In Luciani simium"?[99] It deals with a scoundrel (*o sceleste*). Let us take the word in its true meaning. Dolet had more than one *scelus* to his credit in 1538. On the other hand, Rabelais, as far as we know, never murdered anyone. This scoundrel, far from repenting or listening to the sensible reproofs of those who cared for him, was rushing to his destruction with a kind of frenzied speed. It was just this speed, this frenzy in Dolet, that all who saw him remarked on: "Ah, te / pergis perdere, et in dies furorem / exauges magis ac magis; reprensus / nec mutas, pudor, o sceleste, mentem!" (Oh, you are rushing to your destruction, and every day your frenzy increases; and though you are rebuked you do not change, you scoundrel. For shame!) There is more. The shameless one calls those who do not want to join him in his wrongdoing "the worst of men": "eos qui / nolunt criminibus tuis favere / nec laudare tuas opiniones" (those who do not wish to approve of your crimes or praise your opinions). This is exactly what Ledotus did. The reason for his break with Visagier was that the latter did not want to follow where he would have liked to lead

98. Maittaire, pp. 9–113.
99. *Jo. Vulteii Rhemensis hendecasyllaborum*, fols. 30v–31r.

him: "nam amicos volo quos probare possim!" (for I want friends I can approve of).[100] What he wanted to convince his friends of was that everyone dies for all time, that everyone is subject to fate, that there is neither eternity nor immortality, that there is no God, that man is in no way different from the animals—these were the wretched man's fine doctrines. He taught them to the unfortunates who came to his house every day and listened to him talk: "Quae doces miseros, tuam domum qui / et colloquia qui in dies frequentant."[101] Furthermore, the ape of Lucian was a hypocrite. If someone who was not in his circle ("qui non de grege sit tuo") questioned him, he acted like a good Christian, rejecting Lucian and explaining why he despised him and labored daily to be more pleasing to Christ: "causas / dans cur oderis ipse Lucianum, / Christo cur studeas placere soli."[102] But when one of his own cronies came up to him, they would have a good laugh over it. Belle te simulasse Christianum rides! Enough of such wretched subterfuges, Visagier concludes by saying. If not, God will punish you, so severely that you will have to confess, "Vixi, non homo, sed canis. [I have lived like a dog, not a man.] The poet Visagier foresaw this catastrophe, and he was telling the truth when he predicted it a hundred times. Now it is too late!"

Nothing in this vehement poem suggests Rabelais. Everything about it proclaims Dolet. There is still a fourth piece, in Book I of the Hendecasyllables. It is called simply "In quendam poetam": " 'Christ?' you say. 'I love him more dearly than my own eyes!' His cross is always on your lips; under his aegis you will suffer fire, injury, the cross, the wheel, poison, derision, insults, blows—so you swear. But in truth you are an impious poet. Anyone who really knew what your mind was like, your viper's tongue, your morals, your attempts against the law, your

100. Ibid., fol. 84v.

101. A hasty reading of these lines in "In Luciani simium"—"Adductus precibus meis, parentis / vel Christi potius cruce"—might lead one to think that the Lucianist's father is meant, and that he is adding his prayers to those of Visagier. But parentis goes with Christi. (Persuaded by my prayers or, even more, by the cross of our father, Christ . . .)

102. "Omnia omnibus, omnia interire; / fato obnoxia cuncta; sempiternum et / immortale nihil; Deum esse nullum; / nos nil dissimiles putasque brutis . . . / Sunt haec impia, belluina, vana / quae doces miseros, tuam domum qui / et colloquia qui, in dies, frequentant." Ibid., fol. 31r.

fraudulent acts—in short, all of your life, which is that of a scoundrel—would come to the conclusion that in the whole universe there is no creature more repulsive than you." He then proceeds to his offensive opinions: "To believe that Christ was never born, that Christ never suffered the Passion, that he was neither betrayed nor laid in the tomb—is that loving Christ more dearly than your own eyes?"[103] Finding this invective insufficient, Visagier takes it up again in two pieces that follow, both directed "in eundem": "Can I speak of you as a man? Come now! *Nam tu, nec hominem sapis, nec ipse es!*" (You don't seem like a man, nor are you really one!)

Read and reread these pieces a dozen times. They all obviously refer to the same person. The phrasing, the insults, and the arguments move in and out of one and then another. Every word cries out: Dolet. Dolet, that is, as depicted by his enemies. Not a word suggests Rabelais.

Could he be Rabelais—this brute, this partisan who insulted those who refused to espouse his aggressive and violent materialism? This impassioned propagandist and fanatic who was indoctrinating a group of misguided unfortunates? And how could this foolhardy madman, this propagandist known to everyone, also be Pamphagus, the dog in the *Cymbalum*, who knew the truth but refused to reveal any part of it?

And what of the total silence of contemporaries? They vied with each other to have their say about the falling out between Dolet and Visagier. It was too good a windfall to pass up. Can it be that these men, scandalmongers by nature and by profession, knew nothing about a falling out between Rabelais and Visagier? Read the passages again. They deal with a split between two close friends who were very fond of each other and saw each other often; not merely once did Visagier try to convert his friend, but a hundred times—*centies.* In the small world of the Lyon humanists a startling break occurred between two prominent men, both surrounded by friends and enemies, and was there nothing—no echo, no epigram, no attempt at reconciliation? The silence is inexplicable to anyone acquainted with these men, with their vanity and their naive con-

---

103. "Christum credere non fuisse natum, . . . hoc ne est plus oculis te amare Christum?" Ibid., fol. 28r.

viction that their differences mattered to the universe. Rabelais's atheism, which did not bother the poet Visagier in 1537, revealed itself to his suddenly opened eyes in 1538; can it be that he alone was disturbed by the discovery? Would his friend Sussanneau—pious Sussanneau—who was associated with him in Lyon for a long time, have serenely included in his collection, *Ludi* (of that very year, 1538), the well-known little poem in which he depicted himself as being sick in Montpellier and not expecting any effective treatment except from seeing and being in the presence of his dear Rabelais?[104] And was there no one in Montpellier, where Rabelais practiced from September 1537 to April 1538 in full view of everyone and with general approval, who was capable of noticing the fanatical impiety, propagandistic fury, and contemptible hypocrisy that Visagier denounced in the "Ape of Lucian"? In all truth, it would take strong reasons to enable us to go along with Thuasne's conviction.

5. Rabelais, Rabella, and Chesneau

Yet it will be said that Rabelais has always and everywhere been ritually referred to as the French Lucian. True, the Samosatan's name was often applied to the man from Chinon. All the same, it was hardly a monopoly.

Calvin provides the proof, if any is needed. In 1550 he opened the gates of hell (where he placed the Epicurean Lucianists) not only to Rabelais but also to Des Périers, Antonio de Gouvea, and a number who were not named. He said expressly, "*Paucos nomino* [I name a few], but there are others." The *Excuse aux Nicodémites* of 1544 speaks of Lucianists in the plural, as did the letter of Antoine Fumée earlier. Erasmus was called Lucian, Des Périers was called Lucian, anyone was called Lucian who happened at some time to have thoughts that were a little out of the ordinary or who gave the semblance of so doing. It was a family name, not a personal one.

To see Rabelais as the ape of Lucian Thuasne was indeed moved by other reasons. In a collection of *Inscriptions* by Visagier, published by Colines in December 1538, he came across a piece almost at the beginning of the book entitled "Ad Rabel-

104. *Huberti Sussanei . . . ludorum*, fol. 41.

lam."[105] Rabella! We can just imagine the scholar's heart pound-
ing as he read, in the copy he was looking at in the Bibliothèque Nationale, François Rabelais's own name written in a
sixteenth-century hand opposite the Latin name.[106]

Visagier describes Rabella as a curious man whose curiosity
makes him utterly unbearable. He might be called the king of
snoopers and meddlers. "You want to know everything," Visagier reproves him, "who I am, how I live, who my father is,
where I was born and where my house is. You want to know
my name and my sweetheart's name, my style of life, what I eat
and who works for me, whether I am lucky in love or ever have
been. You want to know—" In the next line Visagier's muse
gets a little too outspoken for us to quote in translation. But immediately after this digression comes the expected conclusion:
"There is nothing that you do not want to know. But in your
rage to know all, Rabella, what you want to know is not enough
and it is too much (*non satis et nimium scire, Rabella, cupis*)."

Rabella, Rabelais—Thuasne gave free rein to his imagination.
It is possible that Rabelais was curious, very curious, *too* curious. It is even probable. In any case, the fact does correspond to
the image we have of his unquenchable thirst for knowledge.
But, to complicate matters, another epigram and another poet
now come into the picture.

◄§ He was a very minor poet, a friend of Visagier and a
native of the same region. Nicholas Chesneau—in Latin, Quer-
culus—was born in Tourteron in the Rhetelois district of the
Ardennes. He had the protection of the Guises, was a Catholic
who was smitten with the Counter-Reformation, and became
dean of the chapter of the church of Saint-Symphorien in
Reims after having perpetrated several works in Latin—notably
two books of *Epigrams* and one of *Hendecasyllables* published
in Paris in 1553 by Richard. Since Visagier's *Hendecasyllables*
are dated 1538, there was an interval of fifteen years between
the two collections. The difference between the two could,
of course, be more than that of publication dates. At any rate,
in Chesneau's *Hendecasyllables* there is also a piece marked

105. *Joan. Vulteii Rhemi inscriptionum,* fol. 6.
106. Thuasne actually says that he found "Rabelaesum" written alongside a poem
by Chesneau. See below. [Translator's note.]

"In Rabellam." Thuasne immediately concluded—with what proof?—that "Chesneau, in league with Voulté, also wrote a little poem that is no more than an extension of Voulté's epigram ... A comparison of the two pieces seems to indicate that the authors consulted with each other before writing them."[107]

Let us be more cautious and say that Chesneau's epigram seems to be an adaptation of Visagier's, expanded, extended, and stretched out, as it were. If you want to know what's going on in town, Chesneau tells us, invite Rabella to dinner. Everything that's happening anywhere, whether at church, in the square, in the great houses—the king's bill of fare, important business transactions, domestic quarrels, marital infidelities, young girls' romances, miscarriages—you will know everything, everything! And what a parasite Rabella is! From this point I shall try to give a literal translation: "He lunches, dines, and sleeps in the house of the great lord next door, who loves a good belly laugh and gathers about him all the Rabellas he can. He allows these robbers of reputations to joke with him, insult him, abuse him—but he cannot sit down to dinner unless he sees at least two or three Rabellas with their elbows on his table!" And then comes the final invective: "Rabella! You are nothing but a babbler, a buffoon, a worthless fellow, a pestilential poisoner of every good and chaste reputation. Your tongue is dripping with viper's venom. Your tongue is more dangerous than the deadliest poison. Your tongue wounds gods and men. Your tongue is leaden, black, and shameless. Believe me, Rabella, you are nothing but your tongue!"

Is this Rabelais? Let us take note of something rather disconcerting. The parasite living off the great, the inquisitive bore, the gossip and slanderer, the viper's tongue, is very much like the Rabelais of "l'enraigé Putherbe." One might think this was a free copy of Visagier's epigram (1538), revised and amended with the help of *Theotimus* (1549).[108] What is its date? Thuasne's assertion is entirely gratuitous. There is nothing that allows us to say Chesneau wrote his piece "in league with Voulté." On the contrary, we know how jealously the poets of

<hr />

107. Thuasne, pp. 322–323.

108. *Gabrielis Putherbei Turonici . . . , Theotimus sive de tollendis et expungendis malis libris, . . . libri III* (Paris: J. Roigny, 1549). On *Theotimus*, see below, ch. 2, sect. 5.

the time guarded their property. Besides, we know nothing of the relationship between Chesneau and Visagier or of any possible relationship between Chesneau and Rabelais. Where would the former have seen the latter? Perhaps in the Guise household—whence many kinds of rivalry might have originated. I am inclined to believe that the piece was written after Visagier's death (1542) and the appearance of *Theotimus* (1549) and was more or less contemporary with Rabelais's death (April 1554?)—Chesneau's *Hendecasyllables* came out in 1553. As for "the great lord next door," if that refers to Cardinal Du Bellay, we should note that his disgrace did not date from the accession of Henry II, as was thought—that is, April 1547. It dated from the spring of 1549 (Romier settled the matter),[109] and it was only after that that criticism of the cardinal could be somewhat more open.

Be that as it may, one thing should be noted. Chesneau's Rabella, no more than Visagier's, is not an atheist or a dogmatic unbeliever. Where does that leave us? Thuasne, later followed by Abel Lefranc, asserted that Chesneau's Rabella and Visagier's Rabella were one and the same. Perhaps. But why should Chesneau's Rabella, identified as Rabelais, also be Visagier's *simius Luciani?* On one hand, we find in one collection three diatribes aimed at an unnamed Lucianist, an enemy of Christ, and a monster of impiety. On the other hand, in another collection of the same year and the same manufacture we find a satirical sketch of a gossip—and this sketch is later taken up by another versifier who turns the gossip into a parasite and calumniator. How can we say that in both cases the same man is the subject and that the man is Rabelais because Rabella is Rabelais? Well, Chesneau also calls his Rabella *Rabula:*[110] "Dico te

---

109. Lucien Romier, *Les Origines politiques des guerres de religion*, I (Paris, 1913), 106 ff. [Translator's note.]

110. On *Rabula* (= shyster), see Dolet, *Commentariorum . . . tomus secundus*, col. 561: "Rabulam a rabie dici volunt, ut is sit rabula qui in negotiis agendis acer est, et rabiosus." (*Rabula* is said to come from *rabies*, because a shyster is one who is sharp in his business dealings, like a mad dog.) The word was in common use among the humanists. Erasmus called Farel a "homo rabula, effreni tum lingua tum calamo" (with unbridled tongue and unbridled pen); P. S. Allen and H. M. Allen, eds., *Opus epistolarum Des. Erasmi Roterodami* (Oxford, 1906–1958), V, 537. Guillaume Postel used the word for the Cenevangelists who fought against the worship of Mary; *Alcorani seu legis Mahometi, et Evangelistarum concordiae liber . . .* (Paris: P. Gromorsius, 1543), p. 35. And so on.

rabulam, Rabella, scurram" (I say you are a shyster, Rabella, a worthless fellow). Chesneau's Rabella has a viper's tongue: "Lingua es vipereo cruenta tabo." Isn't Rabelais *rabie laesus*, and doesn't Visagier's *Luciani sectator* have a hostile tongue, *inimica lingua?* So the chain was forged, as Thuasne saw it. On foundations as feeble as these he erected his "Note sur la rupture de Voulté avec Rabelais."[111] No one has bothered to question his assertions. But wait! There was someone in 1906 who expressed this sensible objection: "It is not certain that the poetic pieces 'Ad Rabellam,' 'In Rabellam,' 'In quendam irreligiosum Luciani sectatorem,' and 'In Luciani simium' refer to the same person." That someone was none other than Abel Lefranc, in his illuminating article on the Sainte-Marthe family and *l'enraigé Putherbe*.[112] There is no question that he was on the right track then, and if he had continued he, too, would have concluded that Visagier's three anti-Lucian pieces refer to Etienne Dolet, not François Rabelais. But if the ape of Lucian and the votary of Lucian refer to the printer at the sign of the *doloire* and not to Master Alcofribas, what is left of Thuasne's edifice? Not only does the edifice collapse, but it is no longer possible for anyone to find in Visagier's epigram "Ad Rabellam" and Chesneau's epigram "In Rabellam" (assuming they really do apply to Rabelais) the slightest pretext for saying, "It is clear that to Visagier, who knew him well, and to Chesneau, who took up his quarrel, Rabelais was above all Rabelais the atheist."

Everything evaporates. No one, as far as we can tell, ever said of Rabelais what Visagier said so clearly of Dolet in 1538: "He is an enemy of Christ, and he denies Christian revelation." This being so, we may wonder: if Thuasne had not started the legend of an anti-Rabelais passage written by Calvin in 1533 and if he had not, on his own authority, applied to Rabelais the epigrams that Visagier wrote in 1538 attacking Dolet's atheism—if he had not been guilty of these serious errors, could anyone possibly have conjured up the figure (original, perhaps, but unreal) of a Rabelais who was a propagandist for atheism in 1532?

111. Thuasne, pp. 315–336.
112. Abel Lefranc, "Rabelais, les Sainte-Marthe et l'enraigé Putherbe," *Revue des Etudes Rabelaisiennes*, 4 (1906), 338, n. 2.

6. From Rabellus to Charidemus

We have already made the acquaintance of Nicholas Bourbon, the copious sayer of Nothings. Thuasne neglected to examine his relationship with François Rabelais, and so did we.

At first glance it was slight—and cold. A single piece was dedicated to the poet-physician by the Apollo of Vendeuvre. It appeared for the first time in the 1538 *Nugae,* and here is a translation: "It is rare nowadays that I meet Du Costé (Lateranus), Du Maine, and Saint-Gelais. Urgent and serious business keeps them busy at court; such are the times. But, dear Rabelais (*mi Rabelaese*), when I have to leave and go where my wishes call me (more accurately, where fate carries me), please greet them for me."[113] That is all, and it is not much—a simple favor for the sake of friendship, or not even that—of politeness. There is not a word of praise for the person of whom the request is made. If one knows anything about the manners of the time, the communication seems quite dry. Still, Bourbon undoubtedly did not lack opportunities to see Rabelais. He lived in Lyon at two different times, both precisely when Rabelais himself was there. The two men had friends and activities in common. They were both present at the banquet for Dolet in Paris. So it is odd that Bourbon addressed nothing more than a versified calling card to Rabelais, distinguished physician that he was. Are there perhaps some pieces by him that refer to *Pantagruel*'s author under a pseudonym? That question arises naturally if one knows anything about the literary customs of these academic Apollos.

❦ Dr. L. de Santi, a well-known scholar from Languedoc (of whom more later), pointed out in an article in 1922 in the *Revue du Seizième Siècle* that there was a rather curious piece, "In Rabellum," in the 1533 version of the *Nugae:*[114] "What is

---

113. *Nicolai Borbonii ... nugarum* (1538), p. 247, no. 67.

114. "Rabelais et Nicolas Bourbon," *Revue du Seizième Siècle*, 9 (1922), 171–175. The piece is in *Nicolai Borbonii ... nugae* (Paris, 1533), fol. 17v; *Nicolai Borbonii ... nugae* (Basel, 1533), I, fol. 7v; *Nicolai Borbonii ... nugarum* (1538), p. 153. De Santi is therefore mistaken in saying that Bourbon substituted the piece "In Rabelaesum" for the epigram "In Rabellam" in the 1538 edition; the former appears on p. 247, the latter on p. 153.

the idea, Rabellus? You keep diverting our pupils from their honorable employment, the study of letters human and sacred. Do you want them to ruin the wholesomeness of youth in your quagmires, your buffoonery wrapped in obscurity, your nonsense, your literature of eating, your shameful barbarism, your excrement, and your filth? Listen to me: allow our schoolboys to remain in good moral health, or else, you frenzied madman, you will have to fear that the very Muses whom you have put to flight will put you to flight, pursuing you across the universe and making you rabid, Rabellus (*ac ne te in rabiem inferant, Rabelle*)!"

Dr. de Santi claims there is no doubt. This is about Rabelais—about his literature in the vernacular, the *Great and Inestimable Chronicles of the Great and Enormous Giant Gargantua* (first known edition, 1532), the *Horrible and Frightful Deeds and Prowesses of the Very Renowned Pantagruel* (1532); perhaps also the *Pantagruelian Prognostication* (end of 1532). These were all books that Bourbon, as a moralizing pedagogue, regarded as dangerous for the young and likely to interfere with their studies. Bourbon, pious and violent, entirely won over to the ideas of the Reformation, could very well have been angered by Rabelais's vernacular writing. As a *vates* infatuated with Greek and Latin he could also very well have refused to brook the scandal of an excellent humanist—a true man of learning, someone capable of preparing for Gryphius editions of Manardi's medical epistles, the aphorisms of Hippocrates, even the testament of Cuspidius—all at once, without the slightest regard for what people would think, getting the idea ("in mentem tibi quid, Rabella, venit") of doing for Nourry, a publisher known for popular jokebooks, a work like *Pantagruel*, something contemptible in the eyes of a moderately intelligent humanist. He could only have done it out of greed (*libri quaestuosi*). Let us recall for a moment all those astonishing assessments of Rabelais's work by critics of the seventeenth, eighteenth, and nineteenth centuries, from La Bruyère to Lamartine, and the lack of comprehension they reveal of its real meaning, value, importance, and (one can say) dignity. "Only a few persons of eccentric tastes pride themselves on understanding and esteeming this work as a whole," wrote Voltaire; "the rest of the nation laugh at the jokes of Rabelais and hold his book in contempt."[115] As for Lamartine, for him Rabelais was "a poisonous, fetid mushroom born in the dunghill of the medieval cloister, the defrocked monks' pig who regaled himself in his dirty sty and loved to spatter his dregs on the face, manners, and language of his age."[116] This is an elegiac indeed! The poet Borbonius in 1538 had no idea he would have such glorious progeny.

If the piece "In Rabellum" refers to Rabelais, as is more than likely, it is a curious, if somewhat grudging, witness to the success of his vernacular publications. In addition, note that the piece ends with the juxtaposition of "Rabellus" and "rabid." This was the theme of the piece Visagier addressed to Rabelais in 1536 and reprinted in 1537, which we referred to earlier. "The man who said that your heart, Rabelais, was infected with rage . . . lied." Who was the man? Dr. de Santi said it was Julius Caesar Scaliger. We will come back to him. Although de Santi called attention to "In Rabellum" he did not think it was Bourbon—who was in any case linked to Scaliger in 1533.

⋙ It is now appropriate to look into collections that were contemporaneous with those of Bourbon. In Paris in 1538 Colines published a volume of *Ludi*, which bore a name we have already come across—Hubertus Sussanneus (Hubert Sussannée or Sussanneau). This Hubert was apparently an unstable and violent man, half scholar, half pedagogue, about whose checkered career little is known. He started out in 1531 rather strangely for a humanist, as thurifer to Pierre Cousturier (*Sutor*). Cousturier was a luminary of the Carthusian order and one of the most aggressive of Our Masters of the Sorbonne against Luther, Lefèvre, Erasmus, and their followers.[117] The

---

115. *Philosophical Letters*, trans. Ernest Dilworth (Indianapolis, 1961), letter XXII, p. 106.

116. Alphonse de Lamartine, *Cours familier de littérature*, 28 vols. (Paris, 1856–1869), III, 424.

117. Bourbon attacked him in his *Nugae:* "In Sutorem Erasmi obtrectarorem" (Against Sutor, the Detractor of Erasmus); *Nicolai Borbonii . . . nugae* (Basel, 1533), fol. 12; *Nicolai Borbonii . . . nugarum* (1538), p. 143. He also appears in the Library of St. Victor: "Sutoris adversus quemdam qui vocaverat eum friponnatorem, et quod fripponatores non sunt damnati ab Ecclesia" (Sutor, Against One Who Called Him a Rogue, Holding That Rogues Are Not Condemned by the Church); *Pantagruel*, ch. 7.

following year Sussanneau paid court to Beda. Then, two years
later, in 1534, he wrote a preface to an edition of Pierre Rosset's
Christus that he dedicated to King Francis; it was packed with
a profusion of scriptural quotations taken from Kings, the
Psalms, St. Paul, St. John, and Proverbs. Two years after that
he told some of his life story to Philippe de Cossé, bishop of
Coutances, at the beginning of a *Dictionarium Ciceronianum*
that Colines published in 1536: how he had expounded Virgil
and Cicero in public in Paris; how he had become acquainted
with the great Macrinus, the French Horace, and through him
with the bishop of Coutances; how he had attached himself to a
Breton gentleman with whom he had voyaged in the West and
after that, returning to Bourges and moving on to Lyon, had
been employed by Gryphius as a proofreader and had made the
acquaintance of Dolet. Still later, passing through the country
of the Allobroges, he went to Turin to expound Cicero, win
over a rector, address the youth of Pavia, and make a Virgilian
pilgrimage to Mantua. It is all accurate, no doubt, but the accuracy is a bit embellished. For example, Sussanneau glides over
his stay among the Allobroges, but we know that he was assis-
tant to the rector of schools in Grenoble and had to flee in August of 1536 after some violent scenes that were in character for
him. Four years later he returned to Grenoble in spite of the
unhappy memories of his first stay, and again had to be dismissed. "He sets a bad example," say the registers. "When he
begins a book he completes only two or three chapters, then
begins another. Besides, he is a blasphemer of God and drunk
most of the time, setting a bad example to those students who
carry swords, since he is always fighting with one or another of
them." It is not at all surprising that he got along well with
Julius Caesar Scaliger and that he became (after a conversation
that he recalls in the preface) the editor of that violent Italian's
second oration against Erasmus. It was completed on September 25, 1535, and was published by Vidouaeus—with Sussanneau supervising the work—probably at the end of 1536, although it bears the date 1537. Erasmus had recently died, and
Sussanneau, whose violent actions never interfered with the
prudence of his pen, dedicated a contrived epigram to him in
his 1538 *Ludi*: "On earth a cloud kept you from seeing part of
the heavens; now you are seeing it all clearly, without clouds"

(divina in terris per nubem ex parte videbas; omnia nunc clare, nunc sine nube vides).[118]

This was a man who hid as best he could under the protective wing of the judge Jean Morin and at the same time communed in Cicero with Dolet (as well as Scaliger), piously invoked the Virgin, and paid a tribute to the medical skills of Rabelais that has often been cited. The piece is "Ad Rablaesum cum esset in Monte Pessulano." "Hubert," he says, speaking of himself, "is languishing in the great city of doctors. There are no drugs that can relieve his illness. You alone have the power, Rabelais—if, as he believes, the only thing that ails him is not seeing you. Your serene countenance will restore his composure and, once he sees you, the languor he feels in all his limbs will disappear." The piece, which is found on folio 41 of the *Ludi*, is more than polite, it is ingratiating. On folios 8, 8 verso, and 29 verso (not to speak of folio 37, where there is a piece called "In Rabulam"), three pieces marked "In Rubellum" or "Ad Rubellum" can be found. Here, to begin with, is the last of these: "Occurris nulla non potus luce, Rubelle; qui te non potum, te bene mane videt!" Ronsard adapted it for his famous *Epitaph for François Rabelais*, published at the end of November 1554:

> Jamais le soleil ne l'a vu
> Tant fust-il matin, qu'il n'eust bu.
>
> Never did the sun come up
> And see him ere he quaffed a cup.

Is it Rabelais? It would be a strange coincidence if Sussanneau's tippler Rubellus were someone else and not the man from Chinon. The two other pieces, one "against," the other "to" Rubellus, express with an absence of invective the sad disapproval of a moralist deploring the conduct of a man who has tendencies that are suspect: "I know more than enough, Rubellus, of what you have perpetrated in your house—things that should be rubbed out with black salt and blotted with cuttlefish

---

118. *Huberti Sussannei . . . ludorum*, fol. 3v.

ink. I know it, but I won't dirty the whiteness of the paper."[119]
Or again: "Austere Cato and Scipio as companions for you?
No, Rubellus. If your style is that of the festival of the Quirina-
lia, that is where you should look. You'll find your true companions there. One or two? No. Three hundred thousand thousand."[120] As for the piece marked "In Rabulam," it has the
same flavor: "You don't like it when people condemn your writings today. I call on the judgment of posterity, is what you say.
And you accuse your times of lacking justice! The Tituses and
the Virgils had no such attitude. Nor did great Apelles, who
wanted to show his painting to the public. But you refuse—because you are the only one who likes what you do."[121]

There are no insults, just the sad tone of a man who had high
hopes of someone and has suddenly seen them vanish. It is the
tone Scaliger would adopt in some of his pieces marked "In Bibinum" and the tone Bourbon himself adopted in his "In Rabellum."

◄§ Is this all? As I was carefully rereading Nicholas Bourbon's *Nugae* (1538 version) I came across a curious piece. As
far as I know, it has never attracted the notice of Rabelais's
friends. It concerns a certain Charidemus—which can be translated Dear to the Plebs, something very close, perhaps, to La
Bruyère's *charme de la canaille*.[122] Here is a rendering of it:

> Many people who have seen you lately, Charidemus, have re-
> ported that you want to publish a new book. And why not?
> It used to be your wont to publish books, and you have a
> great reputation. But there is not a soul who can say what the
> subject of this new work is, Charidemus. Some are looking
> forward to arcane secrets on the name of Jesus, the magic
> arts, evil spirits. Others believe it will be revelations about
> the properties of precious stones, the stars, the days when

119. "Plus satis scio quae domi, Rubelle, / patrasti, sale defricanda nigro / et loli-
ginis allinenda succo. / Sed nolo niveam inquinare chartam." Ibid., fol. 8r.

120. "Cum Catone gravi atque Scipione / non satis tibi convenit, Rubelle. / Quiri-
nalia si sapis, requires. / Illic, reperies tuos sodales." Ibid., fol. 8v.

121. "Reprendi non vis hodie tua scripta, sed inquis: / judicium melius, postera
secla ferent. / Et quasi judicio careant, tua saecula damnas. / Mens diversa / Titis Ver-
giliisque fuit," and so on. Ibid., fol. 37r.

122. "Fit only to delight the rabble." La Bruyère on Rabelais in "Des Ouvrages de
l'esprit." [Translator's note.]

one should seek or avoid Venus. One group speaks about mushrooms and about chard and its virtues; another about beans and other vegetables. Some people claim that you are dealing with leprosy, or with the horrible mange—two diseases well known to you. Believe me, anything is better than singing of the horrific wars of giants or of mountains piled on mountains. But it is not about any of these. Listen to my guess and, please, for your own sake, let me tell you what it is. You are going to treat of the cranes and how, once upon a time, your ancestors the Pygmies valiantly took them captive.[123]

All this about giants and their horrific battles, about a voracious curiosity that moves from magic to botany by way of astronomy, medicine, and any number of other mysteries—it brings the name Rabelais to our lips. Note that Bourbon's piece does not appear in the 1533 *Nugae*. It was therefore probably written between 1534 and 1538. At that point Rabelais, who had not published anything since *Gargantua* (which undoubtedly went on sale in October 1534), may have been thinking of another book.

More arrows are then let fly at "Charme de la Canaille," to render the name à la La Bruyère. He is a Hellenist. He is a Platonist, or at least he claims to be. He says he is a new Hippocrates—three pieces that were included in the 1533 *Nugae* tell us that. One of them advises: "Charidemus has christened himself Hippocrates. He would do better to become Harpocrates." Harpocrates, with his finger on his lips, personified silence. The second teases: "Charidemus has produced a Greek grammar. He

---

123. "Multi qui nuper tecum, Charideme, fuerunt / edere velle novum te retulere librum / Credibile est isthuc: quid ni? Nam emittere libros / consuesti jam olim, magnaque fama tua est. / Sed quo argumento . . . / adhuc dicere nemo potest. / Arcana exspectant alii de nomine Jesu, / de magica arte alii, de cacodaemonibus / de geniis alii gemmarum . . . / Crede mihi, hoc melius quam si horrida bella Gigantum / aut caneres montes montibus impositos." *Nicolai Borbonii . . . nugarum . . .* (1538), p. 417, no. 132. See the piece that follows: "Scribere te dicis, Charideme, immane volumen / qualeque viderunt secula nulla prius / Set tibi scribenti quum saucia mens sit in aegro / corpore, quod veluti putre cadaver habes." (You say, Charidemus, that you are writing an immense volume the like of which no previous generations have seen, but when you have an unsound head in an unsound body you may as well have a decaying corpse with you as you write.) Ibid., p. 418, no. 133.

praises it in public, shows it to everyone, reads out parts of it."
The third scolds: "Son of Folly, person without cultivation, incorrigible one! When you are with grammarians you act the
Platonic philosopher. When they bring in Plato, you revert to
grammarian." These are baffling passages. Hippocrates—that's
Rabelais. Plato—that's Rabelais. But what of the Greek grammar? All right, but those giants, that curiosity about magic, the
botanical lore—it all has to be Rabelais!

◄§ No, it is not Rabelais. Two other pieces in the *Nugae* of
1538 do not appear in the 1533 versions. A certain individual,
says the poet, complains that he is being denigrated in our
verse, an individual whose name sounds something like Charidemus. If his morals, like his name, are like those of Charidemus, so much the worse for him. That's not Bourbon's
fault![124] Who is this individual? The second piece gives his
name. He is Jean Chéradame. This time Bourbon addresses him
by name: "Those who said that I was ruining your reputation
under the name of Charidemus—if they have succeeded in making you believe them, what can I do about it? If you are credu-
lous, am I to blame for your credulity?"[125] The shadows
thicken.

Does the name Chéradame mean anything to us? The man
who bore it was from Normandy. He was a Hebraist with mystical leanings who earned the notice of Imbart de La Tour in
Origines de la Réforme because he published a little treatise on
Dionysian mysticism under the modest title *Hebrew Alpha-
bet.*[126] Searching for symbols, he found them without much effort in the words of the sacred language, and even in the letters
out of which the words were formed. Everything had a meaning: one letter stood for the existence of God, another for

124. "In Quempiam: Si queritur quidam perstringi carmine nostro / nomen habens
ferme quod Charidemus habet. / Nomine si par est Charidemo, et moribus, iste / ne
mihi set vitio vertat uterque sibi." Ibid., VII, p. 391, no. 60. And the next piece: "Jam
cedo tibi; quid tum? tu Charidemus fies / ipsissimus: sic cera est dignus cerite." (Well,
I grant it—what of it? You believe you are Charidemus: it suits low-grade people to be
degraded.) Ibid., p. 391, no. 61.

125. "Ad J. Charadamum: Qui tibi dixerunt Charidemi nomine ficto / carminibus
famam me lacerare tuam / ii fecisse fidem tibi si potuere, quid ad me? / Credule, credu-
litas num tua culpa mea est?" Ibid., p. 460, no. 61.

126. Pierre Imbart de La Tour, *Les Origines de la Réforme.* III: *L'Evangélisme*
(Paris, 1914), 289.

Christ, and so on. He likewise earned the notice of Delaruelle when he was studying the beginnings of Greek learning in Paris between 1514 and 1530.[127] His Greek grammar was published in 1521 by Gourmont, and in 1523 his edition of Craston's Greek lexicon. In the dedication to Guillaume Petit, the bishop of Troyes and the king's confessor, he tells us that he studied medicine before he studied Hebrew and gave himself the cognomen Hippocrates. He also put it in the title of the lexicon, "which has been expanded by the efforts of both Guillaume Du Maine (Mainus) and Jean Chéradame, *Hypocrates, Matheseos et Linguae Professor haud poenitendus.*" We should add that in 1528 he put out the first French edition of Aristophanes (published by Gourmont) and in the same year a translation of Lucian's *Dialogues of the Gods.* Earlier, in 1527, he had published an edition of the *Cratylus.*

And so Rabelais-Charidemus, Rabelais-Hippocrates, and Rabelais-Plato have slipped away, disappeared, vanished into thin air. They are not Rabelais at all, but Chéradame, who came from Argentan in the diocese of Sées and had relatives in Troyes and Langres who could have involved him in controversy with Bourbon, who was from Champagne.[128] But what of the giants? They are gone, too, as well they might be. The expression, after all, can be merely proverbial, a simple reference to piling Pelion on Ossa, about which there is nothing particularly Gargantuan. We are dealing with facts: Jean Chéradame was no myth. Furthermore, there is another piece entitled "In Charidemum" that places him before our eyes in living colors. A while ago when he was paying court to a fashionable young woman, Charidemus went about and was charming and witty in company. Now that he is in possession of the wife he sought, he remains in hiding. When neighbors ask her, as is customary, what she thinks of her husband and whether he is behaving handsomely, the poor thing replies: "I don't know! His head is always in the stars!"[129] Can this neophyte in astronomy be Ra-

127. Louis Delaruelle, "L'Etude du grec à Paris de 1514 à 1530," *Revue du Seizième Siècle,* 9 (1922), 132–134.

128. Among these relatives were the bishop of Troyes, Guillaume Petit, and the bishop of Langres, Michel Boudet. Chéradame dedicated one of his works to each of them.

129. *Nicolai Borbonii . . . nugarum* (1538), p. 423, no. 147.

belais? To be sure, there are his almanacs and prognostications—but Charidemus had won himself a wife ("nunc uxore
potitus expetita") after having been her suitor. François Rabelais, priest, apostate monk from 1527 to 1536, then (Lesellier's
researches have established the facts)[130] a canon of Saint-Maur
for the rest of his days, could have sired natural children; he
only had the right to a concubine—God only knows what
names those companions would have bestowed on her if they
had dealt with the subject—not to a legitimate wife, *uxor*.[131]

A strange trail of invectives winds through the tight little
world of the neo-Latins. Bourbon's *Nugae*, in 1533, brings in
the first batch of contrived slanders "in Charidemum." Open
Visagier's two books of *Epigrams*, published by Gryphius in
1536, and on page 32 we find a little piece called "In Cheradae-
mum" (*sic*), which seems to have constructed in advance a synthesis of Bourbon's two later epigrams: "Dirty, obscene, grue-
some, disreputable and wild, ignorant and worthless—yes, but
Cheradaemus is in love. He makes everyone laugh, he is the
butt of everyone's jokes, he prostitutes himself to the rabble—
yes, but Cheradaemus is in love . . ." This was before Visagier
had his falling out with Bourbon.

⇜§ All the same, the passages in the *Nugae* leave us dissatis-
fied. Chéradame existed, he produced a Greek grammar, he was
curious about magic. But what about those giants? What about
those interests of a botanizing philosopher? And what about the
reservations in those denials made in response to poor Chéradame's complaints? Was Bourbon using a subtle device to kill
two birds with one stone? Having had some fun at Chéradame's
expense in 1533, was he referring to someone else under his
name in 1538, thus giving himself an alibi for slander?

In any case, we should point out that there is nothing in
these pieces that refers to anything but trifles. There is nothing
that refers to a religious or irreligious attitude. And yet for

130. J. Lesellier, "L'Absolution de Rabelais en cour de Rome: ses circonstances, ses
résultats," *Humanisme et Renaissance*, 3 (1936), 237–270; "Deux enfants naturels de
Rabelais légitimés par le pape Paul III," Ibid., 5 (1938), 549–570.
131. Charidemus, who had a beard ("In Charidemum barbatulum," *Nicolai Borbonii . . . nugarum* [1538], p. 383), was also endowed by Bourbon with a person
whom he characterized in cruel terms: "Nihilique homo est Charidemus, et Scortillum
habet, / dignum patella operculum." (Charidemus is not much of a man, and he has a
slut; the cover suits the pot.) Ibid., p. 30.

Bourbon, who was in sympathy with the Reformation and prone to fanaticism by nature and preference, the question did come up. In his 1533 *Nugae* he presented a hypocritical Lucianist who always had Christ on his lips, while Lucian was both in his heart and on his lips: "I know who you are now, *nunc, qui sis, scio; fers in ore Christum, fers in pectore et ore Lucianum.*" This was a phrase that the plagiarizing Visagier repeated in his *Epigrams* of 1537. He, however, applied it to Lefèvre: "Quod fert pectore, fert in ore: Christum."[132] Who was the Lucianist? There is nothing to prove that it was Rabelais, and there is nothing to disprove it. There is neither more nor less reason to think of him than to summon up a dozen others who were his contemporaries and who are known to us—or a mass of unknowns who could have been "Lucianizing" in secret. But what about "Lucianizing"? The meaning of the word varied a good deal with those who used it, it must be said, in those times of religious controversy. A Christian like Erasmus "Lucianized," to the double consternation of a Christian like Luther and a Christian like Beda, who became reconciled in enmity and from their diametrically opposed positions hurled vehement anathemas at the Christian of the *Enchiridion* (that breviary of liberal piety), at the editor of the New Testament, at the man who exerted all his efforts to making the Christianity of his time richer and more vital. Even if the Lucianist of the 1533 *Nugae* were our friend François, like Rabellus in the same work, there would be no need to modify the traditional image of him we have been given by Gebhart, for example. That Evangelical was never in league with fanatics. He did not enter the ranks of the iconoclasts who followed the lead of a Farel. In fact, all his life he made no attempt to hide the fact that he claimed the right to combine in an Erasmian sort of piety Plato's lofty, humane thought and Lucian's clever, gracious wit.

7. Julius Caesar Scaliger and François Rabelais

In addition to the texts pointed out by Thuasne and then by Abel Lefranc, there are others. They raise the same kind of difficulties. In two articles in the *Revue des Etudes Rabelaisiennes*

---

132. *Nicolai Borbonii . . . nugae* (Paris, 1533), fol. C6v; *Joannis Vultei . . . epigrammatum* (1537), I, 73.

a scholar we have already mentioned, Dr. de Santi, called attention to a group of epigrams (unfortunately undated) by the fiery Julius Caesar Scaliger, the literary gladiator, directed against a certain Baryoenus or Baroenus. They are found in the voluminous collection of Scaliger's *Poemata*, which Joseph Scaliger brought out in 1574, after his father's death. There are numerous pieces directed against Dolet in this mélange—four in the *Farrago*, four in the *Hipponax*. They are few compared to the pieces about Baryoenus or Baroenus: nine in the *Farrago* and two in the *Archilochus*, not counting a tirade in the poem *Ata*. Besides, an imposing number of pieces intertwined with the aforementioned refer to a certain Bibinus—a pseudonym from the same barrel, one might say. There are at least four in the *Farrago*, three in the *Archilochus*, and three in the *Hipponax*. If Bibinus, Baryoenus, and Baroenus are all one, this means that more than twenty-five pieces—all violent in the Scaliger manner—seem to have been directed at the same person under different names. He must have been one of the two or three great hatreds of that great hater, Scaliger.

◄§ This witness is not famous. A strutting and shrill peacock, he was born in Riva on the Lago di Garda on April 27, 1484, the son of a Veronese miniaturist named Benedetto Bordone, who lived for a long time in Padua and then in the Della Scala quarter of Venice, whence came the sobriquet which Julius Caesar adopted and which served as the point of departure for his ridiculous pretense that he was descended from the Scaligers of Verona.[133] This adventurer, who did have some gifts, came to France in the entourage of Antonio della Rovere, bishop of Agen, probably around 1524. He married and settled down on the banks of the Garonne. And all at once he began to act like an important person (travelers tell fine tales), invented a heroic past for himself, and described the campaigns he had waged and his exploits in Ravenna, where his father and one of his brothers had been killed. He gave himself ancestors, connections, and a coat of arms. He let it be known that Bordone was the name of a fief, and he turned it into Burden. He most likely

133. On Julius Caesar Scaliger's origins, see Paul Allut, *Etude biographique et bibliographique sur Symphorien Champier* (Lyon, 1859).

furnished himself with a master of arts diploma that was supposed to have come from Padua. In the end he succeeded, by means of his frauds, in getting naturalization papers in 1529 pompously styling him Julius Caesar de Lescalle de Bourdonis, doctor of medicine, native of Verona, and resident of Agen for four years.[134]

It is known how, to make a name for himself, he attacked Erasmus, calling him the son of a prostitute, a drunkard, and some other choice things. He devoted two orations to him. One was sent to Paris as early as 1529 and was printed by Pierre Vidoue on September 1, 1531. The other was finished on September 25, 1535, and printed by Vidoue in 1537, with Sussanneau supervising the work. By the time it appeared, Erasmus was dead. Also, to be fair, Scaliger shed some hypocritical tears for the great man in his *De comicis dimensionibus* of 1539[135] and the same year published an astonishing couplet in his *Heroes:* "Now you are dead, Erasmus. And so you leave me before we could be reconciled in friendship!" (At quid me linquis, Erasme, / ante meus quam sit conciliatus amore?)[136] And one has only to leaf through the little file of letters in Schelhorn's *Amoenitates literariae* that had escaped Joseph's watchful eye and were published by that German scholar[137] to get a clear impression of the way he operated. There one finds two letters that are denunciations of Erasmus by Scaliger. One is addressed to the rector of the University of Paris, the other to Beda personally.[138] Beda is termed *vir doctissimus* and called on to act quickly against an unbeliever who not only wishes to see the flame of our religion extinguished ("religionis nostrae lumina exstinguere") but, in addition, deceives innumerable simple

134. *Catalogue des Actes de François Ier*, ed. Paul Marichal, 10 vols. (Paris, 1887–1908), I, no. 3,352, p. 640. See L. de Santi, "Rabelais et J. C. Scaliger," *Revue des Etudes Rabelaisiennes*, 3 (1905), 12–44; 4 (1906), 28–44; "Le diplôme de Jules César Scaliger," *Mémoires de l'Académie de Science, Inscriptions, et Belles Lettres de Toulouse* (1921), 93–113.

135. *Julii Caesaris Scaligeri liber de comicis dimensionibus* (Lyon: S. Gryphius, 1539), p. 55.

136. *Julii Caesaris Scaligeri heroes* (Lyon: S. Gryphius, 1539), p. 23.

137. "Julii Caesaris Scaligeri epistolia duo . . . nunc primum edita, cura . . . Joachimi Morsi," in Johann Georg Schelhorn, *Amoenitates literariae*, 14 vols. (Frankfort and Leipzig, 1730–31), I, 269–283; "Epistolae nonnullae ex MSto Bibliothecae Zach. Conr. ab Uffenbach," VI, 508–528, VIII, 554–621.

138. Ibid., VI, 512–513, 521–525.

people and leads them into the temptation of heresy ("eius fal-
laciis jam illecti sunt nonnulli qui, quam quod erant, aliud esse
mallent").

This is reprehensible, without even the excuse of fanaticism.
The former disciple of Pomponazzi at Padua could hardly have
put himself forward as an uncompromising Catholic. According
to his son Joseph, he had started out well when he was at Bologna—with Duns Scotus. He had wanted to become a Franciscan, and then pope (*sic*)! But in Agen in 1538 he was prosecuted for heresy, and he died half a Lutheran. All of which, we
see, qualified him to become the aggressive champion of the
most fiercely orthodox sort of Catholicism against Erasmus!
Apart from this, Julius Caesar was an original, a "character."
He had ability: he was as great a polyglot as Panurge (if we are
to believe him, at least), had a passionate interest in rare plants,
which he sent for from Provence so he could draw and paint
them in exact detail, was a physician who loved his calling, engaged in controversy like a madman, was shamelessly suspicious, always tense, excited, vibrant. Joseph wrote of him that
in Agen people feared him rather than liked him. Yet this
shaveling (that's what they had called him at Padua, it seems)
had a presence and authority, a majesty and appearance that
impressed everyone. "He was terrifying," recorded his son naively, "and how he would scream that everyone was afraid of
him!" At this late date we can refuse to fall under his spell, and
we should above all not accept the insane declarations of this
Veronese sycophant as true statements.[139]

What are his verses about? They are about a monk, or rather
an ex-monk who had passed through two orders and deserted
each in turn; a writer and a humanist who composed iambic
verses in answer to Scaliger's iambics; a calumniator, a slanderer, an agitator, and, naturally, for good measure, an atheist.
Furthermore, he was a heavy drinker; his pseudonym would
seem to indicate this. Does a man of imagination like Dr. de

139. See Joseph Scaliger, *Scaligerana ou bons mots . . . de J. Scaliger* (Cologne,
1695): Scaliger's family and pretensions, p. 72; sympathy for the Reformation, pp. 9,
357; relations with Erasmus, p. 140; multilingualism, p. 239; Pomponazzi, his teacher,
p. 320; ecclesiastical ambitions, p. 353; botanical passion, p. 359. In Henry Patry, *Les
Débuts de la Réforme protestante en Guyenne, 1523-1559* (Bordeaux, 1912), there is a
lively picture of Scaliger's Reformed circle in Agen (p. xxxii).

Santi need anything more to assert that Baryoenus, "the Sot," is Rabelais?

◆§ At first glance, the parallels are disconcerting. The Sot, *oinobarēs* or Baryoenus, who was Scaliger's target, had been a monk and dead to the world at the beginning of his career—like Rabelais. He was one of those "odious monks" for whom Scaliger—he who had come under suspicion in 1538—entertained a sturdy hatred. They do the world less good than corpses, he informs us; a corpse at least enriches the earth, but a monk exhausts it with his sterile gluttony ("mortuus impinguat steriles laetamine sulcos; / at monachus, segetum munera rodit, iners"). What is more, Baryoenus was a monk twice—like Rabelais. Scaliger says so specifically, with some details that de Santi did not use, perhaps because he had divined the author's meaning from just a verse or two. Epigram 5, for example, correctly translated, gives us the following details: "The renegade friar Baryoenus, dressed in brown, now puts on black. The bad man was not able to be a good Franciscan. Now that he has become a black monk, has he only changed his color? No. He is and will always be black at heart."[140] This is a disconcerting detail. Master Francis, as a Franciscan, first wore the cord and brown habit (*phaios*) of that order; after that he took the black habit of the Benedictines.

Let us go on. This twice-defrocked monk has become an atheist. In the convent he was dead to the world only. Now he is dead, totally dead, to everything ("At nunc, cum est atheos, jam vero est mortuus orbi / atque orbi, atque Deo, corporeque atque anima").

Further on, Scaliger repeats: "bis monachos, tandemque atheos."[141] And in the funeral oration, in which he makes insinuations about Baryoenus's birth, he likewise alludes to the

---

140. "Fit niger ex phaeo Baryaenus transfuga funis; / Nequam homo non potuit chordiger esse bonus." *Julii Caesaris Scaligeri . . . poemata in duas partes divisa . . .* (n.p., 1574), part I, p. 194. De Santi gave an odd translation of this: "B. has dressed himself in black with a cowl." *Phaeus* is the Greek word *phaios*, which Liddell and Scott's Greek-English lexicon defines as "dusky, dun, gray, Lat. *fuscus*." De Santi translates the next line: "Never has a friar been able to be an honest man." I'm afraid he mistook *nequam* (good for nothing) for *nunquam* (never). De Santi, "Rabelais et J. D. Scaliger," 24.

141. "Twice a monk and finally an atheist."

wicked man's atheism. For his worst characteristic is his wickedness. Not only was he—as boy, youth, and old man—a steady patron of taverns and brothels, but rage (*rabies*) is his distinguishing mark. He vents it in defamatory verse, poisonous iambics that he hurls at one and all, sparing neither God nor the devil ("qui mundum, atque Deum laceravit vocibus atris; / si bonus est, bonus et Cerberus esse potest").[142] In short, he is a specialist in satire and libel. If someone sends him some sharp verses, his first reaction is to ask, "Did I write these?" Dr. de Santi immediately thought of that epigram by Visagier which we spoke of earlier: "The man who said that your heart, Rabelais, was infected with rage . . . lied." There is no doubt about it—Zoilus was Scaliger. If de Santi had been better acquainted with the small world of academic Apollos, he would have thought of pointing out—we will do it for him— that Nicholas Bourbon seems to have been closely associated with Scaliger around 1533–34. He bestowed a garland of eulogies on him at the beginning of the collection of Scaliger's *Epigrams* published by Vascosan in 1533, and he seconded the dedications of "The Gladiator" to Charles Sevin and the epitaphs for Louise of Savoy with pieces from his own pen. Bourbon—Visagier's adversary, the "victim" of his plagiarism in 1538—is always sure to turn up in this small world.[143]

We should point out, on the basis of an uncontestable text— the so-called letter to Salignac—that Rabelais had become acquainted with Scaliger before 1532.[144] Since Scaliger "did not

142. Literally, "If anyone who has slandered the world and God with his vicious words is a good man, then it is possible for Cerberus to be good." *Poemata*, part I, p. 194.

143. Scaliger to Bourbon, Agen, Dec. 1, 1533, first letter: *Julii Caesaris Scaligeri epistolae et orationes, nunquam ante hac excusae* (Antwerp: C. Raphelangius, 1600), epistle 84, p. 265. See the verso of the title page of *Julii Caesaris Scaligeri novorum epigrammatum liber unicus. Ejusdem hymni duo. Ejusdem Diva Ludovica Sabaudia* (Paris: M. Vascosanus, 1533): "Nicolai Borbonii . . . ad R. D. Ioannem Salazarium, Archid. Senonen. . . .: En tibi Scaligeri mitto nova carmina, Praesul, / Carmina quae mira dexteritate fluunt. / Et quae Nasoni tenero si lecta fuissent, / Dixisset, Salve frater, et alter Ego . . . (Paris, College of Beauvais, X Cal. April, MDXXXIII)." (Nicholas Bourbon to the Reverend Lord John Salazar, archdeacon of Sens: I send you herewith Scaliger's new poems, O leader of the chorus—songs that flow with a wondrous skill; if they had been read to sweet Ovid he would have said, "I greet you as a brother, as my alter ego.") These gracious words did not prevent Joseph from saying, "Doletus et Borbonius, poetae nullius nominis." (Dolet and Bourbon were poets of no reputation.) *Scaligerana*, p. 127.

144. Since he denounced him to Erasmus as an atheist. See below, ch. 2, sect. 6.

leave Agen from 1524 to 1558, the year of his death," it must be
that Rabelais passed through the city, probably during the period (1527–31) when, as he himself says in his *Supplicatio pro
Apostasia* of 1536, "he carried on the practice of medicine for
several years in a number of places in the garb of a secular
priest."[145] Everything is thus explained, when one knows Scaliger and his furious jealousies, his unending attacks on local
physicians, for "there was no medical reputation in France,
from Fernel down to the most obscure practitioner in Agen,
that he did not vilify."

Rabelais the physician did not escape the common fate of all
his brothers in Hippocrates.[146]

↝ One has to admit this is all very impressive. Still, there
are some problems. The first is that in the ten epigrams on
Baryoenus mentioned by de Santi and examined by him there
is, if I am not mistaken, not a word to indicate that Baryoenus
was a doctor.

I know the learned man thought otherwise. In the very first
article, commenting on one of Scaliger's epigrams (*Archilochus*,
p. 350),[147] he concluded, "Rabelais is very evidently treated
here not only as a man of letters but as a physician, as a charlatan." Well, no. This is my translation:

> Baryoenus says: Caesar, with no concern for gain, devotes
> himself to letters. Caesar is an ass, neglecting gain in order to
> study literature! But drawing blood, that is how to draw
> money, even if the blood is only incidental—much more so if
> it is the central, the only concern. Nevertheless, in his arro-
> gance Caesar neglects it. Who would regard as sound the
> brain of a man who impoverished himself in order to pore
> over books? Thus does Baryoenus trumpet with puffed-out

145. "Presbyteri secularis habitu assumpto, medicinae praxim in multis locis per
annos multos exercuit." *Les Oeuvres,* ed. Charles Marty-Laveaux, 6 vols. (Paris,
1868–1903), III, 337.

146. Scaliger had the audacity to write to a doctor, Nicholas Boustius, that he was
on the closest of terms with all his colleagues, with a single exception! *Julii Caesaris
Scaligeri epistolae,* epistle 50, p. 171.

147. Febvre cites the collections of poems contained in Scaliger's posthumous 1574
Poemata (Archilochus, Farrago, Hipponax, and so on) and gives the page number in
the *Poemata.* [Translator's note.]

cheeks on streets and squares, flanked by those quacks, Brucus and Syrus, whose every word and deed are for sale. Baryoenus cheerfully rails on, filling the forum with his laughter. But when he sees that Caesar takes no account of this insolent Demosthenes' fury and listens to the vituperation with an expression one usually has when listening to praise, poor Baryoenus explodes with vexation!

You can turn this piece every which way and you will not find anything that says Baryoenus was a doctor. It is, after all, possible to walk between two quacks and not belong to their guild. In the other pieces there is total silence. They say renegade monk, furious calumniator, and atheist, but it is impossible to add quacksalver or charlatan to the litany—at least, with any certainty.

There is another thing. Two of the epigrams, if they refer to Rabelais, are strange. One (*Farrago*, p. 194) gives us an unexpected detail about Baryoenus's origins: the two-time renegade was the son of a butcher: "e lanio, inter grunnitusque boumque cruores / natus."[148] Was Rabelais the son of a butcher? That is news. And in this connection I recall (I am a little ashamed of seeming to be so familiar with these pathetic works) an epigram by Visagier in his *Inscriptiones*, published by Simon de Colines in Paris in 1538. It refers to a doctor named Rullus: "Your father was a butcher. You are no different from him, except that in his case it was animals he sacrificed and in your case it is men."[149] This anodyne morsel was printed in the collection just before the epigram on Rabella the hypercurious: "scire cupis qui sim."

No less remarkable is the end that Scaliger ascribes to his Baryoenus in a piece in the form of an epitaph: "Here lie the bones of Baryoenus, conquered by the purifying flames. Water could not dissolve this black villain; a dog had to devour him with his sharp teeth."[150] This passage is obscure. De Santi, intrepid as always, assures us that it shows "what legends circu-

---

148. "Born of a butcher, amid the groaning and blood of cattle."

149. *Joan. Vultei Rhemi inscriptionum*, fol. 6r.

150. "De Baryaeno Monacho: Hic domita ossa piis Bariaeni sunt sita flammis. / Tetrum non potuit diluere unda nefas. / Omnia dente canis rosit." *Poemata*, part I, p. 194.

lated in the provinces after the death of Pantagruel's creator."
"In the provinces" is a charming anachronism—but any explanation would help. In Agen, "where Scaliger collected the gossip," it was said that "Rabelais had drowned, but the water had
taken offense and rejected his body, which was finally devoured
by a dog." Very possibly, but we would prefer to learn the gossip of Agen in some other way than through a passage that the
gossip is supposed to explain. And now comes the moment to
bring up an important objection.

◄§ Why did Dr. de Santi, when reading Scaliger's boring
poems, linger over some of them? Why did he associate them
with Rabelais? Because he took Baryoenus to mean Sot, Sac-à-
Vin (literally, heavy with wine), and immediately the Rabelais
of legend occurred to him: never did the sun come up and see
him ere he quaffed a cup. But what about the spelling?

Up to now we have intentionally written "Baryœnus," like de
Santi.[151] Actually, Julius Caesar Scaliger had it printed as
Baryænus every time the word appeared in his writings. That is
how it appears in the titles in roman, which shows the ligature
æ with perfect clarity. That is how it appears in the text in
italic. And if one had any doubt, one would only have to look at
line 11 on p. 191 of the *Poemata* ("Male pœnitere . . . artis et
operæ") and compare the œ in "pœnitere" with the æ in
"operæ." Or the line "Quem Gangrænarum fœtida prostibula"
(p. 194, l. 22) and compare the æ in "gangrænarum" with the œ
of "fœtida." Could this mean the Sot is no more? Could a name
made up from the Greek words *barus* and *oinos* ever have become "Baryœnus" in the hands of a Hellenist like Scaliger?

Indeed, de Santi did pay attention to the word, but it was
only to speculate that Scaliger had written "Rabiœnus" in his
manuscript, not "Baryœnus," and that "it was very likely Joseph Scaliger, following his practice of piously pruning his father's writings, who transformed 'Rabiœnus' into 'Baryœnus' to
avert suspicion." This is a totally gratuitous hypothesis. Why
Rabiœnus and not Rabienus, if it was a question of evoking Rabelais's *rabies?*

151. There is a piece by Gouvea entitled "Ad Barenum Ciceronianum," unknown
to de Santi, which, otherwise insignificant, gives another spelling of the name. *Antonii
Goveani . . . epigrammaton,* p. 10.

Still, "fit niger ex phaeo Baryænus transfuga funis"—the line written by the self-important Scaliger keeps echoing in the memory. We reach for the fat octavo volume of his *Poemata*, annoyed to find ourselves faced with documents that are un-dated, having been sent to the printer in no particular order, at a late date (1574), by an heir who was not too sure of himself. There we find the pieces marked "In Bibinum."

◄§ Who is Bibinus? Is he the twin of Pimpinus, the subject of Antonio de Gouvea's bacchic song in his *Epigrams* of 1539?[152] Or is he a real person who was well known? De Santi had no hesitation. He is Rabelais—again.

Indeed, on pp. 445 and 446 of the *Hipponax* there are two diatribes directed against this wicked Tippler that seem to es-tablish his identity with Baryaenus. Like the latter, Bibinus— "Bibinus ille, factiosus et durus"[153]—is a rebellious monk who has cast off his habit. Scaliger depicts him as having shone with brilliance when he was a monk, like the flame of a lamp. He be-came an apostate, and now, "cuculla cum pudore deposita,"[154] is no more than the feeble candle in a horn lantern. Finally, he is shown as a pig in manure: "opimis porcus auctus in sacris," gorging himself on benefices, meat, and overindulgence—a lan-tern still, but the light has gone out. The same theme is found further on (p. 455); this epigram even has one verse in common with the earlier one: "diris monota cum lateret in claustris."[155] Scaliger contrasts the religious who, when he was in the monas-tery, controlled himself (or, rather, was controlled), listened to the voices of educated men and their exhortations, and refrained from scandal and strife with the defrocked monk who is now outside the cloister and never stops roaming in disreputable al-leyways, wallowing in filth, or drinking "like a monk" until he is totally inebriated. This same Bibinus should probably also be connected with the epigram "In quendam," on p. 456 of the *Hipponax*. "Are you astonished," asks Scaliger, "that the learned men who not so long ago covered you with garlands

152. Ibid., p. 19.
153. "Bibinus, he that is factious and wild."
154. "Having shamefully laid down his cowl."
155. "When he was solitary, hidden in the dread cloister."

now heap the worst opprobrium on you? But then you were peaceful, sober, pious, and gentle, and you drew men's hearts to you; now—" Scaliger shows us the wretched man with his shameless tongue, his constant thirst, always running after women, playing at dice, hanging about bars, a troublemaker. What is left? "Are you astonished that those whom you put to flight flee from you?" (Quos tu fugasti, te fugare miraris?)

One or two of these pieces are not without some wit. Here is Bibinus raising his arms to heaven in supplication (*Hipponax*, p. 448): "You have made the age of gold, the age of silver, the age of bronze, the age of iron. When, oh Lord, are you going to make the age of good wine?" But mostly Scaliger's vehemence is unpleasant. "Bibinus? You don't know him? Here is a description of him: a liar, a rascal, a boor, a traitor, a sot, and an infidel. He denies God by his words and even more by his deeds" (*Farrago*, p. 211). Aren't these the very characteristics of Baryaenus, and of the Rabelais of legend, with wickedness thrown in? We can even find a remarkable parallel. We saw that Thuasne said certain pieces by Visagier and Chesneau referring to a monster of curiosity applied to Rabelais. One of Scaliger's epigrams on Bibinus (*Archilochus*, p. 356) is entitled "The Curious Man": "Bibinus judges everyone. Rare are those he approves of, numerous those he maligns." And Scaliger denounces the worthlessness of a man who is always thinking about other people but is like a perpetual exile inside himself: "regnans foris, sic intus est exul sibi." Furthermore, de Santi discovered in one of Scaliger's works of scientific criticism[156] an attack on a charlatan, *quidam semimonachus*, half a monk, who, when he could find nothing else in his pack to use against the physician Scaliger, picked up a calumny that had already been used against himself, as Scaliger had heard with his own ears. It had to do with a fine point in medicine, the virtues of giving gold to a patient in the form of an electuary. Naturally, Scaliger handled his colleague with his usual asperity, calling him a mountebank and a charlatan. This, suggests Dr. de Santi, may have been the opposition of an innovative doctor, one who prided himself on belonging to no school, to a doctor who was a Ga-

---

156. *Julii Caesaris Scaligeri exotericarum exercitationum lib. XV de subtilitate ad Hier. Cardanum* (Paris: F. Morellus, 1554).

lenist and a conservative—Rabelais. If, then, the *semimonachus* of Scaliger's controversy with Cardano is Bibinus, and if Bibinus is Baryaenus, we have to revise our opinion of a few moments ago. Baryaenus may indeed have been a doctor.

◄§ Once established on medical terrain, Dr. de Santi pressed his advantage. There was still much more for him to do. In the *Hipponax* (p. 401) there are two diatribes against Galenists. One is named Cossus, the other Rubellius. "De Rubellio, altero galenista" is the title of the piece. Rubellius is a classical name; it is found in Juvenal (Satire VIII, l.39). So is Cossus (l.21). Surely Julius Caesar Scaliger knew his Juvenal. But it is, after all, not so far from Rubellius to Rabelais as from Baryaenus to Rabelais. This Rubellius—who, if Galen had said, "Two and two are five," would have taken it for gospel truth, *sic atque si Deus mandet*—felt sorry for poor Scaliger. "Foves adhuc ne barbaros Avicennas?" he asked him. "Et sordidatos atque hirtos?"[157] Read a little hastily, these obscure passages might even make one think that Scaliger found fault with the Galenist for sharing the errors of Scotus—which would certainly be applicable to an ex-Franciscan like Rabelais: "nec excidere mente de tua, durus / fallacia argumenta quae Scotus fudit; / nigris et in recessibus lates stulte" (nor have you the fortitude to excise from your mind the fallacious arguments that Scotus poured into it; you foolishly hide in dark corners). But, on rereading, it turns out that these are the Galenist's words, and it is Scaliger who stands charged with Scotism—which will not surprise readers of *Scaligerana*.[158]

What of this Rubellius? Was he Rabelais, or was he rather a

---

157. "Are you still fond of those Avicennas, those filthy, hairy barbarians?"
"Julius Scaliger recommended as essential that all doctors read Avicenna, nor did he think anyone could become a great doctor unless he had read this learned work."
(Julius Scaliger, Avicennae medicis omnibus tanquam pernecessariam commendabat, nec quenquam in magnum medicum evadere posse existimabat, qui tam doctum opus non legisset.) *Scaligerana*, p. 41.
158. "What caused Julius Scaliger to become so learned in logic and scholastic theology was his intention of becoming pope so he would have the means of waging war against the Venetians and removing his principality of Verona from their hands. For he considered becoming a Franciscan and hoped that from a Franciscan he would become a cardinal, and from a cardinal, pope. As a result, while he was at Bologna he diligently applied himself to the reading of Scotus's works." Ibid., p. 353.

celebrated physician of the time, one whom Dolet called Ruellius[159] and who was perhaps Visagier's Rullus, the Rullus whose father was a butcher? We are getting lost. De Santi remembered that Scaliger, in his *Poemata*, had given some of his fine treatment to a certain Calvus. He accused him of everything, of impiety first and foremost: "Tartara dissidiis, coelum impietate lacessit," proclaims the *Farrago* (p. 156).[160] In *Scaligerana*, Joseph Scaliger tells us about this Calvus. He was Jean Escurron, "the famous physician, Scurron" of *Book Four* (ch. 43), who died in 1556 as regent of the University of Montpellier after having been Margaret of Navarre's physician for a long time. "Scirrhonius ignarissimus vir," Joseph wrote, having inherited his father's animosities. "Pharmacotriba, id est, Pileur de Drogues, verius quam medicus."[161] Escurron practiced in Agen at the same time as Scaliger—*inde irae*.[162] Like him, he conducted classes, writes de Santi, and "took away his pupils, or his patients." Here is a flash of light! Rabelais came to Agen, began by associating with Scaliger, then left him and attached himself to his rival; when Escurron went away to teach in Montpellier at the end of 1528, Rabelais followed his master— de Santi assures us of all this. On September 7, 1530, Rabelais enrolled himself in the university register, stating he had taken as his master "egregium dominum Joannem Scurronem, doctorem regentemque in hac alma Universitate."[163] This may like-

---

159. "Ex medicorum Scholis ad certamen concurrunt Symphorianus Campegius; Jacobus Sylvius; Joannes Ruellius; Jo. Copus; Franc. Rabelaesus; Carolus Paludanus." (The following who come from the schools of medicine vie with each other . . .) *Commentariorum linguae latinae tomus primus* (Lyon: S. Gryphius, 1536), col. 1158.

160. "He disturbs Tartarus with his quarrels, and heaven with his impiety." *Poemata*, part I, p. 156. Other references to Calvus are in part I, pp. 99, 151, 161, 169, 185, 197, 390, 392, 637, 639, 643, 645, 647, 652, 653; part II, p. 192.

161. "Escurron was a very ignorant man, a pounder of drugs rather than a physician." He goes on, "Is est Calvus, ille carminibus patris decantatissimus." (This is the Calvus who is constantly referred to in my father's poems.) *Scaligerana*, p. 364. The spelling Escurron comes from *Catalogue des Actes de François Ier*, V, no. 15,079, p. 8.

162. Vulteius dedicated a laudatory piece to a "Jo. Ischyronium: De Henrico Rege Navarrae Lutetiae febricitante" (On King Henry of Navarre's Having a Fever in Paris). *Joan. Vulteii Rhemi inscriptionum*, fol. 4v. Two years earlier, in his first collection of epigrams, he had got off a shot at Scaliger: "With the arrows from his bow the archer pierces his targets; with the darts from his mouth Scaliger murders the universe." *Joannis Vultei . . . epigrammatum* (1536), II, 163.

163. "The distinguished Master Jean Escurron, teacher and regent of this beneficent university."

wise explain the piece "In Bibinum" on p. 451 of the *Hip-ponax:* "When Bibinus came to my house, we were of one voice, one mind, one heart. We were brothers in our friendly quarrels. Since he has gone away, that strange wicked man, we are no longer brothers, no longer sons of the same father. We have no bad quarrels or disharmony between us. He does not want to come, and I don't want him to come."

All of this, we must admit, constitutes a rather disconcerting little fiction, full of plausible episodes and documented verisi-militude. How gratifying it would be if it were all true! It would throw light on the darkness that surrounds Rabelais. And de Santi is so insistent, so persuasive, that we feel we are about to be won over at any moment. The defrocked physician, the half-monk, the curious slanderer, once a respected humanist, now a barfly, *is* Rabelais. It has to be Rabelais. Joseph Scaliger, however, has nothing to say about it. He gives us the clue to the pseudonym Calvus, but he is silent on Baryaenus. Then there is this short piece in the *Archilochus* (p. 356): "Why does Bibinus act friendly to all wicked people? Is it mere coin-cidence? His uncle, his brothers, his father, his sister, and his nephews act friendly to all wicked people—to Tulla, Cynon, Fereguinus, Luscius . . ." Here we are introduced to Bibinus's family. Baryaenus's butcher father has already given us pause. But where and how would Scaliger have gotten to know Rabe-lais's uncle, brothers, father, sister, and nephews? And who are the famous unknowns to whom these people of Chinon are so friendly? The Italian humanist transplanted from the Lago di Garda to the banks of the Garonne could not have been running into them every day on the arcaded streets of Agen. The pas-sage raises a number of problems, and de Santi does not even mention them.

Finally, in the piece directed against Bibinus there are no more allusions to medical matters than in the pieces directed against Baryaenus. If the *semimonachus* of the *Exercitationes* is Rabelais, the differences between him and Scaliger were of a scientific nature, disputes about schools and theories. There is not a single allusion to these questions in the pieces against Bi-binus. Furthermore, there is no allusion either in these pieces or in the pieces against Baryaenus to Rabelais's vernacular writ-ings, *Gargantua* and *Pantagruel*. Bibinus and Baryaenus wrote;

they even wrote too much: "Uno Baryaenus plus die facit scripti / quam bis trecentis a viris legi possunt."[164] It would be possible to apply the three verses that follow to Rabelais's satire: "nam dictionis fluctuantis insanae / si membra contempleris atque suturam / furiosa Orestae somnia esse jurabis."[165] But we learn soon afterward that what Baryaenus wrote were verses: "Quin, de seipso subdidit sibi versus / nomen suorum inscriptitans amicorum."[166] Another piece about Baryaenus, in the *Archilochus* (p. 354), also speaks of verses—"De mutuis laudatoribus."[167] Rabelais did produce some Latin verse. We know that there was quite a collection at Fontevrault in the seventeenth century. Still, were they what made him a prominent person?

The fact is that it is impossible to avoid the impression that Baryaenus and Bibinus were part of Scaliger's immediate circle. They lived in Agen; this would explain the use of pseudonyms. Scaliger used the correct names of persons who lived elsewhere. He said "Erasmus" and "Dolet." Pseudonyms were reserved for individuals he might run into every day.

⊷§ Having made this reasonable statement, we are not very happy. It is so tempting to fill up the great lacuna in Rabelais's biography by using passages that are especially expressive and lively, and to give the Rabelais legend a plausible origin in a grudge of Scaliger. We must, however, not let go now of a prudent axiom: a tempting hypothesis is not the same thing as a demonstrated truth.

Rabelais went to Agen—that I believe. He knew Scaliger there—the famous letter "to Salignac" presupposes that.[168] His medical point of view was displeasing to that Hippocrates of Agen—the contrary would be surprising. Escurron brought the two men together, then was the cause of enmity between them—that is possible. I am mindful of Scaliger's allusions to

---

164. "Baryaenus put more into writing in one day than could be read by twice three hundred men."

165. "If you examine the parts of his wild, insane style and the way the parts are sewn together you will swear that they are the mad dreams of Orestes."

166. "Indeed, he made up verses about himself to which he affixed the names of his friends."

167. "On Those Who Praise Each Other."

168. On this letter, see below, ch. 2, sect. 6.

the new Lucians and kitchen Diagorases of his time; I will come
back to them later. De Santi points out these allusions in the
1554 *Exercitationes,* which repeat phrases used by "Putherbe."
I am equally mindful of Scaliger's statements in the dedication
to Councillor d'Alesme of his commentary on the treatise on
dreams. They refer to men who have nothing in their hands
and hearts but the works of Lucian and Aristophanes and appreciate them, not for the beauty of their style, but for the
sharpness of their ideas: "propter acerbitatem sententiarum,
si modo sententiae eae, ac non venena sint vocanda."[169] This
Nestor of Agen, who had barely managed to escape from the
clutches of the Furred Law-cats,[170] who had called for the just
prosecution of the impious under the law, he whose appeals for
help to Briand Vallée were so bland—here he is, cynically uttering smug bromides: "Nimis secure vivimus hodie . . . Hanc
vocamus libertatem!"[171] Nor have I forgotten that this very
commentary by Scaliger provided the material for chapter 13 of
Book Three, on divination by dreams (Plattard pointed this out
in his 1929 edition of Rabelais's complete works). Having said
all this over and over, I still come up against epigrams that offer
resistance, statements that need to be justified, and silences that
must be explained. If anyone could "prove" that these passages
really had nothing to do with Rabelais, what a lesson in critical
judgment he would have learned—and taught!

8. Conclusion: The Rabelais Legend

We have come to the end of a long digression—perhaps too
long. But since we did a lot of tedious work we did not want
anyone to feel it was necessary to do it over for some time to
come; furthermore, how could we come to a conclusion without
exhausting all the sources that came under our scrutiny? Well,
what sort of conclusion can we come to?

It is clear. The "poets" whose writings we have minutely
combed bequeathed us some incontestable evidence about Ra-

169. ". . . if indeed they should be called ideas and not poison."
170. On these proceedings, see Patry, p. xxxix.
171. "We live in too much security these days . . . This we call liberty!" *Hippocratis liber de somniis cum Julii Caesaris Scaligeri commentariis* (Lyon: S. Gryphius,
1539), dedicatory epistle.

belais for the period after 1532. It consists of the pieces dedicated to Rabelais, in so many words, or concerned with him
under his real name. This evidence is all favorable, whether it is
Visagier's defense of Rabelais against the accusation of rage or
the handsome eulogy by Macrinus in his odes of 1537 or
Dolet's well-known piece on Rabelais's public dissections in
Lyon, his inclusion of Rabelais in the list of the six greatest humanist physicians of his time, and the flattering remark in the
equally well-known piece about the banquet for Dolet. We can
add to the list Sussanneau's effusive note on the Aesculapius of
Montpellier, the last resort of desperate invalids; the magnificent eulogy of Rabelais the philosopher by Gilbert Ducher in
1538; and even Bourbon's note, without warmth but correctly
familiar, in his 1538 *Nugae*. In none of these pieces authentically devoted to Rabelais is the question of religion raised.

Several poets, on the other hand, gave us pieces that seem to
refer to Rabelais under an assumed name and undoubtedly do
refer to him. Such, for example, is Bourbon's 1533 piece "In
Rabellam": it expresses perhaps the outrage of a humanist
against an illustrious colleague who so far forgot himself as to
write in the "vulgar" Romance tongue for "poor idiots"; it certainly does not express the indignation of a believer, a semi-
Lutheran, against an infidel: Bourbon would have been alone in
1533 in refusing to see *Pantagruel* as a powerful ally of anti-
Sorbonne Evangelism. Such, for example, are also Sussanneau's
three pieces marked "In Rubellum" or the "In Rabulam" in his
Ludi of 1538. Such is even the portrait of Rabella the curious in
Visagier's *Inscriptiones* of 1538: he wants to know everything,
but he doubts nothing, in any case not Christianity. Furthermore, if we find ourselves asking unanswerable questions with
regard to Bourbon's pieces of 1533 and even more those of 1538
directed against Charidemus, and if there are more unanswerable questions with regard to Scaliger's undated pieces directed
against Baryaenus and Bibinus—we must similarly state that
not for a moment is Charidemus called to task for his religious
opinions. And if Baryaenus and Bibinus are called atheists two
or three times, that could be stylistic license without any other
significance, or repayment in kind.

There remain several epigrams—not many—aimed at infidels,
generally doubling as hypocrites (not otherwise designated than

as Lucianists, votaries of Lucian, or atheists). These men use the name of Christ but in their inner selves swear only by Lucian. Bourbon was on the lookout for these monsters as early as 1533. His denunciation of them was in vague terms. It was only when he returned to them in his 1538 *Nugae* that he was specific in his objections. "God does not exist," proclaim these evil men. "There is nothing after death (p. 449). If there were a God, how could evil exist? (p. 303). There is, finally, no Providence; everything here below is subject to the whims of chance (p. 477)." In 1536 Visagier, for his part, wrote a "tombeau" for an unbeliever named Anthony (I, 24) and apostrophized another—or two others, if Caneus and Canosus, who attacked Christ, are two different people (I, 46; II, 159). Finally, in 1538 in his *Hendecasyllables* he hurled three great diatribes against "quemdam irreligiosum Luciani sectatorem" (fol. 10), "Luciani simium" (fol. 30v), and "Luciani sectatorem" (fol. 71v). That is all. There is nothing in Dolet, nothing in Ducher, nothing in Gouvea's *Epigrams* of 1539 and 1540, nothing in Sussanneau. Of the few passages we have, only those by Visagier in the *Hendecasyllables* are susceptible of an exact attribution. And everything seems to indicate that one of these at least (if they do not all apply to the same person) is aimed at Etienne Dolet, of whom Visagier used to be extremely fond but was at the moment pursuing with vigorous animosity; his animosity could either have opened his eyes to the true spiritual condition of his old friend or inspired him to hurl some especially grave accusations at his new enemy. Can they have been aimed at Rabelais? Why would they have been? If he was the Rabella of Visagier's *Inscriptiones*, nothing suggests that Rabella was an atheist or an unbeliever. Why him more than anyone else? Surely there was no lack of Lucianists in Lyon circles. We will mention only one, without making too much of him, since we will come back to his case later on. It was a strange case indeed, that of Bonaventure Des Périers, whose *Cymbalum mundi* was the object of vigorous attacks. Bonaventure is surrounded by a silence that is total, mysterious, and truly abnormal. Let us speak only of his possible connections with Visagier. In his admiration, Visagier had brooded like a mother hen, so to speak, over Dolet's *Commentaries*. He made himself their official panegyrist and almost went off his head over them. Bonaventure, for his part, was doing the same thing—and yet there is not a thing, not even one couplet, to Bonaventure in Visagier's prolix output. When Marot went into exile Visagier was his ardent champion. Bonaventure for his part entered the fray for his teacher, beseeched King Francis, prayed, interceded, was active—and yet there is not a thing, not even one couplet, to Bonaventure in Visagier's garrulous output. Visagier, like Bonaventure, was a visitor to Parmentier the bookseller-publisher and to the shop of Sebastian Gryphius. Visagier, like Bonaventure, was acquainted with the lovely nun Scolastica Bectonia. And yet there is not a single thing, not even one couplet, to Bonaventure, or against Bonaventure, in Visagier's opportunistic output. It is really a very strange silence. Instead of making up romances out of whole cloth, it would be as well (much better, even) to see Bonaventure rather than Rabelais behind one or more of the unspecific pieces by the Apollo of Vandy. But that would be whole cloth, too.[172]

◄§ If we now put the pieces together, linking Sussanneau's pieces against Rubellus or Rabula, Bourbon's portrait of Rabella, the inflated copy by Chesneau, and, finally, the Scaliger pieces discovered by Dr. de Santi, we obtain a fairly coherent picture. It is that of a monk whose life was at first admirable and who was esteemed by all (a *rara avis!*), and who then abandoned his habit and liberated himself, changed his behavior and his style of life, gave himself up to drinking and debauchery, wrote—instead of learned works—books that were, well, Rabelaisian, and, while giving free rein to insatiable curiosity, indulged an impassioned animosity, malice, envy, and wicked rage. In short, it is like a caricature of Rabelais in undress, something very close to the Rabelais of legend. Is it legitimate, however, to build up a composite portrait from photographs of unknown persons, and then compare it with a legendary image that is itself—? Yes, when all is said and done, the Rabelais legend is a remarkable problem in retrospective psychology.

◄§ Let us, after all, be brave enough to admit that, in spite of all the discoveries, ingenious hypotheses, and excellent research, we cannot see Rabelais clearly, either with the body's eye or

172. On all this, see Lucien Febvre, *Origène et Des Périers, ou l'énigme du Cymbalum Mundi* (Paris, 1942).

Antho. Matharel.   Iean Fernel.   Iacques Siluius.   Francois Rabelais   Guill. Rondelet.

Portrait of Rabelais in the *Chronologie Collée* (no. 99). The caption calls him "the doctor of Cardinal Du Bellay, outstanding in his profession, rare in learning, merry and witty. Having discarded the habit of a Franciscan, he died as priest of the parish of Meudon near Paris. He translated the *Aphorisms* of Hippocrates." Rabelais is included among outstanding French physicians of the sixteenth century. Note Jean Fernel (no. 97) and Guillaume Rondelet (no. 100).

the mind's eye. What was Rabelais like physically? Some paintings exist that are fanciful and executed without much talent. Or there is the sad picture in the *Chronologie Collée:* a little old man, gaunt, frowning, his eyes bright, his expression somewhat foxy.[173] What was Rabelais like mentally? Something of a buffoon, a sponger who paid his way with noisy farces, all the while boozing his fill and, in the evening, writing obscenities? Or, perhaps, a learned physician, a humanist scholar who fed his prodigious memory with beautiful passages from the an-

173. The work usually referred to as the *Chronologie Collée* is a large early seventeenth-century volume containing several series of engraved portraits in chronological order. Among these are Old Testament patriarchs, Roman emperors, kings of several European countries, and "portraits of some illustrious men who thrived in France from the year 1500 to the present." The title page is different in different copies. The copy at the New York Public Library calls itself *Chronologie et sommaire des souverains pontifs, anciens pères, empereurs, rois, etc. jusqu'en l'an 1622.* [Translator's note.]

cients and the inquiries of his consuming curiosity? Or, better yet, a great philosopher, acclaimed as such by the likes of Theodore Beza and Louis Le Caron—the prince of philosophers, according to Gilbert Ducher:

> In primis sane Rabelaesum, principem eumdem
> Supremum in studiis Diva tuis Sophia.[174]

Our ancestors were more fortunate than we are. They did not choose between the two images. They accepted them both at the same time, the respectable one along with the other. They were all the better able to do so because they did not hold them up alongside each other to compare them.

They would come across a learned individual named Master François Rabelais, associated with the d'Estissac family or the Du Bellay family, or at Aigues-Mortes in the entourage of the king, an individual whom Claude Chappuys included among the masters of requests:

> Et Rabelais, à nul qu'à soy semblable,
> Pour son sçavoir partout recommandable.[175]

> And Rabelais, whose equal no one seems,
> He whose skill and learning everyone esteems.

There, and in a hundred other impressive places, finding themselves in the presence of a Hellenist, a physician, a poet acclaimed and celebrated in verse and in prose, in Greek and in Latin by the greatest literary and scholarly men of his time— from Guillaume Budé to Joachim Du Bellay, with the young Theodore Beza, fiery Dolet, and a score of others equally famous in between—they took off their hats, made a respectful bow to "Messire le Docteur" and waited for noble aphorisms to fall from his eloquent lips. If they subsequently happened to read *Gargantua* or *Pantagruel* and it invited them to laugh, then laugh they did—good-naturedly and without constraint,

---

174. "Indeed, in the forefront of those engaged in thy pursuits, O Holy Wisdom, is Rabelais, their most exalted prince." *Gilberti Ducherii*, p. 54.

175. *Discours de la court* (1543). Quoted in Rabelais, *Les Oeuvres*, ed. Marty-Laveaux, V, xxxii–xxxiii.

like strollers at a fair being diverted by a lively pitchman. They laughed a lot, and they quite naturally inferred what the man was like from his work. He who sang the praises of the holy bottle had to be a mighty boozer. We should point out that Rabelais himself kept encouraging naive readers to be led from the book to the author. Wasn't he always saying "I"? This is not the impersonal narrator of Panurge's lofty deeds, but a vaudeville entertainer, the barker at a sideshow: "Good people, God save you and keep you! Where are you? I can't see you: stay— I'll saddle my nose with spectacles—oh, oh! it will be fair anon, I see you." And in turning Rabelais into a drunkard and a clown they were not making a mistake. Even less were they putting a piece of authentic evidence into the file of History. The Rabelais they were thinking of was indeed a drunkard and a clown, since he was the incarnation of all the heavy drinking, the ribaldry, and the buffoonery in Rabelais's fiction. The "real" Rabelais—whether moderate or intemperate in the tavern and when other occasions for sensual indulgence arose—had no existence for them. The only Rabelais whose existence they recognized was their creation. They fashioned him themselves in the image of his book and his heroes. Rabelais begat Gargantua, Pantagruel, and Panurge. *Genuit autem Gargantua:* Gargantua in turn begat a Rabelais in his own image. He was the only one, the real one for these readers. They were not at all blasé; they were grown-up gullible children, entirely innocent of ideas about the processes of literary creation, a subject that hardly occurred to them, even if their names were Ronsard or Du Bellay.

    ∾ We have some testimony from these two. In the last months of 1553 or early in 1554 Rabelais died. Ronsard immediately dedicated an epitaph to him:

> Au bon Rabelais qui boivoit
> Tousjours, cependent qu'il vivoit.
>
> He loved the grape, did Rabelais,
> And drank his fill both night and day.

He described in devastating terms a gallant stretched out among the cups:

Et parmi les escuelles grasses
Sans nulle honte se touillant
Alloit dans le vin barbouillant
Comme une grenouille en la fange.[176]

Among the dirty cups he wallowed,
Bespattered by the wine's red stain;
He had no shame, he felt no pain,
Contented like a frog in mud.

The description sounds realistic, we think. We forget that in speaking of himself, in "Odelette to Corydon" in the *Mélanges* of 1555, Ronsard depicts himself in a similar position, lying "à la renverse": "Entre les pots et les fonchées" (Mid pots and heaped-up flowers).[177]

As for Du Bellay, a discussion of "learned men in France" who did not "despise their vulgar tongue" acclaims one "who has made Aristophanes to be born again, and so well reproduces the delicate wit of Lucian." It makes a careful distinction between this great writer's inimitable style and that of his lowly imitators, who try to "steal the bark of him of whom I speak, to cover therewith the worm-eaten wood of I don't know what heaviness, so ill-pleasing that no other receipt were necessary to remove from Democritus all desire to laugh." It compares the man it praises so highly to those two French luminaries, Guillaume Budé and Lazare de Baïf: great minds and great personages as well, of high social rank.[178] A year later the same author, reviewing the troop of *enfants poétiques*

---

176. For a detailed discussion, see Margaret de Schweinitz, *Les Epitaphes de Ronsard, étude historique et littéraire* (Thèse de doctorat ès lettres, Paris, 1925); Paul Laumonier, "L'Epitaphe de Rabelais par Ronsard," *Revue des Etudes Rabelaisiennes,* 1 (1903), 205–216; Hugues Vaganay, "La Mort de Rabelais et Ronsard," ibid., 143–150, 204.

The epitaph appeared first in *Bocage,* which was published on Nov. 27, 1554, and was reprinted, with variations, in 1560, in Book I of Ronsard's *Poèmes.* There is a facsimile in Vaganay, pp. 145–146.

177. Curtis Hidden Page, *Songs and Sonnets of Pierre de Ronsard* (Boston and New York, 1924), p. 60.

178. Joachim Du Bellay, *Deffence et illustration de la langue française,* Book II, ch. 12; trans. Gladys M. Turquet (London, 1939), p. 105.

Qui en sonnets et cantiques
Qui en tragiques sanglots
Font revivre les antiques
Au sein de la mort enclos

Who in songs and sonnets
And in tragedy's tears
Resurrected the ancients
We thought dead all these years

authoritatively includes in their ranks—after the three favorites of the Graces, Carle, Héroët, and Saint-Gelais—the *utile-doux* Rabelais.[179] Nothing would have obliged him to refer to Rabelais in this way if he had been a disgusting buffoon, an object of public contempt and revulsion. He praises him as the man

Qui si doctement escrit
Ayant premier en la France
Contre la sage ignorance,
Faict renaistre Démocrit.[180]

Who can with so much learning write
That now we have at last in France
Democritus reborn, whose lance
Cuts through the schoolmen's murky light.

Then Rabelais died. And no sooner was he dead than the critic who had praised him with such sensitivity, the poet who had rendered him such great homage, put some ironical Latin verses into his mouth, making him say, "Here am I, Pamphagus, the devourer of all. See me lying under the crushing weight of my immense belly ... Sleep, gluttony, wine, women, and jest: these were my gods, my only gods, when I was alive."[181]

179. Joachim Du Bellay, "La Musagnœomachie," in *L'Olive*, 2d ed. (Paris, 1550).
180. Du Bellay, "Discours sur la louange de la vertu et sur les divers erreurs des hommes," 1552.
181. *Joachimi Bellaii poematum libri IV* (Paris: F. Morel, 1554), fol. 56v. The poem continues: "Who does not know the rest? I was dedicated to the art of healing, and, even more, of making people laugh. So do not shed any tears, voyager. Laugh, if

This is astounding. We find it amazing because we do not understand, and we start dreaming up stories about rancor and rivalry, as if we were dealing, not with literary images of the Good Tippler, described in realistic detail in the performance of his duties, but with a police file on the improper conduct of one Rabelais, François, profession: doctor of medicine. And, I should add, as if Clément Marot, another grand jester of the time (to name only one), had not been honored with quite a similar legend that came about in exactly the same way.

Let us conjure up François Rabelais's contemporaries—their violence and capriciousness, their inability to resist surface impressions, their extraordinary changes of mood, their astonishing quickness to anger, to take offense, to draw the sword and then kiss and make up. All of which explains those frequent quarrels over nothing, those awful accusations of theft and plagiarism, those appeals to God and man for justice—followed without pause by terrible gushes of flattery and the most insane comparisons to Homer, Pindar, Virgil, and Horace. These are the natural products of a life full of contrasts, much sharper than we can imagine: the contrast of day and night, unknown to us in our electrically lit homes; the contrast of winter and summer, tempered for us in normal times by a thousand devices, whereas they were subjected to the seasons' rigors and necessities practically without letup, for weeks and months at a time. The equalization of the conditions of life is followed by an equalization of moods; the two are conditioned by each other. At the same time, our nerves have been deadened. We have eaten too much of fruit that has, in the words of the Bible, set our teeth on edge. *They* were not deadened, God knows. To give just one example, they were defenseless against a violent and extreme onslaught of sound. We should keep in mind the passage in the *Contes d'Eutrapel,* where Noël Du Fail describes the effect on men of his time of the famous descriptive choral work by Clément Janequin, *The Battle of Marignano.* There was no one who was not overwhelmed by this powerful, puerile

---

you wish to be pleasing to my shade." Need I say that it is very hard for me to see the head of the little old man depicted by Léonard Gaultier perched above an "immense belly"? Of course, we get thinner as we get older ... [The engravings in the section of the *Chronologie Collée* in which the portrait of Rabelais appears are attributed to Gaultier.—Translator.]

music, with its harmonies that imitated the noise of battle. There was no one who, roused by the sounds, did not "look to see if his sword was in its scabbard and did not rise up on his toes to make himself taller and more dashing."[182]

They were simple people who gave in to their feelings. We repress ours.

&⁊ This is something to think about at the very outset in a book that purports to be at least as much a study of historical psychology as a work of scholarly history. We have already been alerted to the fact that there is really no common measure between sixteenth-century men's ways of feeling, thinking, and speaking and our own. We hold back, they let go. Since the seventeenth century and the time of Descartes generations of men have made an inventory of space, analyzed it and organized it. They have bequeathed us a well-ordered world in which every object and every being has perfectly marked boundaries. Generations of men during the same period worked at making time, which was being measured with greater and greater precision, the rigid framework of our actions. This great undertaking had hardly begun in the sixteenth century. Its results had not yet engendered in us, in consequence, our overriding need for logic, coherence, and unity: this *or* that, not this *and* that at the same time. Here or there, not here and there both at once. We should find some cautionary advice in these observations to use in the investigations we have yet to make.

182. Noël Du Fail, *Oeuvres facétieuses*, ed. J. Assézat, 2 vols. (Paris, 1874), II, 124–126. See below, ch. 12, sect. 3.

2. Theologians and Controversialists

ET US LEAVE the small world of the Latin poets, a bit disappointed perhaps, our curiosity having been aroused rather than satisfied. These academic Apollos have presented us with riddles more than they have provided us with information. Let us now knock at the door of the theologians and controversialists, a different sort of men, even if some of them may occasionally have importuned the Latin muse. They had different temperaments and different habits, and we have to take different precautions if we want to understand them and assess their testimony properly. When we confront them we perhaps feel we are better alerted to their sort of professional bias. It remains to be seen whether we do not need to be reminded that, to begin with, like their contemporaries the poets, they were sixteenth-century men. They belonged to a century far removed from our own, despite appearances—far removed most of all in its mental structure.

1. A Letter from Calvin

In the troubled autumn of 1533 people in the circles of Paris that were tinged with evangelism were beginning to take notice of a young man fresh from the universities of Orléans and Bourges. His name was Jean Cauvin, and he was from Noyon. He had lately affixed the Latinized form of his name—Calvinus—to a commentary on Seneca's *De Clementia*.

It was no longer a time for irenicism. The Sorbonne was mo-

[101]

bilizing its supporters against the *mal sentans*. In the university quarter one could sniff the air of battle. In May, Beda and several doctors of like mind had been sent into exile by order of the king. Calvin was often at the house of the rich merchant Etienne de La Forge, who was later burned for heresy. He was also often at the houses of the liberal members of the university who grouped themselves around one of the king's physicians, Guillaume Cop of Basel; his son Nicholas, suspected of holding new ideas, had just been elected rector of the university for the year. Having become a part of these active and well-informed circles, Calvin wrote a richly detailed letter in the last days of October to his friend François Daniel of Orléans:[1] it is an account of one of the memorable sessions—the one of the twenty-fourth—in the course of which the university, under coercion by the king, harshly repudiated its theologians because they were guilty, the sovereign said, of having included in their list of suspect books the *Miroir de l'âme pécheresse* (a work that had already been out for two years) by Margaret of Navarre, King Francis's own sister.[2] In this letter, Thuasne believed, as he stated categorically (and Lefranc was just as emphatic), was proof that as early as 1533 Calvin with his sharp eye had penetrated Rabelais's secret intentions and had unequivocally denounced him as the worst enemy that Christ had at the time.

In 1533 Calvin was twenty-four years old. He had not yet broken with the church of his childhood—that was not how the

---

1. *Joannis Calvini opera quae supersunt omnia*, ed. Baum, Cunitz, Reuss, and Erickson (*Corpus Reformatorum*), 59 vols. (Brunswick, 1863–1900; facsimile reprint, New York, 1964), X, col. 29. Also in A. L. Herminjard, ed., *Correspondance des Réformateurs dans les pays de langue française*, 9 vols. (Geneva, 1866–1897; reprint, Nieuwkoop, 1965–66), III, 106–111 (collated with the original).

2. On this incident, see Léopold Delisle, "Notice sur un registre des procès-verbaux de la Faculté de Théologie de Paris pendant les années 1505–1533," *Notices et extraits des manuscrits de la Bibliothèque Nationale et autres bibliothèques*, 36 (1899), 315–408. The first time, on October 27, the masters declared their innocence under oath *in facie Facultatis*: they had never condemned the book nor known it to be worthy of condemnation ("nunquam condempnasse neque scire condempnatum librum"). It was signed at the top by Le Clerc, immediately after the dean. They took the matter up again on November 3 and 8: "The Faculty has unanimously concluded that it did not condemn, disapprove, or approve the said booklet by its own action or that of its representatives [*Facultas ... unanimiter conclusit ... non condempnasse, reprobasse neque approbasse dictum libellum per se aut deputatos ejusdem*]." *Pantagruel* does not come into it. What is more, I do not believe there was a condemnation of *Pantagruel* in 1533. See below, sect. 3.

problem presented itself to him. But he undoubtedly already
had in his head the speech that his friend, Rector Cop, would
solemnly deliver on the following All Saints Day, a speech that
would shock the theologians, not because of its heresies (it contained none), but because of its sharp attack on the scholastics.
Besides, the young man lacked neither drive nor fire. We would
even have said he had charm as well up until fairly recently,
while the fashionable portrait in the possession of the Consistory of the Walloon church in Hanau was still regarded as an
authentic likeness of the youthful Calvin—or even the famous
enamel by Léonard Limousin.[3] As for the man to whom the future Reformer was writing, François Daniel of Orléans, he was
not a fanatic, an enthusiast, or an ascetic. He would not follow
Calvin in his later development. He would stay in Orléans, remain a Catholic—and have as a friend another François whose
name is not associated with sadness, François Rabelais himself.
One cannot help wondering whether at this period it would not
have been possible for Rabelais and Calvin, through the inter-
mediary of Daniel, to have met in Orléans, or at least to have
heard each other spoken of with affection.

Whatever one makes of these obscure details, in October
1533 Calvin sent Daniel a letter to be read by him and by his
friends, a youthful letter full of pugnacity. According to Thuasne, it condemned *Pantagruel* as obscene and impious. This
was a scholarly blunder, and others have been too quick to take
him at his word. Actually, Calvin was summarizing the argument of Nicholas Le Clerc, the priest of Saint-André des Arts,
an intractable foe of the new ideas and leader of the intransi-
gents in Noël Beda's absence (in exile since May 18 and not to
return to Paris until the end of December).[4] Writing in indirect

3. Both were still taken to represent Calvin by Emile Doumergue in *Iconographie
calvinienne* (Lausanne, 1909). There is no other picture of the youthful Calvin besides
the mediocre portrait acquired in 1929 by the Musée Historique de la Réformation in
Geneva. Cf. "IVᵉ centenaire de la formation de la première Eglise réformée par Calvin
à Strasbourg (1538)," *Bulletin de la Société de l'Histoire du Protestantisme Français*,
87 (1938), 379.

4. This was in connection with the sermons of Gerard Roussel. Cf. Delisle, p. 346;
Fernand Bournon, ed., "Chronique parisienne de Pierre Driart, chambrier de Saint-
Victor (1522–35)," *Mémoires de la Société de l'Histoire de Paris et de l'Ile de France*,
22 (1895), 163 etc. Le Clerc was arrested in March 1534, at the same time as Beda;
ibid., p. 166.

discourse, Calvin had him say that, in drawing up a list of dangerous books, he certainly had not regarded a work by a woman of irreproachable character as among the books on the list that were condemned but rather a bunch of obscene books—and he gave their titles: *Pantagruel, Sylva,* and so on ("se pro damnatis habuisse obscaenos illos Pantagruelem, Sylvam Cunnorum, et ejusdem monetae").[5] On which Calvin remarked: "Omnes tamen fremebant obtendere ignorantiae speciem," which must be translated, "Everyone was indignant to see him call on the excuse of pretended ignorance."

The meaning is clear. It was not Calvin who attacked *Pantagruel,* contrary to what Lefranc, unfortunately following Thuasne, said.[6] It was Le Clerc, whom Calvin ridiculed. To be sure, nothing gives us the authority to ascribe to Calvin a lively instinctive sympathy for Alcofribas, although at that date many a delusion was still possible. While rejoicing to have found such a learned physician and skillful Hellenist as an ally in his campaign against the abuses of scholasticism, Calvin might sometimes have been tempted, if he read *Pantagruel,* to mutter to himself, "Du bist nicht fromm!" as Luther had said when he measured Erasmus against himself. It is some distance, it must be said, from that to enlisting him in the ranks of the supporters of Le Clerc, a man he attacked and denounced in the letter destined for the indignant perusal of the young men of Orléans. Especially since Le Clerc had attacked *Pantagruel* not as impious, but as obscene. This showed considerable rigidity and touchy prudishness for a man of the time,[7] even for a Sorbonist. Yet it was undoubtedly his being a Sorbonist that made the fiery priest of Saint-André des Arts so strict. Le Clerc sensed no whiff of atheism in *Pantagruel.* His nose simply detected a formidable adversary's hatred for the habitués of the Library of Saint Victor—and a liberal spirit's sympathy for the

5. What was this unseemly *Sylva?* Could it have been *Sylva nuptialis* by Nevizzano, as Jacques Pannier suggested? See his review of Rabelais's *Oeuvres,* V, in *Bulletin de la Société de l'Histoire du Protestantisme Français,* 80 (1931), 550, n. 2.

6. "Calvin mentions *Pantagruel* along with numerous other books *he characterizes as obscene.*" "Etude sur *Pantagruel,*" in Rabelais, *Oeuvres,* III (Paris, 1922), liv. And later on the same page: "Everyone knows Calvin's first evaluation, already so hostile."

7. See a note on this subject by Thuasne, "Un Passage de la correspondance d'Erasme rapproché de passages similaires de Rabelais," *Revue des Bibliothèques,* 14 (1904), 290–304. He cites the *Colloquies* of Erasmus, sermons, and other works.

evangelicals. The latter (although never particularly known to promote obscenity) espoused the vengeful book as soon as it appeared. They praised it, promoted it, put it in their libraries, and kept it there.

◄§ When Olivétan—native of Noyon, friend and relation of Calvin, who did the first French version of the Reformed Bible, published by Pierre de Vingle in Neuchâtel in 1535—died in 1539, he left six works "in the vulgar tongue" in his library. Among the six was a copy of *Pantagruel*.[8] But as early as August 1533 (and by the time Calvin wrote to his friends in Orléans in October he may have seen it at the home of Etienne de La Forge or elsewhere) there had appeared "in Corinth" one of those little anticatholic pamphlets that the presses in Neuchâtel would turn out in great numbers, which Théophile Dufour catalogued some time ago in a famous *Notice*.[9] It was the work of Antoine Marcourt, a well-known preacher and the author of the placards of 1534. And what was its title? *The Book of Merchants, right necessary unto all folks, newly made by the Lord Pantapole, right expert in such business, near neighbor unto the Lord Pantagruel*.[10]

"Near neighbor unto the Lord Pantagruel"—the phrase is rather symbolic. It was the Reformers, the innovators, the anti-Catholics at that period who felt they were (and said they were) close neighbors of Rabelais and his giant hero. And in spite of Calvin's subsequent anathemas, it was not easy for them to give up the claim. Henri Pirenne, in a note in *Revue des Etudes Rabelaisiennes*, was right to recall the popularity en-

8. Herminjard, VI, 23; *Calvini opera*, X, col. 367. [This letter describing Olivétan's library actually says "Gargant."—Translator.]

9. Théophile Dufour, *Notice bibliographique sur le Catéchisme et la Confession de foi de Calvin (1537) et les autres livres imprimés à Genève et à Neuchâtel dans les premiers temps de la Réforme (1533–1540)* (Geneva, 1878; reprinted 1970).

10. *Le Livre des Marchans, fort utile à toutes gens, nouvellement composé par le sire Pantapole, bon expert en tel affaire, prochain voysin du Seigneur Pantagruel*. [An English translation was published in London in 1534.—Translator.] On Marcourt, see Jacques-Charles Brunet, *Manuel du libraire et de l'amateur de livres*, 5th ed., 6 vols. (Paris, 1860–1865), III, col. 1,123; Jean Calvin, *Le Catéchisme français, publié en 1537*, ed. Albert Rilliet and Théophile Dufour (Geneva and Paris, 1878), pp. 46, 106; and especially Gabrielle Berthoud, *Marcourt et Rabelais* (Neuchâtel, 1929). Berthoud attributes the elimination of any reference to Rabelais in *The Book of Merchants* after 1534 to the efforts of Viret.

joyed by Rabelais's works in the Netherlands,[11] the land of the Beggars, where Pantagruel's creator would later find an imitator—practically a plagiarizer—in the person of Philippe de Marnix de Sainte-Aldegonde. Marnix had connections with the Franche-Comté, and I have spoken of a number of "Burgundian" things that, more than once, were linked with things "on the other side." Similar links would be found, according to Marcel Bataillon, in the Spain of unorthodox believers around 1550.[12] All of this is evidence to support the thesis that Rabelais was not anti-Christian. He was, rather, sympathetic and valuable to the Reformation, or at least to its forerunner in France, the evangelical movement.

So it is jumping to conclusions to say that Calvin made an accusation against Rabelais. He did not—at least not in 1533. It was a Sorbonne theologian, Our Master Le Clerc, who accused Rabelais, and in so doing made a public avowal of his boorishness and hypocrisy: "omnes fremebant eum obtendere ignorantiae suae speciem." *Omnes*, Calvin included, who was indignant from outside.

When we put this document aside, the oldest piece of evidence brought forward to establish Rabelais's atheism dates only from 1538. What must be proved, then, is not that Rabelais was a rationalist, a propagandist for impiety, and a leader of the coalition against Christianity, but that he was all of these things in 1532, through the instrument of *Pantagruel*. As for documents of 1538 or later, we will deal with them if there are

11. "Rabelais dans les Pays-Bas," *Revue des Etudes Rabelaisiennes,* 4 (1906), 224–225.

12. See Gustave Cohen, "Rabelais et Marnix de Sainte-Aldegonde," *Revue des Etudes Rabelaisiennes,* 6 (1908), 64–65; A. Delboulle, "Marnix de Sainte-Aldegonde plagiaire de Rabelais," *Revue d'Histoire Littéraire de la France,* 3 (1896), 440–443; Lucien Febvre, "Une question mal posée," *Revue Historique,* 161 (1929), 1–73, reprinted in *Au coeur religieux du XVIᵉ siècle* (Paris, 1957), pp. 3–70, and translated as "The Origins of the French Reformation: A Badly-Put Question?" in Peter Burke, ed., *A New Kind of History: From the Writings of Febvre* (New York, 1973), pp. 44–107; Marcel Bataillon, *Erasme et l'Espagne, recherches sur l'histoire spirituelle du XVIᵉ siècle* (Paris, 1937).

For example, a canon in Valencia in 1556 brought in *Pantagruel,* "libro francès," along with works by Erasmus; a scene in Laguna's *Voyage to Turkey* set in the period 1552–1556 is an imitation of *Pantagruel* (one of the characters is named Panurge, for instance). In France, Jean de l'Espine, a prominent Reformer, constantly invoked the authority of Rabelais in his *Excellens Discours,* written in 1548 and published in 1588; see Louis Hogu, "L'Opinion d'un protestant sur Rabelais," *Revue des Etudes Rabelaisiennes,* 8 (1910), 376–377.

any, but the world had moved between 1532 and 1538. And it
had moved very rapidly. October 1533: the meeting of the king
and the pope at Marseilles. March 1534: the excommunication
of Henry VIII. October 1534: the Placards. January 1535: the
edict that suspended printing. June 1535: Olivétan's Bible.
March 1536: the publication of the *Institutio Christiana* in
Basel. July 1536: the death of Erasmus. We don't have to go on.
We will not go up to Morin's publication of the *Cymbalum* in
January or February of 1538 in Paris or, at the other extreme,
Calvin's organization of the mother church of the French Reformation in Strasbourg at the end of that year. These few facts
are enough. They serve as a warning that for those troubled
years of the sixteenth century, when men were living on the
double and ideas were causing things to move with unaccustomed rapidity, it makes no sense to mix up different conditions.

2. The Fantasies of Guillaume Postel

From 1532 to 1543—now that we have put Calvin's letter
aside—the silence of theologians, philosophers, and controversialists on the subject of Rabelais's work and its impiety was
total. And parenthetically, it would seem that if the Latin verses
cited by Thuasne and Lefranc are really about Alcofribas and
his fictions, then uninitiated laymen were way ahead of the doctors and clerics of every persuasion—something, after all, that
would be surprising. The passages from Visagier, Bourbon, and
Sussanneau that we have discussed were concentrated between
1536 and 1538. During that period there was dead calm, silence,
among the learned. Only in 1543, the great year that saw the
appearance of both Copernicus's *De revolutionibus orbium coelestium* and Vesalius's *De corporis humani fabrica*, did one of
them speak. Guillaume Postel attacked several well-known rene-
gades of the Reformation who had recently become confirmed
atheists. Villanovanus was one—the abominable author of the
abominable treatise on *Three Prophets*. The author of the *Cymbalum* was another, as were the author of *Pantagruel* and the
author of *The New Islands*. They were a foursome of infidels
and riffraff.[13]

13. "Addam secretiora mysteria et scopum ad quem tota isthaec nova professio col-
limet, palamque fiet non satis habere quicquid usquam terrarum perfidi dogmatis asser-

"Villanovanus" we take to be Michel de Villeneuve, that is, Michael Servetus, who at just that time — 1542—had had Hugues de La Porte in Lyon publish his edition of the Bible, with a Latin text by Santi Pagnino and annotations that caused it to be suppressed. Poor Servetus—he continues not to be recognized by this name, or to be confused with that other Villanovanus, Simon de Neufville, who was Dolet's teacher at Padua. About *him* we know nothing, however, and it was not to him but to Servetus that the mythical *Treatise on the Three Impostors* was attributed. Not only to Servetus, of course, but to many others, from Averroës and Frederick II to Giordano Bruno, Campanella, and Milton, with Boccaccio, Machiavelli, Aretino, Pomponazzi, Ochino, and Rabelais in between—a sizable number of fathers for a mythical treatise. What is fascinating is that it has also been attributed to Postel. He had no inkling of that in 1543.

The *Cymbalum* we know, and its author as well. As for the enigmatic treatise on *The New Islands*, are we dealing with some (unknown) French adaptation of *Utopia* (*Libellus vere aureus de optimo reipublicae statu, de que nova insula Utopia*)? Or should we be thinking of *Le Disciple de Pantagruel*, which appeared at least as early as 1538 and kept reappearing? It was subtitled *The Voyage and Navigation Made by Panurge, Pantagruel's Disciple, to Unknown and Strange Islands*.[14] Only we have no evidence of any French adaptation of *Utopia* that might figure here, and *Le Disciple de Pantagruel* is an insipid hodgepodge with nothing in it, it seems to me, to arouse the passions of a Postel. In his book on American exoticism in the sixteenth century, Chinard refers in passing to a work pub-

---

tum fuit, id modicus tutari hanc factionem, nisi etiam tam directe quam indirecte (ut aiunt) neget Deum atque de suo Caelo ejicere conetur ... Id arguit nefarius tractatus Villanovani de Tribus Prophetis, Cymbalum Mundi, Pantagruellus et Novae insulae, quorum authores olim erant Cenevangelistarum antesignani." (I shall also mention cults that are more secret and the end to which all of this new creed is directed. It is well known that this faction is not content to defend with all its might whatever perfidious dogma has been uttered anywhere on earth but it also, both directly and indirectly (as they say), denies God and tries to eject him from his heaven ... This is evident in the abominable treatise by Villanovanus on *Three Prophets, Cymbalum mundi, Pantagruel,* and *The New Islands,* the authors of which were once in the forefront of the Cenevangelists.) *Alcorani, seu legis Mahometi, et Evangelistarum concordiae liber ...* (Paris: P. Gromorsius, 1543), p. 72.

14. *Le Voyage et navigation que fist Panurge, disciple de Pantagruel, aux isles incongneues et estranges.*

lished in Paris in 1533 by Colines: *Epitome or Compilation of the Islands Newly Found in the Great Ocean Sea*.[15] It is a French version, by a certain Antoine Fabre, of the first three *decades* of Pietro Martire d'Anghiera's *De novo orbe*, along with a summary of the fourth and two accounts of Mexico drawn from the letters of Cortez; the book as a whole is dedicated to the Duke of Angoulême, and the two accounts are dedicated to My Lady Margaret of France.[16] Several passages in the book caught Chinard's attention. He especially points out a rather curious digression on the aboriginal inhabitants of Hispaniola (p. 23), whom Fabre raised to the dignity of being ancestors of a long line, that of the noble savage. The natives of the great island "live in the golden age." Good by nature, not knowing any bad men, they "do not bury their possessions or put fences around them." Quite the contrary—they "leave their gardens open, without laws, without books, without judges. But of their own nature they pursue what is just and deem evil and unjust one who enjoys doing harm to another."

Is that what caught Postel's attention? It is at least possible to think so. To his attacks on the impious he added, two pages later in the same chapter, a categorical denunciation of libertines who invoke the Gospel "as long as they can live without it in total license and do not have to forgo any of their pleasures." What he was talking about he stated in so many words: Theleme ("as the Scourge of Christ made clear with his Abbey of the Thelemites and its tennis court").[17] Still, it is hard to see how a French translation of a work by the Catholic Pietro Martire deserved to be classified among books by Reformers who had recently turned into fomenters of impiety. Evidently, with

15. Gilbert Chinard, *L'Exotisme américain dans la littérature française au XVIᵉ siècle* (Paris, 1911), p. 261.

16. *Extraict ou recueil des isles nouvellement trouvées en la grand mer océane.* The book is in the Bibliothèque Nationale (Rés. P15). Did Rabelais read it? There is a passage in it on the Indians who "put more value on iron hatchets than on a quantity of gold pieces" that puts one in mind of Rabelais's story of Tom Wellhung in the prologue to *Book Four*.

17. The whole passage reads: "Qua enim Luterani habent ecclesia, eadem habent authoritate ab ecclesia traditum posteritati Evangelium impii verbis crebro Evangelii professionem sibi adscribentes, ut sub eo tamen ita vivant (ut interpretatus est Christomastix in Abbatia Thelemeton ludoque pillae palmariae) ut velint, nec libidini quicquam substrahant." *Alcorani*, p. 74. Here again Postel places Theleme's Scourge of Christ in the ranks of the *Luterani*. It was Lefranc who pointed out this passage of Postel's in 1913 ("Rabelais et Postel," *Revue du Seizième Siècle*, 1, 259).

Postel almost nothing is surprising. If we want to assess the force of this passage singled out by Abel Lefranc, it is absolutely necessary to start by reimmersing it in its setting.

We should read from cover to cover the curious work from which it is taken: *Alcorani seu legis Mahometi et Evangelistarum concordiae liber.* It is not much fun. Postel's Latin is particularly repellent. In the first few pages the Orientalist relates how he put together his large work, *De orbis concordia*, in the phenomenally short space of two months,[18] during a winter so severe that if he had not blown on his pen all the time the ink would have frozen and he would not have been able to write. Poor hardworking men of that difficult age! We get the feeling that there are still quite a few pieces of ice sprinkled over the prose of *Alcorani concordia*. What is more, the book was printed at Postel's own expense by a second-rate printer and looks unimpressive—there are no paragraphs, there is no air in the little pages crowded with italics, and above all, no punctuation. Nevertheless it is an important work. It has not been granted the place it should have in the century's history of ideas. Hardly anyone today is interested in these obscure thoughts or makes an effort to read what was written by that odd, original, intelligent man, Postel.

⁀§ To achieve the moral unity of the universe: to induce all men of every sect, every country, and every continent to feel they were brothers in the ample bosom of a completely ecumenical church; to bring about by the power of persuasion alone, the power of self-evident reason[19] (*ratione evidentiae*, Luther's term), that Protestants and Catholics, Jews and Muhammadans, pagans and idolators from the new world of America, the new world of Africa, and the mysterious empires of the Orient, that all these men provided with the same organs should share without reservation or hostility in a Catholicism so broad that it could be taken for the natural, innate religion that

18. *Alcorani*, p. 5. "I will be blamed for this haste," Postel adds, "but I work to be of service and not for glory" (estimationi non studeo; juvandi animo non gloriae causa acceleravi). In any case, he was not working for readers who were in a hurry.

19. On the meaning of *ratio* in Postel, there are numerous passages in Jan Kvacala, *Postelliana: urkundliche Beiträge zur Geschichte der Mystik in Reformationszeitalter*, Acta et commentationes Imp. universitatis jurievensis (olim dorpatensis), XXIII, no. 9 (Tartu, 1915). See, for example, pp. 27, 29, 34.

a just God had put into the hearts of his creatures; to go beyond the contradictory diversity of dogmas and appeal to the basic feelings and propensities of every human being, such as the out-pouring of gratitude toward his Creator and the yearning (more powerful than death) that made him conceive and desire as his supreme reward the possession of God in immortality; finally, to curse, excommunicate, or reject no one but to create a new Golden Age in which regenerated Catholics would be united with Protestants freed of their errors, with unbelievers restored to belief, with the Turks (so charitable and so tolerant), and above all with the Jews, who were in possession of so large a part of natural law—in short, to reconcile all differences under the rule of a Reason that was identical with the Law of Christ and that had always inspired the founders of religions, the prophets, the magi, the philosophers, every age of history, all the races of the earth, all the religions of the age. This was Guillaume Postel's beautiful dream, if we leave out the chi-meras of his naive illuminism. Postel was a cosmopolite who enriched the old universalistic dream of the Middle Ages with all the daring notions engendered by the geographical discover-ies, the development of Christian missions, and the renewal of religious life that the proliferation of heretical sects attested to.

He made his way toward this mirage, convinced that one day in Syria, at Adam's tomb (which would become the base of the Apostolic See), there would be heard the beating of but a single heart belonging to all peoples, mingled in one church and one nation under the rule of Jesus, King of Kings. He wore himself out with work, with travel, with petitions—this son of a peas-ant, orphaned at twelve, in turn schoolmaster and farm laborer in the Beauce, then in 1525 at the age of fifteen a servant at the Collège Sainte-Barbe. He went from Francis I to Ferdinand, from Margaret to Loyola, hunted down here, listened to there, dragging about with him everywhere the burden of a poverty-stricken, undernourished youth, deprived of all comfort and rest. Little wonder he had a nervous disorder, all too natural in such unhappy heroes of solitary thought.[20] In Venice he was

20. Father Desbillons makes the humane observation that Postel in his youth was burdened by all the miseries of poverty. His constitution, weakened by an eighteen-month siege of dysentery, had been sustained only by his glowing strength of character

acquitted as insane; in Rome he was imprisoned for four years by the Inquisition; in Lyon he was prosecuted on a complaint of the ministers. He finally found himself in Paris, kept under confinement in the priory of Saint-Martin-des-Champs. One of the rare writers of the time who knew how to sketch a profile, Florimond de Raemond, reveals him to us in this setting, with his long white beard, his majestic air, his eyes darting flames like carbuncles, and the smoke rising from his hoary head at the moment of consecration when he celebrated mass (for he was a priest)—"so intently did he concentrate on this mystery."[21]

All in all, he was an unbalanced genius, partly a visionary, partly a raving lunatic—he believed he was immortal and kept proclaiming that Christ spoke through him—but in his fertile and murky brain who knows what Saint-Simonian dreams were germinating ahead of their time, mingled with an obscure presentiment of a kind of Christian socialism. He was presented to King Francis, to whom he owed his departure to the Orient in 1534 with Ambassador Jean de La Forest. He traveled through all of Greece and Asia Minor and part of Syria. He learned demotic Greek, Turkish, Arabic, Coptic, and Armenian. At the cost of countless dangers and hardships he went in search of manuscripts in monasteries. When he returned, Francis I appointed him, on March 6, 1538, reader in Greek, Hebrew, and Arabic letters at the Collège de France. That same year he published, in the form of a study of twelve alphabets, a first fumbling attempt at a comparative grammar. He produced an Arabic grammar. He became the unchallenged master of Oriental studies and the prince of the Paris Orientalists.

It was not for long. Since returning from the Orient he had been plagued by religious problems, rather than linguistics and Orientalism. Not only did he suffer, as did so many men of his time, from the fragmentation of Christianity into sects, which with every passing day were more and more determined to oppose each other; but ever since he had traveled in the Orient his

---

and by a fierce love of learning that was like a burning fever, stimulating and destructive at the same time. *Nouveaux Eclaircissements sur G. Postel* (Liège, 1773), p. 96.

On Postel's dreams, see the passages collected by Kvacala. They throw light especially on the visionary, who was destined to live a thousand years (p. 19) and serve as Christ's herald (p. 4).

21. Florimond de Raemond, *L'Histoire de la naissance, progrez et décadence de l'hérésie de ce siècle* (Rouen, 1624).

suddenly expanded vision was discovering a world divided between a Christian minority and religions that, no matter what
statistical data were lacking, had to be perceived as having far
more adherents and covering an area far vaster than the religion
of Christ. The problem therefore was not merely to bring the
confessions that acknowledged Christ together in unity on one
side. It was to bring all of humanity together.

And so, quite soon and very naturally, Postel became a precursor of those seekers after the universal of which Bodin
would be the lay prototype.[22] Bodin was occupied with the
realms of political institutions (see his *Republic*), comparative
law (see his *Juris universi distributio*), and religion (see his
Heptaplomeres). For a Catholicism that seemed to him to be in
ruins he wanted to substitute a universalism based on scientific
knowledge and the comparative study of facts—in a word,
based on humanity. He thus forged the first links in a long
chain that connected him first to Leibniz, with his dream of a
worldwide politico-religious organization, and then, beyond
that, to Enfantin and the Saint-Simonians, who were also obsessed by a great dream of the Orient. Postel came before any
of them. From 1540 on, as a lovely line in a mediocre sonnet in
a collection by Thevet says, "Il méditoit en lui la Concorde du
Monde." (He meditated much upon a world in harmony.)

◄§ The *Alcorani concordia* of 1543, then, is directly connected with Postel's grand design. It is a vigorous indictment of
the Reformers, who fomented schism and furnished material for
unbelief. In the title Postel calls them Evangelists. In the text
he calls them Cenevangelists. He explains this in his dedicatory
epistle to Bishop Claude Dodée: "I use the word *Evangelists* as
the Germans do; that is how the new sect christens its preachers. I also say *Cenevangelists*, and according to whether I adopt
one or the other spelling, I interpret it as *Cenevangelistas, id est
vanos* [those who are empty] or *Caenevangelistas, id est novos*
[those who are new]."[23] The double play on words fitted right
in with the pedantic taste of the period.

22. On this aspect of Bodin see Lucien Febvre, "L'Universalisme de Jean Bodin,"
Revue de Synthèse, 7 (1934), 165–168.
23. "Utor ea voce more germanico. Concionatores enim suos Evangelistas nuncupat
novi cultus factio. Ad quem vocem adludens, nunc Cenevangelistas, id est vanos, nunc
Caenevangelistas, id est novos, appello." *Alcorani*, p. 4.

Alcorani concordia was to have been part of Postel's huge work, *De orbis concordia,* which he counted on to accomplish the first of his projects. This he defined in the dedicatory epistle of his *Cosmographicae disciplinae compendium.* It was to supply a rational demonstration, one that was perfectly clear and self-evident, of the fundamental dogmas of Catholicism.[24] The first book was to be devoted to proving several difficult truths: the Trinity; the creation ex nihilo; and the resurrection and immortality of the soul. The second book was to contain a systematic refutation of the errors of Muhammad, the most dangerous of Christ's adversaries. The third book would educe the principles common to all peoples and all religions. A fourth book, finally, would raise the question of ways and means. How could the obdurate adherents of Islam be led to the truth? And the pagans, the peoples of India? And the Jews? And the schismatics as well, that new Christian sect of Cenevangelists, which was so formidable because it was so close to true Christianity? *Alcorani et Evangelistarum concordia* constituted this last part of the fourth book. Postel separated it from the main work only because the latter had been subject to terrible transformations in Paris under pressure from the Sorbonne—he gives a detailed account on pp. 8–11. Finally Johann Oporinus offered to publish it. But Postel points out (p. 12) that it did not seem proper to send to a Reformer in Basel a systematic attack on the Reformation. He therefore had it printed in Paris at his own expense, and also at his own risk and peril.

These details are far from pointless. Not only for understanding Postel or Rabelais but, even more and beyond that, for un-

24. "Primum, ut toti orbi terrarum, sed ante omnia Latini Romanive regni alumnis redderem rationem earum rerum quae, hactenus, credendae fuere, postea autem intelligendae sunt, et in Religionis toti generi humano clarissimae, qualis sola christiana est, unione et consensu sunt habendae. Alterum, ut illis gentibus quae sunt Latinae hujus (aut Japetinae) linguae usu destitutae, arabicae videlicet atque syriacae (ipsius Christi propriae) usu coactae, hoc ipsum rationis beneficium, cum Evangelii per typographiae artem multiplicati luce, etiam conferatur." (First, I want to explain to the whole world, and especially to those under Latin or Roman sway, the rational basis of all those things that until now they have had to believe but henceforth will have to understand and that they will be able to possess through union with and assent to a religion that is perfectly intelligible to the entire human race, such as only Christianity is. Second, I want the same benefit of rational demonstration to be conveyed to those nations deprived of the use of the Latin (or Japhetic) tongue, i.e., those limited to the use of Arabic and Syriac (Christ's own tongue), along with the light of the Gospel, which the art of printing makes available in many copies.) Postel, *Cosmographicae disciplinae compendium* . . . (Basel: Oporinus, 1561), dedication.

derstanding the whole intellectual development of the century, it is important to know that *Alcorani concordia* was not a work directed against the "Paduans," as we have lately come to call them—the atheists deriving from Aristotle, especially Pomponazzi and his followers, with whom, ever since the success of a fine book, we are tempted to lump every nonconfessional intellectual movement of that era, as epitomizing them all.[25] Postel concerned himself with these Aristotelians later, especially in 1555 in the *Liber de causis . . . contra atheos* and the *Eversio falsorum Aristotelis dogmatum;* but in 1543, when he indicted *Pantagruel,* it was the Reformation, or as he said, the Evangelists—the Cenevangelists—that were bothering him. This point should be kept in mind from now on.[26]

So Postel at first undertook to show the marvelous agreement that he perceived between the teachings of the Koran—the prototype of all condemned books—and those of the Cenevangelists. The spiritual sons of Luther were for this Orientalist no more than the bastard offspring of Muhammad, and we learn with the help of many citations everything that connects these infidels to each other: "quid inter Mahumetanos et Cenevangelistas intersit." Postel gives a rather disorganized list of twenty-eight propositions (p. 21) taken from the Koran, all of which the Cenevangelists could subscribe to: "non valent aut prosunt ulli aliena opera; patroni et intercessores non valent apud deum; Mariam non debere coli aut honorari . . ."[27] But some propositions are more interesting, and Postel's explanations of them are not without interest. Right off I note the tenth ("nullis miraculis opus esse ad confirmationem religionis") and the twenty-seventh ("Hominem frequenter destitutum libero arbitrio dicit et fatum non raro fortunamque cum Deo confundit [Muhamedes].")[28]

25. Henri Busson, *Les Sources et le développement du rationalisme dans la littérature de la Renaissance (1533–1601)* (Paris, 1922). [Translator's note.]

26. I do not therefore share Renaudet's opinion, when he writes that in 1542 Postel undertook in his *De orbis concordia* to refute the Averroist Vimercati, who had been appointed professor at the Collège Royal—and along with him Pomponazzi and the Italian Averroists. See Henri Hauser and Augustin Renaudet, *Les Débuts de l'âge moderne: la Renaissance et la Réforme,* 4th ed. (Paris, 1956), p. 568.

27. "No one can be helped or benefited by another's good works; patron saints and intercessors are of no use before God; Mary ought not to be worshipped or honored."

28. No. 10: "No miracles are needed to confirm religious belief." No. 27: "[Muhammad] often said that man was deprived of free will, and he not infrequently confused Fate and Fortune with God."

◆§ If the Cenevangelists, like the Muslims, professed such im-
pieties, one could understand how easily their doctrine, which
they claimed was Christian, could pass over into the most obvious kind of impiety. Postel condemned this slide. The Cenevangelists, he declared, profess not only heresy, but impiety. This
is even the title of his second part. And it is precisely in this
second part that he points out the secret goal toward which the
new sect was moving and while doing so takes Rabelais to task
along with Villanovanus (Servetus), Des Périers, and the author of *Novae insulae*—all of them Reformers of long standing
and distinction: "quorum authores olim erant Cenevangelistarum antesignani." Rabelais's impiety, for Postel, was therefore
nothing original or exceptional. Rabelais, who had been
nourished by Evangelism, was simply one of the outstanding
manifestations of a development that he condemned, the slide
from Evangelism to impiety.

But what did impiety consist of for Postel? On reading his
arguments we are somewhat surprised. Or rather, we are surprised if we have no knowledge of the way men of that time
thought and reasoned. First of all, we learn that to proclaim, as
the Evangelists did, "A Christian must believe only what is
contained in the canonical Scriptures," and to say with a sneer,
as the atheists did, "You should not believe in the Gospel,"
were the same thing.[29] There is, to be sure, ingenuity, not to
mention perspicacity, in Postel's argument on this point. I am
going to reproduce it, because it probably reproduced some of
the secret objections of freethinkers of the time. "Everything

---

Postel discusses no. 10 on p. 37. For him, the Cenevangelists' affirmation that miracles were false miracles, miracles of the devil, meant they were exalting the Demon's
power. The twenty-seventh proposition is discussed on p. 70 ff.

29. "Prima ea adsertio, nil praeter ea quae in Canonicis Scripturis habentur, esse
credendum, statim Evangelium non esse credendum suadet." *Alcorani*, p. 73.

Postel reasons as follows: "If nothing is to be held as an article of faith that is not
written in the New Testament, nowhere there will you find that that is the Gospel
rather than something else ... Therefore before we can believe in the Gospel we must
believe in the Church. Otherwise God would be denied, which is what those who are
more skilled in the mysteries secretly do in their very words." (Nam si nil est tenen-
dum pro articulo fidei praeterquam quod est in Novo Testamento scriptum, nusquam
ibi reperias hoc esse Evangelium potius quam quidvis aliud ... Est igitur prius quam
Evangelio Ecclesiae credendum, alioqui negaretur Deus, quod secreto faciunt etiam
verbis qui sunt mysteriorum peritiores.)

that is in the New Testament? So be it. But nowhere does it say in the New Testament that it, rather than some other text, is the Gospel . . . And so? Conclusion: belief in the Church comes before belief in the Gospel." The only thing is that such reasoning makes us think that the impiety of *Pantagruel* condemned by Postel was more an impiety that was deduced than an impiety that was glaringly obvious. And deduced by a long reach, by men who set themselves in opposition to scholasticism but, as we see, were familiar with the resources of the most subtle sort of logic and used them skillfully to lend weight to their intuitions. It was Postel's constant procedure, for we see him further on, as he pursued his case against the Reformers, enumerating the most glaring abominations of these emulators of Muhammad—for example, rejecting the traditions of the Church, making God the author of sin, declaring that there were things in the Church that needed to be corrected (the worst of all the ways in which God was denied, Postel commented, since everything was tied together), and, finally, denying free will, stripping the creature of all merit and discouraging him from good works.[30] These were some of the more horrible doctrines of these veritable Antichrists. *Pantagruel* was thus a public and manifest profession of impiety. But Luther's *De servo arbitrio* was no less so. It is this that unquestionably limits the significance of Postel's accusations against Rabelais. At any rate it is this that keeps us from believing that Rabelais was unlike many other men of his time—a man of fearless mind, of solid good sense, with little inclination to mystical effusions or theological subtleties, who at the same time rested firmly on a cluster of commonly accepted ideas that he criticized and that helped him in criticizing others. He was no revolutionary far in advance of his entire century on the path of negativism. He was not something that was, literally, unheard of. That was not what Guillaume Postel, as perspicacious as he

---

30. "Falsa in sacris esse adseverare, Deum negare est. Si enim, vel in iota una, gratia spiritus sancti permisisset aberrare non tantum Evangelistas, sed legitime coacta Concilia, falsa Christus promisisset." (To assert that there are errors in the religion is to deny God. For if the grace of the Holy Spirit allowed not only the Evangelists but also legitimately convened councils to deviate in even the slightest detail, Christ would have made false promises.) *Alcorani*, p. 75.

was, saw in Rabelais. His attacks did not set Alcofribas apart;
they placed him among the ranks.

◄§ We should not be afraid to pursue this point. Postel has,
after all, been called as a witness in the great trial of Rabelais
for militant anti-Christianism. Testimony of such weight must
be made as clear as possible. Postel tells us that *Pantagruel's*
author was entirely won over to Evangelism, that he was one of
the sect's leaders (*antesignani*). This is perhaps not quite true,
or, rather, it does not make distinctions. But does this statement
in any case support the thesis that Rabelais had been an atheist
since 1532? Postel adds that even in *Gargantua*, which came
after *Pantagruel,* Rabelais was leaning on the Gospel—and giving it a liberal interpretation. He was indeed, and that is what
we are going to try to establish in a slightly different form. Postel accuses him, finally, of maintaining that Nature is good in
herself, and of preaching to those who were "free and well-
born" the scandalous morality of DO WHAT THOU WILT. I understand how, if one begins with these premises, one can deduce an infinitude of consequences, and Postel does not fail to
do so. Do they, however, give us any right to accept an aggres-
sively freethinking Rabelais in place of Gebhart's Rabelais, who
did not claim to be revolutionary—or Stapfer's Rabelais, who
appeared to be a Reformer?[31]
We should add that Postel was fairly late in perceiving any
danger in Rabelais. The date of *Alcorani concordia* is 1543.
Five years earlier, in 1538, when dedicating his *De originibus*
to Cardinal Du Bellay, Postel extolled his patron's generosity
toward all the fine minds of his time: "As evidence of your so-
licitude," he told him, "I will mention only the most distinguished men in the various branches of human knowledge.
They have turned to you every time misfortune assailed them
... Why recall here that good will, so many impressive tokens
of which have been received by such as Paolo Giovio, Rabelais,
Bigot, and many other men of perfect erudition?"[32] This is an

31. See Emile Gebhart, *Rabelais, la Renaissance et la Réforme* (Paris, 1877); Paul
Stapfer, *Rabelais, sa personne, son génie, son oeuvre* (Paris, 1889). [Translator's
note.]
32. "Nolo hic attingere propensum illum tuum animum in Jovium, Rabelaesum, Bi-
gotium ac tales absolutae eruditionis viros." *De originibus, seu de Hebraicae linguae et
gentis antiquitate* ... (Paris: D. Lescuier, 1538), fol. Aii.

interesting passage. At the very least it shows that in 1538 Rabelais—the Rabelais of *Pantagruel* and *Gargantua*—was not an object of scandal to Postel. Otherwise he could have made him part of the anonymous mass of Du Bellay's numerous clients. Between 1538 and 1543 Postel changed his mind about Rabelais, or more precisely, about his books—for he does not mention the name of their author. Would it be possible to find some personal reasons for the change?

In the very interesting preface to *Grammatica arabica*, which was brought out in Paris by the same publisher and no doubt in the same year as *Alcorani et Evangelistarum concordia*, we take note of a curious passage.[33] With the boldness of thought that he often appeared to have, the exact significance of which it is difficult to measure, Postel shows us the vast, "catholic" extent of Islam.

That religion, he says, is so spread throughout the universe that, if you look at the three parts of the world, there is hardly one of them that has escaped it. It has possession of all of Africa except for the Nubia of Prester John; all of Asia, from one end to the other; and see how it is nibbling away at Europe in the East and along the Mediterranean—it already has Greece. It is a quasi-universal religion. The language it expresses itself in, Arabic, is therefore a universal language. Knowledge of it is indispensable, however, not only for traveling in so many countries of the globe and conversing with these masses of men; scholars cannot ignore a tongue that gives them the key to Oriental science. We owe so many things to the Arabs! First and foremost, astrology and the practice of medicine. Here Postel delivers a forceful attack on the Galenists: "Let them mock as much as they want, these 'neoterists' who claim for themselves the distinction of being greatly learned while taking pleasure in disparaging others. For myself, I hold that no man of our time who is concerned about science and its application will not pay

---

33. "Usque adeo orbem totum occupavit [Muhamedica religio] ut, si trifariam in que aequalia totam habitabilem divides vix una pars extra hanc possit reperiri. Habet totam Africam, praeter Nubianam illam regionem quae a Praestano Christiano incolitur. Tota Asia, a nostris litoribus per antipodes usque ad illam partem quae in occidua nostri hemispherii parte est, hac uti. Quos enim primos hominum sua navigatione orbem totum ab occidente per antipodes in ortum lustrando Magellanus ultra Americam reperit in majoribus Moluccarum insulis—illi nugas Muhamedis observant . . . Jam et in Europam haec pestis grassatur, occupatque totam Graeciam." *Grammatica arabica* (Paris: P. Gromorsus, [1538?]).

tribute, after imbibing theory from Galen, to the Arabs in matters of practice."[34] Rabelais, as we know, had a deep admiration for Galen. And we may wonder whether there is not in this passage a hidden allusion to controversies, or at any rate conversations, in Paris or at Saint-Maur between the man who was in the service of the Du Bellays and the protégé of Chancellor Guillaume Poyet.[35] But we recall that Gargantua, in his letter to Pantagruel, told his son to peruse the Greek, *Arabian,* and Latin physicians, and, at a time when no one in France studied Arabic, urged him to learn, along with "the Chaldee," Arabic likewise. And Rabelais himself in another place spoke of a bishop of Caramith "who in Rome was his tutor in the Arabic tongue."[36]

In any case, we should guard against seeing in Postel's judgment of Rabelais's Christianity—and this is our final observation—the authoritative verdict of a strictly observant Catholic. It is impossible to understand anything written by Postel without looking at it from the very special vantage point of this precursor of Campanella who was a propagandist for a natural religion that would embrace in a unified, expanded Christianity all that was best (and fundamentally identical) in Judaism, Islam, and Christianity. The irony, the "Lucianism" of *Pantagruel* could not fail to shock a philosopher with the temperament of a prophet and apostle, as Postel was. He no doubt held it against Rabelais that he made bad use of the intellectual powers he possessed and did not devote his efforts to the positive task of religious reconstruction. Above all, he held it against him that he

34. "Astrologiam et rei medicae praxim illis debemus. Nugentur quicquid velint nescio qui *neoteristae* qui, maledicendi quadam libidine sibi nomen redimere eruditionis volunt, quum tamen ... nullus sit hodie virorum doctorum et in melioris notae praxi exercitatorum, quin postquam egregie a Galeno hausit ipsam theoriam versetur in Arabibus?" And, further on: "Quam multa ... Arabibus solum, non Galeno debemus? Nolo recitare omnium medicinarum temperamentum: saccharum, rhabarbarum turbit, sene, manna, etc." (How many things we owe to the Arabs alone, and not to Galen! I do not wish to go through the compounding of every medicine: sugar, rhubarb root, turpeth, senna, manna, and so on.)

35. These controversies were energetically carried on in medical circles from about 1530. See, for example, *Novae Academiae Florentinae opuscula adversus Avicennam et medicos neotericos qui, Galeni disciplina neglecta, barbaros colunt* (Lyon: S. Gryphius, 1534). Or *Joannis Mesue ... adversus neotericos multos medicos defensio,* G. Puteano Blangiaco medico autore (Lyon: Rose, 1537).

36. "Briefve Déclaration d'aucunes dictions plus obscures contenues on *Quatrième Livre.*" [Translator's note.]

had pledged himself to the Reformation, which Postel—and later Campanella and many others—detested from the bottom of his heart because it split the old Christian world into warring factions and so made more difficult the task of unification to which this strange apostle had dedicated his life. But should his characterization of Rabelais as *Christomastix* be taken very seriously? After all, to him Luther was the "Prince of Antichrists."

    On the other hand, we should not conclude that Postel's judgments were absurd. It may well be that the development he condemned, the slide of many Reformers into more and more liberal doctrines, has been hidden from our view because of Calvin's achievement. It was no less real for that. There was someone who knew it, who saw it, just as Postel did, and who also condemned it in his own way—not Postel's way, because it was not to be expected of him that he would raise doubts about the Reformation. That person was John Calvin.

The *Excuse aux Nicodémites* follows *Alcorani et Evangelistarum concordia* by an interval of a year. I do not think I am the victim of a delusion in thinking that Calvin was not unaware of Postel's violent attack on the Reformation and his very dangerous conclusions. Postel was a remote but direct precursor of Canon Janssen, and he maintained the same thesis that Janssen did, point for point and word for word, in a passage in *Alcorani corcordia* in which he extolled the Germanic innocence and purity of the times preceding the Reformation, and contrasted them with the moral decadence and the torrent of nameless vices and crimes that followed it—the discernible transformation, for example, of the lansquenet, who was once honest and pious, into a raging beast by the new doctrines.[37] For, with a shrewd sense of his adversary's weaknesses, Postel laid his stress on the *morality* of the Reformers. And in what he says of

37. "Caeterum, quis non novit inter Germanos, longe ante isthaec tempora, fuisse summam innocentiam? Certe . . . antequam isthaec concionatorum licentia ita grassaretur . . . Erat ante hanc factionem Germanus miles non saepe in alieno rapiendo abstinentior quovis sanctissimo monacho . . . O utinam pereant, aut convertentur, qui, quicquid erat in Europa generosi una commisere. Ve, ve Germaniae et ejus vicinis!"
(Besides, who does not know that before these times the Germans were the height of innocence? Yes, indeed, before the license of the preachers progressed as it did . . . Before the time of this faction the German soldier did not often engage in rapine but was

the courtier Cenevangelists, who used the theory of justification by faith alone to serve the cause of their vices, some perspicacious observations are mixed in with a host of unfair accusations.[38] The observations allow us to reconstruct in a plausible way a religious development that was rather common then and, most particularly, to question the old theory that it was easy to pass from Catholicism, but not from Evangelism, to a kind of indifferent rationalism. Postel's *aulici Cenevangelistae*, I can't help thinking, were in every characteristic the forerunners by a year of the "delicate protonotaries" whom Calvin violently rejected as tainted with Nicodemism. And, truth to tell, I would be very surprised if *Alcorani concordia* were not one of the sources, and, by provoking a reaction, one of the causes, of the *Excuse de M. Jean Calvin.*[39]

3. A Condemnation by the Sorbonne (1543)

Let us not be so naive as to be astonished that Postel, and others along with him, saw fit in 1543 to regard neither *Pantagruel* nor *Gargantua* as irreproachable, reliable catechisms. There was a well-known authority that had undertaken to instruct everyone in this matter—the theology faculty of the Uni-

---

more abstinent than the holiest monk. Oh, if they would only perish, or be converted—those who have won over everything that was noble in Europe. Woe, woe to Germany and her neighbors!) *Alcorani*, p. 70. Postel as the precursor of Janssen is quite an odd phenomenon. [Johannes Janssen (1829–1891) was the author of *Geschichte des deutschen Volkes seit dem Ausgang des Mittelalters.*—Translator.]

38. In *Alcorani*, p. 112, there is a lengthy discourse on the *aulici Cenevangelistae* who ridicule the Last Judgment: "Ubi est promissio aut adventus ejus?" (Where is it promised or where is it to happen?) they jeer; "ex quo enim patres dormierunt, omnia sic perseverant ab initio creaturae nil aliud familiarius hodie audias ab aulicis Evangelistis qui jam virus suum toto in orbe Cristiano fere sparsere" (for if our fathers have been asleep then all things have continued to exist from the beginning of creation: you hear nothing more commonly said by the courtier Evangelists, who have now spread their poison over the entire Christian world). Further on, Postel attacks the bad morals of those "qui Evangelium in libertatem convertant, interpretationibus contorqueant" (who transform the Gospel into freedom, distorting it with their interpretations). There was another interesting objection to the Last Judgment: "Omnia semper sic fuisse, et Christum nil in orbe immutasse praeter verba. (Everything has always been as it is, and Christ made no change in the world except verbally.) P. 105.

39. Postel was widely read—by Luther, who mentioned him frequently; by Calvin, as we shall see; and by Rabelais. The story of the great god Pan is told by Postel in chapter 7 of Book I of *De orbis concordia*, and it seems likely that this was one of the sources for Rabelais's stories of demons.

versity of Paris. Therefore, if Postel (to speak only of him) gave a long account of his conflicts with that illustrious body in his *Alcorani concordia* and had some harsh and bitter words to say about it, he seemed nonetheless to be very preoccupied with proclaiming and displaying his orthodox associations. Not only did he praise pious bishops like George de Selve, the bishop of Lavaur, or Robert Ceneau, the bishop of Avranches, not to mention Claude Dodée, to whom the book was dedicated, but he spoke of his excellent relations with Doctor "Mallarius" (Maillard), the famous Dominican Orius (that is, the Inquisitor Mathieu Orry), and another well-known Catholic doctor, "Godofridus Titelmanus," *insigni vir pietate.*[40] His conflicts with the Sorbonne had led him to be assiduous in cultivating Catholic theologians. And he was no doubt not surprised when he saw included in the list of dangerous books examined and classified by the theology faculty from Christmas 1542 to March 2, 1543 (according to our way of reckoning) the following item: "64. Grandes Annales très véritables des gestes merveilleux du Grand Gargantua, et Pantagruel Roy des Dipsodes."

◄§ Who drew the attention of the Sorbonne at that date to these works of Rabelais, which had been out for some time? A hypothesis immediately suggests itself. At the end of July or the beginning of August 1542 Dolet had been arrested in Lyon and thrown into the prisons of the archdiocese by order of the Inquisitor. A trial took place, and on October 2 he was sentenced to the stake. The case was appealed to the Parlement of Paris, which considered it. There was a letter of pardon from the king: the humanist printer would be saved, on condition that he abjure his errors and be a witness to the burning of the dangerous books printed by him or found in his possession.[41] Indeed, Du Plessis d'Argentré prints a decree of Parlement for the date of February 14, 1543, ordering, in view of the Inquisitor's request and the decree attendant on the letter of pardon, eleven books printed by him (their names are given), along

40. On de Selve, *Alcorani*, p. 62; Ceneau and Titelmanus, p. 76; Dodée, p. 2; Maillard, p. 9; Orry, p. 10.

41. Christie, p. 414 ff. What Christie says about Dolet's trial is, however, limited and out of date.

with Melanchthon's works, a Geneva Bible, and a copy of Calvin's *Institutes*, to be ceremoniously burned on the square in front of Notre Dame.[42]

Neither the *Gargantua* nor the *Pantagruel* printed by Dolet in 1542 was included among these books, which the investigators must have found copies of at the sign of the *doloire* on Rue Mercière in Lyon. But it was Dolet's case that drew the Sorbonne's attention to two works that the Parlement did not hold to be dangerous but that could have seemed so to the Sorbonne.[43] At any rate, it was not on the basis of Dolet's publications that the Sorbonne made its condemnation. The title given by d'Argentré is proof of that; it is exactly the same as that of the edition with no place of publication that was issued in Lyon in 1542 and appears as no. 42 on p. 98 of Plan's bibliography.[44] It is precisely this edition that contains the "Printer's Note to the Reader" in which Dolet is abused so roundly. Isn't it strange that Dolet's edition (which, we are told, infuriated Rabelais because Dolet had copied an unexpurgated text) did not provoke a harsh response when it was seized and that the judges of the Sorbonne, on the contrary, based their condemnation on the revised and, so to speak, edulcorated text of the 1542

42. See Du Plessis d'Argentré, *Collectio judiciorum de novis erroribus*, 3 vols. (Paris, 1724–1736), II, part 1, 133–134. The decree was directed at *les Gestes du Roy* (no. 19 in Christie's list of books printed by Dolet); *Epigrammes de Dolet* (no. 1); *Caton* (no. 3); *Chrispian; l'Exhortation à la lecture de la Sainte Ecriture* (no. 50; see also René Sturel, "Notes sur Etienne Dolet d'après des inédits," *Revue du Seizième Siècle*, 1 [1913], 55–98); *la Fontaine de Vie* (no. 54); *les Cinquante-deux Dimanches composées par Fabre Stapulense* (no. 44); *les Heures de la Compagnie des Penitens* (no. 53); *le Chevalier Chrétien* by Erasmus (no. 48); *la Manière de se confesser d'Erasme* (no. 49); *le Sommaire du Vieil & Nouveau Testament* (no. 43).
  The Sorbonne's catalogue for December 1542 to March 1543, which follows the above in d'Argentré, mentions in addition the French New Testament printed by Dolet (no. 36 in Christie's list) and *Brief Discours de la Republique françoys desirant la lecture des livres de la Saincte Escripture* (no. 61; see also Sturel). The Latin *Cato* (*Cato Christianus*) had been censured separately, on Sept. 23, 1542. D'Argentré, II, 229.

43. We should note, without making too much of it, that in 1541 and 1542 the abbess of Fontevrault, who was consulting the Sorbonne on a point of doctrine, sent representatives to Paris at various times. See d'Argentré, II, 132–133. It is always a good idea to perk up our ears when Fontevrault is mentioned and our concern is with Rabelais.

44. This is the title: *Grands Annales ou Croniques / Trèsvéritables / des Gestes merveilleux du grand / Gargantua et Pantagruel / son fils. Roy des Dipso / des: enchroniquez par / feu Maistre Alcofribas abstrac / teur de quin / te essen / ce. 1542.* The Sorbonne merely copied it, shortening it a little.

Lyon edition? Furthermore, why did the Sorbonne at that time reissue a condemnation that, according to the opinion prevailing today, it had already made against *Pantagruel* in 1533? Now that the occasion has presented itself, I must confess that the story of the 1533 condemnation, which was accepted as certain by Abel Lefranc, has always seemed suspect to me.[45] It may be that it had been decided in Le Clerc's head, but what keeps puzzling me is how it could have been made real and official by means of a decree that no one has seen and how a book condemned in 1533 could have been reprinted so many times in so many different places without the slightest difficulty. I would prefer to go along with the opinion expressed by Desmaizeaux in his critical notes to Bayle's *Dictionary*. When Le Clerc was assigned to investigate the booksellers, he catalogued the new books he found in the shops. "He divided them into two categories—one of bad books, the other of books that were merely suspect because they were without authors' names and had been printed without the faculty's approval, in defiance of the decree of Parlement . . . He had put the *Miroir* on his list, including it with the books in this second category."[46] Need one add: and *Pantagruel* as well, which undoubtedly benefited from the case of the *Miroir?*

A final observation. All the books that appear in the "Catalogue of Reviewed Works" drawn up by the Sorbonne in 1542 were books by authors who were Reformed or at least in sympathy with the Reformation. *Gargantua* and *Pantagruel* appear along with works by François Lambert d'Avignon, Calvin, Erasmus, Marot, Oecolampadius, Bucer, Johann Brenz, Bugenhagen, Zwingli, Melanchthon, and numerous French translations of sacred books. Thanks to the efforts of the Sorbonne, Rabelais's place is once again not in the ranks of the freethinkers but on the general staff of the Reformation—*Cenevangelistarum antesignani.* The same is true of Dolet. It was not an

45. See above, n. 2. Undoubtedly the distinction applied by Delisle to the *Miroir* can be applied to *Pantagruel:* "It is likely that some doctors had actually censured the book, but it seems certain that an official condemnation had not been pronounced." That was said almost explicitly by the faculty about the *Miroir* on November 3. Delisle, pp. 349–50.

46. Pierre Bayle, *Dictionnaire historique et critique*, 5th ed., 5 vols. (Amsterdam, 1734), IV, 961.

"atheist" who was being persecuted in 1543 but, clearly, an instigator of Reformation heresy.

4. Was Rabelais a Nicodemite?

The following year, however, in 1544, there appeared a polemical work by Calvin: *Excuse à Messieurs les Nicodémites sur la complainte qu'ilz font de sa trop grand' rigueur.*[47] In it there is a well-known passage that Abel Lefranc interpreted as applying to Rabelais.

The *Excuse* (which takes up fifteen pages in Volume VI of the *Calvini opera*, starting with col. 600) consists essentially of a critical description of the Nicodemites, men of little faith. There were those who preached the Word only in order to fish for good benefices in troubled waters. There were the "delicate protonotaries," who were content to discourse on the Gospel before the ladies as long as their zeal "does not impede them from living according to their pleasure"—almost a literal echo, let us note in passing, of Postel's vituperative attack on the impious in *Alcorani concordia.* Conversing with ladies about the Gospel—the phrase has a "Thelemite" ring to it. There were also the bookish ones, who "half transformed Christianity into philosophy"; they relaxed in front of the fire, waiting for a reformation to take place but "taking care not to be actively involved." Here (col. 602) there is a sudden explosion of rage that reveals Calvin's inner feelings: "This band consists almost entirely of men of letters; not that all men of letters are in it; for I would rather that all human knowledge were eradicated from the earth than that it should be the cause of cooling the zeal of Christians and turning them away from God!" Finally, there were "the merchants and the common people, who, comfortable at home, are displeased if anyone comes to disturb them." Having ended his review of those enrolled under the banner of Nicodemus, Calvin makes a brief allusion to "Lucianists or Epicureans, who make a show of cleaving to the Word and in their hearts mock it and think it to be no more than a fable."

No doubt about it, Abel Lefranc tells us, it is Rabelais whom Calvin was referring to. Wasn't he described twenty times, a

---

47. *Answer to the Nicodemites Against Their Complaint of His Too Great Rigor.*

hundred times, as the "French Lucian"? Maybe. But the same thing is true of these passages by Calvin as was true somewhat earlier of Visagier's epigrams. We should not make Lucianism a monopoly of Rabelais. And we should above all be cautious and not write that Calvin "was clearly referring" to Rabelais "in a whole series of passages" in the *Excuse*.[48] What passages? Either Calvin was thinking of Rabelais in speaking of the Lucianists, so there is no point in looking for several passages referring to the author of *Pantagruel* because Calvin spoke about the Lucianists in only one place, and then only to say that he would not speak about them anymore; or else Calvin was referring to Rabelais in other parts of the *Excuse*. Did he therefore regard him as a Nicodemite and not as a Lucianist? Again, there is no mention of Rabelais by name in the *Excuse*. Calvin's polemic of 1544 did not descend to personalities. It stayed with generalities.

And again we sing our old refrain. Let us concede that Calvin was thinking of Rabelais in 1544 when he denounced the "contemners of God"—1544, that is to say, twelve years after the appearance of *Pantagruel*. A book published in 1532 did not look the same in 1544 as it did on the day of its birth; an extraordinarily important development had had an opportunity to take place in the minds of many humanists between those two dates; someone like Calvin, aware of the rapid progress made by anti-Christian rationalism in certain circles, among Epicureans with their easygoing slogan "Eat, drink, and be merry" (no one knows, Henri Hauser pointed out, whether Antoine Fumée[49] in referring to them as *panourgoi* meant to call them "scoundrels" or "Panurges"), reacted by being deeply disturbed, and his disturbance translated itself into retroactive judgments on works of which he could have had a different opinion at first. There is nothing impossible in all of this. The whole question, to be precise, is whether in 1533 and 1535 Calvin was already seeing *Pantagruel* and *Gargantua* with the vision of 1544 and 1550.

5. "L'Enraigé Putherbe" and "De Scandalis" (1549)

Five years passed, and then, in 1549, came the celebrated passage in *Theotimus*. Following Postel and the Sorbonne, Brother

48. Lefranc, p. lv. [Translator's note.]
49. In his letter to Calvin in 1542 or 1543. See *Calvini opera*, XI, cols. 490–494.

Gabriel de Puy-Herbault accused Rabelais of radical impiety and, at the same time, sent him packing to Geneva, his true homeland, without troubling to find out whether Master John Calvin was ready or not to celebrate the return of such prodigal sons to the fold. The point, however, was to strike at Rabelais with every kind of weapon, even if the shots went off in different directions. Atheist and Lutheran—if one had strong feelings one had no hesitation in the sixteenth century in linking these two contradictory epithets with the name of an adversary one wanted to destroy. The fiery monk of Fontevrault vehemently denounced the scandalous books of the ex-Franciscan. Still, he did not reproach him for apostasy; all he found fault with was his philosophy.

"What Diagoras has misunderstood God worse? What Timon has slandered humanity more?" But Putherbeus was not very interested in Diagoras. His preferred theme was calumny. Rabelais was a cheap pamphleteer, a defamer of honest folk—and a cynic to boot.

A maker of clever phrases, living on his tongue, a parasite. One might tolerate him if one had to, except that he also condemns himself. Every day he gets drunk and stuffs himself. He lives like a Greek. He sniffs out the aromas of every kitchen, imitates a monkey with a long tail, and, what's more, dirties paper with his infamies, vomiting forth a poison that little by little infects every place. He hurls calumny and abuse at all orders indiscriminately. He attacks honest folk and pious study and the privileges of honor. He mocks without shame, without a trace of decency. Can he be tolerated? It is a thing unheard of that a bishop of our religion, the first in rank and learning, protects and feeds and admits to the intimacy of his table and his conversation a man who lives in contempt of public morality and decency—one might say he is their worst enemy, a filthy and rotten person, possessing so many words and so little reason![50]

---

50. This passage, printed in italics in a book that is all in roman, is found on pp. 180–183 of *Theotimus* (*Gabrielis Putherbei Turonici . . . , Theotimus sive de tollendis et expungendis malis libris, . . . libri III* [Paris: J. Roigny, 1549]). Lefranc translated it in *Revue des Etudes Rabelaisiennes,* 4 (1906), p. 339.

The diatribe is impressive. It was, however, Rabelais's morals and his mocking effrontery that "l'enraigé Putherbe"[51] particularly found fault with. Impiety was barely mentioned in passing. And it was not God but the "honest folk" who had been shamelessly attacked by satire that Brother Gabriel most of all wanted to avenge. As a matter of fact, by defining the true meaning of the attack, someone has taken it upon himself to reduce its importance considerably. Abel Lefranc established the fact that the Fontevrault monk was the instrument of private enmities—those of the Sainte-Marthe family, whose headquarters were at Fontevrault, where Gaucher de Sainte-Marthe was the abbey's physician. This man, who was buried in the choir of the abbey church in 1551, seems during his life to have had a deep hatred for Antoine Rabelais, François's hypothetical father. Perhaps he was the model for the portrait of the irascible Picrochole. At any rate, when "l'enraigé Putherbe" inveighed against Rabelais he was not playing the role of a historian of religious doctrine. In his entire book on bad books he named—or rather indicated—only one author: Rabelais. It is really impossible to have any doubt that this was for personal reasons.[52]

◄§ The violent language of *Theotimus* came a little before the indictment—just as fierce but more disinterested—by Calvin's *De scandalis* in 1550. This time Rabelais's name was spelled out by "the impostor of Geneva." The latter tells us that he was not one of the obdurate, like Agrippa or Simon de Neufville or Dolet, who always treated the Gospel with haughty disdain, poured vile blasphemies on the Son of God, and maintained that men were no different from dogs and pigs.[53] Like Des Périers and like Gouvea, Rabelais had started out by tasting the Gospel. Only later did blindness strike him and his fellows. It was their sacrilegious laughter that led them to atheism and materialism.

Let us go no further. This is the whole passage, *the* passage. The passages that follow add nothing, they only repeat. They

51. See "les enraigéz Putherbes," *Book Four*, ch. 32.

52. Apart from the article by Lefranc, just cited, see his note on p. 347 of the same volume of *Revue des Etudes Rabelaisiennes*. It leaves no doubt whatever about the participation of Charles de Sainte-Marthe in the attack on Rabelais.

53. *Calvini opera*, VIII, col. 44.

are no more conclusive—indeed, less so. Calvin's appearance of fairness when he takes into account Rabelais's past history as a man in sympathy with the Reformation makes the accusations at the end more impressive. And how precise they are! The goal of Rabelais, Gouvea, and Des Périers is "to abolish all reverence for God"; they do not hesitate to say that "all religions have been formed in the brains of men; that we think there is a God because we like to believe it; that hope of life eternal is something to amuse idiots with; that everything said about hell is done to frighten little children." The indictment is thorough, the prosecutor sure of himself.[54] Afterward there may have been two—or a dozen—others who repeated Calvin's remarks, but it makes little difference. Estienne, Castellio, and others added nothing to what the Reformer enumerated with unmatched energy, ferocity, and certainty in 1550.[55]

It was all said—but for whom? Up to now we have taken the testimony that has been offered, witness by witness. We have weighed the words and informed ourselves about the circumstances of publication, about the personality and intellectual bent of the authors. Some testimony we have rejected as irrelevant—that of 1533 and 1538, and other pieces as well. What are we to do with this "important text" of 1550? Shall we once again point out its late date? Shall we again state that for Calvin, as for Postel, Rabelais had begun by "tasting the Gospel"?

---

54. Too sure—else why Gouvea? Joseph Scaliger wondered why: "Goveanus fuit doctus Lusitanus. Calvinus vocat illum atheum, cum non fuerit. Debebat illum melius nosse." (Gouvea was a learned Portuguese. Calvin calls him an atheist, which he was not. He ought to have known him better.) *Scaligerana ou bons mots . . . de J. Scaliger* (Cologne, 1695), p. 175. See also the following section.

55. His third sermon on ch. 13 of Deuteronomy (Oct. 16, 1555) adds nothing to this. "Say there is a man," says Calvin, "a bigot who wants to establish a new religion in a state"; such a one should (what terrible conviction!) "be put to death at once: it is God's command!" Say, too, there is a man who, out of mistaken devoutness, is disposed to pervert truth and turn it into falsehood: "Such a one must die!" But "say there is a rustic who makes vile jokes at the expense of Holy Writ, like that devil called *Pantagruel* and all such filth and knavery." He and others like him "do not claim to be setting up a new religion, but are mad dogs who disgorge their filth in opposition to the Majesty of God out of a wish to pervert all religion. Should such as they be spared? Indeed! They have cardinals to support them, they have their approval . . . The lord cardinals' names are to be seen emblazoned in those fine books, which ridicule God as much as they do Muhammad!" Those cardinals sound a lot like *Theotimus*. *Calvini opera*, XXVII, col. 261.

This is a secondary issue. Calvin's words raise another question, a theoretical, or if you will, a methodological one.

6. What the Accusation of Atheism Meant in the Sixteenth Century

In Paris around 1936 if a man of the lower middle class made speeches and went to a lot of political meetings his neighbors said, "That's a dangerous man." Then they lowered their voices and, in the same tone in which they would have said "anarchist" in 1900, they uttered the words, "He's a communist!" It is a remark that belongs to our age, which is preoccupied more than anything else with social problems. In the sixteenth century it was religion that colored the universe. If a man proclaimed that he did not think about things exactly the way everyone else did, if he was bold in speech and quick to criticize, people said, "He is impious. A blasphemer." And they finished with, "An atheist!"

So there was an author—or two or a dozen—of that time who declared, "That man? He's an atheist! His book is a manifesto of pure atheism!" Are we going to conclude without further ado that they said it and they ought to know? And that therefore the man *was* an atheist?

Let us listen to the opinion of a serious man—Viret, the Lausanne Reformer. He was a prudent and balanced minister, and throughout his long life he maintained a rather original touch of Swiss-French wiliness. In 1564, like so many of his colleagues, he was troubled by the advances of rationalism. He made a sharp attack on them in an "Epistle to the Church of Montpellier," which appears at the beginning of Volume II of his *Instruction Chrestienne*.[56] There exist, he said, monsters so abominable that they have no belief in Jesus and profess that after the death of the body there is neither eternal life nor eternal death. Among them are some who call themselves "deists." By this they mean they are not atheists, because atheist, they claim, means without God, whereas they recognize a god, the creator

---

56. The passage is reproduced in *Pierre Viret d'après lui-même* (Lausanne, 1911), p. 235. On pp. 236–237 there is a curious excerpt from Viret's *Interim* (1565) about atheists who pretend to be good Catholics.

of heaven and earth; however, they know nothing of Christ and his teachings. Well, Viret pointed out, these men deceive themselves. They certainly are atheists. "For when Saint Paul, in the Epistle to the Ephesians, called the pagans 'atheists' he declared that not merely those who denied all divinity were without God but also those who did not know the true God and followed strange gods instead of Him."[57]

Nothing is clearer than this passage, or more striking. Let us translate it as follows: "Atheist," declares Viret, is the superlative of "deist." What good are all the protestations of those who profess human philosophy? They have a God, and some of them, according to what they say, profess "some conviction of the soul's immortality."[58] That means little to us. Their God is not our God. They are not of our religion. A curse on them, and an end to empty subtleties. If we put them into the superlative it will make a bigger impression: they are atheists! That is how all controversialists in the sixteenth century reasoned—and even in other centuries. I say controversialists, because we should not always assume that men like Viret, Calvin, Estienne, Castellio, and, in the other camp, "l'enraigé Putherbe"—all these witnesses of ours with their clenched fists—were serious and careful historians of ideas, conscientiously seeking to define their contemporaries' opinions. They were all propagandists. I nearly said preachers, preachers who knew their trade. They knew that it was a good idea to cry "Wolf!" at the top of your voice if you wanted to move your audience, even when—especially when—the wolf was at most a stray dog. "Atheist" is a word that carries us into the heart of the sixteenth century. It did not have a strictly defined meaning. It was used in whatever sense one wanted to give it. Viret tells us so unambiguously. He goes so far as to state in the passage that we quoted above that "it would be possible to call the superstitious and the idolatrous 'atheists.' " Ronsard echoes this when he treats the Hu-

57. A little later on, Viret adds, "It is common to call by this name [atheists] not only those who deny all divinity, if indeed anyone so wretched can be found among men, but also those who make fun of all religion, like the deists."

58. Atheism and the denial of immortality—these were the only two attitudes detested by More's Utopians. Yet they restricted themselves to excluding atheists from public functions and preventing them from spreading their errors. See the section on religion in Book II, *De optimo reip. statu deque nova insula Utopia libellus ... Thomae Mori ...* (Basel: Froben, 1518), p. 140.

guenots as atheists, and so does Antoine de La Roche-Chandieu (A. Zamariel) when he replies to Ronsard:

> Athée est celuy que la coustume emporte
> Ores croyant ainsi, ores d'une autre sorte;
> Celluy là croit en Dieu qui y croit nonobstant
> Que l'homme pour cela l'aille persecutant.[59]

> An atheist is one whose faith conforms
> To what mere custom dictates as its norms,
> But those whose faith in God is real persist
> Though worldly power demands that they desist.

Or, still addressing Ronsard and paying him back in the same coin, he declares:

> Athée est qui, mentant, maintient la Papauté
> De laquelle il se moque et voit la fausseté!

> An atheist tells lies: out loud invokes
> The pope, the butt of all his private jokes.

It is still not very easy to give an accurate definition of the word atheist, or, to be more exact, the precise characteristics of atheism. It was a subject that inspired the learned Bayle (to speak only of him)—inspired him to our delight, since he was rarely wittier than when he put his clawed hand, with the points of the claws barely showing, on the hierarchy of the various degrees of atheism "according to the learned men of Hall"[60] or on the harm done to faith by holding with too much vigor and conviction that philosophy and culture inculcate disbelief and are the natural enemies of religion.[61] But "atheist" as

---

59. Quoted in Nathanaël Weiss, "Clément Marot, Ronsard, d'après quelques publications récentes," *Bulletin de la Société de l'Histoire du Protestantisme Français*, 74 (1925), 361, n. 1.

60. Bayle, V, 324, s.v. "Thales." The learned men of Hall distinguished three atheisms. The first maintained that there was no God, the second that the world was not God's work, and the third that "God created the world by a natural determination, and without being prompted to it by any free impulse." In English, Bayle, *A General Dictionary, Historical and Critical*, 10 vols. (London, 1734-1741), IX, 529.

61. Bayle, V, 287, s.v. "Takidden"; III, 358, s.v. "Hobbes."

The so-called letter to Salignac, written by Rabelais to Erasmus on November 30, 1532. Note the mixture of Latin and Greek, and the signature, "François Rabelais, physician."

a kind of obscenity meant to cause a shudder in an audience of the faithful? It is probably a little silly to ask for a precise definition of that.

◄§ If we do not see the matter in this way we cannot understand anything about the astonishing contradictions of sixteenth-century men. To start with, we cannot explain the really comical way they shamelessly used the supreme insult "Atheist!" against each other.[62]

Rabelais was an atheist, you say? Very well. But in 1532 a Frenchman in Lyon, a humanist, wrote a famous letter to Erasmus. This is the celebrated letter "to Salignac," whose real recipient is known today beyond any doubt.[63] What does it contain, apart from an effusion of respect, admiration, and filial gratitude lavished on Erasmus by its author? A curious passage about Julius Caesar Scaliger. That impostor had just hurled a ferocious bill of particulars at the great humanist. Erasmus did not know his attacker and had taken his grandiloquent name for a pseudonym, thinking that Aleander was the author of the attack. "Undeceive yourself," wrote his correspondent. "I know this Scaliger. He really exists. He is practicing as a physician at Agen. The devil (*diabolos ekeinos*) is in bad repute. Not as a doctor—he is not without knowledge in medical matters. But as a believer: he is an atheist such as no man ever was (*atheos hos ouk allos popot' oudeis*)."

The author of that letter was Rabelais. And so in 1532, the very year of *Pantagruel*, Rabelais, shielding his eyes in horror,

62. Henri Estienne knew of a worse one. See his anecdote about Pasquin, who had been insulted by someone. "What did he say?" asked his friends. "Robber? Liar? Poisoner?" "Much worse!" answered Pasquin. "Blasphemer, then? Parricide? Bugger? Atheist?" "Much worse, much worse. He called me 'Pope'!" *Apologie pour Hérodote*, ed. P. Ristelhuber, 2 vols. (Liseux, 1879), II, 373. For Estienne "atheist" was, however, supreme among "normal" insults.

63. The original is in the Municipal Library of Zurich in the Thesaurus Hottingerianus, XI, 569. See Herminjard, III, 413–414; Théodore Ziesing, *Erasme ou Salignac?* (Paris, 1887), with a facsimile at the front; Arthur Heulhard, *Une Lettre fameuse, Rabelais à Erasme* (Paris, 1904); Joseph Förstemann and Otto Günther, eds., *Briefe an Des. Erasmus*, Beihefte zur Zentralblatt für Bibliothekswesen, 27 (Leipzig, 1904), p. 216; Louis Talant, *Rabelais et la Réforme* (Cahors, 1902), p. 265 ff. See also Rabelais, *Les Oeuvres*, ed. Marty-Laveaux, III, 322. There is an English translation in *The Works of Francis Rabelais*, ed. Albert Jay Nock and Catherine Rose Wilson, 2 vols. (New York, 1931), II, 890–891.

accused Scaliger of atheism! Scaliger, however, was not long in
retaliating, and he did not overwork his imagination to do it.[64]
"Me? An atheist? Not as great a one as you!" These are Ciceronian rhetorical devices.

Let us go on to Dolet, who, when he saw "Lutherans" being
burned alive in Paris in 1534 after the posting of the Placards,
was content to shrug his shoulders in disdain: the poor fools,
how could they attribute so much importance to worthless religious quarrels as to get themselves killed like that! But with
what did the same Dolet, so above the fray here, strenuously reproach Erasmus a year later—Erasmus, to whom Rabelais had
shortly before communicated his scandalized discovery that
Scaliger was an atheist; Erasmus, who could hardly have been
unaware of Dolet's reputation or, perhaps, of the curious letter
that his secretary, Gilbert Cousin of Nozeroy, had received at
the end of 1535 from an unknown young man, Johannes An-
gelus Odonus?[65] Yes, Dolet—suspect, a Paduan, "the atheist
Dolet"—in 1535 Dolet accused Erasmus of atheism.[66] And what
a scandalized tone he used! "As for his ideas, where did he get
them, if not from Lucian, the most cutting and impudent of all
authors, a man without religion and without God, disposed to
ridicule everything, religious as well as profane." His indignation is wonderful, isn't it? It is true that I wrote "the atheist
Dolet." I am not using the epithet casually. I am simply reflecting, without further discussion, the accusations of such as Calvin, Estienne, Viret, Castellio, and others. One more name, and
that will do. Briand Vallée, a magistrate in Saintes and later in
Bordeaux, who belongs, on the strength of say-so, in the catalogue of the century's militant rationalists.[67] He was no doubt

64. That is, if Rabelais was meant by the *bis monachus tandemque atheos* we discussed in ch. 1, sect. 7. See also his polemic against Cardano, whose accusation of impiety he returned, and his letter to Beda in Johann Georg Schelhorn, *Amoenitates literariae*, 14 vols. (Frankfort and Leipzig, 1730-31), VI, 523. In the latter he calls
Erasmus "coenum . . . sceleratorum latrunculorum, qui in veram religionem nostram
grassati sunt, caput" (a filthy swine, the chief of the knaves and brigands who have
made attacks on our true religion).

65. See above, ch. 1, sect. 4.

66. *Stephani Doleti dialogus de imitatione ciceroniana adversus Desid. Erasmum
Roterodamum pro Christophoro Longolio* (Lyon: S. Gryphius, 1535), p. 79. See also
Busson, p. 11.

67. Busson, pp. 114-116. The reasons that led Busson to consider Briand a prominent rationalist do not convince me. Ernest Gaullieur, in *Histoire du Collège de
Guyenne* (Paris, 1874), p. 157, considers him Reformed, under the influence of the

only a liberal spirit, a Christian infatuated with Saint Paul and prepared, like Gargantua, to protect "Evangelical preachers." He was, in any case, a friend of Rabelais, who refers to him twice in his narrative. It was Briand who advised that the thorny case of my lords Kissbreech and Suckfist be taken to the King of the Dipsodes for arbitration.[68] And it was he, "that good, virtuous, learned, and just president," who in chapter 37 of *Book Four* was able during a procession to say on which side hunchbacks were deformed, the right or the left, solely on the basis of whether the number of syllables in their names was even or odd. Which, by the way, may not be the most edifying way to participate in a procession. This intellect who was so free of prejudice was also, it seems, afraid of thunder. His friend Antonio de Gouvea presumed to tease him about it on one occasion: "It began to thunder. Vallée at once ran at top speed down to the end of the cellar. The good Lord, he thought, is not found in cellars!" The fascinating thing about this is that Gouvea was one of the atheists mentioned in *De scandalis*,[69] one of the ones whose names Calvin spelled out, along with Rabelais and Des Périers, whose goal was "to abolish all reverence for God." At any rate, his couplet was not very wicked. Briand took it amiss, however. And what did the infidel, the man under suspicion, lose no time in accusing Gouvea of? Of atheism, of course! "Antonio Gouvea, that son of a Marrano! He doesn't believe God is to be found anywhere, either in heaven or in the cellar!"

So you see God played a strange role as a policeman in the prose and verse of these liberated men. And atheists were apparently rather inclined to be scandalized by the atheism of others.

---

court at Nérac; he reminds us that he provided an endowment for the reading of the Pauline Epistles on the first Sunday of every month, for which he alienated part of his fortune; the readings were discontinued by a decree of the court (1540?). Briand's son, a professed Calvinist, was condemned with 546 other Protestants on April 6, 1569, to be humiliated and decapitated.

68. *Pantagruel*, ch. 10: "one amongst them, named Du Douhet, the learnedest of all, and more expert and prudent than any of the rest."

69. On Gouvea's reputation for atheism, see the preceding section. See also Bayle; François Mugnier, *Antoine Govéan* (Paris, 1901); Busson, p. 114. The epigram on Briand Vallée is on p. 9 of Gouvea's collection. The original has *trepido* (anxious instead of *propero* (hasty) *pede* (foot), which scholars have passed along ever since Bayle. [For the phrase translated "at top speed."—Translator.]

◄§ All right, we may say: atheist in the sixteenth century did not always mean atheist. At the very least it signified unbeliever. Can we claim that Rabelais, Scaliger, Dolet, and Briand Vallée were model Christians for their age?

Let us put Rabelais aside, and Dolet, too, perhaps. What about Scaliger? After all, the documents published by Patry tell us that in 1538 he was prosecuted for heresy in Agen. He had chosen as a tutor for his children (so Beza tells us in his *Histoire ecclésiastique*) a Lutheran, Philibert Sarrazin, who had to flee.[70] Scaliger owed his acquittal to the influence of three councillors in the Bordeaux Parlement: La Chassagne, Arnoud Le Ferron—and Briand Vallée. Besides, the words of Joseph, that devoted son, can be cited as evidence. "My father," he said in *Scaligerana*, "at the time of the first burnings harbored those of the Religion, with which he was in sympathy." Later on: "My father, four years before his death, was a semi-Lutheran; every day he saw more and more abuses." And, naturally, "he hated monks."[71] So much for Scaliger. But what about Briand Vallée? An anti-Christian or atheist who in his will endowed a chair for the exegesis of St. Paul? What about Castellio? And Luther? And a score of others of like stature and sentiments?

Let us stop for a moment to consider the case of Castellio. He was one of Rabelais's accusers. In 1554, when Master Alcofribas was no more, shortly after the tragedy at Champel, Castellio came out against those who insisted on making Servetus an atheist. "These calumnies," he wrote in a work that was not to see the light of day until 1614—which considerably lessens its historical impact—"have been so skillfully spread about that numerous Christians see in Servetus another Rabelais, another Dolet, another Neufville, one who has no more faith in God or in Christ than they."[72] Rabelais, Dolet, and Neufville—haven't we encountered this symbolic trio before? Yes, we have: in

---

70. Theodore Beza, *Histoire ecclésiastique des églises réformées au royaume de France*, ed. P. Vesson, 2 vols. (Toulouse, 1882), I, 14–15.

71. *Scaligerana*, pp. 9, 357.

72. "Ita ut putent homines Servetum aliquem fuisse Rabelasii aut Doleti aut Villanovani similem qui nullum Deum aut Christum haberet." There is a noteworthy discussion of this passage in Ferdinand Buisson, *Sébastien Castellion, sa vie et son oeuvre, 1515–1563*, 2 vols. (Paris, 1892), I, 45. It comes from Castellio's *Contra libellum Calvini*, which was written in 1554 but remained in manuscript till 1612; neither Rabelais

Guillaume Postel in 1543 (with Dolet omitted) and in Calvin's *De scandalis* in 1550. The list was passed along from preacher to preacher, with some variations, but very few. Rabelais's name suggested Bonaventure's. Neufville evoked Dolet, unless it was the other way around: the master and the disciple. Especially since Simon de Neufville, Villanovanus (an almost complete unknown), was known practically only through Dolet, and Dolet took care not to call him an atheist. From the disciple, whose opinions were talked about, the totally unknown master was deduced and generously endowed with a "rationalist" creed very similar to the supposed creed of Dolet.[73] This is largesse thrown to us by controversialists. Do we, as historians, have to accept it?

Sebastian Castellio, then, also seriously thought Rabelais was one of those men who believed neither in God nor, a fortiori, in Christ: "Qui nullum Deum aut Christum . . . habent." That could have been only a reconstruction. Well, let us open the *Apologie pour Hérodote* to chapter 14, which contains a fiery denunciation of the new Lucian, Rabelais.[74] Yet another. Let us not restrict ourselves to reading Estienne's diatribe; let us follow his reasoning. In this rather late text of 1566 he was dealing with "blasphemies and curses." He made accusations left and right (p. 182), including both the foul-mouthed, who swore, "I deny God," and the more refined, who called the pope "Most Holy Father." Livid with rage, he told of the abominable jokes made by people who cried out "Sursum corda" when they saw a hanged man; "quia pius es" at a glass of wine (*piot*);[75] or

---

nor his contemporaries were acquainted with it. Of all the pertinent passages collected by Lefranc, the only ones that affected Rabelais directly were those in Postel (1543), in *Theotimus* (1549), and in *De scandalis* (1550). We know how he responded to *Theotimus* and to Calvin.

73. On Simon de Neufville in Hainaut, see Busson, pp. 75–76 and passim. On his relationship with Dolet, ibid., p. 122, and Christie, p. 27 ff.

74. "Our age has seen Lucian reborn as a Frenchman, François Rabelais, with respect to writings that scoff at every kind of religion." Estienne, *Apologie pour Hérodote*, I, 189–190.

75. It was an old joke. See "Calice et doigt le prestre lèche en disant 'quia pius es' " (the priest licks the chalice and his fingers, saying, "Quia pius es"), *La Vérité cachée devant cent ans . . .* (Geneva: J. Michel, 1544), fol. 6r. [The Latin phrases are from liturgy and Scripture: *Sursum corda* = lift up your hearts; *quia pius es* = for thou art holy; *spiritus vitae erat in rotis* = the spirit of the living creature was in the wheels (Ezekiel 1:20).—Translator.]

"Spiritus vitae erat in rotis" at a bottle full of wine from a year when the grapes had had a great deal of sun (*vins rôtis*). Then he brought in Rabelais, associating him, according to the prescribed usage, with Des Périers—two irreligious men who wished to teach others to believe neither in God nor in Providence, "any more than wicked Lucretius had believed"; everything taught by religion was hypothetical; everything one read about eternal life was "written to amuse poor idiots and nourish them with vain hope"; everything said about hell and the Last Judgment was a hobgoblin to frighten little children; in short, "all religions were formed in the heads of men." This was how their terrible teachings could be summed up.

A splendid indictment. Henri Estienne inherited his animosity from his father Robert, who in 1553 bemoaned the fact that Rabelais had not been sent to the stake.[76] When he composed his charge (perhaps in order to display his zeal a bit), he had no idea that one day he himself would be called before the Consistory for having printed a "scandalous" book. The registers of the Company of Pastors, according to Jean Senebier, inform us on that occasion "that in Europe they call him the Pantagruel of Geneva and the prince of atheists"![77] In the sixteenth century one was apparently always someone or other's atheist or Pantagruel. Be that as it may, Estienne's text contains a sentence that Abel Lefranc believed he could leave out without damage, but

76. "Atque hujus modi quidem doctores pro Christi Salvatoris pura doctrina, facile libenterque accipient doctrinam scelerati impiique illius hominis, ac plane athei, *Fr. Rabelesii*, ejusque libros qui non minus impie quam insulse *Gargantuae ac Pantagruelis* nomine sunt inscripti." (There are also some learned men of this sort who freely and easily accept, in place of Christ our Savior's pure doctrine, the doctrine of that vicious and impious man, clearly an atheist, François Rabelais, and his books entitled *Gargantua and Pantagruel*, which were written with as much impiety as bad taste.) Robert Estienne, *In Evangelium secundum Matthaeum, Marcum et Lucam, commentarii ex ecclesiasticis scriptoribus collecti* (Geneva: R. Stephanus, 1553), preface.

77. Jean Senebier, *Histoire littéraire de Genève*, 3 vols. (Geneva, 1786), I, 364. As for what was suspect about Henri with regard to Protestant orthodoxy, see the curious bit of evidence in *Scaligerana*: "Semel erat paratus apostatare. Volebat manere Parisiis ... Rogavit regem ut liberet sibi excedere Geneva, et procuraret infringi testamentum patris Roberti, quo dederat sua bona filio H. Stephano, ea lege ut maneret Genevae. Rex non obtinuit, quia Genevenses voluerunt servare leges suas." (Once he was ready to desert. He wanted to live in Paris ... He called on the king to allow him to leave Geneva and to annul his father Robert's will, by which he had given his goods to his son H. Estienne on condition that he stayed in Geneva. The king did not accomplish this, because the Genevans wished to preserve their own laws.) P. 145.

it is one that is perhaps less insignificant than he thought. The goal of Rabelais, Des Périers, and their associates, Estienne wrote, was, "after slipping in by means of the many jibes and lampoons they hurled at the ignorance of our predecessors . . . to throw stones into our garden too, . . . that is, to strike at the true Christian religion." The true Christian religion is understood of course to be that of Henri Estienne.

The sentence is funny. To begin with, it betrays the embarrassment Estienne felt in accommodating within his scheme all those attacks in *Gargantua* and *Pantagruel* on the "abuses" of the Catholics. It also allows us to perceive a somewhat comical situation. Rabelais was at first congenial to the Reformers, and Beza (though it was before he joined the religion of Geneva) started out by praising his talents and philosophy with much energy and conviction.[78] If Rabelais suddenly became uncongenial and odious to them, it was at the moment he stopped throwing stones only into the pope's garden.

How does chapter 14 of the *Apologie* end? What is its climax? A thoroughgoing attack on another outstanding blasphemer, none other than Sebastian Castellio. Yes, Sebastian Castellio, the disastrous translator of the Bible into French. He had decided to use everyday expressions in his translation— "beggars' words," said Estienne pompously. It was out of pure spite, to cause laughter at the expense of the sacred text, the spite of an unbeliever "who expressly sought out such modes of speaking in order to expose these solemn and holy utterances to derision." Yet Castellio could consider himself lucky: Estienne did not go so far as to treat him as an atheist. Conrad Badius would not show such restraint. When Monsieur de Parvo Castello (a transparent pseudonym) in the *Comédie du Pape Malade* asks, "But what if I am not a papist?" Satan replies at once, "Well, what are you then, my fine atheist?"

And so Monsieur de Parvo Castello—Castellio, the pious Christian—joined Rabelais, Dolet, and Neufville in the atheist hell into which he had been so determined to cast them.[79] As

---

78. Beza's nice couplet—"Quia sic nugatur tractantem ut seria vincat / seria quum faciet, dic, rogo, quantus erit?" (When he who in jesting outdoes those who treat of serious matters shall himself do serious things, how great he will be!)—appeared in the 1548 edition of his poems (*Poemata* [Paris: C. Badius, 1548], p. 16). It was later omitted.

79. On this, see Buisson, II, 254–255.

for Henri Estienne, he did not spend any more time attacking
the author of *De haereticis.* He turned quite soon to another
unbeliever, a man guilty of the worst impiety and crimes. He
was "a knave," this Postel; it was not enough for him "to spew
out his monstrous blasphemies to one and all in private but he
has them printed!"[80]

    ❧ They were all impious, if we are to believe them—unbe-
lievers and, finally, atheists, great and small. We can picture the
big ones eating the little ones, as in the engraving by Bruegel
the Elder—a whole series of fish contained one inside another
in order of their size after being swallowed. We are unquestionably dealing with a device of lawyers or controversialists. And
something else as well, something we too often overlook: a way
of reasoning that was familiar to men of the time. It was a way
of demonstrating their learning. It was the same procedure by
which Father Garasse, for example, revealed to his readers
somewhat later, in *The Curious Doctrine of the Wits of Our
Time*, that Luther had achieved "a perfection of atheism" and
that that man, "corporeal and made entirely of fat," had taught
"that the immortality of the soul is nothing but a pure chimera."[81] There is no doubt about what Garasse was doing; Gui
Patin claimed that the Jesuits were ashamed of him. When he
denounced Pomponazzi and Cornelius Agrippa as devils incar-
nate he cynically added for good measure that he had never
read a line of their writings.[82] Yet consider Cardinal Du Perron,
a serious man, a man of weight and of erudition. Du Perron
said, exactly as Garasse did, "Luther denied the immortality of
the soul and said that it died with the body . . . Among the im-
pieties of the Roman Church he included this: that it believed
in the immortality of the soul."[83]
    Bayle wanted to clear this up. He looked for the apparent

---

80. *Apologie pour Hérodote,* I, 192; II, 187.
81. François Garasse, *La Doctrine curieuse des beaux esprits de ce temps, ou pretendus tels* (Paris: S. Chappelet, 1624), pp. 214, 877. On p. 251 he calls Erasmus and
Zwingli "two hawks of atheism."
82. Garasse, p. 1013. As is only fitting, Garasse himself was accused of atheism; J.
Roger Charbonnel, *La Pensée italienne au XVIᵉ siècle et le courant libertin* (Paris,
1917), p. 351, n. 1. Childish games.
83. Jacques Davy Du Perron, *Perroniana et Thuana,* 2d ed. (Cologne, 1669), p.
202, s.v. "Luther."

reason for these absurdities and concluded that it must have
been Luther's vacillation on the controversial question of the
state of souls after death.[84] Did they remain asleep until the day
of Judgment? Luther, in one of his letters, does not seem to
have totally rejected this view—and for that matter it was held
by several of the fathers. But if they were asleep the souls could
not behold God. Was Luther depriving them of God's visible
presence? That did it. Luther was a denier of immortality; he
treated it with contempt! Was Du Perron telling a cynical untruth, then? Not at all. He had reasoned it out, and correctly, as
he saw it. He had made deductions. He had followed an orderly—hence legitimate—chain of syllogisms, each perfectly
contained in the other. In doing so he was being a man of his
time and his cloth. He had been trained and knew how to
argue. And his contemporaries knew how to argue as he did.
Their minds did not follow the same steps as ours do. They
found nothing surprising about starting from a simple notion
and suddenly finding themselves at the opposite pole from the
starting point. Or, I imagine, about using one of Luther's religious doctrines as a basis for ending with the formulation of an
accusation of materialism or impiety against Luther that he
himself would have found acceptable—since he would have
seen the logical steps by which it had been deduced from contrary premises. These ways of reasoning are surprising to us.
They get in our way when we try to explain all the tragic
events of that time that remain mysteries to us.[85] For example,
to cite only one, the tragic event at Champel.

Some time ago—in 1920, in volume 69 of the *Bulletin de la
Société de l'Histoire du Protestantisme Français*—Hippolyte
Aubert published a disturbing document, a handwritten note
by Guillaume Farel jotted on the first page of a copy of Ser-
vetus's book *De Trinitatis erroribus libri septem*. In this note
Farel expressed his general opinion of the Servetus affair. That

84. See Xavier Marie Le Bachelet, "Ame," in *Dictionnaire de théologie catholique*,
ed. Vacant, Mangenot, and Amann, 15 vols. (Paris, 1908–1950), II, col. 657. Also Noël
Valois, "Jacques Duèse, pape sous le nom de Jean XXII" in *Histoire Littéraire de la
France*, 34 (Paris, 1914), 551 ff. And the references in Marc Bloch, "La Vie d'outre-
tombe du roi Salomon," *Revue Belge de Philologie et d'Histoire*, 4 (1925), pp.
353–354.
85. We will come back to this later.

is to say, he spewed forth a torrent of insults at Calvin's unfortunate victim: heretic; offender against the deity; an editor of sacrilegious writings, who had escaped from Lyon with the complicity and help of atheists ("ope et consilio eorum qui athei sunt"—it would have been surprising if atheists had not been mentioned); a tool of Satan, driven to despair at the death of so zealous a servant ("Satanas, tam selecto se videns privatum ministro"). In short, here are all those charming flourishes of the pen that are found in a letter by Farel that we already knew, the one of December 10, 1553, to Blaurer. It is marvelous and unconsciously tragic.

So much abuse, violence, denunciation—and not one doubt, one regret, one bit of remorse. Let us hear what Aubert says—and there is no need to testify to his competence or impartiality. "As for Servetus's actual doctrine, it seems to us today to have an almost timorous orthodoxy. None of them [the Calvinist theologians] seem to have really understood it. But didn't Servetus try to prove the divinity of Christ and, on the subject of the Trinity, didn't he conclude the existence of a single God in three persons? This view is surely quite mild in its audacity!"[86] No doubt about it. But Farel and Calvin did not reason as we do. They deduced a thousand possible consequences from Servetus's doctrine; they developed *ad absurdum* a thousand propositions that seem anodyne to us. And they quite naturally identified the conclusion to which their sequence of arguments led them with the point of departure. They saw Z in A because they had noted all the intermediate stages between A and Z, and they condemned A in the name of Z without any hesitation whatever.

It was a cruel continuation of the spirit of deductive logic, of the games of the terminists, at once subtle and infantile, which any number of humanists and innovators since the beginning of the century had not been able to treat with enough sarcasm. When reading the ancients they admired different intellectual

---

86. Here is another Genevan authority: in 1926 Eugène Choisy wrote, "Servetus was neither an unbeliever nor a pure denier. If he had some objection to the trinitarian formulation, he did not believe in God the Father any less. He called Christ the Word of God made flesh. He gave the Virgin Mary the title of mother of God. He maintained that Jesus' body was of God's substance and that one could address invocations to Christ as to God." *Calvin éducateur des consciences* (Neuilly, 1926), p. 149.

procedures, ones that were more direct. They were also more human, since they did not, as in more recent times, pit minds against each other to wear themselves out in a constant effort to employ more and more morbid ingenuity and wrap reality in deadly spider webs of syllogisms. Rather, they had men confront each other by looking each other straight in the eye and had intelligences face each other pure and unadorned, contemptuous of all disguise and sincerely hating all guile. There are many useful things to be said about the revival of the dialogue in the sixteenth century. An entire generation was dazzled by these open conversations between creatures endowed not only with reason but with sensibility. Plato had left models composed with an art that was utterly natural. They strove to incorporate in their own language his easy grace and exquisite civility, his sometimes sharp, sometimes deliberate and gentle thrusts. They followed Plato, and also Lucian, who was less of an artist and therefore easier to imitate; we know of Lucian's Erasmian—or Rabelaisian—progeny. Even the Reformation in the beginning made copious use of the free and liberating dialogue form in its propaganda for laymen—the form dear to the father of *Gargantua* and *Pantagruel*. For the old forms of thought, the old modes of reasoning, refused to die. Entrenched in their natural citadels, the schools of theology, which rang with the empty clash of syllogisms, the antiquated methods of argumentation continued to impress themselves on the minds of students pursuing degrees and diplomas. In order to respond to those who continued to make use of these methods, to meet them on their own terrain and fight them with equal weapons, it was necessary for theologians at the very least (but others as well) to be initiates of the old logical mechanics, to use it, and turn it to their advantage. It was a tragic fate and a tragic conflict. At any moment those who were most liberated might slip back into the old servitude. At any moment there might reappear, along with all the excesses and abuses that had been denounced and repudiated hundreds of times, the ridiculous and often odious methods of the "Mateologians" trained at the school of Tubal Holophernes. No one who neglects to take this intellectual drama into account can really understand the men of the time. As for calling them as witnesses—what a train of errors that brings in!

Let us be suspicious of the words of the past. They generally have two meanings, one absolute, the other relative. Even the first is often difficult to define. To say that atheism is the act of denying the deity is not to say anything very precise. But on top of that the relative meaning of the word has changed considerably. In the sixteenth century it implied the most terrible scandal one could decry. This is apparent in a rather general way. What is less apparent is how much the very modes of reasoning were transformed from generation to generation. Let us be suspicious of the words—and even more of the arguments and accusations—of the past.

Conclusion to Part I

Testimony and Modes of Thought

ND NOW, at the end of this long critical
discussion, can we regard as incorrect the
opinion of those who say that as early as
1532 Rabelais was a militant and determined
enemy of Christ, an atheist, or—to avoid an
ambiguous word tinged with deep feeling—a
devious and fanatical propagandist for ratio-
nal deism of the sort enunciated by the libertines of the seventeenth century and the philosophes of the eighteenth? We have
not yet earned the right to do so, nor the right to say the opposite. All we can do is conclude that the testimony of theologians
or controversialists that has been gathered by our predecessors
or by us does not allow anyone to say yes with any certainty.
Or no.

Not one piece of evidence is actually earlier than 1550. I
mean evidence that counts. Not one piece therefore applies exclusively to the Rabelais of *Pantagruel* rather than the various
Rabelaises that came later. Calvin's letter to Daniel does not
have the meaning that has been assigned to it. There is nothing
to prove that Visagier's writings of 1538 are about Rabelais;
everything seems to prove that they concern Dolet. If the passage that has been cited from the *Excuse aux Nicodémites*
(1544) refers to Rabelais, it refers to a good many others at the
same time and in any case is only aimed at a general attitude:
that of a man who pretends to adhere to the Word but makes
fun of it in secret—an attitude that indeed hardly makes him a
formidable foe, for poor "idiots" would see no harm in writings
that were respectful of the Word on the surface, and others, if

they caught a whiff of something suspicious, would be quite capable of taking care of themselves.

In 1543 Postel called *Pantagruel* an impious book. His notion of impiety, however, extended to all the Reformers, and in their army Rabelais was in more than Christian company. Finally, in *Theotimus* Gabriel de Puy-Herbault is universally acknowledged to have been indulging a private grudge. The first conclusive text is, in fact, the one in *De scandalis*. So it is a question of knowing if, when a man in 1550 read a book published in 1532 by an author who afterward did a lot of writing and a lot of living, he looked at it with the eyes of 1532 or of 1550.

Furthermore, none of the testimony comes from a dispassionate mind presenting it impartially as a historian would adduce a piece of evidence. Postel, Calvin, the Estiennes, and Castellio— all of them were controversialists, to some degree. What were their judgments based on? On impressions that were personal and often (if not always) interested. Such a basis sufficed for believers, but does it suffice for historians? Do we even know whether all those men who called *Pantagruel* an atheist manifesto had read it? Buisson pointed out that Castellio spoke of Dolet through hearsay. Why assume he knew Rabelais any better?

What about the exact meaning of their statements? Certainly, if you single out and lift from their writings whatever refers to Rabelais alone, to Dolet alone, or to Des Périers alone, you can draw up an impressive indictment: "Here is all this testimony by contemporaries. The verdict is clear!" But this gives a false impression of what was going on. Does Henri Estienne's testimony carry any weight against Rabelais? Let us pass. What about against Castellio or Postel? The latter tells us that Rabelais was a former Cenevangelist who moved, bag and baggage, into the most confirmed sort of impiety; very well, but he told the same story in connection with Simon de Neufville, and we do not know if Neufville was ever on the side of the Reformation—and, what is more, Postel (like a number of others) generously gave him credit for the paternity of the mythical *Treatise on the Three Impostors*. Let us take Calvin's word when he denounces Rabelais's atheism. I want to. And so Rabelais stands convicted, an evil man who wanted "to abolish all reverence for God" and undermine the foundations of all religion. That is what Calvin said, and Calvin knew—do we dare to doubt that? Of course not, but are we to take Calvin's word when he concludes his response to Servetus by expressly accusing him of having only one aim, "to destroy religion from top to bottom, *totam religionem evertere*"?[1] We should if we trust him. When Calvin charges Agrippa with notorious atheism (which makes quite a few atheists in 1530, so wherein lies *Pantagruel's* supposed originality?), we tell the whole world: "Agrippa was an atheist." But when the same Calvin unleashes an odious accusation of robbery against Castellio?[2] And when, anticipating Henri Estienne—who here, too, was only echoing him—he treats the same Castellio as a clown who subjects religion to jokes: "tu, tu, omnia pietatis principia ridendo, suaviter te oblectas" (you have a fine time laughing at every fundamental of piety)? Poor Castellio, that poor knight of the doleful countenance, who was so austere, rigid, and deathly sad that the son of Utenhove, who had been sent to stay with him, begged his father in desperation to take him away from "Master Castalio," such a saintly man, who never laughed![3]

It is certain that Calvin harbored personal animosity toward Castellio. Animosity, resentment, strong feelings—they were to be found in all these men. They drew themselves up in opposi-

---

1. In his day the Abbé d'Artigny was shocked by the accusation (*Nouveaux mémoires d'histoire*, 7 vols. [Paris, 1749-1756], II, 136). He called upon M. de La Roche to come to the rescue, "though a Protestant," and prove that Servetus "never thought of destroying religion." So much for Servetus—but how many others were there? In May 1537 in Lausanne about a hundred ministers met in a synod. Its purpose was to examine the accusation of antitrinitarianism that had been brought against Viret, Farel, and Calvin by Pierre Caroli, a Sorbonne doctor and a former associate of Briçonnet in Meaux. Calvin rose and addressed Caroli: "I question whether he believes in a God, and I call God and men to witness that there is no more faith in him than in a dog or a pig!" Henri Vuilleumier, *Histoire de l'Eglise réformée du pays de Vaud*. I: *Lausanne* (Paris, 1928), 607.

2. Ferdinand Buisson, *Sébastien Castellion, sa vie et son oeuvre, 1515-1563*, 2 vols. (Paris, 1892), I, 249. [Calvin accused Castellio of using a gaff to steal logs from the river. Castellio admitted taking the logs but said that it could hardly be called stealing to do openly what everyone did.—Translator.]

Is it necessary to say again that Calvin, great as he was, was not an impartial witness when it came to his adversaries? For him anything used against them was good; the saintliness of his own position absolved him.

3. Buisson, II, 89. Castellio stated the question very well in his reply to Beza: "Why would he give a more accurate interpretation of my books than he did of my gaff?" Ibid., p. 260.

tion to each other, ready with an insult on their lips, or a
curse—at least till something better came along. Animosity does
not explain everything, however. There was something else at
the bottom of these quarrels.

What else? Can we say it was a defect in their thinking? Far
be it from us to use such an expression. The men of the sixteenth century no doubt would have used it in speaking of the
"sophists" who came before them, "in those rude times of old,
when the wearing of high round bonnets was in fashion." It is
just that they did not know what some of us know, without that
knowledge having become what really nurtures the general run
of our contemporaries, even the educated ones (even the historians). Every civilization has its own mental tools. Even more,
every era of the same civilization, every advance in technology
or science that gives it its character, has a revised set of tools, a
little more refined for certain purposes, a little less so for others.
A civilization or an era has no assurance that it will be able to
transmit these mental tools in their entirety to succeeding civilizations and eras. The tools may undergo significant deterioration, regression, and distortion; or, on the contrary, more improvement, enrichment, and complexity. They are valuable for
the civilization that succeeds in forging them, and they are valuable for the era that uses them; they are not valuable for all
eternity, or for all humanity, nor even for the whole narrow
course of development within one civilization.

As far as the men of the sixteenth century are concerned, neither their modes of reasoning nor their requirements for proof
were the same as ours. Theirs were not even the modes of reasoning or the requirements for proof of their grandsons, the
contemporaries of Descartes, Pascal, Huygens, and Newton.
The moment has not yet arrived for dealing with these large
questions in a general way. At any rate, from the study to
which we have just devoted ourselves the conclusion seems to
have emerged that in their mode of arguing the men of that
time did not seem to feel either the overwhelming need for precision or the concern for objectivity that we do. We can undoubtedly free ourselves of this need and concern while under
the sway of strong emotions—but at least we apologize for the
liberation, which to us looks like a weakness. We have seen that
in the speculation of men of that time a larger part was played

by contradictions that no longer have a place in our logical systems of thought. And this seems to have emerged equally from
the critical examination of the poetic evidence to which we devoted ourselves in the preceding chapter. That, too, taught us
that man is not Man, but that men change—much more than
we imagine, and at a much faster rate. It taught us, if you will,
that in Rabelais's time (naturally) neither the great revolution
that would end by subordinating logic and mathematics to experimentation was yet in sight—even at a great distance—nor
had the great advances in mathematics whose benefits Descartes
would reap even begun. We cannot ignore these conditions if
we wish to make proper use of human witnesses.

PART II

The Charges of Scandal

3. Rabelais's Pranks

E HAVE collected testimony about Rabelais, testimony about his opinions as interpreted by his contemporaries, from everyone who had anything to say about him—humanists, controversialists, polemicists—whether favorable or unfavorable. We have sifted this testimony with as critical a scrutiny as possible. In so doing we were able to point out errors of interpretation or attribution in the work of our predecessors, some so serious and of such significance that not much of the structure erected by them is actually left standing.

The time has come to interrogate Rabelais himself—that is to say, his work: *Pantagruel* and, to a lesser degree, *Gargantua*. This would seem to be a simple task. If you want to know Rabelais, look at Rabelais. It is, in point of fact, a tricky one. Can a man be known from one work? Hasn't the author covered his face with a mask? Do the mask's features—coarse, exaggerated, caricatural—really represent the true face of the satirist? To what extent is it legitimate to deduce the man from his work? Perhaps the question is not being expressed very well since, after all, it is not the man that has mattered to readers of *Pantagruel* at any time from 1532 to 1926, but the work, or, if you will, what of himself the man put into the work. Getting the proportions right, however, is tricky.

Abel Lefranc will present the evidence, in the passage that served as the point of departure for our reflections on these weighty problems. "What do we find," he exclaims,

at the very threshold of the book? A series of statements that are hardly to be believed. Speaking of the success of the

Grandes Chroniques Gargantuines, the author calls attention to the fact that the readers of those inestimable works believed them, "exactly like the words of the Bible and the Gospel . . ." It is not hard to measure the utter audacity of a parallel so insulting to the Holy Books, in spite of its apparent joking tone. Later the same comparison appears again, when the success of the *Chroniques* is asserted in this famous line: "For the printers have sold more of them in two months' time than there will be bought of Bibles in nine years." Alcofribas, rising to a sort of crescendo, then in a direct attack even calls one of the Evangelists to witness. Claiming to vouch for his own information and truthfulness by means of a burlesque argument, he calmly says, "I speak of it as Saint John spoke of the Apocalypse: *quod vidimus, testamur.*" Has anyone in the realm of religious satire ever gone beyond this degree of scathing irony? There is no possible doubt from the very outset; the Lucianic laughter here conceals strange designs that for centuries no one had dared to form.[1]

Again and again we read this importunate passage, so full of feeling, and we are quite uneasy. Can we have closed our eyes to the evidence? With some apprehension we pick up our copy of Rabelais and open to *Pantagruel.* We start laughing and think no more of the "crescendo" of impiety. Then, putting the volume back on the shelf, we are prepared to swear that there is nothing secret, nothing terrible or sacrilegious in any of those unmalicious obscenities, off-color tall tales, or old, perfectly safe clerical jokes whose inventor was certainly not Rabelais, who took his inspiration where he found it and was satisfied to put the stamp of his own genius on every page. Are we wrong or right?

1. Some Clerical Jests

To decide the matter, we could examine and weigh, one by one, all the scandalous subjects enumerated by Abel Lefranc. But—apart from the fact that scandal has nothing to do with the case

1. Abel Lefranc, "Etude sur *Pantagruel,*" in Rabelais, *Oeuvres*, III (Paris, 1922), xli–xlii.

(*Les Fleurs du mal* and even *Madame Bovary* were once regarded as highly scandalous by the Imperial Prosecutor, but
that does not suffice for us to call their authors pornographers)
—the work has already been done. In 1910 in the *Revue des
Etudes Rabelaisiennes,* Jean Plattard carefully studied the passages of Holy Scripture referred to by Rabelais. And Etienne
Gilson, the historian of medieval philosophy, furnished as his
contribution to the thesis maintained by Plattard, hostile to any
romantic interpretation of Rabelais's jokes, an array of proofs
and arguments drawn from his remarkable familiarity with
scholasticism. The best that we can do is refer the reader to
these definitive studies.[2]

Like Lazare Sainéan, who took the same position in this debate, Plattard clearly saw that Rabelais's jokes belonged to a
clerical tradition and were no different from those that enliv-
ened the genre of *sermons joyeux,* to which Emile Picot drew
our attention some time ago.[3] One can gather a rich crop of
Gospel phrases there, parodied with greater or lesser degrees of
coarseness. And not just any phrases. One sermon took as its
text the very words on which the Lord's Supper was founded:
"Eat and drink."[4] This is much more daring than "Consummatum est," whether said by Panurge or, as Rabelais would have
it, by Saint Thomas Aquinas[5]—and the drinkers' "Sitio" that
Abel Lefranc found so shocking.[6] We should understand that

2. Jean Plattard, "L'Ecriture Sainte et la littérature scripturaire dans l'oeuvre de Rabelais," *Revue des Etudes Rabelaisiennes,* 8 (1910), 257–330; Etienne Gilson, "Rabelais franciscain," in *Les Idées et les lettres,* 2d ed. (Paris, 1955), pp. 197–241.

3. Lazare Sainéan, *La Langue de Rabelais,* 2 vols. (Paris, 1922–1923), II, 371; Raymond Lebègue, *La Tragédie religieuse en France. Les débuts (1514–1573)* (Paris,
1929), p. 77, n. 2, and p. 171; Emile Picot, "Le Monologue dramatique dans l'ancien
théâtre français," *Romania,* 15 (1886), 358–422; 16 (1887), 438–542; 17 (1888),
207–262.

4. Emmanuel Viollet Le Duc, *Ancien Théâtre françois,* 10 vols. (Paris,
1854–1857), II, 5.

5. "... he fairly set it on fire, that he might the better say, *Consummatum est.* Even
just as since his time St. Thomas Aquinas did, when he had eaten up the whole lam-
prey." *Book Three,* ch. 2.

6. "I have the word of the gospel in my mouth, Sitio." *Gargantua,* ch. 5. [*Sitio* = I
thirst (John 19:28).—Translator.] See Plattard, p. 273, which refers to a *Sermon
joyeux de bien boyre* (Lyon, 1540). Also Viollet Le Duc, II, 15: "And God gave us a
rule to follow: / 'Drink well!' Remember when you swallow / That he himself said:
'Sitio.'" The vogue for such clerical jests persisted. When Mme du Boccage inspired
Cardinal Passionei, who was famous for his strict morals, to say something flattering to

these are the drinkers of 1542. Plattard specifically pointed out that this scandalous expression did not appear in the first versions of *Pantagruel;* Rabelais put it in later in the edition published by François Juste—from which he is supposed to have expurgated everything that was too daring! But was it really so daring? No more so than the remark made by Francis I that he was nicknaming Cardinal Louis de Bourbon "Sitio" because, as Claude Haton tells us, "the said Lord always was desirous to drink his good wines, were he as sated as he might be."[7] Should we anathematize the good folk who innocently sang, "Ecce bonum vinum, venite potemus"?[8]

As for Gilson, he pointed out the necessity for anyone studying the development of Rabelais's genius to take into account the years spent in the monastery by the "creator of modern French prose." He could hardly have spent "less than a dozen years of his life—that is, the crucial years of his youth—as a Franciscan." Gilson came to several conclusions, one of which we should look at now: "Since even in a Franciscan monastery not all the time was spent in reading prayers or delving into the philosophy of Scotus, and since they had unrestrained and even merry conversations at certain times of the day, we need to ask ourselves whether something of the sturdy and often popular élan of the Franciscans of the Middle Ages passed into certain passages where lately certain secret intentions have been looked for that Rabelais perhaps never put there."[9] Actually, Gilson had absolutely no trouble in finding any number of merry pages written by Franciscans who were not suspected of heterodoxy. They have the ring of a good Rabelaisian jest—hearty, but often off-color.

Does it do any good to say it? Like Plattard, Gilson, Sainéan, and many others, I cannot get worked up about familiar jokes and clerical pleasantries that some think are full of malicious and subversive intent. They are audacious, to be sure, if we

---

her, Benedict XIV quipped, "Et homo factus est" (and he was made man)—which no one used as a pretext to declare him anti-Christian. See Grace Gill-Mark, *Une Femme de lettres au XVIIIe siècle, Anne-Marie du Boccage* (Paris, 1927), p. 101.

7. *Mémoires de Claude Haton,* ed. Félix Bourquelot, 2 vols. (Paris, 1857), I, 45.

8. "Behold the good wine; come, let us drink." [The allusion is to *Ecce lignum crucis . . . : venite adoremus* (behold the wood of the cross . . . : come let us adore).—Translator.] Sainéan, II, 371.

9. Gilson, pp. 200–201.

judge audacity by our standards. But ours are not the standards of the sixteenth century. That has to be conceded when we deal with pious and mystical Margaret, who wrote the *Heptameron*. We should also concede it in the case of the creator of *Gargantua*.

◄§ I am not scandalized in retrospect by Rabelais's remark about the poor sale of Bibles and the overly good sale of the *Gargantuan Chronicles*. Nothing tells us that Master Alcofribas rejoiced at the former or congratulated himself on the latter. I wonder if his attitude was not the same as that which led him elsewhere to note—and deplore the fact—that in Paris any mountebank in the street could gather a bigger audience than an Evangelical preacher in a church.

I might be more shocked by the lady of Paris's *lama sabachthani* if Masuccio of Salerno or Arnaldus de Villa Nova had not used it before Rabelais.[10] Gargantua's witticism when he is mourning for Badebec in chapter 3 of *Pantagruel*—"she is well, she is in Paradise, at least, if she be no higher"—is one of those artless mockeries that peasants love to use in their stories. Is the genealogy of Gargantua sacrilegious? It was "by the sovereign gift of heaven . . . reserved for our use more full and perfect than any other; I mean not to speak of God, for it belongs not unto my purpose, and the devils, that is to say, the dissembled gospellers, will therein oppose me."[11] Is it an imitation of the genealogy of Christ at the beginning of the Gospel According to St. Matthew? I don't doubt it, all the more since Rabelais takes the trouble to inform us so quite clearly. Nor does he hesitate to tell us in chapter 1 of *Pantagruel* that the genealogy of his hero recalls genealogies that have been handed down to us not only by the Greeks, the Arabs, and the Ethnics but also

10. In chapter 24 of *Pantagruel* the lady sends Pantagruel a ring inscribed "Lama sabachthani." It was the crucified Christ's cry of distress (Matt. 27:46). On its use by Rabelais, see Plattard, p. 269. Jacob Le Duchat (who did the first scholarly edition of Rabelais) pointed out the borrowing from Masuccio; see also Pietro Toldo, "A propos d'une inspiration de Rabelais," *Revue d'Histoire Littéraire de la France*, 11 (1904), 467–468.

11. *Gargantua*, ch. 1. Juste's edition of before 1535 (the first known edition) and Juste's 1535 edition (the second) both have *Dieu*, which was then replaced by *Messias* ("the Messias" in Urquhart's translation). Rabelais also added *calumniateurs* ("false accusers" in Urquhart) to *caffars* ("dissembled gospellers").

"the authors of Holy Scripture, such as my lord St. Luke and likewise St. Matthew."[12] Master Francis, we see, hardly kept things a secret, and he declared all his parodistic intentions quite clearly. Did the parody, however, go beyond the limits, broad as they were, that tradition allowed to jokers in times gone by? That is really the question. And if we answer in the affirmative, why not reproach Rabelais for this scandalous bit of irreverence: when Gargantua (ch. 23) went "into the secret places to make excretion of his natural digestions," his preceptor, who did not intend to lose "any one hour in the day," repeated to him in that secluded sanctuary "what had been read." What had been read, aloud and clearly, with a pronunciation fit for the matter, was "some chapter of the Holy Scripture." Was this a profanation? Or a pious practice?

2. No Church at Theleme?

But there is Theleme: Theleme had no abbey church. Poor Theleme! It lacked a number of other necessities of life. Kitchens, for example, aromatic roasting ovens, and cool, deep cellars—which is rather surprising in Friar John's abbey. So not only did Rabelais not provide Theleme with a kitchen, to the horror of materialists, but he did not provide it with a church, to the consternation of idealists. But next to each room he put a chapel—and what do you do in a chapel if not pray?

Theleme, let us not forget, was the antimonastery. Friar John said so expressly (*Gargantua,* ch. 52): it was instituted deliberately and systematically "contrary to all other" religious orders—that is, to all others in existence. In other abbeys an abbot was in charge. Not at Theleme: "how shall I be able to rule over others, that have not full power and command of myself?" In other abbeys there were walls ("where there is mur before, and mur behind, there is store of murmur"). Not at

---

12. [This passage appears only in the earliest editions of *Pantagruel.*—Translator.] There are other genealogies in the holy books besides that of Christ in Matt. 1. Constructed according to the same scheme, they lend themselves to the same parodies. Gen. 5 gives the descendants of Adam ("and begat Cainan . . . and begat Mahalaleel . . . and begat Jared . . . and begat Enoch . . ."). In chapter 10 is the genealogy of the sons of Noah ("and Cush begat Nimrod," and so on). On the persons in Rabelais's genealogies see Sainéan, I, 478.

Theleme. One could freely enter and leave, come and go. If a chaste woman came into an abbey they swept the ground she defiled. At Theleme, if a monk or a nun had a notion to enter, all the rooms they profaned were cleaned. Let us recall, if it is necessary, the key passage (ch. 57):

"All their life was spent not in laws, statutes, or rules, but according to their own free will and pleasure. They rose out of their beds when they thought good: they did eat, drink, labour, sleep, when they had a mind to it, and were disposed for it ... In all their rule, and strictest tie of their order, there was but this one clause to be observed, 'DO WHAT THOU WILT.' "

Finally, in abbeys there was a church, a large abbey church. One repaired to it at fixed hours, at the sound of relentless bells that cut life up into little pieces. At Theleme there were no common services, no bells, no sun dials, for there is no "greater dotage in the world than for one to guide and direct his courses by the sound of a bell and not by his own judgment and discretion" (ch. 52). How could the Thelemites go to church at set hours if they got up, ate, went to bed—let us add, "and prayed," for that was probably in Rabelais's mind—when they were moved by desire, in accord with their reason? But they only prayed in private chapels and never went to mass, didn't they? For it has been asserted in a scandalized tone that the Thelemites never heard mass.[13]

Who said the Thelemites never went to mass? First of all, they could have attended the parish church—like the king when he was staying at the original château of Versailles, which had no chapel. Or they could have had it said in their chapels. Finally, before we adopt that scandalized tone, let us think. Not only that Rabelais could not cover everything and convert a satire into a dogmatic exercise. But, more than that, what about the mass? Let us not pretend we do not know (it is impossible not to know, we have to know) that in Rabelais's time the mass, vilified by the *mal sentans de la foy*, was not what it became for Catholics in the time of Bérulle and after: the religious act par excellence, the synthesis of all Catholic worship—a sacrament, of course, but even more than that, a sacrifice, *the* sacrifice, the

---

13. "It is clear that the Thelemites, as well as Gargantua, their founder, never heard mass." Abel Lefranc, "Etude sur le 'Gargantua,' " in Rabelais, *Oeuvres*, I (Paris, 1912), xxvi.

essential part of public worship. The great change the seventeenth century made in the mass, the effort to involve the faithful more and more closely with the words and actions of the
priest, had not yet begun. It was part of the immense effort
made by Catholics at the end of the sixteenth century in forcing
themselves to rethink their religion in its entirety in clear opposition to the Reformed religion. And perhaps Master Alcofribas's contemporaries, who observed that great lords ordered
masses by the hundreds in their wills, had reasons that our contemporaries no longer have for feeling that those long sessions
in church were deadly, dear as they were to the hearts of the
collectors of the masses who nodded through the services. That
is what Erasmus thought, like all the others. There is no need
to pile up quotations. Let us just call to mind his expression of
distaste when Gilbert Cousin, his secretary, left him to become
a canon at Nozeroy: *cantabit missam.*[14] Still, the Thelemites
honored Sundays and holidays by being "accoutred in the
French mode, because they accounted it more honourable, and
better befitting the garb of a matronal pudicity." Sundays and
holidays. What holidays? Secular holidays had not yet been invented in 1532, so they must have been religious ones. Let us
not bear down too heavily on tales that are full of spontaneous
fantasy and wit. They are not theologians' abstrusities.

To be sure, Abel Lefranc, in his introduction to *Gargantua*
in 1912, explained the absence of a church at Theleme by Rabelais's "barely dissimulated" sympathies for the innovators. It
was by means of this sign, indeed, as well as some others, that
at that time he saw in Rabelais a believer "seeking to demonstrate his lively and sincere sympathy for the Reformation."
The criterion may not be a perfect one: in places where the

14. "He's going to sing a mass." *Opus epistolarum Des. Erasmi Roterodami*, ed. P.
S. Allen and H. M. Allen, 12 vols. (Oxford, 1906–1958), XI, 259.

Here is a sample of the violent comments on the mass to which the *mal sentans* were
prone, taken from *La Vérité cachée devant cent ans, faicte et composée à six personnages, nouvellement corrigée et augmentée avec les autoritez de la Saincte Escripture*
(Geneva: J. Michael, 1544), fol. 6r: "Tant ne se joue chat à sa rate / Que le prebstre à
son Dieu de paste. / Souffle plus tost de cinq surglou / qu'ung mareschal ne forge un
clou. / Des tours qu'ils en font me sourris / Le mangent après comme chatz souris."
(As a cat with a rat great sport does make / Even more does the priest with his God of
cake. / He huffs and he puffs like a bellows' blast— / No smith can forge a nail so
fast. / How I laugh as they turn it this way and that / Till it's finally downed, like the
mouse by the cat.)

"Reformation" was victorious in 1532 it by no means demanded that large houses of worship be shut down and private worship substituted for public worship. If the Thelemites had been Reformed they would have gone to their abbey church (if they had one), which would have been converted into a "temple," and attended services there. Apart from this, Lefranc made an observation in 1912 that does seem to us to conform entirely to reality: "The sacred word, that is, the Gospel, was the essential element, the sole factor in the spiritual life of the Thelemites." Did the words that inspired this eminently sensible sentence disappear between 1912 and 1923? There was no church at Theleme. Nor was there a Protestant "temple." We can perhaps console ourselves with the thought that the Thelemites would undoubtedly have been able to find one or the other in the nearest town. But doesn't the absence of temple or church mean atheism? There was, to be sure, the Gospel, and there were the chapels. Pooh, those chapels were only for protection! Well, it is true that Theleme had no lightning rods. Still, nine thousand three hundred and thirty-two lightning rods in 1532 were a bit much.[15]

3. Gargantua's Nativity

What else? It's all right if we go slowly—we do not want to miss anything. We may get a sudden flash of light. There is Gargantua's strange nativity, in which he comes into the world by way of the vena cava and the left ear.[16] A curious birth, to be sure. And Rabelais tacks on to the sensational description some pretentious claptrap of his own. "An honest man, and of good judgment, believeth still what is told him, and that which he finds written . . . *Innocens credit omni verbo* . . . *Charitas omnia credit* . . . The Sorbonists say that faith is evidence of things not seen . . . It is not impossible with God; and, if he pleased, all women henceforth should bring forth their children at the ear."

"There is no doubt whatsoever," wrote Lefranc, "that this se-

15. "There were in it nine thousand three hundred and two and thirty chambers, every one whereof had a withdrawing room, a handsome closet, a wardrobe, an oratory, and neat passage, leading into a great and spacious hall." *Gargantua*, ch. 53.

16. *Gargantua*, ch. 6.

quence applies to the Christian doctrine on the birth of Christ."
Is that so? Christ was not born by way of the hollow vein and
the left ear. He was formed in the womb of a virgin by the
working of the Holy Spirit, and he came into the world, according to the early Fathers Irenaeus, Origen, Tertullian, Athana-
sius, Epiphanius, and Jerome, at the end of the normal nine
months of gestation in the most physiologically normal manner.[17] Hundreds of writings describe with antique coarseness of
detail his being born in blood and filth—up until the end of the
fourth century, when the doctrine of the virgin birth was propagated by Saint Ambrose and then by Saint Augustine. Christ
was he who entered the world through a closed door, without
breaking the lock. And so the doctrine of the successive virgini-
ties of Mary was developed. She was a virgin married to a man
whose own outstanding virginity would eventually be proclaimed by the Church, a man whose mission in marrying Mary
was to preserve her virginity.[18] She remained a virgin when she
conceived. She remained a virgin when she gave birth. But she
did not bring her child into the world through her ear. Luke
shows him to us in the embryonic state in her womb,[19] and any
number of Virgins in labor in places of worship presented him
that way to the eyes of the faithful. I find it hard to see, therefore, how Gargantua's strange escapade, his progression from
his mother's vena cava to her left ear, could evoke the idea of
the confinement of the Virgin—a confinement that was represented for centuries in the art of every church in every country
in the guise of a normal confinement, with midwives and experienced women neighbors in attendance.[20]

If only it had been Rabelais who wrote one of the little books

17. S.v. "Jésus-Christ" in *Dictionnaire de théologie catholique*, ed. Vacant, Mangenot, and Amann, 15 vols. (Paris, 1908–1950), VIII, col. 1144.

18. "The first object of Saint Joseph's mission was to preserve Mary's virginity by
contracting a true marriage with the future Mother of God." *Dictionnaire de théologie
catholique*, VIII, col. 1511, s.v. "Joseph."

19. "*Brephos en tē koilia*" (the unborn child in the womb ["the fruit of thy
womb"]). Luke 1:42.

20. Henri Clouzot was sorry he had not taken note of this impious account in his
edition of the *Oeuvres*. It was a sermon on preaching by Bossuet (March 13, 1661)
that opened his eyes. The orator spoke of "her who first conceived the Son of God
through the ear." "Note pour le commentaire: 'L'enfant sortit par l'aureille senestre,' "
Revue du Seizième Siècle, 9 (1922), 219–220.

in the Cycle of Gargantuan Chronicles, *Vray Gargantua nota-
blement omelyé*, to which Pierre-Paul Plan called attention![21]
There, at the beginning, we read the terrifying story of the necromancer Merlin, "begotten without a human father, for his
mother was a nun and conceived by a fantastic spirit who came
in the night to seduce her." This odd tale might eventually lead
an ingenious mind to entertain all kinds of strange suspicions.
Should we, however, conclude that the anonymous author was
carrying out a subversive and conscious plan to ridicule the
conception of Christ, who also was "begotten without a human
father," by a virgin whom a spirit, a breath of air, had come to
impregnate? Once again we have to say that neither the jokes of
the sixteenth century nor its morals were the same as ours. And
if everyone who made licentious references to Mary's virginity
ought to have been burned at the stake, the executioners appointed retroactively by the present day would have had too
much work.[22] Even in 1565, in the midst of Counter-Reformation Italy, a convinced Catholic named Ludovico Guicciardini,
nephew of the historian and author of *Descrittione delli tutti i
Paesi Bassi*, published a little book of spicy tales in Venice,
Hore di recreazione, which was widely read and translated into
several languages. Guicciardini explained that one should drink
before, during, and after a meal because the mother of God was
a virgin before, during, and after the birth of the Lord.[23] It is
anodyne. Yet is is curious to note that, although already purified and refined, the stream kept on flowing—the stream of
good old clerical jokes about religious matters, even the most
delicate ones—especially the most delicate ones. In 1532 this
stream still had all its untamed force.

What of it? Was he unaware of the beginning of the Gospel According to St. John,
from which comes the doctrine that the conception was by way of the organ that is affected by the Word? Not to mention any number of other passages. "*Gaude Virgo,
mater Christi, /quae per aurem concepisti*" (Rejoice, O Virgin, Mother of Christ, who
did conceive by the ear), for example. But what difference do these references make?
The conception of Jesus and Mary's delivery are two events distinct enough not to be
confused with each other.

21. Pierre-Paul Plan, *Bibliographie rabelaisienne: les éditions de Rabelais de 1532 à
1711* (Paris, 1904), no. 4.

22. On the more than licentious jokes of Erasmus, see below, ch. 8, sect. 4.

23. Ludovico Guicciardini, *Hore di recreazione* (Venice, 1594), p. 108.

4. *"Charitas Omnia Credit"*

But Rabelais signed his own condemnation, didn't he? In 1542 he had a revised edition of his works published by Juste, in which he eliminated the scabrous jokes about faith, "evidence of things not seen." The objection to this definition of faith, which is in Saint Paul,[24] would make more sense if Rabelais had not borrowed it from the Sorbonists. It seems likely that the expurgations of 1542 had as their main object the softening or elimination of direct attacks on the Sorbonne. Furthermore, there is a great deal that needs to be said about these expurgations. We often do not entirely understand what they were aiming at. Rabelais in 1542 eliminated a comparison between Panurge and Christ, both hanged in the air.[25] But in that same year he inserted the parodistic use of *Sitio* that Plattard (this time putting on his twentieth-century spectacles) mistakenly declared was the worst of Rabelais's acts of daring.[26] We would do better to call it the tritest of clerical jokes. "Finally, '*Charitas omnia credit* . . . Faith is evidence of things not seen . . .' And the astonishing phrase 'God can do whatever he wishes'! Are these the remarks of a believer humbly submissive to the Church? Can't you feel the irony?" I am suspicious of those who feel the irony too much. Irony is a creature of its time. The expression "God can do whatever he wishes" puts me in mind of another, this one by Erasmus in Latin: "Deus sic potens est, ut quidquid velit, nutu valeat efficere."[27]

This was said by Barbatius in the colloquy "An Examination Concerning Faith."[28] Erasmus took pains to tell us that it was

24. Saint Paul says, "Now faith is the substance of things hoped for, the evidence of things not seen." Heb. 11:1. This was an absolutely classic reference. It cropped up everytime an author in the sixteenth century mentioned faith. See, for example, ch. 1 of Book II of Postel's *De rationibus*, entitled "Fides"; the reference comes up immediately: "Est, inquis, fides sperandarum substantia rerum, argumentum non apparentium." *De rationibus Spiritus Sancti lib. II* (Paris: P. Gromorsius, 1543), II, fol. 26v.

25. The Juste edition of 1533, in ch. 17 of *Pantagruel*, has: "Thou wilt be hanged one time or other. And thou, said he, wilt be interred some time or other. Now, which is most honorable, the air or the earth? Ho, grosse pecore! Was not Jesus Christ hanged in the air?"

26. Plattard, p. 273.

27. "God is so powerful that he is able to bring about whatever he wishes with a nod of his head."

28. The theme was a familiar one in Occam, whom Rabelais as a Franciscan was not unaware of: God can do whatever he wishes; therefore, if it pleased him, despising God, stealing from one's neighbor, fornicating, and so on, would be meritorious acts.

Barbatius—Martin Luther, no less—and he was engaged in the most serious kind of discussion about ideas that had not a trace of irony in them. The theme is indeed that attributed to John Colet in the colloquy "The Whole Duty of Youth": "What I read in Sacred Scripture and the creed called the Apostles' I believe with complete confidence nor do I search further."[29] Luther-Barbatius declares: I am not anxiously concerned how it can be possible for the individual body, after mingling with the elements, to be revived in the same condition it was in during life. I leave it to the supreme spirit: "God can do whatever he wishes." And if he wished, women would no doubt have babies through their ears.

Anyway, who can speak of believers humbly submissive to a Church in 1532? Of course, there were Noël Beda and the most active of the Sorbonne Masters. But apart from them? We should not project into those distant times the conventional type of Catholic who in so many polemical works has served as a contrast to the conventional type of Protestant. Charity believes everything—provisionally, or, to be more exact, by an act of the will. Good sense is less accepting, and chooses. It is right to choose. There is quite a gap between not believing everything and believing nothing. Rabelais, who made fun of the credulity of the "poor idiots" of his time, as they were called, did not tell us what, in his view, the limits of credulity were. What right have we to conclude that they were indistinguishable from those of radical anti-Christianism and thoroughgoing rationalism? Charity believes everything. That is what it is supposed to do. But are we still inclined to believe that "people of the Middle Ages," all of them all the time, were so charitable that they believed absolutely everything? Those poor "people of the Middle Ages"—what a sad picture of them has been painted for generations. Luckily for them, they never existed. And are we any more inclined to believe that the Church ordered the faithful, without distinction, to believe absolutely everything, or that to lay claim to the exercise of good sense and reason meant to become an instant outcast with no hope of return? Rabelais did not believe everything. Nor did thousands

---

And yet Occam was not one of those "dogs" Calvin was so fond of, who "wish to ruin all religion."

29. *The Colloquies of Erasmus*, trans. Craig R. Thompson (Chicago, 1965), p. 41.

of the faithful among his contemporaries who every day protested against "abuses." Are we saying that these men were enemies of religion and fanaticism? Their faith was often passionate, but it was not necessarily blind. "How could I believe,"
wrote Farel in 1528, "what I did not understand?"[30] Every one
of them compiled his own list of "things not seen"—short or
long, sparse or full, according to the men and their minds. What
gives us leave to say that Rabelais's list included the entire content of the Christian faith?

5. The Daring of Origen

I must say I am a little afraid that Abel Lefranc was misled by
an oversimplified notion of what a Christian and, simply from
the point of view of credulity, a Frenchman was in the 1530s.
He makes a great deal, for example, of Rabelais's jokes about
the giant Hurtali and Noah's Ark.[31] These were prodigious acts
of daring, he seems to be telling us, an audacity unheard of in
that era. Well, not really. Rabelais and every one of his contemporaries who wanted to could read every single day, if such was
their pleasure, in a magnificent folio volume devoid of any clan-
destinity passages like that, in which the Genesis stories were
given rather rough treatment.

> What man of intelligence will believe that the first, and the
> second and the third day, and the evening and the morning
> existed without the sun and moon and stars? And that the
> first day, if we may so call it, was even without a heaven?
> And who is so silly as to believe that God, after the manner
> of a farmer, "planted a paradise eastward in Eden," and set in
> it a visible and palpable "tree of life," of such a sort that any-
> one who tasted its fruit with his bodily teeth would gain life?
> ... And what more need I say, when those who are not alto-
> gether blind can collect thousands of such instances, recorded
> as actual events, but which did not happen literally?[32]

30. I could not find this remark where Henri Heyer, who was apparently Febvre's
source, claimed to have seen it. See his *Guillaume Farel: essai sur le développement de
ses idées théologiques* (Geneva, 1872), p. 50. [Translator's note.]

31. *Pantagruel*, ch. 1. See Lefranc, "Etude sur *Pantagruel*," pp. xlii–xliii.

32. Origen, *On First Principles*, trans. G. W. Butterworth (Gloucester, Mass.,
1973), pp. 288–289 (IV, 3).

Who was this rationalist, this blatant Paduan, who then went on to make a myriad of jokes about the story of the Flood and about the Ark that in a few cubits of space was able to contain all the animals in creation; about Sodom and Gomorrah and about Lot and his daughters—all of this with a freedom, audacity, and cynicism not surpassed even by Voltaire? Rabelais's mocking words about Hurtali seem pale beside these direct attacks.

Quite simply, the attacks were made by Origen. Origen, who was printed and reprinted so often in the time of the Renaissance. Origen, whose translation into Latin by a Paris theologian, Jacques Merlin, had been published in 1512 by Jean Petit and Josse Bade in Paris *cum gratia et privilegio regis* in four large folios, the third volume of which began with a sincere "Apology" by the great heterodox theologian.[33] In 1532, the very year of *Pantagruel*, this "Apology" reappeared, still at the beginning of Volume III, in the reissue of the entire translation by Jean Petit, Josse Bade, and Conrad Resch. And in Lyon in 1536 Jacques Giunta reprinted Merlin's translation along with parts of the translation by Erasmus.[34] Not to mention other editions in Italy, France, Switzerland, or Germany. But why speak of Origen?

The passage we have just quoted had been literally translated into Latin and printed exactly as is in one of the most widely known books of the time. Open to Erasmus's adage "Sileni Alcibiadis" and you will have no trouble finding these words, clearly irreverent, turned into good Latin. They were no doubt written to support a classic distinction between spirit and flesh in order to justify reliance on the allegorical method of scriptural interpretation. But, as Jacques Denis remarked in his book on Origen's philosophy, "allegorical exegesis is a form of free thought when dealing with a passage that continues to be re-

---

Anyone who did not read Origen's own words had only to read Erasmus. See Jean Baptiste Pineau, *Erasme, sa pensée religieuse* (Thèse de doctorat ès lettres, Paris, 1924), pp. 111–112.

33. On this translation and the incidents it provoked, see Augustin Renaudet, *Préréforme et humanisme à Paris pendant les premières guerres d'Italie (1494–1517)* (Thèse de doctorat ès lettres, Paris, 1916), p. 618.

34. *Origenis Adamantii operum tomi duo priores cum tabulis et indice generali* (Lyon: J. Giunta, 1536). See Henri and Julien Baudrier, *Bibliographie lyonnaise*, 12 vols. (Lyon, 1895–1921; photographic reprint, Paris, 1964), VI, 171. Also Lucien Febvre, *Origène et Des Périers, ou l'énigme du Cymbalum Mundi* (Paris, 1942).

vered and regarded as the repository of truth."[35] And of all who practiced it, none made bolder use of it than the author of *On First Principles*. So bold that he often found himself agreeing with Celsus and justifying in advance the objections to the Bible raised by the philosophes of the eighteenth century. It was of Origen that Erasmus had no hesitation in writing—in his *De ratione studii*, written in London in March 1506 and on sale in Paris in October 1511—"Among theological writers, after the Scriptures, no one writes better than Origen" (ex theologia, secundum divinas litteras, nemo melius Origene.) When we are acquainted with such passages we hesitate to find Rabelais audacious. We almost want to call him timid.

⋈§ I know, it's a matter of feelings. It will always be impossible to "prove" that when Rabelais told (after many earlier tellings, for he did not make it up)[36] the off-color story of the friar who when he said mass presented an unusual aspect to the faithful, he was not hatching in his inner being the blackest of plots against religion, the plots of a dog (as Calvin so graciously put it) who acted like a clown so he could better subvert all fear of God. All the same, time had moved quickly between 1530 and 1555. When *Gargantua* and *Pantagruel* appeared, between 1532 and 1535, who would have been scandalized by jokes that were shortly to be deemed tasteless and suspect by act of the Reformers themselves? Rabelais had not put into his books the kind of maliciousness that the leaders of the Reformation were loudly attacking around 1545. It was done by men who started to see maliciousness in 1545 where no one a short time before had seen anything but harmless joking.

It was an entirely natural development of ideas—and of manners. On July 25, 1540, Charles Hémard de Denonville, bishop of Mâcon (Rabelais had known him in Rome in 1534 when he was the king's ambassador), died in Le Mans, where he had

35. Jacques Denis, *De la philosophie d'Origène* (Paris, 1884), p. 33.

36. *Pantagruel*, ch. 16. There is an analogous story in the *Cent nouvelles nouvelles* of Philippe de Vigneulles, the hosier of Metz. See Ch.-H. Livingston, "Rabelais et deux contes de Philippe de Vigneulles" in *Mélanges offerts à M. Abel Lefranc* (Paris, 1936), p. 22 ff. There are others of the same stripe in Henri Estienne, *Apologie pour Hérodote*, ed. P. Ristelhuber, 2 vols. (Liseux, 1879), II, 242. Estienne got them from Erasmus, referring to Book II of *Ecclesiastes*, where he recounted the jests of the Franciscan Robert Caraccioli of Lecce.

gone to see Jean Du Bellay. He was given a decent burial. And on August 30, not to prevent dogs from desecrating his tomb—such a concern had not yet arisen, and no one would have been shocked if a whole pack had gone running through the aisles—but rather out of a concern for economy, lest they damage the pall, a protective railing was built around the bishop's sepulcher in the church.[37] A few years later dogs would cause a scandal if they so much as entered the church; and the storytellers of circa 1540, who had reflected the easy manners of their time, would by the same token appear to be cynical jesters—and so they did—with their tales of a time when gentlemen, their hawks perched on their wrists, entered churches "like fat fools" (*comme folz alourdis*) where, according to the translator of *The Ship of Fools,*

> Leurs oyseaulx avec leur sonnettes
> Et chiens meinent terrible bruit.

> Their birds hung with bells and their barking dogs
> Together made a frighful din.

One final citation, out of the many that could be referred to: it will really put us into the mood of the time. Des Périers, in his *Nouvelles Récréations,*[38] recalls the buffoonery of Triboulet, King Francis's remarkable jester. Here is one of many. One evening the king goes to the Sainte Chapelle to hear Vespers. The bishop begins his "Deus in adjutorium," and in the stillness of the lofty nave the sound of voices soon rises; the choir gives its response and the service begins. Triboulet, who is sensitive to noise and furious that the noble silence has been broken, falls upon the bishop at the altar and pounds him with his

---

37. Arthur Heulhard, *Rabelais, ses voyages en Italie, son exil à Metz* (Paris, 1891), p. 178, n. 2.

38. Bonaventure Des Périers, *Oeuvres françoises,* ed. Louis Lacour, 2 vols. (Paris, 1856), II, 320. In addition to Des Périers, numerous passages can be found in collections of sermons. See Olivier Maillard, *Oeuvres françaises, sermons et poésies,* ed. Arthur de La Borderie (Paris, 1877), passim, and especially p. 104, where Maillard attacks those who "with their immodest appearance and unbridled wantonness profane the holy temples and sanctuaries of God as though they were public brothels" (aspectibus impudicis et procacionibus effrenatis sacra Dei templa et aedes tanquam publica prostibula meretricum prophanat)!

fists. Imagine what would happen today if something of the sort took place in one of our churches on Sunday. Now look at Des Périers's account. We see the king, no more than annoyed, summon Triboulet and "ask him why he struck this good man." The jester's answer, given in the church with the service still going on, is unimportant. What matters is the attitude of the characters, the atmosphere.

Neither the story about Triboulet nor the anecdote about the pall is in any way unusual. They simply bear witness, as do so many others, to an attitude we no longer understand—for around 1560 a great revolution began in the behavior of our forefathers with regard to religious objects and places. In Pantagruel's time the ancient freedom was still alive. It was not so distant from the time when an important archdiocesan chapter (that of Besançon) had imposed a fine on members who refused to take part in the procession of the Festival of Fools. Here is a final text, if one is necessary. In a letter to a monk at Steyn (*Religioso Patri Nicolao Wernero*) in 1497 Erasmus calmly recounts something we do not expect. It had been raining without letup for three months. The Seine had overflowed its banks and was ruining everything. The shrine of Saint Genevieve was brought out and it was decided to carry it solemnly to Notre Dame—the bishop in the lead with the university, the abbot in the rear, barefoot, with his monks. The shrine itself was carried by four men who were completely naked: "quatuor, toto corpore nudi, arcam gestabant." And—was it because of this ceremonial costume?—"nunc," devoutly concluded the young Erasmus, "nunc, nihil est coelo serenius!" (Now the sky is perfectly clear.)

6. Rabelais and the Preachers

But why bother with these anecdotes? Let us simply open and reread the sermons of some first-rate witnesses, the "free preachers" of the time. Menot, Maillard—they treated the vices of their time with rough and outspoken contempt. We should not forget that Brother Francis had been able to read them in his monastery as much as he liked. We should not forget that all through his youth he had heard homilies by men who emulated them and had been able to detect echoes of the inspired,

mocking voices of those famous redressers of wrong. We should
not forget that Rabelais himself was a priest and a Franciscan
and—who knows?—may also have preached. And if he did, he
whose prose is that of a speaker—colloquial, rhythmic, always
seemingly meant to be read aloud—he undoubtedly preached in
the style of his order, with the joviality of a learned, down-to-
earth friar. If we reread Menot and Maillard we find they are
the source of hundreds of Rabelaisian jokes and japes. These
may shock our later sense of modesty, but they come, not from
Rabelais, but from his calling.

Is it a matter of vocabulary, of proverbial expressions embedded in the text? There is a prodigious crop of Rabelaisian
phrases in the writers Antony Méray called the free preachers.[39]
"Attired like an apple-gatherer"—Menot used the expression
before Rabelais. "Dressed like a house-burner"—Menot had the
expression first. Long before the valiant captain, Maul-Chitter-
ling (Riflandouille), made his appearance in *Pantagruel* (ch.
29) and *Book Four* (ch. 37), Menot apostrophized the fat
Maul-Chitterlings.[40] Panurge made fun of "my lord the king of
the Three Batches" (*Pantagruel*, ch. 31); Menot laughed at the
abbot of the Three Batches. "When *Oportet* takes its place,
there is no other course to trace"—this is in Menot. "When
Don Oportet taketh place, this is the course which we must
trace"—this is in *Book Three* (ch. 41). Menot's "*Cum venit
mors*, the comedy is over, the game is up" is echoed in the
phrase attributed to Rabelais, "Draw the curtain, the comedy is
over." Further, to Menot's song of the damned, with its six sorrowful notes—to wit, Ut, Re, Mi, Fa, Sol, La—there corresponds the song of Anarchus, become a crier of green sauce
singing, by order of Panurge, "in ge, sol, re, ut" (*Pantagruel*,
ch. 31). What's more, the Rabelaisian device of enumeration,
that incredible numerical precision, comes from Maillard. For
Maillard knew the number of drops of divine blood that fell on
the ground—precisely 47,000. Maillard knew the number of
wounds that covered the body of the Man-God—just about
5,475. Maillard knew that the Lord had taken 1,300 steps

---

39. *Les Libres Prêcheurs devanciers de Luther et de Rabelais: étude historique, critique et anecdotique sur les XIVe, XVe et XVIe siècles* (Paris, 1860). For what follows,
see Joseph Nève, *Sermons choisis de Michel Menot, 1508–1510* (Paris, 1924).
40. Nève, p. 96.

along the Via Dolorosa and that 190,000 persons went up to Calvary.[41]

And there were the satirical jokes.

In Menot, the commendatory abbots were lined up: "commendatarii et potius comedatarii, quia omnia comedunt" (commendatory, or rather, *comedatory*, for they eat up everything). He had asses wearing miters. The streets of Hell were paved with priests' tonsures.[42] He had hypocrites, *caffardi*, the *cafards* beloved of Pantagruel, and he had carriers of indulgences: *isti latores rogationum*.[43] Did Panurge make fun of pardons? He never had as much to say on the subject as Menot did, who was zealous in his pursuit of hypocrites who deceived the people[44] or of sly devils who lost their relics in a tavern and then replaced them with some kindling gathered from the oven, proclaiming, "Come and see a piece of the wood from Saint Lawrence's pyre!" Panurge never had as much to say as Gilles Pépin, who blasted those who sold Paradise at a reasonable price and went about crying, "I have precious stuff to sell!" "What is it?" "The kingdom of heaven!" "How much?"[45] The same Pépin denounced ruffians who dragged the sacrosanct relics of saints around on their horses or carts in order to deceive simple folk with their tricks. This was, again, the preacher's style, the style of churchmen. Rabelais's friend, Brother Antoine Du Saix, one of those "master beggars" of the Order of Saint Anthony whom Rabelais depicts "in quest of hoggish stuff" (*Gargantua*, ch. 17), was not particularly reticent either, in his *Esperon de Discipline* (1532), when it came to blasting monks, "those hypocrites forever making the sign of the cross, mule-drivers with relics, and other common spreaders

41. Abbé Alexandre Samouillan, *O. Maillard, sa prédication et son temps* (Paris, 1891), pp. 156-157.

42. Nève, pp. 344, 343, 354.

43. *Porteurs de rogatons* in Rabelais; see *Gargantua*, ch. 17. [Translator's note.]

44. Nève, p. 258. "Soli caffardi eas predicaverunt cum infinitis mendaciis, ut populum decipiant; qui saepe sunt parvi diaboli quando sunt in taberna, quia non est quaestio nisi de luxuria, de ludo, etc." (Pardons have been preached only by hypocrites with endless lies, in order to deceive the people; they are often very devils when they are in the tavern, since for them it is entirely a question of self-indulgence, enjoying themselves, and so on.) Ibid., p. 259, n. 1. Rabelais was never as harsh as this: "Omnes abusus hodierni sunt in templo. Si quis vult tractare de mercantiis, de luxuria, de pompis, veniat ad ecclesiam." (Every abuse of today is found in places of worship. If you want to negotiate about business, pleasure, festivities—go to church.) Ibid., p. 260.

45. Méray, pp. 132-133.

of lies who set their snares for ninnies by devoting their depre-
dations (I mean predications) to strange subjects that are un-
suitable and off the mark." Again: "My lords the loudmouthed
pilferers—I mean pillars and prelates of the church" are the
rivals in avarice of "Master Simon the Magician, broker of benefices, dealer in prelacies, and grabber of titles, who has used all
that to achieve the rank of burgher."[46] In what way are *Pantagruel* and *Gargantua* different, in tone or spirit, from these
writings of ecclesiastics? Only in having been written by a
great writer.

    ·ᶕ And so we find ourselves inclined to regard Rabelais's
"sacrilegious" jesting as being without venom, and even in
rather good taste when we think of how Martin Luther (that
anti-Christian) addressed Carlstadt in his pamphlet *Against the
Heavenly Prophets:* "You seem to think that Christ was drunk,
having imbibed too much at supper, and wearied his disciples
with meaningless words!" Furthermore, no matter how little
time one has spent in the company of certain ecclesiastics—perfectly respectable as to their lives and worthy of their office—
no matter how slight an opportunity one has had to dine at a
priest's table in the France of bygone days, one can see right
away that the mental outlook of Rabelais, the monk and priest,
was in large part a professional outlook, the outlook of a man of
the Catholic Church who did not think laughing was a sin and
who, when he spoke freely and familiarly about religious matters, was unaware of certain circumspect reticences and faint-
hearted attitudes that were to be found among the Reformed.
Or among unbelievers.

We hasten to say that not everything Abel Lefranc brought
forward in support of his charge that Rabelais was secretly anti-
Christian is struck down by this argument. Two of the passages
he singled out as suggestive deserve to be examined closely.
One, the solemn letter from Gargantua to Pantagruel in chapter
8 of *Pantagruel,* raises the question of the soul and its immortality, a highly controversial question around 1530. The other,
the account of the resurrection of Epistemon by Panurge, raises
the question of miracles. Let us see what Rabelais says and
what Abel Lefranc concluded from that.

46. Nève, p. 229.

4. Gargantua's Letter and the Immortality of the Soul

E KNOW what Gargantua's letter to Pantagruel is: a magnificent manifesto of a Renaissance intoxicated with its splendors. There is no more justly celebrated passage in all of Rabelais's work.

The beginning is taken up with a broad philosophical and moral exposition, a bit long if Gargantua's epistle is considered as a whole, but superb in tone and diction. Heaven only knows what critics—dazzled, no doubt, by the brilliance of Rabelais's prose—have seen in this document and what disparate things they have read into it! In an article entitled "La Lettre de Gargantua à Pantagruel,"[1] Thuasne informs us that "this first part, essentially religious and philosophical in nature, is connected on the one hand to Christian dogma and also to the Protestant doctrine of justification by faith; on the other hand it is connected to Platonic theories of transmutation, to which Plato alludes in many of his writings." Christian dogma. Justification by faith. Platonic theories of transmutation. What else? Let us without further ado look at the famous passage and see what we find there.

1. The Meaning of a Celebrated Passage

To do this, let us begin by translating it. It is in French, of course, magnificent French. Let us put it into words that are

---

1. *Revue des Bibliothèques*, 15 (1905), 99–139. Reprinted in Louis Thuasne, *Rabelais et Villon* (Paris, 1911).

much less beautiful but more immediately accessible to our minds. An excellent practice, by the way; one should never omit availing oneself of it every time it is a matter of interpreting an old document whose message is hard to grasp.[2]

Gargantua, having sent his dear son Pantagruel to school, exhorts him "to profit as well as thou canst." To inflame him with zeal for his studies and make his mind as vigorous and indefatigable among his books as a fire is in dry wood, he appeals to the most profound feelings of a generous heart: to the feelings of love and gratitude that an excellent father should inspire in a well-born son. Since Gargantua has suffered the common lot of men and, as a son of Adam, has through the fault of his first father sadly lost the privilege of immortality that God intended to grant to man when he created him, he must die. Death is the punishment for the fault of Adam and Eve.[3] It is a severe punishment indeed. Pantagruel should mitigate its harshness for his father to the greatest extent possible. The Creator in his goodness has granted to the fallen creatures that he deprived of life enjoyment of a kind of immortality. It is, to be sure, relative, but still highly desirable: that which vouchsafes to parents the procreation of children made in their likeness. Therefore, at the hour when his father's soul will take leave of its human abode Pantagruel should not limit himself to giving his father the illusion of corporeal and physical survival but should in addition strive to make his understanding the reflection, the enduring gleam, of his father's soul. In this way Gargantua will feel relieved of his natural horror of death, and will be able to console himself with the comforting thought that a second self is continuing his life on earth.

This is the intention of a Creator who is sternly just, but

---

2. We have been helped in what follows by Etienne Gilson, "Rabelais franciscain," in *Les Idées et les lettres*, 2d ed. (Paris, 1955), pp. 197–241.

3. "Amongst the gifts, graces, and prerogatives with which the sovereign plasmator God Almighty had endowed and adorned human nature at the beginning, that seems to me most singular and excellent, by which we may in a moral state attain to a kind of immortality, which is done by a progeny issued from us in the lawful bonds of matrimony. Whereby that in some measure is restored to us, which was taken from us by the sin of our first parents, to whom it was said that, because they had not obeyed the commandment of God their Creator, they should die; and by death should be brought to nought that so stately frame and plasmature, wherein the man at first had been created." *Pantagruel*, ch. 8.

good. It was to mitigate the severity of the punishment of death that he willed the sequence of generations that throughout the ages prolongs the life of grandparents through that of their grandchildren. It is a sequence that will end on the Day of Judgment. Then the world will be purified of corruptible bodies and the seeds of sin by a consuming fire. Then death, sin's consequence and its punishment, will cease. Then reproduction, death's consequence and its palliative, will come to an end.[4] There will be no more transmutations of elements into one another; they had no object other than the chain of generation and corruption which, after Rabelais, Ronsard—in his epitaph on Rabelais, in fact—reminded us were profoundly necessary.

> Si d'un mort qui pourri repose
> Nature engendre quelque chose
>   Et si la génération
> Se fait de la corruption:
> Un vigne prendra naissance
> De l'estomac et de la panse
> Du bon Rabelais, qui boivoit
> Toujours, cependant qu'il vivoit.[5]

> If Nature from a corpse that's rotten
> Can cause a thing to be begotten,
>   And if corruption leads to birth
> Everywhere upon the earth:
> Then soon a budding vine will branch
> From Master Francis's rounded paunch.
> He loved the grape, did Rabelais,
> And drank his fill both night and day.

4. "By this means of seminal propagation, there continueth in the children what was lost in the parents; and in the grand-children that which perished in their fathers, and so successively until the day of the last judgment, when Jesus Christ shall have rendered up to God the Father his kingdom in a peaceable condition, out of all danger and contamination of sin; for then shall cease all generations and corruptions, and the elements leave off their continual transmutations, seeing the so much desired peace shall be attained unto and enjoyed, and that all things shall be brought to their end and period." Ibid.

5. This is the text of the first edition, in *Bocage* (Nov. 27, 1554). On the epitaph, see above, ch. 1, sect. 8.

The war of the elements will come to an end. And peace will reign, perfect and absolute, in a universe to which God the Father will restore Jesus the Redeemer. These clearly are the ideas that are rendered in magnificent language in the first part of the letter to Pantagruel. Where do they come from, and what is the spirit animating these pages?

∽§ Generation born out of corruption, transmutation of elements into other elements, an enormous cycle of causes and effects—no wonder that when they read this mysterious and appealing passage in *Pantagruel* hundreds of readers and commentators said the same thing. Rabelais, that great mind shedding light on the darkness of destiny, is here expressing in magnificent language "a general conception of scientific philosophy."[6]

Not really, and there is no need for us to prove it. Gilson has clearly shown that we should not look in this lengthy passage for the original ideas of a great doctor, researcher, and passionate nature worshipper, a man who in his solitary meditations and experiments worked out a nobly ambitious natural philosophy. The most fascinating lines in this difficult text simply give sumptuous illumination to "a conception that is specifically theological or medieval: the state of the world after the Last Judgment." As a whole, the first part of the letter contains no more than a set of ideas that were familiar to all theologians. What is more, they were familiar to all of the faithful—which is to say, to all Frenchmen of the 1530 generation.

The expressions that seem to us so rich and full of scientific thought can all be found in the passages from Saint Thomas and Saint Bonaventure that Gilson contributed to the discussion. As usual, it is learned doctors he cites.[7] For my part, I hope I will be permitted to cite some book peddlers. Let us take one of the popular pamphlets sold by the booksellers who set themselves up under their awnings on the square, and by hawkers and cheapjacks in their wanderings—one of the hundreds of pamphlets put out by the publishers in Lyon every year. Bau-

6. All the terms seem to be from the language of modern science: seminal propagation, contamination, generation, corruption, elements, transmutations, period, and so on.

7. Gilson, p. 201 ff.

drier, I note, mentions one that was published in 1533 by one of the two large Lyon publishers of books "in the vulgar tongue," Olivier Arnoullet (the other was Claude Nourry, the publisher of *Pantagruel*). A copy of it that was printed in April 1537, also by Arnoullet, is in the Bibliothèque Nationale (Rés. D80054). Let us read the title, which is long and explicit: *Prognostication of the coming century, containing three short treatises. The first reveals how death first entered into the world. The second speaks of the souls of the departed. And of the different sorts of Paradise. The third, of the final tribulation. And of the resurrection of bodies, and what will be the time of Judgment, and the day, no man knows thereof.*[8] Here is exactly the same cycle of preoccupations with which the beginning of Gargantua's letter is concerned. And anyone who happened to have the idea of leafing through Baudrier[9]—that mammoth, inexhaustible mine of documents waiting to be sifted through—would have found Benoît Gillebaud's modest pamphlet to be quite a valuable commentary on Rabelais's text.

How death first entered into the world in consequence of Adam's sin, as we are told by the well-known verse in the Epistle to the Romans (5:12); how man "if he had not wished to sin had never died" but "had enjoyed the immortality and blessed eternity of the angels"; how, when the Judgment will be completed, Him whom we had seen "in the form of humanity, we will see in divinity"; how he will offer "his kingdom to God the Father"; by what conflagration, finally, what prodigious and supernatural heat the world will be burned up—these are all exactly the same problems that Pantagruel's high-minded father alludes to in his letter.[10]

---

8. *La Prognostication du ciècle advenir, contenant troys petits traictez. Le premier détermine comment la mort entra premièrement au monde. La seconde parle des âmes des trespassez. Et de la difference des Paradis. Le tiers, de la dernière tribulation. Et de la résurrection des corpz et quel le temps du Jugement, et le jour nul homme ne le sçait.* The final phrase, "and the day, no man knows thereof," is no stroke of originality but a tradition. See, for example, Guillaume Postel, *Alcorani, seu legis Mahometi, et Evangelistarum concordiae liber* (Paris: P. Gromorsius, 1543), p. 116: "De die autem aut hora illa, nemo scit, nisi solus Pater" (and of that day or hour no man knows, but only the Father). This appears in a section entitled *De judicio imminente* that follows the *Alcorani concordia*.

9. Bibliography of Arnoullet's publications in Henri and Julien Baudrier, *Bibliographie lyonnaise*, 12 vols. (Lyon, 1895–1921; photographic reprint, Paris, 1964), X, 1–26; bibliography of Nourry's publications in Baudrier, XII, 72–149.

10. "Se il n'eut voulu pécher, jamais ne fust mort"; "eut ensuivy l'immortalité et

~§ There is, furthermore, another wonderful place in Rabelais's novel that allows us to measure, by way of comparison,
the significance and number of the elements from traditional
Christian theology that are contained in this much-discussed
passage. In chapter 8 of *Book Three* Rabelais again takes up the
theme of the kind of immortality that is assured by procreation.
"Behold," says Panurge, "how nature—having a fervent desire
after its production of plants, trees, shrubs, herbs, sponges, and
plant-animals, to eternize, and continue them unto all succession of ages—*in their several kinds or sorts, at least, although the individuals perish—unruinable, and in an everlasting being*—hath most curiously armed and fenced their buds,
sprouts, shoots, and seeds, wherein the above-mentioned perpe-
tuity consisteth." Man, frail and naked, does not have the good
fortune of the plants. He has had to forge armor to protect himself. Where the work of protecting himself began is suggested
by the title of the chapter: "Why the Codpiece is held to be the
chief piece of armour amongst Warriors." Rabelais explains
with all the crudeness of a physician: it is there, he states, that
"is laid up, conserved and put in store, as in a secessive repository, and sacred warehouse, the semence and original source of
the whole offspring of mankind."
Nothing is more instructive than a comparison of these words
of 1546 with the words of 1532 in *Pantagruel.* Unless we are
entirely mistaken, it completely upsets Abel Lefranc's thesis
about the early appearance of atheism in Rabelais. The fundamental idea is similar in both places, to be sure. But in 1546 Rabelais was not stating a commonplace of Christian theology. He
transposed a famous passage from an author dear to rationalists—Pliny the Elder. "Transposed" is the right word, because
in *Book Three* Rabelais's optimism is substituted for Pliny's
pessimism.[11] And under the inspiration of his model he blends
man with nature, so to speak. He compares him to the plants
and zoophytes; he puts him back into his place in the general

---

benoiste éternité des anges"; "en forme d'humanité, nous le verrons en divinité"; "le
royaulme à Dieu le Père." The quotations can be found in Benoît Gillebaud, *La Prognostication du ciècle advenir* (Lyon: O. Arnoullet, 1537), fols. 2v, 3, 4v, 54v, 55.

11. Jean Plattard, *L'Oeuvre de Rabelais: sources, invention, composition* (Paris,
1910), p. 228; Lazare Sainéan, "L'Histoire naturelle et les branches connexes dans
l'oeuvre de Rabelais," *Revue du Seizième Siècle,* 3 (1915), 201.

category of created beings. Christ disappears, God fades away, and the individual is replaced by mankind. It is no longer a matter of the beneficence of the Creator in mitigating private pain. This time we are indeed in the presence of "a conception of scientific philosophy of a general order."[12] And these pages are no longer animated by the spirit of 1532, a spirit totally imbued with religious traditionalism and an orthodoxy that is, at the very least, literal.[13]

So there is no doubt about the meaning which invests the difficult beginning of Gargantua's letter. But would anyone venture to claim that in order to interpret the obscure details of this controversial passage correctly it is not important to know whether the passage expresses a completely secular, profane philosophic and scientific conviction or an authentically Christian doctrine?[14] Indeed, if Abel Lefranc had known the passages contributed to the discussion by Gilson perhaps he might have hesitated before finding a decisive argument in Gargantua's letter: Rabelais was no longer a Christian in 1532 because he rejected "the Christian dogma of immortality."[15]

12. Abel Lefranc, "Etude sur *Pantagruel,*" in Rabelais, *Oeuvres,* III (Paris, 1922), xliv.

13. To complete the argument, let us turn to fol. 2v of Gillebaud: "My lord Saint Paul the Apostle instructs us and says that it was through a man, to wit our first father, Adam, that sin entered into the world, and through sin, death; and thus death entered into all men, in that all sinned. Our Lord had created the angels and men immortal ... If men had guarded themselves from sinning, they would never have died and would have enjoyed the immortality and blessed eternity of the angels." (Monseigneur Sainct Pol apostre nous enseigne et dit que, par ung homme, c'est assavoir nostre premier père Adam, entra la péché au monde, et par péché, la mort; et ainsi en tous hommes en quoy tous ont péché la mort est entrée. Nostre Seigneur avait créé les anges et hommes immortelz ... Les hommes ... se ilz se fussent gardés de pécher, jamais ne fussent mors et eussent ensuivy l'immortalité et la benoiste éternité des anges.)

14. This Christian doctrine was stated by an authentic Christian, who was, it is true, suspected of being *mal sentant:* Nicholas Bourbon. In a letter to his friend Stella, who feared death, he put it as follows: "Did not the son of God, when he died, abolish our death, and did he not by the same act reconcile us to God and his father, so that he would destroy him who held sway over death—I mean the devil—and thus free all those who were in servitude to the fear of death all their lives?" (Nonne filius Dei moriens mortem nostram destruxit, eademque opera reconciliavit nos Deo et patri suo, ut eum aboleret qui mortis habebat imperium, nempe *ton diabolon;* denique ut liberos redderet eos quicumque metu mortis per omnem vitam obnoxii erant servituti.) *Nicolaii Borbonii Vandoperani nugae. Eiusdem Ferraria* (Basel: A. Cratander, 1533), fol. A3.

15. Lefranc, p. xliv.

2. A Denial of Eternal Life

Look here, says that learned interpreter of Rabelais's work: Rabelais, less explicit than the author of *The Prognostication of the Coming Century,* wrote nothing about the fate of "the souls of the departed." "Any notion of the immortality of the soul is absent from this long account . . . Even the allusion to the 'last judgment' seems strange if looked at a little more closely; it implies, in fact, no idea of eternal rewards or punishments . . . One has only to consider the words, and the conviction that Rabelais did not adhere to the Christian dogma of eternal life is quickly impressed on the mind. The only certain immortality Rabelais envisages is the entirely relative one that derives from 'seminal propagation.' "[16]

Is it really true that in the passage under discussion Rabelais rules out any notion of the immortality of the soul? That was not Gilson's opinion.[17] It is true, he observed, that the idea of the soul's survival is nowhere expressed in positive and dogmatic terms, "and one could, as a result, think that Rabelais ruled it out; but then one needs to explain: (1) what a Last Judgment would be like without resurrection; (2) what the world that Jesus Christ presented to his Father could really be like if souls were not immortal; (3) what the cessation of generations could mean if man had not become incorruptible, since, as Rabelais himself reminds us, there is no reason for generation other than to compensate for death. The simplest interpretation of Rabelais's silence on the immortality of the soul is, therefore, that it is implied in every line of the passage, at least if one would rather not admit that his words make no sense here." This argument by itself is enough. But the problem that has been raised is so important, and the proposed solution so pregnant with consequences, that it is not a waste of time to back up this line of reasoning with additional proof. We are not advancing a thesis; we only want to throw a little light on some obscure questions. Which arguments are the most troubling? They fall into two categories. First, Abel Lefranc finds fault

16. Ibid.

17. Gilson, "Rabelais franciscain," *Revue d'Histoire Franciscaine,* 1 (1924), 270. [In *Les Idées et les lettres,* pp. 230–236, this discussion was reworked and expanded.—Translator.]

with Rabelais for what he does not say, a Rabelais who is silent. Then he finds fault with him for what he does say, a Rabelais who speaks.

Rabelais is silent. Rabelais did not bother to cry out in Gargantua's voice in 1532, "I believe in the immortality of the soul." But what if he did so in his own voice in 1535? If at that date, two years after writing *Pantagruel*, he wrote an entire page that was specific and clear on the subject of personal immortality? This page is to be found everywhere, black on white, in editions that have been in circulation for as long as those of Jannet, Marty-Laveaux, Moland, or Clouzot.[18] It belonged to an *Almanac for the Year 1535, Calculated on the Noble City of Lyons, . . . by Master Francis Rabelais, Doctor in Medicine, and Physician of the Great Hospital of the Aforesaid Lyons.* The *Almanac* is lost, but Antoine Le Roi preserved a curious excerpt from it in his manuscript life of Rabelais.

The author of *Pantagruel* starts out by reminding his readers of one of the proofs of immortality offered by Aristotle in his *Metaphysics:* "All men naturally desire to know." Their desire cannot be satisfied in this transitory life, for (Rabelais quotes Ecclesiastes) "the understanding is never satisfied with learning, as the eye is never satisfied with seeing, nor the ear filled with hearing." But nature has "made nothing without reason nor given appetite nor desire of anything that we may not sometime obtain." Consequently, of necessity "another life comes after this, in which this desire shall be satisfied."[19] Of course, Rabelais does not announce in doctoral fashion: "My good people, this proof is conclusive. It removes all doubts, wins all minds." Who in his place would have said that? Has there ever been a philosopher who thought, and stated, that the "proofs" for the immortality of the soul constituted perfect certitude (I am speaking of intellectual certitude and not that which can be given by faith)? And then let us take note of two things.

"I say this," adds Rabelais,

18. Rabelais, *Oeuvres*, ed. Louis Moland, with a biographical note by Henri Clouzot, 2 vols. (Paris, 1950), I, lxx; *Les Oeuvres*, ed. Charles Marty-Laveaux, 6 vols. (Paris, 1868–1903), III, 257.

19. Trans. W. F. Smith, *The Works of Francis Rabelais*, ed. Albert Jay Nock and Catherine Rose Wilson, 2 vols. (New York, 1931), II, 903.

The argument adopted by Rabelais was one that would be similarly adopted and developed with approbation by such as Descartes, Bossuet, and Spinoza.

inasmuch as I see you in suspense, attentive and desirous to hear from me presently the state and disposition of this year 1535 ... If you wish entirely to satisfy this fervent desire, you ought to wish (as St. Paul said, Philipp. i. [23], *Cupio dissolvi et esse cum Christo*) that your souls should be set free from this darksome prison of its earthly body, and united with Jesus the Christ. Then shall cease all human passions, affections and imperfections; for, in enjoyment of Him we shall have fulness of all good, all knowledge and perfection, as King David formerly sang, Psalm xvi: *Tunc satiabor cum apparuerit gloria tua.*[20] To predict otherwise of it would be ill in me, as it would be simplicity in you to put faith in it![21]

This is a very important passage. Rabelais links what he says about immortality to a theory he was especially fond of and that he enunciated a score of times between 1532 and 1535 in a dozen different forms, both in his novel and in the almanacs. The theory is that of the impossibility of foreseeing future events, notably by the methods of astrology. Rabelais's attitude toward astrology was one of those held most firmly by him and one of the best reasoned. Master Francis expressed himself on the subject many times, with absolute intensity and sincerity.[22] If he joined an argument on immortality to these statements on a subject he treated with such conviction, it is a clear presumption in favor of the seriousness of the argument. To be sure, any human utterance can be based on prudence, or a lie, but these words of 1535 that were issued by Rabelais under his own name, that he used to support a thesis of which he was expecially fond, that one cannot, because of its date, suspect of having been craftily written in response to accusations that were made much later—at the very least they keep us from inferring an alleged silence on the survival of souls that was premeditated

20. "I shall be satisfied, when I awake, with thy likeness." Psalm 17 in King James version. [Translator's note.]

21. *Works*, ed. Nock and Wilson, II, 903.

22. We shall have occasion to come back to this later. For the moment let us be content to refer to chapters 1 and 5 of the *Pantagruelian Prognostication* of 1532; the fragment of Rabelais's *Almanac* for 1533 preserved by Le Roi; various passages in *Pantagruel*, notably, in chapter 8, the famous advice in Gargantua's letter: "As for astronomy, study all the rules thereof. Let pass, nevertheless, the divining and judicial astrology, and the art of Lullius, as being nothing else but plain abuses and vanities."

by Rabelais, with the consequences that were drawn by Henri
Estienne: that in the opinion of Panurge's creator "everything
we read of eternal life is written to amuse poor idiots and nourish them with vain hope." Let us be more scrupulous and not
speak of Rabelais's "opinion." To say that he kept silent on this
serious question of immortality in his writings is simply inaccurate.

◄§ Besides, is it surprising to see Rabelais refer to the psychological proof of immortality in his 1535 almanac? Does the
line of questioning it presupposes take us so far away from his
usual preoccupations? Was man made only for life on earth?
Doesn't his constitution itself give evidence of a higher destiny?
Can't we see, as we observe his life, that, as Pascal said, he was
made for infinity? Isn't there some idea of eternity mixed in
with everything he does, everything he feels, everything he
dreams? Why indeed should he have wings if he is never to fly
up to the heavens, never reach the firmament covered with
stars: "Donec eo ventum est, ubi coelum pingitur astris."[23] Why
has the winged body of Philosophy placed itself on heights[24]
above the moisture-laden clouds from which the ethereal Judge
contemplates the seas covered with sails, the outspread land,
and the abode of the shades? Thus did Gilbert Ducher, in a
piece written before 1538 and dedicated, it so happens, to Rabelais ("Ad Philosophiam, de Francisco Rabelaeso"), evoke philosophical speculation, sweeping its faithful followers up into the
ether. Rabelais was in the forefront:

> In primis sane Rabelaesum, principem eumdem
> Supremum in studiis Diva tuis sophia.[25]

There is, in fact, no shortage of passages in Rabelais's work
that can be connected with the one of 1535. There are even passages after 1535, in *Book Three* and *Book Four*, that date from

23. "Till he arrives where the sky is painted with stars." *Gilberti Ducherii Vultonis Aquapersani epigrammaton libri duo* (Lyon: S. Gryphius, 1538), p. 54.

24. Those of Benoît Gillebaud's third heaven. The first is corporeal, the second
spiritual, the third "is mental and perceived only by thought and so is the abode of the
son of God by whom all things were made." Gillebaud, fol. 14v.

25. "Indeed, in the forefront of those engaged in thy pursuits, O Holy Wisdom, is
Rabelais, their most exalted prince." *Gilberti Ducherii*, p. 54.

a period when, if we are to trust the universal consensus of his interpreters, Rabelais was further from the Church's traditional answers than he was at first. Let us recall the lovely passage in *Book Three* (ch. 13) on the soul awake in the sleeping body. Can we read it without thinking of how Leonardo da Vinci evoked the desire that never ceases to abide in man, that of rediscovering his true fatherland (*ripatriarsi*) and returning to his former state? "It is the flight of a butterfly toward the light; and man, who forever looks forward with unending desire and joyful impatience to the beginning of spring and the beginning of summer, who forever looks forward to the new month and the new year and finds that the things he longs for are too slow in coming—man is not aware that what he desires is his own death. But this desire is the spirit of the elements, the quintessence that is enclosed in the human soul and always yearns to return from the body of Man to Him who placed it there."[26] Thus Leonardo. What about Rabelais? When the body is asleep, and "the concoction is every where accomplished," the soul finds itself as if at liberty, since, till the body "awake, it lacks for nothing." The soul at once "delighteth to disport itself, and is well pleased in that frolic to take a review of its native country, which is the heavens, where it receiveth a most notable participation of its first beginning, with an imbuement from its divine source, and in contemplation of that infinite and intellectual sphere, whereof the centre is every where, and the circumference in no place of the universal world . . . remarketh not only what is preterit and gone . . . but withal taketh notice what is to come." The words of the Florentine artist-philosopher and the Touraine monk-physician are not the same, nor are their intellectual formulations. But doesn't the tone strike the same chord? And by what right can anyone see nothing but hypocritical prudence or vile Tartuffery in these famous passages by Rabelais (and not in the words of Leonardo)? For the great Italian as for the great Frenchman, the true end of man was thought. Thought was the liberator, freeing us from illusory,

26. See J. Roger Charbonnel, *La Pensée italienne au XVIe siècle et le courant libertin* (Paris, 1917), p. 446, n. 1, and p. 447. Erasmus, too, in the *Enchiridion*, is careful not to omit this argument of a soul which, *generis aetherei memor*, reaches out with all its might to things on high and, because it is immortal, loves celestial things. He points out the common source of all these discussions: Plato's *Timaeus*.

vulgar pleasure and responding fully to the basic nobility of our nature. This idea, so strong in da Vinci, was not likely to be any less so in Rabelais, who often described the ecstatic joys of study.[27] In a curious philosophical conversation reported by Charondas Le Caron and brought to light, it so happens, by Abel Lefranc, Rabelais professed just such a lofty doctrine of the Sovereign Good, which was identical with the satisfaction of this ardent desire for knowledge, man's torment and his greatness.[28] But we should also recall how the old French poet Raminagrobis, again in *Book Three* (ch. 21), dies with his eyes fixed on the ideal, whose serene beauty no intrusive vulgarity can prevent him from contemplating: "Go, my lads, in peace,— the great God of the highest heavens be your guardian and pre- server . . . I have this same very day, which is the last both of May and me, . . . chased out of my house a rabble of filthy . . . beasts . . . They went about to . . . call me out of those sweet thoughts, wherein I was already beginning to repose myself, and acquiesce in the contemplation and vision, yea, almost in the very touch and taste of the happiness and felicity which the good God hath prepared for his faithful saints and elect in the other life, and state of immortality."

If there is not a very specific reference to the doctrine of the personal immortality of the soul in this passage, and if there is not a clear affirmation of the soul's survival and its enjoyment of the delights that God has prepared for his elect "in the other life, and state of immortality" in the words uttered by Panta- gruel, Raminagrobis, Gargantua (as we have seen), and, I would add, Dr. Rabelais himself in 1535, in very truth it must be because Rabelais's language is unusually difficult to under- stand.

27. See especially the famous passage in *Book Three*, ch. 31: "Be pleased but to contemplate a little the form, fashion, and carriage of a man exceeding earnestly set upon some learned meditation."

28. Charondas (Loys Le Caron), *Les Dialogues* (Paris: J. Longis, 1556). The Third Dialogue deals with "the tranquillity of the mind and the sovereign good." Charondas reports a conversation that took place, he says, in Saint-Denis at the home of his uncle Valton among Claude Cotterau, a certain Monsieur l'Escorché, and Rabelais. "What can make a man contented?" Rabelais wondered. The wonderful ease and pleasure of the understanding, which, setting out "to know the truth about something, never rests till it has found it and, having arrived at perfect knowledge of it, is then contented." His pleasure is so intense then "that no pain, however sharp and strong, can disturb him." No physical joy even comes close to such mental happiness.

3. Sixteenth-Century Psychology: The Soul

So it may be that Rabelais was not quite so silent on the formidable problem of immortality as has been claimed. In any case, he spoke, and even said too much. In this passage so full of intentional silences, a couple of words seem to have slipped in that say it all. Let us reread it: "When, at his good pleasure, who rules and governs all things, my soul shall leave this mortal habitation, I shall not account myself wholly to die [if thou, my son, doth resemble me morally as well as physically], but to transmigrate[29] from one place unto another, considering that, in and by thee, I continue in my visible image living in the world." Wholly to die: thus does the "dog" declare himself— man dies totally. What an avowal!

An avowal it may be—but of what? Before asking him, it would be helpful to ask ourselves a preliminary question. What did Rabelais and all his contemporaries in 1532—in spite of differences among schools, opinions, and doctrines—generally agree they thought about the human soul? I am not saying about its destiny after death, but, first and foremost, its nature and composition.

⮞ It is quite plain that Rabelais never tells us in dogmatic terms what he thought about the soul. In a score of places, however, he relies on a conception of the soul that is familiar enough so that, with the aid of the guideposts he gives us, we can easily retrace the traditional path of his reasoning. It is a conception that is neither original nor mysterious. It is simply what the doctors of the time, with the help of the ancients— especially Aristotle and Galen—had worked out for their general use. We know that at that time medicine was primarily doctrine, not experimentation; it was based on philosophy. The conception was, to go no further, the one that the great exponent of the standard medical theory of the day, Jean Fernel of

---

29. The first known edition of *Pantagruel* (Claude Nourry, [1532]) has *transmigrer*. All the other editions have *passer*. It was undoubtedly this *transmigrer* that induced Thuasne to detect "Platonic theories about transmutation" in the letter to Pantagruel that are really not to be found there (see above, at the beginning of this chapter). It may be that in replacing *transmigrer* with *passer* Rabelais wished to protect himself from just such an interpretation.

Montdidier, a contemporary of Rabelais,[30] promoted throughout his own century and even throughout the century that followed.

If we open *Book Three* to chapters 13 and 31 we find a very clear summation of the theory of spirits that, following Galen, was unanimously adopted by men of learning in the Renaissance, and, naturally, by Fernel in his *Physiology*.[31] There is a hierarchy of three kinds of wandering spirits attached to the different parts of the body: *natural spirits*, produced by the liver and circulated through the veins; *vital spirits*, or natural spirits that have been refined by the heat of the heart and circulate through the arteries; finally, *animal spirits*, or vital spirits that have been transformed by contact with air after passing through the plexus mirabilis of the brain—they circulate through the nerves.[32] Corresponding to this classification is a division (as universally accepted in the sixteenth century as that of the spirits) of souls into three kinds. Since the soul is, above all, the principle of life, the principle and cause of the living body's functions—as Fernel (in the wake of many others) refers to it—all bodies, all living beings, have a soul proportioned to their specific needs. Plants have a natural soul, animals a sensitive soul; man combines these lower souls with a soul of

30. Fernel died in 1558, Rabelais in 1553. In all probability Fernel was born in 1497, and Rabelais, it seems likely, in 1494. Fernel's doctoral degree in medicine dated from 1530, that of Rabelais from 1537. In fact, however, Fernel did not practice his profession till after 1535, and Rabelais, who was a physician at the great hospital in Lyon in 1532, did not wait for his doctorate to start practicing.

31. See L. Figard, *Un Médecin philosophe au XVIᵉ s.: Etude sur la psychologie de Jean Fernel* (Paris, 1903); Etienne Gilson, "Descartes, Harvey et la scolastique," in *Etudes de philosophie médiévale* (Strasbourg, 1921), pp. 191–246. See also Lazare Sainéan, "L'histoire naturelle dans l'oeuvre de Rabelais," *Revue du Seizième Siècle*, 7 (1920), p. 17 ff.

32. *Book Three*, ch. 13: "The philosophers with the physicians jointly affirm, that the spirits, which are styled animal, spring from, and have their constant practice in and through the arterial blood, refined, and purified to the life within the admirable net, which, wonderfully framed, lieth under the ventricles and tunnels of the brain." Also *Book Three*, ch. 31: "All the arteries of his brain are stretched forth . . . to suppediate, furnish, and supply him with store of spirits, sufficient to replenish and fill up the ventricles . . . and with great alacrity, nimbleness, and agility to run, pass, and course from the one to the other, through those pipes, windings, and conduits, which to skilful anatomists are perceivable at the end of the wonderful net, where all the arteries close in a terminating point: which arteries, taking their rise and origin from the left capsule of the heart, bring through several circuits, ambages, and anfractuosities, the vital spirits, to subtilize and refine them to the aetherial purity of animal spirits."

a higher essence that is specifically his: the intellective soul.[33]
Fernel shows how they appear, one after another, in man. In
the fetus, there is the natural soul; in the child, there is the sensitive soul, which retains the natural soul and adds it to itself;
finally, in the adult, there is the intelligent and rational soul,
which in turn absorbs the sensitive soul, itself containing the
natural soul. There is a whole hierarchy of souls, starting with
nature and the lowliest natural functions, and reaching to God
and divine contemplation. But every time a new stage is
reached a sort of absorption and assimilation takes place.[34] Just
as the soul of animals, the sensitive soul, controls the functions
that these beings share with plants as well as those of their specifically animal life, so on the next higher level does the intellective soul of men simultaneously manifest its power in the natural, sensitive, and intellectual modes.

What happens at death? The vegetable soul of plants and the
sensitive soul of animals are born and die at the same time as
the plants and animals whose vital phenomena they cause. "As
syntheses abstracted from the functions and properties of material, perishable beings," they are material and perishable like
them.[35] What happens to them in man? We have taken Jean
Fernel as our guide, so let us follow him to the end. He is a
guide who is Christian and thoroughly orthodox, whose orthodoxy has never been challenged by anyone. Here he is, then, at

33. Fernel's *Physiologia*, V, ch. 2: "Tres viventium differentias mente complecti-
mur: naturale, sentiens et intelligens; tres quoque animae species iisdem nominibus in-
signitas, quae sunt naturalis, sentiens et intelligens; quibus haec respondent viventium
genera, . . . stirps, brutum, homo." (We understand there are three sorts of living
beings: the natural, the sensual, and the intelligent; and also three kinds of soul, designated by the same names, i.e., natural, sensual, and intelligent; to which there correspond these types of living beings: plant, animal, and man.) In his *Universa medicina*
(first ed. Paris: A. Wechel, 1567).

34. "Dum foetus utero fingitur . . . primum naturalis anima emergit seque prodit;
deinde, vitalis facultatis interventu et conciliatione anima sentiens comparet et elucet.
Haec vero, quanquam simplex est ut in beluis, comitem tamen retinet vim illam natura-
lem, quae tum manens anima dici non potest, ne corporis unius . . . complures formas
. . . fateri cogamur." (While the fetus is taking shape in the womb the natural soul first
emerges and is produced; then, with the intervention and operation of the vital faculty,
the sensual soul appears and shows itself. And it, although it is simple, as in animals,
nevertheless retains as a component this natural force, which then remains but cannot
be called a soul unless we are forced to acknowledge a single body with many forms.)
Physiologia, V, ch. 18.

35. Figard, p. 35.

the crossroads where all his contemporaries hesitated at one time or another. It may be that at death the human soul divides and each part follows its own destiny. Filled with the natural soul, the sensitive soul perishes because it is directly dependent on the body and, located in that body and coextensive with the matter which it animates, is an integral part of the body. The intellectual soul, however, does not perish, for it comes from outside. In the body which it inhabits it lives like the pilot of a ship or, following Fernel's nuances of thought, the artisan in the shop where he works.[36] But it is very hard to conceive of a soul half perishable and half immortal. And it is imprudent to conceive of it as twofold, whereas oneness would necessarily imply immortality, since a simple substance cannot perish either by dissolution or by annihilation. It is, finally, illusory to give man the immortality of an active intellect that is "impersonal, absolute, separate from individuals but participated in by them," whereas everything else is doomed to die, everything that allows a man to say "I" and to distinguish his I from the I of other men. Hence, the tutelary principle of the unity of the soul must be protected above all else; and Fernel goes about doing so with all his ingenuity. For him the intelligence truly absorbs the inferior souls. In man there are no longer distinct and autonomous souls. There are faculties, which the intellective soul, the single true soul of man, uses as intermediaries between itself and the body. These faculties are not the soul, but the instruments of the soul. They are not the body, but the motors of the body. They allow Fernel to maintain the unity and simplicity of the human soul: it is essentially intelligence and, having no need of the body to lift it to intuition and the contemplation of the eternal verities, it escapes the mortal destiny of inferior souls; it never perishes.[37]

36. The simile of the artisan is in *Physiologia*, V, ch. 18: "Ut opifex idoneis instructus instrumentis, si in tenebricosum aut arctum conclave contrudator nequit quae artis suae sunt efficere, sic anima vitioso corpore (quod est tanquam domicilium) coercita, quae sua sunt munia exequi non potest." (Like the artisan equipped with proper tools who cannot exercise his craft if he is forced into a dark, narrow room, so the soul confined in a defective body (its abode, so to speak) is not able to carry out its functions.) If the discomfort becomes unbearable, "tantam illam discrepantiam perhorrescens nec ferre potens, de corpore decedit" (horrified by so much deterioration and unable to bear it, it departs from the body).

37. "Itaque simplex quum sit [anima], nec secerni, nec dividi, nec discerpi nec distrahi potest. Nec interire igitur." (And so, since the soul is simple, it cannot be sepa-

Anyone can see that these half-animal, half-immaterial faculties are stratagems, and poor ones.[38] They anticipate the role played by the famous "plastic medium" of our ancestors. But all of Rabelais's contemporaries, and Rabelais himself, were in the grip of this formidable dilemma and did not know how to get out of it. An exception must always be made of the Alexandrian and Averroist commentators on Aristotle; they vigorously held the position that the personal soul was totally annihilated, and they claimed the benefit of an illusory continuity only for an active intellect that some placed outside man, in God himself, the immortality of the soul thus being nothing but the eternity of God. As for taking the other way out and proclaiming the complete immortality of the soul in all its constituent parts, that was impossible to conceive of. "Thinking the soul of man to be a being which is locally separated from the body the moment a man dies ... was at that time the common opinion of Divines and Philosophers." We take this assessment from that curious page in Bayle's *Dictionary* where he shows us Margaret of Navarre observing the last breath of one of her maids to see if the departure of her soul would or would not be accompanied by a noise or sibilance.[39]

---

rated, divided, broken up, or torn apart. Therefore it cannot perish.) *Physiologia*, V, ch. 18.

38. Especially since Fernel assigns different locations to the three parts of the human soul, in complete contradiction to the opinion of Aristotle, who gave the heart as their only location, common to all (see the discussion in chs. 12, 13, and 14 in Book V of Fernel's *Physiologia*). "Tres quae sunt, non essentia modo sed sedibus quoque et principatu disjectae sunt, neque in eodem possunt solio considere ... Ex propriis operibus, ex medendique ratione, altrix vis et naturalis in jocinore; animalis seu sentiens in cerebro; reliqua vitalis in corde constituenda videbitur." (They are three in number, not only with respect to their essence but also with respect to location. They were separate from the beginning and are unable to reside in the same seat ... Because of its operations and its healing function, the sustaining natural power is in the liver; the animal or sentient force is in the brain; the remaining vital force will be seen to be established in the heart.) *Physiologia*, V, ch. 14.

39. Pierre Bayle, *Dictionnaire historique et critique*, 5th ed., 5 vols. (Amsterdam, 1734), IV, 318, s.v. "Navarre." Bayle took the anecdote from Brantôme's *Vies des dames illustres*. Here is the essential part: "She never stirred from her bed-side, as long as she was agonizing, looking her earnestly in the face, without interruption, till she was dead. Some of her Ladies, who were most familiar with her, asked why she looked with so much attention on that poor dying creature: she answered, that having often heard many learned men assert that the soul left the body the moment it died, she was willing to see if there came from it any wind or noise, or sound on the removal and going out of the soul, but that she could perceive nothing like it ... she added, that if she were not well settled in her faith, she should not know what to think of that re-

We have, as it happens, followed Fernel, but we could just as well have followed any of his contemporaries and would also have found the concept, one he had inherited, of one soul with two levels, unequally immortal. It was found everywhere, even on the stage in the mouths of tragic actors.

> Trois natures en nous, qui toutes s'entretiennent
> Excitent notre vie et vive la maintiennent:
> L'Esprit, l'Ame, l'Anime. Et qui l'une ôteroit,
> Soudain toute la vie ensemble partiroit.

> Three natures grow in us, and all contrive
> To foster life and keep our selves alive.
> Spirit and Soul and Animus are they:
> If one departs, then life itself gives way.

So wrote Charles Toutain in *The Tragedy of Agamemnon*.[40] Animus (*anime*) was a coinage, the same one that was used by an original thinker who was among those who (as we have seen) accused Rabelais of impiety: Guillaume Postel. Indeed, his doctrine, though perhaps a bit more complicated, was not different from Fernel's. It can be found summed up at the beginning of his *Très-merveilleuses victoires des femmes du Nouveau-monde*.[41] In every human creature there are, in addition to the body, two parts: one that is higher, the *animus* (*anime* in

---

moval of the soul and its separation from the body, but that she would believe what her God and her Church commanded her to believe, without any further enquiry." In English, *A General Dictionary, Historical and Critical*, 10 vols. (London, 1734–1741), VII, 733.

40. Charles Toutain, *La Tragédie d'Agamemnon, avec deus livres de chants de philosophie et d'amour* (Paris: M. Le Jeune, 1557), fol. 31v. It goes on: "Nous halletons après cette haleine vivante / Que je nomme l'Esprit, sans cesse respirante. / Mais l'Ame (que je pren comme elle est usitée / En la meilleure part) n'est jamais agitée / De telles passions: car si elle enduroit / Aussi bien que l'Anime et l'Esprit, elle mourroit ... / L'Anime nous avons (autre mot n'a la France) / Qui fait croître et qui donne avec le mouvement / Du ris et du courrous le horsain sentiment." (Our breath derives from Spirit: force untiring, / Sustaining life by endlessly respiring. / These passions do not agitate the Soul, / (So we can learn from those that know its role.) / If great distress should ever come it nigh / Like Animus and Spirit it would die ... / No word for Animus in French exists: / It fosters growth, it makes us move about / And carries wrath and laughter from without.)

41. Paris: J. Ruelle, 1553. We looked at the reprint of this book that was made in the eighteenth century. The quotations can be found there on pp. 13 and 14. See also the edition with biographical and bibliographical notes by Gustave Brunet (Turin, 1869), pp. 15–16.

French); the other lower, the *anima* (*âme* in French). Beyond
that, "there come from without into our animus, anima, and
body *Spirit* and *Mind*, which illuminate, the one the animus,
the other the anima: the philosopher includes the active and potential intellect as well—the one imprints in us the knowledge
of truth as light presents visible things to the eye, while the
other retains it after it has been imprinted, as the air presents
the things shown by light." The anima, then, "is dependent on
the body and is formed within the blood. The animus is immortal, having been divinely created and joined with the anima
into one nature, like the element of earth with water. Mind, or
the higher faculty or the active intellect, corresponds to fire and
is joined with the animus. Spirit, corresponding to air, is joined
with the anima like air with earth."

It is a more complicated system, carrying, if you like, the
stamp of Postel's peculiarities. But it is particularly striking that
we find in him as we do in the standard Fernel both the concept of a human soul formed of elements that are well-nigh het-
erogeneous (so truly distinct that Postel does not hesitate to
coin words to designate them) and the strange mixture of cor-
poreality and immateriality, mortality and immortality, that so
thoroughly baffles our habits of thought. Our habits are post-
Cartesian, it should be said; Bayle pointed that out, and he was
right to do so. In his time theologians and philosophers still
thought like the queen of Navarre; they all held the soul to be
an entity that was separated from its location in the body at the
moment a man expired—all except those who were Cartesians.[42]
Rabelais was not a Cartesian, for obvious reasons. Like everyone else, he held that the intention of the "founder" of the microcosm that is man was "to have a soul therein to be entertained, which is lodged there, as a guest with its host, that it
may live there for awhile. Life consisteth of blood; blood is the
seat of the soul." It was, as a consequence, perfectly natural to
regard the soul as perishable—that is, whatever in the soul cor-
responded to the natural soul and the sensitive soul, and which

---

42. In the article on Margaret of Navarre: "This Princess is very excusable, though
she imagined the soul of man to be a being which is locally separated from the body
the moment a man dies; for this was at that time the common opinion of Divines and
Philosophers, and it is still at this day the opinion of all the Doctors who are not Cartesians."

presided, not only over vegetable functions, but over the exercise of sensation and of the reason that operated with the help of data supplied by the senses or of images that recalled such data.

In short, it was the contribution of the senses that perished, the five external senses along with the four internal ones[43] that Rabelais, faithful to the teaching of Saint Thomas, recognized: common sense, imagination and apprehension, ratiocination and resolution, memory and recollection.[44] This was no small matter, because the sensitive soul, or sensitive part of the soul, which perished was in charge of almost everything that made a person alive, sentient, and active in the world. What was there left to survive? The intellective soul, or the intellective part of the soul. Rabelais proclaimed its immortality in so many words. Open *Book Four* to the famous passage where Pantagruel, referring to the signs shown by "the heavens, as it were joyful for the approaching reception of those blessed souls," on the eve of the death of heroes, cries, "I believe that all intellectual souls are exempted from Atropos's scissors. They are all immortal, whether they be of angels, of demons, or human."[45]

Angels and demons. We must not forget (we are going to return to this later) that for men of that time, and not merely for Rabelais, *unus ex multis*, philosophy, as Ronsard informs us a dozen times,

---

43. Fernel only counted three of them. Cf. *Physiologia*, V, ch. 8: "Sentiens anima duas cognoscendi facultates obtinet, externam, in sensus quinque tanquam in species distributam, et interiorem. Haec porro species habet, vim discernendi communem, vim fictricem et eam quae meminit ac recordatur." (The sentient soul possesses two faculties of knowing—the external, which is divided into five senses, or aspects, and the internal. The latter has as its aspects the common power of discerning, the power of imagination, and the power that remembers and records.)

44. Derived from the following passage in *Book Three*, ch. 31: "You shall see how all the arteries of his brains are stretched forth, and bent like the string of a cross-bow, the more promptly, dexterously, and copiously to suppeditate, furnish, and supply him with store of spirits, sufficient to replenish and fill up the ventricles . . . of common sense,—of the imagination, apprehension, and fancy,—of the ratiocination, arguing, and resolution,—as likewise of the memory, recordation, and remembrance."

45. *Book Four*, ch. 27. The introduction of angels, demons, and heroes was not something dreamed up by Rabelais in an effort to court the Du Bellays, as we might be tempted to think. In Fernel's *De abditis rerum causis*, I, ch. 11 (in his *Universa medicina*), is found the complete theory of angels, demons, and heroes, their history, their origin, their nature, and their functions; and it can be seen that, strictly speaking, Rabelais invented nothing when he wrote the story of the Island of the Macreons.

Cognoit des anges les essences,
La hiérarchie et toutes les puissances
De ces Daimons qui habitent le lieu
De l'air . . .

. . . knows the essence of the angels' nature
And how the demons who inhabit air
Are ranged in order of their different powers.

The demons, by whom dreams are made. The demons, messengers of the deity,

Postes de l'air, divins postes de Dieu
Qui ses segrets nous apportez grand erre.[46]

Couriers of air, the couriers of the Lord,
Who swiftly bring His secret messages.

4. "Wholly to Die"

Having reminded ourselves of this, let us go back to the passage in Rabelais. Let us attempt to clarify all its obscurities. Two of them or, to be more precise, two of its phrases led Abel Lefranc to make a similar objection. One is to "transmigrate" or "pass from one place unto another" and, even more, the other: "wholly to die."[47]

Gargantua, remember, states that at the hour of his death his soul "shall leave this mortal habitation."[48] Why this abandon-

46. See Henri Busson, "Sur la philosophie de Ronsard," *Revue des Cours et Conférences,* 31 (1929–1930), 32–48, 172–185; Albert-Marie Schmidt, *La Poésie scientifique en France au seizième siècle* (Paris, 1940); Pierre de Ronsard, *Hymne des daimons,* ed. Albert-Marie Schmidt (Paris, 1939). The quotations are from "L'Hymne de la Philosophie" in *Le Second Livre des hymnes,* and from sonnet 31 in *Le Premier Livre des amours.*

47. In the passage by Bayle on Margaret that we referred to above we read, "I own it does not follow from thence, that this transmigration is attended with some noise or whizzing, as the Queen of Navarre imagined." Remember that before Rabelais wrote "pass from one place unto another" he too had written "transmigrate." We see how much he made use of traditional language.

48. *Habitation humaine:* exactly how is this to be translated? The learned editors of Rabelais's works do not say. Two meanings seem equally possible. Gargantua means either that his soul will leave the earth, the habitation of men, or that it will forsake the

ment? Obviously, because the body of the good giant is going to die, and the soul must not die with it. But the objection will be made that this is not at all obvious. Rabelais is silent—why make him speak? He specifically wanted to leave some ambiguity hovering over the fate of the soul of which he unquestionably wrote that it departed from the earthly abode of men, and hence Gargantua's body, but leaving the body does not mean to survive. A passenger who leaves a boat when there is a shipwreck is not necessarily saved; there is nothing to prevent him, alongside the ship, from being swallowed by the sea together with it. It is an old comparison, venerable in its antiquity; Saint Thomas made fun of it. In any case, a comparison is not reasoning. Let us simply try to reason. Gargantua begins by speaking of God. It is by him, the great ruler of everything, that the hour of his death will be set. It will be by an act of his absolute will, his "good pleasure," that his soul will leave its "habitation." Can a reader with good sense be found up to this point who imagines that if this all-powerful arbiter of the world thus intervenes directly to separate a body and a soul that were brought together by his efforts it is simply for the pleasure of destroying the soul outside the body, when he might with much less trouble allow it to be destroyed in the body, together with it? The pleasure would be all the more remarkable as this God is the God of the Last Judgment, and once he started destroying souls, what would be left for him to judge? No, we can translate without injury as follows: Gargantua begins by proclaiming that at the hour of his death his soul will be separated from its earthly garment and survive a body destined for destruction.

But what does he add? That only the existence of Pantagruel will make him believe at that final moment that he is passing from one place to another and not wholly dying. That is what seems to be suspect. For if Gargantua's soul does not follow the fate of his body, if it is released from the body in order to survive it, the old giant king has no need of a son for him to be able to say, "I shall pass from one place unto another" and "I shall not wholly die." It is not the existence of Pantagruel, in

---

body in which God placed it "as a guest." I believe the first interpretation is preferable. If the second hypothesis were true, wouldn't Rabelais have written "its habitation," not "this habitation"?

other words, but (if he is a Christian) the existence of his immortal soul that allows him to say with confidence, "My death
will not be a complete annihilation. I shall not wholly die. My
soul will not die. And if I cease to exist here below as a material
person, it will be in order to continue to live in another world
as a spiritual being." I do not think I am misrepresenting these
two statements. On the contrary, I think I am making the ter-
minology more precise and hence giving greater force to the
words on which Abel Lefranc fundamentally relied in order to
tell us: "Extract Rabelais's thought. Leave out the statements
made for show. Get to the bottom. There you will find the twofold and fatal ambiguity that I am revealing for the first time."

Well, I disagree. To argue in this way is to distort the exact
meaning of certain words in Rabelais—by which I mean certain
words in the language of the sixteenth century. "Die" is one of
them. It may seem paradoxical that the word used to designate
a reality that is always the same should have perceptibly
changed its acceptation in the short span of three centuries.[49]
And yet, consider. If we hold spiritualist views, we say that
man does not altogether die. It is a way of speaking, and a perfectly legitimate one, since existence is defined as "that which is
encompassed by thought," and material things are said to exist
because they are in our thoughts; but thought itself is considered even more real, since it gives existence to everything else.
Thus, today it is easy for us to go from the statement "I shall
not altogether die" to "Man does not altogether die." But what
of Rabelais and his contemporaries?

They lived before Descartes and grew up on scholasticism
and theology. Suffice it to say that for them man was not
thought thinking itself. He was the union of two elements that
by their origin and nature had dissimilar fates: a material body
and, in the body "as a guest," a composite soul, more than half
material, located within the body and coextensive with it. Postel
said it very well using a standard formulation: "The soul is not
man. The body is not man. The body and soul together and for

49. Is there any use in saying that no one has ever thought of doing a history of
words and ideas? If anyone did happen to think of it, moreover, he would probably restrict his investigation to ancient societies. Hasn't it been silently and well-nigh universally taken for granted that there is no interest or benefit in doing the history of modern ideas, and even that there is no material on which it could be based?

as long as their union lasts—that is man."[50] Death is, therefore, the breakup of that union. It is not a "natural" phenomenon, but the work of God—a separation.

In other words, at a moment fixed by the wisdom of the Almighty the body undergoes complete annihilation. Men of that time did not yet have the idea expressed by Voltaire two centuries later in the passage in *Micromegas* that marks the advent of our modern scientific and natural conception of death: "The texture of the body is resolved, in order to reanimate nature in another form"; that, he says, is "what we call death."[51] For Rabelais's contemporaries, who could not rely on a totality made up of chemical principles, the body was conceived as subject to annihilation.[52] Its destruction set the soul free. To be more exact, it caused the departure from the body of the soul's finest part and, so to speak, its spiritual essence, while its other parts shared the fate of the body. And that was what death was: the dissolution of a compound—man. And dying of this sort could only be done "wholly."

50. "Nam nec anima per se est homo, nec corpus est homo, sed una ambo homo sunt." Postel, *De rationibus Spiritus Sancti* (Paris: P. Gromorsius, 1543), p. 9.

51. Voltaire, *Micromegas, Histoire philosophique*, ch. 2. [Trans. in *The Works of Voltaire*, 42 vols. (Akron, Ohio, 1905), III, 27.] Consider the distance that separates this passage and its ideas from Ronsard's "L'Hymne de la mort" (in *Le Second Livre des hymnes*): "Ce qui fut se refait; tout coule comme une eau / Et rien dessous le ciel ne se voit de nouveau; / Mais la forme se change en une autre nouvelle, / Et ce changement-là vivre au monde s'appelle, / Et mourir quand la forme en une autre s'en va . . . / Mais notre âme immortelle est toujours en un lieu / Au change non sujette, assise auprès de Dieu, / Citoyenne à jamais de la ville éthérée / Qu'elle avait si longtemps en ce corps désirée." (That which has been revives; the world below / Like moving water streams in steady flow. / Shapes are not fixed, they constantly decay. / Our life on earth means change from day to day, / And death is one more change we undergo . . . / But our immortal soul remains unmoved: / She lives with God, and God is her belovèd. / She dwells forever in His holy city, / For which she yearned when living in the flesh.) The inspiration is clearly pagan; every trace of theological teaching has disappeared; but there is in fact nothing precise, coherent, or scientific behind the beautiful, flowing lines.

52. Rabelais defined death (the letter to Pantagruel) as "the bringing to nought of that so stately frame and plasmature, wherein the man at first had been created." Fernel gives life a definition that is already quite biological: "Est animantium vita facultatum actionumque omnium conservatio." (Life in animals is the conservation of all faculties and motions.) His definition of death has a similar inspiration: "Mors est vitalis roboris omniumque facultatum exstinctio." (Death is the extinction of the vital force and all the faculties.) *Physiologia*, V, ch. 16. These are signs of a purely scientific conception that would little by little triumph over theological doctrine. But note that this definition only applies to animals, and that Fernel ascribes it to Aristotle, whom he is discussing.

The electric current that decomposes water does not destroy the hydrogen it has liberated, but what difference does it make? The water is no less "wholly" dead as a result of the separation of its two components. Similarly, in sixteenth-century orthodox thought, man dies at the very instant the breakup takes place between the soul and the body in which God has housed it. It signifies little that the soul is not altogether subject to the annihilation that overcomes the body. From the moment it takes its leave of its temporary earthly abode, a man is "wholly" dead. This is the punishment desired by God in expiation of original sin. And it depends on God, on his justice and goodness, whether this death will be eternal, or a new life, an eternal life, will follow, through a new union of the surviving soul and the flesh resurrected without corruption. Thus, through divine mercy the elect will, after the ordeal of earthly death, reenter into possession of the "immortality and blessed eternity" which God had intended for man as for the angels, and which sin caused both the rebel angels and all of mankind to lose.[53] Thus death, in the exact meaning of the word, is not the true gateway to life for all men, but only for the just. Man dies wholly. He does not die irrevocably. In forsaking the precarious and brief life here below he knows he will be reborn, if God wishes, to true life, life eternal.[54] It is a magnificent hope, a reward for his faith that mitigates the harshness of the divine punishment, death.[55]

Well, then, what of Gargantua? He knows very well that the spiritual part of his soul will not suffer the fate of his body and that God will summon it to Him. He is without any uneasiness on the subject. And since he has faith, he has hope of being jus-

53. See the work by Gillebaud already cited, fol. 2v: "Nostre Seigneur avait créé les anges et hommes immortelz ... Les hommes ... se ilz se fussent gardés de pécher, jamais ne fussent mors, et eussent ensuivy l'immortalité et la benoiste éternité des anges."

54. Calvin, who held all these views, said, for example, that "the entrance into life is denied to all whom He wishes to deliver to damnation." *The Institutes of the Christian Religion*, Book III, ch. 21.

55. In Erasmus's colloquy, "An Examination Concerning Faith," Barbatius-Luther refers to these conceptions: "death here is twofold, of the body, common to good and bad alike, and of the soul. Now the death of the soul is sin." After the Last Judgment, however ...: "After the resurrection, there will be eternal life both of body and of soul for the righteous ... On the other hand, eternal death, of body as well as of soul, will seize the ungodly; they will have both an immortal body for everlasting torments and a soul perpetually tormented by the goads of sins and without hope of forgiveness." *The*

tified and promoted to eternal life. But what makes him sorrowful, in spite of everything, is the idea of leaving the world he
knows, giving up his present attachments, and breaking the
many tender ties that bind him to men and things on this earth.
It is a weakness, but a very human one. We should be in no
hurry to say, with the magnificent rigidity with which unbelievers call on believers to be superhuman (by virtue of their
principles), that he was scarcely Christian. A Christian is a
man, just a miserable man. And he suffers death because God
willed it. If he did not suffer death it would not be a punishment. The hope of a heavenly reward mitigates its harshness for
the good; it remains no less a trial for them. Therefore, the pain
that Gargantua felt would not be relieved by the survival of his
intellective soul, but rather by the survival of his son, the son
who was the inheritor of his tastes, his thoughts, and his attachments, able to carry on his work and further it among men.
Here is the meaning of those words in the letter: "I am going to
die. The human being, the human personality, that I am going
to cease to be, which has been living in this world, feeling and
doing, and which my friends have known and loved under my
name, is going to die, to die completely and forever. But no. It
shall not, properly speaking, die. I shall not die. I shall simply
change my place. My sensitive soul will, so to speak, change its
material garment. I am still in myself, Gargantua. Tomorrow it
will be as though I were in you, Pantagruel, my son."

No, Gargantua was no unbeliever when he wrote "wholly to
die." Or, if he was, weren't there others like him in the sixteenth century, and even in the seventeenth century? Let me
quote one. What shall we say of the infidel who took it into his
head to pronounce the following audacious words? "The flesh
will change its nature, the body will take another name. Even
that of 'corpse' will not last long. It will become, says Tertullian, a something that has no name in any language. So true is it
that everything dies, even the gloomy words we use to designate our wretched remains."

Colloquies of Erasmus, trans. Craig R. Thompson (Chicago, 1965), p. 188.

This "eternal death" of the damned is a strange one, in which the body and the soul
are eternally revived in order to expiate. To such a degree were ideas of life and death
at that time devoid of any physiological content.

What a magnificent echo of Gargantua's "wholly to die"! We have all by now recognized that this new unbeliever was Bossuet.[56]

5. Rabelais's Offense

We have thus seen once more that we should not read a sixteenth-century work with the eyes of a twentieth-century man and then utter a frightened cry and proclaim the work shocking. Only one thing is shocking: forgetting the small fact that a proposition stated by a man of 1538 does not sound the same when stated by a man of 1938. And that a great deal of work must be done, important and highly intricate work, if we wish to restore to opinions we think we can understand without further investigation the very special meaning they had for the people who held them four centuries ago. Between 1530 and 1930—or '40 or '50—much water has flowed under the high bridges that Descartes and then Leibniz and Kant and all the philosophers of the nineteenth and twentieth centuries, in the way of the technical and scientific revolutions they witnessed, built to span the wide river of our ignorance.

In this sense we might truly say that when Rabelais is summarily charged with free thought (or congratulated for thinking freely—it is the same thing) he is only a victim (or beneficiary) of theology. He knew it too well. He was too aware, for example, of the difficulties raised by the theory of the immortality of the soul. He knew too well how it was stated in the schools and how it was discussed by the learned men of his time. If he had been like most of us today he would have been much more at ease—I mean, that is, if he had been totally and completely ignorant with respect to theology. The question of immortality would have seemed simple to him, instead of being divided and subdivided, as he saw it, into at least a dozen distinct questions, each one susceptible of contradictory solutions. Which meant that the number of possible attitudes was for him not reduced to just two: believing or not believing in the immortality of the soul. There were many more, they were infinitely numerous.

56. J. B. Bossuet, *Sermon sur la mort*, I[er] point.

But there it is. We are not theologians, and the men of the
sixteenth century were—even when they did not spend years in
a monastery, like Rabelais. Rabelais, who was intelligent and a
diligent worker, must have had a considerable amount of theological study imposed on him by his superiors. And it was later
nourished, developed, and humanized by contact with the ancient philosophers, Greek or Roman, who had nurtured Christianity with such a rich and abundant substance. Theologians is
what these men were, with a zeal, a regard for precedents, a respect for traditions, and a burning curiosity that are unheard of
in us. Where does the soul come from when it enters the body?
How and when does it get there? How, when, and in what
form does it leave the body? In what manner is it joined to the
body? By what intermediaries does it act on the organs and
how does it receive their actions? Every new doctor of theology
enriched the long tradition he was heir to by exploring the fine
points of these questions, which to him were exciting, and
which were subdivided into tens, then into hundreds, of secondary problems.

At the same time, moreover, these men were Aristotelians.
Not all of them, it will be said; and those who were belonged to
a number of different factions that were quite far apart. Unquestionably. But even those who were most vigorously opposed to Aristotle's solutions at the very least took from him
the formulation of the problems as he stated them. Caught between Christian dogma and, if you will, Aristotelian dogma,
they did not have much room to move around, to say the least.
With little knowledge of dogma, ignorant of traditions, having
no curiosity about a thousand problems they reject as puerile or
insoluble, and tied to no scholastic metaphysics, contemporary
spiritualists are much more able than their ancestors to give free
rein to their thoughts, dreams, and hopes. The problems have
been simplified. We say "soul," and we regard this soul as the
immaterial principle of life. We are satisfied with this vague expression, or with some other that is its equivalent. The soul for
us is something simple. We know nothing of its parts. We believe it is mortal or immortal in one piece. We do not look for
its seat in the blood, or the brain, or the pineal gland. And we
likewise declare, with the same insouciant simplism, that after
death there is nothing; or, on the contrary, that everything does

not die at death—but always with the feeling that we have established our ground freely and without being bound by hopes and beliefs, and that formal reasoning, distinctions, and the whole arsenal of deductive logic dear to our forebears are only an encumbrance and nuisance.

Hence the sort of demands Abel Lefranc makes on Rabelais. Can Pantagruel, with his intellective soul, be content to make the best of things, to save what can be called the metaphysical immortality of the soul? Can Gargantua be simply assured that one substance, the existence of his intellective soul, will not be destroyed when it comes time for his body to disintegrate? In truth, they are easily satisfied. Some reassurance they give themselves with their immortal substance, if it is true that no one has any conception of a substance, that it is impossible to have any, and if it is true that only the senses and consciousness grasp the attributes and properties of things, if substance is what in each thing is beyond properties and attributes, beyond what is experienced, beyond what can be known. It is something, but we can never say what it is. It is something, but it does not matter if it is called something or nothing: the void, a chimera *bombinans in vacuo.* Some reassurance—as long as they don't try to give it to us. For how could they not see what is so glaringly obvious to us? In any case, what do we, men like them, care about the illusion they are tricking us with: the survival of an impersonal substance that has been joined to the body in an almost fortuitous union and has nothing to do with our real personality? And besides, can they really be orthodox when they speak like that?

These charges are not without merit. But it is right that the case be made, not against Rabelais, but against his whole century. When it passionately raised this question of immortality and constantly turned it over and over, it never raised it without the help of Aristotle—who was sometimes the Aristotle of Saint Thomas, sometimes that of Averroës, sometimes that of Alexander of Aphrodisias. If the answers were not always the same for all these interpreters, the questions were asked in the same way. And how those questions got in the way of the free play of speculation and hope! Perhaps the most daring philosophical intellect of the time, Pomponazzi, did not even know how much his thought was tied up in the knots of an arid scholasticism and lacked elegance and radiance. Now, Rabelais surely did not reason in scholastic language, but the problems that he treated were received, already formulated, from the tradition—and could he completely rid himself of it? Put him on trial. He will seem timid, inadequate, incomplete—so much so that you will attribute to him hundreds of reservations that he undoubtedly never had. So much for Rabelais. But what of Fernel? Fernel was not just one man. He was thousands of men, the cultivated and learned men who docilely followed him and over the course of at least a century and a half drew their ideas and their doctrines from the seven books of his *Physiology* and from his treatise *De abditis rerum causis*.[57] Well, Fernel's doctrine is not so different from that of Rabelais on many points at issue. And no one has seen fit to regard him as an unbeliever because his theory was, after all, disastrous.

The ultimate error, moreover, would be to believe that his theory did not appear disastrous to his contemporaries. Let us remember that their minds were infinitely more subtle and practiced in philosophical discussion than ours. Fernel's contradictions, when he sometimes forgot his own theory and abandoned his official doctrine that the soul was identical with the vital principle in order to make (or proceed as though he made) the vitalist distinction between the soul and life, did not escape them. Nor did the notable lack of success of his efforts to reduce the dualism of thought and life to a unity. Nor did the prudent silence he maintained on the real fate after death of the lower souls that had been transformed into faculties of the intellective soul by means of an adroit but arbitrary renaming. None of this escaped them. But they believed—as we ourselves do— what they wanted to believe. And that is the whole point. Bayle underscored it with a sly bit of mockery in the article we referred to earlier: "The Queen of Navarre," he insisted, "behaved herself in her doubts with all the prudence that was possible; she silenced her natural reason and curiosity, and humbly submitted to the light of revelation."

If the doctrine that we can legitimately ascribe to Rabelais lends itself to the criticism that its views were too easily taken,

---

57. On this continuing popularity of Fernel, see Figard, especially the first chapter. [Cf. Charles Sherrington, *The Endeavour of Jean Fernel* (Cambridge, 1946), ch. 3.— Translator.]

we should not rush to conclude: "Rabelais did not, could not possibly believe what he professed in the giants' words or his own. It was only Lucianism and irony, a trap for the naive." What do we know about it? We have to reconcile ourselves to the fact that the philosophers of the time were painfully caught in a web of difficulties that arose, for the most part, from a desire to bring the doctrines of Aristotelianism into harmony with the teachings of the Church. They could not emerge from such a thicket of brambles without getting scratched. Should we substitute ourselves for them, with our ideas (which will seem strange in another three hundred years), without trying to recover their ideas, and penalize them for not knowing *Cogito ergo sum?* And are we qualified to place them outside the Christian community, against their clearly expressed will, on the pretext that their metaphysical exercises are so weak they must have made them so on purpose? We can do it for a given person, to be sure, but only by arguing as follows: "This man was an unbeliever. We have no proof of it, but we do have a conviction. Therefore he did not believe in immortality." If I remember correctly, this is exactly what is meant by begging the question.

6. *"Unus ex Multis"*

And this leads us to a final reflection. In a dozen—nay, a score—of passages in his introduction, Abel Lefranc extols the impressive acts of daring performed by a Rabelais who was a freethinker. A dozen times he speaks of an "undertaking of such perilous boldness," of his "Promethean allusions," of his statements that are "hardly to be believed." He shows us that the "emulator of Lucian and Lucretius" was a freethinker who went "further than all contemporary writers along the path of philosophical and religious opposition," who as early as 1532 "had ceased to be a Christian," and whose Lucianic laughter concealed designs "that for centuries no one had dared to form."

It is very far from my intention to play the role of a gloomy censor. What is more attractive than this fine enthusiasm, this youthful tone of conviction? But what strikes me is not the loneliness and extraordinary boldness of a man far ahead of the most daring and innovative thinkers of his time; it is, on the contrary, the degree to which Rabelais is a faithful representative of all his contemporaries in their usual modes of thinking, feeling, and philosophizing.

After all, when he wrote *Pantagruel* more than three centuries had passed since the Christian world acquired the revelations of Aristotle's *Physics* and *Metaphysics*. It had been more than three centuries since those revelations provoked an intellectual crisis of singular importance for all men who engaged in speculation. The doctors, faced with a complete and thorough world system for the first time, suddenly perceived, with varied emotions, that "a yawning gulf appeared between so-called natural revelation and true revelation."[58] The denial of the dogma of divine providence, the denial of the dogma of the Creation, the denial of the dogma of immortality, at least of the personal immortality of the soul—such was the tally of the principal injuries that Aristotelian philosophy could do to the Christian religion.

Nevertheless, for many of those who were captivated by the magnitude of a system of thought unequaled at the time but who had no intention of sacrificing their beliefs to it, the obscurity of certain conceptions permitted bridges to be built between faith and Aristotelianism. We know how Saint Thomas made Aristotle the center of his doctrine and used him to combat Averroist pantheism, which claimed, with equal energy, that it authentically conveyed the Greek philosopher's thought. There was in fact a whole school that accepted the Averroist interpretation of Aristotelianism as the embodiment of truth.[59] It was an interpretation that made such an appeal to reason that when profane thought was left to itself it led right to the conclusions of Averroism. And no doubt these men added, "Philosophy is one thing, religion another. The first never prevails over the second. Here is the Greek master's true thought. Does it contradict the teachings of the Church? It goes without saying that for all Christians the doctrine of Christ must prevail." Some made such statements sincerely, others in bad faith—and the bad faith did not fool contemporaries long. By 1277 the Council of Paris had condemned these dissemblers. But the tradition did not disappear quickly; one has only to open Bayle to

58. Etienne Gilson, "La Doctrine de la double vérité," in *Etudes de philosophie médiévale* (Strasbourg, 1921), p. 53.

59. See Pierre Mandonnet, *Siger de Brabant ed l'Averrosime latin du XIIIe siècle* (Fribourg, 1900) and Gilson, *Etudes*, pp. 60–63.

be convinced of it. These things were taught. They were printed. We must therefore suppose that in 1532, when Rabelais wrote *Pantagruel*, there was not a single insignificant young man in the schools, not a single master of arts or apprentice physician who was not aware of the difficulties presented to faith by the Aristotelian theories of a God who knew nothing outside himself, a universe coeternal with God, and a soul that perished with a body of which it was merely the form. What, then, was there for the "real Rabelais" to reveal to his contemporaries, the real Rabelais who has been opposed to the false Rabelais of tradition? Bookish people who knew Latin had no need of *Pantagruel* to learn that the doctrine of the survival of souls did not have the unquestioning approval of all philosophers. If they wanted to be instructed on this point they had only to read Pomponazzi's *De anima*. It was no longer a novelty in 1532; the first edition was dated 1516,[60] and the book caused a sensation in the learned world. After it appeared there were endless works on the soul and immortality. One can consult Henri Busson's book for this great debate, which shook the schools in Italy and elsewhere.[61] The fundamental texts were published and republished in great numbers—notably the *Commentaries* of Alexander of Aphrodisias, who had inspired Pomponazzi and who radically denied the personal immortality of souls.[62] But there were also the works of Averroës, who continued to have his supporters and did not let himself get overwhelmed by the triumphant Alexandrists. In Lyon in 1529 Scipion de Gabiano published the *Commentaries on the Metaphysics* by the Arab master. In Lyon in 1530 Myt published his *Commentaries on the De anima*, with notes and marginalia by the Paduan Averroist Zimara. In Paris in 1530 Simon de Colines printed the *Dialogi* of Leonico Tomeo, which had first appeared in Venice in 1524: two of the dialogues dealt with

60. *De immortalitate animae* (Bologna: J. Ruberiensis, 1516). See the same author's *Apologia pro suo tractatu de immortalitate animae* (Bologna, 1518); *Defensorium, sive responsiones ad Aug. Niphum* (Bologna, 1519), and other works. On the other side, the book by Agostino Nifo: *De immortalitate animae libellus* (Venice, 1518).

61. *Les Sources et le développement du rationalisme dans la littérature française de la Renaissance (1533–1601)* (Paris, 1922), p. 32 ff.

62. Here are some of the editions: his *Enarratio de anima, ad mentem Aristotelis* was printed in Brescia, 1495 (quarto); in Venice, 1514 (folio); in Basel, 1535 (octavo); in Venice, 1538 (octavo); it appeared in Paris, 1528 (folio), shortly after the *Commen-*

the soul, and the second concluded in favor of immortality, but
in an entirely Averroist sense.[63] Let us not go on. We should
not act as if Rabelais, when he summarily and without argumentation denied the survival of intellective souls in 1532 in
books in the "vulgar tongue," revealed anything that was new
or audacious to men who were not at all unaware of the daring
in the ideas of Averroism or its enterprising rival, Alexandrism.[64]

But what about readers who did not know Latin, who were
unaware of all the doctrinal controversies that had been eagerly
pursued for centuries? Couldn't Gargantua's letter to Pantagruel
have had the effect of a revelation on them? A revelation of
what? Imagine Rabelais, eager to cast down religion and destroy
the Christian faith in the minds of men, confronting his audience: a completely new audience of men who had never sat on a
bench at the university and who barely knew Aristotle's name,
if they knew that. Rabelais was about to plant in them the
dangerous idea that the immortality of the soul could not be
proved, that reason was unable to furnish a demonstration of it,
that it was one of the dogmas requiring faith and not critical inquiry. But was Rabelais the first to say such things to these
men?

⋘ Let us picture to ourselves the following arresting but
plausible scene. One Sunday, in some rural church in the
Vendée or Poitou, Brother Francis of the Order of Friars
Minor, a priest, a religious at the monastery of Fontenay-le-
Comte, mounts the pulpit at the request of the parish priest.

---

taries of Themistius. Alexander's own *Commentaries* on the *Metaphysics*, translated
by Sepulveda, appeared in Paris under the imprint of Colines in 1536 (folio) and in
Venice in 1561. The *Problemata* (trans. Valla) appeared in Paris in 1520 (folio) and
trans. Th. Gaza in Paris in 1524, 1534, 1539, and in Lyon in 1551.

63. See Busson, *Les Sources,* passim. We are only taking into account Averroist and
Alexandrist writings. But in addition Averroism was popularized by orthodox authors,
such as Houppelande (d. 1492), who expounded it in order to refute it (innumerable
Paris editions from 1489); and also such as Crockart (*Acutissimae quaestiones,* reprinted many times). See the index in Augustin Renaudet, *Préréforme et humanisme
à Paris pendant les premières guerres d'Italie (1494–1517),* 2d ed. (Paris, 1954).

64. "During the entire Renaissance, in Italy as in France, the question of immortality preoccupied many more minds than the one of miracles. I have discovered no fewer
than sixty special treatises or dissertations on immortality in the course of the century
in France." Busson, *Les Sources,* p. 43, n. 3.

What is his subject? The eternal subject of Christian preaching: death and all that follows it, explaining what it is in Christian eyes and justifying it. The monk expounds the pure doctrine of Duns Scotus, a luminary of his order:[65] "The immortality of the soul, my brothers? We must believe in it. The Church orders us to; but human reason does not convince us of it. How could that feeble reason prove it to us, by what arguments could it make us certain that the rational soul is a form that can subsist by itself, a form capable of existing without the body? And if you are told, on the contrary, that immortality is necessary so that the bad may be punished and the just rewarded, who can prove—how can anyone ever rationally prove—that a Supreme Judge really exists? No. About the personal immortality of souls no more than about Divine Providence is there a real proof to convince us. Reason can demonstrate that immortality is possible, that it is probable, that it is infinitely desirable, and, in a way, necessary. But it is faith, faith alone, that must do the rest."

All of which Brother Francis, when he turned into Alcofribas, could have repeated in his *Pantagruel* with the sly smile of a Bayle. He could have reworked in the ironic mode Perrot d'Ablancourt's *Discourse* to Patru on the immortality of the soul: "You believe in the immortality of the soul because your reason makes you see it thus, and I, against my judgment, believe that our souls are immortal because our religion commands us to believe in this fashion. Consider these two opinions and you will undoubtedly affirm that mine is much the better. Yours is not merely Catholic . . . It is not having perfect confidence in God to rely on our reason for things that He wishes us to believe."[66] In sum, if we suppose he had a proselytizing zeal, a passion for instructing "poor idiots"—which would have made him the exact opposite of an Averroist, by the way—there

65. At the time of the Reformation, Duns Scotus was the official doctor of the Franciscan order. The general constitutions worked out at the chapter in Terni and approved by Alexander VI on April 7, 1501, put him in first place, even ahead of Saint Bonaventure. See Ephrem Longpré, "La Philosophie du B. Duns Scot," *Etudes Franciscaines*, 35 (1923), 610–611. We can understand Gargantua's triumphant exclamation at the end of his enumeration of torcheculs in ch. 13: "And such is the opinion of Master John of Scotland, alias Scotus." It was the last word, the irresistible argument.

66. Printed in Olivier Patru, *Les Oeuvres diverses*, 4th ed., 2 vols. (Paris, 1732), II, 542–544. Cf. Bayle, IV, 605, s.v. "Perrot d'Ablancourt."

was nothing for Rabelais to innovate. He had only to employ the well-known device that freethinkers have always used: cheerfully expound all the difficulties of the doctrine that individual souls are promised immortality, then take shelter behind the dogma. "You see, good friends, you should adore this mystery. In the light of reason, doubt; in the light of faith, believe!" Add a smirk, a smile, a joke if need be. That is the trick, and that is how to hoodwink the Sorbonne at the same time.

Do we see anything like this? The most that this terribly audacious Rabelais could find to do in order to rally the populace to the doctrine of a soul that perishes with the body and of a death that opens up no gates but those of nothingness was to write the beginning of the letter to Gargantua—an account that is serious, moving, and based on perfectly orthodox theory. His greatest act of daring was that, having said that the soul leaves the earth after death, he did not add that it does not die, or slipped into the text the phrases "pass from one place unto another" and "wholly to die," whose poison in the course of precisely three hundred and ninety years not a single commentator had grasped. So clear were Rabelais's intentions that it took four centuries for a man, no doubt a very perceptive one, finally to notice it! Was this Rabelais a man of daring, for occasioning the shudder that passes over so many places in Abel Lefranc's pages? Come on! More likely, the worst of cowards, and the most inept of propagandists. "What power of latent and restrained irony!" exclaimed Abel Lefranc. Latent is weak, restrained is modest. Rabelais's irony, at least here, is visible only to the eyes of faith.[67] In Paris in 1533 a brilliant Italian, a phy-

---

67. I point out only as a reminder a fact that is often overlooked, but we are incorrigible and always ingenuously believe that what seems "quite natural" to us never caused our ancestors more trouble than it does us. The immortality of the soul is an essential element in the Christian structure of man and his fate. This seems so obvious to us that we spontaneously credit Christians of all times with this conception of Christians of today. Nevertheless—this may come as a surprise to many of those highhanded scholars who accuse Rabelais of anti-Christianism with such peremptory assurance— we should remember that belief in the immortality of the soul was "in certain of the earliest Fathers . . . vague almost to non-existence." It was Etienne Gilson who pointed this out (*The Spirit of Medieval Philosophy*, trans. A. H. C. Downes [New York, 1940], p. 172), and he added that "a Christianity without the immortality of the soul is not, in the long run, absolutely inconceivable, and the proof of it is that it has been conceived." The essential thing, really, is that the soul be revived with the body for the Last Judgment, so that man, who is neither the soul alone nor the body alone, but the

sician to Clement VII who entered the service of the king of France and who would later be recalled to Rome by Paul III taught a course on Aristotle's *De anima*. It was a thorny subject. He left us a sort of written profession of faith in the form of twelve couplets, which he read at Bologna in front of Pope Clement.[68] What do we find in them? That the *Mens* is located in the brilliant heights of the celestial world and from there animates, fecundates, and implements its work; that from there it also sees and examines the activities of men; that it has affixed to the spheres spirits and lesser intelligences which it has taught how to direct the movement of those large masses; that the *Mens*, liberated from the body, returns to the ethereal abodes that are proper for eternal spirits (*mentibus aeternis:* Belmisseri does not say *immortalibus*). Let us stop here. If Rabelais is a hero of free thought for having written Gargantua's letter, what should we say of Belmisseri, Pope Clement's physician and later Pope Paul's, who, without thinking he was being revolutionary, serenely limited immortality, or rather eternity, to the active intellect, like a good Averroist?

---

union of the soul and the body, would then be able to know eternal blessedness or eternal damnation. Mortal body, immortal soul, and resurrection of the body reunited with its soul—the idea has not failed to produce a thousand difficulties, called heresies. Must we be reminded that the sixteenth century was not unaware of the ancient Fathers? It read Tertullian and his *De anima* in Froben's edition (1521); it read Justin Martyr's *Dialogue*, or else Irenaeus and Tatian's *Oratio ad Graecos*. It was more learned than we are. And in the arrogance of our ignorance we often sell its real knowledge short. Among other studies on the subject, see Wilhelm Götzmann, *Die Unsterblichkeitsbeweise in der Väterzeit und Scholastik* (Karlsruhe, 1927).

68. On Belmisseri and his theories, see Busson, *Les Sources*, p. 155.

5. The Resurrection of Epistemon and the Miracle

ET US GET to the great and tricky question of the miracle. That is, to chapter 30 of *Pantagruel:* "How Epistemon, who had his head cut off, was finely healed by Panurge, and of the news which he brought from the Devils, and of the People in Hell."

Pantagruel had just defeated Loupgarou in single combat. Remembering the latter's diabolic origins, he had first thrust down his throat "eighteen cags and four bushels of salt." Then, transforming his huge body into a mace, he had used it to assail the giants. A difficult victory, but one that he deserved. When he saw the great peril he was in had he not made a vow to God that, if successful, "in all countries whatsoever, wherein I shall have any power or authority" he would order the preaching of the Holy Gospel, "purely, simply, and entirely"? At which a celestial voice had cried out, "Hoc fac, et vinces!"

But now that the rout of the giants was complete, Pantagruel's companions counted off. Epistemon did not answer. A search began. He was found among the corpses, quite stiff and dead, with his head, all bloody, between his arms. Straightaway Panurge: "My dear bullies all, weep not one drop more, for he being yet all hot, I will make him as sound as ever he was!"

He bathed the wound, replaced the head on the neck with great care, took two or three stitches with a needle, applied an ointment "which he called resuscitative"—and Epistemon began to breathe, to open his eyes, to sneeze and, finally, to demonstrate his return to life by means of a noise that made them say to Panurge, "Now, certainly, he is healed!"

A shocking parody, exclaimed Abel Lefranc. Not only is "Hoc fac et vinces" a grotesque reminder of the "In hoc signo vinces" that foretold Constantine's miraculous victory, but "it is our absolute conviction that we find ourselves here in the presence of a parody of the two most important miracles of the New Testament, that is, the resurrection of Jairus's daughter and that of Lazarus. Certain features have clearly been borrowed from the first of these miracles, certain others from the second."[1]

Our own "absolute conviction" could be that we do not find ourselves in the presence of such a parody. We never have absolute convictions when it comes to historical facts. "Conviction," it has been written, "is one of the most curious manifestations of a priori reasoning. One is only convinced of what cannot be verified, of things that appeal, not to reason, but to faith." Our investigation is in the light of reason alone.

1. The Gospel or "The Four Sons of Aymon"?

Let us dispose of "Hoc fac et vinces." Is it an adaptation of Constantine's "In hoc signo vinces"? Obviously. Yet who in Rabelais's time could resist profaning that prophetic utterance? A while ago the *Bulletin du Bibliophile* announced the discovery of a booklet published in Paris or Antwerp, probably in 1528, with the promising title *The miraculous and greatly admirable day the Turks were defeated by the virtue and power of the Holy Cross: more than one hundred and eighty thousand were left on the field that Friday, Saint Lucy's Day.*[2] Over the title is a woodcut depicting the cross with the promise "In hoc signo vinces!" The booklet is nothing but a vulgar hoax, containing the imaginary account of a battle against the Turks, in which they were attacked simultaneously by Prester John, king of the Ethiopians; the Grand Sophy, king of Persia—and the king of Hungary.

We should add that in *Pantagruel* the context in which the words of prophecy appear is not at all irreverent—quite the

1. Abel Lefranc, "Etude sur *Pantagruel*," in Rabelais, *Oeuvres*, III (Paris, 1922), xlvii.

2. *La Journée miraculeuse et digne de grant admiration de la desconfiture des Turcqz par la vertu et puissance de la Sainte-Croix: plus de cent quatre-vingt mille sont demourez sur le champ, ce vendredy, jour de Saincte Lucie.*

contrary. The voice that comes down from heaven to encourage Pantagruel is responding to a lofty and beautiful prayer. It is not in answer to the solemn promise of some swindler swearing to make a mockery of religion, but of a noble king who promises to see that the Gospel will rule over all of his kingdom. We are either shocked by Pantagruel's prayer (which Abel Lefranc calls beautiful—and indeed it is),[3] or we recognize that the use here of phraseology that imitates the phraseology of the miracle is not at all shocking or even "parodistic."

There is still the main point: chapter 30 of *Pantagruel* is supposed to supply the essential and decisive elements for our conviction about Rabelais's aggressive and militant anti-Christian position. Does this chapter confront us with a travesty of the Gospel written in a spirit (and presented in a form) that leaves no doubt about the author's intention? Has Rabelais, in other words, drawn a completely deliberate satirical caricature here of the two resurrections accomplished by Christ—that of Lazarus, which is related in the Gospel of John, and that of Jairus's daughter, which is related in greater or lesser detail in the other three Gospels?

Let us read the Gospel texts without preconceptions.[4] Rabelais was acquainted with them—that was no miracle for a man of the Church. It is possible that when he was about to portray a miraculous cure he was reminded of Christ's cures; that he responded to the inner pressure of a traditional "literary iconography" of some kind; that the resurrection of Lazarus and of Jairus's daughter came to mind. His account surely owes a great deal to the semiconscious operation of his literary memory. But ought one to force the text of Rabelais, and the Gospel texts as well, fastening on some detail or other and straining the resemblances? It is a futile undertaking. The differences are striking.

In the first place, Lazarus and Jairus's daughter are "completely dead"—dead from illness. Epistemon, however, is not in such bad shape. He has "had his head cut off." And therefore Panurge is to use for this wound par excellence—decapitation—a surgical procedure whose steps are minutely described by Doctor Rabelais. "Then cleansed he his neck very well with

3. Lefranc, p. xlvi.
4. For Lazarus, see John 11:44. For Jairus's daughter, Luke 8:52 and Mark 5:39. The account in Matt. 9 does not add anything.

pure white wine, and, after that, took his head, and into it syn-
apised some powder of diamerdis, which he always carried
about him in one of his bags. Afterwards he anointed it with I
know not what ointment, and set it on very just, vein against
vein, sinew against sinew, and spondyl against spondyl, that he
might not be wry-necked . . . This done, he gave it round about
some fifteen or sixteen stitches with a needle. . . , then on all
sides, and everywhere, he put a little ointment on it, which he
called resuscitative." Not for nothing, we see, did Rabelais edit
for Sebastian Gryphius in that very year of 1532, among other
treatises, the *Ars medicinalis* of Galen ("Cap. XC, Curatio solu-
tionis continuitatis in parte carnosa; cap. XCI, De solutione
continuitatis in osse"). Epistemon's severed head is plainly a
"solution of continuity,"[5] as Rabelais himself says elsewhere in
a jesting tone.

◄§ Can we say that there is anything of the sort in the Gospel accounts? Christ restores Lazarus and Jairus's daughter by
extremely simple means. In the case of Lazarus, after having
prayed to his Father he cries in a loud voice, "Lazarus, come
forth!" and Lazarus gets up. As for Jairus's daughter, he takes
her hand and cries, "Maid, arise!" and the girl gets up. In Rabelais's account no "evocation" of this sort is parodied. But, inversely, there is not the slightest mention in the Gospel of
anointing or of the resuscitative ointment that Abel Lefranc
found so upsetting. To be sure, when Christ restores hearing to
the deaf-mute and sight to the man born blind he touches them
with a substance that comes from himself, charged with his personal magnetism: his saliva. It is not an ointment.

The "resuscitative" medicinal preparation that Panurge uses
does not derive from the Gospel. Lazare Sainéan said, "It comes
from Fierabras."[6] The Saracen giant carried on his saddle two
barrels filled with the balm with which Christ was anointed.
When he was wounded he would drink a little of it and his injuries would instantly be healed. During his fight with Oliver

5. [That is, a *dissolution* of continuity.—Translator.] Parenthetically, the explanation in the critical edition of the *Oeuvres* by Lefranc et al. (IV, 180, n. 43) is not quite
accurate. It is not "a term in scholastic philosophy," but only a term in Galenic medicine.

6. Lazare Sainéan, *La Langue de Rabelais*, 2 vols. (Paris, 1922–1923), I, 335.

he generously offers it to his adversary, whose courage he admires:

> Olivier, car descent lès ceste fonteniele,
> Si buvras de cest basme qui ci pent à ma sele,
> Lors esteras plus sains k'en may n'est arondele.[7]

> ... there been two flagons hangyng on the sadle of my hors
> whyche ben full of the bawme that I conquered in Jherusa-
> lem, & it is the same of whyche your god was enbawmed
> wyth whan he was taken doune fro the crosse and layed in
> hys grave. hye the, and goo drynke therof, & I promyse to
> the that Incontynent thou shalt be hole.[8]

One can think whatever one likes about this parallel. For my
part I do not find it any more convincing than Abel Lefranc's
parallel with the Gospel. But we can thank Sainéan for di-
recting our attention to the romantic literature of the Middle
Ages with which Rabelais was so familiar and which abounded
in extraordinary cures, ointments, miraculous procedures, and
resurrections of the dead. In Marie de France's "Lay of Eliduc,"
for example, there is a girl who has fallen into a mortal slumber
and is recalled to life by a flower that had been used to revive a
slain weasel. In "Amis et Amiles" there is the resurrection by a
divine miracle of murdered children, whose blood cures Amile
of leprosy. In "Jourdain de Blaives" there is a woman left for
dead whose life is restored by an ointment kept behind the
altar.[9] These examples are drawn from relatively early texts.
What we have to do is look at those prose adaptations of medieval romances[10] that the townspeople were flocking to buy and
the printers, especially those in Lyon, to reissue. Rabelais was

---

7. *Fierabras*, ed. Auguste Kroeber and Gustave Servois (Paris, 1860), p. 34.

8. Trans. William Caxton in *The Lyf of the Noble and Crysten Prynce, Charles the Grete*, ed. Sidney J. H. Herrtage, part I (London, 1880), p. 56.

9. For "The Lay of Eliduc" see Karl Warnke's *Die Lais der Marie de France*, 3d ed. (Halle, 1925), pp. clxxv–clxxviii. For "Amis et Amiles" and "Jourdain de Blaives," laisses 165 and 91 in Conrad Hofmann, ed., *Amis et Amiles und Jourdains de Blaives, Zwei altfranzösische Heldengedichte des Kerlingischen Sagenkreises*, 2d ed. (Erlangen, 1882).

10. Emile Besch, "Les Adaptations en prose des chansons de geste au XVe et au XVIe siècle," *Revue du Seizième Siècle*, 3 (1915), 176, n. 2. And Arthur Tilley, "Les Romans de chevalerie en prose," ibid., 6 (1919), 45–63.

acquainted with them, read them,[11] and perhaps wrote some of them.

He was certainly acquainted with one of them, one that his own publisher, Claude Nourry, reprinted many times from the beginning of the century. Baudrier refers to a quarto edition of 1526 in Gothic characters from this source and a large quarto edition of 1531, also in Gothic characters.[12] The presses of Paris also turned it out in large quantities in the same period. Its popularity lasted a long time. We all read *The Four Sons of Aymon* in the Bibliothèque Bleue version when we were children.[13] Open that book[14] to chapter 11, as Rabelais did. It is full of surprises!

Renaud has routed the French, but the victory has been a dear one. Richard, his valiant brother, has been killed; Renaud does not recognize his "horribly mutilated" body and laments, " 'Alas, what shall I do since I have lost my dear brother Richard, the best friend I had in all the world!' And when he had said these words he fell to earth in a swoon from Bayard's back. And when Alard and Guichard saw their brother Renaud who had fallen they began to mourn Richard most lovingly."

Renaud, however, recovers from his swoon. "He began to make great moan, he and Alard and Guichard, over Richard, who lay on the ground, his bowels in his hands." (Like Epistemon: "stark dead, with his head between his arms all bloody.") This ridiculous epic exaggeration is surely in keeping with Rabelais's novel. Whereupon Panurge—I mean Maugis—comes up, "mounted on Brocart, his good steed . . . And then Maugis,

---

11. Besides Besch, see Jean Plattard, *L'Oeuvre de Rabelais: sources, invention, composition* (Paris, 1910). Rabelais often refers to *The Four Sons of Aymon*. See *Gargantua*, ch. 27: "Never did Maugis the Hermit bear himself more valiantly . . . against the Saracens, of whom is written in the Acts of the four sons of Haymon, than did this monk."

12. Henri and Julien Baudrier, *Bibliographie lyonnaise*, 12 vols. (Lyon, 1895–1921; photographic reprint, Paris, 1964), XII.

13. The Bibliothèque Bleue was a series of popular books (with blue covers) which began to be published in the seventeenth century and continued to be reprinted until the middle of the nineteenth century. They were mainly adaptations of chivalric romances. [Translator's note.]

14. We have not been able to lay our hands on one of Nourry's editions. Our references are to the Lyon edition of Jean de Vingle (printing completed Nov. 4, 1497), which is in the Bibliothèque Nationale. Jean (d. 1513) reprinted *The Four Sons* in his workshop four times, with vignettes by Jean Perréal. Cf. Baudrier, XII, 194, 198, 199, 203, 306. He also printed *Fierabras* and *Ogier the Dane*.

seeing Richard so mutilated, was greatly sore at heart, and he looked at the wound, which was most horrible to behold, for through it his liver could be seen." "Promise me," he asks Renaud, "that you will come with me to the tent of Charlemagne and avenge my father's death"; then, "I promise you that I will restore Richard to you *all healed and sound*, free of pain on the spot." It is the same as Panurge's promise: "My dear bullies all, weep not one drop more, for he being all hot *I will make him as sound as ever he was!*" Renaud promises. Maugis gets off his horse, and the magical procedures begin.

Then he took a bottle of white wine. With it he washed Richard's wound right well and took away all the blood that was about. Do not trouble yourselves where he got all the things he needed for his work, for he was the most cunning necromancer that ever was in the world. And when he had done this, he took the bowels and put them inside the body, and took a needle and sewed the wound right gently without causing him great pain; and then he took an ointment which he applied to the wound, and as soon as the aforesaid wound was anointed it was as whole as if there had never been anything amiss. And when he had done all this he took a potion which he had and gave it to Richard to drink. And when Richard had drunk, he jumped to his feet, entirely free of pain, and said to his brothers, "Where did Ogier go? Did all those folk escape from us?"[15]

It is all there—everything Rabelais would retain, everything he would use when he described Epistemon's miraculous cure.[16] Recall that Panurge, holding the severed head "warm fore-against his codpiece, that the wind might not enter into it," also begins by washing the wound with "pure white wine." Since he took lessons from Doctor Rabelais he sinapized into it some

---

15. For an English version, somewhat abridged, see *Renaud of Montauban*, ed. by Robert Steel from William Caxton's translation (London, 1897). The miracle is on pp. 172–173. [Translator's note.]

16. Lefranc cites Luke 8:52, 53. The words are: "And all wept, and bewailed her: but he said, Weep not; she is not dead, but sleepeth. And they laughed him to scorn, knowing that she was dead." I believe it is enough to quote this passage from the Gospel after the one from the medieval romance to show how much further it is from *Pantagruel* in style and intention.

powder of diamerdis, which, the narrator tells us with a precision less naive than that of his predecessor, "he always carried about him in one of his bags." To this he adds the application of "I know not what ointment," joins the head to the neck, and he too sews up the wound with "some fifteen or sixteen stitches with a needle." The whole technique is straight from Maugis.

But nothing has been accomplished yet. Panurge and Maugis have only acted up to now like good surgeons. They have yet to put life back into the corpse that has been repaired and stitched up but is still a corpse. How will they do it? Utter secret words? Call forth? Place on the inanimate being a hand charged with magnetism or moistened with saliva? Maugis has Richard drink a magic potion, and Richard is on his feet at once. If Rabelais had wanted to parody one of Christ's miracles, he had no dearth of possibilities. What does Panurge do? Take the dead man by the hand? Breathe in his face? Call him in a loud voice? Touch him with his saliva? "He cried with a loud voice, Lazarus, come forth. And he that was dead came forth." Or else: "And he put them all out, and took her by the hand, and called, saying, Maid, arise. And her spirit came again, and she arose straightway: and he commanded to give her meat." We have to recognize that if the thought of imitating the Gospel miracles occurred to Rabelais at this moment he succeeded so well in covering it up that it is impossible to detect. Panurge does not even give Epistemon a magic potion. He is content with a fairly prosaic device, rubbing the mended neck with "a little ointment . . . , which he called resuscitative." At that Epistemon opens his eyes.

◄§ When one reads in turn the apostolic accounts of Christ, the miraculous cure of Richard by Maugis, and the resurrection of Epistemon by Panurge, can there be any doubt left in the most exacting of minds? If the reader takes the trouble to refer to the text of the medieval romance, and if, furthermore, he first pays attention to a suggestion by Besch in one of the notes in the article referred to above,[17] he really cannot believe or claim

17. "Cf. the miraculous resurrection of Richard by Maugis," Besch writes, "in *The Four Sons of Aymon* and the resurrection of Epistemon in *Pantagruel*, Book II, XXX. The passage in Rabelais parodies the former almost word for word." Besch, p. 177, n. 1. A long time before us—and before Lefranc wrote his introduction—Besch saw this decisive passage for what it was.

that chapter 30 of *Pantagruel* is a conscious and cynical parody of Christ's personal miracles.

The account in *The Four Sons of Aymon* dispels any difficulties that can be raised. A great mystery has been made of the fact that Rabelais uses *guéri* (healed) instead of *ressuscité* (revived). "[Rabelais] does not dare to say 'revived,' since he wishes to avoid drawing too much attention to the hidden meaning of the episode and feels he has said enough to be understood by the initiate."[18] Rabelais says "healed" like his model: "I promise you that I will restore Richard to you all healed and sound." He says it quite naturally and innocently, without the least hypocritical reservation. If the "initiate" take pride in understanding it, they take pride in a rather simple intellectual feat. I cannot believe anyone thinks Rabelais was a simpleton who was likely to jump out of the frying pan into the fire. Taking pains to substitute *guéri* for *ressuscité* would be peculiar, to say the least, for a man who three lines further down describes (without the least regard for prudence) the miraculous ointment that recalls Epistemon from the dead as "resuscitative."

Besides, there is nothing surprising in the fact that Rabelais was inspired by chapter 11 of *The Four Sons of Aymon* when he wrote chapter 30 of *Pantagruel*. I do not subscribe to the oversimplified assertion of Besch when he writes, "It can be said that *Gargantua* and *Pantagruel* are from beginning to end, but especially in the first two books, nothing but a parody of chivalric romances."[19] It is always well to be suspicious of the expression "nothing but," which gives rise to so many exaggerations and errors. *Gargantua* and *Pantagruel* are something other than what Besch seems to want to reduce them to in a hastily written sentence. "Parody" does not seem to me entirely accurate. Yet, that being said, when Rabelais took up his pen in 1532 he did mean to present his readers with a gigantic *geste* of an apparently new kind, but a *geste* nonetheless, with epic tales of battle, of defeats and casualties—and hence of miraculous resurrections. Is it necessary to recall the names of the heroes of romance, from Fierabras to Morgan and Ferragus, who appear

18. Lefranc, p. xlix.
19. Besch, p. 176.

in Pantagruel's genealogy? To say nothing of the heroes of romance whom Epistemon himself sees in such great numbers in the strange hell he visits while he is dead.[20]

2. The Sixteenth Century and Miracles

All the same, what Panurge accomplished with Epistemon was indeed a miracle, wasn't it? What Rabelais gives us a parodied account of is a miracle. If he was thinking about the miracle of Maugis, it does not, after all, make much difference. What matters are Rabelais's intentions. Can you assure us they were pure?

Let us be careful to give no such assurances. No one will ever—for good reasons—plumb the depths of François Rabelais's conscience. But what can be said without reservation is that the Rabelais who, behind the mask of Panurge, made fun of dupes and simpletons who avidly swallowed humbug and dimwittedly believed every detail of the miracles they were told about (*Innocens credit omni verbo,* and faith is evidence of things not seen) was in 1532 nothing remarkable, heroic, or superhuman.

First of all, about miracles. They were all over the place in that period, they happened every day, every hour, everywhere, on every occasion. And no one was unacquainted with them. The literature was full of them. We have just seen this in the heroic romances. It was even truer of popular booklets, the little pious works that certain publishers issued by the thousands, a whole literature of prodigies, celestial signs, and miraculous cures, only a tiny remnant of which have survived, and which amply satisfied our ancestors' eager credulity and taste for strange adventures.[21] Everyone performed miracles. If God had his miracles—God and the Virgin and God's men (the saints, that is)—the antigod, the devil, had his, too, and they were so much like the former that when the experts, the theologians who were past masters of prodigies as well as diabology, were consulted, they needed to put on their spectacles and have a

---

20. *Pantagruel,* chs. 1, 30.

21. See, for example, Jean Babelon, *La Bibliothèque française de Fernand Colomb* (Paris, 1913), passim. This gives descriptions of booklets purchased by Fernando Columbus in the course of his travels—especially in Lyon.

second look before they expressed an opinion.[22] On this point, the existence of "Satan's miracles," there was absolutely no reservation in the minds of the theologians. Satan's miracles helped them out any number of times when the need arose, providing them with a very simple solution to a great many difficulties.[23] God's miracles were, if I may say so, more normal. There were the great miracles, officially sanctioned by the approval of ecclesiastical authorities and the huge, sudden influx of pilgrims. To mention but one, there was the miraculous transfer by angels to Loreto of the house the Virgin had lived in in Nazareth; we know how the legend grew[24] in the last years of the fifteenth century or the first years of the sixteenth. Around this time a king of France with a childish fear of death sought out a prodigious miracle worker in the depths of Calabria beneath whose feet miracles sprang up by a string of pious incantations, and had him brought to France to keep himself from dying. There were small miracles, too, humble miracles of daily life that are pictured with a great wealth of detail in the *livres de raison* and chronicles of the time: rains that fell after a procession or a vow, mist that miraculously exorcised the effects of a frost, sunshine that reappeared providentially after a season of rain in order to ripen the grain. And there were more sensational ones—hundreds of stories of amazing cures, rescues, improbable resurrections of hanged men.

Is it then—again—any "miracle" that Rabelais had the incli-

22. In *Book Three*, ch. 14, Rabelais makes an allusion to this difficulty: "Truly, I remember, that the Cabalists and Massorets, interpreters of the sacred Scriptures, in treating how with verity one might judge of evangelical apparitions, (because oftentimes the angel of Satan is disguised and transfigured into an angel of light,) said, That the difference of these two mainly did consist in this. The favorable and comforting angel useth in his appearance unto man at first to terrify and hugely affright him, but in the end he bringeth consolation, leaveth the person who hath seen him, joyful, well pleased, fully content, and satisfied. On the other side, the angel of perdition, that wicked, devilish, and malignant spirit, at his appearance unto any person, in the beginning cheereth up the heart of his beholder, but at last forsakes him, and leaves him troubled, angry, and perplexed."

23. Calvin made great use of it. Inversely, the Catholics later used it to restrict the value of the testimony the Protestants wished to derive from the number and constancy of their martyrs. "Satan has his martyrs," was the controversialists' response. See, for example, Florimond de Raemond, *L'Histoire de la naissance, progrez et décadence de l'hérésie de ce siècle* (Rouen, 1624).

24. See Ulysse Chevalier, *Notre-Dame de Lorette: étude historique sur l'authenticité de la Santa Casa* (Paris, 1906).

nation and the wit to make frequent fun of such prodigies? He was not the only one. Let us once and for all stop believing, or acting as if we believed, that just about anyone could make our ancestors of 1530 swallow just about anything under the guise of piety. When all of Paris was in a dither on September 19, 1528, over the miraculous resurrection of Christopher Bueg, hanged on the Place Maubert, who at the last moment commended himself to Our Lady of Recovery, thereupon regaining his senses after being taken down and winning a pardon, the Bourgeois of Paris exclaimed at the miracle;[25] but Pierre Driart, the monk of Saint Victor (who was not a practitioner of free thought), referred to the event under the prudent heading of "miraculous execution, as it is said" and followed his account with three rather significant little words: *Quod pie creditur.*[26] As for the lawyer Versoris, he simply thought that Christopher had not been hanged enough.[27] And if, around this time, a dead woman appeared to the living and informed them that she was damned, the Sorbonne intervened. To be sure, it said, apparitions were possible, but it was necessary not to run the risk that if there were any mistake false miracles might turn people away from believing in true ones: "ne falsorum miraculorum praetextu, veris miraculis detrahatur."

That was how Our Masters the theologians spoke—with caution. In the opposite camp, voices were much louder. Let us not forget that in their work of demolishing the "human inventions" with which Christianity had become weighed down since its earliest years, the Evangelicals always kept coming up against miracles being invoked to sanction the abuses they detested. Soon there were even some entirely new ones directed against them, which were cited shamelessly. They had to respond. Before long they did respond, with an intensity for which they were often reproached.

We called attention earlier to how much there is of interest in

---

25. *Le Journal d'un bourgeois de Paris sous le règne de François Ier (1515–1536)*, ed. V.-L. Bourrilly (Paris, 1910), p. 313.

26. "Which is piously believed." Fernand Bournon, ed., "Chronique parisienne de Pierre Driart, chambrier de Saint-Victor (1522–35)," *Mémoires de la Société de l'Histoire de Paris et de l'Ile-de-France*, 22 (1895), 135.

27. "Livre de raison de Me Nicolas Versoris, avocat au Parlement de Paris, 1519–1530," ed. G. Fagniez, *Mémoires de la Société de l'Histoire de Paris et de l'Ile-de-France*, 12 (1885), 210.

certain discussions in Postel's work *Alcorani et Evangelistarum concordia.*[28] One of the twenty-eight propositions enumerated by the author (common, according to him, to Muslims and Evangelists) is the following: "No need of miracles to confirm religion." (Nullis miraculis opus esse ad confirmationem religionis.) Postel discusses this. On the pretext that priests have abused the simpleminded in recent times with actual impostures, are the Evangelists really going to tell us that miracles in the Church of Christ have the devil as their author? They say this particularly of the miracles recorded at the tombs of martyrs, as if the devil had the power to revive the dead or to bring about the healing of any but those he himself has harmed. If he did, he would be the equal of God himself! Yet, Postel asserts, many Evangelists—or former Evangelists: "qui primum pridemque imbuti ea opinione sunt"—do not go along with such dodges; they state quite clearly that miracles are nothing but magic and illusion. And in another passage in his book he finds fault, curiously, with Oecolampadius. Didn't that learned Evangelist find the Gospel guilty of untruth because he did not believe that Jesus, when he awoke among the dead, would have been able to get back to his companions through locked doors? Postel was furious, shrugged his shoulders, and collected "scientific" arguments in order to accuse Oecolampadius of temerity. In the process, his discussion clearly shows that in the sixteenth century men who took liberties—even very great liberties— with miracles were not necessarily rationalists of a philosophical provenance, if one can call it that, but liberal reformers; and his "qui primum pridemque imbuti ea opinione sunt" reminds us very much of the phrase he applied to Rabelais and Des Périers: "authores olim Cenevangelistarum antesignani."

On this subject as on so many others, Calvin took it upon himself to codify the doctrine of the Reformers. Beginning with the *Institutes* of 1541, in the "Epistle to the King," he grappled with the problem with his usual decisiveness.[29] The miracles

28. Ch. 2, sect. 2.

29. Jean Calvin, *Institution de la Religion Chrestienne,* original 1541 text, ed. Abel Lefranc, Henri Chatelain, and Jacques Pannier (Paris, 1911), p. xvii ff. [The most recent edition is that by Jacques Pannier in 4 vols. (Paris, 1961), I, pp. 7–36. For an English edition see John Calvin, *Institutes of the Christian Religion,* trans. Henry Beveridge, 2 vols. (London, 1962), I, 3–20.—Translator.]

which our adversaries claim support their doctrines against ours, he said, are children's games—or cynical falsehoods. It makes little difference, after all. For a doctrine is either a copy of God's truth, in which case miracles can only confirm it, or it is evil, in which case all the miracles in the world will not make it good. This did not call into question what Postel denounced, the well-known fact that "Satan has his miracles," with which he takes advantage of the simple-minded. In general, and from the very beginning, Calvin clearly showed himself a skeptic on the subject of miracles. Yet no one—today—dreams of putting him among the anti-Christians. He naturally held back on the one really dangerous question, the very one, according to Abel Lefranc, that Rabelais raised, and resolved with a burst of sacrilegious laughter—the question of God's miracles.

◄§ And now we are back at our starting point. In 1532 Rabelais was envious of Maugis's miracles and set out to do much greater ones. The necromancer revived men who were disembowled. Rabelais, with the greatest of ease, put decapitated men back on their feet. This is what you call a miracle—now laugh. But wait a minute. Rabelais did something much worse. He did what no man of his time had ever dreamed of doing: he openly made fun of God. He ridiculed Christ. It was quite simple. He took Panurge, that Panurge of his, that lecher, that joker, that thief, wicked lewd rogue, cozener, drinker, roysterer, and debauched fellow, if ever there was one, and gave him, precisely the most disreputable person in the novel, the job of parodying—whom? The Son of God, the Savior of mankind who restored Lazarus and Jairus's daughter. Thus was carried out, in the guise of farce, the most audacious attack on the power of the creator to intervene in the life of his creatures that could be imagined, as that power was generally treated in the writings of Frenchmen of the sixteenth century—to be precise, Frenchmen who were forty to fifty years old in 1532.

But what proof is there? Can it be proved that Rabelais had the prodigious daring to stand up alone before the God of the Christians and make a sneering and farcical response to the raising of Lazarus, a story that was so dramatic and that for centuries all of Christianity had surrounded with such an aura of faith and feeling? If there is no proof possible (and there is none), is there at least a presumption? The bare words of the passage provide nothing. Would the context help us? What I mean is: is it true that when Rabelais wrote the resurrection of Epistemon in 1532 he was as daring, and as brashly innovative, as has been claimed? The answer has to be no.

3. A Question That Had Been Raised Before "Pantagruel"

It was not chapter 30 of *Pantagruel* that raised the question of miracles. Like the question of immortality, it had been raised in people's minds for quite a long time. The ancient authors had a lot to do with this, and Cicero more than any of them. Not long ago it was realized that if he was read with so much ardor and persistence by prominent humanists, some of whom were of an independent cast of mind, it was not merely for the purity and elegance of his Latin style.[30]

A book like *De divinatione* offered readers of the sixteenth century extraordinarily powerful lessons in rationalism. One of the speakers, Cicero's brother Quintus, defends conservative positions (positions, by the way, that have analogues in Rabelais's books). Quintus believes in prophetic dreams,[31] he holds, like Rabelais, that the souls of men who keep themselves at an equal distance from excesses and deprivations are capable of having visions of the future of an indisputable clarity, and he endows the dying with the spirit of divination and prophecy that Rabelais extolled in Langey on the eve of his death. On the other hand, in Cicero's arguments and the answers he gives his brother there are principles whose application was not limited to pagan superstitions alone. He affirms *fatum*, which is defined as a chain of causes ("fate I call the order and sequence of causes, since a cause linked to a cause makes a thing come about

---

30. Henri Busson, *Les Sources et le développement du rationalisme dans la littérature française de la Renaissance (1533–1601)* (Paris, 1922), p. 17. On Rabelais's borrowings from Cicero, see Plattard, p. 187. Plattard points out an important fact, that Rabelais did not, properly speaking, make use of Cicero in *Pantagruel* or in *Gargantua;* he refers to him only in *Book Three* and *Book Four.*

31. *De divinatione*, I, 29. There are many false dreams, says Cicero, "quia, onusti cibo et vino, perturbata et confusa cernimus" (because when we are full of food and wine we see things that are confused and disordered). There follows a translation of a passage from Plato's *Republic.* Cf. the passage in *Book Three* referred to above, ch. 4, sect. 2.

of itself").[32] He denies, in the name of this determinism, all divination—divination being defined as the presentiment and
prophesying of fortuitous things. He reduces the fortuitous to
what has been eternally known by God. He proclaims the
axiom that everything that happens necessarily has a natural
cause. There must be one; it is impossible that there is none. It
may escape the investigator, but he should remain firmly convinced that it always exists.[33] There are no prodigies. Nor are
there miracles. And he finally concludes: live in peace with religion but make war on superstition.

We do not have to prove that such statements were able to
lead some men of that century to a rationalism that was stead-
fastly hostile to the supernatural. More than ample proof exists
in the extraordinarily daring book that Pomponazzi wrote
around 1520, which was not published till much later, in 1556,
under the title *De naturalium effectuum admirandorum causis,
seu De incantationibus liber*.[34] There is no doubt, however,
that its content was known long before that date.[35] His theory
of miracles comes entirely from *De divinatione*. Either miracles

32. *De divinatione*, I, 55. Here is the crucial passage in its entirety: "Fieri omnia
Fato, ratio cogit fateri. Fatum ... appello ... ordinem seriemque causarum, quum
causa causae nexa rem ex se gignat ... Quod cum ita sit, nihil est factum quod non futurum fuerit, eodemque modo nihil est futurum cujus non causas ad id ipsum effi-
cientes natura contineat." (Reason impels us to recognize that everything is accomplished by Fate. Fate I call the order and sequence of causes, since a cause linked to a
cause makes a thing come about of itself. Since this is so, nothing has happened that
was not going to happen, and by the same token nothing is going to happen unless nature contains the causes that can bring about that very thing.)

33. *De divinatione*, II, 28: "Quidquid oritur, qualecumque est, causam habeat a natura necesse est: ut etiam si praeter consuetudinem exstiterit, praeter naturam tamen
non possit exsistere." (Anything that happens, whatever it is, must of necessity have a
natural cause: so that even if it is unusual it can nevertheless not be unnatural.) And
this statement, ibid.: "Nihil fieri sine causa potest; nec quidquam sit quod fieri non potest; nec, si id factum est, quod potuit fieri, portentum debet videri. Nulla igitur por-
tenta sunt." (Nothing is possible without a cause; nor does anything exist that is impossible; nor, if anything has happened that was possible, should it be seen as an omen.
Therefore there are no omens.) In II, 72, he concludes: "Ut religio propaganda est,
quae est juncta cum cognitione naturae, sic superstitionis stirpes omnes ejiciendae."
(Since the religion that should be promoted is one which is joined to a knowledge of
nature, every trace of superstition should be rejected.)

34. *A Book on the Causes of Wonders in Nature; or, On Incantations*.

35. Cf. Pietro Pomponazzi, *Les Causes des merveilles de la nature, ou les Enchantements*, trans. Henri Busson (Paris, 1930), introduction, p. 26: "Secret Influence of the
Book before Publication." P. 28: "I nevertheless have no proof that *De incantationibus*
was read in France before 1540."

are tricks of magic; or they only exist in and by the imagination of witnesses; or they have natural causes that may escape us but which exist nonetheless. For nothing exists and nothing can be produced which does not have a natural cause. There is no effect without a cause.[36]

Let us put aside this daring book, in view of its publication date. But several months before the appearance of *Pantagruel,* in February 1532, a slim folio volume appeared in Antwerp containing the *De occulta philosophia* of that strange man, Henry Cornelius Agrippa, whose life and thought remain shrouded in such mystery. We know that Agrippa lived in Lyon from the beginning of 1524 until 1528, where he served as royal physician attached to the person of the queen mother, Louise of Savoy. When, in turn, Rabelais arrived in the city at the end of 1531, he surely heard talk about this restless and original colleague, whose books could not have gone unnoticed in the bookshops.[37] The volume published in Antwerp at the beginning of 1532, despite what its title said—*libri tres*—contained only the first book of the treatise. But in chapter 58 of

36. We think we are correct in so interpreting Pomponazzi's difficult words. "Non sunt autem miracula, quia sint totaliter contra naturam . . . sed pro tanto dicuntur miracula quia insueta et rarissime facta, et non secundum communem naturae cursum, sed in longissimis periodis." (There are, moreover, no miracles, for they are entirely against nature . . . but all the same, things are called miracles because they are unusual and extremely rare events which do not follow the ordinary course of nature but occur at very long intervals.) Léon Blanchet rendered this in French as follows: "Ce que les hommes appellent de ce nom, ce sont des événements non pas contraires en réalité au destin astral et au cours de la nature, mais qui sortent de l'ordinaire et ne réappairaissent que de loin en loin, après l'achèvement de très longues périodes astronomiques." Blanchet, *Campanella* (Paris, 1920), p. 290, n. 4.

37. Cf. Abel Lefranc, "Rabelais et Corneille Agrippa," *Mélanges offerts à M. Emile Picot,* 2 vols. (Paris, 1913), II, 477–486. Lefranc recalls that in 1535 Agrippa passed through Lyon and was imprisoned there. He made his way to Grenoble and died there shortly afterward, at the home of de Vachon, president of the Parlement. In 1535 Rabelais likewise fled from Lyon, took refuge in Grenoble, and was de Vachon's guest. Only Lefranc claims that the two men fled for analogous reasons, and that Agrippa left Lyon because his *De vanitate* was condemned by the Sorbonne. There is a serious dating error that nullifies the conclusion of his note. For it was not on March 2, 1535, that the Sorbonne condemned *De vanitate* as "Lutheranist," but on March 2, 1531 (1530 O.S.). Cf. Du Plessis d'Argentré, *Collectio judiciorum de novis erroribus,* 3 vols. (Paris, 1724–1736), II, 85. "Die Secunda Martii 1530" the Sorbonne condemned a book "impressus de novo Parisiis, in vico Sorbonico et prius Coloniae"—that is, it had before it the edition acquired by Jean Pierre: "Parisiis, apud Sorbonam, opera et impensa Ioannis Petri, anno 1531, mense februario."

Book I Agrippa specifically raised the question of the dead returning to life: "De mortuorum reviviscentia, de longeva dormi-
tione atque inedia."[38] Agrippa stated that he admitted the possibility that magi could restore souls to bodies from which they
had already departed.[39] Certain magic herbs and certain ointments (we are reminded of Panurge) are very helpful, he says,
in such resurrections.[40] And no one should protest that this is
only a myth. When a weasel has been killed, can't its father recall it to life with his breath and his voice? When a young lion
is slain, can't its father likewise restore it to life with his breath?
And there are historical examples of bodies taken from the stake
that were revived; of men who were drowned and regained
their senses; of soldiers who were killed in battle and came back
to life—like Epistemon—sometimes after being dead for several
days.[41] Are these miracles? Not at all. Nothing happens except
through the working of natural laws. We must be dealing here
with persons who seem to be dead. The soul has not yet departed. It remains as if hidden in the body—paralyzed and suf-
focated by too violent shaking. There is no longer any life, any
feeling or movement; the man lies senseless.[42] But he is not
dead.

38. "On the Revival of the Dead, and on Sleep and Fasting of Long Duration."

39. "Cum animae hominum omnes perpetuae sint, perfectis quoque animis omnes
spiritus obediunt, putant Magi perfectos homines per suae animae vires alias inferiores
animas jam quodammodo separatas moribundis corporibus suis posse restituere, rursus-
que inspirare, non secus atque mustela interempta spiritu et voce parentis revocatur in
vitam atque leones inanimum partum inhalando vivificant." (Since the souls of men are
all eternal, and all spirits are subject to perfect souls, the magi believe that perfect men
through their spiritual power are able to restore to dying bodies lesser souls that have
somehow already been separated from them, and can put breath back into them, much
as a dead weasel is recalled to life by its father's breath and voice and as lions revive a
lifeless cub by breathing on it.) *Henrici Cor. Agrippae ab Nettesheym a Consiliis et
Archivis inditiarii Sacrae Cesareae Majestatis de occulta philosophia libri tres* (Antwerp: J. Grapheus, 1531), I, ch. 58.

40. Especially those that are made "ex cinere Phoenicis" or "ex serpentum exuviis"
(of the phoenix's ashes or the skins of serpents).

41. "Nam plerosque aqua submersos, alios ignibus injectos et rogo impositos, alios
in bello occisos, alios aliter exanimatos, post plures etiam dies revixisse legimus." (For
we read that many who were submerged in water, others who were thrown into the
fire and laid on a pyre, others who were slain in war, and others who were killed in
other ways were revived, even after several days.)

42. "Oportet moribundas animas nonnunquam in corporibus suis latere vehemen-
tioribus extasibus oppressas et ab omni corporea actione solutas; sic ut vita, sensus,
motus, corpus omne deserant, ita tamen quod homo vere nondum mortuus, etiam per

This is a remarkable—and daring—attempt at a rational interpretation of miraculous events. It is the work of an occultist, and we would be astonished if we did not know that throughout the sixteenth century the inclination of occult philosophy was to get rid of miracles.[43] If you first read in Pico della Mirandola's famous *Apology*, which caused such a sensation in Paris and Rome in 1488, his argument against the theologians in defense of his suspect fourth thesis: "No science gives us better evidence of the divinity of Christ than magic and cabala," in connection with which he raised not merely the question of miracles but of Christ's miracles,[44] and if you then read the pages in which Campanella tried to establish, under the name of natural magic, a web of causes and effects so tightly woven that no supernatural act could possibly slip in between the one and the other,[45] you will then have both ends of a long chain in

---

diuturnum tempus." (Sometimes dying souls find it necessary to conceal themselves in their bodies when they are pressed down by too violent displacements and released from all corporeal activity; it is as though life, sensation, motion, and everything bodily are gone, yet the man is not yet really dead, he is but lying senseless and seemingly dead, even for a long time.) Agrippa thereupon recounts cases of prolonged sleep lasting months or even years, and cases of extraordinary fasting.

43. On this point, cf. Blanchet; also Pomponazzi, intro., p. 20 ff. On Pico della Mirandola's *Apology*, cf. Augustin Renaudet, *Préréforme et humanisme à Paris pendant les premières guerres d'Italie (1494-1517)* (Thèse de doctorat ès lettres, Paris, 1916), pp. 127-129.

44. "Licet nulla sit scientia humanitus inventa quae nos certificare possit de Divinitate Christi, quia certificationem de divinitate ejus ... non habemus, nisi ex modo faciendi miracula quae fecit; quae miracula et esse facta ab eo, et esse taliter facta non nisi ex testimonio scripturae scimus—tamen si quid ad hoc nos possunt adjuvare scientiae humanae, nulla est quae magis nos possit adjuvare quam Magia et Cabala." (Although there is no science discovered by man that could give us certainty about the divinity of Christ, since we have certainty of his divinity only from the way he performed miracles and we know that he performed these miracles and how he performed them only from the testimony of Scripture, nevertheless if human science can be of any help to us in this matter, none can help more than magic and cabala.) *Opera omnia J. Pici* (Basel: H. Petri, 1572), p. 167.

See also ch. 14 of Book IV of his *In astrologiam*, in which Pico asserts that there is a natural course of events which does not allow for miracles: "Est enim ordo rerum a Deo pro naturali cursu institutarum, ita suis finibus inclusus sejunctusque ab his rebus quae, divina virtute et voluntate, fiunt praeter naturam, ut haec omnia si tollantur, nihil sit in rerum natura quod desit, nihil quod supersit." (For there is an order of things that have been set by God on a natural course, which has its own limits and is separate from the things that, through divine power and will, occur outside of nature, so that when all these are left out there is nothing in the universe that is lacking, nothing that is superfluous.) Ibid., p. 546.

45. Blanchet, passim.

which Pomponazzi and Agrippa were only links.

But was Rabelais a link—the Rabelais of 1532, of chapter 30 of *Pantagruel?* Did he, in his desire to free his contemporaries from the yoke of oppressive religion, express in his work a liberated man's conviction that there were no miracles? "All miracles are impossible, even for God. Especially for God, the supreme guardian of the laws of nature. Either the story in the Gospels is a deception, or Lazarus was not really dead, since he could not have been raised from the dead by the intervention of a demiurge. The rule has no exceptions. Whether it is a question of living beings or of inorganic matter, the conditions for the existence of phenomena are determined in an absolute manner." Rabelais could have thought that in 1532. Others were beginning to think like that. Did he really think it? We do not know. But what is certain is that if he thought it he did not write it. And he was not at all an apostle of enlightenment who opened up a hand crammed with truths so they could slip through his fingers and go forth to alight on those of his contemporaries who already happened to be worthy of receiving them. We know more. We know that Rabelais cast no doubt on the veracity, sanctity, or efficacy of the Scriptures, which, according to Pico della Mirandola, were the only proof of Christ's miracles, while the miracles were the only proofs of Christ's divinity. As to the Scriptures, Rabelais has not words enough, in *Gargantua* and *Pantagruel,* to extol their study and pious veneration. At the risk of getting into hot water he proclaims that the Scriptures are the only true basis of religion. He frequently quotes from the Scriptures in French, and the most urgent task he assigns a king is to see that they are preached and taught to all. But did he also, at some point, suggest that the supernatural could be reduced to the natural, as all rational explanations of miracles required? He allowed many serious things to slip into his clowning—did he indicate that such a reduction was imperative for men of reason, and did he point out the grounds on which it could be attempted? No.

If the answer is no, then Rabelais in 1532 was not an early warning of new times, not a superhuman herald of a rationalist faith that was aimed at reducing religion to ashes. For one is not a great thinker—much less a great freethinker or intrepid enemy of revelation—for telling one's contemporaries the story of the soldier with the wooden head, or even the one in which Panurge mimics a miracle of Christ (I mean, of Maugis).[46]

◄§ These are negative conclusions. Can we go further and come to a positive conclusion about Rabelais's attitude toward miracles?

We know Spinoza's saying, which Bayle appropriated for his *Dictionary*,[47] that if he could have convinced himself of the raising of Lazarus he would have been willing to embrace the ordinary faith of Christians. This is one attitude, one opinion. It is shared by a whole family of thinkers who put Christianity into logical terms and claim to place its practitioners on the horns of very serious dilemmas; in this case, in their effort to establish Rabelais as an enemy of Christian dogma, they posit that miracles are the true guarantors of the veracity of Christianity and that Rabelais certainly denied miracles; therefore, having denied them, he ceased to be a Christian. Fine. But if Spinoza uttered the opinion we are recalling at the moment, there was someone who on September 1, 1528, wrote the following sentence worth reflecting on: "Christianity today does not depend on miracles"—*non pendet religio Christianorum a miraculis.* That someone was Erasmus.[48] I think he was a Christian. An objection might conceivably be raised: "Excuse me. Erasmus was not speaking about all miracles. He excepted from his condemnation what can be called the fundamental ones, those of Christ. He stated that those ought to be believed: 'quae sunt in sacris literis tanto firmius credimus, si non quibus-libet hominum fabulas crediderimus.' "[49] But that would simply

46. [The soldier with the wooden head is a character of popular legend said to inhabit the Hôtel des Invalides. He also appears in a humorous story by Eugène Mouton, *Histoire de l'invalide à la tête de bois* . . . (Paris, 1886).—Translator.] Busson writes: "If French rationalism did not rest with Rabelais's laughter, *if it took many problems seriously*, it is partly due to books of this sort (*De incantationibus*)." Pomponazzi, p. 44. I also do not, for my part, share the sort of total contempt for Rabelais's laughter implied in this sentence. Is it necessary to say so?

47. Pierre Bayle, *Dictionnaire historique et critique*, 5th ed., 5 vols. (Amsterdam, 1734), V, 217.

48. Letter to Episcopus (John Longlond). In *Desiderii Erasmi Roterodami opera omnia*, 10 vols. (Leyden, 1703–1706), III, part 1, col. 1100 (epistle 974); *Opus epistolarum Des. Erasmi Roterodami*, ed. P. S. Allen and H. M. Allen, 12 vols. (Oxford, 1906–1958), VII, 462 (epistle 2037).

49. Our belief in the things in Holy Scripture is all the firmer if we do not believe in whatever is said in tales by men.

confirm the fact that here as elsewhere Erasmus did not go as far as Luther did. And Luther was no rationalist, I believe. Luther did not commit the indiscretion of making a journey to Padua. But in the preface that he placed at the beginning of his translation of the New Testament, Luther wrote these memorable lines: "John's Gospel and St. Paul's epistles, especially that to the Romans, and St. Peter's first epistle are the true kernel and marrow of all the books . . . , and it would be advisable for every Christian to read them first and most, and by daily reading to make them as much his own as his daily bread. For in them you do not find many works and miracles of Christ described, but you do find depicted in masterly fashion how faith in Christ overcomes sin, death, and hell, and gives life, righteousness and salvation. This is the real nature of the gospel." And this Christian, this ardent and impassioned prophet, this man of faith, if that word has any meaning, added, in so many words: "If I had to do without one or the other . . . I would rather do without the works than without [Christ's] preaching. For the works do not help me, but his words give life, as he himself says."[50]

This is a crucial passage. It is a useful reminder to anyone who is likely to forget that in the sixteenth century those who denied the validity of miracles were not only the "Paduans" dear to Henri Busson, but also the Reformers, who were not concocting any scheme to destroy the religion of Christ. We have mentioned Luther. There was also Oecolampadius, who scandalized Postel by not believing that after Jesus awoke among the dead he could get back to his companions through locked doors.[51] And how many others were there? Let us not ourselves go beating on an open door. Whether or not it pleases the learned logicians to find fault with them for being illogical and deplore the fact that they had faith in spite of all the rules, when according to logic they should never have had any faith—

50. Martin Luther, *Werke: Die Deutsche Bibel*, VI (Weimar, 1929), 10. English translation in *Luther's Works*, XXXV, ed. E. Theodore Bockmann (Philadelphia, 1960), 361–362.

51. *Alcorani, seu legis Mahometi, et Evangelistarum concordiae liber* . . . (Paris: P. Gromorsius, 1543), p. 15. A discussion follows this statement by a Cenevangelist "adstrictior legibus philosophiae quam Evangelii et rationis" (who owes more to the laws of philosophy than to those of the Gospel and of reason).

the fact is that men who considered themselves Christians, whom hundreds of thousands of their contemporaries took as their guides on the paths of Christianity, professed a Christianity in the sixteenth century that did not place a high value on miracles. *Qui non pendebat a miraculis*—Erasmus's expression is striking. What men are we talking of? Once again as we follow Rabelais our gaze is directed to Erasmus and Luther, and to others in Rabelais's time who were engaged in putting out new, revised, corrected, and updated versions of a Christianity that was more than a thousand years old and were just as inclined to throw miracles overboard (even the miracles of Christ, if necessary) as they were to destroy Purgatory and free the souls confined there. And they did not ask for authorization from scholars who today accuse them of inconsistency and illogic.

If Rabelais had wanted to shake the belief in miracles by frontally attacking it in his books—because in his eyes the possibility of adhering to Christianity depended on the belief—he would have written something other than a parody. He was enough in touch with the philosophical and theological controversies of his time to devote a chapter to Agrippa—"Her Trippa"—whose *De occulta philosophia* had appeared before *Pantagruel.* He did not do it. That is because in his eyes the question undoubtedly was far from having the importance attributed to it today by unbelievers when they somewhat ridiculously (from the historian's point of view) read the illogical believers a lesson they never asked for.

4. Rabelais in the Underworld

Now a couple of words about another episode, which merits no more than a couple of words: we need only reiterate the things we have just been saying when we get to the fanciful Underworld, the infernal caper—also in chapter 30 of *Pantagruel*—that Rabelais has such fun sketching in the margin of a famous little piece by Lucian, "Menippus, or the Descent into Hades."

Among the inhabitants were popes—how scandalous! Boniface VIII and Nicholas III (for the sake of a silly pun)[52] and Pope Alexander and Pope Julius with the "buggerly beard." Let

---

52. "Nicolas pape tiers estoit papetier." [Translator's note.]

us not make ourselves ridiculous by lifting up our hands to heaven over the audacity of such jokes.[53] In the time of King Francis we would have been the only ones to condemn them! But it will be said that there is more. There is no punishment in this underworld, there are no physical torments, no eternal flames. There are good devils, with no trace of viciousness. Quite true. But one would have to be sunk in deep ignorance of the interests, concerns, and preoccupations of the men of the sixteenth century to consider Rabelais's clowning in chapter 30 of *Pantagruel* daring.

Our learned men may be ignorant, but he was not. Much ink had been spilled over these matters for a long time.[54] What about the torments of hell? Many theologians, perfectly confident of being orthodox, absolutely denied that they could specify what those torments were actually like: fire, icy water, the gnawing worm that never dies. There were even some who thought that the damned in hell found themselves having the same feelings they had had on earth. There was no extreme suffering, no perpetual pain—it was simply that they were deprived of God, and of all that was supernatural as well. For the rest, an admirable order held sway in the regions governed by Satan.

We should be fully aware that controversy on this matter was permissible for the learned. It still is. The existence of hell, established for the fallen angels even before the creation of man, may be an article of Christian faith. The same may be true of its eternity. On the other hand, everything that has to do with the layout of the infernal regions—if I may call it that—with their location (in the earth's interior, or elsewhere?), with the kind of existence led by the souls and demons who reside there, with the possibility of their inhabitants' leaving (whether it is a question of demons going to earth on missions of temptation or

53. Attacking Julius II, the pope in the warrior's helmet, was such a ritual that even Gilbert Ducher, who hardly concerned himself with wordly matters, did it in a short poem, "De Julio secundo Rom. pontifice jocus" (*Gilberti Ducherii Vultonis Aquapersani epigrammaton libri duo* [Lyon: S. Gryphius, 1538], p. 109). And why be shocked by these attacks and not by chapter 33 of *Gargantua*: "Our poor Monsieur the pope dies now for fear"? Most of all, why not ask the right question? Was the pope to Gallican France in the years 1515–1520 what he was to French Catholics in 1940?

54. "Enfer," *Dictionnaire de théologie catholique*, ed. Vacant, Mangenot, and Amann, 15 vols. (Paris, 1908–1950), V, cols. 28–120.

of the ordinary damned returning to show themselves to some of the living), all of these problems of detail, suitable for the regaling of children's endless curiosity, have remained the subject of free discussion among theologians. And they made the most of their freedom. We have only to recall Bayle's ironic comments under the entry "Patin" in his *Dictionary*. He goes on at some length with great glee about a passage in Drelincourt's dialogue, *La Descente de Jésus-Christ aux Enfers* (1664 edition, p. 309). He discourses on the four divisions of the infernal territory: one where all the souls of the damned wait for their bodies to arrive after the Resurrection; another, adjacent to this, is Purgatory; the third is the limbo of infants who died without being baptized; and the fourth is the place where the souls of the just were gathered before the Revelation of the Lord. As a result, these regions must be rather extensive, for to gather together—to speak only of them—"all the children who are unbaptised . . . these will no doubt compose two thirds of mankind." This remark was made to a missionary, Bayle adds, who replied: "Embrio's do not take up much room." Had he forgotten that at the hour of the Last Judgment the embryos would be revived as grown men?[55]

Well, this is irony, the irony of an unbeliever. But what of Rabelais? Did he echo discussions he was well aware of? Did he even raise questions in this area? He did not. He was having some fun. I cannot say it was innocent fun, but how malicious was it compared to Bayle's irony? What did Epistemon see in the underworld? Very few actual people, apart from the popes already mentioned. Just as Menippus saw Euripides and Homer, he met two writers, François Villon and Jean Lemaire de Belges; and two court jesters, Caillette and Triboulet. And who were the rest? Heroes from Plutarch, all pagans and therefore destined for hell, from Themistocles to Alexander, from Romulus to Nero, from Hannibal to Scipio, not to mention Caesar, Pompey, Trajan, Nerva, as well as Demosthenes and Cicero; heroes of romance in abundance, from the four sons of Aymon to Ogier the Dane, Huon of Bordeaux, Morgante, and Melusina. It is a carnival. A question had been raised about

---

55. Bayle, IV, 516; English translation in Bayle, *A General Dictionary, Historical and Critical*, 10 vols. (London, 1734–1741), VIII, 184, 185.

"good" pagans—by Erasmus, for example: Saint Socrates, pray for us! And also by Zwingli. Rabelais is not concerned. He is just laughing—and with no fuss at all he puts Cicero and Epictetus among the damned.

As for the romantic heroes of the Round Table, Rabelais does not make them damned. Damned? Let's not be ridiculous—Rabelais does not make the Greeks and Romans he admires in Plutarch damned. He does not make Villon or Lemaire (especially if Lemaire is, as Abel Lefranc would have it, really the prototype of Raminagrobis, the old French poet with the edifying end)—he does not make this bizarre world in any way a world of the damned. He does not present us with souls that, rightly or wrongly (it is debatable), are doomed to eternal torments that need to be specified (that is also debatable). He presents us with untroubled stock characters in a brief and whimsical dialogue of the dead, strolling about Lucianic Elysian Fields for our enjoyment. Great daring, this—but surely the archbishop of Cambrai, Fénelon, forgave Rabelais a long time ago. Indeed, if it were absolutely necessary to derive a lesson from the visit to the underworld, it would certainly not be the one in the old saying, "Sinners always get punished." It would much more likely be the one that the Revolution was later pleased to restate, adapting a biblical text: "Whosoever shall exalt himself shall be abased." Like Lucian, Rabelais sensed the irony of hell, where kings and satraps are "reduced to poverty. . . , selling salt fish on account of their neediness,"[56] where Philip of Macedon sat in a corner mending old shoes. Nothing very astonishing. It was in the tradition of the Franciscan preachers he was familiar with, since he had been one of them. At the very most, it could be said that a little of the egalitarian air that often showed in their speech wafts across this page written by someone who was amusing himself as he wished to amuse others, plying with delight his trade of French Lucian and not thinking of pontificating about the Christian hell any more than the prelate who two centuries later constructed a dialogue in the Elysian Fields—no one bothers to ask whether it is hell or Paradise—between Xerxes, Leonidas, Solon, Alcibiades, Socrates, and

56. Lucian, trans. A. M. Harmon, 8 vols. (Cambridge, Mass., and London, 1961), IV, 103. [Translator's note.]

Pericles (famous pagans) and Louis XI, Cardinal Jean Balue, Cardinal Jiménez, Pope Sixtus V, Good King Henry IV, Riche- lieu, and even (a genuine act of daring under the Bourbons) the Constable Charles de Bourbon.[57]

But in fact Rabelais is laughing at hell, at devils, and at the damned. He is in fact trying "to overturn all fear of God" in the faithful, as Calvin said, "by little gibes and tricks." It is pos- sible. We have no intention, you may be sure, of starting any process of canonization of a saintly Rabelais. Reading chapter 30 of *Pantagruel* in no way supported or fueled the fears that hell inspired in those who by some great and wondrous miracle did not know that it was possible in the France of 1530 to joke about this old theme of popular spoofs. But say that Rabelais la- bored to deliver his contemporaries from some sort of terror, that his aim was to free them from their fear. Was he therefore the only one at the time? Was he therefore so very bold? Was he therefore necessarily an enemy of Christ?

Not to reach any further, I open up the *Enchiridion militis christiani*[58] of Erasmus. The flame that torments the rich man in the Gospel (Luke 16:24), the worm that gnaws at the impi- ous—all the physical tortures described by the poets were spiri- tualized and allegorized by Erasmus.[59] In his way, like Episte- mon, he assured his readers that "the devils were boon companions," and that the torment of the damned was in es- sence only the constant anxiety that accompanies inveterate, ha- bitual sinning. This view is also maintained in a small work published in Lyon in 1542—*De bonorum praemiis et supplicis malorum aeterno*[60]—by a Dominican, Father Ambroise Cath- arin. Such views were held, after mature reflection, by John Calvin, without his thinking they might induce believers to stop believing.

It was possible in 1532 to say that one was a Christian, to be- lieve that one was, and really be one, and to think, along with

57. By Fénelon (1651-1715). [Translator's note.]

58. *Handbook of a Christian Soldier.*

59. "Ut qui injuste dominabatur in vita priori, vita alia in servilem relabatur statum; qui munus sanguine polluerit, talionem subire cogatur." (He who ruled unjustly in his former life is sunk to a state of servility in the next life; he who tainted his office with blood is forced to endure retaliation.)

60. *The Rewards of the Good and the Eternal Torment of the Bad.*

Erasmus, that Christianity did not depend on miracles, or at any rate that it no longer depended on them. It was possible to go as far as Luther and say: Miracles? What do miracles have to do with it? It was possible in 1532 to say that one was a Christian, to believe that one was, and be one, and to think, along with Erasmus, that there was no need for a hell with devils, pitchforks, red-hot tongs, and eternal fires in order to maintain one's faith: *timor inferni, initium fidei.*[61] It was possible in 1532 to say that one was a Christian, to believe that one was, and be one, and to want nothing more than to free the faithful, the ordinary believers, of childish fears and vulgar superstitions. It was possible, and Erasmus was such a Christian—to mention only him. And along with him there were other genuine Christians, none of them Paduans, named Oecolampadius, Zwingli, Luther—even Calvin. We have just caught a glimpse of Rabelais behind these men. We will remind ourselves of this in due course.

61. "The fear of hell is only the beginning of faith." Postel complains about this in his *Libellus de judicio* at the end of the *Alcorani concordia.* Cf., on p. 90: "Quot autem hac tempestate Cenevangelistae volunt paria esse omnium in fide Jesu Christi e vivis decedentium praemia, seu impii, seu pii fuerint, seu boni, seu mali, et par ubique praemium ob solam fidem reponunt: quid aliud, rogo, quam iniquissimum deum constituant?" (How many Cenevangelists nowadays want the rewards of all who die in the faith of Jesus Christ to be equal, whether they be pious or impious, good or bad, and they base this equal reward for everyone on faith alone! What are they doing, I ask, but setting up a god who is very unjust?) Cf. also, ibid.: "Si latro, si praedo, si fur, moechus, impius resipiscat extremo vitae suspirio, erit par Petro, martyribus piisque omnibus. O blasphemiam inauditam! Si haec vera sunt, at quid leges dedit tam divinas quam humanas Deus?" (If a robber, a bandit, a thief, a fornicator, an infidel repents with his last dying breath, he will be the equal of Peter and all the holy martyrs. What unheard-of blasphemy! If this is true, why did God give us laws divine and human?)

Naturally, we should be wary of the phraseology Postel credits the Evangelists with (repenting with one's dying breath, and so on).

BOOK TWO

Belief or Unbelief

PART III

Rabelais's Christianity

6. The Giants' Creed

ITNESSES and testimony have been duly subjected to critical scrutiny, but the fundamental problem remains. What did Rabelais think about things having to do with religion in 1532? Let us turn to the writings we have and put two questions to them. What ideas did Rabelais present to the public in his works? And what, on the other hand, were the philosophical theories on which he relied or which he condemned?

This is a distinction that may cause some surprise. But for men of 1530 it did not yet seem a matter of absolute necessity—necessity arising from conscience—for philosophical opinions to coincide exactly with religious beliefs. Calvin on the one hand and the Tridentine Catholics on the other would achieve that harmony by forging, each in a distinctive way, two perfectly coordinated systems. In 1530 that point had not yet been reached. Without referring any more than we must to the famous doctrine of double truth, "that reduction to absurdity attempted by orthodox theologians against philosophers who were not orthodox,"[1] to clarify this attitude, it is appropriate at this point to take into account a certain state of mind.

Let us put aside conjectures and interpretations for a while, however. Let us take the text of *Pantagruel*, which certainly came off the press at the end of October 1532; the *Pantagru-*

---

1. Etienne Gilson, *Etudes de philosophie médiévale* (Strasbourg, 1921), p. 68.

elian Prognostication, which was put on sale in January 1533 and then was reissued with major additions in 1535; the fragment that has been preserved of the *Almanac of 1533; Gargantua,* which was probably put on sale at the beginning of October 1534; and finally (although the work came a little after the Affair of the Placards) what we have of the *Almanac of 1535.* Let us pick out all the statements about religion and philosophy in this coherent body of material. An important objection to this can be raised, however. What religion and philosophy will they be? The religion and philosophy of Rabelais? Or of Pantagruel, or even of Panurge and Friar John? Didn't Rabelais endow each of his characters with his own set of ideas?

To be sure, we are dealing with passages taken from a novel, and all—or almost all—of them are put in the mouth of Grandgousier, Gargantua, or Pantagruel, the three kings who take on the task of expressing serious thoughts. It is, however, possible to add other passages, ones in which Rabelais speaks for himself. What do we say if they show themselves to be in total conformity with the words he assigns to his kings? And if worse comes to worst, the objection has to apply to all the views expressed. If you argue, "Yes, here are pious words and Christian statements, but they belong to Pantagruel or Gargantua, who function in the novel as noble fathers," you have to allow others to counter, "What of the miracle? Look here—the one who seems to be laughing is not saintly King Pantagruel. It is that thief, that dissolute fellow, that unbeliever Panurge. Panurge speaks only for himself and expresses only the thoughts of Panurge."

Let us be serious and not worry too much about what happens to proper persons who are made terribly unhappy when they read Erasmus's *Colloquies* or Bayle's *Dictionary.* We may not find Rabelais's true thought in the statements we are going to extract from his earliest writings. What is important is not the thought of some individual who is more or less known to posterity, but the thought placed in the public domain by one of the three or four really powerful and original writers France has had. The thought of Rabelais the man I do not know. The thought Rabelais passed off as his own I do quite often know. The thought that Rabelais's readers have found in his writings for centuries and have colored with the changing shades of their own thought as it moved with the times—that is what is essential and what is real.

1. The Giants' God: Creator and Providence

Speaking of Gui Patin, who had hung a handsome portrait of Rabelais, "for which he had once been offered twenty pistoles," on the wall of his study, Bayle wrote: "His creed was not clogged with many articles."[2] Indeed, the derisive physician "admitted only what was contained in the New Testament, and added: *Credo in Deum Christum Crucifixum, etc. . . . De minimis non curat praetor!*"[3] We would pretty much expect that the religious passages gathered from Rabelais's writings by the most diligent cribbler of note cards also would not constitute a very clogged creed. We are surprised: in Rabelais's early books there are whole pages that are patchworks of quotations and allusions from the Gospels and the Bible. God is constantly being invoked in this most profane work. One might say he never ceases to be present either in the thoughts of the kings who rely on him or in the thoughts of the author, who invokes him with a persistence and consistency that are downright surprising.

What God is this? The God of Christians, without any possible doubt, the God in three persons of the strictest orthodoxy. Here, for example, is the Father, to whom Jesus will one day render up his kingdom,[4] the Father "who disposes everything that is and that is done, according to His free purpose and good pleasure"; the *Almanac of 1533*, having thus defined his functions, gives him the title of eternal King.[5] And here is the Son, the "dear Son,"[6] who acts as his father's interpreter among

2. Pierre Bayle, *Dictionnaire historique et critique*, 5th ed., 5 vols. (Amsterdam, 1734), IV, 518. In English, *A General Dictionary, Historical and Critical*, 10 vols. (London, 1734–1741), VIII, 187. The portrait of Rabelais hung next to that of Erasmus in Patin's study: a significant juxtaposition. *Correspondance de Gui Patin* (Paris, 1901), p. 102.

3. "I believe in God, Christ, Crucified, and all that . . . The praetor does not concern himself about trifles!"

4. *Pantagruel*, ch. 8: "when Jesus Christ shall have rendered up to God the Father his kingdom."

5. "But these be secrets of the close council of the eternal King." Trans. W. F. Smith, *The Works of Francis Rabelais*, ed. Albert Jay Nock and Catherine Rose Wilson, 2 vols. (New York, 1931), II, 902.

6. *Gargantua*, ch. 58: "Happy is that man that . . . shall always continue to the end, in aiming at that mark, which God by his dear Son hath set before us."

men. Jesus Christ, Jesus the Christ, Jesus Christ our Lord, Christ the Lord, Our Lord, the living God—under all these titles he is invoked time and again by Rabelais's heroes or by Rabelais himself.[7] And if it was possible to detect in certain theologians of the early sixteenth century—Farel, for example, in his early writings[8]—a preference for the Father, who was more ardently extolled and supplicated than the Son—the giants' religion, on the other hand, like that of Erasmus, was by preference a religion of the Son. Creator, Plasmator, Conservator, Preserver, Protector, Giver of all good; Guardian, Moderator, Just Judge, Redeemer and Savior—not one of these expressions is not said over and over and repeated to satiety throughout Rabelais's work. The Passion is never invoked,[9] but the great episodes in Christ's earthly life are recalled—his death, resurrection, transfiguration, and ascension.[10] Also recalled is his role in the Last Judgment and how, after presiding over that dread ceremony, he will render up to his Father a kingdom at peace and purified of all defilement.[11] On the other hand, the Holy Spirit, which had such an important place in so many doctrines of the time—for example, in Luther—hardly appears in Rabelais. It is barely mentioned except in chapter 40 of *Gargantua:* the giant king informs his companions that the

7. "Jesus Christ," *Pantagruel,* ch. 8; *Gargantua,* ch. 39. "Jesus the Christ," *Pantagruel,* ch. 8 in Juste's edition of 1537 ("je rends par Jésus le Christ grâces à Dieu"); all the other editions from 1533 to 1542 have, "Je rends grâces à Dieu mon conservateur" (I give thanks to God my Savior and Preserver); "that your souls should be . . . united with Jesus the Christ." *Almanac of 1535.* "Christ, our Redeemer," *Gargantua,* ch. 29. "Jesus Christ our Lord," *Almanac of 1533.* "The Lord," *Pantagruel,* chs. 19, 27 [translated as "the great God" by Urquhart]; *Book Three,* ch. 30 [translated as "the Lord God Almighty"]. "Lord God," *Pantagruel,* ch. 14; *Almanac of 1533.* "Our Lord," *Pantagruel,* ch. 8; *Gargantua,* ch. 10; *Book Four,* chs. 4, 19, 20, 24 [variously translated]. "The living God," *Pantagruel,* ch. 28. We should add "the good God of Sabaoth," *Book Three* prologue.

8. Henri Heyer, *Guillaume Farel: essai sur le développement de ses idées théologiques* (Geneva, 1872), pp. 45-46.

9. One does not learn from him that "one drop of the sacred blood is sufficient for us to obtain every grace and every blessing," as Olivier Maillard said.

10. *Gargantua,* ch. 10: "An Evangelical testimony I hope will content you. In Matth. XVII, it is said, that at the transfiguration of our Lord, Vestimenta ejus facta sunt alba sicut lux, his apparel was made white like the light . . . In that color did the angels testify the joy of the whole world at the resurrection of our Saviour, John XX, and at his Ascension, Acts I."

11. *Pantagruel,* ch. 8. See also, on the Last Judgment, *Pantagruel,* ch. 14: "We shall not have the final judgment these seven thousand sixty and seven jubilees yet to come, and so Cusanus will be deceived in his conjecture."

Spirit prays and intercedes with God for Christians, and that God assents to its prayers and is gracious to them. What accounts for this relative obliteration of the Spirit? Erasmus indicated what it was when he wrote the preface to his edition of the works of Saint Hilary. In the Scriptures the Spirit is never called God.[12] And an Evangelical like Farel, totally subsistent on the Word, felt some qualms about professing the divine personality of the Spirit.[13]

We just mentioned the name of Erasmus. And indeed, if he had subjected the giants to the same examination as he did Barbatius in the colloquy "An Examination Concerning Faith" (Barbatius we know is Luther), he would have got them to agree to the very definition that Barbatius provides to Aulus: "When you say 'God,' what do you mean?" "I mean a certain eternal mind that had no beginning and shall have no end; than which nothing can be greater, wiser or better . . . Which by its omnipotent will created whatever exists, visible or invisible; with wondrous wisdom disposes and governs all things; by its goodness nourishes and preserves all things; and graciously restores the fallen race of men."[14] This is indeed the God of the giants, and of Rabelais. But he remains closer to Christian forms and less liberated from the rituals and prayers of traditional Christianity than the God of Erasmus. Moreover, the heroes of Rabelais's novel have every right to invoke the Christian God. Alcofribas Nasier makes us well aware of that. Gargantua and Pantagruel were baptized and are able to swear, like Eudemon, "by the faith of a Christian." It was at his baptism that Pantagruel received his richly significant name.[15] Before him, his father, as soon as he was born and his thirst slaked,

12. "Pater frequentissime Deus vocatur; Filius, aliquoties; Spiritus sanctus nunquam exerte." (The Father is very often called God; the Son sometimes; the Holy Spirit never expressly.)

13. On the other hand, the role of the Holy Spirit is important in Lutheran doctrine. It is what effects works, and inflames the heart so that it will be disposed to do good. It is what makes man reverent toward God. Robert Will, *La Liberté chrétienne, Etude sur le principe de la piété chez Luther* (Strasbourg, 1922), p. 236.

14. "AULUS. Quum Deum dicis, quid sentis? BARBATIUS. Sentio mentem esse quandam aeternam, quae nec initium habuerit, nec finem sit habitura, qua nihil esse potest nec maius, nec sapientius, nec melius . . . quae nutu suo omnipotenti condidit quidquid est rerum visibilium aut invisibilium; quae sapientia mirabili moderatur ac gubernat universa, sua bonitate pascit ac servat omnia, atque hominum genus collapsum gratuito restituit." English translation in *The Colloquies of Erasmus*, trans. Craig R. Thompson (Chicago, 1965), pp. 180–181.

15. *Pantagruel*, ch. 2.

had been "carried to the font, and there baptized, according to the manner of good Christians"[16]—while priests carried his poor mother (a romantic contrast) to the cemetery with many litanies and mementos.[17]

◄§ The omnipotence of God, his infinite power, his almightiness without bounds—it is this that the passages in Rabelais extol above all and in all kinds of ways. It was God, first of all, who created the world. The sky, the stars, the planets, the moon that he placed in the firmament at the beginning of the world to "guide mankind by night"—it was he who "by the effect of his sacred word" brought into being the whole visible universe that dominates our sublunary world. On earth this sovereign plasmator[18] created the first man, Adam, and he continues to produce men "in such form, and for such end, as is most agreeable with his divine will, even as a potter fashioneth his vessels."[19] He is, says Master Alcofribas at some length in the first chapter of the *Pantagruelian Prognostication*, the one "without whose preservation and governance all things in a moment would be reduced to nothing, as out of nothing they were by Him created"—a categorical affirmation of the creation *ex nihilo*, which is likewise proclaimed in a sentence inserted by Rabelais in the *Almanac of 1533* using different words and a different tone: "not what we wish and ask for should be done, but that which pleases [Jesus Christ our Lord] and which He hath determined before the heavens were formed." Of Him, this sovereign Deity, comes, "in Him is, and by Him is made perfect every being, and all life and motion, as says the evangelical trumpet, my lord St. Paul, *Romans xi.*"[20] His intentions are unfathomable. No one is allowed to know the secrets "of the close council of the eternal King[21] . . . These it is better to say

16. *Gargantua*, ch. 7.

17. *Pantagruel*, ch. 3. Picrochole was no less a Christian than his enemies. He said he would spare Barbarossa's life. "Yea," said his counselors, "so that he be content to be christened"! *Gargantua*, ch. 33.

18. *Pantagruel*, ch. 8.

19. *Gargantua*, ch. 40.

20. *Works*, ed. Nock and Wilson, II, 893, 902, 893.

21. The expression was also used by Margaret of Navarre in the *Heptameron*, at the end of Novel 50: Says Geburon, "As we have not been called to the privy council of God, and consequently are ignorant of first causes . . ." *The Heptameron of the Tales of Margaret Queen of Navarre*, 2 vols. (London, 1903), II, 145.

nothing of, and to adore them in silence, as is said *Tob. xii.*, 'It is well done to conceal the secret of the King.' David the prophet saith, *Psalm lxiii,* according to the Chaldaic letter: 'Lord God, silence belongeth to Thee in Sion'; and the reason he gives, *Psalm xvii:* 'For he hath made darkness His secret place'!" In short, it is not only in 1533, the year of the *Prognostication,* but in all succeeding years to the end of the world (for it will come to an end, as it began: "nature produceth nothing that is immortal; for she putteth an end and period to all things by her engendered, according to the saying Omnia orta cadunt, &c."), for as long as the world exists, that it will not have "any governor but God the Creator"; and Rabelais, speaking for himself here, repeats it (ch. 1): "Therefore the ruler of this year, and of all others, according to our authentic solution, will be God Almighty." The *Almanac of 1535* says it again, more specifically: "God Almighty, who has created and ordered everything according to His holy pleasure."[22]

Thus God is the creator and sustainer of the world. He is God-as-Providence as well. He does not remain impassive, inactive, deaf to his creatures' prayers. He is the good Lord, giver of all good,[23] the protector "who doth never forsake those that in him do put their trust and confidence."[24] He is the *servateur* (guardian, savior), and it is by this name that, as the novel progresses, Rabelais's heroes tend more and more to venerate the Almighty. Here the passages are sufficiently numerous to be arranged chronologically in a most interesting way.[25] In short, it

22. *Works,* ed. Nock and Wilson, II, 902, 893, 904.

23. *Pantagruel,* ch. 18: "For whatever comes from Him is good." *Book Three,* ch. 30: "Is not that a mean, whereby we do acknowledge him to be the sole giver of all whatsoever is good?" Ibid., ch. 43: "Almighty God, the giver of all good things."

24. *Pantagruel,* ch. 28.

25. It turns out, surprisingly, that the expression actually appears only once in *Pantagruel,* in ch. 29: "O thou Lord God, who has always been my protector, and my saviour [*mon protecteur et mon servateur*]." In *Gargantua* it is not used at all. In *Book Three* it appears twice. There is a reference to "the advent of that Saviour King, whose coming to this world hath made all oracles and prophecies to cease" (ch. 24) and to "the name of God our Saviour" (ch. 48). But it is in *Book Four* that the use of the expression expands: "the Blessed Saviour" (ch. 4); "this wave will sweep us away, blessed Saviour!" (ch. 18); "Pantagruel, having first implored the help of the great and Almighty Saviour" (ch. 19); "our good Saviour then help us" (ch. 20); "Pantagruel told him that the Almighty Saviour of mankind . . ." (ch. 25); "God, our Creator, Saviour, and Preserver" (ch. 45). [Since Urquhart and Le Motteux sometimes used different words for *servateur* (such as redeemer, deliverer, and preserver), I have altered the preceding phrases to render it as "saviour" every time.—Translator.]

is on his goodness that the stress is placed. He is the one we turn to and implore when we are in danger, in perplexity, in physical or mental distress. To sum it up in a word: he is the one we pray to because we know he heeds, is able and willing to heed, those who place their trust in his protection.

ஃ People pray in Rabelais's novel. They pray copiously, abundantly, and with solemnity. At the first news of Picrochole's attack Grandgousier cries out, "My God, my Saviour [*Sauveur*], help me, inspire me, and advise me what I shall do!" Honest Gallet, on his return from his vain mission to Picrochole, finds the good Grandgousier "upon his knees, bareheaded, crouching in a little corner of his cabinet, and humbly praying unto God, that he would vouchsafe to assuage the choler" of his enemy. When Touchfaucet is vanquished, his conquerers return to the same Grandgousier, "who in his bed was praying unto God for their safety and victory."[26] Pantagruel turns to the divine Savior with just as much fervor and frequency as his grandfather. We know that beautiful long prayer he addresses to him on the verge of engaging in a decisive battle against Loupgarou: "O thou Lord God, who hast always been my protector, and my saviour, thou seest the distress wherein I am at this time."[27] With heavenly assistance, Pantagruel is victorious; but he knows that his victory

> Hangs on the ditty
> Of that committee,
> Where the great God
> Hath his abode.

God does not grant success to the "strong and great,"

> But to his elect, as we must believe;
> Therefore shall he obtain wealth and esteem,
> Who through faith doth put his trust in him.[28]

Pantagruel expresses himself here like his "architriclin" Alcofribas in the *Prognostication:* "If God do not help us, we shall

---

26. *Gargantua*, chs. 28, 32, 45.
27. *Pantagruel*, ch. 29.
28. Ibid., ch. 27.

have our hands and hearts full. But on the other side, if He be with us, nothing can hurt us ... *Si Deus pro nobis, quis contra nos?* If God be for us, who can be against us? In good faith *nemo, Domine,* nobody, an't like your worship; for He is as powerful as He is good." He is so good and so powerful that he never stops entering into life's course in order to sustain men, protect them, and preserve them. "He is wiser than we, and knows what is fit far better than we ourselves."[29] For his part, Gallet asks Picrochole, "Dost thou think that these atrocious abuses are hidden from the Eternal Spirit, and the supreme God? ... If thou do think, thou deceivest thyself; for all things shall come to pass, as in his incomprehensible judgment he hath appointed."[30]

Pomponazzi in his *De incantationibus* attacks prayer. He declares that it is incapable of touching an inflexible deity chained to the laws of *Fatum* like all beings. In Rabelais's novel there is nothing akin to this lofty sentiment. It was not only on solemn occasions but every day that Gargantua and Ponocrates "prayed ... unto God the Creator, in falling down before him, and strengthening their faith towards him, and glorifying him for his boundless bounty."[31] This was a custom "of the primitive Christians," *Book Four* tells us, in a passage that must have been written long before 1546, but which Rabelais had no hesitation in restating at that date. Prayer was "the laudable custom of the primitive Christians,"[32] laudable and beneficial, because the giants' God wanted to heed the faithful. He wanted to because he could.

2. The Omnipotence of God
Opposed to the Determinism of the Astrologers

Not just once but a score of times Rabelais's writings state that there is no law or system of laws that can hamper or restrict God's exercise of his supreme free will. And it is with absolute clarity that they deny that the stars, in particular, have any influence on the destiny of men.

The *Pantagruelian Prognostication* scornfully denounces

29. *Works,* ed. Nock and Wilson, II, 894, 900.
30. *Gargantua,* ch. 31.
31. *Gargantua,* ch. 23.
32. *Book Four,* ch. 1.

"the infinite abuses" arising from Louvain's makers of prognostications, who bemuse the world with false news. If the author
maintains with considerable heat that God is the sole and
unique ruler of the world it is because decent folk have no idea
that "neither Saturn nor Mars, nor Jupiter, nor any other
planet, nor the very angels, nor saints, nor men, nor devils . . .
have any virtue, efficacy, or influence whatsoever" on the things
of this world "unless God of His good pleasure gives it them.
As Avicenna says, second causes have not any influence or action whatsoever, if the first cause did not influence them." Let
us not try, he says elsewhere (the *Almanac of 1533*), to fathom
"the eternal registers," for "it is not lawful for mortal man" to
know them, "as is testified *Acts i.,* 'It is not for you to know the
times and moments which the Father hath put in His own
power.' And this rashness is threatened by His penalty by the
wise Solomon, *Prov. xxv,* 'Whoso prieth out His majesty, shall
be crushed thereby.' " There is the same argument in the *Almanac of 1535:* Predict what is going to happen? "Never as yet,
since the creation of Adam, has there been a man born who has
treated of it or delivered anything in which we ought to acquiesce or rest assured."[33]

This assertion is not a proclamation of ignorance. Rabelais is
careful to inform his readers that he knows as well as anybody
how to turn "over and over all the pantarchs of the heavens,
[calculate] the quadrates of the moon, [hook] out whatever all
the astrophiles, hypernephelists, anemophylaxes, uranopetes,
ombrophores" have thought, and, what is more, to confer "with
Empedocles upon the whole." He does not decline to "extract
from the writers in the art, Greeks, Arabs and Latins" what
their writings contain on the subject. But he only goes so far as
to make extracts: "This is what they say." Rabelais himself does
not say much. He has always protested that he does not wish
"anything in any way whatever to be concluded as to the future
by my prognostications; only that those who in their art have
recorded long observations of the stars, have determined in the
way which I describe." In the final analysis, what directs the
world is the will of God, which is entirely free, a supreme free
will that nothing can fetter. And so do not attempt to grasp the

33. *Works,* ed. Nock and Wilson, II, 893–894, 902, 903.

"invariable decree of God Almighty, who has created and ordered everything according to His holy pleasure."[34] This is the religious foundation of Gargantua's famous instruction to Pantagruel: "As for astronomy, study all the rules thereof. Let pass, nevertheless, the divining and judicial astrology, and the art of Lullius, as being nothing else but plain abuses and vanities."[35] It is also, to cite a personal document, that of the incredulity Rabelais professes when he sends to the bishop of Maillezais from Rome on December 30, 1535, a book of "prognostications" entitled *De eversione Europae* (*Of the Overturning of Europe*): "For my part," he declares, "I give no credit at all to it."[36] This is an attitude laden with a variety of consequences if it is true that at that time it was only through astrology and the theory of "celestial influences" that little by little the notion of natural determinism, so important both for science and philosophy, was introduced. The idea of the absolute omnipotence of the Godhead, without limits or reservations, is unquestionably what is most forcefully, and most frequently, expressed, not only by Rabelais's heroes, but, in the publications where he speaks for himself, by François Rabelais himself.

⋖ This idea is so strong and powerful in him that at times it inspires some rather remarkable reflections. We are not used to seeing in this apostle of human energy and untiring effort a quietist who leaves the care of regulating all human affairs to the goodness of God alone. I am thinking especially of the remarkable passage in *Pantagruel* where a theory of the non-participation of the civil power in matters of faith is clearly enunciated. Men should know they must give way before the omnipotence of God. They should stop coming to the aid of the Almighty in a display of zeal that is truly laughable and almost sacrilegious. A king must engage in combat in order to defend his subjects, "their wives and children, country and family." But to defend the faith? Never.

The faith is God's "own proper cause." In such business, Pantagruel declares as Loupgarou approaches him "with great fierceness, . . . thou, o Lord, wilt have no coadjutors, only a

34. Ibid., pp. 892–893, 904.
35. *Pantagruel*, ch. 8.
36. *Works*, ed. Nock and Wilson, II, 913.

catholic confession and service of thy word, and has forbidden us all arming and defence. For thou art the Almighty, who in thine own cause [which is the faith], and where thine own business is taken in hand, canst defend it far beyond all that we can conceive."[37] A fine protest, by the way, against the persecutive zeal of princes and clerics. It emerges from such a broad view of divine power, power truly absolute and limitless, that we are not surprised to see it lead to the natural consequence pointed out by Erasmus at the beginning of his *De libero arbitrio:* the denial of human free will ("Pugnat ex diametro Dei Omnipotentia cum nostro libero Arbitrio").[38] Indeed, here are some passages. "I do not say, like the cafards," declares Pantagruel in chapter 28 of the novel, *"Help thyself and God will help thee,* for it is the reverse: *Help thyself and God will break thy neck.* For I say to thee, Put all thy hope in God, and he shall not forsake thee."[39] These are remarkably powerful words. Help yourself and God will break your neck! They derive their power, without any question, from the conviction expressed by Grandgousier as he reflects on the situation of his enemy Picrochole. If Picrochole commits many evil deeds, it is because "the eternal God hath left him to the disposure of his own free will and sensual appetite,—which cannot choose but be wicked, if by divine grace it be not continually guided."[40]

Fortunately, Rabelais's God is as supremely good as he is powerful. He does not turn away in horror from sinful man, from man subject to the consequences of Adam's fault—at least, on condition that the sinner earn forgiveness through humility: "we are all of us trespassers, and therefore ought continually to beseech his divine majesty to blot our transgressions out of his memory." Thus are our prayers granted by divine help and grace. Never will God forsake "those that in him do put their trust and confidence." Never will he leave them to the devil's enterprises without any recourse, to the enterprises of "the calumniating spirit" of which Ulrich Gallet speaks, which "by false illusions and deceitful fantasies" attempts to lead men

37. *Pantagruel,* ch. 29.
38. "The omnipotence of God is in diametric opposition to our free will."
39. "Je ne te dys pas comme les caphars: *ayde-toi, Dieu te aydera,* car c'est au rebours: *ayde-toi, Dieu te rompra le col."* This passage appears in the editions published by Juste in 1534 and 1537 but not in later editions. [Translator's note.]
40. *Gargantua,* ch. 29.

astray. Grandgousier, too, fears the effects of "the wicked spirit." If Picrochole wrongs him so much, it can only be because of the evil one's machinations. And many times, in many circumstances, the old king would himself have undoubtedly repeated the classic distinction that the captain of the country bumpkins does not fail to make: "If thou be of God, speak, if thou be of the other spirit, avoid hence, and get thee going!"

No, "nothing is either sacred or holy to those who, having emancipated themselves from God and reason, do merely follow the perverse affections of their own depraved nature." But on the contrary if he is sustained by God and filled with his grace, and knows how to benefit from it, a man can await the hour of Judgment in peace and look forward to the verdict of a God who is "the just rewarder of all our undertakings." He will in the end know the bliss of a soul liberated from "this darksome prison" of the earthly body. "United with Jesus the Christ," the soul will find in its Creator's bosom "the fulness of all good, all knowledge and perfection . . . : *tunc satiabor, cum apparuerit gloria tua.*"

3. A Religion of the Word and of the Spirit

What is the first, and almost the only, duty of man toward a God who is so good? To read, meditate on, and practice the Gospel.

The Gospel—in the early works of Rabelais it is invoked a score of times, quoted, cited, praised, honored, glorified, always in a tone of passionate sincerity and enthusiastic gravity. "Happy is that man," cries Gargantua after having been read the riddle "which was found under the ground, as they were laying the foundation of the abbey" of the Thelemites, "happy is that man that shall not be scandalized, but shall always continue to the end, in aiming at that mark, which God by his dear Son hath set before us, without being distracted or diverted by his carnal affections and depraved nature." For "this life is transitory, but the Word of the Lord endureth for ever." Therefore the first and principal duty is every day to "apply thy mind to the study of the Holy Scriptures"; to get, if possible, the knowledge necessary to read "first, in Greek, the New Testament, with the Epistles of the Apostles; and then the Old Testament

in Hebrew"; to have read every morning "unto him some chapter of the Holy Scripture," not as gibberish mumbled without
comprehension but as a beautiful work of antiquity whose
meaning one wants to fathom.

This is not a benefit limited to literary men. All Christians
ought to participate in the bounty of the Word. Hence the obligation of the shepherds of peoples to see to the spread of the
truth, to support and encourage, not idle monks and ignorant
priests, but good preachers, "Evangelical doctors and schoolmasters," who explain the Sacred Books in sermons that are at
once colloquial and learned. The giant kings felt all the weight
of this obligation. They had no doubt read the impressive
"Epistle of Exhortation to All Christian Men and Women" that
Lefèvre d'Etaples put at the beginning of the second part of his
translation of the New Testament.[41] They, too, no doubt
thought that the children should read "their father's testament"
not once but on a regular basis, "in the chapters of Jesus Christ,
which are the churches where all the people, simple as well as
learned, should gather to hear and honor the holy word of
God." They no doubt wished to imitate in their kingdom of
Utopia "the intention of the good king, Very Christian in his
heart as well as his name . . . , that the word of God be purely
preached throughout his realm, to the glory of the God of
Mercy and Jesus Christ his son"!

We know that Pantagruel proclaims in similar language the
obligation of kings to have the Holy Gospel preached in all
countries "purely, simply, and entirely, so that the abuses of
a rabble of hypocrites and false prophets, who by human constitutions, and depraved inventions, have impoisoned all the
world," should be exterminated in true Christian lands. And
Master Alcofribas first echoes this proclamation of Pantagruel
in one of the four chapters on the seasons added to the 1532
text of the *Pantagruelian Prognostication* in the revised version
of 1534: he attacks those who have not not the slightest belief in
God but "persecute His holy and divine Word, as also those
that stand up for it." After that, in 1535 François Rabelais him-

41. *Les Choses contenues en ce present livre* ... (Paris: S. de Colines, 1523); cf. A.
L. Herminjard, ed., *Correspondance des Réformateurs dans les pays de langue
française*, 9 vols. (Geneva, 1866–1897; reprint, Nieuwkoop, 1965–1966), I, 168 (no.
79).

self, "doctor in medicine, and physician of the great hospital of
. . . Lyons," when he puts out an almanac in his own name,
states: "I say . . . that if the kings, princes and Christian com-
munities have in reverence the holy word of God, and order
themselves and their subjects in accordance with it, . . . we shall
see the face of the heavens, the vesture of the earth and the conduct of the people, joyful, glad, pleasant and kindly, more than
it has been for fifty years."[42] Let us recall that if the inscription
over the great gate of Theleme says,

> Here enter not vile bigots, hypocrites, . . .
> Elsewhere, not here, make sale of your deceits!

we also read—since "it is not now only . . . that people called to
the faith of the gospel, and convinced with the certainty of
evangelical truths, are persecuted"—these words of welcome:

> Here enter you, pure, honest, faithful, true,
> Expounders of the Scriptures old and new,
> Whose glosses do not blind our reason

and this conclusion:

> Come, settle here a charitable faith,
> Which neighborly affection nourisheth.
> And whose light chaseth all corrupters hence,
> Of the blest word, from the aforesaid sense!

4. The Faith and Its Ministers

A religion of the Word is poorly suited to a highly developed
outward form of worship. In Rabelais's writings, too, there is
hardly a question of any but inward worship. It is necessary to
revere God, to worship him, pray to him, and supplicate him,
glorifying him for his boundless bounty. It is necessary to give
"thanks unto him for the time that was past," recommending
oneself "to his divine clemency for the future." It is not forbidden to sing beautiful hymns in his praise. But "to serve, to love,

---

42. *Works*, ed. Nock and Wilson, II, 899–900, 904.

to fear God, and on him to cast all thy thoughts and all thy
hope, and, by faith formed in charity, to cleave unto him, so
that thou mayst never be separated from him by thy sins"—it
is to this that the duties of the true believer are strictly limited.

Away with the superstitions of the promoters of pilgrimages,
carriers of relics, and sellers of mortgages in the beyond. God
alone is enough for a Christian, and God has no need of coadjutors. This is all the more significant since Rabelais had been a
Franciscan, and we know what devotion the Franciscans always
gave to the Virgin. Not once is Mary spoken of in *Pantagruel,*
in *Gargantua,* or, for that matter, in *Book Three* and *Book
Four.* Mary's name appears only once or twice on the lips of
one of Rabelais's heroes. And which one? Panurge the calf, Panurge the whiner, dying of fright in the storm. God without the
Virgin, and without the saints. To be sure, "the sancts and holy
men of God" should be revered. But to ascribe to them the surprising power of healing or the distasteful power of making us
ill, to believe that Saint Margaret comforts pregnant women or
that Saint Sebastian let loose the plague on the universe, to
make a vow at the first sign of danger to Saint John d'Angly,
Saint Eutropius of Xaintes, Saint Mesmes of Chinon and "a
thousand other jolly little sancts and santrels," not to speak of
Saint Guodegrin, "who was martyred with cooked apples"—
these are stupid aberrations of hypocrites without any faith."[43]

"Sweer-to-go," the symbolic pilgrim, should put an end to
his ridiculous journeys and return home with his companions.
He should by his example make all those swagbellies and puff-
bags who traveled in flocks to Saint James of Compostela "in
the year 524" go back to their homes. Look to your families,
Grandgousier preaches to them, "labour every man in his vocation, instruct your children, and live as the good Apostle St.
Paul directeth you: in doing whereof, God, his angels and
sancts, will guard and protect you, and no evil or plague at any
time shall befal you." Do not buy any more indulgences, even
at the low price at which Master John Le Maire, become pope,
sells them in hell: "Get the pardons, rogues, get the pardons,

43. On Rabelais and the saints, see H. Folet, "Rabelais et les saints préposés aux
maladies," *Revue des Etudes Rabelaisiennes,* 4 (1906), 199–216; and Hugues Vaganay, "Les saints 'producteurs de maladies,'" *Revue des Etudes Rabelaisiennes,* 9
(1911), 331–332.

they are good and cheap!" Or at the even lower price that Panurge's cunning manages to pay for them in the churches of
Paris: he takes only a farthing's worth and "in those matters
very little contenteth me." It is not that the true doctrine of the
Church is evil. When Friar John slaughters the pillagers of the
abbey close after they have been duly absolved, he expresses it
correctly in an observation of sinister irony: "These men have
had confession and are penitent souls, they have got their absolution and gained the pardons: they go into paradise as straight
as a sickle!" But, contrary to Friar John, Master John Le Maire
knows that the majority of men think they gain pardons when
they buy them, not when they have repented; and he concludes
that pardons serve only to "dispense with you to be never good
for anything"!

So it is with a number of observances. Holy water is an endless source of jokes. In the year of the great drought when Pantagruel was born there was "work enough to do to save the holy
water in the churches." Thirsty believers ran to drink it at the
fonts, and it was necessary to pass an order, "taken by the
counsel of my Lords the Cardinals, and of our holy Father, that
none did dare to take above one lick."[44] But when Picrochole
sends out sixteen hundred[45] horsemen as scouts under the command of the Count Draw-forth, he does not let them leave till
they are all "thoroughly besprinkled with holy water" and are
wearing the sign of a star in their scarves, "to serve at all adventures in case they should happen to encounter with devils."[46]
This precaution proves to be as vain as saying a prayer before
battle "that will preserve a man from the violence of guns,
and all manner of fire-weapons and engines"; it does me no
good, Friar John states unambiguously, "because I do not believe it."

There is one last feature: in these passages the priest figures
as someone who is useless and lazy, who says masses and
prayers through his nose and mechanically mutters devotions.
He should give way to "Evangelical doctors and schoolmasters." Better yet, monks and nuns, that whole pernicious
race of "eaters of sins," should give way. The time is past when

44. *Pantagruel*, ch. 2.
45. Urquhart has "sixteen." [Translator's note.]
46. *Gargantua*, ch. 43.

a caste of Christians could retire from the world and offer itself as a living sacrifice to the Lord, thus assuring the salvation of its inferior brothers engaged in the grubby business of earning their daily bread. "Yea, but, said Grandgousier, they pray to God for us. Nothing less, answered Gargantua . . . They mumble out great store of legends and psalms, by them not at all understood: they say many pater-nosters, interlarded with Ave-Maries, without thinking upon, or apprehending, the meaning of what it is they say, which truly I call mocking of God, and not prayers." Disguising themselves like masqueraders to deceive the world, pretending to busy themselves with "nothing but contemplation and devotion in fastings, and maceration of their sensuality," in reality "Curios simulant, sed Bacchanalia vivunt!"[47] Gargantua expresses the true doctrine: "All true Christians, of all estates and conditions, in all places, and at all times, send up their prayers to God, and the Mediator prayeth and intercedeth for them, and God is gracious to them." Thus does every creature, standing before God his Creator, answer for his own faults directly. Salvation is an individual matter—a statement that sounds thoroughly modern.

5. The Objection of Sincerity

Thus ends the collection—undertaken with no other purpose than to collect everything and select nothing. Does the result by any chance seem impressive? If so, let us resist the urge to jump to tempting and easy conclusions based on a surface view. A personal doctrine cannot be reconstructed purely from appearances. Let us examine the manifold problems raised by the allusions in Rabelais.

First of all, what note do they sound? A Christian one. However much we may have wished not to interpret, we have had to stress this many times. Furthermore, if we had extended our inquiry our conclusions would have been reinforced. We would have observed how Christian the beautiful image of ideal royalty is that Rabelais delineates in the persons of Gargantua, Pantagruel, and their foil Picrochole.

47. "[They] affect ancestral peasant virtues as a front for their lechery." Juvenal, satire 2; trans. Peter Green, in Juvenal, *The Sixteen Satires* (Middlesex, 1967), p. 75. [Translator's note.]

It is not with arrogance that the giants proclaim themselves to be Christian. Their concern to act in conformity with the doctrine and spirit of Christianity is made clear on every occasion. When he takes up arms to protect his subjects, Grandgousier says, "Reason will have it so; for by their labor am I entertained, and with their sweat am I nourished, I, my children and my family." Reason: but let us make no mistake about the nature of this political "rationalism." Other passages offer guidance: "The time is not now as formerly, to conquer the kingdoms of our neighbour princes, and to build up our own greatness on the loss of our nearest," declares Grandgousier when he is attacked by Picrochole. He could have stopped there; he adds, "the loss of our nearest Christian brother." It is not a notion of some unspoken compact of human solidarity that the old king is expressing here but one of specifically Christian solidarity. Likewise Ulrich Gallet, his envoy, develops the theme of a Holy Alliance, a "sacred league," between Christian princes when he addresses in vain the churlish and troublesome king whose undertakings Grandgousier condemns in a word: "This imitation of the ancient Herculeses, Alexanders, Hannibals, Scipios, Caesars, and other such heroes, is quite contrary to the profession of the gospel of Christ." This is a refinement of the meaning of the quotation from Plato that Rabelais brings forth, following Erasmus and *The Praise of Folly:* "That those commonwealths are happy, whose rulers philosophise, and whose philosophers rule." When Rabelais's rulers philosophize, we should understand that it is primarily with the help of Saint Paul.

What objections are there? I can see three that it would be well to take care of before looking at the "giants' catechism" and assessing its meaning and importance. There is, first of all, the following: "You say these are Christian passages? But all Rabelais did was find them in the game bag of his memory, where they were left from his years as a monk. Many are simply references to religious things and imply no adherence to an active belief. As for the others, don't be naive. Don't you think Master Francis's true purpose was to let some extremely daring notions slip in under the cover of reassuring phrases?" Here, connected with the first objection, we have the second—that of sincerity.

6. Where Rabelais Declares Himself to Be a Christian

We are at the Lyon fair of November 1532. This is where, in all likelihood, *Pantagruel* made its appearance in the great world. Was it an anti-Christian work by the most unrelenting of atheists? But on November 30, 1532 (the same month of the same year), this enemy of Christ sent Erasmus the famous letter "to Salignac." We have seen that it contains an accusation of atheism directed by Rabelais against Scaliger. It contains something else even more curious: the expression Rabelais inscribed in his beautiful, elegant hand at the top of the famous letter: "S.P. a Jesu-Christo Servatore."

Can we say that Rabelais the anti-Christian was in any way constrained here to put himself under Christ's protection? His distinguished correspondent would not have been scandalized by the simple "S. P. D." that Rabelais—the same Rabelais— used in all his letters to the very Christian Budé: "Domino Gulielmo Budae, S. P. D.," used in the letter of March 4, 1521.[48] And if the perpetual argument (which is so convenient) is advanced that Rabelais was being prudent, I reply, "Of what use to Rabelais would have been the assertion of a belief in Jesus Christ the Savior in a letter that was not meant to be made public and that actually took its place in Erasmus's correspondence only much later and under a false name, and what protection would it have given him?"

As for passages that were written to be printed and propagated among men, passages that can always be attacked for hypocritical prudence—there is no lack of these that could be cited. Let us open to the preface of the *Pantagruelian Prognostication,* which appeared in January 1533: "To the courteous reader, greetings and peace in Jesus the Christ." Except for the name of Jesus, it is the closing phrase of Grandgousier's letter to Gargantua: "the peace of Christ, our Redeemer be with thee." Stapfer claimed that the use of "Christ" without the definite article here indicates Rabelais's Protestant tendencies.[49] It

---

48. Facsimile in Abel Lefranc, "Les Autographes de Rabelais," *Revue des Etudes Rabelaisiennes,* 3 (1905), between pp. 348 and 349. ["S. P. D." (*salutem plurimam dicit*) was the salutation used by pagan writers in ancient Rome.—Translator.]

49. Paul Stapfer, *Rabelais, sa personne, son génie, son oeuvre* (Paris, 1889), p. 380. On this subject, cf. Jean Plattard, "Notes pour le Commentaire, XII," *Revue des Etudes Rabelaisiennes,* 10 (1912), 255-257.

would do to be less positive. But at the same time it should be noted that, contrary to what has been said, the phrase "the peace of Christ be with thee," in Latin or in French, was in current use among the Evangelicals. "Gratia et Pax Christi Jesu," wrote François Lambert d'Avignon to the elector of Saxony in 1523, following the example of Luther when, in the same year, he greeted Charles of Savoy with these words: "Gratia et pax in Christo Jesu Domino nostro." In 1526 (December 7) Roussel wrote to Farel, "Gratia et pax Christi tecum." In the same month, also writing to Farel, Toussain used similar words: "Gratia et pax Domini nostri Jesu Christi sit cum omnibus vobis." And as for the reference to the Redeemer made by Grandgousier, I find it in Farel on November 18, 1532, considerably expanded, moreover: "The Grace, peace, and mercy of God our merciful Father, by the sole Savior and Redeemer Jesus!"[50]

All these passages are indications of an atmosphere. No less so are the passages we find in the remnants that have been preserved of another of Rabelais's almanacs. Like the almanac of 1535, it has been lost. It appeared in Lyon, "calculated on the meridian of the noble city" for the year 1533 and "composed by me, Francis Rabelais, doctor in medicine and professor in astrology." A rather short fragment, also preserved by Antoine Le Roi, is to be found in all the editions of Rabelais's works. It is a tissue of sacred passages in French, all perfectly orthodox. A single example will give the flavor: "We ought to humble ourselves and entreat [the eternal King], even as Jesus Christ our Lord hath taught us, that not what we wish and ask for should be done, but that which pleases Him and which He hath determined before the heavens were formed, only that in everything and everywhere His glorious Name should be hallowed."[51] Here, from the pen of this great naysayer, are quite a number of quite fervent invocations of Christ.

I can hear an objection: "They were written for sale, and for the sake of security." Can anyone really show us what might have compelled, not Alcofribas, but Dr. Rabelais to fill an almanac he was preparing for 1533 full of Christian statements?

---

50. For these passages, see Herminjard, I, 112, 152, 458, 464; II, 459.
51. *Works*, ed. Nock and Wilson, II, 902.

Rather than biblical quotations and "beautiful Gospel texts in French," wouldn't resounding, unrestrained buffoonery have served the purpose just as well? If not better, precisely with regard to Rabelais's personal security?

Is it necessary, finally, to mention the quite remarkable wording of the handwritten ex libris that Rabelais put on the first page of his Plato—the 1513 Aldine edition, which was the first edition of the complete Greek text of the philosopher, a large folio in two parts, now preserved in Montpellier? Over the title we read, in Rabelais's hand: "Francisci Rabelesi, medici spoudaiotatou, kai tōn autou philōn christianōn."[52] Abel Lefranc dates this inscription from the years in the monastery—around 1520, he says, when Rabelais was being harassed at Fontenay along with Pierre Amy. Christianōn would have been at once a profession and a precaution. I can see many objections to this theory—first of all, if Rabelais had wanted to stop the investigations with a slightly ingenuous declaration of Christianity on the very first page of his Plato, he would undoubtedly have made an effort to have his enemies, who did not study for fear of the mumps (especially not Greek, the language of the devil), understand him. "Graecum est, non legitur." So he would have written in Latin: "et amicorum ejus Christianorum."

Besides, if the inscription dates from his years as a monk, one word in it is rather startling: medicus. Not that there is any incompatibility between the status of Franciscan and that of medical student. But in fact when Rabelais was in the monastery at Fontenay he was not François Rabelais, physician. He was Brother Francis. I am well aware that the words "Francisci Rabelaesi Chinōnos men to genos, tēn haerēsin de Phrankiskanou Iatrou"[53] are supposed to have been found on a Greek edition of the New Testament. The wording is peculiar. Abel Lefranc, who has catalogued all of Rabelais's handwritten ex libris, has not seen this one.[54] Let us prudently ignore it. If anyone thinks Rabelais had a very early vocation for medicine, let me direct

---

52. "Property of François Rabelais, most excellent physician, and his Christian friends." Facsimile in *Bulletin du Bibliophile* (1901), p. 105, and in *Revue des Etudes Rabelaisiennes*, 1 (1903), 28.

53. "Property of François Rabelais, of Chinon by birth, a Franciscan physician by vocation."

54. See Lefranc, "Les Autographes de Rabelais."

ἌΠΑΝΤΑ ΤΑ᾽ ΤΟῦ ΠΛΆΤΩΝΟΣ.

OMNIA PLATONIS OPERA.

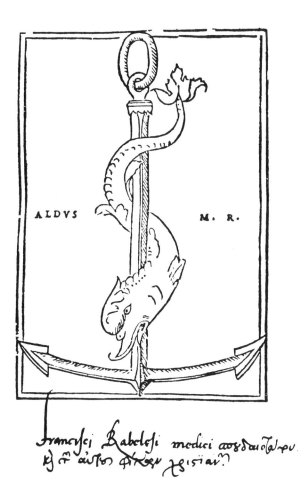

ALDVS   M. R.

The title page of Rabelais's copy of Plato's works, with his ex
libris in a combination of Latin and Greek. The dolphin and
anchor formed the most famous of all printers' marks, that of
Aldus Manutius of Venice.

his attention to the *Reply* that Jean Bouchet wrote to Rabelais at the time when, having changed from a Franciscan to a Benedictine, he was acting as secretary to Geoffroy d'Estissac. The bishop of Maillezais,

> Prélat dévot de bonne conscience
> Et fort sçavant en divine science,
> En canonique, & en humanité,

> A pious prelate, good in heart and soul,
> Learned in holy science, wisdom's goal,
> In canon law and all humanities,

because of his tastes, was seeking out men learned

> En grec, latin et françois, bien estrez
> A deviser d'histoire ou théologie.

> In languages—in Latin, French, and Greek,
> Expert in history and equipped to speak
> On matters theological.

These were the very talents Rabelais had, so Bouchet informs us:

> Dont tu es l'un; car en toute clergie
> Tu es expert. A ce moyen te print
> Pour le servir, dont très grand heur te vint.
> Tu ne pouvais trouver meilleur service
> Pour te pourvoir bien tost de bénefice.[55]

> Of whom you're one; because all scholarship
> You've mastered well. The moment summoned you
> To seize the chance to render service due
> This man. You'll find no better place to serve
> And soon you'll hold the living you deserve.

Greek, Latin, French, history, theology—not a word in the epistle about Rabelais's medical knowledge. If Rabelais was al-

---

55. *Les Oeuvres*, ed. Charles Marty-Laveaux, 6 vols. (Paris, 1868–1903), III, 304–305. There are no allusions to Rabelais's medical studies in Budé's letters either.

ready so specialized in medicine at this period that he could call himself "Rabelais, physician" and ignore every other accomplishment, isn't this silence of Bouchet really astonishing?

◄§ There is another thing. Rabelais had children. There were two at first, for whom evidence has recently been found.[56] Then there was a third, of whom we have known for a long time.[57] A friend of Rabelais, the Toulouse lawyer-poet Jean de Boysonné, left us several pieces of Latin verse on this Rabelais nativity; they remained in manuscript for a long time and are, unfortunately, not dated.[58] The child was born in Lyon, we do not know when. He saw "Roman pontiffs" crowded around his cradle. He died at the age of two. That is all. But what name did Rabelais give his son? Theodule. It was not a common name. It was a deliberately chosen one, quite suitable for the child of a deist who wanted to avoid all saints' names. To be sure—or for the child of an evangelist, no less animated by the same wish. But isn't it interesting that Jean de Boysonné, in one of the poems in his "Memorial to Theodule," addresses him who deserted life so young: "Why leave life?" And the child replies, "It is not from hatred of life, Boysonné. I die to escape the risk of dying forever. To live with Christ—that, Boysonné, is the only life to be desired for virtuous men." But, you say, this has only to do with the poet, Boysonné himself. Yes. Only would he have spoken this way about the son of a non-Christian? "I die to escape the risk of dying forever" is a peculiar statement to ascribe to the son of a confirmed materialist.[59]

In any case, let Rabelais have the word again. Not once but a dozen, nay, a score of times in *Gargantua* and *Pantagruel* the emancipated, the anti-Christian Rabelais speaks of the Gospel and of good Evangelical preachers in terms that are irreproach-

56. J. Lesellier, "Deux Enfants naturels de Rabelais légitimés par le pape Paul III," *Humanisme et Renaissance*, 5 (1938), 549–570.

57. On this child, see Arthur Heulhard, *Rabelais, ses voyages en Italie, son exil à Metz* (Paris, 1891), p. 107 ff.

58. There is an analysis of these poems (seven in number) in *Les Poésies latines de Jean de Boyssoné*, ed. Henri Jacoubet (Toulouse, 1931), nos. 29, 82, 83, 84, 85, 86, 167.

59. We should note that on at least one occasion Rabelais called himself Theodore. In chapter 23 of *Gargantua* Ponocrates requests "a learned physician of that time, called Master Theodorus," to bring Gargantua into a better course. In Juste's Lyon edition of before 1535 (the earliest one known) "Seraphin Calobarsy" appears instead of "Théodore." Seraphin Calobarsy is an anagram of Phrançois Rabelays. Hence Calobarsy = Rabelais = Theodore.

able and, what is more, emotional and colored with an obvious enthusiasm. Need I recall some of these passages, which are so well known, all of them marked by intentional gravity? There is Pantagruel's vow (ch. 29), retained by Rabelais without any change edition after edition: "I will cause thy holy gospel to be purely, simply, and entirely preached, so that the abuses of a rabble of hypocrites and false prophets, who by human constitutions, and depraved inventions, have impoisoned all the world, shall be quite exterminated from about me!" Further on, there is Rabelais speaking for himself, complaining about the spiritual state of the Parisians. A juggler, a mule, a blind fiddler draw more people to crossroads in the big city than a good Evangelical preacher—one of those preachers who, unlike the lazy monks, instruct the world in the whole of Christian truth. We know that on rainy days Gargantua went to hear their salutary sermons. Thanks to them, he plumbed the meaning of those pages of Holy Scripture that every morning "whilst they were in rubbing of him" young Anagnostes read to him with fit pronunciation.[60]

We should point out that such statements were not without danger. They placed a man among the innovaters. They marked him out for the thunderbolts of Parlements, who were little suspected of harboring any fondness for "Luthery." *Pantagruel* came out in 1532. But it was precisely in June of 1532 that Jean de Caturce was burned alive for heresy in Toulouse. To tell the truth, I am unable to understand Abel Lefranc's Rabelais and his contradictions. For a man who was so discreet to commit such indiscretions! He was an implacable enemy of Christianity, yet he exposed himself to serious difficulties for the pleasure of taking up the cudgel for a Gospel he made fun of. Unless he is supposed to have had the mildly paradoxical idea that reading the Gospel in French would serve as an antidote to the poison of Christianity!

I am aware of what Henri Estienne suggested: this evil man wished to use Christian statements calculated to mislead the Evangelicals in order to attract them and, once they took the bait, they would read him without suspicion and then fall victim to his poison. As Machiavellianism goes, this is indeed Ma-

---

60. *Gargantua*, chs. 17, 40, 23, 24.

chiavellian. But the slightest grain of proof would be more to
the point. Moreover, forget the holy water, the holy handker-
chief at Chamberry that burned so well they could not get one
thread of it saved, Saint Eutropius who causes dropsy, Saint
Margaret who does not comfort pregnant women, and finally
the Sorbonne and the Sorbonists. But, once again, what about
those deeply felt passages on the Gospel?

If I had selected from them I might perhaps grant the first
objection. I did not select. The passages I gathered, extending
over three years of literary activity, display a remarkable quality of consistency, coherence, and unity. No, it has nothing to
do with memories brought together by chance. If that were the
case, Rabelais would have kept to strictly orthodox assumptions.
He would not have ridiculed pilgrims, nor would he have
passed over the Virgin Mary in silence. It is a matter of a system, a religion. We find its elements, everywhere the same, in
both *Pantagruel* and *Gargantua,* in the almanacs and the *Prognostication.* In one place and another, it is all of a piece. It
makes the "S. P. a Jesu-Christo Servatore" in the letter to
Erasmus perfectly intelligible, as well as the "greetings and
peace in Jesus the Christ" of the *Pantagruelian Prognostication,* the "peace of Christ our Redeemer" of Grandgousier's letter to Gargantua, the beautiful invocation of "Jesus Christ our
Lord" in the *Almanac of 1533,* and the Christian ex libris in
the 1513 Plato.

What about the second objection?

Rabelais, we are told, was a rationalist, a freethinker, who as
such clearly wished to combat the dangerous influence on the
minds of unlettered men (he wrote in French, don't forget) of a
religion that for centuries had flowed back out of the churches
and monasteries, penetrating and saturating minds, and by constant use slipping into men's every act and thought. And the
means he contrived was to pile up perfectly Christian pro-
nouncements in the most conspicuous places in his books. The
rule he taught was to follow the Gospel, preach the Gospel, and
cling to the Gospel. And when he compiled almanacs for popular use, the wonderful means he discovered for turning the
reader away from Christianity was to fill the pages full of Gospel quotations in French! It was a strange procedure for a cow-
ard. For by following it Rabelais gratuitously exposed himself

to trouble. He placed himself among the supporters of an innovative and suspect Christianity. Let us acknowledge that if the man who quoted Psalm 5 at the beginning of the *Pantagruelian Prognostication* ("Thou shalt destroy them that speak leasing") was lying; if the man who proclaimed, "it is a heinous, foul, and crying sin to tell a damned wilful lie, thereby to deceive the poor gaping world," was lying; if, when he spoke of Scripture with such reverence and ardor, he was lying—to invoke the dangers of the time and the venal cowardice that proceeds from a need that recognizes no moral law would not suffice to make us admire Rabelais for prodigious skill at deception.[61] We would have to say, without admiration—contrary to the custom of our contemporaries, who are always overjoyed to point out that the "rationalists" of the past were all liars and cowards—we would have to say, not without contempt, "He was an arrant knave." But we would have to add, "and an arrogant fool." For he missed the target.

7. If the Giants Were Bluffing, What Was Behind It?

There remains the third objection, the most important one. To tell the truth, I have not found it stated anywhere. But anyone who knows what the conditions of philosophical speculation were like at the beginning of the sixteenth century finds himself immediately impelled to state it. Aren't Rabelais's heroes presenting us with the antidote and the poison side by side? "Here, my clever readers, is the Christian doctrine. I even give it to you in refined form, free of what to many seems like a series of abuses. Alongside it is critical rationalism, the doctrine of the liberated. Here we have truth according to revelation, there the truth based on reason. The author does not intervene. It is up to you to determine that there is an obvious incompatibility." A skillful tactic. But I do not see anything like it in his writings.

Moreover, wouldn't this Rabelais have been connected with

---

61. There are other passages in Rabelais on lying—in the prologue to *Pantagruel*, for example, or *Gargantua*, ch. 6—but it is possible to discount them as claptrap. At any rate he spoke in his own voice on lying in quite a modern tone. On Luther's attitude, which was different, there has, as is known, been a controversy among Heinrich Denifle, Hartmann Grisar, and A. V. Müller.

some known doctrine? Was he, as Postel said of Pomponazzi (quite wrongly), a *philosophicus Lucreticus?* To say that Rabelais was called Lucian again and again but never Lucretius would be a worthless argument. At any rate, it turns out that, unless we are mistaken, not one reference to Lucretius is found in all of Rabelais's output. Jean Plattard does not mention him in his catalogue of sources. And Lucretius denied miracles in the name of natural determinism, but Rabelais's determinism seems to be something rather looser. He denied Providence as a pessimist, but Rabelais was an optimist. He denied the creation while relying on atomism; there is no question of atomism in Rabelais. Finally, he taught that religion, the child of men, engendered by ignorance and fear, was exploited by a caste of scoundrels—can anything like this be seen in Rabelais's writings? Does the God of whom they speak resemble in any way the gods of Epicurus and Lucretius, shown by the Latin poet as indifferent to a universe existing from all eternity and as leading a life in an inaccessible abode untouched by the prayers as well as the passions of men? Was Rabelais an emulator of Lucretius? If so, what becomes of all that has been affirmed about the Platonism of Pantagruel's creator? "We are not sufficiently certain," wrote Lefranc in 1901, "to what extent *Gargantua* and *Pantagruel* are imbued with Platonism." But the fact is that it is not among the Platonizers or Neoplatonizers of the Renaissance that one looks for enemies of Christ. When their doctrine was not weighed down with too heavy a load of occultist fancies and chimeras it easily joined with orthodoxy. In any case, a choice has to be made: Lucretius or Plato. For the time being, I'll say Plato.

Well, what of Rabelais as a Paduan—after all, there *was* a Padua, wasn't there? This is no longer a simple question, and we have already indicated as we have gone along that there are some problems about accepting this epithet. Yet it really is necessary that this Rabelais who was an implacable anti-Christian should have based his anti-Christianism on a system of ideas. In the absence of Lucretian Epicureanism, I can see two that suggest themselves: Averroism and Alexandrism. Again we have to make a choice before going on, and we have to stop talking of Plato. What would a Platonist be doing in the midst of those Paduan Scholastics? But how plausible is an Averroist Rabelais? Averroës's God was a commentary on Aristotle, and it raised no end of difficulties for a belief in the creation *ex nihilo* and the remunerative justice of the deity acknowledged and proclaimed by Rabelais. Averroës's God, not having created the universe, which is without beginning or end, does not even have knowledge of this universe, nor does he bestow any thought on it or, a fortiori, his Providence. Could this God of Averroës, then, be the God of Pantagruel or the God of Gargantua? And as for Alexander, and Pomponazzi his disciple, where are the texts and the proofs, or other evidence in the absence of texts? What about occultism? I understand that Master Francis, man of learning and distinguished physician, knew what he needed to know. He was therefore quite capable of casting a horoscope. If it was a matter of accommodating powerful patrons, he did it. But he believed in it as much as Friar John did in the prayer against gunfire. And he repeated over and over with as much clarity as Henry Cornelius Agrippa in his *De incertitudine* that to attribute to the stars, without any reverence for the divine Majesty, a power that belongs to Him alone, and to place the liberty of men in thrall to the stars, were acts of impiety. And Pico della Mirandola had long since provided everyone with the demonstration of this.

Well, then, where can we look in that period for the adversaries—at least the potential ones—of Christianity if not in the world of the occultists, whose doctrines Rabelais's good sense was unable to follow to their conclusions? We do not have to demonstrate this. It has been done, in particular by Léon Blanchet in his *Campanella*.[62]

But Agrippa had already seen it and said that judicial astrology "removes the faith of religion, destroying miracles, removing providence, and teaching that all things are dependent on the power and virtue of the stars and come about through the fatal and inevitable necessity of their constellations." What is more, "it favors vices, inasmuch as it excuses them as having descended to us from the heavens."[63]

So much for generalities. We do not have to go into detail.

---

62. Paris, 1920.

63. Henry Cornelius Agrippa, *De incertitudine et vanitate scientiarum*, ch. 31. [Febvre quotes from the French translation by Louis Turquet de Mayerne (first published in 1582).—Translator.]

Around 1530 there were a certain number of questions the answers to which were of passionate interest to contemporaries. They were not only debated in the schools before the chairs of celebrated doctors. Good burghers often discussed them after a sermon or in free talk over a drink. Maillard, Menot, and the other preachers frequently testify to this. We have already seen what these problems were. And we have always had to conclude, rightly or wrongly, that if there were some audacious souls who proposed clearly anti-Christian answers to these burning questions, Rabelais in his early writings was far from associating himself with such boldness. As far as the problem of creation went, he never spoke of anything but creation *ex nihilo*, and in a thoroughly orthodox manner. As far as the problem of Providence went, it was the same thing. As for miracles, Panurge laughed, and his laughter was without significance. As for the whole complex of problems raised by the study of the relationship of the divine will with the human will—freedom or necessity, predestination and free will, the origin of evil and the reason for its existence—Olivier Maillard at one point describes people of his time getting hold of some doctors and eagerly questioning them on these important difficulties. "What about Judas? Did the Lord know he was going to betray him? If so, Judas wasn't free. Was he responsible then?" On all these contested points Rabelais either kept quiet or, if he spoke, it was as a Christian.

No, there really are no grounds for setting up in opposition to the giants' religion, which is Christian, a Rabelaisian philosophy that cannot be reconciled with that religion. There is no Gargantuan or Pantagruelian, not to mention Panurgic, metaphysics that categorically denies, without actually saying so but with indisputable clarity, the assertions of a catechism that may be missing some assertions but is strictly orthodox in its positive statements. It is a broad Christian orthodoxy, if not a strictly Tridentine one. To use again the words we used before: no, it does not appear that from 1532 to 1535 Rabelais left the choice to the reader and placed side by side in his writings the poison and the antidote.

◄§ And here we are again, confronting these passages, the collection of religious passages we have taken from Rabelais's early writings and which, as we have seen, form a very coherent whole. Christian texts they are, to be sure, but what sort of Christianity is it? Do they derive from a traditional and conservative outlook? It is impossible to claim that. Should we see in them proof of an adherence to the Reformation that is more or less emphatic and explicit? Or would it be well to look elsewhere?

These are tricky questions, as are all questions of this type. There is nothing harder to resolve than problems of sources and influences when dealing with a religious doctrine, especially in that troubled period. Even when we are faced with a theology fully expounded by a theologian or with a complete doctrine interpreted in a lucid and ample manner by a doctor anxious to conceal none of his personal ideas—even then there are so many uncertainties. Just think, for example, of the huge library of contradictory writings we have on the sources of Luther's thought. But when it is someone like Rabelais and a matter of sentences that are scattered through a bawdy novel that we have to look for among humorous and ribald remarks . . . Let us not get discouraged, and let us begin by locating the giants' religion in relation to the great religions of the time that witnessed its birth.

7. Rabelais, the Reformation, and Luther

HERE IS, as we know, a standard way to resolve the question we have just raised. A number of critics have been in agreement in calling the giants' theology "Reformed."

A number of them—not all. If there are radicals, there are also the moderates. For the latter, Rabelais was not, properly speaking, Reformed. He followed the early campaigns of the evangelists and Reformers with sympathy. He joined his efforts to theirs within limits that everyone says were more or less broad. Weighing his words in his introduction to *Gargantua* in 1912, Abel Lefranc noted that "without entirely adhering to the new religious doctrines, Rabelais sought in this period to manifest toward them an attentive and sincere sympathy that is quite well accounted for by the intellectual preoccupations he was living in the midst of." As for Jean Plattard, he noted that "in his tendencies Rabelais at this date was close to the Reformers. On the Sorbonne, indulgences, the worship of the saints, and observances he was in agreement with the early French Reformers, whose aspirations had been expressed by Lefèvre d'Etaples and whose program had been formulated by him."[1] Let us content ourselves with these two quotations. The opinions are in nearly total agreement.

There are the radicals, however. For them sympathy and tendencies are words that are too vague. Actually, for a time Rabe-

1. "L'Ecriture Sainte et la littérature scripturaire dans l'oeuvre de Rabelais," *Revue des Etudes Rabelaisiennes*, 8 (1910), 300–301.

lais deserved the appellation Reformed. He ought to be listed
under the letter *R* in the second edition of *La France Protestante.* Let us listen to one theologian who goes to battle in some
disarray, but whose conviction is unburdened by either maybes
or probablys. What, he asks, were Rabelais's religious ideas?
"Those of the early French Reformation. They can be summed
up as follows: A Christian should not be ruled by anything but
the teachings of the Gospel; the power of the popes is an excessive and usurped power; monastic life is against nature and
dangerous from the social point of view; the worship of the
saints is in contradiction to the Gospel, and pilgrimages are
nothing but odious and useless journeys; the worship of God
should be a totally internal and personal one, consisting of veneration and prayer; we should put all our trust in the Everlasting and in him alone. Here in a few phrases is what emerges
from his work."[2] And after this enumeration, which is blithely
lacking in rigor, he concludes: "Rabelais was a heretic, he had
lived under the shadow of the stake. But if he deserved to be
burned, 'it was not for his many merry blasphemies [this was
Stapfer writing earlier],[3] which were authorized by the tradition of the Middle Ages and which the profound immorality of
the Catholic Church had never been offended by; it was for
having said that the pure Gospel is superior to all human books
and commentaries, or having had a fondness for quoting Saint
Paul—Saint Paul, the great apostle of the Reformation, the
founder of Protestantism before Luther.' "

Let us forget "the profound immorality of the Catholic
Church," that close relative of its antagonist, the well-known
amorality of Luther's teaching. Let us lay "Saint Paul, the founder of Protestantism" to rest, forever we hope, in Controversy's
catacombs. Stapfer suggests the use of two specific criteria. One
is a poor choice. To quote Saint Paul, to rely on Saint Paul, to
be inspired by Saint Paul—this did not mean to be Reformed,
whatever may have been the predilection of the Reformed for
the apostle. Many Catholics who remained Catholics formed
their religious thought on his writings. Indeed, it is not difficult
to derive two or more different systems from the Pauline texts

2. Louis Talant, *Rabelais et la Réforme* (Cahors, 1902), pp. 100–101.
3. Paul Stapfer, *Rabelais, sa personne, son génie, son oeuvre* (Paris, 1889), p. 329.

when they are interpreted with ingenuity—which is something true theologians never lack. The fact nonetheless remains that Stapfer has pointed out the right way. Let us follow his steps without adopting his prejudices.

1. In the Years Between 1532 and 1535, What Did Being "Reformed" Mean?

We need criteria. But how do we choose them? For *Pantagruel*, the year is 1532; for *Gargantua*, 1535. What, then, was someone who was Reformed in 1532, and again in 1535? It all depends on the country.

At that date a certain number of rulers in Europe—collective rulers (city magistrates, cantonal assemblies) or individual ones (kings, princes, lords)—had already broken more or less completely with the Roman Church and had established Reformed national churches in the territories under their rule. There is no doubt that there were people in those states who were "Reformed": subjects who accepted the decisions of their sovereign in matters of faith and had in effect been separated from Rome together with him. But they were still not very numerous.

Perhaps the situation in this regard was clearest in Switzerland, as we call it today. From 1529—very early—it could be said that the confederated cantons formed two groups. Zurich, Bern, Basel, and Saint Gall had replaced the mass with preaching. There was still much left for the innovators to do, especially in French-speaking Switzerland, the dependency of Bern, before the religious map of the country could be drawn in any kind of definitive fashion. And neither Catholics nor Protestants gave up their efforts to make their faith prevail, by violent means if necessary. On October 11, 1531, Zwingli's bloody body lying on the field of battle at Kappel was dismembered and burned by the Catholics.

What of Germany? The situation was uncertain for a long time, since the Protestant princes were obliged to be cautious. In the aftermath of Pavia and the sack of Rome the emperor was so powerful! It was only in 1527, at the Diet of Speyer, that the princes obtained a kind of provisional freedom to organize the churches in their states according to their ideas and without having to fear endless conflicts with the Reichskammergericht, which up to then had kept everything in confusion. What of England? It was in 1532, the year of *Pantagruel,* that Henry VIII began to put pressure on the decisions of the English clergy; but no one yet knew what this prince, at once anti-Roman and anti-Lutheran, wanted in matters of faith or where he would stop. The Act of Supremacy did not come until 1534; and *Gargantua* appeared, after *Pantagruel,* at the time when Thomas More was decapitated and when the closing of the English monasteries was beginning under the vigorous direction of Thomas Cromwell.

Doctrines were affected by these uncertainties. Rare were the states where doctrines were rigorously defined by official theologians and entered into confessions of faith that were circulated in great quantities—or, I might add, accepted without reservation or dissent by nearly all the faithful. In Germany, in the Electoral Duchy of Saxony, where the direct influence of Luther operated with most force, it was not until 1528 that, in the light of the first results of church visitations, a significant effort was made to bring some order into observances and doctrines. In May of 1529 Luther produced in quick succession his Large and Small Catechisms. But for years (especially after 1525 and 1526) the controversy over Communion was bitterly carried on among Luther, Zwingli, Oecolampadius, and others. Even in states where the rulers had been won over to the Reformation there was a prodigious variety of opinions, there were passionate rivalries between opposing schools, and there was a tremendous sprouting of sects. And among the docile who bent without resistance to their master's will there was a deep attachment, conscious or otherwise, to old ideas and observances.

Everyone was waiting. For what? No one knew exactly. At bottom, many thought that everything would work out. Everywhere people believed in the Council—in Germany perhaps more than anywhere. It can be seen in the manifestations of sympathy that, especially from November 1534 on, greeted Paul III's statements about the next meeting of the parliament of Christendom. Even more, it can be seen in the efforts of princes who were hostile to each other on political grounds to become completely reconciled, whether they were followers of the Schmalkaldic League, of Henry VIII, or of King Francis. Theologians quarreling with each other; princes following now one of them, now another, in the space of a few months; ordinary believers deeply troubled, professing practically all opinions without agreeing on any one of them; half-savage rural masses given over to superstition—these were the disparate elements in a confused situation.

◄§ What of France? There was extreme uncertainty about the intentions of the king. He had not broken with Rome, but he had an understanding with the Lutheran princes: it was a perpetual seesaw. One day he saved Berquin by having the archers of his guard snatch him from the Parlement's clutches. Another day, taper in hand, he took part in the penitential processions of June 1528. He let Berquin, whom he had first saved, die (April 17, 1529), then at the beginning of 1530 he established the *lecteurs royaux*, and in April 1531 he invited Zwingli to present him with a confession of faith. Yet in October 1533 he went to Marseilles, met with Pope Clement, and married the Dauphin to a Medici. But at the end of November 1533, in Avignon, he was considering a project for an alliance with the Lutherans; in January 1534 he negotiated with the Landgrave. The Affair of the Placards (October 18, 1534), which in all probability erupted as *Gargantua* was being put on sale, was needed before the king was driven to the worst extremes—directed against the Lutherans, no doubt, but also against letters themselves, against the printing business, which an edict was supposed to abolish, against humanism and classical languages. What is more, it was not the last about-face of this monarch who was so prolific of whims.

Yes, there was general uncertainty about his intentions. Even more, however, there was a deep uncertainty among the French about doctrines. There was no Martin Luther in France. In no respect did an old man like Lefèvre play the same role as that Augustinian monk, energetic, aggressive, full of plebeian vitality. Of those who were called Lutherans then, how many really embraced Luther's doctrines and were ready to subscribe to the catechisms of 1529? There were many serious discrepancies in their ideas, resulting from a combination of their temperament and experience, as well as from what they read and how their minds responded first to one, then another, of the quarreling doctors in the neighboring countries: Luther, Melanchthon, Bucer, Zwingli, Oecolampadius. Thus there was in France, more than in Germany or Switzerland, a prodigious variety of individual doctrines, not very precise and, since they were not put into practice, under no obligation to adapt themselves to reality. Besides, rare indeed were the doctrines that proclaimed themselves schismatic. Schism was a terrible thing—and equivocation was so tempting!

The Council had not yet spoken. And while it remained silent, who dared to say that the true representatives of true religion were the doctors of the Sorbonne rather than the preachers of the Louvre?

No, to define a person who was "Reformed" in France between 1530 and 1535 is truly not an easy task.

2. Creeds and Criteria: The Scriptures

Henri Hauser, a historian fully aware of these difficulties, has proposed a method. There is no doubt, he tells us, that we must keep readers from believing there existed in France between 1520 and 1530 a single coherent system, linked to "Reformed ideas," that could have been adopted as a creed by all who were called "Evangelicals." The essential fact is that some Evangelicals took certain positions which were rejected by others as too advanced. It is quite evident that included in these very positions were a few, a small number, that preordained their adherents to become true Protestants sooner or later. These were the ones that counted, more than those secondary though conspicuous articles that appeared and reappeared in the writings of the Sorbonne like stock characters: indulgences, pilgrimages, saints.

On the other hand, no matter how inclined one is to be an autonomist on the question of the relations between the French Reformation and foreign Reformations, in particular the German Reformation, the problem in 1530 was no longer so simple. There existed at least one coherent, integrated Reform doctrine that was professed by a body of ministers, who were beginning to form a solid organization, and that was expounded in formal catechisms: the energetic doctrine of Luther. Keeping these observations in mind, if we join Hauser in seeking to determine which of the articles in the various Evangelical professions of faith qualify as irrecusable criteria, we find there are two: the Scriptures are the sole source of religion, and man is justified by faith alone. Now let us go back to Rabelais's writings.

◄§ Are the Scriptures the sole source of religion, the sole standard of belief and conduct? In Rabelais's early works the beneficence and efficacy of the Word are celebrated a score of times. What is more, the sacred texts are quoted in profusion, and frequently in French.

Of course, it is not expressly stated that a Christian must reject everything that is not explicitly prescribed in the Sacred Books. But it is specified that the Gospel will be preached purely, simply, and entirely, purged of all additions—notably the "human constitutions and depraved inventions" that the "hypocrites" (*papelars*, that is, adherents of the papacy) have thought it necessary to add over the course of time to the divine Word and its teachings. It is well to understand that by "Scriptures" is meant, above all, the New Testament. That is what is chiefly alluded to in Rabelais's novel and, apart from frequent quotations from the Psalms, almost exclusively. When Rabelais speaks for himself and when he has his heroes speak, they have in mind almost nothing in all of the sacred writings but those passages which are especially holy, those which Christianity recognizes as its immediate sources—the Gospels, properly speaking, and the canonical Epistles. In other words, the Word of Christ alone,[4] the Word without any exegesis, not even that of the Fathers, who are never cited in Rabelais's writings; the Word of Christ, of the God-Man by whose necessary mediation we have received God's gifts and rendered our homage to God ever since the time he appeared on earth, and even before that.[5] Go back and look at the passages quoted earlier; Rabelais's heroes, like Luther, indeed seem to have espoused the Augus-

4. No exception was made in the case of Saint Paul, who was often quoted. It was God himself who spoke through his mouth. "Jesuchrist dit, parlant en Sainct Pol" (Jesus Christ says, speaking through Saint Paul), wrote Lefèvre in his Psalter.

5. And even before that. Thus Luther could say, "It is Christ who was the God of Israel," and Luther along with countless other Christians in the sixteenth century could find in the Psalms of David the expression of all the fundamental experiences of a Christian. Luther also said, "We cannot praise God otherwise than through Christ. For, just as we have received everything through his mediation, so we must render our homage to God through his mediation." This state of affairs will come to an end after the Last Judgment. Then God will reign by himself, *ipse per se*, and will no longer govern his Church through a human being. The faithful, granted the beatific vision, will see God face to face. Martin Luther, *Werke* (Weimar, 1883–1974), II, 457, ll. 27 ff. This takes us back to the passage from Rabelais that we examined earlier. For the passages from Luther, see Henri Strohl, *L'Epanouissement de la pensée religieuse de Luther de 1515 à 1520* (Strasbourg, 1924), p. 62 ff.

tinian notion of the Trinity, which really knows of only one
God. This seems to be what Rabelais's heroes thought, as it was
emphatically what Luther thought.

We should now be very careful to add that the natural imprecision of passages extracted, not from a *Summa theologica*, but
from a bawdy novel leaves at least one question (a basic one)
without an explicit answer. Not everything is taken care of
when one says, "Return to the Gospel." The Gospel could
stand for many different things to those who commended it. It
could be a code revealed to men by a legalistic God, every word
and letter of which was to be revered. Or it could be the living
word of the "divine Prince of Christian Philosophy" hailed by
Erasmus. Or the "paper pope," as the Anabaptists would jeer,
scoffing at Luther's Bibliocracy—or the great Charter of Liberty granted to the children of God to serve as their guide, their
rule of conduct, and their precept of morality on earth. We
should not be astonished if the passages we have do not provide
us with Rabelais's—or Gargantua's—last word on the Gospel.
There is nothing that allows us to say they provide a conception of the Scriptures divested of orthodoxy. At the same time
it is quite certain that Rabelais did not separate the Gospel from
the literary works of antiquity. If Pantagruel applies his mind
"at some of the hours of the day . . . to the study of the Holy
Scriptures," he takes equal delight, like his father Gargantua, in
reading "Plutarch's Morals" and "the pleasant Dialogues of
Plato," not to mention Cicero, the prince of Latin style. And if
it was necessary to rid the Sacred Books of the additions dear to
the hypocrites, it was not forbidden to supplement with great
ancient ideas the moral teaching they dispensed.

3. Justification by Faith

Rule number two: affirming the "central dogma," as it is sometimes called, or the "essential principle," rather, of the Reformation: justification by faith. But that term needs to be interpreted
and carefully elucidated. Let us ask Luther, among whose concerns the place it occupied is well known, to help us in this delicate task. And since neither for him nor for those who followed
him was it a matter of an objective theological tenet but primarily a personal and profound spiritual state, let us seek to

express ourselves in language that is as simply "human" as possible.

"God," proclaimed Luther, strengthened by the experience that had shaken him to the depths of his being, "is the sole author of salvation. God alone, completely and absolutely, for man can hinder the work of justification, support it, or help it, but he can never collaborate in it in any way whatsoever. God, the father of mercy, gives His grace to man as a gift, a pure gift, freely and without compensation. He gives it to a fallen creature who does not in the least deserve it and whose work cannot possibly be good in His eyes, defiled as it is in advance by the original corruption of Adam's sons. Instead of vainly boasting of his supposed merits, man should acknowledge in his heart the unworthiness of his works and the fact that he is incapable of doing anything for his salvation himself. Then grace will spontaneously fall on him. It will awaken faith—for it too is not born of man's effort. It is also a pure gift of God, the means by which the creature can apprehend Grace and satisfy Justice. Endowed with such faith, man no longer knows the anguish and torture that ravage the consciences of so many who are scrupulous. He no longer anxiously examines himself about his salvation. He no longer makes and remakes those eternal balance sheets of wretched good works and inexpiable sins that always result in a deficit. He has in his heart the intimate and perfect assurance that he has nothing to dread from the anger of God and everything to gain from His mercy."

We know the central position occupied by this doctrine of Luther's, here briefly summarized,[6] not so much in his system as in his conception of Christian life. Can it be compared with what is professed by Rabelais's heroes? There is a difficulty: nowhere in his writings prior to 1535 does Rabelais allude to the doctrine that faith alone justifies. Nowhere does he deal with the question of works in general. Nowhere does he explicitly oppose faith to works.

To be sure, he mocks. He directs his gibes at the belief in the efficacy of certain works supposed to be especially useful for salvation—pilgrimages, for example. But to compose a tirade on

6. For details, see Lucien Febvre, *Un Destin, Martin Luther,* 4th ed. (Paris, 1968) [English trans. by Roberts Tapley (New York, 1929)]; Strohl; Robert Will, *La Liberté chrétienne, étude sur le principe de la piété chez Luther* (Strasbourg, 1922).

Sweer-to-go and his companions is not to join Luther in affirming the radical incapacity of man to earn salvation even by
doing what he calls good; nor is it to give a Lutheran interpretation to "the deeds of the law" in Saint Paul. Rather, it is a remarkable thing that Rabelais, who quotes Saint Paul so copiously in his early works, never quotes the well-known Pauline
texts on which the Lutherans, Evangelicals, and Calvinists in
turn relied in order to proclaim the uselessness of works as the
means of achieving salvation, and the justifying power of faith
alone.

4. Faith Formed in Charity

There is more. In a conspicuous passage in *Pantagruel* there
appears a doctrinal statement that no one up to now seems to
have given the attention it deserves. But wait. Naturally,
Etienne Gilson did not let it go by without an explanation.[7] But
his explanation remains a literal one. Nor did the learned editors of the *Oeuvres* annotate these words, making one think
they were devoid of interest. Here they are: You should, Gargantua tells his son, serve, love, and fear God, and, "by faith
formed in charity, cleave unto him, so thou mayst never be separated from him by thy sins." Faith formed in charity: what
does that mean?

The phrase—*fides charitate formata*—was familiar to the
Scholastics. It was famous. We do not have to trace its history;
only one thing matters to us here, that in taking it for his own
Gargantua took for his own a thoroughly orthodox theory of
the relationship between faith and charity that Luther had interpreted in his own fashion and vehemently repudiated.[8] Moreover, whether Luther's interpretation was correct or not;
whether he was or was not mistaken about the actual doctrine
of those who, to his indignation, made use of that "accursed
term 'formed' " (*maledictum illud vocabulum formatum*), that
is, if we can believe him, those who spoke of a faith whose chief

---

7. Etienne Gilson, "Rabelais franciscain," in *Les Idées et les lettres,* 2d ed. (Paris,
1955), pp. 214–215. Gilson shows with the help of Saint Thomas how much "this
whole passage respects received theology." He does not point out (nor did he have to)
its interest for the "diagnosis" of Rabelais's Reformed tendencies.

8. See Will, pp. 91, 251, 257.

inspiration, whose *forma*, was charity, a faith that charity "informed" in the same way as the soul was said to inform the body—these are theologians' debates. Those who would like to have some idea of them need only read with attention the pages crammed with quotations and references in Denifle.[9] That adversary of Luther long ago devoted those pages to proving the error—or errors—of his adversary, who, he thought, had made a travesty of the Church's traditional doctrine.

For our part, let us limit ourselves to the following assertion: *fides charitate formata* is the very opposite of a Lutheran tenet. And of a Calvinist one, we might add. Calvin's opinion on this question of the relationship between faith and charity appears to be quite similar to Luther's. Let us open his *Institutes* of 1541 to chapter 4, "Of Faith." We read: "By the same reasoning two other lies of the Sophists are overturned. The first is that they believe faith is formed when pious affection is added to the knowledge of God." And further on: "What the Schoolmen teach, that charity comes before faith and hope, is a mere dream, since it is faith alone that first engenders charity in us." The same note is struck, finally, in chapter 6, "Of Justification": "Also in vain do they lay hold of another subtlety, that we are justified by faith alone, which works by charity. We indeed acknowledge with Saint Paul that the only faith that justifies is that which is joined with charity; but it does not take from charity its justifying power. Nay, it justifies in no other way than by bringing us into communication with the justice of Christ."[10] These passages appear eloquent enough.

Rabelais, then, composed with obvious care a dozen great lines with which to close Gargantua's solemn letter in a fitting manner. If he had been imbued with Lutheran doctrine, would he have used an expression that he knew was orthodox beyond any possible doubt and that he also no doubt knew was foreign and antagonistic to Luther's thought? The question can be asked, and it should be asked—at any rate, with caution, and with care for fine shadings. Let us bring in only one example. If

9. Heinrich Denifle, *Luther und Luthertum in der ersten Entwicklung*, 2d ed., reworked by Albert Maria Weiss, 2 vols. plus 2 vols. of supplementary material (Mainz, 1906), I, 658–727.

10. Jean Calvin, *Institution de la Religion Chrestienne*, original 1541 text, ed. Abel Lefranc, Henri Chatelain, and Jacques Pannier (Paris, 1911), pp. 208, 212, 360.

we open up the *Diálogo* of Juan de Valdés, which has been restored to us by the happy find of Marcel Bataillon, we find an
allusion to the faith "ala qual los theologolos llaman fe formada," clearly testifying that for Valdés, who was still an Erasmian in 1529 before he left his first master in order to move
closer to Luther, only *fides formata*, made fecund by charity
and the source of meritorious works, could be called faith.[11] In
this connection, let us apply to Rabelais an observation by Marcel Bataillon. "Valdés," he wrote in his introduction to the
Diálogo, "could not possibly be a Lutheran as long as he regarded Erasmus as an excellent doctor and true theologian."[12]

"Faith formed in charity"—the phrase does not sound like
Luther. It was not, as Juan de Valdés very clearly attests, re-
pugnant to an Erasmian Evangelical, even if he otherwise
admired Luther. This is not the first time our analysis has
brought us to a similar conclusion. Is our analysis too meticu-
lous? There is nothing unusual about it, in any case. When theologians became interested in the men who are sometimes called
the Reformers before the Reformation and examined them with
painstaking care, looking through a magnifying glass, for example, at the opinions of Jan Pupper of Goch, who wrote a treatise
called *De libertate christiana* in 1473 (printed only in 1521),
the doctrine of which no less than the title seems to anticipate
Luther on a number of points, what did they fix their attention
on in order to establish the actual agreement or disagreement
between the two theologians? The earlier of them, Pupper, was
inspired by an Augustianism which he was not alone in having
a preference for in the monastic world of the time. Their analy-

11. Juan de Valdés, *Diálogo de doctrina cristiana*, facsimile ed. with introduction
by Marcel Bataillon (Coimbra, 1925), fol. LXXX r. Here is Juan de Valdés's passage in
its entirety: "mas os digo que porque esta fe de que yo hablo: ala qual los Theologolos
llaman fe formada, es como un bivo fuego en los coraçôes de los fieles, con el qual do-
cada dia mas se apuran y allegan a dios." (Moreover I say to you that because this
faith about which I am speaking and which the theologians call "formed faith" is like a
lively fire in the hearts of the faithful, which day by day purifies them and brings them
closer to God.)

12. Ibid., introduction, pp. 124–125. The phrase about Erasmus comes from Juan
de Valdés himself; see *Diálogo*, fol. XVII v. Marcel Bataillon adds: "Historically speaking, to be a Lutheran was not merely to share with Luther some opinion or other on
grace, the definitive statement of which was already found in Saint Augustine, if not in
Saint Paul; it was to go along with Luther all the way in the violent negations that defined him as much as did the positive content of his thought. In this regard Erasmus is
a good touchstone."

sis proceeded to show that in the midst of phrases that appeared to be strictly Lutheran a Catholic notion of merit stubbornly survived. "It is uniquely the grace of God that assigns merits to man. Nevertheless, God wishes to have to do only with a soul that can appreciate a merit."[13] And furthermore, when Jan Pupper of Goch made a distinction between *fides informis* and *fides caritate formata*—that is to say, "a faith that is not yet itself and a faith that is no longer wholly itself"—he was clearly a long way away from the Reformers' conception. No one as yet has thought of using this criterion in connection with Rabelais. If anyone did apply it he would be justified in concluding that *fides charitate formata* was a phrase foreign to Martin Luther's thought. It was a phrase permeated by Catholic substance, a phrase familiar to many evangelists between 1530 and 1536 and to many devoted readers and disciples of Erasmus.

5. The Question of Works

Let us go on. How is the big question of man's cooperation in his salvation—the question of works—handled in Rabelais's novel? There is no use in showing to what extent it is linked to the question of justification, of merit, and of grace. Rabelais's words, when they are confronted directly, give no clear impression. At first glance we are tempted to think that it was as though two or three rather obvious Lutheran "motifs," effectively handled, had been tacked on to a smooth background of Catholic doctrine. Is this impression correct?

In Rabelais's writings before 1535 we encounter very energetic appeals to a God who judges and rewards, giving man credit for his efforts at achieving perfection. Logicians or theologians—aren't they the same thing?—have not failed to proclaim that the conception in these phrases is one that was foreign to the Reformers, if not abhorrent to them. To make God into immanent justice, to see him as the Supreme Judge who demands punishment or expiation for sins that have been carefully charged to each person's account—it is quite true that in

13. On Pupper, see *Geschriften van Joann Pupper van Goch en Corn. Grapheus; Confutatio determinationis parisiensis contra M. L.*, ed. F. Pijper, Bibliotheca Reformatoria Neerlandica, 6 (The Hague, 1909); Otto Clemen, *Johann Pupper von Goch* (Leipzig, 1896); Will, p. 8.

Luther's eyes this was the worst of errors, the one that was most dangerous for peace of mind and for the Christian life in general. It would therefore seem that when Ulrich Gallet reminds Picrochole that all human actions shall come before God's Judgment, from which nothing is hidden, when he invokes against the brutish and lawless king the supreme God, "just rewarder of all our undertakings," his phrases have a clearly traditional ring. Again we must avoid overstatement. The passages on which such conclusions can be based are quite limited—and they are sentences in a novel.[14]

On the other hand, there is that singular passage already cited above: "Help yourself and heaven will help you," say the cafards. In fact, help yourself and the devil will break your bones—that is the real truth! What strange quietism for the creator and originator of Friar John, we are tempted to say. Or, if you will, for the man who depicted the Storm, the apostle of strong arms and rolled-up sleeves. And there is that other passage on the free will and sensual appetite of Picrochole, "which cannot choose but be wicked, if by divine grace it be not continually guided." Here is pessimism that we are tempted to call Lutheran. It is a surprise in the optimist of Theleme, the apologist of the Thelemites, who were moved by the spur that prompts men who are "free and well-born" to do good.

Must we speak of a contradiction? Would Rabelais as a theologian contradict himself, good scholar that he was? In the first place, this discussion places us in the realm of beliefs, which is not tenanted by pure concepts. And we should not imagine that the didactic thought of theologians at that time—I mean during the great classical centuries of the Middle Ages, the twelfth, thirteenth, and fourteenth, as well as during the fifteenth and sixteenth, centuries of decline and disintegration—penetrated intuitive thought. I am speaking not only of ordinary believers but also of the intuitive thought of preachers and sometimes of theologians. Is this a contradiction? But just think of Luther himself when he dealt with questions of this sort. He contradicted himself and wandered hither and yon. He said categori-

---

14. Never take the words of polemicists as statements by theologians. Here is a clearly innovative work, *La Vérité cachée devant cent ans* (*The Truth Hidden for a Hundred Years*) (Geneva: J. Michel, 1544). In it Truth assigns the faithful as a duty "To do all works of mercy you know of / And act in peace, in harmony, and love!"

cally that man does not do wrong in spite of himself, he does it necessarily, spontaneously, willingly; that he is, by virtue of his corrupt nature, driven by absolute necessity to do wrong. But doesn't it sometimes look as if he recognized, hidden in the depths of human nature, a moral disposition—*recta ratio, bona voluntas,* or, as he said in his preface to the Epistle to the Romans, a free inclination toward the good that God discovers in the depths of the human heart? Didn't he write in the Large Catechism that the Ten Commandments are inscribed in the heart of man and that they have been implanted there by nature? When he identified the Decalogue with natural law, wasn't he admitting an intuitive need of the human mind to do good and be saved? Again, he sharply ridiculed the sacrilegious pretensions of the man who presumes to collaborate with God in the work of salvation. But didn't he sometimes see us as collaborators with a God who, though he can act alone, does us the honor of summoning us to work with him? It seems, therefore, said one theologian, "that alongside the religious state of mind that we are accustomed to observe in Luther there is another in which he seems to admit man's cooperation in accomplishing God's intentions."[15]

Here coexisting in the same man are opposing tendencies, one pulling him in one direction, the other in another. But there is more. As always, anachronism comes into play. For in the end—to get back to Rabelais—we have to reread the words after taking off our modern eyeglasses, the ones of today; we have to read them with the eyes of another time. And what would we say then about the meaning we impose on so many passages in Rabelais—above all, the famous words: "men that are free, well-born, well-bred, and conversant in honest companies, have naturally an instinct and spur that prompteth them unto virtuous actions, and withdraws them from vice"? "Naturally"?

We are so imbued with biological thought that the word "nature" is enough to get us excited. We immediately capitalize it, and without any hesitation acknowledge it to be the Nature of the Naturalists, a deity, the rival of the theologians' God, and the idol (along with Life) of the biological age. If we use it in

15. Will, pp. 230–233, 244, n. 1.

this way for our own purposes, that is our business. To presume to drag Rabelais along with us is too much. For when Rabelais wrote "par nature" in the passage under consideration he did not intend to refer to "spontaneous forces," the mastery and control of which have been the result, if not the aim, of science. He was not setting up over the theologians' God an idol that usurped the powers acknowledged to be his and offered men as an ideal the interplay of needs and instincts that constitute what we call the will to live. What *we* call. But Rabelais was unable either to speak or to think in this way—nor did he want to.

As much of a naturalist as he was for his time, as curious as he was to read Pliny and Theophrastus, to collect seeds and spores, to follow the frolicking of whales in the Bay of Biscay with his Rondelet open in front of him, and by frequent anatomies to get the perfect knowledge of that other world, called the microcosm, which is man—he could not philosophize in the manner of Spencer or, if you will, Haeckel. He philosophized, quite simply, like Aristotle. Like him he thought that virtue was a habit, a good habit, the habit of acting in conformity to one's condition as a man. *Secundum naturam,* by which we understand according to *his* nature, not according to Nature, a goddess who is, by the way, more shackled than free. We should say, further: in accordance with natural law, which does not mean following the laws of Nature. Of those laws Rabelais did not, any more than his contemporaries, have a clear and distinct idea. What is more, he strenuously refused to acknowledge the prefiguration of those laws in the "influences" of the stars and the "deterministic" speculations of the astrologers.

Rabelais philosophized like Aristotle. He had also read Plato, however—read and reread him. And so he did not translate "according to nature," like Aristotle, merely as "according to reason," since man's nature is essentially to be reasonable—that is, in Aristotelian language, since man's form is his reasonable soul. Like Plato, Rabelais also translated "according to reason" as "according to God," since God is the author of Reason. Put it, if you will, as "according to God's own reason," the reason of God, who is an upright God, followed by Justice, carrying in his train men who grow to be like him and whose reward is the happiness of living as just men among the just. But those who think they can be their own guides are abandoned by God.

They can have some success at the very outset—or the appearance of success. But soon Justice exacts vengeance and ruins
them—themselves, their dreams, their supporters, their countries. Justice ruins Picrochole: the book of the *Laws* gives Rabelais absolute assurance of this.[16]

Is this the Rabelais who was a student of Greek and nothing
else? No, indeed. In these deeply resonant passages of Rabelais's work there is what we have just said there is. There is also
something else. There are Christian speculations on grace,
which alone gives value and worth to the accomplishments and
undertakings of men. And running through everything there is
the ambiguity retained for centuries by the word "nature" as
applied to man. On the one hand there is nature as the combination of fundamental properties that serve to define him and,
consequently, everything that is innate, instinctive, and spontaneous in him, whether with respect to God (this is the opposition between corrupt nature and grace) or with respect to humanity (this is the distinction between the state of nature and
the civilized state). In a word, nature in this sense is everything
in man that defines the species man. On the other hand, there is
nature as the character peculiar to each person, what makes one
human being distinguishable from his neighbor, what makes
him himself, a particular man, and not just any man. These are
ambiguities that we are on our guard against, as our analyses
show, and yet we perpetuate them and succumb to them. Every
day, confusing the two senses by slipping from one to the
other, we speak of medical treatment or pedagogy that "con-
forms to nature." All the more reason for men of the sixteenth
century, who had for their instructors in philosophy neither
Descartes nor the long line of experts in philosophical dissec-
tion spawned by the *Discourse on Method.* For them it was
always Plato and Aristotle, a Plato and Aristotle moreover re-
modeled and recast in a more or less Christian form by the
Scholastics. Rabelais and his contemporaries repudiated this effort of the Scholastics, but they did not succeed in extricating
themselves from it. And we should not think that *Physis* in
Greek works or *Natura* in Latin ones has fewer different meanings—and if you will, contradictory ones—than "nature" does

16. Plato, *Laws*, Book IV (716 C–D).

in our own writings. The man of the sixteenth century, however, was hardly equipped to detect these contradictions.

Contradictions: we say the word with a pedantic sniff of disdain. Better to get some intellectual amusement from contemplating all the conflicts in the trends that characterized an agitated, innovative, and prolific era than become involved in chaotic confusion trying somehow to disentangle the naturalist religion of the Renaissance from the revealed religion of the Reformation.

6. Justification, a Tricky Criterion

Let us now come back to that criterion of criteria, justification by faith, which is often called the formal principle of the Reformation. What did Rabelais think about it? Which theory did he support?

All that one can say when relying on passages that are not at all explicit is the following: The three or four sentences that refer remotely, really very remotely, to the complex of problems we call Justification do not, when compared to a coherent and systematic theological doctrine (not the effusions of Luther when he let his heart speak but the doctrine that was called Lutheran by assiduous theologians after they pruned it, polished it, and rid it of his untidiness and his lightning flashes), sound Reformed except intermittently and momentarily. The only thing is, did all Reformers around 1532 profess Luther's doctrine on these questions, the doctrine that Calvin adopted?

Let us leave out Lefèvre, who negotiated a circumspect pact between faith and works in his commentary on the Epistles of Paul: "for faith alone, no more than works alone, does not earn salvation. Works prepare and purify; faith opens to us the approach to God, who alone justifies and absolves. Works make us better; faith converts us; justification illuminates us."[17] But what about Farel? There is no doubt that in his famous *Sommaire*, which had so much to do with the success of Reformed

---

17. Commentary on Rom. 3:28, 29 in *Epistole divi Pauli apostoli: cum commentariis . . . Jacobi Fabri Stapulensis* (Paris: F. Regnault and J. de La Port, [1517]), fols. 75r, 76r. [Febvre uses the French translation in Augustin Renaudet, *Préréforme et humanisme à Paris pendant les premières guerres d'Italie (1494–1517)* (Paris, 1916), p. 628.—Translator.]

ideas between 1530 and 1540, he professed that man needs to be covered by the Justice of Christ before he can dare to present himself before God. But he passed rather rapidly over this point of doctrine, which in Luther's view was so important. To help us understand it, Heyer uses a blander expression, which is all the more telling. "This point of view," he writes, "although little developed, was not foreign to Farel. He enjoins us in his *Sommaire* to put all our assurance in Jesus alone and in his Justice."[18] It is a rather hasty injunction, far removed from the magnificent expositions of Luther when he orchestrates the bare theme of Justification with his usual amplitude. Let us turn to another text, no less celebrated—the summary of the contents of the Sacred Books printed at great length at the beginning of Martin Lempereur's 1534 Bible.[19] We cannot help but make analogous observations about it.

There justification is explained clearly but briefly, in rather conciliatory terms. "Because of this faith and trust in Jesus Christ, which shows itself through charitable works and moves man to do the same, we are justified. That is to say, the Father of Jesus Christ holds us to be just and to be sons of his grace, having no regard for our sins and not reckoning them against us as sins." Here is an answer for Picrochole, one he might have given to Ulrich Gallet; but we note in passing the sentence about charitable works, through which faith manifests itself. This concern to give works and charity a prominent place in Christian life was very French at the time. The summary of the Contents of the Sacred Books develops the suggestion at some length: "Through our good works," it explains, "(to do the which God has prepared us) we demonstrate that we surely have been called by that grace; for whoever does them not shows he has no faith in Jesus Christ." And Farel exhibits the same tendency, if Charles Schmidt's judgment is correct: "The fundamental principle that sums up all his theological opinions is the following: one is only justified by a faith that operates through charity." Gerard Roussel said "a faith that works through charity," which is exactly the same thing: "Where

18. Henri Heyer, *Guillaume Farel: essai sur le développement de ses idées théologiques* (Geneva, 1872), p. 49.

19. *La Saincte Bible en Françoys translatée selon la pure et entière traduction de S. Hiérome* (Antwerp: M. Lempereur, 1534).

there is a living faith that works through charity, there is the observance of all the commandments."[20]

Unquestionably this is not the doctrine of Saint Paul, his assertion (I Cor. 13:13) that charity is superior to faith and hope (an assertion by the way that it is strange to see Calvin scornfully crediting to the doctors of the Sorbonne, in one of the passages cited above). But it does seem to be the doctrine of Saint Augustine: "Without charity faith can exist, but it is of no use."[21] And is it so hard, after all, to move from phrases such as these to those of the scholastics, to the *fides charitate formata* that Gargantua refers to? Especially if it is true that it does not mean, as Luther claimed, that charity perfects a faith that would remain imperfect without it, but that charity, without modifying the essence of faith in any way or changing its substance, gives it a higher perfection, unites it to its final goal, and renders it meritorious.[22]

Let us guard against being too strict. The two criteria that we have adopted following Henri Hauser's lead should not be applied with insensitive rigidity. We should, moreover, note the obvious superiority of the first over the second. Yes, the Scriptures as the sole source of Faith: that was essential. Justification, however, was a controversial issue, and remained so for a long time. We would see Cardinal Contarini at the Colloquy of Regensburg in 1541 proposing to Melanchthon and Bucer a formula for unity—which they accepted—that was regarded as Catholic and correct by Morone, Eck, Gropper, and Pflug. The Lutheran doctrine was therefore susceptible of attenuation on this point, and the Catholic doctrine of modification. For diagnosing opinions we should not use the assertions on justification of a Christian of the first half of the sixteenth century except with care. It was not merely the theology of the giants that when confronted with Luther's pure doctrine—or later with Calvin's pure doctrine—attested to marked divergencies of opinion. Is it necessary to repeat that it was the entire theology—at once audacious and occasionally timid—of those men in France

---

20. Charles Schmidt, *Etudes sur Farel* (Strasbourg, 1834), p. 43; Charles Schmidt, *Gérard Roussel* (Strasbourg, 1841), p. 138.

21. "Sine caritate quippe fides potest quidem esse; sed non et prodesse." Saint Augustine, *De Trinitate*, Book XV, ch. 18, n. 33.

22. Denifle, I, 667.

around 1530 and 1535 who sought their way along new paths, to which they were being summoned by a few powerful minds and the liberal temper of a century fiercely eager for independence?

7. Rabelais and Matters German

Fortunately, we are beginning to know this difficult history a little better. And this we owe to the book by W. G. Moore, which takes up and expands valuable hints provided by Nathanaël Weiss, at the same time transferring them to another plane. It gives us some idea of the huge effort that must have been undertaken, that *was* undertaken, but that remained unknown for a long time because of its clandestine nature.[23]

On the subject of the influence exerted outside Germany by Luther's appeals and their effect in French-speaking countries we are no longer without some hints, inadequate though they may be, in our view. At any rate, no one today can say anymore that French ears heard no echo of that powerful voice whose thunder knocked down so many walls in Germany. The Reformer's Latin writings were in circulation all over the kingdom before the intellectual customs officers could do anything about it. Today we know in some detail how, by what route, and with what precautions suspect booksellers imported an entire heretical literature by the bushel. At their head were Jean Schabler in Paris and Jean Vaugris in Lyon. We know about the role of the Ecu de Bâle,[24] the activity of Froben, the eagerness with which the public sought out the innovative writings, the partiality for them of Lefèvre d'Etaples, the Meaux circle, and, in the background, a princess like Margaret of Navarre. Meanwhile the theologians who were inimical to Luther were popularizing the subversive ideas of the rebellious Augustinian in order to refute them. The burnings of books printed in Ger-

23. Will Grayburn Moore, *La Réforme allemande et la littérature française; recherches sur la notoriété de Luther en France* (Strasbourg, 1930); review by Lucien Febvre, *Revue Critique d'Histoire et de Littérature*, n.s. 97 (1930), 315–318; Nathanaël Weiss, "La Littérature de la Réforme française, Notes sur les traités de Luther, traduits en français et imprimés en France entre 1525 et 1534," *Bulletin de la Société de l'Histoire du Protestantisme Français*, 36 (1887), 664–670.

24. "The Arms of Basel," the sign of Michel Parmentier's shop in Lyon. See Jean Plattard, "A l'Ecu de Bâle," *Revue du Seizième Siècle*, 13 (1926), 282–285.

many and the Rhineland, the fury of those who tracked them down, and the obvious enthusiasm of those who acquired them—all bear witness to a considerable diffusion of Luther's writings in France at the time. Did Rabelais know this literature? No doubt about it.

Let us turn without another word to the famous chapter 7 of *Pantagruel*. It is there that we find the catalogue of the library of Saint Victor. In every item, or nearly every one, we find an avowal of the passionate curiosity with which the young Rabelais followed the drama in the German lands.

First of all, there was the Reuchlin affair—Reuchlin had taught at Orléans around 1475. Here, one after another, are all the heroes of the cabala war, the real ones as well as the imaginary ones: Magister Ortuinus (Master Hardouin de Graës, Ortuin Gratius), a renowned theologian; Magister Jacobus Hocstrates, *hereticometra*,[25] that is, the famous Dominican and Inquisitor Hochstraten of Cologne; Magister Lupoldus Federfusius of the *Epistolae obscurorum virorum*; and all the Cologne doctors whose *Tarrabalationes adversus Reuchlin* was in the library. Furthermore, we see that in the prologue to *Gargantua* Alcofribas makes fun of those who prove that "Ovid, in his Metamorphosis" gave a symbolic prefiguration of the Christian sacraments; at their head was "a certain gulligut friar, and true bacon-picker," who was infatuated with such remarkable parallels. In the *Epistolae* Friar Dollekopf boasts of knowing "unum librum quem scripsit quidam Magister noster Anglicus de Ordine nostro . . . super librum Metamorphoseon Ovidii, exponens omnes fabulas allegorice et spiritualiter."[26] And when Janotus begins his argument, "Omnis bella bellabilis," he ends with "Ergo gluc!"[27] The *Epistolae* has "Quicquid ipsi non intelligunt, hoc comburunt: Ergo . . ."[28]

But what about the "Luther affair" itself? In one of the excellent notes on the catalogue that Jean Plattard included in the

25. Measurer of heretics. [Translator's note.]
26. "A book composed by a certain English Doctor of our Order . . . concerning *Ovid's Metamorphoses*, explaining each story allegorically and spiritually." *Epistolae obscurorum virorum*, ed. Aloys Bömer, 2 vols. (Heidelberg, 1924), II, 50. Translation by Francis Griffin Stokes in *On the Eve of the Reformation: "Letters of Obscure Men"* (New York, 1964), p. 57.
27. *Gargantua*, ch. 19.
28. "What they do not understand they burn; ergo . . ."

edition of Rabelais's works, he pointed out quite rightly that the dispute in Cologne and the quarrels of the Sorbonists with humanism "are echoed in this episode." That is true—but so is the dispute over Luther, which he forgot. For there was a certain Master of the Sacred Palace, the Dominican Thomist Silvester Mazzolini of Prierio, who was appointed by the pope to judge Luther and immediately (1518) wrote a violent and mediocre *Dialogus de potestate papae* directed against the defendant. Moreover, the presses in Lyon had brought out his *Aurea Rosa super Evangelio* in 1524 and 1528 (B. Bonyn for J. and F. Giunta), and the same presses are said to have printed his *Summa Silvestrina* in 1524 and 1533.[29] Rabelais did not fail to send this *Magister noster* off to his theological tipples.[30]

A more considerable personage was Jacobus de Vio of Gaeta, Cardinal of Saint Sixtus, also a Dominican and a Thomist. In October 1518 he tried to bring Luther back into the bosom of the Church. The presses of France, in Lyon and Paris, allowed none of his works to be unknown. His *Summa Caietana*, revised by Daniel, appeared in Lyon in July 1530 (J. Crespin for J. Giunta); it was reprinted there in 1533 and 1539. His *Psalmi Davidici* appeared in Paris in January–February 1532, published by Badius; his *Evangelia cum commentariis* appeared in May; and his *Epistolae Pauli* in May also—an avalanche.[31] We should not be astonished that the monastery library contains the crutches needed to support his lame thinking: *The Whinings of Cajetan.*[32]

Finally—in addition to Hochstraten, already mentioned, who intervened in the Luther affair as well (he published some *Disputationes contra lutheranos* in Cologne in 1526)—there was Luther's principal adversary from the beginning. This was again a Dominican, and perhaps Rabelais the ex-Franciscan got particular delight from being able to draw up such a fine list of

29. Henri and Julien Baudrier, *Bibliographie lyonnaise*, 12 vols. (Lyon, 1895–1921; photographic reprint, Paris, 1964), VI, 114, 129, 152, and other pages.

30. "De brodiorum usu et honestate chopinandi, per Silvestrem Prieratem, Jacospinum" (On the use of soups and the honor of tippling, by Silvester of Prierio, Jacobin). *Pantagruel*, ch. 7.

31. Baudrier, VI, 138; Philippe Renouard, *Bibliographie des impressions et des oeuvres de Josse Badius Ascensius, imprimeur et humaniste, 1462–1535*, 3 vols. (Paris, 1908), III, 355–356.

32. *Les Henilles de Gaïetan.*

prizewinning Friars Preachers. We are talking of Hans Maier from Egg on the Günz in Swabia, whom we know under his Latin name, Eckius—the theologian of Ingolstadt, the preacher of Augsburg, the Fuggers' lawyer in the dispute over lending money at interest, and finally the hero of the Leipzig disputation in 1519. He is no more absent from the library than are his confreres; Rabelais attributes to him a symbolic treatise on chimney-sweeping, "Manera sweepandi fornacellos per Mag. Eccium," but not long before, in 1531, there had appeared in Paris, under the imprint of Gilles de Gourmont, his *Errorum lutheranorum CDIV Catalogus,*[33] which is at the Bibliothèque Nationale (Rés. D80059), and whose title alone is a programmatic statement.

Prierias, Cajetan, and Eck, the three protagonists of the Luther drama, responded to the appeal, as we see—all three of them. As for the Paris theologians whom Rabelais also mentions, they were all declared adversaries of Luther and took positions against him in their writings—from potbellied Noël Beda, qualified to be the author of a substantial treatise *De optimate triparum,*[34] all the way to Nicolas Du Chesne, the suitable adversary of *Pantagruel,* and the Carthusian Pierre Cousturier, called Sutor, an inexhaustible author of prolix works: his *De tralatione Bibliae* of 1525 was an apologia for the Vulgate, followed by a systematic denunciation of the criminals (led by Erasmus and Lefèvre) who wooed simple people by lowering the Scriptures to their level; his *In novos Anticomaritas* at the beginning of 1526 attacked not only those who opposed the cult of the Virgin but also those who disparaged the saints; his *Apologia adversus damnatam Lutheri haeresim de votis monasticis,* more recent (1531), seems to have been the real-life prototype of the apologia that Rabelais noted on the shelves of Saint Victor: "adversus quendam," he tells us, "qui vocaverat eum fripponatorem—et quod fripponatores non sunt damnati ab Ecclesia."[35] *Damnatus ab Ecclesia*—that was just what Luther was, for having righteously denounced the Small Vales of the Indulgences and the horde of Roman tax collectors, those *frip-*

---

33. *Catalogue of 404 Lutheran Errors.*
34. *On the Excellence of Tripe.*
35. *Against One Who Called Him a Rogue, Holding That Rogues Are Not Condemned by the Church.*

ponatores non damnati, those "Crackerades of Bullists . . . , Contrepate Clerks, Scriveners, Brief-writers, Rapporters, and Papal Bull-despatchers" with whom Rabelais would one day deal personally, all those masters of the art of extracting cash from marsupial pockets and raking in those profits from pardons that were sanctimoniously described at Saint Victor by Bishop Boudarin in his *De emulgentiarium profectibus enneades novem, cum privilegio papali.*[36] Thus did Rabelais take sides, putting on no *Spectacles of Pilgrims Bound for Rome* in order to see Christianity and not converted by Marforio's *Apology Against Those Who Allege That the Pope's Mule Doth Eat But at Set Times.* With these bitingly ironic titles he clearly took his place in the camp of the protesters.[37] With a few precautions, however. It is funny no one has noticed that he says nothing about the most active of Luther's French antagonists, that former disciple of Lefèvre d'Etaples, Josse Clichtove, who completely switched over to the offensive against the innovators. He does not make sport of him. On the other hand, two of the titles are somewhat more eloquent. One is *De Purgatorii cosmographia.*[38] Alongside this notable work by Jabolenus, Pantagruel discovers a *De cagotis tollendis*[39] without any pardon, in the singular). And the worst of all is a *De auferibilitate Papae ab Ecclesia*,[40] which Gerson wrote in connection with the schism—but Gargantua's son was not bothered by this kind of precision, and if he took the phrase in its absolute sense, what was the program it advocated?

Indeed, in this catalogue attention is constantly drawn to matters German: let us not forget that final phrase about printing "in this noble city of Tubingen." Should we be inordinately surprised at this? Surely not since the appearance of Moore's wonderful book, not because of the cursory but very judicious section that Moore devotes to Rabelais,[41] not because of the

36. *Nine Enneads on the Profits of Emulgences, with the Papal Privilege.*
37. On all these titles see the notes in the edition of the *Oeuvres* by Lefranc et al., III, 76–97. They are not explicit enough about the "philolutheran" nature of the section.
38. *On the Cosmography of Purgatory.*
39. *On Removing Hypocrites.* [Urquhart calls it *De white-leperotis tollendis.*—Translator.]
40. *On the Possibility of the Pope's Being Deposed by the Church.*
41. Moore, ch. 14 (p. 306 ff.).

parallel he establishes between the ex-Franciscan and the ex-Augustinian, but because he has clearly shown the importance of the relations that brought together humanists and theologians in France and Germany in the first half of the sixteenth century. Moore makes the excellent point that Rabelais associated with the circles that had been won over by the wide, unanticipated distribution of Luther's writings.[42] "And although one has no right to attribute to him reading he may never have done, it would be a methodological error not to point out in his work what seems to be an echo, not merely of the doctrines of the day, but of the voice of the chief Reformer himself."[43]

An echo? For my part, every time I reread *Pantagruel* and *Gargantua* as a historian there is more than one sentence that I pause over in surprise, with the sudden feeling that something like a breath from a long way off is passing over Rabelais's prose. In spite of myself it forces me to turn in the direction of far-off Wittenberg, home of Luther, the ex-friar.

8. The Breath of Luther in Rabelais's Work

What of the strange quietism that was so little a part of Rabelais's temperament but to which he sometimes seemed to abandon himself in his early writings as though in the grip of some powerful influence? It is true that it was professed by a great number of believers at the time. But it was Luther who on many occasions gave it its most powerful expression.

Well, take a look at the curious passage on faith in Pantagruel's prayer when he is obliged to face Loupgarou.[44] Moore's attention was also caught by it.[45] Faith is the special business, the "proper cause," of God, and in order to defend this faith, what need is there for a human coadjutor, or for a prince, exercising a zeal that is at once ridiculous and sacrilegious, to offer his puny aid to the Almighty? The thought, expressed with such power and conviction, has something rather striking about it, and anyway the idea is not banal. Where did Rabelais get it?

42. Don't forget, either, that he was with the Du Bellays, who were so involved in German affairs, that he served them in their political activities, that he once lived briefly in Metz, and so on.
43. Moore, p. 318.
44. *Pantagruel*, ch. 29.
45. Moore, p. 315.

I only know that Pantagruel's ideas on this score are rather remarkably reminiscent of the young Luther's.

In his early writings the Reformer persistently said it a hundred times: temporal power is not qualified to interfere with
faith.[46] Let it serve the Church indirectly by assuring it the fa-
cilities needed for the free exercise of its activity—fine. But
force men to believe? "Let it be satisfied," says Luther in so
many words, "to see that the Gospel is known and to stimulate
faith. But everyone must be allowed the liberty to respond to
this appeal or not . . . Nor must it seek to impose the sacraments. Let him who does not wish to be baptized ignore it. He
who wishes to do without Communion has the right. He who
does not wish to confess likewise has the right." And in his famous treatise of 1523 on temporal power: "They wish to impose belief on men. What madness! For his belief or unbelief
each man is responsible only to his own conscience. And since
his decision cannot harm the State, the latter ought not concern
itself; it should simply attend to its own affairs." But shouldn't
the people be prevented from falling into heresy? No, answers
Luther boldly. It is for God's Word, not the sword, to attempt
conversions. If the Word accomplishes nothing, force will accomplish even less. When you speak of heresy, you speak of
spiritual force, which cannot be struck by iron, burned by fire,
drowned in blood. Let God's Word enlighten hearts and then
all heresies and errors in the hearts will disappear. And for his
part, the giant king proclaims, "In such a business thou wilt
have no coadjutors, only a catholic confession and service of thy
word."[47] But there is a difference. For the defense of the faith
Rabelais adds to the Word "thousand thousands of hundreds of
millions of legions of angels, the least of which is able to kill all
mortal men, and turn about the heavens and earth at his pleasure, as heretofore it very plainly appeared in the army of Sen-
nacherib." One might think there was some irony here, were it
not for the evident seriousness of the sentence that follows; it

46. For what follows, see Strohl, pp. 325, 412.
47. Moore writes (p. 315): "It is impossible not to see in the elements superim-
posed one on the other certain phrasings that bear the sure mark of the Reformation;
they are numerous enough and explicit enough so that one can assume they have an
origin that is, more specifically, Lutheran in the true sense of the word." There is naturally no question of literal borrowing.

contains Pantagruel's vow: to have the holy gospel purely, simply, and entirely preached.

Now look at the long letter from Gargantua to Pantagruel[48] and its evocation of the life of people of honor, interwoven with friendship and conversation, "which conversation of mine," avers Gargantua, "although it was not without sin, (because we are all of us trespassers, and therefore ought continually to beseech his divine majesty to blot our transgressions out of his memory), yet was it by the help and grace of God, without all manner of reproach before men." Where have we read something analogous to this? In Luther's *Sermon on the Ten Commandments*, the Latin text of which was published in 1518.[49] True Christians, said Luther, know and confess that they are poor sinners. They all attribute the good that is in them to their own merit, not to God's grace. And yet if their sins are taken away from them, that is by God's grace; it is surely not by their own merit.

Again, there are the very beautiful passages Rabelais devotes to the problem of peace and war. Gustave Lanson some time ago pointed out his "French way" of treating this great question of social morality—and of individual morality as well. But Luther, too, was preoccupied in his youth with extending the principles of Christian morality into the political domain. This was quite a tricky undertaking in a time when Machiavellianism had gained so many adepts and when politics and morality seemed to be completely divorced from each other. We know how severely Luther criticized the papacy in particular for favoring the disastrous notion that honor and pledges of loyalty have no currency in politics; we know how angered he was by the practices he ascribed to the nuncios, always ready for a price to legitimize unjust possessions, release sovereigns from their oaths, and abrogate treaties. "God orders us to keep our oath and honor a pledge made even to our enemies—and from such a commandment you dare to release us!" But in the sermon on good works, in the treatise on temporal power, above all in 1526 in a short work devoted to examining "whether the career of arms is not incompatible with the Christian faith" he

48. *Pantagruel,* ch. 8.
49. Luther, I, 394–521.

resolved the problem of the military rights and obligations of the sovereign in the same way as Grandgousier. All war for glory and conquest is a crime. The only licit war is defensive war. "He who begins a war is in the wrong; it is only just that he be vanquished and punished for being the first to draw the sword ... *Deus dissipat gentes qui bella volunt* (Psalm 68:31)."[50]

There is still more. "All true Christians," says Gargantua, "of all estates and conditions, in all places and at all times send up their prayer to God, and the Mediator [*l'esperit*] prayeth and intercedeth for them, and God is gracious to them." This is from Saint Paul, from the Epistle to the Romans, the edition of the *Oeuvres* correctly informs us. No doubt of it, and from the Saint Paul who was familiar to the French Evangelicals, it might have added—the Saint Paul to whom Lefèvre d'Etaples specifically refers in his *Epistre comment on doibt prier Dieu:*[51] "Jesus Christ says, speaking through Saint Paul, we do not know how to pray as we ought; but the spirit prays for us, with groanings which cannot be uttered." Yet it is precisely this quotation from Lefèvre that permits us to assess the import of Rabelais's words better and to take note of its very special emphasis. Aren't we tempted on rereading the rich and beautiful sentence the writer assigned to the giant king to remember that one great voice had ever since 1521 been proclaiming the abolition of the disastrous distinction between simple laymen living in the world and chosen and elect Christians who live out of the world and pray to God as their profession, in special places, at special hours, in forms and ceremonies that are equally special?

"By the Holy Spirit," writes a Lutheran theologian, Robert Will, analyzing the young Luther's doctrine of the priesthood of all Christians, "that is to say, by the impulses that the knowledge of Christ awakens in him, the Christian has free access to approach God. He recognizes him as a Father who adopts him. He prays. Prayer for Luther is one of the sacerdotal expressions of Christian liberty."[52] In thus cleaving to God (*adhérer* is a

---

50. "Scatter thou the people that delight in war." King James version, Psalm 68:30. [Translator's note.]

51. *Epistle on How One Ought to Pray to God.* Original reproduced in Alfred Laune, *La Traduction de l'Ancien testament de Lefèvre d'Etaples* (Le Cateau, 1895), p. 3.

52. Will, p. 136.

word Rabelais uses), the justified believer shares in the master's
birthright, his kingship, and his priesthood. He makes himself
master of God himself, the God "who carries out the will of
those who fear him and heeds their prayer." Aren't these lines a
sort of commentary on Rabelais's words, and a fairly accurate
one?

In any case, there is something different, something more, in
this passage than in the many contemporary satires on monastic
morals—in this passage and the one that immediately precedes
it, which reduce to nil the social role of monks, who do not
work like peasants or defend their country like soldiers or cure
the sick like doctors or preach and teach like good Evangelical
preachers.

"Yea, but, said Grandgousier, they pray to God for us. Nothing less, answered Gargantua."[53] Here it is not even the question of vows that is being raised anymore, but one that is fundamental in another way, the question of the sacrifice of some
for all, supported by the doctrine of the reversibility of merits,
which would be accepted by so many minds at the time of the
Counter Reformation. Rabelais's sense of justice was shocked
by it, and he rejected it in the name of an individualism that
was thoroughly modern—and Lutheran in tone. As was the
echo in the speech of the victorious king to the freed prisoners:
"Look to your families, *labour every man in his vocation*
[*Beruf*], instruct your children, and live as the good Apostle
St. Paul directeth you: in doing whereof, God, his angels and
sancts, will guard and protect you."

9. Rabelais Had Tasted the Gospel, But Through Whom?

Thus, we hope, the complexity of the problem is fully revealed.
The problem of the pros, the cons, the innovative statements. It
is not merely the common currency of goodhearted jokesters
making sport of monks, pardons, and priests' maidservants, but
the Gospel proclaimed as the sole source of religion and human

---

53. Which Voltaire, who did not care for Rabelais, seems to have had mind in his
"Man of Forty Crowns": " 'Are they [monks] more useful to the country than I am?
. . Do they cultivate the land? Do they defend the state? . . .' 'No, they pray to God
for us.' 'Well, then, I will pray to God for them in return.' " *The Works of Voltaire*,
42 vols. (Akron, Ohio, 1905), II, 275.

constitutions, doctrinal decisions by popes and councils, even the testimony of the Fathers—all that heavy baggage—rejected with scorn. There is the Christ who abolished the Law, whose Gospel stands for the spirit as opposed to the letter; Christ is practically identified with God: God is our Savior, states Gargantua explicitly. The interceding powers, the Virgin and the saints, are given a very lowly place. Monasticism is condemned, not for its abuses, but in the name of the same principle; the domination of those who arrogate to themselves the right to administer and distribute the grace of God to men is threatened and overturned. These are all important pieces of a religious system that we obviously cannot, in the light of the Tridentine decrees, call "Catholic." Over all of them wafts that breath of Luther.

Rabelais had tasted the Gospel, as Calvin asserted. And in 1532 and 1534 he was well aware of having tasted it. With a sincerity that cannot be doubted in any way, he stood by the side of those whose spiritual life was derived from it. He served the cause of these men in *Pantagruel, Gargantua,* and the short works that have been preserved. He interpreted it and pleaded it with all his talent. Some of the innovators' main themes—not all of them, but almost all—he illuminated and developed in a powerful manner. Did he do this without any illusions? That is the real problem. For it is possible at certain moments to be, in all good conscience, mistaken about one's true nature—to say and think one is an Evangelical when one is the father, creator, and most perfect adept of Pantagruelism.

Rabelais could have said and thought he was an Evangelical. In those troubled years between 1530 and 1535 he could have stood by the side of innovators who, twenty years later, after many changes, were going to recognize Calvin's Geneva as their spiritual homeland. If he had already carefully analyzed himself to the depths of his mind and conscience he would have perceived all the things that separated him from those who were really Protestants. Was it his bawdiness? If you wish, although in the polemical literature of the Reformation that was nothing especially shocking to so many authors of pamphlets written in rather free language. It was much more his fundamental moralism, the huge place he gave to the ideal of moral perfection that his *raisonneurs* never cease to proclaim. Above all, just as strong as his inability to comprehend a penitential attitude was his refusal to be obsessed by sin that defiles everything and radically corrupts human beings. The giants might indeed proclaim the omnipotence of the Creator. But never did those mighty bodies, those judicious minds, experience the sort of stupefied terror before the dread majesty of the Lord that led someone like Luther to flee "like a badger into the cracks of rocks," from the justice of a God who, because of his limitless grandeur, was more frightening than the devil in all his rage.

And so a question arises. The Gospel as the sole source of faith, human constitutions revoked, all those articles of a program of energetic and specific reforms that we enumerated above—would they have been found around the year 1530 in the work of men other than the Reformers? Rabelais had tasted the Gospel, but who had led him to become for a while its resounding herald? Had he tasted it only under the influence of the Reformation and the Reformers and through their activity alone?

8. Rabelais, Erasmus, and the Philosophy of Christ

 R O U N D 1520 Rabelais was a monk in the monastery of the Friars Minor in Fontenay-le-Comte, studying Greek and trying to compose letters in that language. He had as a companion Pierre Amy, who would later introduce him to Guillaume Budé and who, "having escaped the ambush of the hobgoblins," would end his life out of the monastery under strong suspicion of being a follower of the Reformation. At that time the activity of men concerned with religious problems and with the means of bringing about a renewal that all recognized as indispensable oscillated between two poles. It moved back and forth between Luther and Erasmus.

This is an important fact, too often lost sight of, and it explains any number of works and events of the time. Generally speaking, however, the second half of the nineteenth century did not concern itself much with Erasmus. It did not understand him, because its knowledge of him was meager or inaccurate. What is the reason for his being so long out of favor? Undoubtedly the blame must fall on the worship of success, the tendency to be on the winning side that was characteristic of the historiography of an age when physical power was esteemed at the expense of intellectual power.

1. An Erasmus for Our Time

Historically speaking, Erasmus appears as a loser, Luther and Loyola as winners. That is the case. Between the reformed religion ardently preached by Luther and rigorously organized by Calvin and what can be called the Tridentine form of Catholicism, the humanist religion of Erasmus, his "philosophy of Christ," went into an abrupt and total eclipse, no matter what requital may have been in store for it in the near or distant future. To be more precise, the schism, Rome's condemnation of Luther, and the decisive scene at Worms sounded the knell of Erasmus's great designs. It had not been his intention to choose a position equidistant from two lines of battle, between religions in violent opposition to each other, and establish a school of sages who drew their sustenance from antiquity and the Gospel, miraculously reconciling traditional Catholicism, the Protestantism of renewal, and a modicum of critical rationalism. He wanted a select few, who were inspired by his thought and supported his efforts, to prevent not only a fatal schism (which was not the issue when he began to publish his great religious writings, long before the appearance of Luther), but an unfortunate split between two spirits that, according to him, were meant to complement each other, to interpenetrate, and ultimately to be fused in the vital unity of a philosophy of Christ with unlimited possibilities for development and change—the spirit of free and critical inquiry stemming from the Renaissance and the spirit of respectful, trusting adherence to dogma that formed the traditional strength and unity of the Church.

Up to the very moment of the schism and the decisive check to his efforts at mediation, he preached and believed in the possibility of the spiritual reformation of a Church that allowed Christians of all schools to feel like brothers, free of antagonisms and anathemas, and—rejecting useless subtleties, unnecessary obscurities, and a self-infatuated theology's tyrannical as well as dangerous deductions, interpretations, and constructions—that united men of good will and sound conscience around a very few tenets. These were contained in the Apostles' Creed and were to be interpreted purely, so to speak, according to the light of the Gospel. Still, it was necessary to understand the function and exact significance of these tenets. It was not a matter of finding obscure explanations and thus bit by bit creating a theology exactly like the one that was supposed to be destroyed—although on this point Erasmus's ideas seemed quixotic, since a spirit of subtlety should be recognized that was not the special domain of one caste but the common property of countless men. What difference did it make if the Spirit proceeded from the Father, or the Son, or the Father *and* the Son? The main thing was to cultivate the gifts of the Spirit—love, joy, goodness, patience, faith, humility—and to keep the life-giving fountainhead of a spontaneous moral life in one's heart.

It was a beautiful dream, closely related to what Erasmus's friend, Thomas More, had described in 1516 in a famous little book which sketched the broad outlines of the free, simple, and eminently tolerant religion of the Utopians. Erasmus, however, was pleased to conceive another dream, even more beautiful perhaps, if not harder to put into practice. This was to see, through the exertion of broad, humane understanding, the gradual disappearance of the tenets to which he asked unanimous adherence and agreement among the faithful—no matter how few those tenets and how truly basic. Just as he rejected the literal meaning in interpreting the Old Testament, just as he dared to say that even the New Testament—this was one of the boldest statements a man of his time could make—even the New Testament, however historical it seemed, had a life-giving spirit that transcended its literal meaning and its corruptible flesh, so he could envision the possibility that truly superior minds might one day substitute for the imperative-sounding articles of the Creed an interpretation of the higher truths they represented that was at once more profound, more personal, and more humane.

2. This Erasmus and Our Rabelais

So there is nothing astonishing about the fact that for years there was a whole elite that lived off this man, a man full of talent, full of knowledge, full of refinement and brilliance. There were his widely read books: the *Enchiridion*, the *Encomium moriae*, the *Adages*, the *Colloquies*. There was his famous edition of the New Testament, with the wealth of controversies and explanations attached to it. There were all those letters lavished on the scholars of all Europe, which were shown off, copied, and circulated everywhere. These were, between 1500 and 1530, the deep springs of intellectual and spiritual life from which thousands of men scattered all over Christendom drank their fill.

One would then assume, if one did not know, that Erasmus's thought, as it had developed and been conveyed in some remarkable books long before 1517 and the appearance of Luther, was known and savored by Rabelais. Everything existed to create a current of sympathy and prior affection between the beginner and the triumphant master. Think of the striking parallelism of their two lives. While an Augustinian monk at the monastery of Steyn, Erasmus had been ordained a priest. While a Franciscan monk at the monastery of Fontenay-le-Comte, Rabelais had been ordained a priest. At Steyn, Erasmus, with several friends, especially Servatius Rogerus, the closest of all, had secretly read at night the Latin classics, poets, philosophers, and scholars. Little by little there was born in him—along with the feeling that his vocation was primarily literary ("velut occulta naturae vi rapiebar ad bonas litteras,"[1] he would later write) and along with a growing hunger for freedom ("vellem eam mihi vitae libertatem fata sinerent natura quam contulit,"[2] a sigh that speaks volumes)—a feeling of inner protest against the intellectual poverty and lack of polish of those around him. He already called them barbarians at this period, sharpening the darts he would hurl at them in his *Antibarbari* of 1520.[3] This was Erasmus at Steyn. As for Rabelais at Fontenay, he too, with his companion Pierre Amy and the learned men of the district, the judge Tiraqueau and the lieutenant of the baillage Bouchard, had secretly devoured the works of the two ancient civilizations. He had even learned Greek, because times had changed since Erasmus had left Steyn. The age of Pantagruel had succeeded the age of Gargantua.

In short, Tiraqueau could write a eulogy of Rabelais that, word for word, would have fitted the Augustinian of Steyn: "a man superior to his age, superior to his calling as a Franciscan,

---

1. "It was as though I was drawn to literature by some hidden force of nature."

2. "I would that my destiny permitted me the same degree of freedom as nature bestowed on me." *The Correspondence of Erasmus*, trans. R. A. B. Mynors and D. F. S. Thomson, The Collected Works of Erasmus, 1 (Toronto, 1974), p. 16.

3. On Servatius Rogerus, see *Opus epistolarum Des. Erasmi Roterodami*, ed. P. S. Allen and H. M. Allen, 12 vols. (Oxford, 1906–1958), I, 77. It was to him that Erasmus wrote, around 1488, "*vellem*, etc." On Erasmus's life in the monastery, see Jean Baptiste Pineau, *Erasme, sa pensée religieuse* (Thèse de doctorat ès lettres, Paris, 1924), ch. 2, p. 24 ff.

one might well say superior to his status as a monk."[4] Conversely, Rabelais at the monastery could have recognized his own feelings if he had read the plea that Erasmus addressed to the papal chancellery in 1516, in which he recounted his early experiences.[5] Like the future author of the *Colloquies*, didn't the man who was then a religious at Fontenay cherish along with his resolute passion for study a lively horror of ceremonies that ate up time and a no less lively revulsion for the rabble of monks, who were only concerned with tippling and feasting? Having started out like this, Erasmus had left the monastery without fuss or scandal, "permissu atque adeo jussu episcopi ordinarii."[6] Rabelais, meanwhile, feeling the spur that prompts men who are "free and well-born" to fulfill their nature, had for his part quit the monastery of Puy-Saint-Martin, he too with the permission of his bishop, and had entered the Benedictine abbey of Saint-Pierre in Maillezais, whose monks served as canons of the cathedral.

There were similarities in their lives and analogies in their situations; but there were deeper resemblances between the two men. Both the one and the other had early on felt mysterious paths opening up between their Christianity and the wisdom of antiquity. The one like the other was inclined to base his theology on both sacred writings and profane writings, taken together. Both the one and the other were at war with the education they had first received. They were at war with the idiotic basic books, "Papiam, Hugutoniem, Ebrardum, Catholicon, Joannem Garlandum, Isidorum"—the list was compiled by Erasmus,[7] before Rabelais compiled his[8] and after Valla his.[9] For the one as for the other, finally, humanism was not a literary game or mere formal perfection. It was a light that dispelled the darkness. It is not astonishing that sympathy was awakened

4. "Vir supra aetatem, praeterque ejus sodalicii morem, ne nimiam religionem dicam, utriusque linguae omnifariaeque doctrinae peritissimus." Jean Plattard, *L'Adolescence de Rabelais en Poitou* (Paris, 1923), pp. 23–24.

5. This is the letter supposedly to Lambert Grunnius, on which see the note in Allen, II, 292.

6. "With permisison and even by order of the bishop's ordinary."

7. Allen, I, 26, ll. 88–89.

8. "Who read unto him Hugutio, Hebrard's *Grecisme*, the Doctrinal, the Parts, the Quid est, the Supplementum, Marmoret, De Moribus in mensa servandis; Seneca de quatuor virtutibus cardinalibus; Passavantus cum commento . . ." *Gargantua*, ch. 14.

9. In his *Elegantiae linguae latinae*, II.

in the younger of the two men for the elder. Can we find signs of it in his writings?

3. Some Borrowings

To start with (that was quite a while ago), we looked into that marvelous comedy in one hundred diverse acts, the *Colloquies* —a masterpiece of irony, of dialectic (meaning two-person thinking), of prudence sometimes bordering on wiliness, of calculated daring masked by a pretended innocence. It was almost immediately apparent that Rabelais had read the *Colloquies* and had shamelessly taken generous helpings from them. Erasmus denounced the College of Montaigu as an intellectual prison, a den of squalor and unspeakable misery. Rabelais consigned Montaigu to royal prosecution and to his own loathing, but without having had Erasmus's personal experiences or his justified resentment. On the behavior of monks, Erasmus stated the themes and Rabelais developed them. The rapacious flock of black birds who swoop down on the dying in the colloquies *Funus* (*The Funeral*) and *Franciscani* (*The Well-to-do Beggars*)[10] are the same as those who are chased away by the old French poet Raminagrobis, anxious to assure himself some peace in his last hours. In *Ichthyphagia* (*A Fish Diet*) Erasmus tells the story of a nun who becomes ill in the dormitory and refuses to cry out: the rule above all. Rabelais (*Book Three*, ch. 19) is familiar with the scrupulous nun and even knows her name, a Rabelaisian one. The ex-Augustinian sings of the felicity of homes whose thresholds are touched by Franciscan sandals, because there fruitfulness has its abode (*Exequiae seraphicae*, *The Seraphic Funeral*). The former Franciscan of Fontenay goes further (*Gargantua*, ch. 45): "the very shadow of the steeple of an abbey is fruitful." Erasmus in the *Colloquies* makes fun of the abbot who strictly forbids his monks to study (*Abbatis et eruditae*, *The Abbot and the Learned Lady*): "I do not want my monks to spend time reading books." Friar John was familiar with that abbot, who had said to him it was a monstrous thing to see a learned monk (*Gargantua*, ch. 39). He kept his monks from studying "for fear of the mumps." In Erasmus there is indignation, with a personal accent, against the

---

10. Erasmus's title is *Ptochoplousioi*. The English translations are from *The Colloquies of Erasmus*, trans. Craig R. Thompson (Chicago, 1965).

forcing of the will; Rabelais echoes it. The colloquy *The Ship-wreck* (*Naufragium*) presents passengers and sailors in danger of drowning; some invoke the Virgin and the saints, others do not. Rabelais took note and would remember when he wrote about the storm in *Book Four*. The saints? Erasmus shows them as full of vengeance, visiting horrible afflictions on those of the faithful who neglect to worship them. We know what Rabelais thought about such superstitions. What about pilgrimages? Erasmus laughs at the folly of those who abandon wife, children, home, job, and property to go on them. Grandgousier sends these fools back home, back to their wives, their children, and their occupations (*Gargantua*, ch. 45). But this is enough, I think, to show that the French Lucian had not neglected to read the *Colloquies*—and had profited from them.

The French Lucian—before him, Erasmus had been a Lucian, not a Dutch one, but one who was universal. If Rabelais found it so easy to write like Lucian, wasn't it because Erasmus had given him the wherewithal? Or at least had prepared the way? In his catalogue of publications, *Catalogus lucubrationum*, compiled in 1523,[11] the list of his translations of the Greek author can be found: twenty-four dialogues, seventeen works of other kinds. Erasmus kept coming back to Lucian with particular affection. Starting in November 1506 he published a whole slew of Lucian translations at the firm of Josse Badius in Paris: *Toxaris, Timon*, the well-known *Cock*, the essay *On Salaried Posts in Great Houses*, and *Pseudomantis*. Thomas More was associated with him in this great popularizing effort; he himself had translated *The Tyrannicide*.[12] Erasmus would retain his taste for Lucian. He would pass him along to everyone he came in contact with. The first edition of the Greek text of Lucian in its entirety, with complete Latin translation and notes—often reprinted in the sixteenth century and the early years of the seventeenth—was prepared for the Basel publisher Heinrich Petri in 1563 by the humanist Gilbert Cousin of Nozeroy (in the Franche-Comté), who was Erasmus's secretary in his last years, from 1530 to 1533.[13]

11. In a letter to John von Botzheim. Allen, I, 38–39.

12. Erasmus's titles are *Toxaris sive amicitia, Timon sive Misanthropus, Somnium sive Gallus, Libellus de iis qui mercede conducti in divitum familiis vivunt, Alexander seu Pseudomantis*, and *Tyrannicida*. [Translator's note.]

13. A. Pidoux, "Bibliographie historique des oeuvres de Gilbert Cousin," *Le Bibliographe Moderne*, 15 (1911), 132–171.

It is true that Erasmus did not merely stick to the form of Lucian's writings but was inspired by the spirit that guided them and applied Horace's words of praise to the Greek author—"The man who mingles the useful with the sweet carries the day." (Omne tulit punctum, qui miscuit utile dulci.)[14] Nevertheless, when looking for the intellectual connection between Erasmus and Rabelais it is a good idea to go beyond the *Colloquies* and their Lucianic charm and wit. If it is true that Erasmus presented to his learned and studious contemporaries a type of religion that was markedly different from the Lutheran type and better suited to the special needs and natural inclinations of humanists, isn't it proper to search for other sources of Rabelais's inspiration, sources that were deeper and more inward? To search for them, above all, in the *Enchiridion*, one of the most widely read books of the sixteenth century; in *The Praise of Folly*; and in the *Adages*, that treasury of ancient wisdom rejuvenated by a modern author of profound humanity?

4. The Daring of Erasmus and the Daring of Rabelais

When someone who is a little familiar with *Gargantua* and *Pantagruel* takes the trouble to fathom Erasmus's thought as it is encapsulated in these little volumes crammed full of antique pith and living substance, he is struck at once by an obvious fact. Considered in its broad outlines, the giants' catechism is exactly the same as the catechism of Erasmus in the *Enchiridion*, *The Praise of Folly*, and the *Adages*.

There are few articles, in one place and the other. There are no theological subtleties. Christ is at the center of religious life—Christ and the Gospel, interpreted with sincerity. Between this God and man there are no useless intercessors: the Virgin and the saints, reduced to the ranks, play only a secondary and remote role. There is no pessimism. The stain of original sin is learnedly attenuated; confidence is proclaimed in the proper virtue and fundamental probity of human nature; finally, moral duty is placed in the forefront. The sacraments are reduced in number, dignity, and value; ceremonies and obser-

---

14. *Ars poetica*, l. 343. Trans. by Edward Henry Blakeney in *The Complete Works of Horace*, ed. Casper J. Kraemer, Jr. (New York, 1936). [Translator's note.]

vances are judged to be inefficacious by themselves and subordinated to rectitude of conscience; finally, the monastic life is judged mercilessly as to its theory and its practice. This is the basis of Erasmus's religion as described in the *Enchiridion*, *The Praise of Folly*, the *Adages*, and the *Colloquies*. And it is also the basis, as we have seen, of the religion of the giants and of Rabelais. There is not a single religious phrase in *Pantagruel* or *Gargantua* that could not be footnoted with a wealth of sentences from Erasmus. Nor even—I am deliberately using an absurd expression—a single philosophical phrase.

We examined earlier the interpretations that might be given of the famous passage in *Gargantua* on the rule of conduct for the Thelemites (ch. 57): "In all their rule, and strictest tie of their order, there was but this one clause to be observed, DO WHAT THOU WILT. Because men that are free, well-born, well-bred, and conversant in honest companies, have naturally an instinct and spur that prompteth them unto virtuous actions, and withdraws them from vice, which is called honour." In order to examine the passage we confronted it directly, just as it appears in Rabelais, without asking any questions about its origin. We did, however, know its origin. Let us open up Erasmus's second *Hyperaspistes*, which appeared in September 1527 and was directed against Luther. Of it Renaudet wrote: "Never before had Erasmus's religion, his conception of divine grace, broadly and generously offered to all souls, and the instinctive revulsion of his mind and heart against Luther's idea of a fierce and angry God found more human expression."[15] And he added: "Never had Erasmus's rationalism confronted Luther's irrationalism more directly." Now it is possible to read in this book (which apparently was studied closely by Rabelais) the following passage: "Fateor in quibusdam ingeniis bene natis ac bene educatis minimum esse pravitatis. Maxima proclivitatis pars est non ex natura, sed ex corrupta institutione, ex improbo convictu, ex assuetudine peccandi, malitiaque voluntatis."[16] It is not really necessary to translate the Latin. Rabelais provides an elegant trans-

---

15. Augustin Renaudet, *Etudes Erasmiennes (1521–1529)* (Paris, 1939), p. 281.

16. "I confess that in certain well-born and well-bred minds there is very little vice. The greatest component of such a predisposition is not from nature but from corrupt education, wicked company, habituation to sin, and ill will." *Desiderii Erasmi Roterodami opera omnia*, 10 vols. (Leyden, 1703–1706; photographic reprint, Hildesheim, 1962), X, col. 1454.

lation. We should only note that the form used by Erasmus justifies the interpretation we have suggested for it in the form
used by Rabelais.

What is more, this is not an isolated passage. In *De pueris
statim ac liberaliter instituendis*, which he brought out in 1529,
right after he moved to Fribourg, we find the assertion that
human nature is basically good. Of course Christian doctrine,
the *Christiana philosophia*, teaches us the consequences of
Adam's transgression, the inclination to evil residing in us ever
since that time. That is true, but let us not accuse the child's
nature more than it deserves: *praeter meritum accusare naturam*. Of itself that nature is inclined to good, not evil. And
Erasmus specifically says: "The dog is born to hunt, the bird to
fly, the horse to run, the ox to plow; so man is born to love wisdom and fair deeds." The nature of man can also be defined as
"an inclination, a deeply instinctive propensity to good." At
which a critic who was citing these passages exclaimed, "Nothing is more contrary to Christian doctrine."[17] And he quoted
the following remark of Calvin: "Our nature is so prolific of
every sort of evil that it can allow itself no respite." For Luther
he referred to numerous passages that Denifle had interpreted
in this way. But, after all, Calvin and Luther are not "Christian
doctrine," are they? They are Calvinist doctrine, to be sure, and
Lutheran doctrine, but no more. What if we look at Saint
Thomas, for example? He concedes that there subsists in the
fallen nature that derives from original sin a natural inclination
toward the true and the good. As for Rabelais, he was only a
poor little brother of Saint Francis and there is no question of
equating him with the Doctors of the Faith. But it is curious to
see that one of the statements most frequently referred to and
quoted as being among the most characteristic of his way of
thinking comes so clearly from Erasmus. From the Erasmus
who was ultimately to blame for the "naturalist" failure to meet
the exigencies of Christianity so often deplored by non-Chris-
tians. That is, to hear them tell it.

There is more. Rabelais's acts of daring were all committed
by the pen of Erasmus, only in much more accentuated form,
less good-natured, less rustic, more cutting. Here are some ex-

17. Pineau, p. 11, n. 48.

amples that come to mind. Remember Hurtali and the jokes about Noah's Ark? We saw they were rather pale compared to the liberties taken by Origen with the "puerile" accounts in Genesis. But if that high-spirited and heterodox Father made such a harsh mockery of the "biblical fables," it was in order to conclude that we must look for their deep spiritual meaning. Erasmus had read Origen. Luther, following in the wake of Beda, took him much to task for that. He had been urged to read him by the Franciscan Vitrier, partly under whose influence he had written the first draft of the *Enchiridion.* He turned to his own purposes the somewhat shocking jokes of Celsus's famous adversary. But he was less impassioned about searching for the spiritual meaning, and it is quite apparent that, as has been pointed out, Erasmus "leaned on Origen only to go beyond him." Open to the *Enchiridion*[18] or look again at the adage "Sileni Alcibiadis." Adam formed by a divine sculptor with the help of wet clay; the soul breathed into him; Eve manufactured from a rib of the first man; the Garden of Eden; a serpent who speaks a language that can be understood by human beings; the miraculous, nursery-tale tree; a God who strolls in his orchard in the cool of the day; the angel who stands guard with a flaming sword . . . What mythology! exclaims Erasmus. It is what one would say about the fables that came out of old Homer's inexhaustible workshop in such naive abundance. Poor Hurtali turns out to be quite harmless in comparison. And what would all our French critics say if Rabelais had taken it into his head to express similar judgments through his irreverent mouthpiece Panurge? Erasmus is not making fun of some paltry little imaginary giant astride Noah's Ark. He is mercilessly scoffing at all of Genesis, at what he wittily calls,

18. The Fifth Rule: the distinction between literal meaning and spiritual meaning as applied to the stories in Genesis. "Alioqui, si sine allegoria legeris Adae simulacrum de argilla uda formatum eique inspiratam animam, Evam de costa subductam, etc. . . . , non video, quid ita multo magis operae pretium sis facturus, quam si cantaveris luteum simulacrum Promethei, ignem dolo subductum, etc." (Otherwise, if you read without allegorical interpretation of Adam's being moulded out of damp earth and having a soul breathed into him, of Eve shaped from an extracted rib, etc. . . . , I do not see that you would be doing anything much more worth the effort than if you were to sing about the clay image made by Prometheus and how fire, stolen by a trick, etc.) English version in *The Enchiridion of Erasmus,* trans. Raymond Himelick (Bloomington, Ind., 1963), p. 105.

paraphrasing Livy, *totam orbis conditi historiam.*[19] What is Rabelais beside him? A timid and prudent orthodox Christian.[20]

What about the man from Chinon's other bold strokes? The story of Gargantua's mysterious birth, in which he arrived in the world by way of the left ear? And, in general, his not very great reverence for "Our Lady"? But just read Erasmus. Let us point out, to begin with, that if Rabelais restricts himself to not mentioning the Virgin and never directly and openly criticizes her traditional worship, Erasmus, who is infinitely more daring, does not have the same reticence. The Virgin's honorary titles are unsparingly denied to her. Is she the Mother of God? No, simply the mother of Jesus. Strip her of everything she has been given by successive generations of believers, each assiduously outdoing the other. Remove from her the names, the honors, and the achievements of which there is no mention in the Gospel and which have been bestowed on her by men alone. What is left? A simple woman, Erasmus concludes, worthy and virtuous, but who does not require preachers to begin their sermons by invoking her when they do not invoke the Holy Spirit or Christ, or the faithful to worship her images, offer her candles in broad daylight, and make vows to her that are more extraordinary than the ones heard by the Jupiter of Lucian—and of Rabelais.[21] And what about bawdy jokes? During the storm in the colloquy *The Shipwreck* the terrified sailors, not knowing where else to turn, call on Mary and intone a Salve Regina.[22] In Pantagruel's boat in *Book Four* the sailors are less devout. They leave it to Panurge alone to take care of appealing to Our Lady's sovereign benevolence. One of the speakers in the colloquy jibes, "What has she to do with the

19. "The whole history of the founding of the world."

20. "In order to be a Catholic," Renan would write, "it is necessary to believe that the first chapters of Genesis represent a true history. Well, I would wager my life twenty times over that they are only a myth." Ernest Renan, *Fragments intimes et romanesques* (Paris, 1914), pp. 32–33. "In order to be a Catholic"—but that little phrase did not have the same meaning in 1530 as in 1840.

21. *Desiderii Erasmi . . . opera,* IX, col. 942. Cf. Pineau, p. 254.

22. The choice of the Salve was deliberate. We know what polemics it gave rise to. See Sutor, *Apologeticum in novos anticomaritas praeclaris beatissimae Virginis Mariae laudibus detrahentes* (Paris: J. Parvus, 1526), ch. 3, fol. VII v, and the entire discussion in chs. 6–11. Cf. likewise Jérôme de Hangest, *Adversus antimarianos propugnacula* (1526), ch. 1 ("Novorum antimarianorum articuli"). In Rabelais there is no reference to the debate and no mention of the Salve Regina (or of the Ave Maris Stella or the Stabat Mater, which also did not escape criticism).

sea?" To which the other replies, "Formerly Venus was protec-
tress of sailors, because she was believed to have been born of
the sea. Since she gave up guarding them, the Virgin Mother
has succeeded this mother who was not a virgin."[23] There is no
doubt that this is quite an audacious joke. Without making too
much of it or using grandiloquent language, we can reflect that
it was a good thing Erasmus in his later years wrote a mass in
honor of Our Lady of Loreto, *Virgo Lauretana*, to atone for his
youthful irreverence.

The same note was struck elsewhere. This time Saint Bernard was being raked over the coals—the Virgin's knight,
whom she would one day reward for his zeal by offering him
the breast that had suckled the Infant God. You call Saint Bernard a mellifluous doctor? jibes Erasmus. Better call him Doctor
Lactifluous. In yet another place there is a little scene that says
quite a bit. Erasmus had arrived in Besançon from Basel at the
invitation of a powerful dignitary, Ferri Carondelet, the archdeacon of the chapter and the brother of one of Erasmus's pro-
tectors and friends, Jean Carondelet, the archbishop of Palermo.
At the end of one of those terrible Franche-Comté dinners,
washed down with great quantities of wine, that were such
agony for Erasmus's delicate stomach, the guests were finally
about to get up from the table. Someone began to say grace.
But what a grace! It was even more abundant than the meal.
Everything was gone through and gone through again: the Pater
Noster, the Kyrie, all the way to the De profundis. Finally the
speaker stopped, out of breath. Erasmus thought he had been
sprung, put on his hat, and made as if to disappear. But the
speaker suddenly regained his breath. "Et beata Viscera," he
bellowed at the top of his voice. "That's all we need!" groaned
the humanist in despair, in front of the absorbed and startled
canons. There followed scandal, denunciations, protests—a
whole ecclesiastical drama.[24] Indeed, if Rabelais had some ulte-
rior motive when he described Gargantua's strange birth, he

---

23. "Suffecta est huic matri non virgini virgo mater." Translation in Thompson, p.
141.

24. Allen, VI, 288 (no. 1679); Erasmus told the story to Noël Beda in order to ex-
culpate himself (March 13, 1526). "Beata viscera quae meruerunt portare filium Dei"
(Blessed are the bowels which were worthy to carry the son of God), said the Little
Office of the Virgin. On Erasmus's stay in Besançon, see Armand Boussey, "Erasme à
Besançon," *Bulletin de l'Académie des Sciences, Belles-lettres, et Arts de Besançon*, 127
(1896), 48.

was doing nothing new. He had a predecessor in his dubious audacity: that *enfant terrible*, Erasmus of Rotterdam.

So it was with everything. Did Rabelais extinguish the fires of hell? It was not hard, since Erasmus had extinguished them before him. And without even hiding behind a fiction. He had said quite plainly that the infernal flames were only a figure of speech of the Gospel. To follow the path of Christ was to prepare one's entrance into a *felicitas* whose nature he did not tell us about: his Paradise was lacking in imagination. On the other hand, to turn aside from the path of Christ was to prepare one's punishment in the next world. To doubt that, one would have to be neither a Christian nor a man. But what would be the nature of that punishment? It would be entirely moral. The worm that gnaws at the impious is remorse, which does not wait for death in order to begin its work. The flame that torments the rich man of Scripture and all those ingenious tortures that the poets describe (*de quibus multa scripsere poetae*, we have been warned: the descriptions of hell are poetic commonplaces)—we understand by these picturesque words, which we should avoid taking literally, only the constant anxiety of souls that are addicted to the practice of vice. This is an indisputably daring passage. For it caused an outcry.[25] The Sorbonne took note of it, and Erasmus had to declare in 1526 that he had no doubts about hellfire: *de igne gehennae*. He had no doubts; he metaphorized it.

Need I go on? It is not very interesting. For if these audacities of Erasmus (who in many ways was more obvious) correspond to the greatest acts of daring that have been detected in the work of Rabelais, for Erasmus they were only timid audacities. His true acts of daring were of another sort, and no equivalent to them is to be found in any of Rabelais's works. We might therefore do without any allusion to them, but we are, after all, attempting to locate Rabelais's religion in relation to the other religions of his time. A few examples will permit us to assess what the "Christian liberty" was that someone like Erasmus was employing around 1520. It was extreme liberty, so extreme that the Bedas of the Sorbonne and elsewhere were already crying heresy, so extreme that there are subtle doctors

25. For the references, see Pineau, pp. 130–131.

today who, too eager to show themselves sharper than truth, and, besides, totally unconscious of anachronism, write rather persuasive books in which they picture an Erasmus who had "ceased to be a Christian"—just as this has been said of Rabelais. There is no need to say that we are unable to go along with them, since, beyond Rabelais, this whole book is aimed at what we consider to be a distortion of intellectual and religious history.

5. Who Was More Daring?

One becomes a Christian through baptism, that second birth. It is the sacrament that erases original sin and causes the creature to pass from the death of sin to the life of grace. It saves him from the deadly grip of hell in order to number him among the children of God and give him a right to Paradise. Wait a minute, says Erasmus: "You are baptized, but don't think you are a Christian!"[26] What makes a Christian is not the ritual but the right intention. If you do not have it, baptized though you are, you are not a Christian. If you do have it, even though you are a pagan, you are a Christian. Whereupon we should not ask in a somewhat melodramatic voice, "What happens to ritual? To the sacrament? To dogma?" The most elementary of catechisms instructs us that in order to be a good Christian it is not enough to have received baptism. One must, in addition, believe in Christian doctrine and practice the duties it imposes. Let us not ask the question, and let us not discuss the matter. It is a needless effort, after the chapter by Renaudet and after Marcel Bataillon's arguments.[27] Let us simply take note of the boldness of what Renaudet, adopting a parallel I had established earlier, called Erasmian modernism. And then let us refer to the passages from Rabelais that we cited above. Where is the daring, the real and profound daring?

The Christian's food, the substance of his faith, is the Eucharist. Through it he receives the body, the blood, the soul, and

26. "Baptizatus es: ne protinus te christianum putes," says the *Enchiridion*. Cf. Pineau, p. 123.

27. The chapter entitled "Le Modernisme Erasmien" in Renaudet; the entire chapter on the *Enchiridion* in Marcel Bataillon, *Erasme et l'Espagne, recherches sur l'histoire spirituelle du XVIe siècle* (Paris, 1937), especially p. 221.

the divinity of Christ under the species of bread and wine. But what about Erasmus? Let us be on our guard here against false sentimentality. Let us not exclaim that a believer has not words enough with which to celebrate the sacrament's benefits, to describe his hunger and thirst for the divine body, and to testify to his absolute faith that it is God, his God, who is really present in the sacrifice. We would be committing the same error, the same anachronism—and for the same reasons—that we pointed out above in connection with Theleme, when we talked about "the holy sacrifice of the mass." That is what *we* call it, but it is certainly not what the Thelemites called it. The Eucharist has a history. Let us not forget that from the year 1000 until the first years of the sixteenth century it was the practice of very pious persons, the members of the three orders, nuns, even ecstatics, to take communion three or four times a year at most. Father Tacchi Venturi, in one of the few books of any value that we possess on the history of devotions, *La Storia della Compagnia di Gesù in Italia*, clearly establishes this.[28] It was not until after the Council of Trent—less abstractly and with only France in mind, let us say after the *Introduction to the Devout Life*[29]—that frequent communion was established, that a mystique of the Eucharist took hold more and more, and, finally, that Christian perfection was defined as Antoine Arnauld defined it: the possibility of being near the Son of God every day.

With this reservation in mind, what did Erasmus say about the Eucharist that scandalizes some of our contemporaries—who are not in the habit of taking the sacraments themselves but never think anyone speaks emphatically enough of their efficacy? Some things that are really rather surprising. That for him it evoked reminders of antiquity. That bread among the ancients was a symbol of friendship. That they broke bread together when they wanted to form a bond of a sacred character with each other. That this is what Christ did with his disciples. Erasmus said even more. He said that this was the origin of Christ's action in distributing the bread to his disciples and

28. 2d ed., 2 vols. (Rome, 1950–1951). See likewise Henri Bremond, *Histoire littéraire du sentiment religieux en France depuis la fin des guerres de religion jusqu'à nos jours*, 11 vols. (Paris, 1916–1933), IV, where there is an excursus on the subject.
29. By Saint Francis of Sales. [Translator's note.]

consecrating an eternal friendship among them: "unde et Christus, princeps noster, distributo pane, perpetuam inter suos consecrabat amicitiam." Friendship? We know the beautiful definition that Erasmus gave of Christianity: "nihil aliud quam vera perfectaque amicitia."[30] It is surely neither flat nor weak. Of course, a man of our times, borrowing the language of contemporary devotion, might exclaim, "What, for Erasmus, happens to the great mystery of a God who is really present in the host, a God who with his flesh, his blood, and his substance nourishes the avid heart of the believer? What happens to the efficacious power of the sacrament?"

The power of the sacrament? Erasmus immediately replies: "Everything depends on the communicant's attitude." Didn't Christ himself say so? What a contemptible thing it is to eat flesh and drink wine if the physical eating is not joined to spiritual eating! The Eucharist is a danger for someone whose attitude is not what it should be. Indeed, at this point it would be well to point out that Zwingli agreed: he had listened to his master, taken note of his words, and proceeded to make them tougher. The Sacramentarians agreed, and they put Erasmus's words into practice. With regard to baptism, which did not somehow automatically remove sin; or sin, which was nothing but a simple inclination to evil, which man could overcome; or those who were not baptized but well-intentioned, who would be saved; or the Eucharist, finally, which was purely symbolic—they made out of Erasmus's opinions, developing them and systematizing them, a complete body of doctrine. But there were others who also listened—those who felt no overriding need within themselves for a defined faith, who were free in spirit, had been nurtured more on ancient literature than on Christian teaching, and went further in their desire for libera-

---

30. "Nothing but true and perfect friendship." Allen, I, 417 (no. 187); cf. Pineau, p. 115. Alongside Erasmus's brief definition, put this one by Nicholas Bourbon: "Deo servire ex animo et liberaliter / Et credere Christum meruisse aeterni ut Patris / Gens electa sumus et haeredes Filii; / Crucem suam ferre et parere regibus, / Prodesse cunctis et nocere nemini: / Hoc Christianismo quid Christianius?" (To serve God freely and from the heart and to believe Christ obtained leave from his eternal Father that we should be an elect people and his Son's heirs; to bear his cross and be obedient to kings, to do good to all and harm to none—what is more Christian than a Christianity like this?) *Nicolai Borbonii Vandoperani Lingonensis nugarum libri octo* (Lyon: S. Gryphius, 1538), p. 345.

tion. They listened and came to the conclusion that the great power of the Eucharist, without anything more mysterious about it, was the power of commemoration.

Furthermore, Christianity was the religion of Christ, but what was Christ? Under what species was he to be imagined? We know with what ardor the believer exerts himself to imitate his Savior, keeps him before his eyes, and evokes the circumstances of his terrestrial life and dramatic death. We know with what keen compassion he meditates on the cross, contemplates his redeemer as he suffers and dies for him, and kisses the wounds from which the regenerating blood of his God flows. What about Erasmus? At times it could be said that for an explanation of the mystery of the cross he turned, not to the little book that nurtured the chosen Christians in the monastery of his youth, but to an authority who was a little unexpected—Socrates. The explanation, too, was unexpected. Despise external things and, through love of things that are spiritual and invisible, let the soul triumph over the body—that was the lesson of the cross.[31] It was a lesson that was totally abstract and totally moral. As for imitating ordinary Christians who reread the story of the Passion every day, prostrated themselves before the crucifix, decorated their bodies with thousands of crosses, venerated some supposed fragments of the True Cross they kept at home, or for hours on end recalled and meditated on the sufferings of Christ in order to be stirred by a pity that was totally carnal—no, Christ was not the doleful man on the cross, the pathetic victim whom thousands upon thousands of painted and sculptured images in the churches showed to the prostrate faithful, affecting them viscerally. Christ was neither a man nor a person. And it could be said that Erasmus sometimes extended to the New Testament the distinction he made in the Old Testament between the literal meaning and the spiritual meaning of the narrative. He regarded the Savior's passion and death as so many allegories to be interpreted by the elect; the mob, however, bound to the concrete, did not perceive their deep significance. Christ was a precept, a moral doctrine, nothing else but the virtues he preached—charity, simplicity, patience, purity:

31. Pineau, p. 116. On the difficulty of grasping the actual person of Jesus, which Erasmus pointed out, see Renaudet, p. 162.

"Christum ... nihil aliud quam caritatem, simplicitatem, patientiam, puritatem, breviter quicquid ille docuit."[32]

Let it be understood that we are not about to make any literal or summary interpretations, without counterweights or correctives, of an extraordinarily rich mind—and, besides, one that developed over time. We know very well that other passages can be lined up alongside these that are authentically and irreproachably orthodox. We know very well that any sentence separated from its context easily takes on a deceptive prominence, and that any phrase is susceptible of different translations. "Res tanta nihil est [Eucharistia] imo perniciosa, nisi adsit Spiritus"—how is this sentence to be translated so that the thought is not falsified? "This Eucharist, which is of such great value, is nothing but a danger if the Spirit does not give it its efficacy"? Here the very idea of the sacrament has been done away with and destroyed. But suppose we say: "Will this precious Eucharist produce all the beneficial effects we ought to expect and not cause any unfortunate ones if the ground is poorly prepared?" Here is respectable orthodoxy, since the Church teaches that the sacraments sanctify only those who receive them with a good attitude. There is not one phrase that Erasmus employs on these burning issues that is not susceptible of two interpretations thoroughly different in spirit. Which is to say that people find in Erasmus—and this was already true in his own time—what is in themselves. The orthodox found their orthodoxy, the Reformed found their Reformation, the skeptics found their irony. This does not preclude the existence of an Erasmian way of thinking, as it does not preclude the existence of a Rabelaisian way of thinking. Was it a Christian way of thinking? Luther said no. So did Beda. But we know what to make of those anathemas from fanatics or visionaries. Erasmus himself said yes, with all his might. And so did not only Zwingli his disciple, the Sacramentarians, and hundreds of superior men scattered all over Christendom, but—to speak only of them—all those thousands of Spaniards who made the *Enchiridion* the most read, along with the *Imitation*, of all books of piety and who went to it to draw out the pure essence of a

32. Pineau, p. 115. Cf. this other passage from Erasmus: "[Christus] a nobis praeter puram simplicemque vitam nihil exigit." (Christ demands nothing of us beyond a pure and simple life.) Allen, III, 364 (no. 858).

totally spiritual Christianity, a Pauline Christianity that "sought to meet God in a new mood of confidence and freedom."

6. How Far Rabelais Went Along with Erasmus

People found in Erasmus what was in themselves. What did Rabelais find? He has not told us. All he did was proclaim one day in truly moving terms his whole intellectual debt to Erasmus, saying he was truly his spiritual son. This was in the famous so-called letter to Salignac, whose testimony we have already invoked. Was it a showpiece, a stylistic exercise to which it would be foolish to attach any importance? That is easily said. We should note that when Rabelais wrote this extremely handsome testimonial of his gratitude to Erasmus he was no longer at the age of childish enthusiasms, however one dates the events of his life. We should also note that when Rabelais took up his pen Erasmus was an old man, attacked and vilified on all sides—defeated, in short, and no longer the brilliant hero, the champion of Christ, the only possible successor to Luther, the man whom Dürer so touchingly apostrophized in a well-known passage in his journal when he heard false news of the Reformer's death in 1521. Yet the letter to Salignac clearly has only a general application. It is impossible to get out of it what it does not contain.

We have already said that when one looks at passages in Rabelais and compares them to passages in Erasmus one is struck by their timidity. They are several steps behind the latter's least audacious passages. Nowhere does Rabelais indicate that he has seen how a clever man might use the daring interpretations, innuendoes, and sometimes disturbing evasions in Erasmus to plant a series of disquieting doubts in perceptive minds.

All this, of course, on the hypothesis that Rabelais was an enemy of Christ, a "militant freethinker" out to deal formidable blows to Christianity. Freethinker or not, was Rabelais really aware that Erasmus's formulations, skillfully reworked, might lead far afield, undermine revelation, make the Gospel story more rational and human, and substitute a Christianity of the brotherhood of man for a Christianity of redemption? For my part, I do not believe that Rabelais or any of his contemporaries could have perceived as clearly as men in the twentieth century can the train of conclusions that four centuries of work in philosophy, philology, and history allow us to draw from a few statements when they are stretched to their limit and pushed in a particular direction. In any case, no passage in Rabelais says anything of the sort. Most of what he is known to have borrowed from the author of the *Colloquies* has to do, as we have seen, with ideas for dialogue, repartee, jokes, and social satire that is only skin-deep. Of innuendoes, the kind of innuendoes that never stop once they have started on their way and about which one has no idea how far the person who started them meant to go, there is not a sign. Not if one does not accept— and we do not—the interpretation Abel Lefranc has suggested for Gargantua's "wholly to die" and Epistemon's absurd resurrection.

There is more. If a cursory look at Erasmus's great religious writings leads us to regard Rabelais's daring as somewhat pallid compared to the bold innovations of the philosophy of Christ, by the same token we can better appreciate and take all the more seriously the pious declarations of the giants and their chronicler. Is this a paradox? There is a certain Rabelaisian tone that is not of the Reformation—is it Erasmian?

Certainly Rabelais and his heroes have in common with Erasmus a concern for morality that distinguishes them from Luther. In the case of Rabelais, there is no need to demonstrate this. In the case of Erasmus, it is quite apparent that his main interest is in suggesting sound and honest rules for men to live by. He would gladly sacrifice theology—all theologies[33]—on the altar of ethics, the only altar he really cares about. A long time ago Melanchthon had the intelligence to notice this; Pineau has taken care to preserve his testimony: "What do we ask of theology? Two things," said Luther's friend. "Consolation in the face of death and the Last Judgment—that is what Luther gives. Instruction in morality and good behavior—that is Erasmus's business." And then, a direct hit: "But haven't the gentiles already provided us with this? And what do Christ and the phi-

33. See his remark to Conrad Pellican (August 1526), complaining of the Reform theologians, who were as intolerant as the Catholics: "Est mihi cum conjuratis theologis omnibus bellum internecinum." (Between me and the whole league of theologians there is internecine warfare.) Allen, VI, 38 (no. 1737).

losophers have to do with each other?"[34] The conclusion is that those who follow Erasmus preach charity, not faith. And if charity does not spring from faith it is only Pharisaism, not charity.

This is very good, even if Melanchthon was not, of course, an objective historian of ideas but a controversialist doing battle for his church. In any case, if Rabelais's moralism naturally agrees with Erasmus's moralism we should not reduce the doctrine of the giants to this moralism alone. For theirs is a Christian doctrine, and we would be off the mark. It is a curious thing that *Gargantua* and *Pantagruel* give evidence of a special concern and respect for the Almighty that are not found in Erasmus, at least not in the same form. It is no less certain that Erasmus does not have the lovely prayers and effusive Christian exhortations of Rabelais's kings; he wrote nothing like them.

Warm effusiveness, radiant sympathy—these are not words in Erasmus's vocabulary.[35] The center of the man from Rotterdam's sphere lay somewhere in the intellect; its circumference was small, its radius very short. We should not expect to find in him a man of effusions and powerful sentiments overflowing from a tender heart. Erasmus's dryly sardonic comments on the Passion shock even unbelievers in our own day. His manner of ridiculing occasional illuminations of the Spirit, the inspiration experienced by mystics, places him far from the mood of Rabelais, far from the tone of a final chord like "And the Mediator prayeth." The author of the *Colloquies*, that pure intellect, was unable to be tender—or to resist making a witty point. He was the same man who, at the monastery of Steyn, took almost all his delight in the polished refinement and somewhat feeble sensibility of Terence's heroes. Rabelais, at Fontenay, read Plato.

7. The Religion of the Giants and the Religion of Erasmus

These are shadings. We must not transform them into violently contrasting colors. It is nonetheless true that the giants' piety seems, I won't say much more sincere, but livelier and richer, warmer and at times more persuasive than the piety of Erasmus. Let us recall that on two or three occasions it is possi-

34. Pineau, p. 131.
35. Pineau, p. 23, n. 37. Erasmus never employed certain religious phrases that come spontaneously to the pen of a sincere Christian.

ble to detect in Rabelais's words something like an echo of the great prophetic, impressive voice of Luther—and Luther himself, with a sure sense of psychological realities, made no bones about the irremediable contrast between his piety and that of Erasmus.[36] Furthermore, on many important questions, political or religious, Rabelais's thought seems to be more in harmony with Luther's than with that of Erasmus. Rabelais was no cosmopolitan. He was a Frenchman, a patriot, devoted to his king. It is known with what hatred he regarded those who fled from the battle of Pavia. He was a "nationalist," in the historical sense of the word. His pacifism recognized, with a forcefulness unknown in Erasmus, the primordial necessity of defending oneself against aggression. Between the author of the *Colloquies* and the author of *Pantagruel* there were obvious differences of temperament and character, and they should be pointed out. But their importance should not be exaggerated.

On the whole, the giants' religion surely remains closer to Erasmus's religion—interpreted literally and without exaggerating its peculiarities—than to the religion of the Reformation. Closer in its concern with morality, as we have seen. Closer in its profound humanity. Closer in its optimism and its repudiation of all asceticism, all violence done to nature. As for particulars, let us recall all of Rabelais's raillery, his criticisms, his attacks directed against theologians, monks, and nuns, against abuses and observances. These are in Erasmus, and they actually came from Erasmus, even if they were also in the thought and writing of the "Evangelicals" and Reformers of the time. What about the giants' catechism? Its essential articles could have been endorsed as enthusiastically by Erasmus as by the Evangelicals and the Reformers. It could be said that he had endorsed them in advance. Of the two criteria that might be used to find out whether a doctrine was or was not fully "reformed," one—the appeal to the Gospel as the sole source of religion—applies to Luther, Erasmus, and Rabelais alike. The other—justification by faith, Luther's personal contribution that passed from him to Calvin—applies neither to Erasmus nor to Rabelais.

It is not a matter of satisfying ourselves with a clear-cut

---

36. Lucien Febvre, *Un Destin, Martin Luther*, 4th ed. (Paris, 1968), p. 170 ff.; Roberts Tapley, trans., *Martin Luther, a Destiny* (New York, 1929), p. 269 ff.

phrase or two, or of stating (because we do not know) that Rabelais's religious ideas came from Erasmus and no one else. Let us simply assert that for a man who was nurtured on Erasmus to adopt the articles of the giants' catechism he had no need of the far-off Luther or of a Lefèvre, a Roussel, or a Farel closer to home. Nothing stands in the way of all the articles—or almost all—having come from Erasmus. Nothing compels us to believe that they all came from him. We are in the domain of possibility, or at most of probability, not certainty. We are not about to minimize "the role of the Reformation" (to use a conveniently imprecise phrase) in Rabelais's religious development between 1530 and 1535. On the contrary, in the specifically religious passages of his earliest works there is a kind of seriousness, of gravity, of thoughtful and touching conviction that evoke memories of the French Biblicists, of Lefèvre's disciples, of those who listened to Roussel, if not Farel. We even believe—and this has not been noticed till now—that there are quite clear echoes of Luther in these passages. Rabelais had tasted the Gospel— that is certain. But in our ignorance as to the details of his reading and his associations, we should not give credit only to the "Reformers" of France or Germany. Let us remember the letter to Salignac and take Erasmus into account, at least as much as Luther or the French "Lutherans."

8. Was Rabelais an Erasmian to the Last?

Furthermore, I can see an additional benefit in this. We do not need a large number of notecards when picking out the "religious" passages in *Book Three* and *Book Four*. The matter of breviary wore itself thin in the work of a man hardly haunted anymore by the memory of his years as a monk. The quotations from the New Testament and the Psalms became rare, the properly philosophical digressions frequent. The Rabelais of 1546, 1548, and 1552 seems to be far from the Rabelais of 1532 and 1534. In any case, he was very far from the Reformation.

In addition, let us recall that in *Book Four*, in the dialogue of Panurge and Dingdong, he may have been parodying the repetitious "Yea, verily, yea, verily" (*voire, voire*) of Calvin's French catechism,[37] and in any case he certainly had his say, in

37. So Arthur Heulhard would have it. *Rabelais, ses voyages en Italie, son exil à Metz* (Paris, 1891), p. 252.

rough language, about the Reformer of Geneva when he wrote the myth of Physis and her enemy, Antiphysis, that old woman who lived in a shoe whose children were "the hypocritical tribes of eaves-dropping dissemblers, superstitious pope-mongers, and priest-ridden bigots, the frantic Pistolets, the demoniacal Calvins, impostors of Geneva, apparitors with the devil in them, and other grinders and squeezers of livings, herb-stinking hermits, gulligutted dunces of the cowl, church vermin, false zealots, devourers of the substance of men, and many more other deformed and ill-favored monsters, made in spite of nature." So there he was, positioned between the Chitterlings and Shrovetide in a state of rather philosophical indifference. Already in 1542, when revising *Pantagruel* for a new edition, he had inserted in the prologue a reference to "predestinators" between "abusers" and "seducers of the people"; and this allusion to the Calvinist doctrine of predestination must surely not have gone unnoticed in Geneva. In short, this was the break, a clear and public one, between Rabelais and the Protestants that had been announced by third parties before being proclaimed in categorical fashion by the two interested parties, Calvin and Rabelais.

Open *Book Four* again. In this same book in which the hypocritical dissemblers are given such rough treatment, there is, after the great silence of *Book Three,* a sheaf of references to Christianity. It is not much, but it comes after a famine. There was an invocation to God in the old prologue: "May we never do aught without first praising his holy name." In the new prologue there is a reference to the Gospel, to which we had become unaccustomed: "Such is the Lord's will, which I obey, and whose most holy word of good news I revere, that is the Gospel, where it is said, Luke IV, in great derision to the physician neglectful of his own health, Physician, heal thyself." And the giant kings recover a few of their Christian chancellery habits and some of their faith in the power of prayer. "I have this hope in the Lord, that he will hear our supplications, considering with what faith and zeal we pray," says Pantagruel.[38] And Gargantua says, "The peace of the Lord [*l'Aeternel*] be with thee." Not much. But this reticence makes all the more surprising an episode like that of the *Thalamege* (ch. 1).

38. Actually, Rabelais himself, in the prologue. [Translator's note.]

Pantagruel is embarking on his voyage. Before setting sail he calls together the crew of his flagship, the *Thalamege*. First he makes "a short but sweet exhortation, wholly backed with authorities from Scripture upon navigation." When this is ended, "with an audible voice prayers were said in the presence and hearing of all the burghers of Thalassa, who had flocked to the mole to see them take shipping." And "after the prayers, was melodiously sung a psalm of the holy King David, which begins, *When Israel went out of Egypt*; and that being ended, tables were placed upon deck, and a feast speedily served up. The Thalassians, who had also borne a chorus in the psalm . . . drank to them."

"There you have," wrote Abel Lefranc, "a perfectly accurate account of a meeting of the faithful in a Reformed church . . . Rabelais's religious sympathies [for the Reformation] are thus, contrary to the assertions of recent commentators, clearly affirmed in the course of the fourth book as in the three preceding ones."[39] The three preceding ones? For my part I would rather say "the first two," for the evidence of sympathy toward the Reformation in *Book Three* completely escapes me. There is more. I can quite well imagine what the scruples of those "recent commentators" were. It was 1548. At that time Rabelais's sympathies for the Reformation had long been spoken of in the past tense. Postel, to cite only him, spoke of them in the past tense in 1543. The Genevans saw Pantagruel's creator as nothing but an adversary. And all of a sudden, when he had to describe an embarkation, he described beyond a shadow of a doubt an embarkation of Evangelicals in a port of Evangelicals! Isn't there a contradiction here?

More simply, it is possible to see here the protest of an unrepentant old Evangelical against the new direction given to the Reformation by Calvin, the expression of a tacit but hearty loathing for the intolerance, the excommunications, the stake, and no less for the inhuman strictness of a doctrine that tempered neither the deadly burden of sin on the creature nor the mysterious injustice of predestination. Rabelais seems to be saying no to Calvin, but yet to be saying yes to the wonderful ideal of the men of 1530. And the episode of the *Thalamege* asserts an unflagging loyalty to a youthful dream, a persistent

39. Abel Lefranc, *Les Navigations de Pantagruel* (Paris, 1905), p. 46.

taste for a humanized Christianity that sets before a fatherly God free beings who, without rituals or intermediaries, give voice to the harmonious song of a quiet faith. It is possible. But I am able to understand this loyalty much better, after the philosophical daring of *Book Three* and its silences as well, if I connect it, not with a vague Protestant doctrine predating the Reformation, but with an intellectual ideal formed largely with the help of Erasmus.

The protest of an old Evangelical it may have been. But where did this Evangelism come from? From the group at Meaux? In 1548 it had long been only a memory, and was not even a name. Of the followers of Briçonnet, Lefèvre, and Roussel, some had returned to a Catholicism that was more and more intransigent but allowed them to end their lives in peace at the price of external and formal concessions. Others had attached themselves to the Church of Geneva and left their Pantagruelism far behind, if it had ever existed. But for a long time there also remained some Erasmians, men who had been nourished by the broad and free thought of the *Enchiridion*, *The Praise of Folly*, the *Adages*, and the *Colloquies*.

The time had undoubtedly arrived which Erasmus had had a premonition of ever since 1521, when he foresaw that as a result of the schism the yoke of the faithful would become twice as heavy and the conjectures of theologians would be transformed into truths of faith that it would be necessary to profess under pain of death. It was now dangerous—needlessly dangerous— for someone to preach the Gospel who did not adhere to one of the opposing creeds that competed for consciences. The religious wars were on the horizon. The Erasmians were silent, as Erasmus had fallen silent. But in the secret recesses of their consciences they remained loyal to the intelligent and generous Erasmianism of their youth. They continued to read the Philosopher of Christ with all the more pleasure, as the ideas of Erasmus—simple as they were, lacking in dogmatism and expressed in sensitive language by a mind that professed a horror of grand statements, the cultivation of irony, respect for decorum, and above all else a sort of timid and audacious opportunism—were wonderfully adapted to the necessities of an age dominated by religions that were pitted against each other but were equally official and allowed ideas to be expressed only within the framework of their own tenets.

PART IV

The Limits of Unbelief in the Sixteenth Century

9. Religion's Domination of Life

S WE START OFF on a new track, let us avoid wrong turns. For example, let us not begin by inquiring whether a break with Christianity—with the various forms of Christianity we have just enumerated—was easy or not. To put the matter in terms of easiness is a mistake. In all periods there have been heroes, or hotheads, who were unconcerned about difficulty—and in the sixteenth century such hotheads often had heat applied to their bodies. But the prospect did not frighten them. The number of martyrs who faced suffering without fear attests to that—martyrs of the Reformation or the Counter Reformation, martyrs of Anabaptism and Antitrinitarianism, martyrs of all the sectarian doctrines and even of what was then called atheism. Let us not inquire whether a break was *easy*, but whether or not conditions were met that could have made a break *possible*. To do that, let us start by assessing the place that religion actually continued to occupy in men's lives.

It is not an easy task. We do not have an equivalent for the sixteenth century of the remarkable ninth volume of Henri Bremond's *Histoire littéraire du sentiment religieux en France*, entitled *La Vie chrétienne sous l'Ancien Régime*—which means Christian life in the seventeenth century.[1] There is not the slightest work of a general nature on the history and practice of piety in the sixteenth century. It is a blank page. And, I may add, there is a great lack, a great gap, in our knowledge of the

1. Henri Bremond, *Histoire littéraire du sentiment religieux en France depuis la fin des guerres de religion jusqu'à nos jours*, 11 vols. (Paris, 1916–1933).

[335]

men and things of that time. So all we can do is provide a quick sketch, perhaps suggest some topics for research, and in any case make two or three generalizations.

Today Christianity is one religion among many—the most important of all, to our Western eyes, but only to ours. We usually define it as a body of definite dogmas and beliefs associated with observances and rituals that have been fixed for a long time. We are not entirely correct when we do so. For, whether we like it or not, the climate of our Western societies is still a profoundly Christian one. In the past, in the sixteenth century, it was all the more so. Christianity was the very air one breathed in what we call Europe and what was then Christendom. It was the atmosphere in which a man lived out his entire life—not just his intellectual life, but his private life in a multitude of activities, his public life in a variety of occupations, and his professional life no matter what his field. It all happened somehow automatically, inevitably, independently of any express wish to be a believer, to be a Catholic, to accept one's religion or to practice it.

Today we make a choice to be a Christian or not. There was no choice in the sixteenth century. One was a Christian in fact. One's thoughts could wander far from Christ, but these were plays of fancy, without the living support of reality. One could not even abstain from observance. Whether one wanted to or not, whether one clearly understood or not, one found oneself immersed from birth in a bath of Christianity from which one did not emerge even at death. Death was of necessity Christian, Christian in a social sense, because of rituals that no one could escape, even if one rebelled before death, even if one mocked and scoffed in one's last moments. From birth to death stretched a long chain of ceremonies, traditions, customs, and observances, all of them Christian or Christianized, and they bound a man in spite of himself, held him captive even if he claimed to be free. And first and foremost they pressed in on his private life.

1. Private Life

A child was born, and it was living. It was carried without delay to the church and baptized while bells rang which themselves had been solemnly baptized by the bishop, anointed with holy oil, and scented with frankincense and myrrh, and were not rung on secular occasions. If the child was sickly and it was necessary to be quick for some compelling reason, nobody waited; the priest or, in his absence, a relative or a friend of the family pronounced the words of the sacrament, and there you had it, automatically: one more Christian in the world. It was automatic because the question never arose whether it could be done differently. Even the name given the newborn child, its baptismal name, was a Christian one. Among Catholics it was most often the name of a saint, assuring the child it would have a patron in heaven; among Protestants, later, it was some Hebrew name taken from the Old Testament. Of course everyone in France in the sixteenth century already had, in addition to his personal name, a "surname" (what we call the family name), but in many cases it was still the Christian name that came first. If you go through the catalogue of the authors of his time prepared by old Gesner, the bibliographers' illustrous progenitor, you find that the authors are listed by him in alphabetical order, not by their family names but by their Christian ones: all those named Jacobus, then those named Johannes, Paulus, Petrus. Furthermore, the Church was not content merely to suggest the name for the parents' approval. Once it was given, it was the Church that registered it; the parish priest or the priest who officiated entered in his book "of Catholicity" the birth of the new little parishioner along with the names of the godfather and godmother.

A child was born, but it was dead when it came into the world or else it died before receiving holy baptism. Was it doomed to limbo, and thus to enduring the most severe of all punishments—to be eternally deprived of God? The parents said no. With stubborn hope they carried it to the church, too, and placed it on the altar of some revered "sanctuary of respite."[2] There, through the intercession of a powerful worker of miracles (Saint Claudius or Saint Gervase, Saint Christine or Saint Ursus), or more often through the intercession of the Virgin Mary herself, who was specially invoked, God would not of course bring the dead child back to life—nobody dared to hope

2. P. Saintyves, *En marge de la Légende dorée* (Paris, 1931), p. 167 ff.

for that—but perhaps in His goodness He would perform the miracle of restoring life for one brief moment, just long enough for the child to be christened and saved from limbo. The mother and the relatives watched anxiously and intently for a movement of the eyes or legs or the appearance of a few drops of sweat on the tiny corpse—sufficient signs of life, they believed, for baptism to be administered. And administered it was, despite the careful precautions of the ecclesiastical authorities. Was this what everyone believed? Of course not. But when the situation arose, how many could resist the temptation of obtaining such a miracle, which would triumph over any possible aversions?

◄§ A man died. Whether or not he had arranged the details of his funeral in his will (and those who shirked this obligation were rare indeed), he was buried "in the right way," in a Christian fashion, in his family tomb, most often in some monastery church of the Dominicans, the Franciscans, or the Carmelites. This was done without social distinctions, whether it was a matter of a baron or an ordinary craftsman. Could one take it on oneself to refuse Christian burial? It was impossible— and unthinkable.

As soon as a sick man felt he was in danger, he sent for the priest. If, because he was unaware of his condition, he at first neglected this pious duty, his kinfolk stepped in. In their absence, it was the doctor. For him this was an obligation that would become more and more stringent; in the time of Louis XIV if a doctor neglected to warn a patient on the second or third visit that he should put his conscience in order, it was a serious offense which, if repeated, led to loss of the right to practice medicine.[3] Let us not forget that until the Revolution the permanent secretary of the French Academy had to perform a similar duty for his colleagues when their lives were in danger.[4] So the priest arrived. Sometimes he brought the invalid

---

3. S.v. "Malade," Durande de Maillane, *Dictionnaire de droit canonique et de pratique bénéficielle*, rev. ed., 6 vols. (Lyon, 1787), IV, 489–492.

4. It is true that when the permanent secretary was Charles Duclos he neglected to warn himself. See the letter of April 5, 1772, from Mlle de Lubert to M. de Gémeaux, *Les Lettres du Président de Brosses à Ch.-C. Loppin de Gémeaux*, ed. Yvonne Bézard (Paris, 1929), p. 338, n. 1.

some relics to touch. In any case, with great ceremony he brought him the Holy Sacrament, surrounded by rows of kneeling believers, while a choir boy rang a bell. A crowd gathered at the believer's door. Relatives, friends, neighbors, sometimes passersby and strangers came up the stairs and crowded into the bedroom, soon to be the death chamber,[5] in obedience to these appeals to Christian solidarity, to the mystique of the communion of the whole Church, which Erasmus did not fail to mention in his *De preparatione ad mortem.*

The drama was brought to its conclusion. The consecrated bell rang again when the funeral procession entered the church. The divine service was recited, and a requiem mass was said for the deceased. Or masses were said. For the deceased often stipulated that before being buried in the monastery church where his grave was to be, his body was first to be brought to the parish church, accompanied by fine processions of Friars Preachers, Friars Minor, and Carmelites. At the parish church there was a requiem mass, to music, with deacon and subdeacon participating. At the monastery church mass was said again—or several masses, rather: a mass of the Holy Spirit, a mass of Our Lady, a requiem mass. The next day and the days following other masses were said, high ones or low ones, and at night there were vigils of nine psalms and nine lessons. All of this was somehow done routinely, done customarily and traditionally—as a matter of course. And without anyone ever dreaming of shirking a single one of these duties, which were such a part of everyone's life that they seemed to be virtually inseparable from it.

The refusal to bury in Christian ground those who were excommunicated for debt, which I have pointed out was frequent in certain areas—in the Franche-Comté in particular[6]—infuriated the faithful, who compared the enormity of the punish-

---

5. On the technique of preparing for death in the seventeenth century, see ch. 5, "L'Art de bien mourir," in Bremond, IX. For the *ars moriendi* of the fifteenth century and its popularity in the sixteenth, as well as mortuary monuments, see Emile Mâle, *L'Art religieux de la fin du Moyen Age en France,* 2d ed. (Paris, 1922), p. 381 ff., pp. 391–437.

6. Lucien Febvre, "L'Application du Concile de Trente et l'excommunication pour dettes en Franche-Comté," *Revue Historique,* 103 (Jan.-April, 1910), 225–247; 104 (May-Aug., 1910), 1–39; trans. in *A New Kind of History,* ed. Peter Burke (New York, 1973), pp. 160–184.

ment and the humiliation it caused with the often small amount of the debt that occasioned it. The practice was, however, quite widespread. One has only to look at the *Journal d'un bourgeois de Paris* to realize that.[7] In addition, the corpses of men who had been condemned to death, of those who had been executed for terrible crimes, and of suicides as well, were sometimes subjected to verbal abuse and, after thousands of outrages, thrown onto the rubbish heap.[8] But some protests were already being raised. They show us how strong the Christian burial customs were. To refuse the Eucharist to men condemned to death seemed an inhumanly harsh decision. In the middle of the seventeenth century Jean Chifflet discussed the matter and took a position against the custom.[9] He was humane, more humane than the hard-hearted men of the sixteenth century.

⋖§ Birth and death. Between these two extremes everything a man did in the normal course of life was marked with the stamp of religion.

A man ate, and religion surrounded his food with rules, rituals, and prohibitions. He sat down to his table; whatever the formula, whether the *Agimus gratias* of good Catholics or the *Père éternel* of the Huguenots, the head of the family recited the blessing, and everyone made the Christian sign, the sign of the cross. After that the father took the loaf of bread and before cutting it marked the Christian cross on the crust with his knife. When everyone got up from the table a child said grace and all left after crossing themselves.

What about the food itself? It was eaten partly on the Church's orders. According to whether the Church said so or not, one had a collation or a regular meal, one ate fat or one ate lean, one helped oneself to butter or not, one included eggs or did without them. Even the utensils sometimes felt the effects of prohibitions. Felix Platter tells us that in Montpellier at the beginning of Lent the pots that had been used for cooking meat

7. *Le Journal d'un bourgeois de Paris sous le règne de François Ier* (*1515–1536*), ed. V.-L. Bourilly (Paris, 1910), p. 374.

8. What is more, the bodies of the excommunicated did not decay in the ground—which allowed evil spirits to take possession of them. On the other hand, it is true that incorruptibility was often taken as a sign of sanctity. See Saintyves.

9. *Joannis Chifletii J. C. Vesontini consilium de sacramento Eucharistiae ultimo supplicio afficiendis non denegando* (Brussels: Typis Mommartianis, 1644).

were broken and all new ones bought to be used for fish and Lenten food.[10] Moreover, secular law reinforced religious law in these matters. Eating bacon in Lent or cooking a capon on Friday was tantamount to a crime and was punished by secular judges with the most severe penalties: lashing, beating, public humiliation at mass while holding a heavy taper, confiscation of one's goods, banishment, and sometimes even death. And don't think these were exceptional. Similar regulations and prosecutions of this sort were normal and frequent in troubled times.[11] There is no collection of legal documents that does not attest to this.

People got married. For Catholics marriage was a sacrament that conferred grace. It was a sacrament in which it was generally admitted that the ministers were the couple themselves, but the priest added the blessing of a church ceremony, the nuptial benediction. This had already been preceded by another ceremony, that of betrothal—it was so important that before the Council of Trent's prohibitions, a betrothal "in words of the present," as it was called, constituted a real and valid marriage. All that was needed, without the parents' consent being required, was a mutual exchange of promises between the bride and groom in the presence of a priest.[12] There is no doubt that in the sixteenth century the Church had ceased to have the only jurisdiction over the legal problems raised by marriage. It nevertheless continued to be actively involved, and, in any case, it is fitting that in its registers, the registers of "Catholicity," are to be found the records of marriages, as well as births or deaths.

Someone was sick, or was afraid of becoming ill. The doctor was of course available to comfort his patients, but real healing

10. *Beloved Son Felix, the Journal of Felix Platter, a Medical Student in Montpellier in the Sixteenth Century*, trans. Seán Jennett (London, 1961), p. 53.

11. Let us recall Marot and his misdeeds: "Why, I declare, it's Clement himself: / Arrest that man for eating bacon!" "Ballade contre celle qui fut s'amye" (1525) in *Les Oeuvres de Clément Marot de Cahors en Quercy*, 5 vols., ed. Georges Guiffrey (Paris, 1875-1931; photographic reprint, Geneva, 1969), V, 80. For court cases, look, for example, through Lucien Febvre, *Notes et documents sur la Réforme et l'Inquisition en Franche-Comté; extraits des archives du Parlement de Dôle* (Thèse de doctorat ès lettres, Paris, 1912), especially pp. 208, 232, 240, 275.

12. Whence the famous question of clandestine marriages, on which Rabelais also had his say. See Jean Plattard, "L'Invective de Gargantua contre les mariages contractés 'sans le sceu et adveu' des parents," *Revue du Seizième Siècle*, 14 (1927), 381-388.

came from God, directly or through the mediation of the saints in Paradise. Was there an epidemic, in particular the plague? All at once there were pilgrimages and vows to Saint Sebastian—hadn't God let him recover from all those wounds inflicted by the arrows of the Roman archers? That was reason enough for him to be able to save men from the arrows of the plague. All at once there were pilgrimages and vows to Saint Adrian, to Saint Macarius of Ghent, to Saint Christopher—yes, and to Saint Louis, who was acquainted with the plague because he died of it, or to Saint Roch of Montpellier.[13] Was it an individual illness? All at once there were personal pilgrimages and vows, either to some great and world-famous shrine—Saint James of Compostela or Mont Saint Michel or Our Lady of Loreto or Saint Peter's in Rome—or else to one of those local pilgrimage sites that aroused a fervor no less zealous: they had an advantage for simple folk in being specialized in one or another kind of cure. And if in the end a cure did not take place, one started thinking about one's will. The notary was sent for— or else the priest, who took his place when necessary. And one dictated one's final wishes.

◄§ There was not a single will in all of Christendom that did not begin with an invocation and the sign of the cross. "In the name of the holy and indivisible Trinity, of the Father, of the Son, and of the Holy Ghost, amen. Firstly, as to my soul, at present and when it shall depart from my body, I give it up and commend it to God, its sovereign creator and redeemer; to the glorious Virgin Mary, His mother; to my lord Saint Martin, my glorious patron, and to the whole heavenly Host in Paradise": this was the standard formula for wills in the Franche-Comté.[14] "Knowing that in the course of nature it is fitting for every creature to end in death . . . , of his own free will, to the honor of God the creator and the glorious Virgin Mary His mother and all the saints in Paradise, the said Claude has willed and

---

13. References in Lucien Febvre, "Une Question mal posée," *Revue Historique*, 161 (1929), p. 29 ff.; reprinted in *Au coeur religieux du XVIe siècle* (Paris, 1957), p. 27 ff.; and translated as "The Origins of the French Reformation: A Badly-put Question?" in *A New Kind of History*, p. 60 ff. See also Mâle, p. 185 ff. On post-Tridentine continuities, see Mâle, *L'Art religieux après le Concile de Trente* (Paris, 1932), p. 375 ff.

14. Ulysse Robert, *Testaments de l'Officialité de Besançon, 1265–1500*, 2 vols. (Paris, 1902–1907), II, 208.

disposed of himself, his goods, his rights, and his actions which God has lent and given to him ... And firstly, as a good Catholic and Christian, making the sign of the cross and saying *In nomine Patris et Filii et Spiritus Sancti, Amen*, he has commended and does commend his soul to God the creator and to the whole heavenly Host in Paradise": that was the formula for wills in Savoy, no less standard.[15] Let us not pass all the provinces of France in review; the procession would be far too monotonous, and the Christian rhetoric far too trite. But no one was exempt from it. No one even thought of being exempt from it.

After this, the testator made arrangements for a Christian burial, then for his funeral rites: ordering masses, arranging for anniversaries, making a long list of gifts and pious donations, and of charities that were stipulated as being in honor of God. Sometimes there were reparations. In Paris in 1527 a councillor of the Cour des Monnaies killed his brother-in-law. He was beheaded; but in addition the Parlement ordered 400 *livres* to be deducted from his estate to order masses for the victim.[16] In the collection of wills in the official's court of Besançon it is common to find in every four columns of type at least two that represent Christian formulas and stipulations.

There is no need to press the point. Every activity, every day was seemingly saturated with religion. It was true of the thoughts of those who stayed at home and of those who went abroad. It was even true of the interest in the exotic. Geoffroy Atkinson, who has catalogued and then summarized the geographic literature of the French Renaissance in the sixteenth century, asserts that there were still thirty-five *Voyages to Jerusalem* published between 1480 and 1609 as against forty *Voyages to the New World*. The proportion reveals to us the secret, persistent desire of all these men: to walk in the streets of Jerusalem, to behold the Holy Sepulcher or, at the very least, to feast their imaginations on some such dream while reading accounts of voyages to the holy places.[17]

In a word, everything still seemed to depend on the Church.

15. Gabriel Pérouse, *Etude sur les usages et le droit privé en Savoie au milieu du XVIe s.* (Chambéry, 1913), p. 200.

16. *Le Journal d'un bourgeois de Paris*, p. 307 ("14 8bre 1527").

17. Geoffroy Atkinson, *Les Nouveaux Horizons de la Renaissance française* (Paris, 1935), p. 11. The Stations of the Cross, which came into being at this time, were a response to this desire. See Febvre, "Une Question mal posée," pp. 30–31.

Even time. Time was not yet pocket watches, which were still very rare. It was not even town clocks that cut up the passage of time into regular slices. It was church bells, proclaiming a succession of prayers and services from morning to evening at recognized hours. And at night, when the bells were silent, a melancholy chant sounded through the quiet streets to punctuate men's sleep. But it was a religious cry, a reminder of the Christian faith: "Awake, awake, you Christians who sleep, and pray for the dead, that God may forgive them!" Thus the town crier in Besançon in the middle of the sixteenth century. Even the calendar spoke in Christian language. It was not on November 13 that the courts of law resumed their work, but on the day after the feast of my lord Saint Martin. It was not on October 9 that the short workdays for artisans began, but on Saint Remy's Day. And there was the countrymen's calendar: if there was ice on Saint Matthias's Day it would crack; fair weather on Saint Maurice's Day meant storm and wind; if it rained on Saint Médard's Day it would not stop for forty days. There were easily a hundred days out of the 365 that were thus referred to by a saint's name and not by an abstract date.

2. Professional Life

"For the gratification and glory of God the creator, and the most glorious Virgin Mary His most holy mother, and my lord Saint Stephen, my most revered patron, and the whole heavenly host in Paradise, I have collected and brought together several of the choicest masters in this art . . . together with a small addition on what little I have discovered and experienced during the time I have practiced it." Thus begins *Arithmetic, Newly Written by Master Etienne de la Roche, called Villefranche, a native of Lyon on the Rhone* (1516).[18] It was one of the standard arithmetics for use by merchants. This formula, more or less abbreviated, can be found at the beginning of all account books of the period and most books on science. It is quite rare not to find it at all.

As for university life, we know that the ceremonies of the

---

18. *L'Arisméthique nouvellement composée par maistre Estienne de la Roche, dict Villefranche, natif de Lyon sur le Rhône.*

universities at any rate were not yet secularized in the sixteenth century and that the great bodies, the elements of which they were composed—faculties, nations, colleges, and so on—always wore a half-secular, half-Christian look that is revealed not only in the testimony of those who attended them at the time (and even somewhat earlier in the century, in the case of Felix Platter and Lucas Geizkofler), but by the official documents emanating from the universities. The universities were composed of men, some of whom were laymen but who partly retained the appearance of clerics and some of whom were clerics but were partially secularized. There is no question of concluding that sixteenth-century universities were totally Christian organizations. One might as well claim that the Collège de France, the Collège Royal, was nothing but a Christian institution because in 1775 the notice of a course in chemistry still began: "*With the help of God,* Jean d'Arcet announces the inauguration of the chair in Chemistry with a lecture . . ." On the other hand, it is very true—and that is what matters to us here—that the universities, as institutions, continued to be bathed in a sort of Christian atmosphere that no one could possibly dispel or make disappear at will.

Academic degrees to us merely mean examinations. For men in the sixteenth century they were ceremonial acts. In Platter's University of Montpellier as in Geizkofler's University of Dôle[19] they took place in a church, amid great pomp, to the sound of the organ, between a mass and a thanksgiving, with the candidate giving his defense in front of the altar—even if he was a Lutheran. Education and the church: the connection was so strong that when Francis I in 1521 was contemplating the establishment of a college in the Hôtel de Nesle for the teaching of Greek he provided for a chapel staffed by four canons and four chaplains. It was an unlikely setting for Greek instruction.

What of the life of a "nation" of the university? It was endowed with a patron saint, distinct from the university's patron saints, whose image appeared on its seal. Its life in the sixteenth

---

19. *Mémoires de Luc Geizkofler, tyrolien (1550–1620)*, trans. Edouard Fick (Geneva, 1892), p. 182 ff. At Bourges examinations took place at first in the Cathedral of Saint Stephen, "but, as the chancel was often disturbed by noise, it was soon decided that only the doctors and licentiates would be admitted." René Gandilhon, *La Nation germanique de l'Université de Bourges* (Bourges, 1936), p. 8. It should be noted that Geizkofler was a Protestant, as was Platter.

century was punctuated at regular intervals by a series of religious festivals and services on the occasion of which it was compulsory for all the masters, licentiates, and determinants to meet in the nation's church. There the nation's coffer, filled with religious objects, sacred vessels, and ritual ornaments, was kept, and the burial vault with the nation's coat of arms was to be found, the place provided for the burial of foreigners who died in the course of their studies.[20] It is unnecessary for us to point out that attendance at services, religious ceremonies, and festivals did not involve people's feelings, that after the gathering in church there was a gathering in the tavern—*fieri festum in ecclesia et in taberna* was the program in full of the Anglo-German nation in Paris. True, but *in ecclesia* came first. And who would bother to say anything in favor of ceremonies when their observation was universal and obligatory and when they were enveloped in general respect and unanimous approval?

◄§ It is too easy to score points here. Let us look elsewhere—first of all, at the craft guilds.

No need to recall that all of them were coupled with confraternities, which had been created for the purpose of uniting the guild's members in an identical feeling of devotion to God and the guild's patron saints, but also for the practical purpose of having masses said for the living and the dead or distributing alms and charity to needy fellow members and the poor. And of course these religious activities of the guilds were directed on occasion to quite secular ends. Let us, for example, recall the weavers mentioned in a 1358 ordinance who used the cover of a mass they ordered to be sung with the greatest devotion because they were eager to postpone the hour they started work. The possibility of such behavior quickly ended when the confraternities became the masters' affair. But then the journeymen's confraternities came into being, where the customs of journeymen originated. In the beginning their framework was also provided by the Church. There was no journeymen's confraternity without a chapel, the lighting of which was paid for

20. Gandilhon, p. 8; Madeleine Toulouse, *La Nation anglaise-allemande de l'Université de Paris* (Paris, 1939), p. 137.

by the members in common. Or without a mass that they heard in a body before going to their confraternity dinner. Elections were even held in the chapel, when mass was over. The clergy did not disapprove. In the middle of the eighteenth century, as Henri Hauser has shown in his book on journeymen's guilds in Dijon in the seventeenth and eighteenth centuries, the religious orders—the Carthusians, Benedictines, and Franciscans—were still eager to protect journeymen.[21] The eagerness was perhaps mercenary, but it persisted in any case. But there was more.

Work itself proceeded in a Christian framework. If work was forbidden on Sunday, under threat of serious penalties, it was not from any secular concern about hygiene. Nor if work was similarly forbidden on feast days—and not merely those we call the major ones: Christmas, Easter, Ascension, Pentecost, Assumption, All Saints. In Paris, for example, there were the Feast of Saint Genevieve and Epiphany in January, the Purification of the Virgin in February, the Annunciation in March, Saints James the Lesser and Philip and the Invention of the Cross in May, the Nativity of Saint John the Baptist in June, in July the Feast of Saint Mary Magdalen, the Feast of Saint James the Greater, and the Feast of Saint Christopher—let us not go on, but we should naturally add to the list the feast of the confraternity's patron saint and the feast of the saint of the parish. We should also add the shortened workday on Saturdays and the eves or vigils before nonworking feast days, for reasons that were equally religious. The framework was there all the time—and there, too, the atmosphere was Christian.[22]

3. Public Life

What about public life? Is it necessary to remind ourselves how saturated with Christianity the state still was—in nature, spirit, and structure? Is it necessary to remind ourselves that all man-

21. Henri Hauser, "Les Compagnonnages d'arts et métiers à Dijon aux XVIIᵉ et XVIIIᵉ siècles," *Revue Bourgignonne*, 17, no. 4 (1927), 23 ff. See likewise Etienne Martin Saint-Léon, *Histoire des corporations de métiers*, 3d ed. (Paris, 1922), pp. 255–258. Also Georges Espinas, "Métiers et confréries," *Annales d'Histoire Economique et Sociale*, 10 (1938), 437–438.

22. On the time spent at work, see Hauser, p. 136, and Martin Saint-Léon, p. 261, which calculates that in the sixteenth century, in addition to Sundays, there were about sixty nonworking feast days.

agers of men in the sixteenth century, as soon as they started reflecting on the problem of politics, tended by a natural inclination to create theocracies? Even—perhaps especially—those who most energetically disengaged themselves from their surroundings and seemed to display a determined spirit of innovation. In the Calvinist Christian state of Geneva everyone had to bow to the sovereign authority of God and Jesus Christ.[23] Before every election a minister of the Word was called on to address a prayer to God and an exhortation to the general council, to remind the burghers and citizens of the favors God had granted to them, and urge them to bow down before His sovereign authority. Anyone who wished to be received as a burgher of the city had to take an oath to live "according to the reformation of the Holy Gospel"; and everyone who lived in Geneva had to attend compulsory public worship every Sunday and participate in the Lord's Supper four times a year. In Catholic countries, though the modalities were quite different, there was the same joint participation in the state by the temporal and the spiritual.

France was headed by a king anointed with holy oil that had been miraculously brought by a dove for the baptism of Clovis.[24] He was not a king who was purely secular; by his touch he repeatedly performed miraculous cures authenticated by the faith of the healed. He was a king who of course did not make his policies serve the Church all the time and in all ways, but, along with all his contemporaries, he saw it as a genuine public institution. He even made its precepts be respected by regular or secular ministers of that religion when they behaved badly. Furthermore, he made sure that orthodoxy was respected, he prosecuted those who violated it, he repressed blasphemy as a crime, and sacrilege as the crime of crimes. There was permanent accord and constant support between secular courts of law and the Church, between judge and priest. There was no need for ecclesiastics to ask for help from courts in which, moreover, numerous clerical counsellors often participated; such help was natural, a matter of course. If a man committed some misdeed of consequence, one that involved the

23. Eugène Choisy, *Calvin éducateur des consciences* (Neuilly, 1926), p. 60 ff.
24. Marc Bloch, *The Royal Touch: Sacred Monarchy and Scrofula in England and France*, trans. J. E. Anderson (London, 1973).

commandments of Our Mother Holy Church, secular law ordained that before any other punishment he was to be led into a
church and there, during mass, on his knees, with a heavy taper
in his hand, cry out for mercy to God, the glorious Virgin
Mary, the saints of Paradise, the Church, and the law. Often
even a pilgrimage to Rome or to Our Lady of Loreto or to Saint
James of Compostela or to Saint Nicholas of Bari served as a
penalty in the secular law's regular arsenal of punishments.[25]

◄§ And so the Church involved itself in everything, or, to be
more exact, it found itself involved in everything. If there was
an outbreak of plague—processions, masses to Saint Sebastian,
masses to Saint Roch paid for by the towns along with compulsory contributions from the citizens. If the fruits of the earth
were in danger from drought or excessive rain—processions,
statues taken down, prayers at shrines. If insects, rats, or mice
were infesting the countryside—the bishop directed a monitory
against them, the animal counterpart to excommunication,
which bowed the heads of humans under the fulminations of
the Church, punishing them for past faults, compelling them to
atone, and keeping them from ever repeating the offense. For
the Church often became an auxiliary of the law—of its own
law as well as the king's law. If it was a question of finding out
who had made off with some movable property, of getting a
debt paid or rights restored that had been usurped by third parties, the church judge was asked for letters that were publicly
proclaimed from the pulpits or posted on church doors. Under
threat of excommunication the requested information was obtained (maybe).

At any rate, great collective expressions of emotion were cen-
tered in the church. Festivals, ceremonies, masses, and processions—often even entertainments—unfolded there. The theater,
religious in origin, for the most part remained religious in fact.
Rabelais was full of the savage, popular diableries and mysteries
that sought to edify by making people laugh. Margaret of Navarre had a beautiful manuscript copy made for her of the *Mystery of the Acts of the Apostles*, which had been performed
with solemnity in her good town of Bourges. And her own the-

25. Etienne Vancauwenberg, *Les Pèlerinages expiatoires et judiciaires dans le droit
communal de la Belgique au Moyen Age* (Louvain, 1922).

atrical writing is all religious. It had not been so long since the Chapter of Besançon, to speak of nothing else, levied a fine on those of its canons who refused to "ride" on the day of the Festival of Fools.[26] The church was, moreover, the center for news. It was there that one learned of events in the parish—christenings, betrothals, marriages, and deaths. It was there that all, great and small, sanctified or commemorated the most solemn acts and most precious memories of their lives or the lives of those near to them. It was in the church, the parish church, that one likewise found out what one had to know about public events: that peace had been made or war declared, that the king had been victorious or had been routed, that a son had been born to him, that he was ill, that he was dying. Each time there were processions, prayers, the ringing of bells, Te Deums, funeral services, masses, and ceremonies of all kinds. This was true in the city, and it was perhaps even truer in the country.

The church tower (*clocher*) was such an effective symbol of the community and its bells that even today we French speak of *l'esprit de clocher*, but without quite understanding anymore what depth of meaning was expressed by this expression, which is now becoming obsolete. What did it mean? A configuration of very strong feelings, of realities that no longer exist: the church as theater and center of festivities; the church constructed of stone, the only solid building and the only beautiful one in the village, along with the fortified house of the small local lord, perhaps. It was a building made by craftsmen, mostly patched up again and again to conform to fashion—the fashion of yesterday if not the day before yesterday—by master masons from the neighboring town. When times were not too calamitous it meant candles, images, paintings, singing, incense, and gilt—ceremonial that was managed passably well in the villages, managed better in the towns, and arranged perfectly in the city. Sometimes on feast days it meant the zest of a sermon seasoned with jokes and spiced with satire against the great of this world.

But the church was also a refuge and asylum in time of

26. On "31 Xᵇʳᵉ 1437" the chapter demanded an apology from the canons who did not ride on Innocents' Day. On January 8, 1444, there were fines of 10 and 5 *sols* for canons and chaplains who had shirked the same duty. Archives Départementales du Doubs, Series G, nos. 179, 180.

war—a structure with thick walls, sometimes with a crenellated tower, that protected the inhabitants, their goods, and their flocks from even a brutal razzia. The church was a meeting place, used for elections and gatherings of all sorts, sometimes as a school. Its bell was the property of the community of the faithful, and it rang for rest and for work, for prayer and consultations, for baptism and burial—everything that left a mark on men's existence: their joys, their festivals, or their fears. If there was danger from lightning, the bellringer hurled the full peal of the bell at the unleashed elements. If there was danger from fire, the bell became the sinister tocsin that summoned the parishioners to help. If there was danger from brigands or a disturbance of the peace, the bell was such a symbol of the community that sometimes there were inflicted on it the sanctions that the latter was supposed to suffer—a practice that lasted till the eighteenth century, when an intendant in the Bourbonnais in 1737 could be seen ordering the bells taken down from a church tower and flogged by the executioner. The traitors had betrayed their duty and sounded the tocsin against the royal guards, who had been engaged with some salt smugglers.

All of which shows that the church was situated at the heart of men's lives—their emotional lives, their professional lives, and their aesthetic lives, if one can use that imposing word—of everything that was beyond them and everything that bound them together, of their great passions and their minor concerns, of their hopes and their dreams. All of this again attests to the insidious and total domination of men by religion. For it all happened without anyone's thinking about it, without anyone's even raising the question of whether it ought to be done differently. And it was so strong, so necessary, that no one at that time said to himself, "So our life, the whole of our life, is dominated by religion, by Christianity! How tiny is the area of our lives that is already secularized, compared to everything that is still governed, regulated, and shaped by religion!" This religion, this Christianity, was like the mantle of the Madonna of mercy, which was so frequently depicted in churches at that time. All men of all estates were sheltered under her mantle. Did anyone want to escape? Impossible. Nestled in its maternal folds, men did not even feel that they were captives. For them to rebel it would first have been necessary for them to question.

4. The Problem of a Precursor

Let us, however, presuppose an exceptional man—one of those men, few in number, who show they are capable of being a century ahead of their contemporaries, of stating truths that will not be taken as such till fifty, sixty, or a hundred years later. What support would he have found to free himself from this universal, this multiform domination of religion? And where would he have found it? In philosophy? In the science of his time? This is the first question, the one that has to be asked before any other. For if, after studying the matter, our conclusion leads us to think that neither in philosophy nor in sixteenth-century science could a contemporary of Rabelais (or Rabelais himself, if we make him a man of abnormal intellectual powers) find sufficient support for such a liberation, we will then be forced to accept two further conclusions.

One of them is that whatever this man could say against religion did not matter, historically speaking. Because denials that rest solely on personal impulses and moods are without social significance, without exemplary value, and without any compelling force to those who hear them. To deny, to deny effectively, no matter what the denial is directed against, is not simply to say, out of caprice, whim, or a vain wish to attract attention, "I deny." To deny is to say deliberately and calmly, "For such and such reasons, which are valid for every man and every normally constituted intellect, it appears impossible to me, truly impossible, to accept such and such a system." For such and such reasons . . . and when the system in question was as broad and powerful as Christianity, a system that for centuries dominated the whole moral, emotional, aesthetic, political, and social life of what was not without historical reasons called Christendom, these could not be fragmentary reasons or special reasons. They had to form a veritable cluster of coherent reasons lending each other support and resting, every last one of them, on a cluster of concordant scientific verifications. If this cluster could not be formed, if the concordant reasons could not be found, the denial was without significance. It was inconsequential. It hardly deserves to be discussed, any more than the sneers of the drunkard in the tavern who guffaws when he is told that the earth is moving, under him and with him, at such a speed that it cannot even be felt.

Was Rabelais a denier of Christianity in 1532? If Rabelais could not be supported by such a cluster of reasoning and duly worked out verifications (whether or not they might, by the way, be subject to a variety of interpretations), then Rabelais as a denier in 1532 purely out of the liberality of his spirit is a Rabelais whose thought is deprived of all historical and human meaning, value, and importance. And as a consequence there is nothing for the historian to do but pass over him in silence, to leave him alone.

And what is the other conclusion? It is no less clear. To speak of rationalism and free thought when we are dealing with an age when the most intelligent of men, the most learned, and the most daring were truly incapable of finding any support either in philosophy or science against a religion whose domination was universal is to speak of an illusion. More precisely, it is to perpetrate, under the cover of fine-sounding words and an impressive vocabulary, the most serious and most ridiculous of all anachronisms; in the realm of ideas it is like giving Diogenes an umbrella and Mars a machine gun. If you prefer, it is bringing Offenbach and his *Belle Hélène* into the history of religious and philosophical ideas—where he perhaps has no business being.

10. A Possible Support
for Irreligion: Philosophy

HE PHILOSOPHY of the sixteenth century is not in very high repute with the philosophers of our own time. The best authors insist on finding it chaotic and defective: "A multiplication of doctrines," says Emile Bréhier in his recent history, "a multiplication of doctrines and thoughts which had been incubating throughout the Middle Ages but which had previously been repressed. This confused mixture might be called naturalism, for generally it subjected neither the universe nor human conduct to a transcendental rule, but simply sought to identify their immanent laws."[1] And with an expression of contempt this historian of philosophy (is contempt really a historian's response?) makes a somewhat disconcerting value judgment on the "confused naturalism" he has diagnosed. After all, it is hard enough for a historian to understand without having to worry about making weighty judgments. This magma, he tells us, contained, "alongside the most viable and fruitful ideas, the worst monstrosities." And that is that.

Actually, before raising difficult problems and taking in at a glance, if that is possible, the philosophy of the men of the Renaissance, perhaps it would be better to remind ourselves that the history of the sciences and the history of thought are made up of fragments of violently contrasting designs and colors, a series of theories and attitudes that not only are distinct from one another but oppose and contradict each other. Each has its

1. Emile Bréhier, *The History of Philosophy: The Middle Ages and the Renaissance,* trans. Wade Baskin (Chicago, 1965), p. 215.

share of truth, considering the circumstances of time, place, social structure, and intellectual culture that explain its birth and its content. To the extent that we are thus able to justify these contrasts and oppositions, we can understand why, as circumstances changed, each of these theories and attitudes had to give way to others. Only to that extent can we evaluate the persistent effort of human intelligence as it responds to the pressure of events and the impact of circumstances. This is what the historian's task really is.

I. Mental Tools

Let us begin, then, by asking some questions about the setting, conditions, and possibilities. And to get at what is essential, let us state a problem that looks simple but about which, in connection with the sixteenth century, no one has bothered to bring the facts together: the problem of knowing what clarity, comprehension, and, finally, efficacy (in our estimation, of course) men's thought was capable of. Frenchmen engaged in speculation without as yet having at their disposal in their own language any of the usual words that automatically come from our pens as soon as we start to engage in philosophy. The absence of these words entails not only inconvenience but actual inadequacy or deficiency of thought.

1. Missing Words

Not "absolute" or "relative," "abstract" or "concrete," "confused" or "complex," not "adequate" (which Spinoza was fond of, but in Latin), not "virtual" (which Chapelain would use, but only around 1660), not "insoluble," "intentional," "intrinsic," "inherent," "occult," "primitive," "sensitive" (all words of the eighteenth century), not "transcendental" (which would adorn the periods of Bossuet around 1698)—none of these words, which I have chosen at random, belonged, according to dictionaries and Ferdinand Brunot, to the vocabulary of sixteenth-century men. Let us say, in order to pin the notion down, to the richest vocabulary of all, that of Rabelais.

Yet these are only adjectives, a handful of them. What about nouns? How many of them were absent from the roll? Neither "causality" nor "regularity," "concept" nor "criterion," nor "condition," neither "analysis" nor "synthesis" linked together, before *The Port-Royal Logic*, neither "deduction" (it still meant only "narration") nor "induction" (to emerge only in the nineteenth century), not even "intuition" (to come into existence with Descartes and Leibniz), not "coordination" or "classification" ("that barbarous word invented lately," Féraud's dictionary was still saying in 1787)—none of these common words either, which we really would not be able to do without in order to do philosophy, figured in the vocabulary of Rabelais's contemporaries. They did not even have a word for expressing what we presume to call, only since the middle of the seventeenth century, a "system." Naturally, they also did not have words for labeling or enumerating (hence for being able to call to mind immediately and efficiently) all the "systems" that meant most to men of the time, especially those who have been granted the name of rationalists: "Rationalism" itself, to start with, which would not be christened till very late, in the nineteenth century; "Deism," which hardly began its career before Bossuet, who was one of the first to use it; "Theism," which the late eighteenth century would briefly borrow from the English; "Pantheism," the name for which would be found at the time of the Regency in the work of John Toland; "Materialism," which had to wait for Voltaire (1734), La Mettrie, and the Encyclopedia before getting the run of the place; "Naturalism" itself, which appeared only in 1752 in the *Dictionnaire de Trévoux* and, before that, in La Mettrie (1748); "Fatalism," too, is found in La Mettrie, although Diderot's novel was able to launch "fatalist" only in 1796; "Determinism" is a latecomer, with Kant; "Optimism" (*Trévoux*, 1752); its opposite "Pessimism": "pessimists" would not come onto the scene till 1835 in the dictionary of the French Academy, and "Pessimism" was to appear even later; "Skepticism" began, with Diderot, to replace the older "Pyrrhonism," Balzac's brainchild and a favorite of Pascal; "Fideism" would emerge only in 1838 from a conflict among theologians. And there are any number of others: "Idealism" (*Trévoux*), "Stoicism" (La Bruyère), "Quietism" (Nicole, Bossuet), "Puritanism" (Bossuet). Before passing judgment let us keep in mind that none of these words were, in any case, at the disposal of Frenchmen in 1520, 1530, 1540, or 1550 if they wanted to think and then translate their thoughts into French for other Frenchmen.[2]

If they were nonconformists ("conformist" is one of Bossuet's words), they did not even have a convenient name for designating themselves and bringing them together. "Libertine" appeared later in the century, "libertinism" only in La Noue and Charron. "Esprit fort" would not be launched till the eighteenth century, when Helvetius made much use of it, and "libre penseur" only with Voltaire and the appearance of his *Treatise on Tolerance* (1763). But "tolerance" itself did not triumph (also thanks to Voltaire) until the middle of the century of *tolérantisme*, a product of the eighteenth century from the beginning; it had been preceded by "intolerance" in Montesquieu and Argenson. Let us remember that "irreligious" was part of Port-Royal's style, and "controversialist" belonged to Pascal's usage; "orthodoxy" first appeared in Naudé and "heterodoxy" in Furetière.[3]

No need to add—it goes without saying—that the ancestors of the libertines of Louis XIII's time had (for good reason) no names in their sixteenth-century language for observatory, telescope, magnifying glass, lens, microscope, barometer, thermometer, or motor. Of course not, since an idea that seems to men at any point in history to be a valid explanation of things—and hence is for them confused with truth—is what accords with the technical means available for modifying and predicting the behavior of those things. These technical means are acquired from the sciences. So we have good reason for making such a point of the as yet hardly defined vocabulary of the sciences that were contemporary with *Pantagruel*, whether we are dealing with chemistry, which was still entirely involved in alchemy; or the biological sciences, which would hardly get going until the nineteenth century; or astronomy, which was still immersed in astrology and, before the seventeenth century or, more often, the eighteenth, did not have words in French for "attraction" (used by Cyrano de Bergerac) or orbit or ellipse or

2. At least in a systematic manner and with their philosophical meaning. It is possible to detect the presence of one or two of them in the writing of some precursor, but these remained isolated instances; they were not in the mainstream.

3. François de La Noue (1531–1591); Pierre Charron (1541–1603); Gabriel Naudé (1600–1653); Antoine Furetière (1619–1688). [Translator's note.]

parabola or revolution or rotation or constellation or nebula. At the same time, the French vocabulary of mathematics—I am speaking of the simplest and commonest terms—was still so unrefined, so poor, and so vague that one day in July 1654 Pascal, who could not arrive at the formulation of a problem in French, restated it in Latin, for, he said in so many words, "French is worthless."

That is a serious assertion. The words that presented themselves to these men when they reasoned about the sciences in French—or simply when they reasoned—were not words made for reasoning, for explaining and demonstrating. They were not scientific words but words that belonged to the language of all, to the common, living language. They were accordion words, if I may say so. Their meaning expanded, contracted, altered, and evolved with a freedom that scientific words have ceased to exercise. The latter have the immobility of signposts. They have been blamed (by Charles Nicolle) for creating devotees and slaves, for irrevocably binding and chaining. Perhaps. But without them, how could anyone's thought be given a truly philosophical vigor, solidity, and clarity?[4]

2. Syntax and Perspective

All this was true of vocabulary. What about syntax?

Certainly old French, the concrete, impressionistic, and naive French of the twelfth century, in which the verb was in charge, enthroned in the second position, from which it contemplated the other elements as they turned around it like so many satellites—that French was far removed from the opening of the sixteenth century, with its anarchic freedom and the perfect disorder of its constructions and (what is so annoying to us) its constant mixing of simple and compound tenses:[5]

4. For all of this, see Ferdinand Brunot, *La Pensée et la langue*, 2d ed. (Paris, 1926). See also Arsène Darmesteter and Adolphe Hatzfeld, *Le Seizième Siècle en France: tableau de la littérature et de la langue*, 16th ed. (Paris, 1934), pp. 183–301.

5. For what follows, consult volumes II (*Le Seizième Siècle*), III (*La Formation de la langue classique*, part I, book II), IV (*La Langue classique*, part I, book IV), and VI (*Le XVIIIe Siècle*, part I) of Ferdinand Brunot, *Histoire de la langue française des origines à nos jours*, new ed., 13 vols. (Paris, 1966-1979). Also Edmond Huguet, *Etude sur la syntaxe de Rabelais comparée à celle des autres prosateurs de 1450 à 1550* (Paris, 1894) and Lazare Sainéan, *La Langue de Rabelais*, 2 vols. (Paris, 1922-1923).

La dame le veut retenir,
Par le mantel l'avait saisi,
que les ataches en rompit.

The lady wishes to hold on, had seized him by the cloak,
whereof the strings broke.

This gives an impression of jerkiness and incoherence. It
makes us think of those novice filmmakers who never stop
jumping around and changing their position as they run back
and forth with the camera in front of the scene they are shoot-
ing, but the impression is no less disagreeable when a picture-
maker decides to use a single tense (a decision often made in
the Middle Ages) to narrate events that did not always all tran-
spire on the same plane.

In a word, there is no perspective, and so there are difficulties
in interpreting the confused design of the old authors. They
evoke an object, a person, or a scene in a few imprecise words.
It is up to the reader to do the rest if he feels the need—to arrange, put in order, make specific.

There is no doubt that at the end of the fifteenth century
great progress had been made. There was an increase in forms
subjected to the leveling process of analogy; the system of two
cases (subject-object) was abolished, and as a consequence a
more rigorous word order was introduced into the sentence, allowing subject to be distinguished from object with certainty;
the verb little by little yielded its sovereignty to the subject. In
short, translated into grammatical actions, there were clear indications of a progressive organization of thought, an organization
at once reflected in these synthetic transformations and facili-
tated by them. And just as perspective—*che dolce cosa!*—little
by little became a necessity and then an instinct for artists, just
as their whole view of the world (*our* view of the world) found
itself imperceptibly changed, so the more regular, more harmonious use of tenses progressively allowed writers to introduce
order into their thoughts, and perspective—depth, if you will—
into their narratives.

Obviously, everything was not yet perfect at the end of the
fifteenth century and the beginning of the sixteenth. Ferdinand
Brunot was fond of quoting a wonderful sentence from Comines's account of the beginning of the Battle of Montlhéry.

"Cette artillerie," wrote the chronicler, unperturbed, "tua une trompette en apportant ung plat de viande sur le degré."[6] Any number of others might also be taken from Comines. There is the following sentence, for example, a few pages away: "Et, cette ymagination, leur donnoit l'obscurité du temps."[7] Or this impressionistic observation: "Le roy vint ung matin par eaue jusques viz à viz nostre ost, largement chevaulx sur le bort de la rivière."[8] But let us not imagine that the sixteenth century made everything clear and orderly:

> Jeanne, en te baisant, tu me dis
> Que j'ai le chef à demi-gris.
>
> Ah, Jane, I kiss you—and you say
> My hair is turned by half to gray.[9]

That is from Ronsard.[10] But here is something from Brantôme: "Je m'étois proposé aussi, comme quand j'en discourus au comte de Rochefoucaut, seulement de demander congé au Roy, pour n'estre dit transfuge, par un de mes amis, pour me retirer ailleurs où je trouverois mieux qu'en son royaume." (I had also resolved, as when I spoke of it to the Count de Rochefoucaut, only to ask the king for leave, so as not to be called a deserter, through one of my friends, to retire elsewhere where I would find it better than in his kingdom.) The sentence does not tes-

6. Philippe de Commynes, *Mémoires*, ed. Joseph Calmette and G. Durville, 3 vols. (Paris, 1964–1965), I, 61 (book I, ch. 9). Literally, "This artillery did slay a trumpet while bringing up a dish of meat on the step." The sentence appears in a recent English translation as, "This artillery . . . killed a trumpeter on the stairs as he was bringing up a dish of meat." *The Memoirs of Philippe de Commynes*, ed. Samuel Kinser, trans. Isabelle Cazeaux, 2 vols. (Columbia, S.C., 1969–1973), I, 127. [Translator's note.]

7. Commynes, I, 73 (book I, ch. 11). "It was the obscurity of the weather which led them to imagine these things." *Memoirs*, trans. Cazeaux, I, 134. The literal translation is, "And this imagining to them gave the darkness of the weather." [Translator's note.]

8. Commynes, I, 75 (book I, ch. 12). "One morning the king came by water to a spot facing our army; he had many horsemen on the bank of the river." *Memoirs*, trans. Cazeaux, I, 135. The literal translation is, "The king came one morning by water to just face to face with our host, largely horses on the bank of the river." [Translator's note.]

9. Literally, "Jane, kissing you you say to me that I have a head at half-gray." [Translator's note.]

10. *Odes*, IV, 31.

tify to much of an ability to arrange thoughts in an orderly way.

What about agreement of tenses? It remained irregular, sometimes *very* irregular. "Ils dirent qu'ils n'iront point":[11] this alarmed no one. And a sentence like this one from Jean d'Auton seems to be a sort of gamble: "Lesd. lettres que lui envoyoit led. lieutenant du Roy, desquelles choses fut très animé contre les Boullongnoys, disant qu'il les destruira, s'il faut qu'en armes aille sur le lieu, et que, à bon droit, avoit deservy cruelle pugnition."[12] It makes one think of a child playing with a telescope, looking now through the big end, now through the little end, and changing the focus all the while. Similarly, word order is not always strictly fixed; often the verb still comes before the subject. "Provoqué l'ont ses fils et ses filles"—that is from Des Périers. And "Là bauffrant attendit les moines l'abbé"—from Rabelais. Similarly, the object often comes before the verb: "un mesme teint avoient l'aube et les roses"—from Des Périers again. A sentence like the following, which René Sturel found in the liquid prose of the translator of Plutarch,[13] is a good demonstration of how sixteenth-century French, even in the hands of its best practitioners, continued to have a tendency to put everything on the same plane, both the main idea and the secondary details. Here it is through an almost complete lack of subordination:

> Quand les Romains eurent defait Antiochus, ils commencèrent de plus en plus à gagner et ancrer sur les Grecs, de sort que leur empire environnait déjà les Achéens de tous côtés, même les gouverneurs des villes se rangeoient et s'inclinoient fort sous eux pour s'insinuer en leur bienveillance et déjà tendait la puissance de l'Empire romain le grand cours,

11. "They said they will not go." [In French, as in English, normal modern usage is, "They said they would not go."—Translator.]

12. Jehan d'Auton, *Chroniques de Louis XII*, ed. R. de Maulde La Clavière, 4 vols. (Paris, 1889–1895), IV, 85. An English rendering in the same period style would be: "The said letters the which the said lieutenant of the king sent him, of what things he had been most aroused against the Boulognese, saying that he will destroy them if it be that he might go in arms upon the place and that for good reason had it deserved a cruel punishment." [Translator's note.]

13. René Sturel, *Jacques Amyot, traducteur des Vies parallèles de Plutarque* (Paris, 1908), p. 201.

avec la faveur de fortune, à la monarchie du monde universel
et approchait bien fort le but où les dieux vouloient tout faire
tourner.[14]

It was a long-winded, verbose language, too often lacking in
rhythm and style, a language of peasants who spoke rarely, but,
when the occasion presented itself, spoke endlessly, losing
themselves in explanations and tangents, in details and circumstances, because they were inept at untangling the thread of
their thought, because they had time, lots of time, all the time
in the world, and, finally (we will come back to this aspect
later), because everything in language mattered, everything was
loaded with consequences and heavy with secret magic.[15] It is
not astonishing, therefore, that they were incapable of rendering
the conciseness of ancient writing. Quite the reverse. They
stretched it out, they added to it. When Amyot found *dynamin*
in the original he translated it any number of times as "his
power and his army." Similarly, *oikon* became "his house and
his estate." In short, work had only begun on what would end
as the Louis XIII style of which Lanson spoke, a solidly based
sentence that unfolded slowly, a sentence meant for thought
"that strove to make itself orderly and sought before all else to
reveal how it made connections. The words were packed into a
logical framework built of relative pronouns, conjunctions, and
present participles." It recalled "the dressing that frames the
brickwork of the buildings in the Place Royale."[16]

These were severe constraints and heavy shackles on thought.
Nobody escaped. Edmond Huguet, with some naiveté, has
asked the following question about Rabelais: "How did it hap-

14. In English, with the same arrangement of independent and subordinate clauses:
"When the Romans had defeated Antiochus, they began more and more to win out and
establish themselves over the Greeks, in such a way that their empire already surrounded the Achaeans on all sides, even the governors of the cities came over to their
side and succumbed to them in order to insinuate themselves into their good graces,
and already the power of the Roman Empire was pursuing its great course, with the
favor of fortune, toward the monarchy of the entire world and was fast approaching
the goal to which the gods wished everything to be directed." [Translator's note.]

15. See below, ch. 11, sect. 3. See likewise the remarks of Jean-Richard Bloch in
"Langage d'utilité, langage poétique," *Encyclopédie française*, 21 vols. (Paris,
1935-1966), XVI, 16'50-8-16'50-16.

16. Gustave Lanson, *L'Art de la prose* (Paris, 1880; photographic reprint, 1968), p.
58.

pen that this great writer did not take as much liberty with syntax as he did with vocabulary?"[17] Well, it was because he
couldn't—not, as Huguet said, because "it is ordinarily not in
syntax that originality is sought" (which means nothing), but
because syntax does not depend on one man, even if he is a genius. It is a social institution, in a way. It is something that belongs to and reflects an era and a group, not just a single writer.
And every era, every group in large measure has the syntax it
deserves—I mean a syntax that corresponds to its level of intellectual development and scientific knowledge.

There are action and reaction. The state of the language impedes the free play of ideas, but in spite of everything the
pressure of ideas causes linguistic frameworks to crack; it breaks
them, enlarges them. If the men of the sixteenth century had
had at their disposal a language that was better adapted to the
needs of philosophical and religious speculation, what would
they have done with it, in the absence of a better and more
highly developed science? Some good judges of such things
have recently accused Copernicus of spoiling his system by
wishing to make it too precise. Others, no less qualified, have
insisted on "the benefits of imprecision," adding that "Kepler
would not have discovered his laws if he had had more precision."[18] Obviously, the conditions for speculation are not the
same in all periods. There are periods in which it is necessary
to know how to take risks, invent, step out in front first and
look (or take another look) afterward. Language and thought:
the problem is like that presented to a tailor by a garment that
never wears out and has to be constantly refitted to the body
of a customer in a perpetual process of transformation. Sometimes the garment is too roomy, at other times the customer
feels too tight in it, yet it is necessary that they should accommodate themselves to each other, and accommodate themselves
they do. They are always accommodating, but there is a lag.
Language has often acted like a barrier, if not a dam; whence,
in intellectual history, all those quantities of backed-up water
that one day suddenly break through and sweep everything
away.

17. Huguet, introduction.
18. Remarks of Alexandre Koyré in *Le Ciel dans l'histoire et dans la science*, Huitième semaine internationale de synthèse (Paris, 1940), p. 85.

3. The Argument from Latin

At this point no one should say, "You are playing with words. Didn't they have Latin in the sixteenth century? And when they happened to do philosophy didn't they do it in the language of Cicero, who served as their instructor not only in writing but also in thinking?"

Undoubtedly, all men of that time who speculated—all, or nearly all ("nearly" being added merely to be scrupulous, or out of deference to Bernard Palissy)—were bilingual. If they were not, they lost face. One man among many who did not let them forget it was Ronsard:

> Les François qui mes vers liront
> S'ils ne sont et Grecs et Romains
> Au lieu de ce livre ils n'auront
> Qu'un pesant faix entre les mains.

> Frenchmen who would read my book
> Romans and Greeks should be.
> Or, when in their hands they look,
> Not verse but empty bulk they'll see.

Since they spoke Latin, weren't they therefore able to think in Latin? Yet even when they attempted to revive Latin thought, to make it live in them as much as they could, it remained dead thought. To the extent that it intruded itself on them, it was only able to hold back their free flights. It kept them in bondage to ways of thinking and feeling that were archaic, obsolete, or, if you prefer, out of date and out of tune. Their civilization, as we have seen, was totally imbued and saturated with Christianity, with Christian ideas and feelings. And they were putting all their effort and zeal into painfully worming their way into ideas and feelings that were partly in opposition to their own or, if you wish, the ones they should have had, the ones they were able to have.

Let us then try translating into Latin most of those concepts for the expression of which sixteenth-century French had no words. Absolute? But *absolutus* means complete, finished, no more than that; it is not used philosophically. Abstract? But *abstractus* signifies isolated or distracted. Cicero had no doubt found a good way of putting it: "quod cogitatione tantum percipitur";[19] that was what it was, and yet it was not. Besides, when one is speaking and writing it is like being at a market: better to have a hundred-franc note than to count out a hundred coppers one by one. The same thing goes for "relative." *Pertinans ad?* But that means something else. And late Latin *relativus* has hardly anything but a grammatical meaning. Let us say nothing of "transcendental"(and scarcely mention "transcendent" in its philosophical sense of superior, excellent, sublime). And what of the series of names of systems ending in "ism"?

It is possible to find ways of "putting it," I realize that—to look for equivalents, use paraphrases, translate with a dozen words what we express clearly and objectively with one. But let us note that in order to translate an idea in this way we must already possess it, that the sign of possession in such matters is the word, that if a person does not have the word in his vernacular tongue it is quite obvious he cannot go looking for a way to render it in his Latin, and finally, that if we can, strictly speaking, try to express the idea of determinism with a long paraphrase (Henri Goelzer endeavored to do so in his French-Latin dictionary: "doctrina qua rerum universitas ex causis aliis ex aliis nexis necessario constat"),[20] it is because nineteenth- and twentieth-century Frenchmen like us have attended classes in philosophy and our teachers have conveyed to us along with the word the concept that it expresses. The men of the sixteenth century, however, would have been quite hard put to make the concept explicit in order to translate it, because they had not had our courses in philosophy or mathematics; and there could never have emerged from their solitary efforts the common notion of determinism, the ordinary and almost vulgar notion that all of us have had in our possession without trying ever since we were sixteen. The effort of more than one man was needed for that.

People always go on about the new acquisitions (the compass, the cannon, printing) for which the Latinizers of the sixteenth century were able to find Latin names only at the price

19. "What is only grasped by thought."
20. "The doctrine according to which absolutely everything depends on causes that are necessarily linked together one after the other."

of subtle and considerable effort and veritable contortions of language. There is quite a bit of exaggeration and delusion in this. In fact, no one in the schools or universities—none of the masters, I mean—had any objection in such cases to clothing words from the most vulgar of "vulgar" speech in Latin dress. They created sentences like "Placuit nationi remediare et obviare abusibus commissis vel committendis per nuntios nationis" and "Vult specialiter quod fiat una distincta tabula omnium dioceseon."[21] This was professor's Latin. And "Capis me pro alio," "Parvus garsonus bavat super sese," "Ego bibi unum magnum vitrum totum plenum de vino"[22]—which was student's Latin,[23] *Maturino Corderio teste:* see his *De corrupti sermonis emendatione*[24] of 1530. Let us simply note that these student usages had a tendency to take away from Latin its character as an international language. A student in Tübingen would have been just as surprised at "bavat super sese" or "faciam te quinaudum"[25] as Pantagruel was when he heard the sibylline speech of the Limosin.[26] But that was not where the real difficulty lay. That started when it was necessary to take a turn "dedans le clos des occultes idées" (in the garden of occult ideas), as the poet of *Les Regrets* said somewhere.[27]

Beret was *birretus* or *birrus* in student jargon. Bombard was *bombarda* in the jargon of military strategists. Shoes with laces were *solutares ad laqueos,* and felt caps were *capellae de fultro* in the jargon of the dandies at the Collège de Navarre. All these proper objects were there, really there, waiting to be called by some name or other. But what about ideas? What about concepts? Were they there, at the disposal of thinkers? It was a vicious circle: if they were actually there, at least potentially, just on the threshold of philosophical consciousness, was Latin—a

---

21. "The nation was pleased to remedy and obviate the abuses that had been or were being committed by the nation's emissaries"; "It especially desires that a separate list be made of all the dioceses."

22. "You take me for someone else"; "The little boy is dribbling on himself"; "I drank all of a big glass full of wine."

23. For all this, see Louis Massebieau, *Les Colloques scolaires du XVIᵉ siècle et leurs auteurs, 1480–1570* (Thèse de doctorat ès lettres, Paris, 1878), pp. 27, 210.

24. Mathurin Cordier, *On the Correction of Corrupt Speech.*

25. In French, "je te ferai quinaud" (I shall put you to shame).

26. *Pantagruel*, ch. 6.

27. Joachim Du Bellay. [Translator's note.]

language made to express the intellectual processes of a civilization that had been dead for a thousand years—capable of bringing to life ideas on the verge of being born?

To be sure, it had served theologians and scholastics to express ideas that the Romans and Greeks had never conceived of—although as soon as those ideas emerged from the nest they tried to return to the ancient fold and find shelter under Aristotle's wing as far as they could. New requirements had come into being, however, requirements of purity and correctness. A strict concept of "barbarism" was added to the no less strict one of "solecism." The philologists had begun their work of picayune criticism. We can be sorry about that if we like, but it would be a bit naive. Those men knew what they were doing. I am speaking of men like Lorenzo Valla, Erasmus, and Budé. And after all, in forcing their contemporaries (who asked for nothing better and, nine times out of ten, made themselves the willing accomplices of their designs) to return to the purity and correctness of classical Latin, they got rid of an ambiguity. They returned ancient philosophy to antiquity, to the past. They cleared the way for new construction. Without wishing to do so, they made it easy for living, vigorous languages to come on the scene. They opened the door to "modern" philosophies.

4. An Example: Infinity

Of the difficulties that men of the sixteenth century ran up against, we will take only one example, but a good one. We know the statement made by Malebranche in his *Search for Truth:* "the finest, highest, firmest, and first proof for the existence of God is that which presumes the least; it is the idea we have of infinity."[28]

Infinity: it was of course possible to speak in Latin of *infinitas* or *infinitio*. "Infinitio ipsa quam *apeirian* vocant," says Cicero in *De finibus*.[29] It was possible. But let us take a closer look.[30]

At one extreme were the Greeks. Since the Eleatics, more or

28. Book III, ch. 2, sect. 6.
29. *De finibus bonorum et malorum,* I:6.
30. Albert Rivaud, "L'Infini: histoire de l'idée," in *Le Ciel dans l'histoire*, pp. 213–233; Charles Serrus, "L'Infini: le problème," ibid., pp. 235–260.

less, they had declared that what was finite in space, what was limited, indeed what was perfect, finished in that respect—that was the only conceivable form of being, since thought and knowledge always set limits. Then came the Romans. All of them had a similar feeling that the universe was bounded and limited in time, since the series of causes was broken off by a first term with no cause. All of them had the same aversion to the infinite and the boundless, which was also indefinite and, as such, bore the marks of imperfection; indeed, the realm of the perfect was that of the bounded, and the ancient gods themselves, being perfect, were finite and bounded. In sum, for two thousand years infinity was the sign of defectiveness and imperfection, of virtuality.

At the other extreme were the Scholastics and their idea of an infinite God—which was the fruit of another idea, that of a boundless universe or an infinite void surrounding the universe. The idea was perhaps not entirely strange to the early Greek thinkers, but it did not take hold until a short while before the Christian era. It served to introduce the notion of an infinite being, with which metaphysical and theological reflection was endlessly engaged from the beginning of the first century: a being infinite not only in quantity but also in power; it contained within itself a superabundance of energy and force that went beyond anything we could imagine, being first and foremost a grandeur, a might, an intelligence, and a will that were all equally infinite. Starting with this, scholastic thought proceeded to delineate the argument that Kant would call the ontological argument, the use of which in the seventeenth century gave such a curious boost to metaphysical speculation (while the skeptics, for their part, made use of the obscurities in the concept of infinity in their attempt to overturn reason).

So if the men of the sixteenth century had continued to place their feet carefully in the footsteps of the men of the twelfth, thirteenth, and fourteenth centuries; if they had continued to express themselves like them, with the words of a scholastic Latin that was moving further and further away (in body and soul) from classical Latin; if they had not declared war on precisely the ways of thinking and writing that had belonged to their fathers and grandfathers; if they had not wished to break with those modes of reasoning and a language they labeled bar-

baric (whether they actually succeeded in doing so is another question); if they had not undertaken to go beyond Christianity, theology, and scholasticism and return to the sources, the real sources of ancient thought, to Cicero first of all, who was more than ever esteemed and followed as a philosopher, more than ever studied and imitated as a writer—there would perhaps have been no problems, or not many. But in fact they did want something else. They dreamt of a total revolution. With remarkable forcefulness, they declared war on the recent past, the past of the Christian Middle Ages, in order to reimmerse themselves directly and completely in the more distant past, that of pagan antiquity.

There was, in truth, only one way out of all these difficulties. And there was one person who did not deceive himself about it. "If I write in French," said Descartes, "which is the language of my country, rather than in Latin, which is that of my teachers, it is because I hope that those who rely purely on their natural intelligence will be better judges of my views than those who believe only what they find in the writings of antiquity." It is with this explanation that the *Discourse on Method* ends.[31] Indeed, there was no better way to contrast the deadly sterility of traditional thought, embedded in its Latin matrix, with the revolutionary fecundity of pure "natural intelligence" making use of an instrument suited to its needs. But it was necessary for that instrument to be invented. And it is no accident that it was only around 1600 that philosophy included two men of consequence who expressed themselves in French, Guillaume du Vair and Pierre Charron. After them came the real philosopher: René Descartes. From then on there were no more philosophers in France who used Latin.

Theology had already become aware of this tremendous change. For the determination with which the Evangelicals and then the Protestants of the sixteenth century insisted on the right of each believer to read the most sacred books of his religion, its fundamental texts, in his own "vulgar French" and no longer only in the Latin of the Vulgate is to us at times startling and astonishing. At bottom it revealed an uneasiness.

---

31. René Descartes, *Discourse on Method*, trans. Laurence J. Lafleur (Indianapolis and New York, 1950), p. 50.

These men sensed obscurely that additional barriers between the Word and the living people they were inviting to receive it could be raised by the screen of a language that was not only dead but was precisely the language that for centuries had conveyed and transmitted thought that was profoundly hostile to everything that that Word preached, the thought of Christianity's persecutors, men who when Christianity appeared had wanted to stamp it out once and for all.

II. Two Kinds of Thought

Having said this, we can now go back to our philosophers of the sixteenth century with greater means of understanding them. We can put aside disparaging remarks that are perhaps a bit oversimple and in their place ask some specific questions.

Specific, yet not overly ambitious. We should not be asking the meaning of "the philosophy of the Renaissance," which would be to settle with one word a very big question, *too* big a question. We should rather ask what common meaning (if there is one) is to be derived from all those "burgeoning and multiplying" philosophies (as Bréhier said) that we see bursting out in the West at the end of the fifteenth century and the beginning of the sixteenth. Even when limited in this way and stripped in advance of any illusions about a "synthesis," the question still seems enormous and meaningless. Yet it has been raised, and we should not discard it without a serious examination. After that we will grapple with another one, no less formidable. On the practical level, it is simply stated, yet it is a particularly hard one to resolve. This time, however, it has to do with logical and rational, not psychological and emotional, complexity. To be more precise, it has to do with a great problem about sincerity.

How did these philosophies from which we are about to try to derive common tendencies and state general directions, if such a thing is possible, reconcile themselves, not theoretically but practically, with Christianity—the Christianity whose constant domination over the life and the men of that most Christian age we have described? And if it appeared that in essence these philosophies were not Christian, how could the men who professed them and promoted them reconcile their speculations as philosophers with their submission to the Church as believers? Must it be said, bluntly, that they reconciled them only with the help of hypocrisy? That they lied, and that their apparent submissiveness to Christianity was only cowardice, prudence, and pretense?

1. Greek Thought and Christian Faith: Was There a Conflict?

Any synthesis of Renaissance philosophies appears difficult. This is to be expected. Already in 1920 Léon Blanchet, a historian of philosophy whose early death was unquestionably a loss for this field of study, asked in his *Campanella* how it was possible to sum up in a single statement "the thought of an age of transition that was still finding its way and did not succeed in imposing on its ideas the order and harmony appropriate to ages of organization and equilibrium."[32]

Still, it has been tried, more than once. Especially in Italy, where particular attention has always been given, quite naturally, to the movements of the Renaissance. Thus in 1868, in a study on Pomponazzi, and again in 1872, in one on Bernardino Telesio, the occasions of two volumes of *studi storici* on the idea of nature in the Renaissance, Fiorentino believed he was able to observe all through the Middle Ages, reaching out in every direction, "a coherent effort to seek everything in the other world: genus and species beyond the individual, matter and form beyond their union, God beyond things, the intellect beyond the soul—and true virtue beyond life."[33] In short, Fiorentino defined the Middle Ages as the realm of transcendence and the Renaissance, by contrast, as the restoration or establishment of immanence. In a vast fresco he showed the whole train of thinkers who could be called medieval—from Proclus, their ancestor, all the way to Occam—striving to cancel out nature to the advantage of spirit, after which, beginning in the fourteenth century, the thinkers of the Renaissance appeared, moving in the opposite direction and proclaiming the spirit that was at the heart of nature.

Oh, those great machines, true and false at the same time, as

---

32. Léon Blanchet, *Campanella* (Paris, 1920), p. 126.
33. Francesco Fiorentino, *Pietro Pomponazzi, studi storici su la scuola bolognesa e padovana del secolo XVI* (Florence, 1868), p. 143.

is all this playing with massive, poorly analyzed conceptions: *the* Middle Ages, *the* Renaissance, to say nothing of Transcendence and its kindred enemy Immanence. At least they generally have the merit of posing problems and stimulating reflection, of soliciting a reply or further exposition. This is what happened, again in Italy, when Giovanni Gentile asserted in a new essay on Telesio and a general study of the problems raised by the relationship between scholasticism and philosophy that, to tell the truth, the conflict was not between immanence and transcendence, those entities of thought, but between Greek philosophy and the whole aggregate of Christian concepts.

⋘ It was a historian's view and, as such, should not leave us unmoved. The fact is that "the men of the Renaissance"—to use that convenient cliché—took the ancients, and the Greeks above all, as their instructors in philosophy to whatever extent they engaged in it. The Greeks came to them through the interpretative translations of their original systems bequeathed to us by the Romans. That is to say, Lucretius adopted and adapted the physics and psychology of Epicurus; Cicero in his brilliant dialogues transmitted an academic eclecticism adorned in beautiful language ("verba tantum affero, quibus abundo");[34] finally, Seneca popularized Stoic ethics, whose rigors he was able to temper in a humane way. But the Greeks were also apprehended directly, in their writings in Greek, by men who were avid to broaden their horizon, return to the sources, and read the real Plato or the real Aristotle in his own words. The existence of the Greeks was not a sudden discovery for these men. It is no doubt superfluous to say that Greek thought had permeated Scholastic systems for a long time, and Etienne Gilson has been able to see in the Renaissance, not Greek thought taking its revenge on Christian dogma, but, with the aid of Erasmus in his *Enchiridion* and *Paraclesis,* an attempt to purify a Christianity in which too many inroads had been made by the various philosophies of Hellas: Platonism and Pythagoreanism, Academicism and Stoicism.[35] It is, however, precisely the words of Erasmus that bear witness to the wide range of interests that fed the intrepid appetite of the humanists, in-

34. "I bring you only words, in which I abound." *Ad familiares,* VIII, 63.
35. Etienne Gilson, *Héloïse et Abélard, étude sur le Moyen Age et l'humanisme* (Paris, 1938), p. 185 ff. (appendix).

terests that in any case went beyond their immediate object. For those crude men of sixteenth-century France—crude in their ferocious will to work, their astonishing autodidactic asceticism, their fervor that triumphed over all difficulties, poverty, and deprivation—were not in search of Aristotle or Plato, Plutarch or Epictetus in the *Moralia* or the *Enneads*, the *Organum* or *Timaeus*. It was themselves they were looking for in those works, which were at once clear and difficult, obscure and brilliant—themselves and their reasons for living, believing, and acting in a world that was being built by them, for them, and in front of their very eyes. Yes, they wanted to assimilate Greek learning, but in order to go beyond it. And let us not reproach them for adopting Empedocles' synthesis and making it their own, his theory of the four elements of water, air, earth, and fire, not forgetting love and hate and adding the concept of the four fundamental opposing qualities: dry and wet, cold and hot, which for centuries marked the victory of quality over quantity. No, let us not reproach them, since it was what was invoked for almost two millennia, as much in physics as in cosmology or alchemy. And for two more centuries (until Lavoisier) it would continue to govern chemistry and rule over medicine. No reproaches on that score. But rather let us see that it was to them, the Greeks, that Copernicus, though concerned with innovation, came in search of the first germ of his hypothesis, the point of departure for his reflections. To go beyond the Greeks, yes; but by first letting them carry him to the outermost limits of their universe.

◄§ This philhellenism of the "Renaissants" caused a big problem—precisely the one stated by Etienne Gilson when he showed the distress of Erasmus at seeing himself surrounded by so many Greeks and so few Christians[36] and his anger at those who impiously compared Aristotle and Christ. He was angered by the corruption by the Greek spirit of Christian wisdom, of which Saint Paul said that it made foolish the wisdom of this world. It was precisely this problem that Gentile had already attempted to state in the works we mentioned earlier—and to deal with.

Greek philosophy, he wrote, is "thought that sees beyond it-

36. Gilson, p. 188.

self [*il pensiero che si vede fuori di se*] and sees itself thus either as Nature, immediately perceived, or as Idea. But the idea is not [for the Greeks] the act of thought thinking; it is a thing to which thought is attached and which it assumes to be eternal truth, the eternal cause of all reality and of knowledge itself, paralleling the vicissitudes of things. In one and the other hypothesis the idea is a reality that is itself what it is, independent of the relationships that thought has with it when it apprehends it."[37]

It is a tragic concept, remarks Gentile, "the most sorrowful of any that the human soul can have about its own existence in the world," since the soul lives on truth or, if you will, on its faith in the real existence of what it thinks and affirms. According to the Greek concept, however, truth—real truth, the truth that truly exists—is not in man's soul. It is outside man, who is driven, as in Plato's myth of Eros, by an immense desire to seize it and embrace its true essence; but it eludes his grasp. It remains a stranger to reality, as though unattainable in its immutable perfection.

And as a consequence, science—the science whose conditions were marvelously analyzed in Aristotle's *Logic*—was not what our science is, learning acquired by man, the instrument of knowledge and mastery forged by an active, conquering intelligence. It was not a science constantly remaking itself throughout history but a science that emerged directly from principles that contained all the concepts, perfectly interconnected, which together constituted what was knowable. It was a science that did not evolve, that neither grew nor diminished, and that excluded history, since it was from the beginning and for all time identical to itself in all its absolute perfection.

Christianity, properly speaking, denied such concepts, however. In bringing God down to man and bringing man down into the world it restored to man the full measure of his worth. It placed God inside his creature, thus letting it participate in the divine nature. God even made himself man, undergoing all human sufferings down to the last one, death. Love was no longer, as in Plato's myth, the avid contemplation of the incommunicable; it was the very work of man, his perpetual forging

37. Giovanni Gentile, *Bernardino Telesio* (Bari, 1911), p. 12.

of himself. It was no longer the ecstatic celebration of a world that is, but a worker's celebration of a world being forged and reforged by man, who was indeed not so much intelligence and learning as love and will. This man was the creator of his own truth, a truth that was confounded with the good and, far from being external to us, became ours when we sought it with a pure heart and good will, with sincerity and innocence. Here was a great transformation. Man was no longer a spectator, he was a participant. He found himself, rediscovered himself, in the bosom of Christianity.

Was there therefore an antagonism? There were two doctrines or, if you wish, two conceptions, and they did not agree. Was it necessary to choose between them? No, because there were not two philosophies here but only one, and on the other side was a faith, the revelation of a truth that did not necessarily, of itself and all at once, have to be integrated into the system of speculative thought. So a compromise could be reached. It was reached. And instead of freeing itself from Aristotelian logic, the logic of transcendence, Christian thought during the whole Middle Ages remained linked to the concepts of the Greeks.

Before everything else it should have relied on God made man, on the Son. In fact, it preferred to rely on the Father. As though of its own accord, it let itself be ensnared again and again in the net of Aristotelian metaphysics, which maintained that the principle of reality lay beyond reality itself. And it was in vain that it tried to fill the ever-yawning gulf that opened between the cause of motion, which was not motion, and a motion that could not find sufficient reason in itself; between the principle of becoming, which never became, and nature, which could not find in itself the reason for its generations or its corruptions—let us say, in short, between the soul on the one hand and the body on the other, and within the soul between the intelligible soul, which was understanding in actuality, and the natural soul, the potential intellect, incapable of knowing anything by itself.

There was a divorce of matter, the potentiality of all, from form, the realization of all. There was a separation of life from the aspiration to life. There was the insoluble agony of those— Aristotelians or Platonists, Nominalists or Realists, Averroists or Thomists—who endeavored during the Middle Ages to conceive of reality and, led astray by the very way they stated, or restated, the problem, never succeeded, nor could they ever succeed. For all of them it was truly a mental torture of Tantalus. Therefore, in spite of those efforts, the Middle Ages never managed to bring into harmony, on the one hand, the tendencies of a mysticism that affirmed the direct presence of God and Truth in the human spirit but at the same time denied science and the kind of knowledge that developed and was systematic and, on the other hand, the tendencies of an intellectualistic philosophy that presupposed a reality beyond the mind that sought it and devoted all its attention to the construction, rich in form and empty of substance, of what could not possibly be the truth.

2. Greek Philosophy and Christian Faith: An Interchange

As a consequence, it is easy enough for us to say that the task of the Renaissance was clear, if not simple. It was to put an end to Scholastic logic, psychology, and physics and restore truth, that child of the times recognized at last for what it was, to its rights in the depths of the human soul, and not only truth but also virtue and perfection, taken over by man and cut to his measure. It was to proclaim and declare the absolute value of both nature and humanity. Yes, and we even have the right to add that the Renaissance undertook the task manfully. Manfully, yes—but with perfect lucidity? In the same spirit as our own today? That is another matter.

There is nothing simple about anything that affects man, so let us be on our guard against simplism of any kind. And let us not go about saying—or believing—that the Renaissance set up, or was able to set up, in opposition to Christianity a rival system conceived of as such and aimed at it like an engine of war. That is a falsification of history.

Not merely because—to return to the terms in which we ourselves stated the debate—it is to believe that the men of that time, without any difficulty, through some kind of stupendous miracle, were able to break the thousands of chains in which their thought, their sensibility, and their will were bound by Christianity. But because—a much more serious matter—it is to conceive of Christianity itself and its relations with philosophy (let us not call it Greek philosophy if you will, but a philosophy descended from Greece) in a singularly elementary fashion. It is to refuse to comprehend the constant play of interchanges and borrowings that bound together these two terms that are said to be antagonists. It is not to see that the great syntheses, such as those of a Marsilio Ficino or a Pico della Mirandola, which we call Hellenic—Aristotelian or Platonic in inspiration—were all permeated by Christianity and, although they often seemed suspect to the doctors of the Church, the rigid guardians of orthodoxy, they were all animated in their Grecism by the spiritual breath of the Gospel. It is, above all, to close one's eyes to something that played a remarkably illogical role—but logic is precisely what has nothing to do with these things—in this history of medieval thought in its decline and modern thought in its beginnings: the central role played by the rebirth of Platonism, of which Rabelais in particular was one of the artificers and protagonists.

◄§ For if it is true—the formulation is Bréhier's, and it is not very far from what Gentile thought—that "in spite of a vast number of divergences and diversities there was throughout the Middle Ages but one image, or rather one single frame in which could be fitted every possible image of the universe" (and Bréhier, giving this scheme the name of Theocentrism, describes it as follows: "from God as the principle to God as the end and consummation, following the passage through finite beings," a formula that can fit, he says, "the most orthodox of the *Summae* as well as the most heterodox of the mystics, for the order of nature and the order of human conduct take their place as if by necessity between the principle and the end"), the return to Platonism, as can be vouched by so many philosophers of the Renaissance, served only to reanimate and bolster in them the notion that "the great task of philosophy was to organize everything in the material world and in the world of the spirit in terms of God as the principle and God as the end."[38]

It was at precisely this moment that their thought was being joyously nourished by new elements of remarkable energy and power. It was the moment when, to assist the effort of the Oc-

38. Bréhier, pp. 217, 218.

camists, who since the fourteenth century had resolutely undertaken the study of the facts of nature in and for themselves, a
mass of new information poured in, the byproduct of the explorations and discoveries. They widened enormously in a single stroke the old concepts in the *Mirrors of the World*, the
whole *Weltanschauung* of the men of the Middle Ages. It was
the hour when the contemporaries of Columbus and Magellan,
venturing forth on the high seas thanks to the compass and various other technical advances, were beginning to measure the
unprecedented consequences of these gains—or observed that
some among them had already measured them—with a kind of
fearful, exultant amazement. It was the time when their technical skills and, in the first place, their firearms assured them
easy, decisive, and lasting superiority over peoples armed with
bows and clubs, and they began the exploitation of the lands
they conquered by making inventories of treasures that culmi-
nated not only in prodigious journeyings of plants and animals
around the world but even in the direct acquisition of any number of beings and any number of forms. Under this impetus the
ancient framework, handed down from generation to generation
with closed eyes by conformists without any curiosity, would
be irremediably shattered, would fall apart and disappear. It
was, finally, the moment when the emerging philological spirit
began to apply itself to the exegesis of texts that had not only
been restored to their literal content but whose spirit was permeated with a sense—still tentative—of what would be called
history.

It was a contradiction. Or, more simply, a compromise, since
no one at the time saw any contradiction. It was the hour when
what can be called the documents of nature joined with the
documents of humanity that constituted the beautiful works of
antiquity. It was the hour when technological skills were beginning to be seen not merely as ways to earn a living but as so
many tools for reworking reality, diverting natural phenomena,
and interpreting them in order to bend them to man's youthful
power. It was the hour when it was finally possible profitably
to begin—and indeed a beginning was made—to organize the
great investigation of nature that would allow systems foreign
to the theocentrism of which Bréhier spoke to be worked out.
And at that hour a few of the most zealous among those who

were able to conduct investigations, at that hour someone like Rabelais (to mention only him) still stubbornly organized his thought around the ancient schema we have been told about: God as principle, God as end, and every thing and every spirit carefully arranged between this principle and end.

Why this singular mental attitude? Why this illogicality? A number of causes that might be alleged suggest themselves. And among them is the following: philosophy then was only opinions, a chaos of contradictory and wavering opinions. They wavered because they still lacked a steady, solid base, the firm base that would make them secure: science.

11. A Possible Support for Irreligion: The Sciences

HERE ARE times when we sneer at the science of the period. We make fun of this one's unicorn horns, that one's old wives' remedies, everyone's superstitions, ignorance, and credulity. At other times we feel respect. We extol a heroic effort and find ourselves agreeing with the old myth of the Renaissance. And we are right to fluctuate in this way.

1. The Old Myth of the Renaissance

It is an old myth that is still alive, despite much criticism. It starts with antiquity and the science of the ancients, the fertile Hellenic inventiveness that created the geometry of Euclid, the mechanics of Archimedes, the medicine of Hippocrates and Galen, the cosmography and geography of Ptolemy, the physics and natural history of Aristotle—an entire body of knowledge that was able to pass from the Greeks to the Romans. After that, a descent into night, the dark night of the Middle Ages. The ancient treasure was forgotten, if not lost. For centuries, nothing but syllogistic reasoning and sterile deduction. Not one fruitful achievement in doctrine, not one technological discovery of any importance.

This lasted until once again, at the end of the fifteenth century, a revolution was set in motion. Men became aware of their intellectual impoverishment and set out in search of the vanished treasures. One by one the scattered pieces were found in attics. To make use of all these riches they once more, through a superb effort, learned how to read real Latin, classical Greek, and, beyond that, even Hebrew, which had no utility for scientific knowledge but was indispensable for biblical exegesis. Then there was a drunken orgy. Gorging themselves on all this ancient provender suddenly placed within their reach, the humanists set to work. They were helped by printing, which had just come into existence. They were helped by the new geographical maps they had recently acquired that suddenly expanded their mental horizons as much as their physical ones. Copernicus grafted himself onto Pythagoras, Kepler onto Copernicus, and Galileo onto Kepler, while Andreas Vesalius added to the fruits of experimentation those of the Hippocratic tradition.

All of this, which seems logical, simple, and coherent, we hardly believe anymore.[1] Not that it is enough for us to know that "the men of the Middle Ages" were far from ignorant of all of ancient culture. What counts in our eyes is not that Brother John or Brother Martin of the Dominican order or the venerable Benedictine brotherhood might have been acquainted with some manuscript fragment or other of an ancient classical text around the year 1280. What counts is the way Brother John and Brother Martin read that fragment, the way they really were able to read it. Did they read it as we do? Certainly not. Their Christianity did not limit itself to putting to rest all the great metaphysical anxieties troubling the faithful. It animated and inspired the great *summae* of the time, its *Mirrors of the World, Faces of the World,* and so on, and took man over completely, accompanying him in all the undertakings of his life, public as well as private, religious as well as secular. It armed him with coherent conceptions about nature, science, history, morality, and life. And it was through these conceptions, without worrying about putting in place historically what he read, that he read, interpreted, and appropriated the ancient texts. Sometimes, by accident, he rather amazingly managed to understand a fragment or remnant of them.

And, on the other hand, what about the humanist revolution? What exactly were the effect and influence of humanism on sci-

1. See, in volume XVI of the *Encyclopédie française,* 21 vols. (Paris, 1935–1966), the articles by Joseph Bédier on "Le Moyen Age" (pp. 16'10-3–16'10-9) and by Lucien Febvre on "La Renaissance" (pp. 16'10-13–16'12-1).

entific concepts and their revival in the time of the Renaissance? Many knowledgeable people—Thorndike, to name but one[2]— have believed it possible to reduce that effect to nothing, or almost nothing. They have maintained the thesis—a plausible one—that humanism and science developed separately, without any direct reciprocal effect. On one side was humanism, nurtured by books and authors—nurtured exclusively by books and authors. Humanism read Pliny the Elder just as it read Pliny the Younger, citing both the one and the other with veneration, referring with just as much respect to the uncle's knowledge as to the nephew's graceful pen, and creating alongside the scholastic tradition of Bartholomew the Englishman and Albert of Saxony (who vied with each other in being printed and reprinted by the best publishers) a classical tradition, above all an Aristotelian tradition, that was no renewal, that renewed nothing. On the other side was reality: discoveries, inventions, and technology, along with the skills and reflections they set in motion, which would later become the skills and reflections of authentic scientists.

Thus there were few or hardly any contacts between bookish knowledge and practical knowledge. Yet there was the example of cartography, of the comparison presented in atlases between the detailed and accurate drawings along the sides, provided by the portolanos, those masterworks of navigation, and the scholarly Ptolemaic maps based on a network of coordinates. Wasn't there something in this example to give encouragement to the men of the time? There was nothing, however—or almost nothing. We are given over to astonishment and wonder when we find in a book devoted to the Venetian navy of the fifteenth century[3] an unexpected reference to an attempt made at the beginning of the century to marry theory and practice. Even more astonishing, it was an attempt that succeeded. In 1525 and 1526, when the Venetian Senate was deliberating about a type of vessel suitable for the destruction of pirates, Matteo Bressan, a venerable master of the trade who had been brought up entirely on

2. Cf. Lynn Thorndike, *Science and Thought in the Fifteenth Century* (New York, 1929).

3. Frederic C. Lane, *Venetian Ships and Shipbuilders of the Renaissance* (Baltimore, 1934). Reviewed by Lucien Febvre in *Annales d'Histoire Economique et Sociale,* 7 (1935), 80–83.

practice, presented them with a type of round boat. But Victor Faustus, public lecturer on Greek eloquence in the city of Saint Mark—Victor Faustus the humanist, brought up on Greek mathematics and Aristotelian mechanics—dared to venture on practical ground and submitted to the Senate his learned plans for a quinquereme. And the marvel was that in the competition the quinquereme carried off the prize against the boats made by artisans—this, as one can imagine, to the great enthusiasm of the humanists, eager to extol the new Archimedes.

It was practically a unique example, until the day that Vitruvius began to dictate the projects of master masons—who suddenly became "architects." In 1539 Robert Estienne included the word in his dictionary, thus giving his approval to the development.[4] No matter that Faustus's quinquereme was, incidentally, unable to stay in favor with the Venetian sailors for long. A tradition had been established. And when the problem once again presented itself later on, the Venetian Senate turned, not to the master craftsmen, but to a learned professor of mathematics. The name of that professor was Galileo Galilei.

◆§ That was a different time. While waiting for it to arrive slowly, nothing changed. Bold explorers and daring sailors had long since crossed and recrossed the equator (1472–1473), but the learned physician Alberti Carrara, who died in 1490, was still teaching in 1483 and 1490, in his *De constitutione mundi,* that on this very equator there existed a barren, empty zone, quite uninhabitable, the preface, as it were, to a southern hemisphere completely covered by water. It was the same with the scholar Alessandro Achillini, who did not die until 1512. He seriously considered in his turn the question of how to know whether the equatorial regions were inhabited or not, and it was with the help of ancient and medieval citations (Aristotle, Avicenna, Pietro d'Abano) that he imperturbably resolved it, without any reference to the Portuguese explorations. Then there was Jacques Signot's *Description du monde,* which was pub-

4. Earlier the word had been used by Lemaire de Belges (1510) and Geoffroy Tory (1529). Rabelais launched its use in *Pantagruel.* Francis I conferred the title on Serlio in 1541. Likewise see references from Amiens in Lucien Febvre, "Ce qu'on peut trouver dans une série d'inventaires mobiliers," *Annales d'Histoire Sociale,* 3 (1941), 51; trans. in *A New Kind of History,* ed. Peter Burke (New York, 1973).

lished by Alain Lotrian in 1539; the book was reprinted in
1540, 1545, and 1547 in Paris and in 1572 and 1599 in Lyon.
There is no mention of America in it. And in the same year,
1539, there was the *Recueil de diverses histoires des trois
parties du monde*, translated into French from a work by
J. Boemus. It was, as the title said, about the three parts of the
world. There was no mention of America in this often reprinted
compilation. The question of the equatorial zone was not to be
resolved in accordance with experience until 1548, when Contarini's posthumous *De elementis* appeared.

These were closet geographers and cosmographers, who
lagged behind the open-air geographers and cosmographers.
But, as Duhem has clearly shown, it was the same in the domain of what was then called, in a poorly defined term, physics.
The humanists were actually behind the Paris scholastics who
based their study of dynamics on fruitful principles: Jean Buri-
dan, Albert of Saxony, and others. The humanists continued to
swear by Aristotle. They stayed with his physics—for example,
among the French, Lefèvre d'Etaples and the men of his circle.
If it was necessary to give it some support (and it was), they
turned to the metaphysics of Nicholas of Cusa. Later, when the
disciples of Melanchthon felt the same need, they would invoke
the words of Holy Writ, further prolonging the era of confusion.

Having said this, there you have it. Today we hardly speak at
all anymore, we speak less and less, of the Dark Night of the
Middle Ages—and this has been so for some time now. Nor do
we speak of the Renaissance as if it were poised like some victorious archer scattering the shadows of that night once and for
all. This is because good sense has prevailed and we are no
longer really able to believe in the total suspensions we used to
be told about: the suspension of human curiosity, of the spirit
of observation and, if you will, of invention. It is because we
have finally told ourselves that when an epoch had architects
with the breadth of those who conceived and built our great
Romanesque basilicas (Cluny, Vézelay, Saint-Sernin, and so
on) and our great Gothic cathedrals (Paris, Chartres, Amiens,
Reims, Bourges) and the powerful fortresses of the great barons
(Courcy, Pierrefonds, Chateau-Gaillard)—what with all the
problems of geometry, mechanics, transportation, hoisting, and

handling of material that such construction presented, and the whole wealth of successful experiments and observed failures that this work both necessitated and encouraged—it is contemptuous to deny to such an epoch, en masse and indiscriminately, the spirit of observation and the spirit of innovation. On closer examination, the men who invented—or reinvented or adopted and introduced into our Western civilization—the chest harness, the horseshoe, the stirrup, the button, the watermill, the windmill, the carpenter's plane, the spinning wheel, the compass, gunpowder, paper, printing, and so on, served the spirit of invention, and humanity, with distinction.[5]

2. Printing and Its Effects: Hearsay

So when we are told that the spirit of observation was reborn in the Renaissance we can answer: No, it did not need to be reborn, to reappear. It had never disappeared. It only took new forms, perhaps. And it certainly equipped itself mentally. For in order to construct great summations, theories, and systems it is first necessary to have material, a great deal of material. The Middle Ages never had such material at its disposal.

For them the tremendous effort of the ancient compilers had been as good as lost. Here and there a manuscript preserved a few portions, a manuscript known to a small number of men. There may have been another manuscript a hundred leagues away. There was no way of bringing them together, comparing them, setting one alongside the other, without a dangerous, precarious journey.

Then came the birth of printing. At the same time, the scattered fragments of ancient learning were beginning to emerge a little everywhere. Thereupon printing got to work. It reassembled, collected, and transmitted. As early as 1499 the basic collection of the "old astronomers," Greek and Latin—*Scriptores astronomici veteres*—was published in Venice by Aldus Manutius. The same Aldus had already published his five folios of the Greek text of Aristotle between 1495 and 1498. Volume III contained the *De historia animalium*, volume IV the *Historia*

5. See Marc Bloch, "Les 'Inventions' médiévales," *Annales d'Histoire Economique et Sociale*, 7 (1935), 634–643, and, in general, the whole November issue of that year on technology, "Les Techniques, l'histoire et la vie."

A realistic depiction of a gutted dolphin in Guillaume Rondelet's *De piscibus marinis* (*Fishes of the Sea*), 1554–1555.

By permission of the Houghton Library, Harvard University.

plantarum of Theophrastus together with the *Problemata* and
Mechanica. Ptolemy's *Cosmography* had already come off the
presses in 1475, minus the charts, then in 1478 in Rome with
the charts wonderfully engraved on copper. In turn, Hervagius
in Basel issued the first edition of Euclid's *Elements* in 1533 and
then the first edition of Archimedes' works in 1544. Galen had
been published in Greek by Aldus in the form of five small
folios in 1525, and the Greek text of Hippocrates had been published in 1526, also by Aldus. They had been preceded by Avicenna (1473, 1476, 1491), and Pliny, published in Venice by
Johannes de Spira in 1469 (then in 1470, 1473, 1476, 1479, and
so on), had come ahead of everyone else. Thus the geometry,
mechanics, cosmography, geography, physics, natural history,
and medicine of the ancients were brought within everyone's
reach. One was armed, equipped for study. One worked on
solid foundations. From now on one could interpret, perfect,
and comment on what the old masters had taught. Or, rather,
one could have done so if one did not venerate them so.

The work of altering, completing, and readapting started.
With a passion that was at once furious and calm, Konrad von
Gesner of Zurich undertook to catalogue all the animals he
found mentioned in any work. It was an enormous undertaking,
thankless and a little naive, since it placed real beings and fabu-
lous ones side by side. He filled four huge folios that were published in Zurich in the middle of the century (1551). There

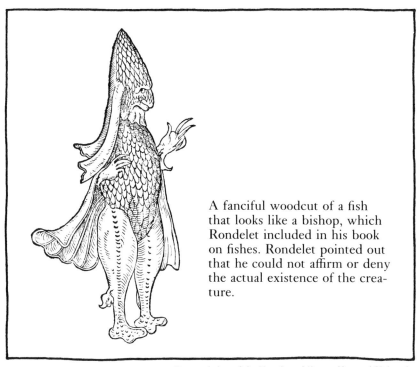

A fanciful woodcut of a fish
that looks like a bishop, which
Rondelet included in his book
on fishes. Rondelet pointed out
that he could not affirm or deny
the actual existence of the creature.

By permission of the Houghton Library, Harvard University.

were others who catalogued plants with the same passion. In
1530 in Strasbourg appeared the first volume of the earliest il-
lustrated flora, the wonderful collection by Otto Brunfels, *Her-
barum icones ad naturae imitationem effigiatae.*

This was followed in Basel in 1542 by the *De historia stir-
pium* of Leonhard Fuchs, and soon afterward by Rondibilis's
Fishes—the learned Rondelet—first in Latin, as was proper
(1554), and then in French (1558) with its wonderful wood-
cuts. At almost the same time (1555) Pierre Belon of Le Mans
published his *Fishes* and his *Birds*, "together with their descriptions and true portraits drawn from nature." The whole of living nature. To this Georg Agricola added inanimate nature, the
minerals. In 1546 his *De ortu et causis subterraneorum* appeared in Basel. In 1555, also in Basel, appeared the magnificent
folio of *De re metallica.* Scholars were able to put in long working days. They now knew their labor would not be in vain;
printing was there to make it bear fruit throughout the world.

And Rabelais, who stoutly counted himself among these great makers of inventories, who when he was in Rome felt the urge to catalogue all the ruins and remnants of antiquity, was able in his *Gargantua* and his *Pantagruel* to intone a hymn to science, to men's limitless knowledge.

That was Rabelais in *Gargantua* and *Pantagruel*. But in 1564 *Book Five* of *Pantagruel* appeared, and we will no doubt never know to what extent it was or was not the reworking of what had been sketched out by Rabelais. In *Book Five*, chapter 31, we find the astonishing allegory of Hearsay, the misshapen old fellow who is blind and palsied but all covered with ears that are always wide open and supplied with seven tongues that move at once in his furnace-door mouth. Through all his ears he receives incongruous and crude information from books and newspapers, and through all his tongues he communicates it to gaping listeners who never verify, criticize, or examine it, no matter what it is. "And all by hear-say" is the refrain of the passage, punctuating the nasty remarks—a Molière-like refrain we would say if it were not Rabelaisian. Is the irony forced? No, this is both ironic and fair. For if the men of that time made compilations, if they made compilations above all and to the exclusion of almost everything else, it was because for conquering the world's secrets, for forcing nature out of her hiding places, they had nothing—no weapons, no tools, no general plan. They had only a tremendous will—their will, and nothing else.

3. The Lack of Tools and of a Scientific Language

As far as physical tools are concerned, they were still unacquainted with the most ordinary instruments of today, those that are familiar to everyone and, furthermore, those that are the most simple. For observing they had nothing better than their two eyes, aided at the most, if they needed it, by eyeglasses that were necessarily rudimentary. Certainly neither the state of optics nor of glassmaking made any others possible. There were no lenses of either glass or cut crystal that were suitable for enlarging very distant objects like the stars or very small ones like insects and seeds. It was not till the beginning of the seventeenth century, in Holland, that the astronomical telescope would be invented and Galileo would be able to observe the stars, discover the mountains of the moon, add to the number of stars, count thirty-six Pleiades instead of seven, and contemplate the ring of Saturn or the moons of Jupiter. And it was likewise not till the seventeenth century, also in Holland, that Leeuwenhoek of Delft, with a magnifying glass and then with a rudimentary microscope, was able to conduct the first research on the internal structure of tissues and reveal to astounded naturalists the amazing fecundity of the Infusoria. But once an observation was made, what was there to measure it with? There was no clear and well-defined nomenclature, there were no guaranteed, precise standards adopted and cheerfully assented to by all. What there was was an incoherent multitude of systems of measurement that varied from city to city and village to village—whether dealing with length, weight, or volume. As for taking temperatures, that was impossible. The thermometer had not come into existence and was not to do so for a long time.

And just as it had no tools, science had no language.[6] It is, of course, true to say that in its final glow before being extinguished the Greek genius had created algebra. But it was an algebra for calculating, an algebra whose ambitions were limited to guaranteeing conveniently automatic calculations, whereas to us algebra is only secondarily a mechanical means of solving problems, and is also only secondarily a way of calculating with symbols. If algebra can be defined as the point where mathematics contemplates relation in all its nakedness without any support other than the symbol for the relation itself, the point where arithmetic is transformed into logic, a logic more exact, richer, and deeper than that of the dialecticians, then algebra had not come into existence in Rabelais's time. It was not to come into existence until the very end of the sixteenth century, with François Viète's *Isagoge*. Viète was from Poitou, born in Fontenay-le-Comte, where that other François had lived for so long in a monastery. At any rate, it was Viète who took a tech-

6. On what follows, see Moritz Cantor, *Vorlesungen über Geschichte der Mathematik*, vol. II: *Von 1200–1668*, 2d ed. (Leipzig, 1900), especially ch. 53 on counting boards, ch. 57 on Pacioli, ch. 58 on Chuquet and Lefèvre, ch. 68 on Viète. See likewise W. W. Rouse Ball, *A Short Account of the History of Mathematics*, 4th ed. (London, 1908), chs. 11, 12; and Augustin Cournot, *Considérations sur la marche des idées et des événements dans les temps modernes*, ed. François Mentré, 2 vols. (Paris, 1934), I, ch. 3; II, ch. 1.

nique, a collection of practical rules and recipes for the use of
those who liked mathematical games, and made of it, not a true
science (that was the work of the Italians Tartaglia, Cardano,
Ferrari, and Bombelli), but a language linked to a science,
linked in such a way that every improvement in the science
brought about an improvement in the language, and vice versa.

Of course, anyone who opens up the *Summa de arithmetica,
geometria, proportioni et proportionalità* by Lucas Pacioli,
published in Venice in 1494—the first mathematical treatise
that printing made widely known—will find some algebraic
concepts there: *algebra, almucabala, arte maggiore*, presented
as a method of calculation necessary for arithmetic and geometry. But it is a strange algebra, still ignorant of mathematical
signs $(+, -)$, whose place is taken by letters; of the very convenient use of x and y; of the practical symbols x, x^2, x^3, x^4, whose
place is taken by expressions like *cosa* to mean the unknown or
censo to indicate the unknown squared.[7] To Viète goes the
honor of having introduced the use of letters to indicate both
known and unknown quantities, and of having likewise adopted
a practical notation for expressing powers. In anticipation of
this, Pacioli did teach how to solve quadratic and certain
higher-degree equations with rudimentary tools, but the general
solution of third-degree equations remained unknown to him. It
would be the collective achievement of a whole series of great
Italians, among them Tartaglia and Cardano.

There was no algebraic language. There was not even an
arithmetic language that was convenient, regular, and modern.
The use of the numerals we call Arabic because they are Indian, the gobar numerals that came into western Europe from
Spain or Barbary, was far from common, although Italian merchants had been acquainted with them ever since the thirteenth
and fourteenth centuries. If there was a rapid spread of the
practice of using these symbols in calendars for ecclesiastics and
in almanacs for astrologers and physicians, it met strong resistance in everyday life from Roman numerals—or, to be more
exact, the slightly modified minuscule Roman numerals that
were called *chiffres de finance*. They appeared grouped accord-

7. Which he abbreviated as *co* (*cosa*), *ce* (*censo*), and *cu* (*cubo*). Regiomontanus
(1436–1476), for his part, called the unknown *res* and its square *census*. To solve a
problem *per artem rei et census* meant to solve it by means of a quadratic equation.

ing to categories, separated by dots: tens, twenties superscribed by two X's, hundreds superscribed by a C, and thousands superscribed by an M—all as poorly contrived as possible to permit the execution of any arithmetical operation no matter how elementary.

There were also no written calculations—those procedures that seem so convenient and simple to us and that still seemed fiendishly difficult to men of the sixteenth century, suitable only for the mathematical elite. Before laughing, let us remember that in 1645, more than a century after the appearance of *Pantagruel*, Pascal was still insisting on the extreme difficulty of written calculations when he dedicated his calculating machine to Chancellor Séguier. Not only do they constantly force us "to keep or borrow the necessary sums," whence come innumerable errors (and he might have added that it was precisely because of these errors[8] that the Arabs had invented checking by casting out nines), but moreover they demand of the unfortunate calculator "deep attention that tires the mind in a short time." Actually in Rabelais's time counting was done mostly and almost exclusively with the help of counting boards or "exchequers" (which gave their name to the ministers of the treasury on the other side of the Channel) and counters, which were used with greater or lesser dexterity in the Ancien Régime up to its decline.[9]

In any case, did those men figure better in their heads than with pen in hand? I am always reminded of the lovely story about the secretary of a president of the Chambre des Comptes who was rudely called upon by a gang to open his door: "If you don't open, there are fifty of us here, and we will each beat you a hundred times." He who was summoned answered at once, in terror. "What? Five thousand blows!" And Tallement des Réaux, who tells the story, is filled with wonder: "I admire the

8. "Errors in calculation were the general rule. It was exceptional for an addition to be correct. The divergences were often considerable, sometimes exceeding 100,000 *livres*." Roger Doucet, *L'Etat des finances de 1523* (Paris, 1923), p. 12.

9. On these usages see, in addition to Cantor, Albert Dupont, *Formes des comptes et façons de compter dans l'ancien temps* (Paris and Vienne, 1928). The whole development of arithmetic and even of elementary algebra took place in association with advances in bookkeeping. On these, see Raymond de Roover, "Aux origines d'une technique intellectuelle: la formation et l'expansion de la comptabilité à partie double," *Annales d'Histoire Economique et Sociale*, 9 (1937), 171-193, 270-298.

man's presence of mind, and it seems to me one needed to be secretary to a president of the Comptes to make the calculation so adroitly!"[10] The impossible calculation: 100 × 50.

Moreover, the techniques and methods of written calculation were still far from uniform. Addition and subtraction were done from left to right. Our present procedure only started to be used, in part, around 1600. Pacioli, the great authority, gave his readers a choice of three methods of subtraction and eight of multiplication, each having its own name. Their difficulty seemed to be such that efforts were bent to find mechanical means that would allow novices to avoid them—for example, Napier's famous "bones" at the beginning of the seventeenth century. But it was division that of all the operations had the worst reputation. Rival methods made claims on the student, and the one we use today was not the one held in most re-pute—far from it.

There were no established methods, there were insufficient symbols. In 1489 the signs + and − were found, to be sure, in Johannes Widman of Eger's *Mercantile Arithmetic*, but as ab-breviations, not operational symbols. In 1484 the Parisian Nic-olas Chuquet, working for the merchants of Lyon, was still using the notations *p* and *m* to abbreviate "plus" and "minus" in his *Triparty*.[11] As a matter of fact, Viète was the first author who is really known to have employed these signs consistently, starting in 1591, and little by little he promoted their use. The equals sign =, introduced in 1557 by Robert Recorde in a trea-tise that remained in manuscript for a long time, was not in general use, either, until the seventeenth century. The "multi-plied by" ×, employed by Oughtred in 1631, did not prevail right away; Leibniz still indicated multiplication by the sign⌢. As for the sign ÷ (divided by), it also dates from 1631. Need I add that logarithms were not invented until 1614 by Napier— and that Rabelais's contemporaries had not the slightest notion of any of this?

10. Gédéon Tallement des Réaux, *Historiettes,* ed. Antoine Adam, 2 vols. (Paris, 1960–1961), II, 470.

11. On Chuquet, see Cantor, II, 318, and Aristide Marre, "Notice sur Nicolas Chu-quet et son *Triparty en la science des nombres,*" *Bulletino di Bibliografia e di Storia delle Scienze Matematiche e Fisiche, Pubblicato da B. Boncompagni,* 13 (1880), 555–592, followed by a reproduction of the text of the *Triparty* (593–659, 693–814).

At which we ought not smile and ask: Is it really necessary to possess these signs in order to reason correctly?[12] It is surely not by divine right that the cross means "plus" and the Saint Andrew's cross "multiplied by." The reverse convention could have been adopted. But to do arithmetic or algebra in a useful way without some such system of signs is impossible. And a man who does not have them at his disposal, who is therefore living in a world in which mathematics is still elementary, has not had his mind formed in the same way as one who, even though he may be ignorant or unable—or unconcerned—to solve an equation himself or do a more or less complicated problem, lives in a society that is on the whole subjected to the rigor of its modes of mathematical reasoning, to the precision of its modes of calculation, and to the correctness and elegance of its ways of giving proofs.

"All of our modern life is as though impregnated with mathematics. Men's everyday actions and their structures bear its mark—and we do not escape its influence even in our artistic pleasures or our moral life." A man of the sixteenth century would not have been able to subscribe to this statement by Paul Montel. We are not surprised by it. It would have caused him, quite rightly, to be totally incredulous.

4. Fluid Time, Stagnant Time

Let us apply these reflections to the measurement of time. People were often still content to approximate it as peasants do—estimating daytime according to the sun and nighttime, or rather the end of night, by listening for the rooster's crow. It is interesting to read from the prolific pen of the Reformer of Lausanne, Viret, words of praise for the roosters that men-at-arms always took with them when they went off to war: "which at night served them as clocks."[13]

The fact is that there were very few real clocks, most of them

12. See the observations by Abel Rey on this subject in his *La Science dans l'antiquité*, 5 vols. (Paris, 1930–1948), III, 371 ff. Which is not to overlook the important reflections in Cournot, I, 35: "If, however, the Greeks had been acquainted with our arithmetical notation, there is no doubt this would have given a different direction to their studies, even the purely speculative ones."

13. Pierre Viret, *Instruction chrestienne*, II: *Exposition de la foy chrestienne* (Geneva: Rivery, 1564), p. 179 (dialogue IX).

for public use. Furthermore, it was a rare town that could pride itself on a true clock, either without chimes or, wondrous to behold, with chimes, like the oldest one of all, the one ordered by Charles V and placed on the tower of the palace in 1370—it still gives its name to the present-day Quai de l'Horloge. They were sturdy, rudimentary machines. It was necessary to wind them several times in the course of twenty-four hours. We would know that from Froissart's *Horloge amoureuse* even if city archives from the end of the fourteenth century did not speak a great deal about the one who "regulates the clock" (*gouverne le reloige*) and about his consumption of grease, iron wire, wood, and rope for the said clock, its hammer, and its wheels: "A clock cannot go by itself or move, unless it has one to watch it and care for it: a clockmaker, who administers to it carefully when necessary, lifts its weights, returns them to their duty, and makes them move in an orderly way."[14]

There is no need to say that those clocks did not sound the hours. Every time the hand passed a new hour, a pin fixed to the driving wheel released a lever that set in motion a hammer that sounded an alarm on a bell. The watchman, thus alerted, with the aid of the hammer then struck the necessary number of strokes on the bell of the tower. But there was no question of indicating the hour's subdivisions. And besides, in many instances the night watchmen were provided with the hour only approximately, by means of hourglasses using sand or water that they were responsible for turning. They cried out from the tops of towers the information these furnished them, and guards repeated it on the streets. As for individuals, how many in Pantagruel's time owned a clock? The number was minimal, outside of kings and princes. They were proud and considered themselves privileged if they possessed, under the name of clock, one of those hourglasses that used water rather than sand, to which Joseph Scaliger offered pompous praise in his second *Scaligerana*: "horologia sunt valde recentia et praeclarum inventum."[15]

<hr/>

14. [Paraphrase of ll. 927–934 of Jean Froissart, "Li Orloge amoureus" in *Oeuvres de Froissart: poésies*, ed. Auguste Scheler, 3 vols. (Brussels, 1870–1872), I, 79–80. —Translator.] See Alfred Franklin. *La Vie privée d'autrefois*, 23 vols. (Paris, 1887–1901), IV: *La Mesure du temps*, passim.

15. "Clocks are very recent, and a wonderful invention." He goes on: "The water clock, *hydrologium*—I have one . . . Those using water are less durable and more accurate, since the sand sometimes piles up or gets damp ·. . Finely broken enamel is better

On the whole, they were the ways of a peasant society, which accepted the fact that it would never know the exact time except when the bell rang (assuming it was set properly) and otherwise referring to plants and animals, to the flight or song of some bird. "Around sunrise" or else "around sunset": these are the most frequent indications by Gilles de Gouberville, a gentleman of Normandy, in his diary.[16] Sometimes, rather curiously, he refers to the behavior of a bird he calls a *vitecoq*, which must have been a kind of woodcock. "It was the time of the *vitecoqs'* flight," he will say, "when I came home" (November 28, 1554) or, again, he will note that on January 5, 1557 (O.S.), after vespers the bachelors of the parish started playing pall-mall with the married men; they were at it "till the *vitecoqs'* flight."[17] And yet Gouberville had a clock, a great rarity, which he sent to an armorer in Digoville in January 1561 (O.S.) for repairs.[18] And he delighted in taking note of the hours, always prefacing this with a modest and prudent "around": they returned "around an hour before daybreak" or "we came to take several glasses, around half an hour"—which has a precision that was entirely abnormal.

Thus we find fancifulness, imprecision, inexactness everywhere, the doing of men who did not even know their ages precisely. Countless are the historical personages of the time who have given us a choice of three or four birth dates. When was Erasmus born? He did not know, only that the event took place on the eve of Saints Simon and Jude. What year was Lefèvre d'Etaples born? We try to deduce it from very vague hints. What year was Rabelais born? He did not know. Luther? We are in doubt. The month was generally known—a month in a year that was itself poorly organized, since the vernal equinox had moved back little by little from March 21 to March 11. The family and the parents remembered that the baby had come into the world at haymaking time, at the time of the wheat harvest or grape harvest; there had been snow, or else it was the

than sand ..." S.v. "Horloge," *Scaligerana ou bons mots ... de J. Scaliger* (Cologne, 1695), p. 198.

16. For example, "about an hour after sunrise" (Aug. 1553), *Le Journal du Sire de Gouberville*, ed. Eugène de Robillard de Beaurepaire (Caen, 1892), p. 28; "It was about sunset when we arrived" (Sept. 1553), ibid., p. 34.

17. Ibid., pp. 139, 398. On January 4, 1562, Gouberville presented a friend with "a brace of *vitecoqs*" (p. 857).

18. Ibid., p. 747.

month "when the ears of wheat began to come out ... and the
stalks were already starting to grow": these rustic details are in
John Calvin.[19] So a family tradition was established: François
was born on November 27, and Jeanne on January 12 (how
cold it was when she was carried to the font!). Sometimes even
the hour was known, in a more or less general way—"around,"
as the Sire de Gouberville would say. The mother did not forget the hour; it was the date, an abstract notion, that went beyond the sphere of ordinary concerns. To find birth certificates
in good order we have to turn to the world's great—or the sons
of doctors and learned men, those for whom a horoscope was
cast and whose birth, as a consequence, was surrounded with
astonishingly accurate details. They knew (or rather their astrologers provided for them) the year, the day, the hour, and
the minute, not only of their birth, but of their conception. We
are informed of this by Brantôme, who was an intimate of Margaret of Navarre through his mother and grandmother. The
princess had been born "under the 10th degree of Aquarius
when Saturn was separated from Venus by the quartile aspect
on the 10th of April, 1492, at 10 o'clock in the evening at the
castle of Angoulême—and had been conceived in the year 1491
at 10 hours and 17 minutes before midnight on the 11th of
July."[20] Now, that is being precise! Cardano himself was no less
well informed about his entry into the world. He gives the
year, day, and hour, but to within the quarter.[21]

With these exceptions, the great mass gave up all concern for

19. "Quand les blés commencent à jeter, ... que déjà le tuyau commence à s'élever,"
Joannis Calvini opera quae supersunt omnia, ed. Baum, Cunitz, Reuss, and Erickson
(Corpus Reformatorum), 59 vols. (Brunswick, 1863–1900), XXVII, col. 371. There
was a strange step backward: at the height of the century of scientific precision, of the
measurement of the meridian and the invention and strict definition of the meter, a
"quantitative" [Febvre probably means qualitative—Translator] calendar was again to
be seen, and by the grace of Fabre d'Eglantine the months greened ʾnd flowered:
Floréal, Prairial, Messidor. And the ten days of the decade were given rustic names:
grape, saffron, chestnut, horse or colchicum, and so on.

20. Pierre de Bourdeille, Seigneur de Brantôme, *Vie des dames illustres* in *Oeuvres
complètes*, ed. Ludovic Lalanne, 11 vols. (Paris, 1864–1882), VIII, 123.

21. Jerome Cardan, *The Book of My Life*, trans. Jean Stoner (New York, 1930), p.
4. The hour's subdivisions were poorly organized. Systems varied: 4 points, 10 minutes, 15 parts, 40 movements, 60 ostenta, 22,560 atoms, said Hrabanus Maurus; 4
points, 40 movements, 480 ounces, 5,640 minutes, said a thirteenth-century text cited
by Littré (s.v. "Minute"); 4 points, 10 minutes, 40 momenta, 22,560 atoms, said Jean
Michel Albert (d. 1450). See Thorndike, p. 221.

precision. "There is nothing," wrote Thomas Platter in his memoirs, "that I can vouch for less than the exact time of each circumstance of my life"—which did not prevent him from telling wonderful stories about his mother's father, who lived to the age of 126 and at over 100 married a girl of 30 by whom he had a son, but naturally no one knew the date of his birth.[22] What good was such precision to a Valais mountaineer? Men had not yet been forced to precision by the harsh discipline of time that we know: civil time, religious time, school time, military time, factory time, railroad time—so much so that in the end everyone has to have a watch. Just think, in 1867, at the time of the Paris International Exposition, there were still barely four million watches in France, and twenty-five million in the whole world. That was very few, but it was already a lot, since it had been necessary to overcome so much resistance and instinctive aversion. "I never tie myself to hours," solemnly declares the abbot of Theleme, Friar John. "They are made for the man, and not the man for them."[23] But a hundred years later Sorel's Francion, describing his arrival at the College of Lisieux, groans, "I was obliged to appear at divine services, at meals, and at lessons at certain hours, to the sound of the bell, by which all things were marked."[24]

In the main in the sixteenth century, in the great longstanding duel fought between experienced time and measured time, it was the first that kept the advantage. "Chapter XXIII. How Gargantua was instructed by Ponocrates, and in such sort disciplinated, that he lost not one hour of the day." Not to lose an hour a day: horrible ideal of new times! How much happier good King Charles V had been; he had a taper that was divided into twenty-four parts, and from time to time someone came to tell him "to what point the candle had burned down."

Chronology imposes a tough abstract rule. Can we ourselves claim to have submitted to it fully and rigorously? When we evoke our own past and then compare our memories with the calendar, what disharmony there is! It is obvious that we re-

22. Thomas Platter, *Lebensbeschreibung*, ed. Alfred Hartmann (Klosterberg and Basel, 1944), p. 24.
23. *Gargantua*, ch. 41.
24. Charles Sorel, *Histoire comique de Francion*, ed. Emile Roy, 4 vols. (Paris, 1924–1931), I, 172.

make the past according to our dispositions, often telescoping the years and constructing out of events that are sometimes very widely separated in time coherent wholes that we find pleasing. If this is true of us, men of today, who do not know how to live without a watch, a watch carefully set according to astronomical time, what was it like in the sixteenth century? For how many men had the astronomical calendar already become the true measurement, the true regulator, of time? Even in the religious realm? Can we really believe that for measuring time, for slicing it up, peasants then had any means of measuring and marking but particular circumstances that were important to the life of the group and capable of arousing it to paroxysms of activity or of passion?

Just think how even today the concept of time easily becomes hazy, despite the number and rigor of the marks we have with which to measure it. It takes the child a while to pin it down, while a sick person easily makes mistakes about it. As we go back a dozen generations we find ourselves in the midst of the era of fluid time. Among the uneducated, "before" and "after" were two concepts that did not yet strictly exclude each other. Death did not prevent the dead from living and coming back. It was the same with space. In Rabelais's time many objections were raised to accepting the idea that a man could occupy two places at once—two spots in a space that was still poorly organized, where each thing was not yet the rightful occupant of an exclusive place, a place that could be instantly located at any moment.

Are we therefore surprised that men of the past lacked a historical sense? That, to take only one example, they never raised the problem of the age of the world in any of their writings? That the absolute figure of 4004 years from the creation of the world to the birth of Christ was never a subject for discussion?[25] And that, finally, it was with no discomfort at all that they saw their painters depict the besiegers of Jericho in the garb of the men-at-arms of Marignano or clothe the bystanders at Golgotha in slashed doublets? The great step backward, the great movement in reverse as humanity gradually retook pos-

25. Geoffroy Atkinson, *Les Nouveaux Horizons de la Renaissance française* (Paris, 1935), pp. 270, 416–417.

session of the trenches from which it first set out to conquer what it calls progress, had not begun. It is still going on before our eyes and scores new successes every day. For many men of that time the historical was confused with the mythical. In the indefinite past that they called "former times" or "olden times" or "a very long time ago" without more precision, who knows how many still accepted without much difficulty the presence of mythical personages existing side by side with "mythified" (if I may say that) historical personages in a sort of fluid promiscuity that shocks us but did not bother any of them? All of this went a very long way; it involved all of life and the total behavior of the era.

Do we need one last indication? If time was not measured with accuracy, if no one bothered to keep track of it, reckon it, or regard it in an exact way, how could it have been treated as a precise commodity to be saved, managed, or used effectively? In its works the sixteenth century, the heir of the fifteenth century in this respect, was in fact one of the biggest wasters of time that a century ever was. That was the period when the architects of churches, castles, and palaces squandered a prodigious outlay of days, months, and years in complicated ornaments, tracery, and flourishes; when buildings in the Flamboyant style, carved Burgundian chests, and cut and slashed garments—even dishes cooked with a knowing, cruel slowness—seemed like so many huge strongboxes in which men who kept no reckoning hid away bundles of time that did not produce interest.[26] It was a far cry from our unadorned, sleek buildings, all flat surfaces without moldings or sculpture, rising into the air in three weeks—the air into which a skyscraper rises in three months is the same air in which the Tour Saint-Jacques, with its festoons and arches, could be seen growing for years, course upon course, every day becoming more and more carved and ornate.

It would take much time, much research that is now lacking,

26. The cage in which the Duke of Nemours was kept at the castle of Pierre Scize in Lyon by order of Louis XI (1476) had required, apart from the ironwork that took the largest expenditure of time, 139 days' work by master and journeyman carpenters, we are told by Deniau. See Arthur Kleinclausz, *Histoire de Lyon*, 3 vols. (Lyon, 1939–1952), I, 348. On all of this see Adolf Loos, "Ornament and Crime," (1908), in Ludwig Münz and Gustav Künstler, *Adolf Loos, Pioneer of Modern Architecture*, trans. Harold Meek (New York, 1966), pp. 226–231. What was a paradox then is a truism today.

tools we have not been provided with, to complete this picture of the conditions of thought of a century we think we can still reach out and touch but which is, however, already so far away both in its mental habits and its social structure. Yet are we not well enough informed by now to think, without too much presumption, that if these were the conditions of existence to which the men of that time were subjected, their thought could not really have had conclusive force nor their science compelling power?

5. Hypothesis and Reality: The World System

The philosophy of the past was opinions, which were worth whatever the speaker was worth in the eyes of his followers or critics. There was no checking by facts, no recourse to realities that allowed one to make a valid choice between the rival opinions of A and B, so long as both of them stood up equally well to the logician's critical examination. As for the science of the past, it too was opinions.

Let us take just one example, but an important one. On the general motion of the stars, a question debated for thousands of years, a contemporary of Rabelais found himself confronted by several different theories. To be brief and not go into minute detail, he could number himself among the champions of Ptolemy's cosmology or the diehard Averroists. He could choose between the *Almagest*—with its learned geometric constructions, its complicated epicycles and eccentrics that were meant to account for the motions of the sun and the planets—and the theories of al-Bitruji, Averroës's contemporary, who like him opposed the Ptolemaic complexities: for him as for Aristotle nine homocentric spheres, nine spherical shells, fitted exactly one inside the other, turned around the earth's center. And their motion was uniform, since that was postulated by Greek metaphysics. The fact that observation had, however, revealed certain stars to be sometimes closer to the earth and sometimes farther away mattered little to those who followed the Arabs.

What choice was there between Arab realism and Greek imagination, and how could one choose? Let us not, with some ingenuousness, say: pick what is true. In the overwhelming majority, the men of the sixteenth century would have answered that what was true or even, more modestly, what was plausible, mattered little here. The problem that presented itself to the astronomer, as Duhem established to perfection in a remarkable treatise in 1908, was a mathematical one.[27] It was a question of "saving the phenomena." A long time before, Simplicius, commenting on the four books of Aristotle's *De caelo*, had written that the whole question was the very one Plato had asked the mathematicians, putting it as follows: "What are the circular motions, uniform and perfectly regular, that can be conveniently adopted as hypotheses so we can 'save appearances'?" Whether they described reality was another question. Of course, if several satisfactory hypotheses could be formulated that equally allowed appearances to be saved, it is quite plain that only one of them would be "true," that is, would respond to the fundamental nature of things. But what did such conformity matter to the astronomer? It was only of interest to the physicist. It was for him alone to establish which of the hypotheses that had been formulated was *katà phýsin*, it being only by accident that the others saved the phenomena.

Let us refrain from showing surprise at such an attitude. For, after all, when the geometrical astronomers professed the ideas about the role and value of hypotheses in mathematics that we have just spoken of, they were in a direct line with modern science. They already sensed in a confused way the justice of Bertrand Russell's quip that mathematics is "the subject in which we never know what we are talking about, nor whether what we are saying is true." And of course the scholars of the sixteenth century were incapable of developing the theme as Jacques Hadamard did in his wonderful introduction to mathematics in the *Encyclopédie française*.[28] But their attitude was a sensible one. Besides, it was not their fault if, when the question of reality was raised, the physicists of the time found themselves incapable of choosing between the hypotheses on valid— valid in our opinion, that is to say—grounds, the grounds of observation and experimentation.

When Rabelais's contemporaries got involved in such questions there really was some basis for their remaining in a quan-

27. Pierre Duhem, *To Save the Phenomena, an Essay on the Idea of Physical Theory from Plato to Galileo*, trans. Edmund Doland and Chaninah Maschler (Chicago, 1969). Originally published as a series of articles in *Annales de Philosophie Chrétienne* and then as a book, *Sozein ta phainomena, Essai sur la notion de théorie physique de Platon à Galilée* (Paris, 1908).

28. I, 1´52-1-1´58-7.

dary. There was no doubt that Ptolemy, with his eccentrics and epicycles, saved appearances in an excellent fashion. His learned and complicated system permitted calculations and, as a consequence, predictions. The Arabs boasted of the same excellence, but since they had not carried their deductions to the point of constructing tables and ephemerides that would permit calculation and prediction, it was possible to have some doubt about the validity of their assertions. So the debate had to be resolved in terms of physics. And those among Pantagruel's contemporaries who felt in themselves a profound need for realism were firm adherents of a physics they believed to be Aristotelian. They picked the Arabs—the Paduan Averroists are an example. The others remained in a quandary, torn between their admiration for Ptolemy's constructions and the resistance that physics offered to those constructions. It was, however, not so great that in the end they did not become adherents of the *Almagest*'s cosmology.

6. Copernicus's Point of View

In this book we could leave it here. For the man who was about to transform all these theories through his genius had no influence on the general current of ideas before the middle of the century. The lesson to be drawn from his scientific "adventure," however, is one we cannot overlook.

Copernicus: the first man to prove that the moving earth turned around the stationary sun; the man who thereby dethroned the earth and, in so doing, assured "the triumph of Truth." Maybe. But just listen to him speak. At the very beginning of his book is a dedicatory letter to Pope Paul III. The author marked his point of departure in a word: how to choose between the Averroists and the Ptolemaists. He chose to ignore both of them and formulate a new hypothesis, something that was perhaps "impossible" in the eyes of a physicist, but no hypothesis was impossible in the eyes of a geometer as long as in formulating it and relying on it he succeeded in saving appearances and making rigorous calculations possible.

Copernicus modestly claimed he had borrowed this hypothesis from the ancients. Indeed, they had passed it on to various Pythagoreans, but it had seemed so shocking to them that no one after those daring souls had taken it up again. It was the hypothesis of a moving earth around a stationary sun. "The opinion seemed absurd," said Copernicus to the pope, "but I knew that my predecessors had been granted freedom to imagine all kinds of fictitious circles with a view to saving the appearances of the heavens. I therefore thought that I might no less easily be granted the right to make an attempt, to try whether, by attributing some motion to the earth, stronger proofs might not be discovered on the subject of the revolutions of the heavenly spheres than those of my predecessors." The hypothesis was indeed found to confirm all the appearances, to "save all the phenomena." The case had been decided: it could be adopted.

That was Copernicus speaking like an astronomer-geometer. But in secret he added something to his statements, which was that his hypothesis, first formulated in his mind before 1515 and at that time expressed in preliminary form in a manuscript called *Commentariolus* (it was then reworked from 1523 to 1532, then recast one last time in 1540–41 on the eve of the publication of *De revolutionibus*), a hypothesis that was the fruit of thirty-six years of scholarly research, meditation, calculation, and observation, was "true." For it gave a better account of appearances than previous hypotheses and, besides, it had the advantage over them of simplicity. Copernicus thus placed himself in the ranks of the realists. As Abel Rey has justly observed, Copernicus had spent nine years in Italy studying medicine rather than mathematics and so shared the state of mind of the doctors, who since the fourteenth century had been animated by a spirit of experimentation, still rudimentary but already active.[29] And moreover, although Copernicus limited himself to allowing this to be glimpsed from his general tendencies, his pupil Rheticus proclaimed it at the top of his voice in 1540. His master, he explained, did not intend to be satisfied with giving a better account of appearances. He was actually constructing a new physics, one that Aristotle himself would have embraced if he had still been on earth.[30]

Copernicus thought it, Rheticus said it. But for both of them it was an act of faith. For the proof was lacking. And not

29. "All the great precursors, all the early scientists of the Renaissance, were doctors." Rey, III, 453.

30. Georg Joachim Rheticus, *Ad clariss. v. D. Jo. Schonerum de libris revolutionum Nic. Copernici narratio prima* (Gdansk, 1540).

merely the proof, but also the means of establishing it. That is why, once *De revolutionibus* appeared, many who admired it continued to claim that nothing obliged them to a real belief in the earth's motion and the sun's immobility. The genius of Copernicus was no less great in their eyes if his hypothesis was only a wonderful device, an incomparable way of saving appearances. That is what allowed theologians—and Melanchthon in the first place—to urge young people to be prudent. "Men of science, with subtle minds," he wrote in 1549 in his course in physics, *Initia doctrinae physicae,* "like to discuss a lot of questions on which they exercise their ingenuity, but the young should be aware that these scientists have no intention of affirming such things."

Furthermore, this prudence did not prevent Melanchthon from paying tribute to the Copernican theory of lunar orbits. Nor did it induce the astronomer Reinhold to refuse to lend his support to the new system in 1551 with the astronomical tables he computed, the *Prutenic Tables,* which did much to spread the new theories. For these men, however, and for many others of the time, saving the phenomena was one thing and grasping the actual truth of reality was another. And once again: how could they have reasoned otherwise?

They could not be ahead of their times. They could not fill the yawning gap between the physics of the heavenly bodies—stars and spheres that ever since Aristotle had consisted of a simple substance distinct from the four elements and incapable of generation or corruption—and the physics of sublunary things, not eternal and subject to the work of corruption and generation. To be sure, for a few precursors the distinction between the two physics had tended to disappear. Cusa and da Vinci had already dared to liken the earth to the planets. This was again opinion, opinion pure and simple. In order for real progress to take place, it was necessary to have experimental, decisive proof. It was necessary for observation to establish clearly and indisputably the analogy between the composition of the planets and that of the earth. But the telescope had not come into existence. It was necessary for the mechanical explanation of the celestial motions to become more complicated, for Copernicus's circular orbits to become elliptical, for the old Platonic concept of uniform motion to give way to the concept of speed varying in inverse proportion to the distance separating each planet from the sun. All of this would be the work of Kepler. It was necessary for Galileo, discovering the spots on the sun, to refute the Peripatetic dogma of the eternity of the heavens and, seeing the mountains of the moon with his own eyes, fill up the abyss separating our sublunary world from the celestial moon. In a word, it was necessary to achieve the fusion into a single physics of the two physics that had been separate for so long.[31]

And when that happened let us not imagine that everything became clear to everybody—all men of science and philosophy, I mean. It took Campanella a while to adhere to the new system. And when Galileo converted him, when he was led to make the assertion, on August 5, 1632, that Galileo's discoveries were the starting point of a new era—*son principio di secol novo*—Campanella nevertheless did not immediately give up his theory of 1604 and 1611 about the sun as the seat of love rushing toward our earth, the seat of hate, in order to consume it—at a speed he believed it was possible to determine. It makes us smile. Campanella was not smiling, and nobody around him was smiling, either. He did not ask that science be Science but rather that it confirm his views of men's destiny, his predictions about the end of the world, all his apocalyptic and millenarian dreams.[32]

7. World System: Certainty or Fear?

We should not underestimate the significance of these facts. Whether the men of the sixteenth century were or were not settled in their minds with regard to such astronomical and cosmo-

31. Cournot had already said this before Duhem, in sober and excellent fashion: "In other respects one can say that Copernicus and Tycho perfected but did not innovate, since for them as for their forerunners astronomy had no other object but the geometric theory of celestial motion, the development of a geometric hypothesis or the substitution of one geometric hypothesis for another—without coming to grips with celestial mechanics, a theory of the forces that produce celestial motion, except by conjectures that were not at all scientific; without, as a consequence, being able to *furnish decisive proof of the truth or error of the hypothesis.*" Cournot, I, 110. This was written in 1868 and first published in 1872.

32. For Campanella's attitude toward the new astronomy, see Léon Blanchet, *Campanella* (Paris, 1920), p. 241.

graphical problems was important for something quite apart
from advances in any particular science. Who can ever measure
with accuracy the importance that the firm and confident back-
ing of a society's world system, based—that is, held to be
based—on immutable foundations, has for that society's good
health and functioning, for its faith in itself and its equilibrium,
and for its dynamism as well?

For three generations the system of Laplace provided a really
astounding kind of certainty, security, and moral outlook. Together with the abnormal stability of the monetary system for
more than a century, it consituted one of the agents, one of the
primordial elements, of that moral climate of confidence and
stability—false confidence and false stability—in whose sweetness Europe slumbered till its bloody awakening. "The system
of Laplace," we said, but for Rabelais's contemporaries there
was not even the system of Copernicus. Not only because we
know the publication date of De revolutionibus, the date that
all the new things it promised its eager readers began to be circulated: "Motus stellarum, tam fixarum quam erraticarum,
cum ex veteribus tum etiam ex recentibus observationibus in-
stitutos, et novis insuper ac admirabilibus hypothesibus or-
natos."[33] But also because when contemporaries were able to
get hold of this work of genius that summed up the effort of a
lifetime, they acted with rather significant discretion. A second
edition was not required till twenty-three years later, in 1566;
and in the beginning of the seventeenth century two more editions appeared, one after the other, in 1617 and 1640 in Holland.

A while ago Jean Plattard expressed surprise, somewhat naively, at how slight its influence was. He might have considered
that such radical and profound changes as physics has under-
gone before our eyes in the last thirty or forty years have still
had no effect—to speak with more precision, they have not
made any conscious impact—on the system of ideas of our own
contemporaries. Abbé Bremond could have told him how much
time was needed—a century—for Bérulle's Oratory to bring
about a "Copernican revolution," on the model of astronomy, in

---

33. The motions of the stars, the fixed as well as the wandering ones, established
from both old and recent observations, and in addition furnished with new and admirable hypotheses.

the realm of belief, a lag that is dealt with so intelligently in his history of religious sentiment.[34]

While Our Master Janotus waited, in the '30s of the sixteenth century, comfortably seated at his table in front of his theological tipple, he was firmly convinced that the sun still went around him and that the night sky was a star-pierced vault that bounded the world. Like Voltaire, he was better able to conceive "nature limited than nature infinite." And who could blame him? A good thesis was a fine thing. It was always nice, when one was the first licentiate at Paris, to take a thesis and prove it in opposition to another that was no less capable of being proved. Things went no further than that. They could not go further. For that to happen it would be necessary for the experimental method to come into being, it would be necessary to have not only discourses on method but also applications of method. That point had not yet been reached. Those were not times of a critical spirit. The times of credulity continued to roll on—and of fear as well.

For fear, the child of ignorance, was always lodged in the hearts of those strong men. "Around 11 o'clock at night, when it was very clear and serene, the sky over the highest tower of the fortress appeared so red and inflamed that it greatly frightened our people"—from *Notes on Japan* by the Jesuit Fathers Froës, Rogier, Cabral, and others, not in 1520 or 1530, but in 1587.[35] Oh well, Jesuits. But no, it was everybody, a whole nation, a whole literature: *Wonderful Visions of Diverse Shape and Aspect Appearing over the City of Saint-Amour in the Free County of Burgundy*—published in Lyon for B. Rigaud, 1575, 8vo, 14 pp.; *Summary Description of the Awful Meteor and Wonderful Vision Lately Seen in the Air over the Castle of Aubépin near the City of Saint-Amour in the Free County of Burgundy,* by Monsieur Himbert de Billy, native of Charlieu in the Lyonnais, pupil of the worthy Corneille de Montfort called de Blockland, published in Lyon by Benoist Rigaud, 1577, 4to, 15 pp.; *Discourse on What Is Threatened to Be Seen to Befall by the Comet Appearing on the 12th of the Present Month of November 1577, the Which Is Still to Be Seen Today*

---

34. Henri Bremond, *Histoire littéraire du sentiment religieux en France depuis la fin des guerres de religion jusqu'à nos jours,* 11 vols. (Paris, 1916–1933), III, 25 ff.

35. *Avvisi del Giapone . . .* (Rome, 1586).

in Lyon and Other Places, published in Lyon for François Didier, 8vo, 8 fols.; *Summary Discourse on the Vision and Omen of the Comet*—we could go on.[36] Within four or five years in this small corner of France alone there were twenty to thirty odd little books: omens, apparitions, and wondrous signs, descriptions of hairy or bearded stars, a discourse on "great and frightening fires appearing in the sky" or "a wondrous vision of two armies appearing in the air over Chatel-Chalon in the Free County of Burgundy" (1590). All of it was the work of distinguished astrologers and astrophiles, in the guise of scientists, who were richly entertained at the courts of great lords who believed in their science and were shaken by the same fears as they themselves were. It evokes a world that has disappeared, it evokes its fears and its credulities, based on the naive worship of authorities and the unshaken prestige of Hearsay.[37] But why all these odd writings?

"My heart still trembles within me, when I think on the many dreadful prodigies we saw five or six days before [the learned and valiant Chevalier de Langey] died." So wrote Rabelais in chapter 27 of *Book Four*. And Guillaume Du Bellay's physician shows us the distressed "family" of the dying man, all his dismayed relatives, friends, and servants gazing at each other without uttering a word before these dreadful prodigies "that thwart the order of nature." All were overcome by fear—

36. *Visions merveilleuses de diverses forme et figure, apparues sur la ville de Saint-Amour en la Franche-Comté de Bourgongne; Sommaire description de l'effroyable météore et vision merveilleuse naguères veüe en l'air au-dessus du chasteau de l'Aubépin, proche de la ville de Saint-Amour en la Franche-Comté de Bourgongne; Discours sur ce que menace de voir advenir la Comète apparue le 12 de ce présent mois de novembre 1577, laquelle se voit encore aujourd'hui à Lyon et autres lieux; Sommaire discours sur la vision et présage du comète.*

37. We should not proceed to believe that the seventeenth century did not have these fears. "Apprehension of the eclipse has so universally troubled men's minds," wrote Bénigne Bouhier in 1676, "that there are few who are exempt from it. Some are frightened to death—and the others are at the feet of the confessionals." Augustin Jacquet, *La Vie littéraire dans une ville de province sous Louis XIV* (Paris, 1886), p. 42. Bayle's *Letter on the Comet* (1680) was written specifically to overcome these fears. That they were, moreover, not absolutely universal in the sixteenth century is established in a nice passage by Dolet in his *Genethliacum* of 1539: "His notis securus ages, nec territus ullo/portento, credes generare cuncta sagacis/naturae vi praestante, imperioque stupendo." (If you know this, you are free of care, nor are you frightened by any portents; you believe everything is produced by the excellent force, the overwhelming power, of wise nature.)

the great fear of the comet that had appeared in the sky some days before the departure of a soul "so noble, so precious, and so heroic."

Thus Rabelais. Here is Ronsard on bad dreams, the Ronsard of the *Hymne des daimons:*

> Et lors une grande peur va nos coeurs assaillant.
> Le poil nous dresse au chef et du front, goutte à
>   goutte,
> Jusques à nos talons la sueur nous degoutte.
> Si nous sommes au lit, n'osons lever les bras
> Ni tant soit peu tourner le corps entre les draps.[38]

> And then a mighty fear assails our fainting hearts.
> Our hair stands up in fright, and drop by drop the
>   sweat
> Pours down from brow to heel and leaves our body
>   wet.
> If we're asleep in bed we dare not lift an arm
> Or stir between the sheets, lest we come to harm.

And these were nothing but frightening visions, dead men in their shrouds, drownings in rivers, bears tearing us to pieces, lions gobbling us up, bandits killing us: a saga of absurd but panic terror.

Their autobiographies were a procession of fears. Look again at the memoirs of Thomas Platter, the founder of the dynasty.[39] In them are fear of spirits, whose exploits are constantly recounted by old wives; fear of the night, which is haunted; fear of the specks of dust dancing in a beam of light. Panic fear: might it not be one of the monsters who bite off children's heads? Fear always and everywhere. Even reading an almanac was a source of terror. And the "propaganda" of the sixteenth century was already alerted to it. Look at Montaigne's *Essays* (I:11). He is talking about the Marquis de Saluces, who was so

38. Pierre de Ronsard, *Oeuvres complètes*, ed. Paul Laumonier, 18 vols. (Paris, 1914–1967), VIII, 122.

39. The passage referred to seems actually to be in the memoirs of Felix Platter, Thomas's son. See Felix Platter, *Tagebuch (Lebensbeschreibung) 1536–1567*, ed. Valentin Lötscher (Basel and Stuttgart, 1976), p. 59. [Translator's note.]

terrified by the predictions in his almanacs that he changed his party and deserted the king for the emperor. The latter was, however, no innocent in the matter. Had he not given money, a great deal of money, to increase the number of disastrous prophecies proclaiming the ruin of the king of France? Montaigne wisely concludes, "I see some who study and comment on their almanacs and cite their authority in current events. With all they say, they necessarily tell both truth and falsehood."[40] But that was wise Montaigne.

8. Doubt in the Sixteenth Century

In an examination of Malgaigne's edition of the works of Ambroise Paré[41] it has been carefully calculated that this man, one of the most independent men of his time, relied on written texts 2,274 times; he invoked 301 different authorities, of which the principal one was Galen, whom he cited 543 times, and the second was Hippocrates, 426 times. It was Paré who wrote, "Although learning may be important, so also is it that the mind be grounded in experience." But it was also he who discoursed absurdly on the venom of cats.[42]

Those poor souls, torn between contradictory concerns, and reduced to begging as a favor what to us seems a matter of common sense! Thus Jean de Léry, speaking of a pilot he had watched at work, wrote: "Although he knew neither A nor B," he had nevertheless "through his long experience with his charts, astrolabes, and jacob's staffs profited so well in the art of navigation that at every turn he silenced a learned personage on our ship who always triumphed in speaking of theory." Thereupon Jean de Léry very reverentially denied he was finding fault with "the sciences that are acquired and learned in schools and through books." He simply asked, humbly, that "without sticking too much to the opinion of anyone in particular," no one should ever "urge on me a reason that goes against my experience of a thing."[43]

40. *The Complete Essays of Montaigne*, trans. Donald M. Frame (Stanford, Calif., 1958), p. 29.

41. *Oeuvres complètes d'Ambroise Paré*, ed. J. F. Malgaigne, 3 vols. (Paris, 1840–1841).

42. M. A. Chaussade, "La Méthode scientifique d'Ambroise Paré," *Revue de Synthèse Historique*, 44 (1927), 37.

43. Atkinson, pp. 286–287.

This was in 1578, long after Rabelais. At that time (within two years) a simple artisan who had himself not learned much from books, "deprived as he was of the Latin tongue," created a dialogue between the two everlasting enemies, Theory and Practice, in his various treatises, headed by the *Admirable Discourse on the Nature of Waters and Fountains* (1580). Protesting against "Sciences written in the study by an imaginative or biased theory" or "taken from some book written from imagination by those who have practiced nothing," he contested the pernicious doctrine that "theory begat practice."[44]

He went so far as to dare to contradict a doctor like Cardano, "a famous physician, who has been a regent at Toledo, and has written many books in Latin,"[45] but to do so it was necessary for him to defend himself and silence those who would say, "How is it possible for a man to know something and to speak of natural things without having seen the Latin books of the Philosophers?"[46]

Hence the cockiness and bravado affected by Palissy, starting with his "Warning to the Reader." And it was justified, although the fellow quickly reached his limits, which were those of good sense relying on itself without help or assistance. A thesis: "Rocks cannot harden unless there is abundant water. And ordinarily, the hardest ones are found in cold, rainy countries." The proof: Fine marble is found in the Pyrenees, a region flowing with water, and cold and rainy. It is likewise found in Dinant, "a cold and rainy region" where the Meuse flows. Finally, the last proof: It is known that in Freiburg im Breisgau beautiful crystal is found "in mountains in which there is snow nearly all the time."[47] And that must be why all the women of that region are redheads.

Certainty, uncertainties: let us not now proceed to think (this must be said in order to complete the description of this moral climate) or give ourselves the idea that their uncertainties, when they were clearly conscious of them (which naturally was not all the time), seriously disturbed the men of the sixteenth

44. Bernard Palissy, *Oeuvres*, ed. Benjamin Fillon, 2 vols. (Paris, 1888), II, 6 (avertissement); English version, *The Admirable Discourses of Bernard Palissy*, trans. Aurèle La Rocque (Urbana, Ill., 1957), p. 26.

45. *Discours admirable des pierres* in Palissy, *Oeuvres*, II, 160–161; trans. in *Admirable Discourses*, p. 156.

46. Palissy, *Oeuvres*, II, 6; trans. in *Admirable Discourses*, p. 26.

47. Palissy, *Oeuvres*, II, 186; trans. in *Admirable Discourses*, p. 177.

century or touched them deeply. It was the Savoyard vicar who complained, with eloquence, of the torments of doubt. "Doubt about the things it is important for us to know is too violent a state for the human mind, which does not hold out in this state for long. It decides in spite of itself one way or the other and prefers to be deceived rather than to believe nothing."[48] We are all to some degree the vicar's children in this matter. The men of the sixteenth century were not of his lineage—those, that is, who liked to doubt. But not all of them did—far from it.

These were for the most part dogmatic and weighty persons, Our Masters the theologians. Molded over a long period by a logic built on the law of identity and the law of contradiction on the one hand, and the law of the excluded middle on the other, they were led by their intellectual method itself spontaneously to take a clear-cut position in every debate, to construct dilemmas: either this or that, we know or we do not know. We should not put it as "what we say is true or what we say is false." These questions of truth and error are more complex than they seem—Copernicus was our witness to that—and we will come back to them in a moment. Let us say, more simply, that in argumentation there was no middle term; of two contradictions one was necessarily true, the other no less necessarily false. These tough adversaries were skilled at such fencing (and, besides, they were used to changing parts, taking turns at being, with the same facility and the same assurance, the one who said, "I affirm," and the one who answered, "I deny"). Without always admitting it to themselves they found in the end that they preferred—very much preferred—a violent and rough adversary like Luther, whom they recognized as one of their own, one who had become an infidel, to be sure, but one of their own all the same, to the subtle, vacillating, and discriminating Erasmus. Erasmus was ungraspable, a slippery eel, the chief object of their virtuous wrath. In 1528 in his *Apologia for the Monastic Orders*, directed against Erasmus, Carvajal wrote, "Luther releases his anger openly. Erasmus stays in the shadows, lying in ambush. The one is as fierce as a lion, fearing no one. The other, with the cunning of a serpent, always remains

48. Jean-Jacques Rousseau, *Emile, or On Education*, trans. Allan Bloom (New York, 1979), p. 268.

hidden so he can shoot his poison with more accuracy."[49] Carvajal did not add (but he thought), "And he takes shelter in the
alibis of the Dialogue, that cursed genre, the Lucianic genre par
excellence."

Here was a conflict between two methods: the old dogmatic
method of reasoning, on the one hand, and on the other, the
dialectical method, the art of conversing, of discussing, which
unfolded with such ease, liveliness, and civility in Plato's dialogues. At times his dialogues were broken up into responses
meeting head on, at times they stretched out in long mono-
logues taking turns on opposing sides. It was reincarnated in
another form in the mocking, witty prose works of Lucian of
Samosata—and it was there that Erasmus discovered it and was
inspired by it before Rabelais was. Rabelais succeeded in making a perfect, original, and lively adaptation of the Greek dialogue in his novel, one of the two or three most French books
of all time. This horrified and infuriated the theologians, who
saw red when they encountered, not a great, heavy ox fattened
on the syllogisms of the cathedral schools, who did not frighten
them, but an agile banderillero with fiery darts, dressed in a
slim, scarlet layman's doublet, whom they could never get at as
he flew, danced, and smiled, knowingly eluding them with a
nice little bow and an ironic smile.

There were those who liked classical fencing according to the
rules: two men facing each other at either end of a platform,
with matched weapons. And there were those who preferred a
duel of three, four, or more, a melee, a fully armed assault.
There were those who were placid and traditional, and those
who liked disquiet. The latter were sensitive to the beauty of
form; the others were indifferent to the music of sentences and
the harmony of periods, taking up arms against those who opposed the saying of Cicero in the *Tusculan Disputations,* which
Carvajal used against the Erasmians: "Saepe est, etiam sub pal-
lio sordido, Sapientia"[50]—a somewhat sad consolation, to be
sure. There were those who closed their doors and stayed

49. Luis de Carvajal, *Apologia monasticae religionis diluens nugas Erasmi . . .* (Salamanca, 1528). See Marcel Bataillon, *Erasme et l'Espagne, recherches sur l'histoire
spirituelle du XVIe siècle* (Paris, 1937), p. 350.

50. "Wisdom is often to be found even in a shabby cloak." Bataillon, p. 347. There
is a good example of self-satisfied syllogistic argument on this page.

quietly at home, claiming to enjoy undisturbed peace; and there were those who had an appetite for taking chances and, in any case, opened their windows and welcomed everything new, vibrant, and alive that was brought to them by the sun's rays after first crossing eternal silences and then the earth's swirling atmosphere. And also, if one looks at it carefully, the former gave the name doubt not to the suffering described by Rousseau's vicar, but to an indiscriminate taste for the most contradictory opinions, provided they were well presented and made a case for themselves. It was academic doubt, resting not on truth but on plausibility, and in the end it was resolved painlessly and effortlessly by observing customs and traditions, if in the end it became necessary to make a decision in order to act or a choice in order to live.

Moreover, to doubt was to learn. And what joy there was in learning! What pleasure, therefore, in doubting! In Ambroise Firmin Didot's book on Aldus Manutius there is a wonderful letter from Marcus Musurus to his brother-in-law John Gregoropulos in which he describes how sweet life is in proximity to the great lord who is his protector, a pious, humane prince incapable of evil. When, after performing his duty as a reader once each day, Marcus is free to retire to his room: "there I enjoy all sorts of books," he remarks, "that deal with the pro and the con, and I take my leave of these only to surfeit myself with others, even more numerous."[51] He would no doubt have responded to anyone who expressed surprise at his state of mind, "Who can have learned enough to stop doubting?" How can one affirm anything? And why affirm anything? There are, alas, men who affirm violently, implacably, with a mailed fist as their final argument. No, let us not become narrow like that. Let us be curious. Let us take from everyone. From among all the delights we owe to our curiosity let us avoid choosing narrowly, like fanatics.

9. Veracity in the Sixteenth Century

Besides, how could those men have suffered from uncertainty of a scientific order? Among all those ideas of ours missing to them was one more we never find.

---

51. Ambroise Firmin Didot, *Alde Manuce et l'hellenisme à Venise* (Paris, 1875), pp. 34–35.

The idea that truth is the common property of all men; that if any man possesses a piece of it, however tiny it may be, he should immediately communicate it to all as soon as he can, without reservations or calculation; that if he does not do so he is guilty of a crime against the collectivity—this idea of ours (in any case, of our scientists, totally disinterested and generous with their contributions) was scarcely held by men of the sixteenth century, or was not articulated by them. As far as I can tell, it is necessary to go all the way to Palissy—that is, to 1580—to find a clear statement, and a curious one besides, on this subject. Practice is speaking, the antagonist of Theory in the everlasting dialogue: "I am sure that a good remedy against a plague or some other pernicious disease must not be kept secret. The secrets of agriculture must not be kept secret ... The sciences that serve the whole state must not be kept secret. But with my art of the earth and many other arts, that is not so."[52] And Palissy says why. Glass is no longer a secret; as a result, it is made everywhere, and gentlemen glassmakers, even though they are gentlemen, "live more poorly than the porters of Paris." Take enameled buttons; they sold at first at three francs a dozen, but those who invented them did not keep the thing secret, and hence there are so many made today that people are ashamed to wear them. As for the enamels of Limoges, it is the same thing. You pay three *sols* a dozen for plaques to decorate caps, perfectly welded on copper!

These were economic considerations, which made craftsmanship and its "secrets" a separate, distinct sphere. But Palissy had at least proclaimed the obligation not to conceal "the sciences that serve the whole state." It was a new concern. I would have said it showed him to be a Protestant, if Saint Francis Xavier, in a "Letter from the Indies" of 1545 cited by Atkinson, had not been overcome by a sudden rage against the University of Paris from a distance and denounced those who would rather study in order to know a great deal than "by their science to produce some benefit to others who are in need of it."[53] Which amounts to almost the same idea—but likewise conveyed by a man with no authority. The scientists themselves sang a different tune. Not one of them, it seems, had an

52. *Discours admirable de l'art de terre* in Palissy, *Oeuvres*, II, 202–203; trans. in *Admirable Discourses*, pp. 188–189.

53. Atkinson, pp. 45–46.

apostle's temperament. They were all like the dog Pamphagus
in the fourth dialogue of Des Périers's *Cymbalum mundi*: they
refused to talk. In his preface to Paul III, Copernicus declared
that he had doubted for a long time whether he ought to write
his book, whether it would not be enough, following the example of the Pythagoreans, to transmit the secrets of philosophy
only to his friends by word of mouth. Did the cosmographers
who, forty years after the publication of Vespucci's voyages in
French, continued simply to pass over the two Americas in silence in books devoted to the description of the globe, follow
the same course? We tend to think that the discovery of the
new continent brought about in all of Europe a sort of intellectual and philosophical revolution that was without precedent—
just as, moreover, we think, equally incorrectly, that Galileo's
contemporaries must have felt moved almost immediately by
the immensity of the new heavens. That required Pascal and
"the eternal silence of these infinite spaces that terrifies me"—
the new, scientific form of the Great Fear. Indeed, Molière did
not make fun of anti-Copernicans, even if it is true (Montesquieu tells us it is) that "it was necessary for Molière to make
Monsieur Diafoirus speak in order to make doctors believe in
the circulation of the blood: ridicule applied at the right moment has great power." That power was not yet being exercised
in the sixteenth century. And the contemporaries of the con-
quistadors and Copernicus, and later those of Kepler and Galileo, were all silent, all unaware of America, of both Americas, at
least in their books. They were all unaware of the moving earth.

And then, it is fine to be concerned about truth, but was
there for these men always a certain, exclusive truth? We have
already briefly indicated that in scholastic jousting the two adversaries were always ready to change places, roles, and theses.
Those were the rules of the game. Form—the texture of the argument, the quickness of the repartee, the rattle of the words—
was important, more important than matter. These were tour-
naments, not mortal combats. And the men who were trained in
this way were, quite naturally, victims of the kinds of professional bias we sometimes see in lawyers. They accommodated
themselves rather easily to a true and a false that were well
trimmed, equally plausible, and equally specious under their
carapace of syllogisms and familiar arguments. Just as long as
the job was well done.

Complete agreement between their reasoning and their innermost thoughts was not something for which they even felt a
need. Pierre Rousselot's observation about Saint Bernard and
the Victorines is an accurate one: "At a time when speculation
was still totally scholastic, defined concepts were easily out of
harmony with deep intuitions. The pious effusions of sermons
or didactic works contained an implicit philosophy that was not
in agreement with the explicit doctrine of their works that were
properly didactic."[54]

And this would continue. All the better for someone who
succeeded in uncovering the truth. It was his own dear little
treasure; he hugged it to his bosom and jealously fondled it behind closed doors. Neither Descartes nor Malebranche nor
Spinoza behaved otherwise. All the more reason for those in the
sixteenth century to behave so. They knew what truths cost,
how hard they were to unearth. They tasted the triumph of
success, the solitary, acute, and rare pleasure of a mind that
with difficulty and with practically no guide or teacher makes
a discovery. They also knew that these joys and successes belonged to an elite and were its reward. The members of that
elite continued to amuse themselves by playing tricks on
colleagues and rivals, by hiding important results from competitors.[55] These were the ruses of grownup children. Archivists
and librarians throughout the nineteenth century still took absurd delight in them. And in the sixteenth century Copernicus
waited until the end of his life to publish his system. A century
later Huygens would still keep his way of conceiving the rings
of Saturn secret for several years; he contented himself with
staking a claim, at any event, by having a line in cabalistic style,
to which he had the key, printed at the bottom of a report:
"A. C. N. C. A. E. I."—which translates as *Annulo Cingitur
Nusquam Cohaerente Ad Eclipticam Inclinato.*[56] Was this prudence? Was it possessive jealousy? For things to change somewhat the eighteenth century and its passion for proselytizing

---

54. Pierre Rousselot, *Pour l'histoire du problème de l'amour au Moyen Age* (Munster, 1908), pp. 4–5.

55. When Felix Platter was at Montpellier he stole at night into the room where his
landlord, an apothecary, kept volumes full of *remedia. Beloved Son Felix, the Journal
of Felix Platter, a Medical Student in Montpellier in the Sixteenth Century,* trans.
Seán Jennett (London, 1961), p. 83.

56. It is surrounded by a completely detached ring that is inclined toward the ecliptic.

were needed. As far as the sixteenth century is concerned, let us look again at the story in Ambroise Paré's *Discourse on the Unicorn* about Charles IX's physician, Chapelain, who did not believe in the healing power of the unicorn's horn any more than Paré did. Called on to explain this and to use his authority in the service of truth, "he replied that never in his lifetime would he expose himself to be picked on by envious slanderers." But he added that after his death "what he had left behind in writing would be found."

Truth: in the realm of the sciences there would be one truth on the day when, of two opinions that were merely opinions, it would be possible to ascertain that one was verified by facts and the other was negated or not confirmed by them. That day did not come in the sixteenth century. It had not yet arrived even at the beginning of the eighteenth. "I shall espouse no opinions, except those in the books of Euclid," wrote the Montesquieu of the *Notebooks*.[57] Here we see that while this powerful intellect set a limit, as far as he was concerned, to the sway of opinions that were merely opinions, the limit was mathematical, not experimental. It was Claude Bernard who was able to write, "I shall espouse no opinions except those verified by facts." That is the correct formulation—but it was to undergo onc last transformation on everyone's lips. "Verified by facts" was finally rendered as "true." Conception and term have glided into each other in the course of a slow evolution. We have allowed it to happen ever since there have been sciences equipped with the material for their proof. Ever since there has been a Science.

10. An Artisanal Mentality

In the final analysis, how can these attitudes be explained, the attitudes of not just a few but of the bulk of the learned men of the time? Essentially, I believe, by the individual character assumed by scientific work then. It was the finest moment of what I have called the small scientific craftsman.[58] That is what he can be called. A scientist worked on a project for which he

57. Montesquieu, *Cahiers (1716-1755)*, ed. Bernard Grasset (Paris, 1941), p. 11.
58. Lucien Febvre, "De 1892 à 1933: examen de conscience d'une histoire et d'un historien," *Revue de Synthèse*, 7 (1934), 93-106.

had first conceived the idea and drawn up the plan, seated alone in his study, with the door closed, like a cobbler in his shop, equipped with tools he had made for himself—without assistance, without contacts, without collaborators. What was his chief preoccupation? To carve the truth as Cellini carved some precious saltcellar for King Francis, and display all his skill, all the resources of his art and his talent, in a masterwork of craftsmanship. The time of collective effort had not yet come into existence, of collaboration and teamwork for the greatest good of the community, the kind of teamwork that makes for comradeship, that desires comradeship, and does not permit dissimulation, intentional error, cheating, and forgery; collective work that makes of veracity a virtue that is as commendable and necessary in the area of scientific research as it is in the area of legal contracts and stipulations, of judicial testimony and evidence. But in order for this development to take place, for the interests of truth to come to surpass all other interests for the scientist, even the most personal ones, some other things were necessary. The mystique of spreading education over the masses like a blessing. The new concept of the power of science: the idea, which was still so strange to our sixteenth-century forefathers, that knowledge is power—not merely power over oneself, one's conduct, moods, and passions (know thyself, said Socrates, and Rabelais's contemporaries did not spurn the advice), but power over things, which have to be known to be mastered. And also the penetration of technology by science, so slow to be realized—the penetration that Rabelais had a glimpse of, but from a distance, and that alone would, by bringing about the reconciliation of *homo faber* and *homo sapiens*, finally endow science with social virtue.

Science: the singular noun comes to our lips effortlessly in 1941. Or, rather, if we must make an effort, it is to keep ourselves from using it when speaking of Rabelais's time. Because that in itself is an anachronism. Let us guard against projecting this modern conception of science onto the learning of our ancestors. It is an impossible fit. For two thousand years the old sciences, limited and traditional, were cultivated solely in the flowerbeds of a sheltering philosophy, the philosophy of the Concept. And in the sixteenth century the revolution had hardly begun, the revolution that would come about at various times in different compartments of learning and would not really take place until the nineteenth century.

There was still nothing of that *Francesco primo regnante.* Nothing but scientists enjoying their truth in private. That in itself would be enough to render illusory Abel Lefranc's proselytizing Rabelais, the author and ringleader of a great conspiracy to *écraser l'infâme.*

12. A Possible Support for Irreligion: Occultism

HE QUICK LOOK we have just taken at the state of science, of scientific theory and practice, in the sixteenth century allows us now to grasp and really understand what it was that was painful and incomplete in the destiny of the men of the time—naturally, I mean the most intelligent and best educated of them—and so avoid some errors of judgment that, frequent as they are, are nonetheless dangerous.

1. A Century of Precursors

Cournot already observed in his *Considérations* that it is easy for us to extol the modernism of the Paduan Averroists and, for example, place in an attractive light their notion of an active universal intellect that perpetuates itself and stays alive in the human race as a whole, in collective humanity.[1] Its flame is never extinguished and every man in the course of his individual and perishable existence experiences its temporary illumination; it is this flame that lights the torch of each personal existence, so that it may shine as it is consumed. Can't we find in this a presentiment of a great modern idea, that of the collective life of humanity? Yes, if we wish, but the important thing is to observe that since the Averroists were without any scientific support for the elaboration of their notions, finding none either in what was then known of biology (even the word is impossi-

1. Augustin Cournot, *Considérations sur la marche des idées et des événements dans les temps modernes*, ed. François Mentré, 2 vols. (Paris, 1934), I, 132.

ble to apply to those times) or in the social sciences, since nothing was yet known about the structure of societies and the
stages of mankind, and locked as they were in the circle of an
empty Peripatetic ontology, they could only end in verbal subtleties, without real issue or significance.[2]

And the political philosophers of the time, above all those
who were freest in spirit, the most curious, and the most intelligent, those of the Italian school (Pomponazzi was one, as was
Machiavelli before him and Cardano or Campanella after him),
had no idea of any general pattern of human history, of any
overall direction in the advance of progress. What was history
for them? A succession of cycles, brought about by chance or at
least by the mysterious influence of the celestial spheres, which
presided over the formation of empires and religions, raised up
exceptional men, and gave them a fitting ascendancy over the
mob.[3] After that the institutions they founded followed the general law of advance and decline, and so every political order,
every civic virtue, every religious faith disappeared and sank
into disorder and corruption—until the day when, through the
action of some propitious influence, order and a new faith were
reborn. It was a simple theory, and it had a long life—after all,
there was Vico. But it was not a theory of history. And there
can be no political doctrine if history is absent or if it is led
down paths that are not its own. Humanist history is unquestionably the most remarkable of all the illustrations of this law.

And so it was with everything. The men of the sixteenth century were bubbling with ideas, and their whole century along
with them. But they were confused ideas that they did not
know how to convey clearly, that they could not find the words
to express distinctly; brief ideas that they did not know how to
expand, extend, or orchestrate. Once in a while, in a sudden
burst, they emitted a flash of light. A spark pierced the night
darkness and then went out. And the darkness seemed blacker
than ever.

The sixteenth century was a century of precursors—that is,
of men without a posterity, men who produced nothing. Leonardo and Palissy, enticed by the mysteries of a globe that up

2. Ibid., passim.
3. For Machiavelli, see Augustin Renaudet, *Machiavel, étude historique des doctrines politiques* (Paris, 1942), p. 153 ff.

to then had not seemed to present a single scientist with a single problem about its inmost structure, revived Greek ideas that had gone unnoticed for two thousand years. They provided a foretaste of what would some day be geology and paleontology. It was too early. Those ideas did not really revive and become productive until two hundred years later. Servetus and Sarpi prowled around that great mystery which had already so strongly aroused the curiosity of Dr. Rabelais: the circulation of the blood. There is no point in recalling that wonderful fresco in *Book Three*, Panurge's astonishing lyrical celebration of the exchanges of blood. It was too early. The time of Harvey and the *De motu cordis* would come, but later, in 1628. In the assortment of ideas belonging to Giordano Bruno there was one we are struck by; it is one of ours, the idea of the infinity of the world or, more precisely, of an infinite number of worlds. It was too early. It had to wait for Galileo and his telescope, for Herschel and the modern telescope. Then and only then would Fontenelle be able to write his *Plurality of Worlds.*

Leonardo, Servetus, Palissy, Bruno, and any number of others were precursors full of presentiments, but they did not gain a public following. They simply attest to the strength, the vigor, and the tumultuous burst of energy of a time when powerful minds were searching blindly, always bumping into the walls of their dark prisons, for what they could not find and would not be able to find without the light science alone could shed. But in their growing uneasiness they could no longer be satisfied with what had contented their fathers and grandfathers. They escaped from their dungeon in spirit. And to survive, in the absence of a "clear" science that had not yet come into existence, they happily immersed themselves in the murky waters of their occult sciences.

2. Smells, Tastes, and Sounds

Those murky waters repel rather than attract us. Not for nothing have we become used to clarity ever since Descartes established its conditions. And when someone tries to plunge us into a world where we would not know where to apply any of the tools that have become not merely familiar but natural to us— analysis and synthesis, to start with—we feel uncomfortable, ill at ease, disquieted. Not so the men of the sixteenth century, and this has to be said. "Where thought was confused, it must be presented as confused"—that is the historian's first duty. Henri Berr, who said it, is right. Rabelais's contemporaries, so seemingly close to us, are quite far removed from us in every aspect of their intellectual equipment. Its very structure was not the same as ours.

I have said elsewhere that we are hothouse plants; those men grew out of doors.[4] They were men close to the earth and to rural life, who encountered the countryside even in their cities, its plants and animals, its smells and noises. They were open-air men, seeing nature but also feeling, sniffing, hearing, touching, breathing her through all their senses—

> Le gouster, le toucher, l'oeil, l'oreille et le nez
> Sans lequels nostre corps seroit un corps de marbre

> The taste, the touch, the eye, the ear, the nose,
> Without which we'd have bodies made of stone—

and resisted having to decide, among these organs of connection and protection,

> Lesquels, pour présider en la part plus insigne
> Sont de plus grand service et qualité plus digne.[5]

> Which, playing a role of greater prominence,
> Do higher service and deserve more praise.

But their "affective" senses, as we call them, taste and touch, and hearing as well (in spite of Du Bellay and his hymn to

4. Lucien Febvre, "Les Principaux Aspects d'une civilisation: quatre leçons sur la première Renaissance française," *Revue des Cours et Conférences*, 26, 2d ser. (1924–1925), 193-210, 326-340, 398-417, 577-593; trans. Marian Rothstein, *Life in Renaissance France* (Cambridge, Mass., 1977).What I wrote there does not contradict the apt remark by René Millet in his *Rabelais* (5th ed., Paris, 1921), denouncing the effect on sixteenth-century poetry "of a false ideal." These sanguine men, he observed, "who fought like mercenaries, dressed in magnificent fabrics, and lived through the body and the eyes as much as through the mind—as soon as they started to write they no longer had sight, senses, or touch" (p. 85).

5. Joachim Du Bellay, "Hymne de la surdité, à P. de Ronsard Vand." (*Divers jeux rustiques*, XXXVIII) in *Oeuvres poétiques*, ed. Henri Chamard, 6 vols. (Paris, 1908–1931), V, 187.

deafness), were exercised much more and were more highly developed (or less atrophied) than ours, and their thoughts existed in a more clouded and less purified atmosphere.

Read the beginning of this ode by Ronsard:

> Je suis troublé de fureur,
> Le poil me dresse d'horreur,
> D'une ardeur mon âme est pleine,
> Mon estomac est pantois,
> Et par son canal ma vois
> Peut se dégorger à peine.[6]

> I'm swept by fury's might,
> My hair stands up in fright,
> And fire my soul surrounds,
> My breast heaves all entangled
> While in my throat is strangled
> My voice, which makes no sounds.

Or these lines, no less expressive, from the "Ode to Calliope":

> La bouche m'agrée
> Que ta vois sucrée
> De son miel a pu,
> Laquelle en Parnasse
> De l'eau de Pegase
> Gloutement a bu.[7]

> How dear those lips
> O'er which there slips
> Your voice so honey-sweet,
> They've drunk their fill
> From the Muses' rill
> Where Pegasus touched his feet.

Surely you would not say this is visual poetry. Observe also the following evocations of phantoms. Are these pale silhouettes

6. *Odes*, I, 2, in Pierre de Ronsard, *Oeuvres complètes*, ed. Paul Laumonier, 18 vols. (Paris, 1914–1967), I, 65.

7. *Odes*, II, 2, ibid., I, 175.

traced on an inky background, in the manner of Romantic litho-
graphs? No, rather noises and hissing:

> La nuit, les fantausmes vollans,
> Claquetans leurs becs violans,
> En sifflant mon âme épovantent.[8]

> The phantoms fly about at night;
> With beaks that loudly clack and fright
> My soul with dreadful hisses.

Such was the hell described by Lemaire de Belges, as dictated to him by the Lover in Green. It was a hell filled with
"terrifying cries,"

> Fiers hurlements de bêtes redoutables . . .
> Bruits de marteaux, chaînes et ferremens,
> Grands tumbemens de montagnes et ruine
> Et grands soufflis de vents avec bruine.[9]

> Enormous howls that come from fearsome beasts . . .
> The clank of hammers striking chains and iron,
> The crash of mighty mountains to the plain
> And mighty gusts of wind with chilling rain.

Here, again by Ronsard, is the evocation of a kiss:

> Baiser, fils de deux lèvres closes.

> A kiss, the child of two closed lips.

What the poet wishes to suggest is not the pure shape of a
mouth, the color of two lips, the gleam of a row of sparkling
teeth; paradoxically, it is voices again, and fragrances:

> Je sens en ma bouche, souvent,
> Bruire le soupir de son vent . . .
> Resouflant l'âme qui pendoit
> Aux lèvres où ell' t'attendoit,

---

8. *Odes*, III, 8, ibid., II, 18.
9. "Les Deux Epistres de l'amant vert," at the end of the first book of his *Illustrations*. Cf. Arsène Darmesteter and Adolphe Hatzfeld, *Le Seizième Siècle en France:
tableau de la littérature et de la langue*, 16th ed. (Paris, 1934), p. 173.

Bouche d'amome toute pleine
Que m'engendre de ton haleine
Un pré de fleurs en chaque part
Où ta flairante odeur s'épart.[10]

Within my mouth I often hear
The sighings of that zephyr dear.
My soul would breathe and rise up free
To hang upon my lips for thee,

Oh mouth that's filled with spices rare.
Thy breath doth make a meadow fair
And flowers spring on every side
Where'er thy perfume's scattered wide.

And all of this poetry is full of sounds and laden with fragrances like this, whether it speaks of "the sea sounding from its cavernous depths,"[11] or populates the murmuring forest with voices,

Sainte Gastine, heureuse secrétaire
De mes ennuis, qui respons en ton bois
Ores en haute, ores en basse voix,
Aux longs soupirs que mon coeur ne peut taire[12]

Blessèd Gastine, who guards my secret pain,
Your woods re-echo to my endless sighs,
At times with shouts, at times with whispered cries,
Recording thus my heavy heart's refrain

10. "Le Baiser de Cassandre," *Odes*, III, 16, *Oeuvres*, II, 43. And further on (p. 55): "Aux mouches à miel, pour cueiller les fleurs sur la bouche de Cassandre" (To the Honeybees, to Gather the Flowers on Cassandra's Mouth), *Odes*, III, 20: 'Autour de sa bouche alenée / De mes baisers tant bien donnés." (Around her mouth where wafts the air / Of all those kisses that we share.)

Also see on p. 127 (these are all chosen at random) Ode 14 from Book IV: "Nymphe aux beaux yeux, qui souffles de ta bouche / Une Arabie à qui près s'en approche . . . / Cent mille baisers donne-moi / Donne-les moi, ça, que je les dévore." (Your mouth breathes forth, oh nymph with eyes so fair, / A very Araby of perfumed air . . . / Give me a hundred thousand kisses! / Yes, give me them that I may eat them up.)

Or Ode 7 from Book II (I, 197): "Cassandre ne donne pas / Des baisers, mais . . . / Du nectar, du sucre doux / de la cannelle et du baume." (Cassandra does not give kisses, but nectar, sweet sugar, cinnamon, and balm.)

11. "La mer qui sonne contre les gouffres." Ronsard, *Bocage*, 8, in *Oeuvres*, II, 181. Cf. *Odes*, IV, 16, in *Oeuvres*, II, 133: "Et par les palais humides . . . / Hucha les soeurs Néréides / Qui ronfloient au bruit des flots." (Across those moist abodes she cried . . . / And watery nymphs to her replied / With echoes of the billows' roar.)

12. *Les Amours*, CXXII, *Oeuvres*, IV, 128.

or, when describing walks in the country, refers only to smells and sounds:

> J'aime fort les jardins qui sentent le sauvage,
> J'aime le flot de l'eau qui gazouille au rivage.

> I love the smell of country gardens where wildflowers
>   grow,
> I love the sound of babbling brooks that swiftly flow.

I hear an objection about the type of writing and the date. This was Ronsard; it was 1560 or 1570; Ronsard was a true poet, a great poet; he had his own individual temperament, his personal characteristics. Well, what about the others? Let us not search very far. Look again at the *Reply* written by Bouchet in the first quarter of the century to "Master François Rabelais, distinguished man of Greek and Latin letters."[13] The title assures us it will give us "the description of a beautiful abode." We therefore expect lines, colors, patterns, and vistas—all the pleasures of the eye. But no, we get sounds, noises, voices—the pleasures of the ear. All the divinities of water and woods appear in turn. Are they beautiful shapes, goddesses by Jean Goujon come to life in nature? There is not a word about their appearance, their form, their bodies. Their voices are heard, that is all:

> Car d'une part les Nayades y sont,
> Dessus le Clan doulce rivière,

> There is one place where Naiads make their home,
> Upon that lovely river called the Clan,

the Naiads who frolic "on green, moist meadows" with their sisters the Hymnids. In another place disport

> Aultres qui font résonner hault leurs voix
> C'est assavoir les silvestres Driades . . .
> Et davantage Oréades aux mons
> Dont bien souvent on oyt les doulx sermons,

---

13. Rabelais, *Les Oeuvres*, ed. Charles Marty-Laveaux, 6 vols. (Paris, 1868–1903), III, 304.

Et puis après les gentilles Nappées
Qui rage font par chansons decouppées
De bien chanter aux castallins ruysseaux
Par les jardins nourrissans arbrisseaux.

Others whose voices ring out loud and high:
The Dryads, nymphs who dwell in deepest woods . . .
And mountain-living nymphs are also heard,
The Oreads, so sweet in every word,
And now a gentle throng of Napaeae
Bursts forth in notes of clear-cut melody;
They sing beside Castalian brooks that flow
Through verdant gardens where thick arbors grow.

But dawn is coming. How will the poet, "making his way beneath the verdant shades," distract himself from his cares? By looking at the frolicking nymphs? No, by listening:

Pour oublier les ennuyeux encombres
Tu puis ouir des nymphes les doulx chans
Dont sont remplis bois, boucages et champs.

Forget your sorrows, ease your troubled mind
And listen to the nymphs' melodious strains
That fill the forests, bosky dells, and plains.

As for the rest,

Après y sont les bons fruictz et bons vins
Que bien aimons entre nous Poictevins.

To eat the ripened fruit, good wine to drink
Is great delight, we men of Poitiers think.

Not one word about "seeing." These are auditory charms. And so it was with all of them. When Marot describes the grounds of the Temple of Cupid, the garden is not planted with brightly colored flowers. It is a garden to delight not the eye but the nose. From it comes the fragrance of

> Marguerites, lys et oeillets,
> Passeveloux, roses flairantes
> Romarins, boutons vermeillets
> Lavandes odoriferantes,
> Toutes autres fleurs apparentes
> Jettans odeur très adoucie.

> Fair daisies, pinks, and lilies tender,
> Of cockscombs, roses sweetly blooming,
> Rosemary, buttercups in splendor,
> And lavender the sense illuming,
> With all the other flowers perfuming
> The air that from the garden blows.

The most "visual" of all, relatively speaking, were only slightly so. It is true that Du Bellay, describing a "living fountain," writes:

> Là sembloit que Nature et l'Art eussent pris peine
> D'assembler en un lieu tous les plaisirs de l'oeil.

> It seemed that Art and Nature both took pains
> To bring together things that please the eye.

But he immediately adds:

> Et là s'oyoit un bruit incitant au sommeil
> De cent accords plus doux que ceux d'une Sirène.

> One heard a sound inviting sleep, a sigh
> Of music tuned like Sirens' sweet refrains.

It is interesting that the France he evoked with such fervor from the depths of his Roman exile was never a physical form for him, a body, a face, an image. It was always a voice, only a voice and a certain sweetness:

> France, France, respons à ma triste querelle.

> Oh France, my France, please answer my sad plaint.

Thus does he cry out to his "mother" when the Roman winter

> D'une tremblante horreur fait hérisser la peau.

> Makes my skin with quaking terror bristle.

And yet he was not devoid of a plastic sense, nor was he incapable of perceiving true greatness, if he could write:

> Et ne sont mes portraits auprès de vos tableaux
> Non plus qu'est un Janet auprès d'un Michelange.

> My pictures placed beside your own
> Are Janets next to Michelangelo.[14]

Never mind. What of Du Bellay sticks in our minds are never pictures but always sounds, whether he is noting "the long sad howl of watching dogs" or, struck by their voices and not their graceful lines, hears "two swans lamenting" on a mirror of water.

Is it poetic temperament we are dealing with? But it was not only the poets.[15] It is interesting to see that Paracelsus, in insisting that medicine be preeminently a matter of physical observation, had recourse to a whole set of acoustical and olfactory images that are somewhat surprising to us. He wanted it to be "no less resounding to our ears than the cascade of the Rhine or the roar of waves on the Ocean." He wanted the nostrils to be used, too, to "distinguish the smell of the object under study."[16] And is it necessary to remind ourselves that the men of the time quite frequently studied a great many things by means of

---

14. "Janet" was the painter Jean Clouet (d. 1541). [Translator's note.]

15. Profane or sacred. For here we should bring in the appeals of the Old Testament ("Hear, O heavens, and give ear, O earth") and the exhortations of the Psalms ("Let thine ears be attentive to the voice of my supplications" or "O God, in the multitude of thy mercy hear me"). We should call to mind what the Reformers, following Luther's lead, said about the Word taken in by the ear; thus Luther would write the well-known "Solae aures sunt organa Christiani" (Only the ears are Christian organs) in his *Commentary on the Epistle to the Hebrews.* This is not contradicted by the assertion in his *Table Talk* (for there the poet was speaking): "Oculi sunt donum praestantissimum omnibus animantibus datum." (The eyes are the most excellent gift that has been given to all living things.)

16. Léon Blanchet, *Campanella* (Paris, 1920), p. 194 and n. 2.

the ear? That they were read to instead of reading themselves? And that the great were surrounded by talkers who communicated oral knowledge to them by means of the ear?

But let us return to the sphere of the abstract. Abel Rey has recently shown very well in some remarkable passages how Greek mathematics was established "solely by way of geometry." The plastic intuition of the Greeks, he said, to which they owed all the wonders of their architecture and its structural miracles, impelled them to fit everything they most valued— "perfect understanding, perfect intelligence, the clarity and distinctness of ideas, the conclusive power of their interconnection"—not into the category of imageless thought and pure logic (as we would be tempted to do), but on the contrary into that of geometry, the category of forms. Forms "alone were truly clear and distinct for the Greeks, because they were *seen*, and because through vision, physical as well as mental, every structure could be fathomed to its depths."[17]

This is a fact that historians of sixteenth-century mathematics, first Cantor and then Rouse Ball, have insisted on. The sixteenth century did not see first: it heard and smelled, it sniffed the air and caught sounds. It was only later, as the seventeenth century was approaching, that it seriously and actively became engaged in geometry, focusing its attention on the world of forms with Kepler (1571–1630) and Desargues of Lyon (1593–1662).[18] It was then that *vision* was unleashed in the world of science as it was in the world of physical sensations, and the world of beauty as well.

3. Music

For the same was true of music, which did not rise above the concrete, the given, and the immediate, and loved to reproduce the myriad confused noises of battle, the boom of cannons, the

---

17. Abel Rey, *La Science dans l'antiquité*, 5 vols. (Paris, 1930–1948), III, 389. See likewise p. 27, and particularly, in II, 445 ff., his important reflections on the role of sight in the evolution of thought. "The passage from the qualitative to the quantitative is essentially linked to advances in the predominance of visual perception."

18. W. W. Rouse Ball, *A Short Account of the History of Mathematics*, 4th ed. (London, 1908), pp. 254–258; Moritz Cantor, *Vorlesungen über Geschichte der Mathematik*, vol. II: *Von 1200–1668*, 2d ed. (Leipzig, 1900), p. 608 ff. (ch. 71).

song of the lark, or the cries of Paris. And we should stop acting as if music were *our* prize, *our* recent conquest, *our* discovery. The Romantics knew and said the opposite. Victor Hugo, in May 1837, wrote (in the thirty-fifth poem of *Les Rayons et les Ombres*, "That Music Dates from the Sixteenth Century"):

> Puissant Palestrina, vieux maître, vieux génie,
> Je vous salue ici, père de l'harmonie.
> Car ainsi qu'un grand fleuve où boivent les humains
> Toute cette musique a coulé de vos mains!
>
> Oh mighty Palestrina, ancient genius,
> Harmony's father, I salute you, master,
> For like a river where mankind can drink
> All music since has flowed from your great hands!

and Michelet echoed him in his book on the Renaissance: "And so a new mother of the human race came into the world: the great enchantress and consoler, Music, was born."[19] Actually, for the men of the sixteenth century it was as much a part of their lives as it is of ours—more so, no doubt. And not only were they actively interested, surrounding themselves whenever they had the means with fine singers and musicians, but they fell under the spell of sound and, unresisting, surrendered their ingenuous souls to the onslaught of voices, strings, and woodwinds. There is plenty of evidence. The fair elder Limeuil, one of Queen Catherine's ladies, was not the only one of her time to summon her favorite musician when death was approaching: " 'Julian, take your viol and keep playing *The Defeat of the Swiss* as well as you can until you see that I am dead, for I see the time is near. And when you get to the words "All is lost,"

19. Jules Michelet, *Histoire de France*, 16 vols. (Paris, 1898), VIII, 85. Michelet, too, evoked Palestrina, but he associated him with his teacher, Claude Goudimel of the Franche-Comté, who set Marot's *Psalms* to music. And he traced this whole musical development back to Luther: "Luther opened the way, and from then on the whole world sang—everyone, Protestants and Catholics alike. From Luther came Goudimel, . . . the teacher of Palestrina . . . It was a song that was true, free, and pure, a song that came from the bottom of the heart." Naturally, I do not accept the opinions of the Romantics as my own. Today we know that the freeing of polyphony from plainsong— that is to say, "music"—goes back (at least) to Adam de La Halle.

go over them four or five times, as pitiably as you can.' Which the other did, and she herself helped with the voice. And when it came to 'All is lost,' she repeated it twice and, turning to the other side of the bed, expired."[20] This is what Brantôme, recounting her end in his *Fifth Discourse*, calls in his coarse language "a joyous and pleasant death." So much for Brantôme. But his testimony is joined by that of Noël Du Fail in *Contes et discours d'Eutrapel*. He tells us in chapter 20 ("Eutrapel's Music") what happened at court "when they sang before great Francis the song of war made by Janequin on the victory he had won over the Swiss. There was no one who did not look to see if his sword was in its scabbard and who did not rise up on his toes to make himself taller and more dashing."[21] In fact, in Le Roux de Lincy's *Recueil de chants historiques* we can read the text, or a fragment of it, of this famous *Battle of Marignano*, Clément Janequin's great musical fresco, which was distributed by the publisher Attaignant beginning in 1527. By itself and without the help of the music it has a headlong rhythm, a rhythm that evokes I know not what dances of Negroes furiously rousing themselves to battle:

> Soufflez, jouez, soufflez toujours,
> Tournez, virez, faictes vos tours,
> Phifrez, soufflez, frappez tabours . . .

> Tournez, tournez, brayez, tournez,
> Gros courtault et faucons,
> Pour resjouir les compagnies,
> Pour resjouir les compagnons . . .

> Donnez des horions, pati patac,
> Tricque, tricque, tricque, tricque,
> Trac, tricque, tricque, tricque,
> Chipe, chope, torche, lorgne,
> Chope, chope, serre, serre, serre . . .

20. Pierre de Bourdeille, Seigneur de Brantôme, *Les Dames galantes*, ed. Henri Bouchot, 2 vols. (Paris, n.d.), II, 86; also in his *Oeuvres complètes*, ed. Ludovic Lalanne, 11 vols. (Paris, 1864–1882), IX, 416.

21. Noël Du Fail, *Oeuvres facétieuses*, ed. J. Assézat, 2 vols. (Paris, 1874), II, 124–126.

Nobles, sautez dans les arçons
Armés, bouclés, frisques et mignons,
La lance au poing, hardis et prontz . . . [22]

After this, no one should be surprised to see that men of the sixteenth century showed concern for musicotherapy. The *Quintessence*, in *Book Five* (ch. 20), "cured the sick with a song." It is true that this was in order to outdo kings ("you have kings in your world that fantastically pretend to cure some certain diseases, as for example, scrofula or wens, swelled throats, nick-named the king's evil, and quartan agues, only with a touch"). Something political is lurking there. But there is nothing political in chapter 7 of Book XX of *Magia naturalis* by B. Porta (Naples, 1588): "De Lyra et multis quibusdam ejus proprietatibus."[23] He goes into the finest points, taking note of the properties of the various woods from which instruments are made. These were matters for sick people and doctors, but any number of healthy men understood and approved when Etienne Dolet proclaimed in his *Commentaries* of 1536: "To music I owe my life itself; to it I owe all the success of my literary efforts . . . I could never have supported the incessant, immense, endless labour of compiling these *Commentaries* unless by the power of music I had not sometimes been soothed."[24] Ronsard echoed this in the preface to the *Mellange de chansons, tant de vieux autheurs que des modernes,* which appeared in Paris in 1572: "Sir, he who hears the sweet harmony of instruments or the sweetness of the natural voice and does not rejoice, is not moved, and does not tremble from head to foot as though sweetly ravished and lifted I know not how out of himself—it is a sign he has a twisted, vicious, and depraved soul, and it is well to be on one's guard against him, as against one inauspiciously born."[25] But music went beyond the sphere of individuals and, inasmuch as the taste for it was universal, it constituted

22. Antoine Le Roux de Lincy, ed., *Recueil de chants historiques français,* 2 vols. (Paris, 1841–1842), II, 65–67. [Janequin's works have recently been published in six volumes by Editions de l'Oiseau-Lyre, and this song has been recorded by The King's Singers.—Translator.]

23. Of Song and Its Many Sorts of Properties.

24. Richard Copley Christie, *Etienne Dolet, The Martyr of the Renaissance* (London, 1899; reprint, Nieuwkoop, 1964), p. 294.

25. *Oeuvres,* VII, 337.

a powerful bond among the men of all nations who felt its joys deeply. In France and outside France. Marcel Bataillon has written some perceptive and accurate things about this in his study of the cosmopolitanism of Damião de Góis.[26] And who knows how many came by this route into the movement for renewal which, in Protestant lands as in countries that remained Catholic, would culminate with the introduction into worship of a kind of music that was more stirring than plainsong?

4. Underdevelopment of Sight

We should have no fear of stressing all this. A series of fascinating studies could be done on the sensory underpinnings of thought in different periods. When one has become familiar with the writers of the sixteenth century one thing is striking in every case: with very rare exceptions they did not know how to draw a sketch, catch a likeness, or place a flesh-and-blood person before the reader. Rabelais could, but he was Rabelais. And when, in *Book Four* (ch. 12), he shows us "an old fat ruddy Catchpole" with "his large greasy spatterdashes, his jaded hollow-flanked mare, his bag full of writs and informations dangling at his girdle" and "the large silver hoop on his left thumb," we certainly do not accuse him of lacking a visual sense. But apart from the one and only Rabelais, who was there? Did anyone depict *him*? Did anyone care enough to let us see him? He was abused, not portrayed.

What we would give to see Rabelais at table, as Léon Gozlan has given us Balzac, painted from life.[27] After all, who knows? Perhaps we would be in for some surprises: a dyspeptic, disagreeable Rabelais who could not discriminate among wines—a misfortune visited on many a gourmet with or without a license. What we would give to have Margaret of Navarre sketched by a master in four pointed sentences that evoke her and allow us to see her, making us say, "We can just feel it's her!" But what can we do? Saint-Simon did not come along until much later. As for Margaret, no one wrote more than that sister of King Francis, no one saw more great ladies and great

---

26. *Le Cosmopolitisme de Damião de Góis* (Paris, [?]), p. 35 ff.
27. Léon Gozlan, *Balzac intime*, new ed. (Paris, n.d.). [Translator's note.]

personages whom we would so much like to *see* ourselves. But
she had absolutely no power to evoke them—not princes or
kings, not her brother, not her mother, not her two husbands,
or the imaginary characters that populate the seventy-two tales
of the *Heptameron* (several hundred, and not a single one with
any shape). We might add, not landscapes either, not even the
Pyrenees torn by raging torrents. We can count the rare living
sketches left us by an age that was quick to write, that was on
the whole wordy in its story-telling. Take Brantôme. No more
than clichés: generous queens, beautiful and accomplished
ladies, courtly and gallant gentlemen. When we have cited a
rather startling Theodore Beza in old age, pulling the covers
around his chilly body with his skinny old man's hands—it was
Florimond de Raemond who, not without talent, drew him in
this way, the Florimond who was the "chief Author whom the
Roman Catholick writers transcribe when they speak of the Reformers," as Bayle said in his article on Ochino[28]—we have
taken note of nearly everything.[29]

Like their acute hearing and sharp sense of smell, the men of
that time doubtless had keen sight. But that was just it. They
had not yet set it apart from the other senses. They had not yet
tied its information in particular in a necessary link with their
need to know. This is important, if it is true that "the passage
from the qualitative to the quantitative is essentially linked to
advances in the predominance of visual perception, of what we
might call the visualization of perception." Abel Rey makes this
observation, and a little later he adds, "Sight and, within sight,
pattern constitute the scientific sense par excellence."[30]

In short, if I may venture to say so, there was no Hotel Fair-
view in the sixteenth century, nor any Prospect Hotel. They
were not to appear until the age of Romanticism. The Renaissance continued to put up at the Rose, the Wild Man, or the
Golden Lion, refugees from heraldry that had stumbled into the
hotel business.

28. Pierre Bayle, *A General Dictionary, Historical and Critical,* 10 vols. (London,
1734–1741), VIII, 9.

29. Another spirited sketch by him is that of Postel celebrating mass. See above, ch.
2, sect. 2.

30. On sight and the evolution of thought, see Rey, II, 445 ff.; III, 27. See also Abel
Rey, "De la pensée primitive à la pensée actuelle," *Encyclopédie française,* 21 vols.
(Paris, 1935–1966), I, 1′10-11.

5. The Sense of the Impossible

It put up there just as it was, with all its baggage, which was quite often not in the latest fashion. Everything is connected. The intellectual sense par excellence, sight, had not yet taken first place, outdistancing all the others. But "intellectual" and "intelligence" are words that require, if not to be defined, at least to be dated. And having read Lévy-Bruhl's wonderful books, we do not need to have that conclusively demonstrated.

Yes, the books of Lévy-Bruhl.[31] Exactly: there is no one who has lived for long among those men of the sixteenth century, studying their ways of thinking and feeling, who is not struck by everything that evokes the "primitive mentality" which that philosopher has so interestingly reconstructed for us. Their world was a fluid one where nothing was strictly defined, where entities lost their boundaries and, in the twinkling of an eye, without causing much protest, changed shape, appearance, size, even "kingdom," as we would say. And there were all those stories about stones that breathed, came to life, stirred, and moved; trees that came alive without causing astonishment to those readers of Ovid:[32]

> Escoute, bucheron, arreste un peu le bras,
> Ce ne sont pas des bois que tu jettes à bas.
>
> Stay, woodsman, stay thy hand awhile, and hark—
> It is not trees that thou art laying low![33]

There were the old legends, forever young: the one about the *anatifera*, a crustacean from which a bird was born, the barnacle goose; the one about the Vallisneria, an aquatic plant with a strange method of fertilization, which had been used in the decoration of Mycenaean vases—its legend continued to flourish in the middle of the sixteenth century, and it explains the stories

31. It is understood that when we refer to these books we are not taking a position in the great debate on his theory of antilogical, or at any rate alogical, prelogical thought. These are matters for philosophers, for which see Rey, "De la pensée primitive à la pensée actuelle," p. 1'10-7 ff.

32. Isn't there a whole study to be done from this point of view on the popularity of Ovid's *Metamorphoses* in the sixteenth century?

33. Ronsard, *Oeuvres*, XVIII, part 1, p. 144; trans. in Curtis Hidden Page, *Songs and Sonnets of Pierre de Ronsard* (Boston and New York, 1924), p. 94.

so frequently told of leaves falling from trees into a stream and changing into birds.[34] Finally, there were animals that behaved like men, and men who changed into animals at will. The typical case was the werewolf, a human being who could be in two different places at once, to no one's surprise: in one place he was man, in the other he was animal.[35] How can we be astonished, after this, at the ease with which these men, accustomed to wallowing in imprecision, accommodated themselves to situations that were murky, ambiguous, and poorly defined, that seem absurd to us and would irritate us? They did so even in a realm where, for us, strict regularity is required more than in any other. Just think, for example, of France's borders, full of enclaves and exclaves; the country had no strict boundaries and was surrounded by villages that were divided in two, or three, uncertain to whom they belonged. In the face of so much uncertainty Rabelais's contemporaries felt none of the discomfort that for us would soon become unbearable—logically unbearable.

But it will be said that those were poor people, the ones who truly believed they were present at a witches' sabbath all the while they were at home sitting in a corner of their dreary hearth or lying on their pallet, that I have deliberately chosen people like that. Poor people? But what about their judges? They were not poor people, and they were not unlettered. Did they have any more difficulty with stories of werewolves than the witches themselves did? No, they did not. They went along with the stories. They were taken in by words. The only difference was that perhaps they sometimes felt a certain amount of

34. Frédéric Houssay, "La Légende du *Lepas anatifera*, la *Vallisneria spiralis* et le poulpe," *Comptes Rendus Hebdomadaires des Séances de l'Académie des Sciences*, 132 (Jan.–June 1901), 263–265; "Les Théories de la genèse à Mycènes et le sens zoologique de certains symboles du culte d'Aphrodite," *Revue Archéologique*, 3d ser., 26 (1895), 1–27; "Nouvelles Recherches sur la faune et la flore des vases peints de l'époque mycénienne et sur la philosophie pré-ionienne," *Revue Archéologique*, 3d ser., 30 (1897), 81–105. On stones that were alive, walked, drank, bathed, and so on, see the investigations of P. Saintyves, particularly "Le Thème des pierres qui boivent ou se baignent," *Revue de Folklore Français et de Folklore Colonial*, 5 (1934), 213–216.

35. Lucien Lévy-Bruhl, *The "Soul" of the Primitive*, trans. Lilian A. Clare (London, 1928), p. 158 ff. There is no worthwhile book that studies witchcraft from this point of view. On lycanthrophy, see among others J. de Nynauld, *De la lycanthropie, transformation et extase de sorciers* (Paris: Millot, 1615), and Beauvois de Chauvincourt, *Discours de la lycantropie ou de la transmutation des hommes en loups* (Paris: J. Reze, 1599).

intellectual outrage in the presence of demonstrations of sorcery. Naturally, the sorcerer did not; he might be terrified, but he was not surprised at anything he did, said, confessed, or explained. Is it necessary to recall that the author of the *Heptaplomeres*, Jean Bodin, one of the most open-minded, intelligent thinkers of the time, was also the author of the *Démonomanie des sorciers* and that he believed in the exploits of witches with all his heart?

Nothing gives us the right to accuse well-known and respected magistrates of any special credulity, foolishness, or mental weakness in comparison with their contemporaries—men like Boguet, Rémy, and Lancre, who were not only the chroniclers but the judges and destroyers of the witches in their respective jurisdictions, the Franche-Comté, Lorraine, and Labourd. Their way of responding to facts was not the same as ours.[36] They were struck by similarities that for us are devoid of interest and meaning. Resemblances that we overlook as fortuitous or superficial or arbitrary seemed to them to arise from connections that were full of mystery. They did not restrict themselves to accepting them. They investigated them with great interest. Theologians had long since accustomed them to moving painlessly and effortlessly in what Ferdinand Lot in his fine book on the end of the ancient world calls (though that is not why I like the book!) a "dangerous folly," of which he gives several examples taken from hundreds of others "equally entertaining or equally melancholy,"[37] as he insists on saying, momentarily forgetting his role as a historian. Folly is a word without meaning. Their mode of thinking was not ours, that is all. And much later in the century men of intelligence and knowledge continued, on the basis of comparisons we find unlikely, to engage in reasoning like that of Molière's Dr. Diafoirus. There was Fauchet, for example, the author of a book on the origins of the French language, who claimed to demonstrate that "the temperate regions were the first to be inhabited," Mesopotamia and Palestine being the proof—which was plausible, "for just as the heart and liver (according to a good number

36. The law of the time recognized no boundary between man and beast. The pig that killed a man or ate a child was tried like a criminal and hanged in accordance with the law.

37. *The End of the Ancient World and the Beginnings of the Middle Ages*, trans. Philip and Mariette Leon (New York, 1961), p. 376.

of physicians) were formed in man before the arms and legs, so those regions in the center of the earth were the first to have been inhabited."[38]

Indeed, no one then had a sense of what was impossible. No one had a concept of the impossible.

We are told that a man who had been beheaded took his head in his hands and started to walk down the street. We shrug our shoulders and inquire into the fact no further—we would feel ridiculous. In 1541 men did not say it was impossible.[39] They did not know how to have doubts about the possibility of a fact. For them there was no tyrannical, absolute, compelling concept of *law* that limited the unlimited power of nature, creating and producing without restraint. Criticism of facts was not to begin until precisely the moment when this concept of law took effect universally, when because of that the concept of the *impossible*, so fruitful in spite of its negative appearance, began to mean something, when to every mind *non posse* brought about *non esse*.

In the sixteenth century that moment had not arrived. A prophetic dream, an apparition, a deed or a communication from a distance—all were facts. And how could one doubt facts? I saw that phantom or ghost. I heard the noise of chains and squealing and weeping in the haunted house I slept in. As I came back in the evening from hunting I saw Hellequin's Hunt go by in the sky with a loud shout.[40] All facts, no doubt about it. I saw, I heard, I trembled. How could my friends have any doubt? My testimony is reliable. I never make up stories. And I honestly feel confident about my experience.

In the sixteenth century no one had yet uttered Cyrano's profound, human remark: "We do not have to believe all things of a man, since a man can say all things. We only have to believe of him what is human."[41] Beautiful words. But their date is 1641.

We were speaking of experience. Why is there no history of

38. Claude Fauchet, *Les Oeuvres* ... (Paris: David Le Clerc, 1610), fol. 534r.

39. On "cephalophoria" and cephalophoric saints, see P. Saintyves, *En marge de la Légende dorée* (Paris, 1931), p. 219 ff.

40. There are numerous references to Hellequin's Hunt in Gouberville. See *Le Journal du Sire de Gouberville*, ed. Eugène de Robillard de Beaurepaire (Caen, 1892), p. 210 (Aug. 14, 1553), for example. See likewise Ronsard (below, sect. 7).

41. "Contre les sorciers." In Cyrano de Bergerac, *Oeuvres comiques, galantes et littéraires*, new ed., ed. P. L. Jacob (Paris, 1858), pp. 53–54.

this word, either, which in French also has the meaning of "experiment"? For us *expérience* is a technique, especially familiar to men who work in laboratories. It is an intervention, carefully thought out and calculated in advance, into the realm of naked facts, the result of a choice—and a choice made in order to allow either the verification of an already formed hypothesis or the formation of a new one. For them it was an act of feeling, observing, and recording a phenomenon just as it was, an event that happened by itself, entirely apart from any intervention or particular wish to bring it about or not.

6. Natural and Supernatural

And no more than they possessed our concept of possible in relation to impossible did the men of the sixteenth century possess our concept of natural as opposed to supernatural. Or, rather, for them there was normal and constant communication between the natural and the supernatural. They retained a mystical vision of the universe, a primitive vision that did not look, as we do, for the causes of what they got from subjective experience, with a concern for locating each event within the network of phenomena, for explaining it by what preceded it, for making it the necessary consequence of given conditions and the no less necessary cause of easily predicted consequences. They claimed to find causes, simple and powerful ones, in a world that by definition eluded experience, a world peopled by invisible powers, by forces, spirits, and influences that surround us on all sides, besiege us, and rule our destiny.

A thunderbolt was not a "natural phenomenon" but the voluntary and conscious act of the Deity suddenly intervening in human affairs.[42] A comet appearing in the sky was not a "natural phenomenon." It was an omen, an announcement—the announcement of a death. In Rouen in 1600 there appeared a book by Taillepied: *Treatise on the Appearance of Spirits, to Wit, Disembodied Souls, Phantoms, Prodigies, and Marvelous Acci-*

---

42. Of the execution of a Huguenot in Montpellier in January 1554 Platter remarked, "An extraordinary phenomenon occurred . . . Immediately after the execution it began to thunder violently. I heard it plainly, and so did many others with me." *Beloved Son Felix, the Journal of Felix Platter, a Medical Student in Montpellier in the Sixteenth Century,* trans. Seán Jennett (London, 1961), p. 72.

*dents Sometimes Preceding the Death of Great Persons or Sig-
naling a Change in the State.*[43] It was an extension into the seventeenth century of Rabelais's chapter on the death of Langey,
of which we will speak in a moment. An eclipse, the fall of a
meteorite, a gray sunset—all were signs, interventions of heavenly powers.

In the whole fabric of life nature and supernature were perpetually intertwined, astonishing no one or making anyone uneasy. It was exactly like the cosmographies of the time, in
which the incoherent appears alongside the plausible, the true is
tied in with the fanciful, and offspring of the bestiaries' absurd
fauna crop up in the midst of "real" animals painted from life:
here the catoblepas is eating its feet with a stupid expression on
its face, there a genuine monkey is slyly scratching itself.

So it was with everything. We think they were not serious
when they asserted that if the corpse of a victim were brought
into the murderer's presence it would start to bleed. But Felix
Platter saw it being done in Montpellier very late in the century. Although he was a learned physician Platter did not
scoff.[44] If we are to believe Jobbé-Duval, the wounds of corpses
were opening and bleeding in front of killers in Brittany until
the seventeenth century in the principal jurisdictions and until
the Revolution in the others.[45] We do not understand that even
if a culprit was caught in the act the justice of the time still required a confession and admission of guilt. An admission destroyed, or at least counteracted, the noxious influence of what
was being admitted. By destroying a secret, a confession reduced its evil effect to naught. We ask ourselves against whom,
what mental defectives, Rabelais could have taken offense when
he became so angry with unspeakable persons who attributed to
the saints the repulsive idea of sending illnesses that they
agreed to cure after they were prayed to. The fact is, however,
that for us illness is only a physical disorder. For them it remained a curse. Just as the healing action of simples was not a

43. *Traité de l'apparition des esprits, à sçavoir des âmes séparées, fantosmes, prodiges et accidens merveilleux, qui précèdent quelquefois la morts de grands personnages ou signifient changement de la chose publique.*

44. *Beloved Son Felix,* p. 127 (Dec. 1556).

45. E. Jobbé-Duval, "Les Idées primitives dans la Bretagne contemporaine," *Nouvelle Revue Historique de Droit Français et Etranger,* 33 (1909), 550–593, 722–773;
35 (1911), 257–330; 37 (1913), 5–56, 421–473; 38 (1914), 5–60, 343–389.

"natural" act but took effect only if the ritual of gathering, in particular, was done according to form.[46] Every medical prescription in those days was a strange mixture of magical practices and the facts of experience. It was necessary to drink a certain decoction, to anoint oneself with a certain ointment— but at the same time, and more than anything else, it was necessary to make a certain gesture and utter a certain phrase: then, and only then, would the remedy take effect. "He who can cure a malady has this power only because he has been able to give it." That is not an observation by some commentator in the margin of the text of *Gargantua*. It is a statement by Lévy-Bruhl explaining the notions of his primitive peoples.[47] It plunges us back into a world which we had the illusion of having left for good.

The fact is that all of us today, educated men, are used to moving in the midst of an intellectualized nature whose various manifestations rest on a framework of necessary laws and fixed forms that correspond to certain conceptions. *They*, however, were at home in a peculiar world where phenomena were not located precisely, where time did not impose a strict sequential order on events and existences, where what came to an end could nevertheless continue, where death did not prevent a being from still existing and entering into other beings, as long as they showed some similarities to it. All of them, to a greater or lesser degree—not merely the uneducated, the foolish, and the ignorant. They did not have our instinctive certainty at all times and in all places that there are laws. Their scientists did not as yet think that their task, their proper calling, was precisely to discover laws and, immersing themselves in a mass of facts that were seemingly unconnected, to impose on them an order, classification, and hierarchy, the absence of which would

46. There were countless survivals in the sixteenth century (and after) of the state of mind described in Armand Delatte, "Herbarius: recherches sur le cérémonial usité chez les Anciens pour la cueillette des simples et des herbes magiques," *Bulletin de la Classe des Lettres et des Sciences Morales et Politiques de l'Académie Royale de Belgique*, 5th ser., 22 (1936), 227–348. On the ritual of gathering medicinal plants (Saint-John's-wort), see also Saintyves, *Légende dorée*, p. 246 ff. On saints who inflicted illness, see Hugues Vaganay, "Les saints 'producteurs de maladies,' " *Revue des Etudes Rabelaisiennes*, 9 (1911), 331–332.

47. Lucien Lévy-Bruhl, *Primitives and the Supernatural*, trans. Lilian A. Clare (New York, 1935), p. 158.

leave their minds unsatisfied. And what we in our language call a mystery is the impossibility of relating a fact to a law. For them there was no mystery. A will, the will of a good being or an evil one, a will that was beneficent or malevolent, expressed itself with the help of something they did not explain. And yet let us not forget that this was an advance. The appeal to the supernatural was the first step, and a considerable one, taken by man in mastering the confused jumble of facts in which he was submerged and imposing some human order on them.

7. A Universe Populated by Demons

How, then, could their universe, their tiny, orderly universe surrounding the earth, have resembled our incomprehensible, dizzying universe? They had not the slightest inkling of the infinite multiplication of unknown worlds, a concept familiar to us all. Instead they peopled their celestial space, which was still within the reach of a human imagination that made no attempt to rise out of itself, with a strange population:

> Quand l'Eternel bâtit la grand' maison du monde,
> Il peupla de poissons les abîmes de l'onde,
> D'hommes la terre, et l'air de Démons et les Cieux
> D'anges, à celle fin qu'il n'y eut point de lieux
> Vagues dans l'Univers, et selon leurs natures
> Qu'ils fussent tous remplis de propres créatures.[48]

> Th'Eternal in His wisdom built the world
> And stocked with swimming fish the ocean's depths;
> He peopled earth with men, the air with demons,
> And filled the heavens with angels, lest there be
> An empty space in all the universe:
> The world was full of creatures proper to their place.

Thus Ronsard in his *Hymne des daimons*.[49] In these lines he seems to have borrowed the rhythms of Victor Hugo. Poetic fantasy? That is not at all certain. Was he not adapting a state-

---

48. Ronsard, *Oeuvres*, VIII, 119.

49. See commentary in the edition of the *Hymne* by Albert-Marie Schmidt (Paris, 1939), p. 14 ff.

ment by Pico della Mirandola in his *Dignity of Man:* "God the Father, the supreme architect, had already built this cosmic home that we behold, the most sacred temple of His godhead, by the laws of His mysterious Wisdom. The region above the heavens He had adorned with Intelligences, the heavenly spheres he had quickened with eternal souls, and the excrementary and filthy parts of the lower world He had filled with a multitude of animals of every kind"?[50] Anyway, who in the sixteenth century lacked familiarity with angels and demons? Who did not carry inside himself a strange, phantasmagorical universe haunted by strange species?

Ronsard was a poet, Pico a dreamer. True, but then there was Fernel, an illustrious representative of the profession that lately moved a historian of ideas to say, "All the great precursors, all the early scientists of the Renaissance, were doctors."[51] Fernel was the standard of standards, the light and guide of the sons of Hippocrates for generations. Open his great summa, *Universa medicina,* to the treatise *De abditis rerum causis.*[52] What *causae abditae* it reveals! Here again, in Fernel, are spirits in abundance, spirits wandering over the world. Wandering spirits were so convenient, so good for doing everything and explaining everything. They were originally good, having been made in their creator's image, but one day one of them, Lucifer, drunk with pride, uttered the sacrilegious words, "In caelum conscendam, super astra Dei exaltabo solium meum, et sedebo in monte Testamenti."[53] Hell received him, together with his companions. Ever since, the band of fallen angels has stood in opposition to the shining band of the loyal angels, arrayed in nine choirs around the divine throne. This was Christian mythology, but, good Renaissance philosopher that he was, Fernel informs us that its sources were pagan: "de Daemonibus quicquid sum dicturus, e Platonicorum fontibus exhauriam."[54] And

---

50. "Oration on the Dignity of Man," trans. Elizabeth Livermore Forbes in *The Renaissance Philosophy of Man,* ed. Ernst Cassirer, Paul Oskar Kristeller, and John Herman Randall, Jr. (Chicago, 1948), p. 224. See Schmidt, p. 15.

51. Rey, III, 453, and the whole discussion that follows on the contribution of doctors to the development of experimental science.

52. *On the Hidden Causes of Things.* It was first published in 1548.

53. "I shall ascend to heaven, I shall raise my throne higher than the stars of God, and I shall sit on the mountain of the Testament."

54. "Whatever I shall have to say about demons I shall take from Platonic sources."

to the angels and demons he adds the heroes, whom Plato describes in the fourth book of the *Laws*. All are intermediaries between God and men, since God does not mingle with his creatures in his own person: "Deus quidem homini non miscetur, sed per id medium, commercium omne atque colloquium inter Deos hominesque conficitur, et vigilantibus nobis atque dormientibus."[55]

So we should cease being astonished when we come upon that strange chapter 27 in *Book Four*, in which the physician of "the learned and valiant Chevalier de Langey" discourses on "the decease of heroic souls" and remembers "the dreadful prodigies that happened before the death of the late Lord," when "the heavens, as it were, joyful for the approaching reception" of some "noble, precious, and heroic" soul, seemed "to make bonfires by . . . comets and blazing meteors"—not to mention "prodigies, monsters, and other foreboding signs, that thwart the order of nature." And we should above all not think that Rabelais is speaking lightly and having fun. He uses his most serious tone, which is a clear sign, and he solemnly calls his witnesses to the stand: "the Lords D'Assier, Chemant, one-eyed Mailly, St. Ayl, Villeneufve-la-Guart, Master Gabriel, physician of Savillan, Rabelais" and many other friends—"God take me presently if I tell you one single syllable of a lie in the matter."

A strange chapter—at any rate, that is what we say. But what about the men of the time? "The precious squad of angels": Ronsard was not alone in seeing it ranged around God in silent attention, the angels who were without bodies or passions, the true citizens of Heaven and, "no less than Him, immortal,"

Car ilz sont qu'Esprits, divins, parfaits et purs.[56]

For they are spirits, pure, divine, and perfect.

And as for the disorderly mob of demons, scattered beneath the moon, inhabiting

---

55. "Indeed God does not mingle with man, but it is through this medium that all intercourse and conversation between Gods and men is accomplished, when we are awake as well as when we are asleep."

See Jean Fernel, *De abditis rerum causis*, I, ch. 11.

56. *Hymne des daimons*, l. 69, in Ronsard, *Oeuvres*, VIII, 119.

L'air gros, épais, brouillé qui est de toutes parts
Toujours rempli de vents, de foudres et d'orages,[57]

The thick, heavy, murky air that's filled
With winds, with storms, with thunderclaps, and
        lightning,

the poet was not alone in seeing it as it passed through the midst of the clouds, with its light bodies, its beings of air and not of earth—but having weight nevertheless, weighing "just a little," so that if they were carried too high those bodies would not give up the place "the will of God had destined them to stay in."

They were odd creatures, those demons, partaking of God and of humans at the same time: of God as immortals, and of us as "filled with all the passions":

Ils désirent, ils craignent,
Ils veulent concevoir, ils aiment et dédaignent
Et n'ont rien propre à eux que le corps seulement.[58]

They wish, they fear,
They yearn to understand, they love and hate,
And nothing but their body is their own.

Some are good and some bad:

Les bons viennent de l'air, jusques on ces bas lieux
Pour nous faire savoir la volonté des Dieux
Puis rapportent à Dieu nos faits et nos prières
Et détachent du corps nos âmes prisonnières.[59]

The good fly down to earth from up on high
To tell us what the Gods demand of us
And then take back to God our deeds and prayers;
They free our fettered souls from body's prison.

It is also they who bring us dreams, and it is they from whom come Prophecy and the dark art

57. Ibid., l. 74 ff.
58. Ibid., p. 123, l. 159 ff.
59. Ibid., p. 126, l. 209 ff.

De savoir par oiseaux augurer le futur.[60]

Of using birds to learn about the future.

The bad ones, on the other hand, bring the earth

Pestes, fièvres, langueurs, orages et tonnerre.
Ils font des sons en l'air pour nous espovanter.[61]

Plagues and wasting fevers, storms and thunder.
They fill the air with sounds to make us fearful.

And they do quite a few other things. All the tragic signs
that appear in the sky—double suns, dark moons, bloody rain,
in short everything monstrous occurring in the air—were recognized as their work. And it is likewise they who visit haunted
houses. They are the Incubi, Larvae, Lemures, Penates, Suc-
cubi, Empusas, and Lamias who are always prowling around
our homes. They are goblins, sprites, and the kobolds of Nor-
way. They are the Naiads and the Nereids who still the waves
or raise storms. Yet they are timid and easily put to flight: they
are afraid of light and of a torch's gleam. All of them are afraid
of a sword's iron most of all, and they flee from it

De peur de ne sentir leur liaison coupée.[62]

Fearing it might cut apart their tight-knit band.

Indeed the classic image of the Magician showed him armed
with a naked sword. And Ronsard tells us how one night, as he
was going to see his mistress, "all alone beyond the Loir," he
saw the infernal hunt pass through the air and would have
fallen down dead if he had not had the idea

De tirer mon épée et de couper menu
L'air tout autour de moi, avecques le fer nu.[63]

Of drawing out my sword and all around me
Cutting the air to bits with naked steel.

60. Ibid., l. 218.
61. Ibid., l. 224 ff.
62. Ibid., p. 134, l. 344.
63. Ibid., p. 135, l. 369 ff.

Let us not surround these passages of poetry with all the analogous texts that could support, confirm, and augment them, but simply ask the question that immediately comes to mind:

Was this a scientific knowledge of reality? Was it, in the first place, an objective study of the living beings and inanimate objects "in nature" and of the countless secrets of their structure, function, and behavior? But how would that have satisfied the contemporaries of Rabelais—and Ronsard—when knowledge was communicated to men by the aerial and planetary demons, acting as messengers and couriers:

> Couriers of air, the couriers of the Lord
> Who swiftly bring His secret messages.[64]

The demons were intermediaries whose duty was to instruct terrestrial creatures on

> Les chemins de la nature
> Ou la musique des cieux.[65]
>
> The pathways nature follows
> Or the music of the heavens.

And these demons existed only to serve humanity, to give it the power to act on beings and phenomena in the bosom of a nature created for its needs and to allow it to have a sure grasp of the universe, thanks much more to their magically induced interventions than to the action of the mechanic arts.

So they all believed, the masters of ancient demonology which the Renaissance revived—from Marsilio Ficino (d. 1499) to Johannes Trithemius (d. 1516) to Cornelius Agrippa (d. 1536) to Paracelsus (d. 1541) and Ronsard (d. 1585). All were immersed in the same everyday phantasmagoria at the heart of a universe populated by spirits, demons, and semidivine creatures who were the agents and instruments of causality, manipulating (at a time when the machine had not come into being) natural forces, producing phenomena and then linking them to each other. Under a diversity of constantly fluctuating forms,

64. *Le Premier Livre des amours*, 31, in *Oeuvres*, IV, 34. See above, ch. 4, sect. 3.
65. "Ode à la Reine" in Ronsard, *Oeuvres*, I, 69.

which beings and objects put on and which were always changing, since

La matière demeure et la forme se perd,

Their matter stays unchanged, the form is lost,

they perceived one reality, single and multiple, physical and spiritual, that always continued to exist and to circulate. It was a deep conviction, and the World Soul of the Stoics, a concept dear to the men of the Renaissance, allowed it to have a philosophical form that was not only recognized but prestigious.

8. Occultism and Religion

There has been much discussion in recent years about the role, the value, and the reputation of the "occult science" that developed on the fringes of humanist science through the efforts of astrologers, physicians, and seekers of the philosophers' stone. It has been shown (and on opposing sides) how the confused effort of these men, their obscure ideas, and their adventurous speculations mixed with dreams rendered perhaps more service to modern science in certain areas and contributed more to its birth and formation than the standard knowledge of the doctors whom the universities turned out. The question for us right now is an entirely different one. We want to know if the mental state we have tried to describe did or did not predispose men in the sixteenth century to free themselves from the tutelage of religion, to break with the revealed, organized religions to which they belonged by birth, environment, or choice.

We are instinctively led to think it did. We are men of the twentieth century, provided by scientists daily with such a collection of miracles authenticated by facts and tested by experiment that the hypothetical or fanciful miracles proclaimed or predicted by the occultists seem pale by comparison. At any rate, we consider them naive. We no longer need to be told by some outsider that our science does not know everything and does not tell us everything, that it can at any moment be overtaken and transformed by a mass of new information and ideas. Yes, the marvelous is an everyday commodity. But, in a rather

peculiar shift, it is no longer the magus, the alchemist, or the as-
trologer who holds the monopoly on it. Far from it. It is the li-
censed, qualified, official scientist who holds the monopoly and
delivers to the public. Far more phantasmagorical than the
phantasmagorias of the past, today's phantasmagoria comes out
of laboratories, is honored, decorated, crowned, and looked on
as true, as the most authentic of truths. Outside of this there are
only the simple-minded and the charlatans, who have no standing among serious people. And therefore, quite naturally, it
seems to us that the speculators on the fringes of the sixteenth
century—the Cabalists, Hermetists, and occultists of every persuasion—must have erected opposite the orthodoxies of science
and religion little chapels that threatened churches and universities alike. There seems to be every indication that we should
regard them as the vanguard of what the seventeenth century
would call the army of *esprits forts*.

This too is an illusion. Obviously today, when we lay out in
front of us on one side the confused heap of pantheistic doctrines from every age and every provenance preserved for us by
the Cabala, the Hermetic books, and numbers of other obscure
sources, and, on the other side, a Christianity whose dogmas are
quite fixed and accord quite well with the needs of men endowed by their whole training and background with logical, rational minds, the disharmony seems glaring to us and concilia-
tion impossible. Either one or the other—a choice must be
made. *We* have to make a choice. But they did not choose. And
it was always for the same fundamental reasons.

They were not struck by the contradiction, they were not
bothered by it, and it did not present them with inexorable dilemmas. Can we say they were occupied with harmonizing
them? This has been said. They have been shown to be engaged in reconciling Plato with Aristotle, and Greek philosophy
with the Gospel. "Reconcile" is a word that should be pro-
scribed here. For reconciliation, as we understand its meaning,
is an activity that is still completely logical. To tell the truth,
they did not reconcile. Saurat has put it well: they made a
"synthesis of desires,"[66] the desires of men who, like the mys-

66. Denis Saurat, *Literature and Occult Tradition*, trans. Dorothy Bolton (New
York, 1930), p. 4.

tics but in a different way, reacted against a dogmatic theology that was too friendly to logic and whose delimitation, which was becoming more rigid every day, prevented refractory natures from wandering freely in pursuit of myths that were dark, alluring, and attractive and assuaged a primitivism whose demands were still felt. Thus they eagerly and voraciously used occultism to satisfy needs they had little notion of how to control and which they controlled only by their appetite. They ate without counting calories. They ate like undernourished men who do not have much in reserve. And they pursued their dreams along the edges of the Cabala, Trismegistus, and Proclus as they did along the edges of Pseudo-Dionysius, Raymond Lull, and the Rhenish mystics. All provided sustenance, both the former and the latter—sustenance for souls much more eager to feel and believe than to reason, criticize, and make judgments. This was true of all of them. To begin with, there was Pico della Mirandola, who undoubtedly was at times disturbing, and profoundly so, to the orthodox and who after propagating in humanist circles the most wonderful assortment of ideas that were alien, if not hostile, to Christianity, had himself piously buried in the habit that had been worn by Savonarola. He would have been quite astonished if he had been asked if he felt he was a Christian or not when he was setting forth his musings in all those thick volumes. As would, no doubt, our own devout Lefèvre (to take the only example among us), Jacobus Faber Stapulensis, editor of Saint Paul, commentator on the Gospels, and to a great extent the forerunner of the Reformation in France, who, with the same fervor which he felt for the Gospels, extolled, translated, edited, and popularized, among many others, the work of Trismegistus, for which he wrote a handsome preface.

Later, no doubt, the libertines would turn to the masters of occultism and seek an alibi for their own skepticism in their confused doctrines. Or, feeling revulsion at the orderly dryness of classicism, would look to them for the assistance obscurity might give them and the nutritional abundance muddy waters might provide. It was a natural reaction against a religion that was too civilized, a Christianity that was too logically coherent. The time had not arrived in the sixteenth century, for the profound reasons of which we have spoken. One fed one's dreams as one could. One looked to find oneself in others, without worrying about logical harmony or noncontradiction. That was the time when Martin Luther discovered the *German Theology* and found Martin Luther in it on every page and in every line. He enthusiastically had it published, acclaimed, and distributed throughout Germany. He had seen none of what was not Luther in that mystical treatise or of what contradicted Luther. Here, too, was "underdevelopment of sight." He was content to "feel"—like his whole age.

Conclusion

A Century That Wanted to Believe

 A V I N G   S A I D all this, we can go back to the problem this book wished to consider: the problem of unbelief, of its extent and possibility as far as the men of the Renaissance were concerned.

To believe or not to believe. The naive, simplistic notion that the problem is without mystery, the antihistorical notion that we can deal with it with regard to the men of the sixteenth century in the same way we tend to deal with it with regard to ourselves—this illusion and these anachronisms are what this whole book has been directed against. Let us now put aside the first term, "to believe." What about the other?

⟞ Not to believe. Would you say the problem was simple? Was it so easy for a man, as nonconformist as he could conceivably be in other respects, to break with the habits, the customs, even the laws of the social groups of which he was a part, at a time when those habits, customs, and laws were still in full force; when, on the other hand, the number of freethinkers who were trying to shake off the yoke was infinitesimal; when there was no material in his knowledge and the knowledge of the men of his time either for forming valid doubts or for supporting those doubts with proofs that, on the basis of experimentation, could have the force of real, veritable conviction?

But let us not remain in the abstract. "Not to believe" is a phrase that is inadequate. What concerns us at the moment is not some kind of abstract belief, the attitude of a man who does not believe in the existence of a God endowed with certain attributes and granted certain epithets: Creator, Preserver (Rabelais's *servateur*), or Providence, just and good, the guardian of a morality decreed by Him. What primarily concerns us is the attitude of a man who, born a Christian and totally involved in Christianity, could extricate his mind and shake off the common yoke—the yoke of a religion unfalteringly and unreservedly professed by nearly every one of his contemporaries.

Anyway, one must have some reasons for shaking off the common yoke. Good reasons—I mean reasons that would appear sound to whomever they were meant to satisfy. To assume that it could be done almost gratuitously, other than as a witty exercise or the pleasure of scoffing and showing off, is by the same token to ascribe to innovators a spiritual frivolity that immediately deprives their initiatives of any interest. One must have reasons. But reasons of what order? As men of the twentieth century, we are tempted to say historical and scientific reasons in the first place, with metaphysical reasons only third in line.

◆§ Not to believe for reasons of a historical order: was that possible for Rabelais and his contemporaries? But did anyone at that time grapple with the text of the Gospels as he grappled with the text of some writer—or rather with the juxtaposed texts of several different writers for the purpose of authenticating them, dating them, and establishing their reciprocal relationships? No one had thought of it. Or, if the idea had occurred to some, to a few men of particularly subtle and penetrating intellect, it had retained the status of an unverifiable idea, vague and without force.[1] How could it have been otherwise?

To the extent that the Gospel was seen as a block, to the extent that its divine inspiration was not disputed, to the extent that the examination of questions of date, provenance, and filiation had not been undertaken, to the extent that the history of Christianity's beginnings had not been handled in the same way as profane history—to just that extent was no disruption of

---

1. On the criticism of Erasmus, see Augustin Renaudet, *Etudes Erasmiennes* (*1521–1529*) (Paris, 1939), p. 136 ff.

Christianity possible, anywhere or by anybody, at least on the
basis of historical data. Only Euhemerism was available to the
men of the time; taken from Cicero by ardent Ciceronians, it
made the gods into deified men.[2] And we can have no doubt
that in France around 1550 hardy intellects were to be found
who slipped over from the pagan gods to the Christian God and
stopped limiting to Jupiter (and Venus and many others—Euhemerism was not, however, particularly feminist) the application of a doctrine that was simple, and economical besides, in
that it required no physical proof. Nor can we doubt that bold
intellects were to be found who applied the doctrine—at least in
secret meetings and small, extremely small, groups—to Jesus
himself. Calvin specifically tells us so in *De scandalis*, as did the
letter of Antoine Fumée, which preceded it chronologically. But
this was the middle of the century, after all. And did it go very
far? Could it go very far?

No further, you may say, than Renan's *Life of Jesus*. A specious analogy. Because behind Renan's *Jesus* lay years and
years of historical and philological study of the Gospels. Behind
the opinions of the "Achristians" of 1550 lay nothing but arguments that were no arguments; idle observations about Jesus'
morality as it was believed it could be drawn from the Gospels,
whose historic and documentary value was untouched by any
critical doubt; or other observations, no less idle, on the style of
the Gospels, to the advantage of the divine Plato's style. There
was nothing—only assertions by personalities whom Calvin and
the controversialists naturally called proud, arrogant, and over-
bearing. Nothing. There was not even, at the time of Rabelais,
the argument we would have expected to see exploited by the
contemporaries of Columbus, Cortez, Cabral, and Magellan:
that Christianity did not extend over the ecumene but kept outside its authority and its benefits, and, above all, outside salvation, eternal salvation, a mass of men and peoples whom the
navigators had suddenly revealed to the Old World.

"Not even." We cannot help saying it. How could those new
lands they discovered, unknown lands that did not know Christ

2. On Euhemerism in the sixteenth century, see Henri Busson, *Les Sources et le
développement du rationalisme dans la littérature française de la Renaissance
(1533–1601)* (Paris, 1922) and especially my study, *Origène et Des Périers, ou
l'énigme du Cymbalum Mundi* (Paris, 1942), in particular p. 129 ff.

and that Christ did not know, not have raised obstacles in their minds, serious and insurmountable obstacles to Christianity? But as far as they were concerned, what the discoveries engendered in their messianic souls was an old-fashioned, amazing zeal for proselytizing. Portuguese, Spaniards, Italians, and Frenchmen for years and decades all vied with each other not in boasting that they were traveling all over the world as merchants, but that they sailed, fought, and braved all sorts of dangers primarily and above all in order to extend the boundaries of Christianity: to make the king of the Congo a Christian, to allow the great king of Abyssinia to send ambassadors to Rome and negotiate the resumption of relations between his Christian people and the Vicar of Christ, to open up at last to the teachings of the divine Master the shores of the Indian Ocean, of India, of the East Indian islands, and beyond them, the shores of China and, before long, Japan.

That was what was on their minds. They were not us. Obviously, it was not the same for all of them, and some very quickly and very early had unorthodox thoughts. Guicciardini, for example, was among the very first.[3] What the others, even those who were very intelligent and well educated, felt most of all was a mounting fever for propagating, converting, and proselytizing. It was this fever that at first inflamed Ignatius of Loyola and his early companions, and drove Francis Xavier to India. These were men of action, not critics. Like Postel, of whom we spoke earlier, they were thoroughly obsessed with the great dream of unifying the Christian world, of incorporating into a renewed Christianity peoples who until then had been strangers and enemies to Christianity. They worried about the Lapps, the Ethiopians, and the Indians before they borrowed arguments against Christianity from their religious histories. As for the rest, they were not interested in what we are.

---

3. "Per queste navigazioni si è manifestato essersi nella cognizione della terra ingannati in molte cose gli antichi . . . , ma dato . . . qualche anzietà agli interpreti della Scrittura Sacra." (These voyages have made it clear that the ancients were deceived in many ways regarding a knowledge of the earth . . . They have given some cause for alarm to interpreters of the Holy Scriptures.) Francesco Guicciardini, *La Storia d'Italia*, ed. Alessandro Gherardi, 4 vols. (Florence, 1919), II, 110–111; English version, *The History of Italy*, trans. Sidney Alexander (New York and London, 1969), p. 182.

Just as the system of Copernicus remained without philosophical significance for a long time, so the discovery of a New World, a fourth "part of the world," for several decades caused only moderate amazement. That is a fact, and one that says a great deal about a state of mind.[4]

◄§ As to unbelief on a scientific foundation, let us first observe that it could not have been directed against Christianity as such (and indeed was not directed against it when it did come into being). It would at the same time have been directed against any religion teaching first and foremost that the universe, everything in the universe, depended on the will of a creator and lawgiver God.

Armed with the mighty concept of law, it gradually strove to reduce the powers of such a God. In the first place it strove to establish that if it was strictly possible to admit the original intervention of a *primum movens*, an initial divine motor, there was in any case no longer room, once the machine was started, for an interventionist God, for his miracles, or even, quite simply, for his Providence. After which the same unbelief on a scientific foundation, this time attacking any religion that posited the necessity of the initial action of a creator and lawgiver God at the beginning, opposed to it the concept, in various guises, of an autonomous nature that was subject to nothing but its own laws. But we have seen that precisely neither the concept of law nor the concept of nature was included among those worked out in the sixteenth century. Not that it had no sense of necessary regularity, no curiosity about a rational order in the world—but this was in connection with the Good and, later, the Beautiful.

So what was left? The unbelief of despair, expressed in the shout of a poor man covered with bruises, in poor Villon's cry of anguish:

> En mon pais suis en terre lointaine,
> Lez un brasier frissonne tout ardent,
> Nu comme ung vers, vestu en président,
> Je ris en pleurs et attens sans espoir.

4. Cf. Geoffroy Atkinson, *Les Nouveaux Horizons de la Renaissance française* (Paris, 1935).

In my own country I'm in a distant land
Beside the blaze I'm shivering in flames
Naked as a worm, dressed like a president
I laugh in tears and hope in despair.[5]

Or perhaps the unbelief that was a revolt against the triumph of injustice: "If there is a God and he is good, how can he let evil be done?" But does that question really go very far? In any case, it is one of the questions to which religions—above all Christianity—have a ready answer and one that is to the point.

As historians we should gather a very clear impression from this: unbelief changes with the period. Sometimes it changes very rapidly—just as concepts change, those on which some people rely in order to make denials, while their neighbors use others in order to prop up the systems under attack. We know how very rapid the change can be. The attitude of a scientist in 1940 with regard to the determinism of natural laws can no longer be that of Claude Bernard or, not going back so far, that of accredited scientists in 1900.

It is absurd and puerile, therefore, to think that the unbelief of men in the sixteenth century, insofar as it was a reality, was in any way comparable to our own. It is absurd, and it is anachronistic. And it is utter madness to make Rabelais the first name in a linear series at the tail end of which we put the "free-thinkers" of the twentieth century (supposing, moreover, that they are a single bloc and do not differ profoundly from each other in turn of mind, scientific experience, and particular arguments). This whole book has shown that, or else it is worth nothing.

⋙ For his time Rabelais was a free intellect. He was a man of sturdy intelligence and vigorous good sense, and he was untrammeled by many of the prejudices that circulated around him. I believe this, and I want it to be so. But I said "for his time"—which pretty much implies that between his freedom of intellect and ours there is not a difference of degree but one of kind, and that they have nothing in common except a certain mental disposition, a certain temperament, a certain way of be-

5. François Villon, "Ballade du concours de Blois"; *The Poems of François Villon*, trans. Galway Kinnell (Boston, 1977), p. 177.

having. As for his ideas, let us not, for goodness' sake, place them at the head of the series, the starting point for our own ideas. A savage who makes fire by energetically twirling a stick in the hollow of a piece of dry wood is extremely ingenious. And if he thought up the technique himself he is a savage of genius. For all that, we are not going to list him as one of the inventors of the electric stove.

So we can without hesitation answer the two questions we asked when we began. If a man like Rabelais, even supposing him endowed with a prodigious precursor's intelligence, undertook to conduct the kind of furious crusade we have been told he did—no, it would not have been possible for a man like him to undertake such a thing in a truly serious way. He had no ground on which to stand. And his denials could at best have been no more than opinions—paradoxical ways of thinking and feeling that nothing from outside came to the support of or propped up in any real or substantial way, nothing in either the science or philosophy of his time. And, on the other hand, no, a coherent rationalism was not yet in existence at the time of *Pantagruel*, a well-organized rationalist system that was dangerous for that very reason, because it was based on valid philosophical speculations and scientific discoveries. It could not have been in existence yet.

For the men of that time directed their ambition, their highest ambition, to being tributaries of the Greeks and Romans. Sometimes they picked up along the way some new fact or other unknown to the ancients which, when reflected on, could not be brought into their system of ideas without damaging it. But through a sort of intentional paradox they refused to see the contradiction. They remained faithful to the ancient doctrines, even though these had for them only the force of opinion, or opinions, and even though the doctrines did not agree with each other. Some had a materialist flavor, others a spiritualist one; these led to deism, those to genuine atheism; certain ones were optimistic, others pessimistic. Rabelais was like all his contemporaries in letting himself hear these contradictory voices—beautiful voices, moving, supple, full of eloquence and charm. Could he choose? Could he become the champion of one doctrine and the furious adversary of the others? Why? And how?

All opinions are of equal value when they are based only on impressions, prejudice, or vague analogies. In the face of such opinions neither Rabelais nor his contemporaries had the touchstone yet, the only touchstone that could have allowed them to choose, the right scale on which to weigh opinions: a strong scientific method. Let us give it both of its names: the experimental method and the critical method. They hesitated, they wavered, they finally got on one side and clung to it, striking hard at those on the other side. Meanwhile, above them, on the altars of easiness, Hearsay triumphed.

Obviously at the time of the Renaissance passionate and curious men felt a sort of suffocation and paralysis in the face of all the contradictory and vehement clamor of the ancient philosophies. Where could one begin? Whom was one to listen to first? Aristotle or Plato? Epicurus or Marcus Aurelius? Lucretius or Seneca? What a predicament! It was better to hold back, to take refuge in a smile and a "maybe." Beyond that, one put the spiritual meaning alongside the literal one, as Erasmus did when he edited the New Testament, and one made use of allegory in one's interpretations, together with all the transpositions that allegory allowed.

All of which is, to our taste, not very clear or decisive, and is often accused by us of being hypocritical. But no, let us be fair to the men of that time. To be fair is to understand. What they wanted, what they were attempting to do, was to restore the unity of thought—the dream of all men. It was to establish harmony between their growing knowledge of the facts of nature and their conception of the deity. But how could they have realized the harmony at that time, at that stage of science and philosophy? Those who made the attempt in spite of everything foundered in contradictions, and we can take pity on them. Those who recoiled at the task were the ones who violently opposed the method of Erasmus and (at least to the extent they were capable of doing so) put an abrupt end to the development of what he was trying to do. And they had a name. They were the Reformers.

◄§ One last word. Wanting to make the sixteenth century a skeptical century, a free-thinking and rationalist one, and glorify it as such is the worst of errors and delusions. On the authority of its best representatives it was, quite to the contrary, an inspired century, one that sought in all things first of all a reflection of the divine.

Take aesthetics. What hidden passions there were in the time of that Renaissance saturated with Platonism! "I think," wrote Bembo to Giovanni Francesco Pico della Mirandola, "that, just as there is in God a certain divine form of justice, temperance, and the other virtues, so there is also found a certain divine form of the best style [*recte scribendi speciem quamdam divinam*], an absolutely perfect model that was kept in sight, as far as they were able to do so by means of thought, by Xenophon and Demosthenes and in particular Plato and, more than any other, Cicero, when every one of them wrote. To this image that they conceived in their minds they added their own genius and style. I believe we should do as they did: strive to approach, to the best of our ability and as closely as possible, this image of beauty." Strive—while anticipating that the reward for our efforts will be the mysterious communication of this divine form. For without special help from on high—*non sine divino numine*—Petrarch would not, according to Despauter,[6] "have either declared war on the barbarians or recalled the Muses from exile or revived the cult of eloquence."

Take philosophy. It was the same thing. They reasoned, certainly. And sometimes it was more than reason. We can say it went as far as unreason. An aggravated scholasticism had stamped them all. It had trained them for disputation, and it is hard to shake off training like that. But were they satisifed with it?

As far as Aristotle was concerned, after untold efforts they found a subtle means of reconciling him not only with Plato, but with Plotinus. As far as metaphysics was concerned, they imbued it with a mystique that conferred on the pure ideas a sort of physical solidity and living warmth—so much so that some among them let themselves be tempted either by the distraction of a sensual idealism that added a new touch of perversity to the charms of paganism or else by the daydreams of a visionary credulity that blindly followed the labyrinths of occultism. The majority inhabited in their minds and desires,

6. Jan Despauter (d. 1520), grammarian. [Translator's note.]

not the trivial and noisy sphere of the senses, and not even the rarefied sphere of pure reason, but the third sphere, the one where God resided and made himself felt by his creatures, where those who searched with complete purity of mind would occasionally catch sight of a less cold and uncertain light—here again, a reflection of a higher illumination.

Hence their unquestionable nobility. Hence also their weaknesses, inasmuch as their moral life remained anchored in matter while their mental effort lifted them, ecstatic Epicureans that they were, to the contemplative sphere. On the whole, those were exceptions. The basic mysticism of most of them kept to straight and safe paths. Almost too much so, if we consider the example of the man in whom the century at its outset was truly most pleased to see itself mirrored: Erasmus, whose irony was at times a bit Voltairian.

All in all, the deep religiosity of the majority of those who created the modern world, a phrase that applies to someone like Descartes, was, I hope I have shown, applicable a century earlier to Rabelais, and to those whose deep faith he knew how to express superbly.

BIBLIOGRAPHY

INDEX

Bibliography

Author's Note

The bibliographic entries that follow do not constitute an exhaustive bibliography of a subject whose limits are difficult to define. We have included only books we actually used and, more precisely, ones from which we quoted in the body of the work. Books and articles, of course. Four pages are sometimes more useful than some compilations in four volumes. So let no one accuse us of careless omissions. Conscious omissions, yes. It is with deliberate intent that a number of works that were of practically no use to us are not listed.

Translator's Note

This bibliography is essentially Lucien Febvre's own, as it appears in the 1962 reprinting (which contains some changes that were made in the 1947 reprinting), except for the updating of some items, the inclusion of English translations, the substitution of original works for their French translations, and the addition of works cited in the text that were omitted from the original bibliography. The most recent editions are given whenever appropriate.

Plan of the Bibliography

Abbreviations of Frequently Cited Periodicals

BSHPF   *Bulletin de la Société de l'Histoire du Protestantisme Français*
RER   *Revue des Etudes Rabelaisiennes*
RSS   *Revue du Seizième Siècle*

I. Working Tools

A. Bibliographic Collections and Indexes; Printers and Booksellers

(*Bibliographic Collections and Indexes*)

Baudrier, Henri, and Julien Baudrier. *Bibliographie lyonnaise. Recherches sur les imprimeurs, libraires, relieurs et fondeurs de lettres de Lyon au XVIᵉ siècle.* 12 vols. Lyon, 1895–1921; photographic reprint, Paris, 1964.

Brunet, Jacques-Charles. *Manuel du libraire et de l'amateur de livres.* 5th ed. 6 vols. Paris, 1860–1865. Two-vol. supplement, Paris, 1878–1880.

Buisson, Ferdinand. *Répertoire des ouvrages pédagogiques du XVIᵉ siècle.* Paris, 1886; photographic reprint, Nieuwkoop, 1962.

Caillet, Albert Louis. *Manuel bibliographique des sciences psychiques ou occultes.* 3 vols. Paris, 1913.

Clouzot, Etienne, and Henri Martin. *Revue des Etudes Rabelaisiennes, Tomes I-X, 1903–1912. Tables générales.* Paris, 1924.

Coyecque, Ernest. *Recueil d'actes notariés relatifs à l'histoire de Paris et ses environs au XVIᵉ siècle, 1495–1545.* 2 vols. Paris, 1905, 1924.

Giraud, Jeanne. *Manuel de bibliographie littéraire pour les XVIᵉ, XVIIᵉ, et XVIIIᵉ siècles français.* 2d ed. Paris, 1958.

Lanson, Gustave. *Manuel bibliographique de la littérature française moderne, XVIᵉ, XVIIᵉ, XVIIIᵉ, et XIXᵉ siècles.* New ed., rev. and corr. Paris, 1931.

Mattaire, Michael. *Annales typographici ab artis inventae origine ad annum MDCLXIV.* 5 vols. in 9. The Hague, Amsterdam, and London, 1719–1741; photographic reprint, Graz, 1965–1967.

Pichon, Jérome, and Georges Vicaire. *Documents pour servir à l'histoire des libraires de Paris, 1486–1600.* Paris, 1894.

Renouard, Philippe. *Documents sur les imprimeurs, libraires, etc. ayant exercé à Paris de 1450 à 1600.* Paris, 1901.

——— *Imprimeurs parisiens, libraires, fondeurs de caractères et correcteurs d'imprimérie depuis l'introduction de l'imprimérie à Paris (1470) jusqu'à la fin du XVIe siècle.* Paris, 1896.

——— *Les Marques typographiques parisiennes des XVe et XVIe siècles.* Paris, 1926.

Reusch, Franz Heinrich, ed. *Die Indices librorum prohibitorum des sechszehnten Jahrhunderts.* Bibliothek des Stuttgarter literarisches Vereins, vol. 176. Tübingen, 1886; photographic reprint, 1961.

Short Title Catalogue of Books Printed in France and of French Books Printed in Other Countries from 1470 to 1600 Now in the British Museum. London, 1924.

Silvestre, Louis Catherine. *Marques typographiques ou recueils des monogrammes, chiffres, enseignes . . . des libraires et imprimeurs . . . depuis l'introduction de l'imprimérie, en 1470, jusqu'à la fin du XVIe siècle.* 2 vols. Paris, 1867.

(*Individuals*)

Arnoullet, Olivier
  Bibliography of publications in Baudrier, *Bibliographie lyonnaise*, X, 28–91.

Badius, Josse
  Renouard, Philippe. *Bibliographie des impressions et des oeuvres de Josse Badius Ascensius, imprimeur et humaniste, 1462–1535.* 3 vols. Paris, 1908.

Colines, Simon de
  Renouard, Philippe. *Bibliographie des éditions de Simon de Colines, 1520–46.* Paris, 1894.

Columbus, Fernando
  Babelon, Jean. *La Bibliothèque française de Fernand Colomb.* Paris, 1913.

The Estiennes
  Renouard, Antoine A. *Annales de l'imprimérie des Estienne.* 2d ed. Paris, 1843.

Gryphius, Sebastian
  Bibliography of publications in Baudrier, *Bibliographie lyonnaise*, VIII, 11–286.

Nourry, Claude, dit Le Prince
  Bibliography of publications in Baudrier, *Bibliographie lyonnaise*, XII, 72–149.

B. Dictionaries, Encyclopedias, Biographical Indexes

Bayle, Pierre. *Dictionnaire historique et critique.* 5th ed. 5 vols. Amsterdam, 1734.

———— *A General Dictionary, Historical and Critical.* 10 vols. London, 1734–1741.

Dictionnaire de théologie catholique. Ed. Vacant, Mangenot, and Amann. 15 vols. Paris, 1908–1950.

Dictionnaire d'histoire et de géographie ecclésiastiques. Ed. Baudrillart, Aigrain, Richard, and Rouziès. 19 vols. to date. Paris, 1912– .

Durand de Maillane. *Dictionnaire de droit canonique et de pratique bénéficielle.* Rev. ed. 6 vols. Lyon, 1787.

Encyclopédie française. General ed. Lucien Febvre. 21 vols. Paris, 1935–1966.

Eubel, Conrad. *Hierarchia catholica medii et recentioris aevi.* 2d ed. vols. I and II. 8 vols. Regensburg, 1901–1978; reprint of I and II, Padua.

Gams, P. B., ed. *Series episcoporum Ecclesiae catholicae.* Regensburg, 1873–1886; reprint, Graz, 1957.

Haag, Eugène, ed. *La France Protestante.* 10 vols. Paris and Geneva, 1846–1859. 2d ed. 6 vols. (incomplete). Henri Bordier, ed. Paris, 1877–1888.

Hurter, Hugo. *Nomenclator literarius theologiae catholicae, theologos exhibens aetate, natione, disciplinis distinctos.* 5 vols. Innsbruck, 1909–1926; reprint, New York, 1962.

Lalande, André. *Vocabulaire technique et critique de la philosophie.* 4th ed. 3 vols. Paris, 1932–1938. 10th ed. 1 vol. Paris, 1968.

Marchand, Prosper. *Dictionnaire historique.* 2 vols. in 1. The Hague, 1758.

Picot, Emile. *Les Français italianisants au XVIe siècle.* 2 vols. Paris, 1906–1907.

Realencyclopädie für protestantische Theologie und Kirche. Ed. J. J. Herzog. 3d ed. rev. by Albert Hauck. 24 vols. Leipzig, 1896–1913.

Vindry, Fleury. *Les Parlementaires français au XVIe siècle.* 2 vols. Paris, 1909, 1912.

C. Some Documentary Texts and Collections

Auton, Jehan d'. *Chroniques de Louis XII.* Ed. R. de Maulde La Clavière. 4 vols. Paris, 1889–1895.

Catalogue des Actes de François Ier. Ed. Paul Marichal. 10 vols. Paris, 1887–1908.

Driart, Pierre. "Chronique parisienne de Pierre Driart, chambrier de Saint-Victor (1522–35)." Ed. Fernand Bournon. *Mémoires de la Société de l'Histoire de Paris et de l'Ile de France,* 22 (1895), 67–178.

Geizkofler, Lucas. *Mémoires de Luc Geizkofler, tyrolien (1550–1620).* Trans. Edouard Fick. Geneva, 1892.

Gouberville, Gilles de. *Le Journal du Sire de Gouberville.* Ed. Eugène de Robillard de Beaurepaire. Caen, 1892.

———— *Journal manuscrit d'un sire de Gouberville et du Mesnil-au-Val, gentilhomme campagnard.* Ed. Alexandre Tollemer. 2d ed. Rennes, 1879.

Grin, François. "Journal de François Grin, religieux de Saint-Victor (1554–1570)." Ed. Baron A. de Ruble. *Mémoires de la Société de l'Histoire de Paris et de l'Ile de France,* 21 (1894), 1–52.

Haton, Claude. *Mémoires de Claude Haton.* Ed. Félix Bourquelot. 2 vols. Paris, 1857.

Le Journal d'un bourgeois de Paris sous le règne de François Ier (1515–1536). Ed. V.-L. Bourrilly. Paris, 1910.

Le Roux de Lincy, Antoine, ed. *Recueil de chants historiques français.* 2 vols. Paris, 1841–1842.

Léry, Jean de. *Histoire d'un voyage faict en la terre du Brésil dite Amérique.* [La Rochelle]: pour Ant. Chuppin, 1578.

Platter, Felix. *Beloved Son Felix, the Journal of Felix Platter, a Medical Student in Montpellier in the Sixteenth Century.* Trans. Seán Jennett. London, 1961.

———— *Tagebuch (Lebensbeschreibung) 1536–1567.* Ed. Valentin Lötscher. Basel and Stuttgart, 1976.

Platter, Thomas. *Lebensbeschreibung.* Ed. Alfred Hartmann. Klosterberg and Basel, 1944.

Schelhorn, Johann Georg. *Amoenitates literariae.* 14 vols. Frankfort and Leipzig, 1730–1731.

Versoris, Nicolas. "Livre de raison de Me Nicolas Versoris, avocat au Parlement de Paris, 1519–1530." Ed. G. Fagniez. *Mémoires de la Société de l'Histoire de Paris et de l'Ile de France,* 12 (1885), 99–222.

D. Some Works and Observations on Methodology

Berr, Henri. *En marge de l'histoire universelle.* Paris, 1934.

Febvre, Lucien. *Combats pour l'histoire.* Paris, 1953.

———— *A New Kind of History, from the Writings of Febvre.* Trans. K. Folca. Ed. Peter Burke. New York, 1973.

———— "De 1892 à 1933: Examen de conscience d'une histoire et d'un historien." *Revue de Synthèse,* 7 (1934), 93–106. In *Combats pour l'histoire,* pp. 3–17.

———— "De Spengler à Toynbee, quelques philosophies opportunistes de l'histoire." *Revue de Métaphysique et de Morale,* 43 (1936), 573–602. In *Combats pour l'histoire,* pp. 119–143.

———— "Psychologie et histoire." In *Encyclopédie française,* VIII, 8′12-3– 8′12-7. Reprinted in *Combats pour l'histoire,* pp. 207–220. Trans. as "History and Psychology" in *A New Kind of History,* pp. 1–11.

———— "Les Recherches collectives et l'avenir de l'histoire." *Revue de Synthèse,* 11 (1936), 7–14. In *Combats pour l'histoire,* pp. 55–60.

———— "La Sensibilité dans l'histoire." *Annales d'Histoire Sociale,* 3 (1941), 5–20. In *Combats pour l'histoire,* pp. 221–238. Trans. as "Sensibility and History" in *A New Kind of History,* pp. 12–26.

II. Rabelais: The Man and His Work

A. The Writings of Rabelais: Bibliographies and Editions

Boulenger, Jacques. "Etude critique sur les rédactions de *Pantagruel*." *RSS*, 6 (1919), 201–275. Reprinted in Rabelais, *Oeuvres*, ed. Lefranc, III, lxxi–cxxvii.

Plan, Pierre-Paul. *Bibliographie rabelaisienne: les éditions de Rabelais de 1532 à 1711*. Paris, 1904.

Rabelais, François. *Les Oeuvres*. Ed. Charles Marty-Laveaux. 6 vols. Paris, 1868–1903.

———— *Oeuvres complètes*. Ed. Jean Plattard. 5 vols. Paris, 1929.

———— *Oeuvres*. Critical ed. by Abel Lefranc, Jacques Boulenger, Henri Clouzot, Paul Dorveaux, Jean Plattard, and Lazare Sainéan. 6 vols. Paris, 1912–1955.

———— *Oeuvres*. Ed. Louis Moland. With a biographical note by Henri Clouzot. 2 vols. Paris, 1950.

———— *The Works of Francis Rabelais*. Ed. Albert Jay Nock and Catherine Rose Wilson. 2 vols. New York, 1931.

B. General Studies: The Man and His Work

Bibliothèque Nationale. *Rabelais, exposition organisée à l'occasion du quatrième centenaire de la publication de Pantagruel*. Paris, 1933.

Boulenger, Jacques. *Rabelais à travers les âges*. Paris, 1925.

Febvre, Lucien. "L'Homme, la légende et l'oeuvre." *Revue de Synthèse*, 1 (1931), 113–133. In *Combats pour l'histoire*, pp. 247–262.

Gebhart, Emile. *Rabelais, la Renaissance et la Réforme*. Paris, 1877.

Heulhard, Arthur. *Rabelais, ses voyages en Italie, son exil à Metz*. Paris, 1891.

Lote, Georges. *La Vie et l'oeuvre de François Rabelais*. Aix-en-Provence, 1938.

Millet, René. *Rabelais*. 5th ed. Paris, 1921.

Plattard, Jean. *L'Oeuvre de Rabelais: sources, invention, composition*. Paris, 1910.

———— *La Vie de François Rabelais*. Paris and Brussels, 1928.

Stapfer, Paul. *Rabelais, sa personne, son génie, son oeuvre*. Paris, 1889.

Thuasne, Louis. *Etudes sur Rabelais*. Paris, 1904.

C. Partial Studies: Biographical Episodes

Bourrilly, V.-L. "Rabelais à Lyon en août 1537." *RER*, 4 (1906), 103–134.

Clouzot, Henri. "Chronologie de la vie de Rabelais." In *Oeuvres*, ed. Lefranc, I, cxxviii–cxliii.

De Santi, L. "Le cours de Rabelais à la Faculté de Montpellier 1537–38." *RER*, 3 (1905), 309–310.

———— "Rabelais à Toulouse." *RSS*, 7 (1921), 42–62.

Grimaud, Henri. "Généalogie de la famille Rabelais." *RER*, 4 (1906), 228–234.

Lefranc, Abel. "Les Autographes de Rabelais." *RER*, 3 (1905), 339–350.

———— "Rabelais et le pouvoir royal." *RSS*, 17 (1930), 191–202.

———— "Le Vrai Visage de François Rabelais." *RSS*, 13 (1926), 308–310.

Lesellier, J. "L'Absolution de Rabelais en cour de Rome: ses circonstances, ses résultats." *Humanisme et Renaissance*, 3 (1936), 237–270.

———— "Deux Enfants naturels de Rabelais légitimés par le pape Paul III." *Humanisme et Renaissance*, 5 (1938), 549–570.

Picot, Emile. "Rabelais à Lyon en août 1540." *RER*, 4 (1906), 45–48.

Plattard, Jean. *L'Adolescence de Rabelais en Poitou.* Paris, 1923.

Zeller, Gaston. "Le Séjour de Rabelais à Metz." *RSS*, 14 (1927), 141–149.

D. Partial Studies: Works and Relations

Berthoud, Gabrielle. *Marcourt et Rabelais.* Neuchâtel, 1929.

Busson, Henri. "Rabelais et le miracle." *Revue des Cours et Conférences*, 30, no. 1 (1929), 385–400.

Clouzot, Henri. "Note pour le commentaire: 'L'enfant sortit par l'aureille senestre.'" *RSS*, 9 (1922), 219–220.

Dubreme, Claude. "L'Accouchement de Gargamelle par l'oreille senestre." *Chronique Médicale*, 40 (1933), 74. (Part of a continuing discussion.)

Folet, H. "Rabelais et les saints préposés aux maladies." *RER*, 4 (1906), 199–216.

Fusil, C.-A. "Rabelais et Lucrèce." *RSS*, 12 (1925), 157–161.

Gilson, Etienne. "Notes médiévales au Tiers Livre." *Revue d'Histoire Franciscaine*, 2 (1925), 72–88.

———— "Rabelais franciscain." *Revue d'Histoire Franciscaine*, 1 (1924), 257–287. Slightly revised in *Les Idées et les lettres*, pp. 197–241.

Hogu, Louis. "L'Opinion d'un protestant sur Rabelais." *RER*, 8 (1910), 376–377.

Lefranc, Abel. "Etude sur le 'Gargantua.'" In Rabelais, *Oeuvres*, ed. Lefranc, I.

———— "Etude sur *Pantagruel.*" In Rabelais, *Oeuvres*, ed. Lefranc, III.

———— "Etude sur le Tiers Livre." In Rabelais, *Oeuvres*, ed. Lefranc, V.

———— *Les Navigations de Pantagruel.* Paris, 1905.

Livingston, Charles H. "Rabelais et deux contes de Philippe de Vigneulles." In *Mélanges offerts à M. Abel Lefranc*, p. 22 ff.

Marcourt, Antoine. *Le Livre des marchans, fort utile à toutes gens, nouvellement composé par le sire Pantapole, bon expert en tel affaire, prochain voysin du Seigneur Pantagruel.* Neuchâtel, 1533.

———— *The boke of marchauntes, right necessary unto all folkes, Newly made by the lorde Pantapole, right expert in such busynesse, nere neyghbor unto the lord Pantagrule.* London: Thomas Godfraye, 1534.

Pannier, Jacques. Review of Rabelais, *Oeuvres*, ed. Lefranc, V. *BSHPF*, 80 (1931), 548–551.

Pirenne, Henri. "Rabelais dans les Pays-Bas." *RER*, 4 (1906), 224–225.

Plattard, Jean. "L'Ecriture Sainte et la littérature scripturaire dans l'oeuvre de Rabelais." *RER*, 8 (1910), 257–330.

—— "L'Invective de Gargantua contre les mariages contractés 'sans le sceu et adveu' des parents." *RSS*, 14 (1927), 381–388.

—— "Notes pour le Commentaire, XII." *RER*, 10 (1912), 255–257.

—— "Les Publications savantes de Rabelais." *RER*, 2 (1904), 67–77.

—— "Rabelais et Mellin de Saint Gelais." *RER*, 9 (1911), 90–108.

—— "Rabelais réputé poète par quelques écrivains de son temps." *RER*, 10 (1912), 291–304.

Sainéan, Lazare. "L'Histoire naturelle et les branches connexes dans l'oeuvre de Rabelais." *RSS*, 3 (1915), 187–277.

—— "L'Histoire naturelle dans l'oeuvre de Rabelais." *RSS*, 7 (1920), 1–45.

Talant, Louis. *Rabelais et la Réforme*. Cahors, 1902.

Thuasne, Louis. "La Lettre de Gargantua à Pantagruel." *Revue des Bibliothèques*, 15 (1905), 99–139. Reprinted in Thuasne, *Rabelais et Villon*.

Toldo, Pietro. "A propos d'une inspiration de Rabelais." *Revue d'Histoire Littéraire de la France*, 11 (1904), 467–468.

III. Predecessors, Contemporaries, and Adversaries of Rabelais

A. Humanists and Writers

Amis et Amiles

Hofmann, Conrad, ed. *Amis et Amiles und Jourdains de Blaives, Zwei altfranzösische Heldengedichte des Kerlingischen Sagenkreises*. 2d ed. Erlangen, 1882.

Arlier, Antoine

Gerig, John L. *Antoine Arlier and the Renaissance at Nîmes*. New York, 1929.

Puech, Dr. "Un Ami d'Etienne Dolet (1506–1545)." *Revue du Midi*, 12 (1892), 382–401.

Beza, Theodore

Beza, Theodore. *Poemata*. Paris: Conrad Badius, 1548.

—— *Histoire ecclésiastique des églises réformées au royaume de France*. Ed. P. Vesson. 2 vols. Toulouse, 1882.

Bouchet, Jean

Hamon, Auguste. *Un Grand Rhétoriqueur poitevin: Jean Bouchet, 1476–1577?* Thèse de doctorat ès lettres, Paris, 1901.

Haskovec, P. "Rabelais et Jean Bouchet." *RER*, 6 (1907), 56–60.

Plattard, Jean. "Une Oeuvre inédite du grand rhétoriqueur Jean Bouchet." *RSS*, 9 (1922), 80–82.

Bourbon, Nicholas

Nicolai Borbonii Vandoperani nugae. Paris: apud Michaelum Vascosanum, 1533.

Nicolai Borbonii Vandoperani nugae. Eiusdem Ferraria. Basel: per And. Cratandrum, 1533.

Nicolai Borbonii Vandoperani opusculum puerile ad pueros de moribus, sive Paidagogeion. Lyon: apud Seb. Gryphium, 1536.

Nicolai Borbonii Vandoperani Lingonensis nugarum libri octo. Lyon: apud Seb. Gryphium, 1538.

Carré, G. *De vita et scriptis N. Borbonii Vandoperani.* Thèse de doctorat ès lettres, Paris, 1888.

De Santi, L. "Rabelais et Nicolas Bourbon." *RSS,* 9 (1922), 171–175.

Boysonné, Jean de

   Les Trois Centuries de Maistre Jehan de Boyssoné. Ed. Henri Jacoubet. Bibliothèque méridionale, 2d ser., XX. Toulouse, 1923.

   Les Poésies latines de Jean de Boyssoné. Ed. Henri Jacoubet. Toulouse, 1931.

   La Correspondance de Jean de Boyssonè. Ed. Henri Jacoubet. Toulouse, 1931.

   "Lettres inédites de Jean de Boysonné et de ses amis." Ed. Joseph Buche. *Revue des Langues Romanes* (1895), 176–190, 271–278; (1896), 71–86, 138–143, 355–372; (1897), 177–197.

   Bousquet, Fernand. "Compte-rendu du séance du 27 avril 1923." (Text of two unpublished letters by Boysonné and Melanchthon presented by Fernand Bousquet.) *Bulletin de la Société des Sciences, Arts et Belles-Lettres du Tarn,* 1 (1921–1927), 177–180.

   Jacoubet, Henri. "Alciat et Boyssoné, d'après leur correspondance." *RSS,* 13 (1926), 231–242.

   ——— "Les Dix Années d'amitié de Dolet et de Boyssoné (Toulouse 1532, Lyon 1542)." *RSS,* 12 (1925), 290–321.

   ——— *Jean de Boyssoné et son temps.* Toulouse and Paris, 1930.

   ——— "Quelques Conjectures à propos de Boyssoné." *RSS,* 11 (1924), 302–319.

   Mugnier, François. *La Vie et les poésies de Jean de Boysonné.* Paris, 1897.

Brantôme, Pierre de Bourdeille, Seigneur de

   Brantôme. *Oeuvres complètes.* Ed. Ludovic Lalanne. 11 vols. Paris, 1864–1882.

   ——— *Les Dames galantes.* Ed. Henri Bouchot. 2 vols. Paris, n.d.

   ——— *Vie des dames illustres.* In *Oeuvres complètes,* VIII.

   Bouchot, Henri. *Les Femmes de Brantôme.* Paris, 1890.

Britannus (Robert Breton)

   Roberti Britanni epistulae. Roberti Britanni carmina. Toulouse, 1536.

   Rob. Britanni Atrebatensis epistol. libri II. Paris: G. Bossozelius, 1540.

   Roberti Britanni de optimo statu reipublicae liber. Huic adjuncta Gul. Langei Bellaii deploratio. Paris: ex officina Christiani Wecheli, 1543.

Brixius (Germain de Brie)

   Germani Brixii Altisseodorensis gratulatoriae IV. Ejusdem epistulae IV. Paris, 1531.

Budé, Guillaume

   Delaruelle, Louis. *Guillaume Budé, les origines, les débuts, les idées maîtresses.* Bibliothèque de l'Ecole des Hautes Etudes, Sciences historiques et philologiques, no. 162. Paris, 1907.

   ——— *Répertoire analytique et chronologique de la correspondance de*

Guillaume Budé. Thèse de doctorat ès lettres, Paris, 1907; reprint, New York, 196?.

Champier, Symphorien

Allut, Paul. *Etude biographique et bibliographique sur Symphorien Champier*. Lyon, 1859.

Chappuys, Claude

Roche, Louis P. *Claude Chappuys, poète de la cour de François Ier*. Paris, 1929.

Charondas (Loys Le Caron)

Charondas. *Les Dialogues*. Paris: chez Jean Longis, 1556.

Pinvert, Lucien. "Un Entretien philosophique de Rabelais, rapporté par Charondas (1556)." *RER*, 1 (1903), 193–201.

Chesneau, Nicholas

Nic. Querculi epigrammatum libri II. Ejusdem hendecasyllaborum liber unus. Paris: T. Richard, 1553.

Comines, Philippe de

Commynes, Philippe de. *Mémoires*. Ed. Joseph Calmette and G. Durville. 3 vols. Paris, 1964–1965.

The Memoirs of Philippe de Commynes. Ed. Samuel Kinser. Trans. Isabelle Cazeaux. 2 vols. Columbia, S.C., 1969–1973.

Cousin, Gilbert

Gilberti Cognati Nozereni opera multifarii argumenti. Basel: Henri Pierre, 1562.

Febvre, Lucien. "Un Sécrétaire d'Erasme: Gilbert Cousin et la Réforme en Franche-Comté." *BSHPF*, 56 (1907), 97–148.

Pidoux, A. "Bibliographie historique des oeuvres de Gilbert Cousin." *Le Bibliographe Moderne*, 15 (1911), 132–171.

Des Masures, Louis

Ludovici Masurii carmina. Lyon: apud J. Tornaesium et G. Gazeium, 1557.

Oeuvres poétiques des Louis des Masures. Lyon: J. de Tournes et G. Gazeau, 1557.

Vingt Pseaumes de David traduits selon la vérité hébraïque et mis en rime françoise par Louis des Masures, tournisien. Lyon: J. de Tournes et G. Gazeau, 1557.

Des Périers, Bonaventure

Des Périers, Bonaventure. *Oeuvres françoises*. Ed. Louis Lacour. 2 vols. Paris, 1856.

———— *Le Cymbalum Mundi*. Facsimile of Paris ed. by Jean Morin, 1537. Intro. by Pierre-Paul Plan. Paris, 1914.

Becker, Philip-August. *Bonaventure des Périers als Dichter und Erzähler*. Vienna, 1924.

Chenevière, Adolphe. *Bonaventure des Périers, sa vie, ses poésies*. Thèse de doctorat ès lettres, Paris, 1886.

Febvre, Lucien. "Une Histoire obscure: la publication du 'Cymbalum Mundi.'" *RSS*, 17 (1930), 1–41.

———— *Origène et Des Périers, ou l'énigme du Cymbalum Mundi*. Paris, 1942.

Walser, Ernst. "Der Sinn des *Cymbalum Mundi:* Eine Spottschrift gegen Calvin." *Zwingliana*, 4 (1922), 65–82.

Dolet, Etienne

Stephani Doleti orationes duo in Tholosam. Ejusdem epistolarum libri II. Ejusdem carminum libri II. Ad eundem epistolarum amicorum liber. Prob. Lyon: S. Gryphius, 1534.

Stephani Doleti dialogus de imitatione ciceroniana adversus Desid. Erasmum Roterodamum pro Christophoro Longolio. Lyon: ap. Seb. Gryphium, 1535.

Dolet, Etienne. *Commentariorum linguae latinae tomus primus.* Lyon: apud Seb. Gryphium, 1536.

——— *Commentariorum linguae latinae tomus secundus.* Lyon: apud Seb. Gryphium, 1538.

Stephani Doleti Galli Aurelii liber de imitatione ciceroniana adversus Floridum Sabinum. Confutatio maledictorum, et varia epigrammata. Lyon: ex officina Auctoris, 1540.

Bayle, Pierre. "Dolet." In *Dictionnaire historique*, II, 647–649.

Boulmier, Joseph. *Estienne Dolet. Sa vie, ses oeuvres, son martyre.* Paris, 1857.

Chassaigne, Marc. *Etienne Dolet, portrait et documents inédits.* Paris, 1930.

Christie, Richard Copley. *Etienne Dolet, the Martyr of the Renaissance.* London, 1899; reprint, Nieuwkoop, 1964.

Desmaiseaux, Pierre. "Dolet." In Bayle, *Dictionnaire historique*, II, 984–987.

Douen, O. "Etienne Dolet, ses opinions religieuses." *BSHPF*, 30 (1881), 337–355, 385–408.

Febvre, Lucien. "Dolet propagateur de l'Evangile." *Bibliothèque d'Humanisme et Renaissance*, 6 (1945), 98–170. Reprinted in *Au coeur religieux du XVIe siècle*, pp. 172–224. Trans. as "Dolet, Propagator of the Gospel" in *A New Kind of History*, pp. 108–159.

Maittaire, Michael. "Dolet." In *Annales typographici*, III, part 1, pp. 9–113.

Née de la Rochelle, Jean François. *Vie d'Etienne Dolet.* Paris, 1779.

Procès d'Estienne Dolet. Paris, 1836.

Sturel, René. "Notes sur Etienne Dolet d'après des inédits." *RSS*, 1 (1913), 55–98.

Du Bellay, Guillaume

Bourrilly, V.-L. *Guillaume du Bellay, Seigneur de Langey.* Paris, 1904.

——— "Rabelais et la mort de Guillaume du Bellay." *RER*, 2 (1904), 51–54.

Du Bellay, Jean

Jo. Bellaii Cardinalis . . . poemata aliquot . . . ad eundem Matisconum Pontificem. In same volume as Odes of Macrinus. Paris: ex officina Rob. Stephani, 1546.

Bourrilly, V.-L. "Le Cardinal Jean du Bellay en Italie (juin 1535–mars 1536)." *RER*, 5 (1907), 233–285.

Du Bellay, Joachim
  Du Bellay, Joachim. *Oeuvres poétiques*. Ed. Henri Chamard. 6 vols. Paris, 1908–1931.
  Joachimi Bellaii poematum libri IV. Paris: Fred. Morel, 1558.
  Du Bellay, Joachim. *Deffence et illustration de la langue française*. Ed. Henri Chamard. Paris, 1904.
  ——— *The Defence and Illustration of the French Language*. Trans. Gladys M. Turquet. London, 1939.
Ducher, Gilbert
  Gilberti Ducherii Vultonis Aquapersani epigrammaton libri duo. Lyon: apud Seb. Gryphium, 1538.
Du Fail, Noël
  Du Fail, Noël. *Oeuvres facétieuses*. Ed. J. Assézat. 2 vols. Paris, 1874.
  Philipot, Emmanuel. *La Vie et l'oeuvre littéraire de Noël du Fail*. Thèse de doctorat ès lettres, Paris, 1914.
Du Saix, Antoine
  Plattard, Jean. "Frère Antoine du Saix, 'commandeur jambonnier de St. Antoine' de Bourg-en-Bresse." *RER*, 9 (1911), 221–248.
  Texte, Joseph. *De Antonio Saxano*. Thèse de doctorat ès lettres, Paris, 1895.
Erasmus, Desiderius
  Desiderii Erasmi Roterodami opera omnia. Ed. Joannes Clericus. 10 vols. Leyden, 1703–1706; photographic reprint, Hildesheim, 1962.
  Opus epistolarum Des. Erasmi Roterodami. Ed. P. S. Allen and H. M. Allen. 12 vols. Oxford, 1906–1958.
  The Correspondence of Erasmus. Trans. R. A. B. Mynors and D. F. S. Thomson. Vol. I, The Collected Works of Erasmus. Toronto, 1974.
  Förstemann, Joseph, and Otto Günther, eds. *Briefe an Des. Erasmus*. Beihefte zur Zentralblatt für Bibliothekswesen, 27. Leipzig, 1904.
  Erasmus, Desiderius. *Colloquia familiaria*. Ed. O. Holtze. Leipzig, 1872.
  ——— *The Colloquies of Erasmus*. Trans. Craig R. Thompson. Chicago, 1965.
  Smith, Preserved. *A Key to the Colloquies of Erasmus*. Harvard Theological Studies. Cambridge, Mass., 1927.
  Erasmus, Desiderius. *The Enchiridion of Erasmus*. Trans. Raymond Himelick. Bloomington, Ind., 1963.
  Bataillon, Marcel. *Erasme et la cour de Portugal*. Coimbra, 1927.
  ——— *Erasme et l'Espagne, recherches sur l'histoire spirituelle du XVIᵉ siècle*. Paris, 1937.
  ——— *Les Portugais contre Erasme à l'assemblée théologique de Valladolid, 1527*. Coimbra, 1928.
  Boussey, Armand. "Erasme à Besançon." *Bulletin de l'Académie des Sciences, Belles-Lettres, et Arts de Besançon*, 127 (1896), 48.
  Carvajal, Luis de. *Apologia monasticae religionis diluens nugas Erasmi . . .* Salamanca, 1528.
  Delaruelle, Louis. "Ce que Rabelais doit à Erasme et à Budé." *Revue d'Histoire Littéraire de la France*, 11 (1904), 220–262.

Febvre, Lucien. "Augustin Renaudet et ses 'Etudes Erasmiennes.' " *Annales d'Histoire Sociale*, 1 (1939), 407-410.

——— "Une Conquête de l'histoire: l'Espagne d'Erasme." *Annales d'Histoire Sociale*, 1 (1939), 28-42. In *Au coeur religieux du XVIᵉ siècle*, pp. 93-111.

——— "Crises et figures religieuses: du Modernisme à Erasmisme." *Revue de Synthèse*, 1 (1931), 357-376. In *Au coeur religieux du XVIᵉ siècle*, pp. 122-136.

——— "L'Erasmisme en Espagne." *Revue de Synthèse Historique*, 44 (1927), 153-155.

Ferrère, F. "Erasme et le cicéronianisme au XVIᵉ siècle." *Revue de l'Agenais*, 51 (1924), 176-182, 283-294, 342-357.

Heulhard, Arthur. *Une Lettre fameuse, Rabelais à Erasme*. Paris, 1904.

Mann, Margaret. *Erasme et les débuts de la Réforme française*. Paris, 1934.

Mestwerdt, Paul. *Die Anfänge des Erasmus, Humanismus und Devotio Moderna*. Studien zur Kultur und Geschichte der Reformation, Verein für Reformationsgeschichte. Leipzig, 1917.

Pineau, Jean Baptiste. *Erasme, sa pensée religieuse*. Thèse de doctorat ès lettres, Paris, 1924.

Renaudet, Augustin. *Erasme, sa pensée religieuse et son action d'après sa correspondance (1518-1521)*. Paris, 1926.

——— *Etudes Erasmiennes (1521-1529)*. Paris, 1939.

Smith, W. F. "Rabelais et Erasme." *RER*, 6 (1908), 375-378.

Thuasne, Louis. "Un Passage de la correspondance d'Erasme rapproché de passages similaires de Rabelais." *Revue des Bibliothèques*, 14 (1904), 290-304.

Ziesing, Théodore. *Erasme ou Salignac?* Paris, 1887.

Estienne, Henri

   Estienne, Henri. *Apologie pour Hérodote*. Ed. P. Ristelhuber. 2 vols. Liseux, 1879.

   Clément, Louis. *Henri Estienne et son oeuvre française*. Thèse de doctorat ès lettres, Paris, 1898.

   Lefranc, Abel. "Rabelais et les Estienne; le procès du Cymbalum de Bonaventure des Périers." *RSS*, 15 (1928), 356-366.

Estienne, Robert

   In Evangelium secundum Matthaeum, Marcum et Lucam, commentarii ex ecclesiasticis scriptoribus collecti. Geneva: Oliva Roberti Stephani, 1553.

Fabre, Antoine

   Fabre, Antoine. *Extraict ou recueil des isles nouvellement trouvées en la grand mer océane*. Paris: Colines, 1533.

Fierabras

   Fierabras. Ed. Auguste Kroeber and Gustave Servois. Paris, 1860.

   The Lyf of the Noble and Crysten Prynce, Charles the Grete. Trans. William Caxton. Ed. Sidney J. H. Herrtage. Part I. London, 1880.

The Four Sons of Aymon
   Les Quatre Fils Aymon. Lyon: Jean de Vingle, 1497.
   Renaud of Montauban. Ed. Robert Steel. London, 1897.
Froissart, Jean
   Oeuvres de Froissart: poésies. Ed. Auguste Scheler. 3 vols. Brussels, 1870–1872.
Góis, Damião de
   Bataillon, Marcel. *Le Cosmopolitisme de Damião de Góis.* Paris, n.d.
Gouvea, André de
   Bataillon, Marcel. "Sur André de Gouvea, principal du Collège de Guyenne." *O Instituto,* 78 (1929), 1–19.
Gouvea, Antonio de
   Antonii Goveani Lusitani epigrammaton libri duo. Lyon: apud Seb. Gryphium, 1539.
   Antonii Goveani epigrammata. Ejusdem epistolae quatuor. Lyon: apud Seb. Gryphium, 1540.
   Antonii Goveani pro Aristotele responsio adversus Petri Rami calumnias. Paris: apud S. Colinoeum, 1543.
   Antonii Goveani opera juridica, philologica, philosophica. Ed. Jacobus van Vaassen. Rotterdam, 1766.
   Mugnier, François. *Antoine Govéan.* Paris, 1901.
Gouvea, Diogo de
   Bataillon, Marcel. *Un Document portugais sur les origines de la Compagnie de Jésus.* Paris, 1930.
Guicciardini, Francesco
   Guicciardini, Francesco. *La Storia d'Italia.* Ed. Alessandro Gherardi. 4 vols. Florence, 1919.
   ———— *The History of Italy.* Trans. Sidney Alexander. New York and London, 1969.
Guicciardini, Ludovico
   Guicciardini, Ludovico. *Hore di recreazione.* Venice, 1594.
Héroët, Antoine
   Héroët, Antoine. *Oeuvres poétiques.* Ed. Ferdinand Gohin. Paris, 1909.
   Larbaud, Valéry. *Notes sur Antoine Héroët et Jean de Lingendes.* Paris, 1927. Reprinted in Larbaud, . . .*Ce vice impuni, la lecture* . . . *Domaine française* (Paris, 1941).
La Borderie, Bertrand de
   Livingston, Charles H. "Un Disciple de Clément Marot: Bertrand de La Borderie." *RSS,* 16 (1929), 219–282.
Machiavelli, Niccolò
   Renaudet, Augustin. *Machiavel, étude historique des doctrines politiques.* Paris, 1942.
Margaret of Navarre
   Les Marguerites de la Marguerite des princesses. Ed. Félix Frank. 4 vols. Paris, 1873.
   Les Dernières Poésies de Marguerite de Navarre. Ed. Abel Lefranc. Paris, 1896.

L'Heptaméron des nouvelles de Marguerite d'Angoulême, reine de Navarre. Société des bibliophiles français. 3 vols. Paris, 1853–54.

L'Heptaméron des nouvelles de Marguerite de Navarre. Ed. Antoine Le Roux de Lincey and Anatole de Montaiglon. 4 vols. Paris, 1880.

The Heptameron of the Tales of Margaret Queen of Navarre. 2 vols. London, 1903.

Becker, Philip-August. "Marguerite, duchesse d'Alençon, et Guillaume Briçonnet, évêque de Meaux, d'après leur correspondance inédite (1521–1524)." *BSHPF,* 49 (1900), 393–477, 661–667.

Febvre, Lucien. *Autour de l'Heptaméron; amour sacré, amour profane.* Paris, 1944.

Jourda, Pierre. *Marguerite d'Angoulême, duchesse d'Alençon, reine de Navarre (1492–1549).* 2 vols. Paris, 1930.

——— "Le Mécénat de Marguerite de Navarre." *RSS,* 18 (1931), 253–271.

——— *Répertoire analytique et chronologique de la correspondance de Marguerite d'Angoulême.* Paris, 1930.

——— "Tableau chronologique des publications de Marguerite de Navarre." *RSS,* 12 (1925), 209–255.

Lefranc, Abel. "Les Idées religieuses de Marguerite de Navarre d'après son oeuvre poétique." *BSHPF,* 46 (1897), 7–30, 72–84, 137–148, 295–311, 418–442.

——— "Marguerite de Navarre et le Platonisme de la Renaissance." *Bibliothèque de l'Ecole des Chartes,* 58 (1897), 259–292; 59 (1898), 712–757. Reprinted in Lefranc, *Grands écrivains de la Renaissance,* pp. 139–249.

Marie de France

Die Lais der Marie de France. Ed. Karl Warnke. 3rd ed. Halle, 1925.

Marnix, Philippe de, Seigneur de Sainte-Aldegonde

Cohen, Gustave. "Rabelais et Marnix de Sainte-Aldegonde." *RER,* 6 (1908), 64–65.

Delboulle, A. "Marnix de Sainte-Aldegonde plagiaire de Rabelais." *Revue d'Histoire Littéraire de la France,* 3 (1896), 440–443.

Marot, Clément

Les Oeuvres de Clément Marot de Cahors en Quercy. Ed. Georges Guiffrey. 5 vols. Paris, 1875–1931; photographic reprint, Geneva, 1969.

Marot, Clément. *Oeuvres complètes.* Ed. Pierre Jannet. 4 vols. Paris, 1873–1876.

Becker, Philip-August. *Clement Marot, sein Leben und seine Dichtung.* Sächsische Forschungsinstitut, Leipzig. Romanische Abteilung, 1. Munich, 1926.

——— *Clement Marots Psalmenübersetzung.* Berichte über die Verhandlungen des sächsische Akademie der Wissenschaften, Leipzig. Philosophisch-historische Klasse, 72, no. 1. Leipzig, 1921.

Pannier, Jacques. "Une Première Edition (?) des psaumes de Marot, imprimée par Etienne Dolet." *BSHPF,* 78 (1929), 238–240.

Plattard, Jean. *Marot, sa carrière poétique, son oeuvre.* Paris, 1938.

Villey, Pierre. "Recherches sur la chronologie des oeuvres de Marot." *Bulletin du Bibliophile et du Bibliothécaire* (1920), 185-209, 238-249; (1921), 49-61, 101-117, 171-188, 226-252, 272-287; (1922), 263-271, 311-317, 372-388, 423-432; (1923), 48-54.

―――― "Tableau chronologique des publications de Marot." *RSS*, 7 (1920), 46-97, 206-234; 8 (1921), 80-110, 157-211.

Weiss, Nathanaël. "Clément Marot, Ronsard, d'après quelques publications récentes." *BSHPF*, 74 (1925), 360-371.

Montaigne, Michel Eyquem de

The Complete Essays of Montaigne. Trans. Donald M. Frame. Stanford, Calif., 1958.

More, Thomas

De optimo reip. statu deque nova insula Utopia libellus . . . Thomae Mori . . . Basel: Froben, 1518.

More, Thomas. *L'Utopie ou le traité de la meilleure forme du gouvernement.* Latin text, ed. Marie Delcourt. Paris, 1936.

Bremond, Henri. *Thomas More.* Paris, 1904.

Dermenghem, Emile. *Thomas Morus et les Utopistes de la Renaissance.* Paris, 1927.

Omphal, Jakob (Omphalius)

De elocutionis imitatione ac apparatu liber unus, auctore Jac. Omphalio jurecons. ad Cardinalem Bellaium Episco. Parisiensem. Paris: apud Simonem Colinoeum, 1537.

Omphal, Jakob. *Epistolae aliquot familiares.* (Following *De elocutionis imitatione . . .*) Cologne: Theod. Baumianus, 1580.

Pasquier, Etienne

Pasquier, Etienne. *Les Oeuvres contenant ses Recherches de la France, etc.* 2 vols. Amsterdam, 1723.

Pellicier, Guillaume

Zeller, Jean. *La Diplomatie française d'après la correspondance de Guillaume Pellicier, ambassadeur à Venise.* Paris, 1881.

Puy-Herbaut, Gabriel du

Gabrielis Putherbei Turonici, professione Fontebreldaei, Theotimus sive de tollendis et expungendis malis libris, iis praecipue quos vix incolumi fide ac pietate plerique legere queant, libri III. Paris: apud Joannem Roigny, 1549.

Ronsard, Pierre de

Ronsard, Pierre de. *Oeuvres complètes.* Ed. Prosper Blanchemain. 8 vols. Paris, 1855-1867.

―――― *Oeuvres complètes.* Ed. Paul Laumonier. 18 vols. Paris, 1914-1967.

―――― *Hymne des daimons.* Ed. Albert-Marie Schmidt. Paris, 1939.

Page, Curtis Hidden, trans. *Songs and Sonnets of Pierre de Ronsard.* Boston and New York, 1924.

Busson, Henri. "Sur la philosophie de Ronsard." *Revue des Cours et Conférences,* 31 (1929-30), 32-48, 172-185.

Laumonier, Paul. "L'Epitaphe de Rabelais par Ronsard." *RER,* 1 (1903), 205-216.

Schweinitz, Margaret de. *Les Epitaphes de Ronsard, étude historique et littéraire.* Thèse de doctorat ès lettres, Paris, 1925.

Vaganay, Hugues. "La Mort de Rabelais et Ronsard." *RER*, 1 (1903), 143–150, 204.

Rosset, Pierre

Petri Rosseti poetae laureati Christus, nunc primum in lucem editus. Paris: apud Sim. Colinaeum, 1534.

P. Rosseti, poetae laureati, Paulus nunc denuo in lucem aeditus, et emaculatius explicatus a F. H... Sussannaeo. Paris: ap. Nicol. Buffet, 1537.

Petri Rosseti poetae laureati Christus. 2d ed. Paris: ap. Simonem Colinaeum, 1543.

Rousselet, Claude

Claudii Rosseletti jurisconsulti patritiique Lugdunensis epigrammata. Lyon: apud Seb. Gryphium, 1537.

Sainte-Marthe, Charles de

La Poésie françoise de Charles de Saincte Marthe, natif de Fontevrault en Poictou, divisée en trois livres ... Plus un livre de ses amys. Lyon: chez le Prince, 1540.

Lefranc, Abel. "Picrochole et Gaucher de Sainte-Marthe." *RER*, 3 (1905), 241–252.

———— "Rabelais, les Sainte-Marthe et l'enraigé Putherbe." *RER*, 4 (1906), 335–348.

"Pièces rélatives au procès de Gaucher de Sainte-Marthe avec les marchands fréquentant la rivière de Loire." *RER*, 9 (1911), 133–140.

Ruutz-Rees, Caroline. *Charles de Sainte-Marthe (1512–1555).* New York, 1910.

Salmon, Jean (known as Macrin)

Salmonii Macrini Juliodunensis lyricorum libri duo. Epithalamiorum liber unus. Paris: ex officina Gerardi Morrhii Campensis, 1531.

Salmonii Macrini Juliodunensis, cubicularii regii, odarum libri VI. Lyon: Seb. Gryphius excud., 1537.

Salmonii Macrini Juliodunen. cubicularii regii hymnorum libri sex ad Jo. Bellaium S. R. E. Cardinalem ampliss. Paris: ex officina Roberti Stephani, 1537.

Salmonii Macrini Juliodunensis odarum libri tres ad P. Castellanum Pontificem Matisconensem. Jo. Bellaii Cardinalis ... poemata aliquot ... ad eundem Matisconum Pontificem. Paris: ex officina Rob. Stephani, 1546.

Salmonii Macrini Juliodunensis cubicularii regii epigrammatum libri duo. Poitiers: ex officina Marnefiorum fratrum, 1548.

Salmonii Macrini Juliodunensis cubicularii regii epitome vitae Domini Nostri Jesu Christi ad Margaritam Valesiam. Paris: ex typographia Matthaei Davidis, via Amygdalium, 1549.

Scaliger, Julius Caesar

Julii Caesaris Scaligeri oratio pro M. Tullio Cicerone contra Des. Erasmum Rot. N.p.: Venundantur a Vidoveo, 1531.

Julii Caesaris Scaligeri novorum epigrammatum liber unicus. Ejusdem hymni duo. Ejusdem Diva Ludovica Sabaudia. Paris: apud Michaelum Vascosanum, 1533.

Julii Caesaris Scaligeri adversus Des. Erasmi Rot. dialogum Ciceronianum oratio secunda. Paris: P. Vidouaeus, 1537.

Julii Caesaris Scaligeri in luctu filii oratio. Lyon: apud Seb. Gryphium, 1538.

Hippocratis liber de somniis cum Julii Caesaris Scaligeri commentariis. Lyon: apud Seb. Gryphium, 1539.

Julii Caesaris Scaligeri heroes. Lyon: apud Seb. Gryphium, 1539.

Julii Caesaris Scaligeri liber de comicis dimensionibus. Lyon: apud Seb. Gryphium, 1539.

Julii Caesaris Scaligeri de causis linguae latinae libri tredecim. Lyon: apud S. Gryphium, 1540.

Julii Caesaris Scaligeri poematia. Lyon: apud G. et M. Beringos fratres, 1546.

Julii Caesaris Scaligeri exotericarum exercitationum lib. XV de subtilitate ad Hier. Cardanum. Paris: Fred. Morellus, 1554.

Julii Caesaris Scaligeri viri clarissimi poemata in duas partes divisa, pleraque omnia in publicum iam primum prodeunt: reliqua vero quam ante emendatius edita sunt . . . 2 vols. in 1. N.p., 1574.

Julii Caesaris Scaligeri epistolae et orationes, nunquam ante hac excusae. Antwerp: Ex officina Plantiniana, apud Christophorum Raphalangium, 1600.

Julii Caesaris Scaligeri adversus Desid. Erasmum orationes duae eloquentiae romanae vindices. 4 vols. in 1. Toulouse: typ. R. Colomerii, 1620.

Electa Scaligerana, h. e. Julii Caesaris Scaligeri sententiae. Hanover, 1624.

"Julii Caesaris Scaligeri epistolia duo . . . nunc primum edita, cura . . . Joachimi Morsi." In Schelhorn, *Amoenitates literariae*, I, 269–283.

Scaliger, Julius Caesar. "Epistolae nonnullae ex MSto Bibliothecae Zach. Conr. ab Uffenbach." In Schelhorn, *Amoenitates literariae*, VI, 508–528; VIII, 554–621.

Scaliger, Joseph. *Scaligerana ou bons mots . . . de J. Scaliger.* Cologne, 1695.

De Santi, L. "Le Diplôme de Jules César Scaliger." *Mémoires de l'Académie de Science, Inscriptions, et Belles-Lettres de Toulouse* (1921), 93–113.

——— "Rabelais et J. C. Scaliger." *RER*, 3 (1905), 12–44; 4 (1906), 28–44.

Magen, Adolphe. *Documents sur J. C. Scaliger.* Agen, 1873.

Scève, Maurice

Oeuvres poétiques complètes de Maurice Scève. Ed. Bertrand Guégan. Paris, 1927.

Scève, Maurice. *Délie object de plus haulte vertu.* Ed. Eugène Parturier. Paris, 1916.

Baur, Albert. *Maurice Scève et la Renaissance lyonnaise.* Paris, 1906.

Larbaud, Valéry. *Notes sur Maurice Scève.* Paris, 1925. Reprinted in Larbaud, . . . *Ce vice impuni, la lecture . . . Domaine français* (Paris, 1941).

Parturier, Eugène. "Maurice Scève et le Petit Oeuvre d'amour de 1537." *RSS,* 17 (1930), 298–311.

Sussanneau, Hubert

Dictionarium ciceronianum authore Huberto Sussannaeo suessionensi. Epigrammatum eiusdem libellus. Paris: apud Simonem Colinaeum, 1536.

Huberti Sussannei, legum et medicinae doctoris, ludorum libri nunc recens conditi atque aediti. Paris: apud S. Colinaeum, 1538.

Quantitates Alexandri Galli, vulgo de Villa Dei, correctione adhibita ab Huberto Sussannaeo locupletatae. Additus est elegiarum eiusdem liber. Paris: S. de Colines, 1542.

Tartas, Jean de

Courteault, Paul. "Le Premier Principal du Collège de Guienne." In *Mélanges offerts à M. Abel Lefranc,* pp. 234–245.

Tiraqueau, André

Barat, J. "L'Influence de Tiraqueau sur Rabelais." *RER,* 3 (1905), 138–155, 253–270.

Bréjon, Jacques. *Un Jurisconsulte de la Renaissance, André Tiraqueau (1488–1558).* Paris, 1937.

Plattard, Jean. "Tiraqueau et Rabelais." *RER,* 4 (1906), 384–389.

Polain, M.-L. "Appendice bibliographique à 'L'Influence de Tiraqueau sur Rabelais.' " *RER,* 3 (1905), 271–275.

Toutain, Charles

Toutain, Charles. *La Tragédie d'Agamemnon, avec deus livres de chants de philosophie et d'amour.* Paris: Chès Martin le Jeune, 1557.

Villon, François

Villon, François. *Oeuvres.* Ed. Louis Thuasne. Paris, 1923.

The Poems of François Villon. Trans. Galway Kinnell. Boston, 1977.

Thuasne, Louis. *Rabelais et Villon.* Paris, 1911.

Visagier, Jean (Vulteius)

Joannis Vultei Remensis epigrammatum libri II. Lyon: apud S. Gryphium, 1536.

Joannis Vultei Remensis epigrammaton libri III. Ejusdem Xenia. Lyon: apud Michaelem Parmanterium, 1537.

Jo. Vultei Rhemensis hendecasyllaborum libri quatuor. Paris: apud Simonem Colinaeum, 1538.

Joan. Vulteii Rhemi inscriptionum libri duo. Xeniorum libellus. Paris: apud Sim. Colinaeum, 1538.

B., M. "Quel est le véritable nom du poète remois . . . ?" *Revue d'Histoire Littéraire de la France,* 1 (1894), 530.

Bourilly, V.-L. "Documents inédits: J. Voulté et le Cardinal du Bellay." *Revue de la Renaissance,* 2 (1902), 192–195.

B. Philosophers and Scholars

Agrippa, Henry Cornelius

> *Splendidae nobilitatis viri et armatae militiae equitis aurati ac utriusque juris doctoris sacrae caesareae majestatis a consiliis et archivis inditiarii Henrici Cornelii Agrippae ab Nettesheym de incertitudine et vanitate scientiarum et artium atque excellentia verbi Dei declamatio.* Antwerp: Joan-Grapheus excudebat, 1530.

Agrippa, Henry Cornelius. *Déclamation sur l'incertitude, vanité, et abus des sciences . . .* Trans. Louis Turquet de Mayerne. N.p.: par Jean Durand, 1582.

> *Henrici Cor. Agrippae ab Nettesheym a consiliis et archivis inditiarii sacrae cesareae majestatis de occulta philosophia libri tres.* Antwerp: Joan. Grapheus excudebat, 1531.

> *H. Corn. Agrippae . . . opera in duos tomos digesta. Cum figuris.* Lyon: .per Beringos fratres, [1531].

> *Henrici Cornelii Agrippae ab Nettesheym a consiliis et archivis inditiarii sacrae cesareae majestatis de occulta philosophia libri tres.* [Cologne], 1533.

Chapuys, Eustache. *Correspondance avec Henri Cornelius Agrippa de Nettesheim.* Ed. Léon Charvet. Lyon and Geneva, 1875.

Daguet, Alexandre. *Agrippa chez les Suisses.* Paris, 1856.

Lefranc, Abel. "Rabelais et Corneille Agrippa." In *Mélanges offerts à M. Emile Picot*, II, 477–486.

Maillet-Guy, Luc. "Henri Corneille Agrippa, sa famille, ses relations avec Saint-Antoine de Viennois." *Bulletin de la Société d'Archéologie et de Statistique de la Drôme*, 60 (1926), 120–144, 201–225.

Orsier, Joseph. *Henri Cornelis Agrippa, sa vie et son oeuvre d'après sa correspondance.* Paris, 1911.

Prost, Auguste. *Les Sciences et les arts occultes au XVIᵉ siècle, Corneille Agrippa, sa vie et ses oeuvres.* 2 vols. Paris, 1881–1882.

Saint-Genois, Jules de. *Recherches sur . . . Corneille de Schipper.* Ghent, 1856.

Belon, Pierre

Delaunay, Paul. "Un Adversaire de la Réforme, les idées religieuses de Pierre Belon, du Mans." *Bulletin de la Commission Historique et Archéologique de la Mayenne*, 38 (1922), 97–117.

——— "L'Aventureuse Existence de Pierre Belon du Mans." *RSS*, 9 (1922), 251–268; 10 (1923), 1–34, 125–147; 11 (1924), 30–48, 222–232; 12 (1925), 78–97, 256–282. Reprinted as a book, Paris, 1926.

Bérault, Nicholas

Delaruelle, Louis. "Nicole Bérault." *Revue des Bibliothèques*, 12 (1902), 420–445.

——— *Nicole Bérault. Publications du Musée Belge: Revue de Philologie Classique*, 8. Louvain and Paris, 1909.

——— "Notes complémentaires sur deux humanistes (Bérault et Lascaris)." *RSS*, 15 (1928), 311–323.

Bodin, Jean

Colloque de Jean Bodin des secrets cachez des choses sublimes entre sept sçavans qui sont de differens sentimens. Trans. of extracts from *Heptaplomeres.* Ed. Roger Chauviré. Paris, 1914.

Bezold, Friedrich von. "Jean Bodins Colloquium Heptaplomeres und das Atheismus des sechszehnten Jahrhunderts." *Historische Zeitschrift,* ser. 3, 17 (1914), 260-315.

Chauviré, Roger. *Jean Bodin, auteur de la République.* Paris, 1914.

————— "La Pensée religieuse de Jean Bodin (d'après des documents nouveaux)." *La Province d'Anjou,* 4 (1929), 433-451.

Diecman, L. J. *De naturalismo cum aliorum, tum maxime Jo. Bodini schediasma inaugurale.* Leipzig, 1684. Discussed by Bayle in his *Nouvelles de la république des lettres;* in *Oeuvres diverses,* I, 65 ff.

Febvre, Lucien. "L'Universalisme de Jean Bodin." *Revue de Synthèse,* 7 (1934), 165-168.

Hauser, Henri. "Un Précurseur: Jean Bodin, Angevin (1529 ou 1530-1596)." *Annales d'Histoire Economique et Sociale,* 3 (1931), 379-387.

Mesnard, Pierre. "La Pensée religieuse de Jean Bodin." *RSS,* 16 (1929), 77-121.

Ponthieux, A. "Quelques Documents inédits sur Jean Bodin." *RSS,* 15 (1938), 56-99.

Bouelles, Charles de

Bouelles, Charles de. *Liber de sapiente.* Ed. Raymond Klibansky. In Cassirer, *Individuum und Kosmos,* pp. 299-412.

Campanella, Tommaso

Blanchet, Léon. *Campanella.* Paris, 1920.

Cardano, Geronimo

Hieronymi Cardani Mediolanensis medici de subtilitate libri XXI. Basel: ex officina Petrina, 1560. (The copy in the Bibliothèque Nationale is the one owned by Ronsard.)

Cardan, Jerome. *The Book of My Life.* Trans. Jean Stoner. New York, 1930.

Copernicus, Nicholas

Copernicus, Nicholas. *De revolutionibus orbium coelestium libri VI.* Nuremberg: Joh. Petreius, 1543.

————— *Des Révolutions des orbes célestes.* Trans. Alexandre Koyré. Paris, 1934.

Rheticus, Georg Joachim. *Ad clariss. v. D. Jo. Schonerum de libris revolutionum Nic. Copernici narratio prima.* Gdansk, 1540.

Plattard, Jean. "Le Système de Copernic dans la littérature française au XVIᵉ siècle." *RSS,* 1 (1913), 220-237.

Prowe, Leopold. *Nicolaus Coppernicus.* 2 vols. in 3. Berlin, 1883-1884.

Cusa, Nicholas of

Cusa, Nicholas of. *Liber de mente.* Ed. Joachim Ritter. In Cassirer, *Individuum und Kosmos,* pp. 204-297.

————— *De concordantia catholica libri III.* Facsimile ed. Bonn, 1928.

—— *De docta ignorantia.* Ed. Paolo Rotta. Classici della filosofia moderna . . . a cura di B. Croce e G. Gentile, 19. Bari, 1913.

—— *De la docte ignorance.* Trans. L. Moulinier, with intro. by Abel Rey. Paris, 1930.

Rotta, Paolo. *Il cardinale Nicolo di Cusa, la vita ed il pensiero.* Pubblicazioni della Università cattolica del Sacro Cuore, ser. 1: scienze filosofiche, 12. Milan, 1928.

Vansteenberghe, Edmond. *Le Cardinal Nicolas de Cues.* Paris, 1920; reprint, Frankfurt-am-Main, 1963.

Fernel, Jean

Fernel, Jean. *Universa medicina.* Paris: Andreas Wechel, 1567.

Figard, L. *Un Médecin philosophe au XVIe siècle: étude sur la psychologie de Jean Fernel.* Paris, 1903.

Sherrington, Charles. *The Endeavour of Jean Fernel.* Cambridge, 1946.

Ficino, Marsilio

Festugière, Jean. "La Philosophie de l'amour de Marcile Ficin et son influence sur la littérature française au XVIe siècle." *Revista da Universidade de Coimbra,* 8 (1922), 396–564. Reprinted in *Etudes de Philosophie Médiévale,* 31 (1941), 1–168.

Pusino, Ivan. "Ficinos und Picos religio-philosophische Anschauungen." *Zeitschrift für Kirchengeschichte,* 44 (1925), 504–543.

Leonardo de Vinci

Duhem, Pierre. *Léonard da Vinci, ceux qu'il a lus, ceux qui l'ont lu.* Paris, 1906.

Séailles, Gabriel. *Léonard de Vinci.* 4th ed. Paris, 1912.

Palissy, Bernard

Palissy, Bernard. *Oeuvres.* Ed. Benjamin Fillon. 2 vols. Paris, 1888.

The Admirable Discourses of Bernard Palissy. Trans. Aurèle La Rocque. Urbana, Ill., 1957.

Paracelsus, Philippus Aureolus

Koyré, Alexandre. "Paracelse." *Revue d'Histoire et de Philosophie Religieuse,* 13 (1933), 46–75, 145–163.

Paré, Ambroise

Oeuvres complètes d'Ambroise Paré. Ed. J. F. Malgaigne. 3 vols. Paris, 1840–1841.

Chaussade, M. A. "Ambroise Paré." *Bulletin de la Commission Historique et Archéologique de la Mayenne,* 2d ser., 43 (1927), 290–316; 44 (1928), 117–138.

—— "La Méthode scientifique d'Ambroise Paré." *Revue de Synthèse Historique,* 44 (1927), 35–50.

Pico della Mirandola, Giovanni

Opera omnia J. Pici. 2 vols. Basel: Henric Petri, 1572.

Pico della Mirandola, Giovanni. "Oration on the Dignity of Man." Trans. Elizabeth Livermore Forbes. In Cassirer et al., *The Renaissance Philosophy of Man,* pp. 223–254.

Dorez, Léon, and Louis Thuasne. *Pic de la Mirandole en France.* Paris, 1897.

Liebert, Arthur. *Giovanni Pico de la Mirandola: Ausgewählte Schriften.* Jena, 1905.

Pusino, Ivan. "Der Einfluss Picos auf Erasmus." *Zeitschrift für Kirchengeschichte,* 46 (1928), 75–96.

Semprini, Giovanni. *Pico della Mirandola.* Todi, 1921.

Pomponazzi, Pietro

Pomponatii opera. Basel: Henric Petri, 1567.

Pomponazzi, Pietro. *De immortalitate animae.* Bologna: per Justinianum Ruberiensem, 1516.

—— *De immortalitate animae.* Ed. Giovanni Gentile. Messina, 1925.

—— *Apologia pro suo tractatu de immortalitate animae.* Bologna, 1518.

—— *Defensorium, sive responsiones ad Aug. Niphum.* Bologna, 1519.

—— *Les Causes des merveilles de la nature, ou les Enchantements.* Trans. Henri Busson. Paris, 1930.

—— "On the Immortality of the Soul." Trans. William Henry Hay II. In Cassirer et al., *The Renaissance Philosophy of Man,* pp. 280–381.

Busson, Henri. "Pomponazzi." *Revue de Littérature Comparée,* 9 (1929), 308–347.

Fiorentino, Francesco. *Pietro Pomponazzi, studi storici su la scuola bolognesa e padovana del secolo XVI.* Florence, 1868.

Nifo, Agostino. *De immortalitate animae libellus.* Venice, 1518.

Postel, Guillaume

Postel, Guillaume. *De originibus, seu de hebraicae linguae et gentis antiquitate deque variarum linguarum affinitate liber.* Paris: apud Dionysium Lescuier, 1538.

—— *Grammatica arabica.* Paris: apud . . . P. Gromorsium, [1538].

De rationibus Spiritus Sancti lib. II, Gulielmo Postello Barentonio authore. Paris: excudebat ipsi authori P. Gromorsius, 1543.

Postel, Guillaume. *Alcorani seu legis Mahometi, et Evangelistarum concordiae liber, in quo de calamitatibus orbi christiano imminentibus tractatu. Additus est libellus de universalis conversionis judicio.* Paris: excudebat P. Gromorsius, 1543.

Quatuor librorum de orbis terrae concordia primus, Gulielmo Postello Barentonio math. prof. regio authore. Paris: excudebat ipsi authori Petrus Gromorsus, [1543].

De orbis terrae concordia libri quatuor . . . Gulielmo Postello Barentonio, mathematum in academia lutetiana professore regio, authore. [Basel: Oporin, 1544.]

Eversio falsorum Aristotelis dogmatum, authore D. Justino Martyre . . . Gulielmo Postello in tenebrarum Babylonicarum dispulsionem interprete. Paris: apud Seb. Nivellium, 1552.

Liber de causis seu de principiis et originibus naturae utriusque . . . Contra atheos et huius larvae Babylonicae alumnos qui suae favent impietati ex magnorum authorum perversione . . . authore G. Postello. Paris: apud Seb. Nivellium, 1552.

Postel, Guillaume. *Les Très-Merveilleuses Victoires des femmes du nou-veau-monde; et comment elles doibvent à tout le monde par raison commander, & mesme à ceulx qui auront la monarchie du monde vieil. A Madame Marguerite de France . . . La Doctrine du siècle doré . . .* Paris: chez Jehan Ruelle, 1553.

———— *Les Très-Merveilleuses Victoires des femmes du nouveau-monde suivi de la doctrine du siècle doré . . .* With a biographical and bibli-ographical note by Gustave Brunet. Turin, 1869.

———— *Cosmographicae disciplinae compendium, in suum finem, hoc est ad divinae Providentiae certissimam demonstrationem, conductum.* Basel: Oporinus, 1561.

Desbillons, François. *Nouveaux éclaircissements sur G. Postel.* Liège, 1773.

Kvacala, Jan. *Postelliana; urkundliche Beiträge zur Geschichte der Mys-tik in Reformationszeitalter.* Acta et commentationes Imp. universi-tatis jurievensis (olim dorpatensis), 23, no. 9. Tartu, 1915.

———— "Wilhelm Postell; seine Geistesart und seine Reformgedanken." *Archiv für Reformationsgeschichte,* 9 (1911–12), 285–330; 11 (1914), 200–227; 15 (1918), 157–203.

Lefranc, Abel. "Rabelais et Postel." *RSS,* 1 (1913), 259.

Ravaisse, Paul. "Un Ex-libris de Guillaume Postel." In *Mélanges offerts à M. Emile Picot,* I, 315–333.

Weill, Georges. *De Guilelmi Postelli vita et indole.* Paris, 1892.

Ramus, Petrus

Waddington, Charles Tzaunt. *Ramus (Pierre de La Ramée), sa vie, ses écrits et ses opinions.* Paris, 1855.

Telesio, Bernardino

Fiorentino, Francesco. *Bernardino Telesio, ossia studi storici su l'idea della natura nel risorgimento italiano.* 2 vols. Florence, 1872–1874. Review by Adolphe Franck in *Journal des Savants* (1873), 548–560, 687–701.

Gentile, Giovanni. *Bernardino Telesio.* Bari, 1911.

IV. Rabelais's Age

A. Conceptual Problems and Intellectual Life

1. Sixteenth-Century Language and Linguistic Questions

Bloch, Jean-Richard. "Langage d'utilité, langage poétique." In *Encyclopédie française,* XVI, 16′50-8–16′50-16.

Brunot, Ferdinand. *Histoire de la langue française des origines à nos jours.* New ed. 13 vols. Paris, 1966–1979.

———— *La Pensée et la langue.* 2d ed. Paris, 1926.

Darmesteter, Arsène, and Adolphe Hatzfeld. *Le Seizième Siècle en France: tableau de la littérature et de la langue.* 16th ed. Paris, 1934.

Estienne, Robert. *Dictionnaire françois-latin.* Paris: Robert Estienne, 1539.

Huguet, Edmond. *Dictionnaire de la langue française du seizième siècle.* 7 vols. Paris, 1925–1967.

——— *Etude sur la syntaxe de Rabelais comparée à celle des autres prosa-teurs de 1450 à 1550.* Paris, 1894.

——— *Le Langage figuré au seizième siècle.* Paris, 1933.

Lanson, Gustave. *L'Art de la prose.* Paris, 1880; photographic reprint, 1968.

Massebieau, Louis. *Les Colloques scolaires du XVIᵉ siècle et leurs auteurs 1480–1570.* Thèse de doctorat ès lettres, Paris, 1878.

Nève, Joseph. "Proverbes et néologismes dans les sermons de Michel Menot." *RSS,* 7 (1920), 98–122.

Sainéan, Lazare. *La Langue de Rabelais.* 2 vols. Paris, 1922–1923.

Sturel, René. *Jacques Amyot, Traducteur des Vies parallèles de Plutarque.* Paris, 1908.

Wartburg, Walter von. *Evolution et structure de la langue française.* 2d ed. Chicago, 1937.

2. The Middle Ages, the Renaissance, and Humanism

Atkinson, Geoffroy. *Les Nouveaux Horizons de la Renaissance française.* Paris, 1935.

Bloch, Marc. *Feudal Society.* Trans. L. A. Manyon. 2 vols. Chicago, 1961.

Burckhardt, Jacob. *The Civilization of the Renaissance in Italy.* Trans. S. G. C. Middlemore. Many editions.

Didot, Ambroise Firmin. *Alde Manuce et l'hellénisme à Venise.* Paris, 1875.

Febvre, Lucien. "Les Principaux Aspects d'une civilisation: quatre leçons sur la première Renaissance française." *Revue des Cours et Conférences,* 26, 2d ser. (1924–1925), 193–210, 326–340, 398–417, 577–593. Reprinted in Febvre, *Pour une histoire à part entière* (Paris, 1962), pp. 529–603.

——— *Life in Renaissance France.* (Trans. of the preceding work.) Trans. Marian Rothstein. Cambridge, Mass., 1977.

——— "La Renaissance." In *Encyclopédie française,* XVI, 16′10-13–16′12-1.

Gilson, Etienne. *Héloise et Abélard, étude sur le Moyen Age et l'Humanisme.* Paris, 1938.

Huizinga, Johan. *The Waning of the Middle Ages.* Trans. F. Hopman. New York, 1949.

Lot, Ferdinand. *The End of the Ancient World and the Beginnings of the Middle Ages.* Trans. Philip and Mariette Leon. New York, 1961.

Michelet, Jules. *Histoire de France.* 16 vols. VII: *La Renaissance.* VIII: *La Réforme.* Paris, 1898.

Nordström, Johan. *Moyen Age et Renaissance: essai historique.* Trans. from Swedish by T. Hammar. Paris, 1933.

Renaudet, Augustin. *Préréforme et humanisme à Paris pendant les premières guerres d'Italie (1494–1517).* Thèse de doctorat ès lettres, Paris, 1916. 2d ed., Paris, 1954.

Strowski, Fortunat. "La Philosophie de l'homme dans la littérature française." *Revue des Cours et Conférences,* 26 (1924–1925), 1: 3–14, 233–242, 395–403, 490–500, 682–694; 2: 13–25, 289–303; 27 (1925–1926), 1: 20–42, 144–153.

3. Literary History

Besch, Emile. "Les Adaptations en prose des chansons de geste au XVᵉ et au XVIᵉ siècle." *RSS*, 3 (1915), 155–181.

Chinard, Gilbert. *L'Exotisme américain dans la littérature française au XVIᵉ siècle*. Paris, 1911.

Delaruelle, Louis. "L'Etude du grec à Paris de 1514 à 1530." *RSS*, 9 (1922), 132–148.

Gachat d'Artigny, Antoine. *Nouveaux Mémoires d'histoire*. 7 vols. Paris, 1749–1756.

Gilson, Etienne. *Les Idées et les lettres*. 2d ed. Paris, 1955.

Ilvonen, Eero. *Parodie des thèmes pieux dans la littérature française du Moyen Age*. Paris, 1914.

Jacquet, Augustin. *La Vie littéraire dans une ville de province sous Louis XIV*. Paris, 1886.

Lamartine, Alphonse de. *Cours familier de littérature*. 28 vols. Paris, 1856–1869.

Lebègue, Raymond. *La Tragédie religieuse en France. Les débuts (1514–1573)*. Paris, 1929.

Lefranc, Abel. *Grands Ecrivains français de la Renaissance*. Paris, 1914.

Mélanges de littérature, d'histoire et de philologie offerts à Paul Laumonier. Paris, 1935.

Mélanges offerts à M. Abel Lefranc. Paris, 1936.

Mélanges offerts à M. Emile Picot. 2 vols. Paris, 1913.

Murarasu, D. *La Poésie néo-latine et la Renaissance des lettres antiques en France (1500–1549)*. Paris, 1928.

Picot, Emile. "Le Monologue dramatique dans l'ancien théâtre français." *Romania*, 15 (1886), 358–422; 16 (1887), 438–542; 17 (1888), 207–262.

Sainéan, Lazare. *Problèmes littéraires du XVIᵉ siècle*. Paris, 1927.

Senebier, Jean. *Histoire littéraire de Genève*. 3 vols. Geneva, 1786.

Tilley, Arthur. "Les Romans de chevalerie en prose." *RSS*, 6 (1919), 45–63.

Vianey, Joseph. "Les Grands Poètes de la nature en France: Ronsard-La Fontaine." *Revue des Cours et Conférences*, 27 (1925), 3–19.

——— "La Nature dans la poésie française." In *Mélanges de littérature . . . offerts à Paul Laumonier*, pp. 171–188.

Villey, Pierre. *Marot et Rabelais*. Paris, 1923.

Viollet Le Duc, Emmanuel. *Ancien Théâtre français*. 10 vols. Paris, 1854–1857.

4. Intellectual Institutions and Centers

Collignon, Albert. "Le Mécenat du Cardinal Jean de Lorraine (1498–1550)." *Annales de l'Est*, 24 (1910), 7–175.

Dawson, John Charles. *Toulouse in the Renaissance*. New York, 1923.

De Santi, L. "La Réaction universitaire à Toulouse: Blaise d'Auriol." *Mémoires de l'Académie des Sciences, Inscriptions et Belles-Lettres de Toulouse*, 10th ser., 6 (1906), 27–68.

Du Boulay, César Egasse (Bulaeus). *Historia universitatis parisiensis*. 6 vols. Paris, 1665–1673.

Gandilhon, René. *La Nation germanique de l'Université de Bourges.* Bourges, 1936.

Gaullieur, Ernest. *Histoire du Collège de Guyenne.* Paris, 1874.

Irsay, Stephen d'. *Histoire des universités françaises et étrangères.* 2 vols. I: *Moyen Age et Renaissance.* Paris, 1933.

Lefranc, Abel. "Les Commencements du Collège de France, 1529–1544." In *Mélanges d'histoire offerts à Henri Pirenne*, I, 291–306.

———— *Histoire du Collège de France.* Paris, 1893.

Lefranc, Abel, et al., eds. *Le Collège de France (1530–1930), livre jubilaire composé à l'occasion de son quatrième centenaire.* Paris, 1932.

Plattard, Jean. "A l'Ecu de Bâle." *RSS*, 13 (1926), 282–285.

Quicherat, Jules. *Histoire de Sainte Barbe.* 3 vols. Paris, 1860–1864.

Toulouse, Madeleine. *La Nation anglaise-allemande de l'Université de Paris.* Paris, 1939.

5. Art and Iconography

Bibliothèque Nationale. *La Musique française du Moyen Age à la Révolution.* Ed. Emile Dacier et al. Paris, 1934.

David, Henri. *De Sluter à Sambin. Essai critique sur la sculpture et le décor monumental en Bourgogne au XVe et au XVIe siècles.* 2 vols. Thèse de doctorat ès lettres, Paris, 1933.

Fauré, Elie. *History of Art.* Trans. Walter Pack. 5 vols. III: *Renaissance Art.* New York and London, 1921–1930.

Febvre, Lucien. "Histoire de l'art, histoire de la civilisation." *Revue de Synthèse*, 9 (1935), 7–17. In *Combats pour l'histoire*, pp. 295–301.

Loos, Adolf. "Ornament and Crime." Trans. Harold Meek. In Ludwig Münz and Gustav Künstler, *Adolf Loos, Pioneer of Modern Architecture.* New York, 1966.

Mâle, Emile. *L'Art religieux de la fin du Moyen Age en France.* 2d ed. Paris, 1922.

———— *L'Art religieux après le Concile de Trente.* Paris, 1932.

B. The Sciences and Philosophy

1. The Sciences in the Sixteenth Century

Cantor, Moritz. *Vorlesungen über Geschichte der Mathematik.* II: *Von 1200–1668.* 2d ed. Leipzig, 1900.

Le Ciel dans l'histoire et dans la science. Huitième semaine internationale de synthèse. Paris, 1940.

De Roover, Raymond. "Aux origines d'une technique intellectuelle: la formation et l'expansion de la comptabilité à partie double." *Annales d'Histoire Economique et Sociale*, 9 (1937), 171–193, 270–298.

Duhem, Pierre. *Les Origines de la statique.* Paris, 1905.

———— *Le Système du monde. Histoire des doctrines cosmologiques de Platon à Copernic.* 10 vols. Paris, 1913–1959.

———— *To Save the Phenomena, an Essay on the Idea of Physical Theory from Plato to Galileo.* Trans. Edmund Doland and Chaninah Maschler. Chicago, 1969.

Dupont, Albert. *Contribution à l'histoire de la comptabilité: Luca Paciolo.* Paris and Vienne, 1925.

—— *Formes des comptes et façons de compter dans l'ancien temps.* Paris and Vienne, 1928.

Encyclopédie française, I: *L'Outillage mental.* 1: Abel Rey, "De la pensée primitive à la pensée actuelle," pp. 1′10-3–1′20-11. 2: Antoine Meillet, ed., "Le Langage," pp. 1′32-1–1′48-8. 3: Paul Montel, ed., "La Mathématique," pp. 1′50-5–1′96-6.

Marre, Aristide. "Notice sur Nicolas Chuquet et son *Triparty en la science des nombres." Bulletino di Bibliografia e di Storia delle Scienze Matematiche e Fisiche, Pubblicato da B. Boncompagni,* 13 (1880), 550–659, 693–814.

Rouse Ball, W. W. *A Short Account of the History of Mathematics.* 4th ed. London, 1908.

Thorndike, Lynn. *Science and Thought in the Fifteenth Century.* New York, 1929.

2. The Philosophy of the Renaissance and Its Antecedents

Bouché-Leclerq, Auguste. *L'Astrologie grecque.* Paris, 1899; reissued, Brussels, 1963.

Bréhier, Emile. *The History of Philosophy: The Middle Ages and the Renaissance.* Trans. Wade Baskin. Chicago, 1965.

—— *La Philosophie du Moyen Age.* Paris, 1937.

Brunschvicg, Léon. *Les progrès de la conscience dans la philosophie occidentale.* 2 vols. Paris, 1927.

Busson, Henri. *Les Sources et le développement du rationalisme dans la littérature française de la Renaissance (1533–1601).* Paris, 1922.

Cassirer, Ernst. *Individuum und Kosmos in der Philosophie der Renaissance.* Leipzig and Berlin, 1927.

Cassirer, Ernst, Paul Oskar Kristeller, and John Herman Randall, Jr., eds. *The Renaissance Philosophy of Man.* Chicago, 1948.

Charbonnel, J. Roger. *La Pensée italienne au XVIe siècle et le courant libertin.* Paris, 1917.

Cournot, Augustin. *Considérations sur la marche des idées et des événements dans les temps modernes.* Ed. François Mentré. 2 vols. Paris, 1934.

Denis, Jacques. *De la philosophie d'Origène.* Paris, 1884.

Desjardins, Albert. *Les Sentiments moraux au XVIe siècle.* Paris, 1886.

Febvre, Lucien. "L'Histoire de la philosophie et l'histoire des historiens." *Revue de Synthèse,* 3 (1932), 97–103.

Fusil, C. A. "La Renaissance de Lucrèce au XVIe siècle en France." *RSS,* 15 (1928), 134–150.

Gilson, Etienne. "La Doctrine de la double vérité." In *Etudes de philosophie médiévale,* pp. 51–75.

—— *Etudes de philosophie médiévale.* Strasbourg, 1921.

——— *La Philosophie au Moyen Age*. 2d ed., rev. and augmented. 2 vols. Paris, 1952.

——— *The Spirit of Medieval Philosophy*. Trans. A. H. C. Downes. New York, 1940.

Götzmann, Wilhelm. *Die Unsterblichkeitsbeweise in der Väterzeit und Scholastik*. Karlsruhe, 1927.

Jundt, Auguste. *Histoire du panthéisme populaire au Moyen Age et au XVIe siècle*. Paris, 1875; reprint, Frankfurt-am-Main, 1964.

Lasserre, Pierre. *La Jeunesse d'Ernest Renan; histoire de la crise religieuse au XIXe siècle*. 3 vols. Paris, 1925–1932.

Lefranc, Abel. "Le Platonisme et la littérature en France à l'époque de la Renaissance (1500–1550)." *Revue d'Histoire Littéraire de la France*, 3 (1896), 1–44. In *Grands Ecrivains de la Renaissance*, pp. 63–137.

Longpré, Ephrem. "La Philosophie du B. Duns Scot." *Etudes Franciscaines*, 34 (1922), 433–482; 35 (1923), 26–66, 241–278, 499–531, 582–614; 36 (1924), 29–62, 225–253, 337–370.

Mandonnet, Pierre. *Siger de Brabant et l'Averroïsme latin du XIIIe siècle*. Fribourg, 1900.

Mesnard, Pierre. "Du Vair et le néostoicisme." *Revue d'Histoire de la Philosophie*, 2 (1928), 142–166.

Origen. *Operum Origenis Adamantii tomi duo priores. Tertius et quartus tomi, quorum tertius complectitur apologiam*. 4 vols. in 2. Paris: Jo. Parvus et Jod. Badius Ascensius, 1512.

——— *Origenis Adamantii operum tomi duo priores cum tabulis et indice generali*. 4 vols. Lyon: Jacques Giunta, 1536.

——— *On First Principles*. Trans. G. W. Butterworth. Gloucester, Mass., 1973.

Renan, Ernest. *Averroès et l'Averroïsme*. 8th ed. Paris, 1925.

Rey, Abel. *La Science dans l'antiquité*. 5 vols. Paris, 1930–1948.

Rougier, Louis. "La Mentalité scolastique." *Revue Philosophique de la France et de l'Etranger*, 97 (1924), 208–232.

——— *La Scolastique et le Thomisme*. Paris, 1925.

Rousselot, Pierre. *Pour l'histoire du problème de l'amour au Moyen Age*. Munster, 1908.

Saurat, Denis. *Literature and Occult Tradition: Studies in Philosophical Poetry*. Trans. Dorothy Bolton. New York, 1930.

Schmidt, Albert-Marie. *La Poésie scientifique en France au seizième siècle*. Paris, 1940. Review by Lucien Febvre in *Annales d'Histoire Sociale*, 1 (1939), 278–279.

Zanta, Léontine. *La Renaissance du stoïcisme au XVIe siècle*. Paris, 1914.

C. Religious Problems

1. Beliefs, Traditions, and Survivals

Beauvois de Chauvincourt. *Discours de la Lycantropie ou de la transmutation des hommes en loups*. Paris: J. Reze, 1599.

Bloch, Marc. *The Royal Touch: Sacred Monarchy and Scrofula in England and France.* Trans. J. E. Anderson. London, 1973.

——— "La Vie d'outre-tombe du roi Salomon." *Revue Belge de Philologie et d'Histoire,* 4 (1925), 349–377.

Chevalier, Ulysse. *Notre-Dame de Lorette; étude historique sur l'authenticité de la Santa Casa.* Paris, 1906.

De Brosses, Charles. *Les Lettres du Président de Brosses à Ch.-C. Loppin de Gémeaux.* Ed. Yvonne Bézard. Paris, 1929.

Delatte, Armand. "Herbarius: Recherches sur le cérémonial usité chez les anciens pour la cueillette des simples et des herbes magiques." *Bulletin de la Classe des Lettres et des Sciences Morales et Politiques de l'Académie Royale de Belgique,* 5th ser., 22 (1936), 227–348.

Gillebaud, Benoît. *La Prognostication du ciècle advenir contenant troys petis traictez.* Lyon: cheulx Olivier Arnoullet, 1537.

Hansen, Joseph. *Quellen zur Geschichte des Hexenwahns und der Hexenverfolgung im Mittelalter.* Bonn, 1901; reprint, Hildesheim, 1963.

——— *Zauberwahn, Inquisition und Hexenprozess im Mittelalter.* Munich, 1900; reprint, Aalen, 1964.

Houssay, Frédéric. "La Légende du *Lepas anatifera,* la *Vallisneria spiralis* et le poulpe." *Comptes Rendus Hebdomadaires des Séances de l'Académie des Sciences,* 132 (Jan.-June, 1901), 263–265.

——— "Nouvelles Recherches sur la faune et la flore des vases peints de l'époque mycénienne et sur la philosophie pré-ionienne." *Revue Archéologique,* 3d ser., 30 (1897), 81–105.

——— "Les Théories de la genèse à Mycènes et le sens zoologique de certains symboles du culte d'Aphrodite." *Revue Archéologique,* 3d ser., 26 (1895), 1–27.

Jobbé-Duval, E. "Les Idées primitives dans la Bretagne contemporaine." *Nouvelle Revue Historique de Droit Français et Etranger,* 33 (1909), 550–593, 722–773; 35 (1911), 257–330; 37 (1913), 5–56, 421–473; 38 (1914), 5–60, 343–389.

Lévy-Bruhl, Lucien. *Primitive Mentality.* Trans. Lilian A. Clare. London and New York, 1923.

——— *Primitives and the Supernatural.* Trans. Lilian A. Clare. New York, 1935.

——— *The "Soul" of the Primitive.* Trans. Lilian A. Clare. London, 1928.

Nisard, Charles. *Histoire des livres populaires ou de la littérature du colportage.* 2d ed. 2 vols. in 1. Paris, 1864; reprint, Paris, 1968.

Nynauld, J. de. *De la lycanthropie, transformation et extase de sorciers.* Paris: Millot, 1615.

Saintyves, P. *L'Astrologie populaire, étudiée spécialement dans les doctrines et les traditions relatives à l'influence de la lune.* Paris, 1937.

——— *En marge de la Légende dorée.* Paris, 1931.

——— "Le Thème des pierres qui boivent ou se baignent." *Revue de Folklore Français et de Folklore Colonial,* 5 (1934), 213–216.

Taillepied, Noël. *Traité de l'apparition des esprits, à sçavoir des âmes séparées, fantosmes, prodiges et accidens merveilleux, qui précèdent quel-*

quefois la mort des grands personnages ou signifient changement de la chose publique. Rouen: Romain de Beauvais, 1600; first ed., Paris: G. Bichon, 1588.

Vaganay, Hugues. "Les Saints 'producteurs de maladies.' " *RER,* 9 (1911), 331-332.

Valois, Noël. "Jacques Duèse, pape sous le nom de Jean XXII." In *Histoire Littéraire de la France,* 34 (Paris, 1914), pp. 391-630.

Vancauwenberg, Etienne. *Les Pèlerinages expiatoires et judiciaires dans le droit communal de la Belgique au Moyen Age.* Louvain, 1922.

Wagner, Robert Léon. *Sorcier et magicien, contribution à l'étude du vocabulaire de la magie.* Thèse de doctorat ès lettres, Paris, 1939.

2. The Religious Life and the Life of Piety

Bremond, Henri. *Histoire littéraire du sentiment religieux en France depuis la fin des guerres de religion jusqu'à nos jours.* 11 vols. Paris, 1916-1933; new ed., 1967-1968.

Chifflet, Jean. *Joannis Chifletii J. C. Vesontini consilium de sacramento Eucharistiae ultimo supplicio afficiendis non denegando.* Brussels: Typis Mommartianis, 1644.

Gilson, Etienne. "Michel Menot et la technique du sermon médiéval." *Revue d'Histoire Franciscaine,* 2 (1925), 301-350.

Maillard, Olivier. *Oeuvres françaises, sermons et poésies.* Ed. Arthur de La Borderie. Paris, 1877.

Méray, Antony. *Les Libres Prêcheurs devanciers de Luther et de Rabelais: étude historique, critique et anecdotique sur les XIVe, XVe et XVIe siècles.* Paris, 1860.

Nève, Joseph. *Sermons choisis de Michel Menot, 1508-1510.* Paris, 1924.

Pourrat, Pierre. *Christian Spirituality.* Trans. W. H. Mitchell and S. P. Jacques. 3 vols. London, 1922-1927.

Samouillan, Alexandre. *O. Maillard, sa prédication et son temps.* Paris, 1891.

Watrigant, Henri. *La Méditation fondamentale avant S. Ignace.* Enghien, 1907.

3. The Reformation and the Reformers
a. Biblical Texts

La Saincte Bible en Françoys translatée selon la pure et entière traduction de S. Hiérome. Antwerp: par Martin Lempereur, 1534.

La Bible qui est toute la Saincte Escripture. Neuchâtel: par P. de Vingle, dict Pirot Picard, 1535.

La Bible. New French translation with intro. and commentary by Eduard Reuss. 16 vols. Paris, 1874-1881.

b. Reformation, Pre-Reformation, and Anti-Reformation

Clerval, Jules A. *Registre des procès-verbaux de la faculté de théologie de Paris.* I: 1505-1523. Paris, 1917.

Delisle, Léopold. "Notice sur un registre des procès-verbaux de la faculté de théologie de Paris pendant les années 1505-1533." *Notices et Extraits des*

Manuscrits de la Bibliothèque Nationale et Autres Bibliothèques, 36 (1899), 315-408.

Dufour, Théophile. *Notice bibliographique sur le Catéchisme et la Confession de foi de Calvin (1537) et les autres livres imprimés à Genève et à Neuchâtel dans les premiers temps de la Réforme (1533-1540)*. Geneva, 1878; reprinted, 1970.

Du Plessis d'Argentré, Charles. *Collectio judiciorum de novis erroribus*. 3 vols. Paris, 1724-1736.

Febvre, Lucien. *Au coeur religieux du XVIe siècle*. Paris, 1957.

———— "L'Application du Concile de Trente et l'excommunication pour dettes en Franche-Comté." *Revue Historique*, 103 (Jan.-April, 1910), 225-247; 104 (May-Aug., 1910), 1-39. In shortened form in *Au coeur religieux*, pp. 225-250. Trans. as "Excommunication for Debts in Franche-Comté" in *A New Kind of History*, pp. 160-184.

———— "Un Bilan: la France et Strasbourg au XVIe siècle." *La Vie en Alsace* (1925), 239-244; (1926), in no. 2.

———— "Ce qu'on peut trouver dans une série d'inventaires mobiliers; de la Renaissance à la Contre-réforme: changements de climat." *Annales d'Histoire Sociale*, 3 (1941), 41-54. In *Au coeur religieux*, pp. 274-290. Trans. as "Amiens: from the Renaissance to the Counter-Reformation" in *A New Kind of History*, pp. 193-207.

———— *Notes et documents sur la Réforme et l'Inquisition en Franche-Comté; extraits des archives du Parlement de Dôle*. Thèse de doctorat ès lettres, Paris, 1912.

———— *Philippe II et la Franche-Comté, étude d'histoire politique, religieuse et sociale*. Thèse de doctorat ès lettres, Paris, 1912.

———— "Une Question mal posée: les origines de la Réforme française et le problème des causes de la Réforme." *Revue Historique*, 161 (1929), 1-73. In *Au coeur religieux*, pp. 3-70. Trans. as "The Origins of the French Reformation: A Badly-put Question?" in *A New Kind of History*, pp. 44-107.

Feret, Pierre. *La Faculté de théologie de Paris et ses docteurs les plus célèbres. L'Epoque moderne*. 7 vols. Paris, 1900-1910.

Gaullieur, Ernest. *Histoire de la Réformation à Bordeaux et dans le Parlement de Guienne*. Bordeaux, 1884.

Hauser, Henri. *Etudes sur la Réforme française*. Paris, 1909.

Hauser, Henri, and Augustin Renaudet. *Les Débuts de l'âge moderne: la Renaissance et la Réforme*. 4th ed. Peuples et civilisations, 8. Paris, 1956.

Herminjard, A. L., ed. *Correspondance des Réformateurs dans les pays de langue française*. 9 vols. Geneva, 1866-1897; reprint, Nieuwkoop, 1965-1966.

Hyma, Albert. *The Christian Renaissance: a History of the "Devotio moderna."* 2d ed. New York, 1925.

Imbart de la Tour, Pierre. *Les Origines de la Réforme*. 4 vols. Paris, 1905-1935.

Patry, Henry. *Les Débuts de la Réforme protestante en Guyenne, 1523-1559, arrêts du Parlement*. Bordeaux, 1912.

Piaget, Arthur, ed. *Les Actes de la Dispute de Lausanne* (*1536*). Neuchâtel, 1928.

Raemond, Florimond de. *L'Histoire de la naissance, progrez et décadence de l'hérésie de ce siècle.* Rouen, 1624.

Romier, Lucien. *Les Origines politiques des guerres de religion.* Vol. I. Paris, 1913.

Tacchi Venturi, Pietro. *La Storia della Compagnia di Gesù in Italia, narrata col sussidio di fonti inedite.* 2d ed. 2 vols. Rome, 1950–1951.

Vuilleumier, Henri. *Histoire de l'Eglise réformée du pays de Vaud.* I: *Lausanne.* Paris, 1928.

c. Reformers, Pre-Reformers, and Counter-Reformers

Beda (or Bédier), Noël

    Barnaud, Jean. "Lefèvre d'Etaples et Bédier." *BSHPF*, 85 (1936), 251–279.

    Caron, Pierre. "Noël Béda." *Ecole Nationale des Chartes, Positions des Thèses* (1898), 27–34.

    Hyrvoix, Albert. "Noël Bédier, d'après des documents inédits (1533–34)." *Revue des Questions Historiques,* 72, new ser., 28 (1902), 578–591.

Calvin, John

    Joannis Calvini opera quae supersunt omnia. Ed. Baum, Cunitz, Reuss, and Erickson. 59 vols. Corpus Reformatorum. Brunswick, 1863–1900; facsimile reprint, New York, 1964.

    Calvin, Jean. *Institution de la religion chrestienne.* Original 1541 text. Ed. Abel Lefranc, Henri Chatelain, and Jacques Pannier. Paris, 1911.

    Calvin, John. *Institutes of the Christian Religion.* Trans. Henry Beveridge. 2 vols. London, 1962.

    Calvin, Jean. *Des scandales.* Geneva: J. Crespin, 1550.

    ——— *Le Catéchisme français, publié en 1537.* Ed. Albert Rilliet and Théophile Dufour. Geneva and Paris, 1878.

    Calvin, John. *Instruction in Faith.* Trans. Paul T. Fuhrmann. London and Philadelphia, 1949.

    Sermons de M. Jean Calvin, sur le V. livre de Moyse nommés Deutéronome. Geneva: de l'imprimérie de Thomas Courteau, 1567.

    Choisy, Eugène. *Calvin éducateur des consciences.* Neuilly, 1926.

    Doumergue, Emile. *Iconographie calvinienne.* Lausanne, 1909.

    ——— *Jean Calvin, les hommes et les choses de son temps.* 6 vols. Lausanne, 1899–1905; Neuilly-sur-Seine, 1926.

    Jarry, L. "Une Correspondance littéraire au XVIe siècle, Pierre Daniel et les érudits de son temps d'après les documents inédits Berne." *Mémoires de la Société Archéologique et Historique de l'Orléanais,* 15 (1876), 343–430.

    "IVe centenaire de la formation de la première Eglise réformée par Calvin à Strasbourg (1538)." *BSHPF*, 87 (1938), 341–381.

Castellio, Sebastian
  Buisson, Ferdinand. *Sébastien Castellion, sa vie et son oeuvre,*
    1515–1563. 2 vols. Paris, 1892.
Cousturier, Pierre (Sutor)
  Sutor. *Apologeticum in novos anticomaritas praeclaris beatissimae Vir-*
    ginis Mariae laudibus detrahentes. Paris: in officina Joan. Parvi,
    1526.
Du Perron, Jacques Davy
  Perroniana et Thuana. 2d ed. Cologne, 1669.
Epistolae obscurorum virorum
  Epistolae obscurorum virorum. Ed. Aloys Bömer. 2 vols. Heidelberg,
    1924.
  On the Eve of the Reformation: "Letters of Obscure Men." Trans.
    Francis Griffin Stokes. Ed. Hans Hillebrand. New York, 1964.
Farel, Guillaume
  Farel, Guillaume. *Sommaire: c'est une briefve declaration d'aucuns lieux*
    fort nécessaires à un chacun chrestien pour mettre sa confiance en
    Dieu et à ayder son prochain. Facsimile of original 1525 ed. Ed.
    Arthur Piaget. Paris, 1935.
  Comité Farel. *Guillaume Farel, 1489–1565; biographie nouvelle écrite*
    d'après les documents originaux par un group d'historiens, profes-
    seurs et pasteurs . . . Neuchâtel and Paris, 1930.
  Heyer, Henri. *Guillaume Farel: essai sur le développement de ses idées*
    théologiques. Geneva, 1872.
  Schmidt, Charles. *Etudes sur Farel.* Strasbourg, 1834.
Garasse, François
  Garasse, François. *Le Rabelais réformé par les ministres, et notamment*
    par le P. Du Moulin. Brussels: Chr. Gerard, 1620.
  ———— *Les Recherches des recherches et autres oeuvres de Me Estienne*
    Pasquier. Paris: Seb. Chappelet, 1622.
  ———— *La Doctrine curieuse des beaux esprits de ce temps, ou pretendus*
    tels. Paris: chez Sébastien Chappelet, 1624.
Lefèvre d'Etaples, Jacques
  Epistole divi Pauli apostoli: cum commentariis . . . Jacobi Fabri Stapu-
    lensis. Paris: in edibus Francisci Regnault: et Joannis de la Porte,
    [1517].
  Lefèvre d'Etaples, Jacques. *Commentarii initiatorii in IV Evangelia.*
    Meaux: impensis S. Colinaei, 1522.
  ———— *Les Choses contenues en ce present livre. Une epistre exborta-*
    toire. La S. Evangile selon S. Matthieu . . . La S. Evangile selon S.
    Jehan . . . Paris: Simon de Colines, 1523.
  Laune, Alfred. *La Traduction de l'Ancien testament de Lefèvre d'Eta-*
    ples. Le Cateau, 1895.
Luther, Martin
  Luther, Martin. *Werke.* Kritische Gesamtausgabe. Weimar, 1883–1974.
  Luther's Works. General eds. Harold J. Grimm, Helmut T. Lehmann,
    Jaroslav Pelikan, et al. 54 vols. St. Louis and Philadelphia,
    1955–1976.

Denifle, Heinrich. *Luther und Luthertum in der ersten Entwicklung.* 2d ed., reworked by Albert Maria Weiss. 2 vols., plus 2 vols. of supplementary material. Mainz, 1906.

Febvre, Lucien. *Un Destin, Martin Luther.* 4th ed. Paris, 1968.

—— *Martin Luther, a Destiny.* Trans. Roberts Tapley. New York, 1929.

Moore, Will Grayburn. *La Réforme allemande et la littérature française; recherches sur la notoriété de Luther en France.* Strasbourg, 1930. Review by Lucien Febvre in *Revue Critique d'Histoire et de Littérature,* new ser., 97 (1930), 315–318.

Strohl, Henri. *L'Epanouissement de la pensée religieuse de Luther de 1515 à 1520.* Strasbourg, 1924.

—— *L'Evolution religieuse de Luther jusqu'en 1515.* Strasbourg, 1922.

Weiss, Nathanaël. "La Littérature de la Réforme française, notes sur les traités de Luther, traduits en français et imprimés en France entre 1525 et 1534." *BSHPF,* 36 (1887), 664–670.

Will, Robert. *La Liberté chrétienne, etude sur le principe de la piété chez Luther.* Strasbourg, 1922.

Pupper of Goch, Jan

    Geschriften van Joann Pupper van Goch en Corn. Grapheus; Confutatio determinationis parisiensis contra M. L. Ed. F. Pijper. Bibliotheca Reformatoria Neerlandica, 6. The Hague, 1909.

    Clemen, Otto. *Johann Pupper von Goch.* Leipzig, 1896.

Roussel, Gérard

    Schmidt, Charles. *Gérard Roussel.* Strasbourg, 1841.

Valdés, Juan de

    Valdés, Juan de. *Diálogo de doctrina cristiana.* Facsimile ed., with intro. by Marcel Bataillon. Coimbra, 1925.

La Vérité cachée

    La Vérité cachée devant cent ans faicte et composée à six personnages: nouvellement corrigée et augmentée avec les autoritez de la saincte escripture. Geneva: J. Michel, 1544.

Viret, Pierre

    Viret, Pierre. *Instruction chrestienne.* II: *Exposition de la foy chrestienne.* Geneva: Rivery, 1564.

    Pierre Viret d'après lui-même. Lausanne, 1911.

    Barnaud, Jean. *Pierre Viret, sa vie et son oeuvre.* Saint-Amans, 1911.

D. Miscellaneous Questions

Archives départementales du Doubs, series G, nos. 179, 180.

Bayle, Pierre. *Oeuvres diverses.* 4 vols. The Hague, 1727.

Bloch, Marc. "Les 'Inventions' médiévales." *Annales d'Histoire Economique et Sociale,* 7 (1935), 634–643.

Coornaert, Emile. *Les Corporations en France avant 1789.* Paris, 1940.

Cyrano de Bergerac, Savinien de. *Oeuvres comiques, galantes et littéraires.* New ed. Ed. P. L. Jacob. Paris, 1858.

Descartes, René. *Discourse on Method.* Trans. Laurence J. Lafleur. Indianapolis and New York, 1950.

Doucet, Roger. *L'Etat des finances de 1523.* Paris, 1923.

Esmein, A. *Le Mariage en droit canonique.* 2d ed. Ed. R. Génestal and Jean Dauviller. 2 vols. Paris, 1929–1935.

Espinas, Georges. "Métiers et confréries." *Annales d'Histoire Economique et Sociale,* 10 (1938), 432–438.

Fauchet, Claude. *Les Oeuvres . . .* Paris: par David Le Clerc, 1610.

Franklin, Alfred. *La Mesure du temps.* La Vie privée d'autrefois (23 vols.), IV. Paris, 1888.

Gill-Mark, Grace. *Une Femme de lettres au XVIIIᵉ siècle, Anne-Marie du Boccage.* Paris, 1927.

Gozlan, Léon. *Balzac intime.* New ed. Paris, n.d.

Halévy, Ludovic. "Trois diners avec Gambetta; récit public par M. Daniel Halévy." *Revue des Deux Mondes,* 52 (July 1, 1929), 67–91.

Hauser, Henri. "Les Compagnonnages d'arts et métiers à Dijon aux XVIIᵉ et XVIIIᵉ siècles." *Revue Bourgignonne,* 17, no. 4 (1927), entire issue.

Horace. *The Complete Works of Horace.* Ed. Casper J. Kraemer, Jr. New York, 1936.

Juvenal. *The Sixteen Satires.* Trans. Peter Green. Middlesex, 1967.

Kleinclausz, Arthur. *Histoire de Lyon.* 3 vols. Lyon, 1939–1952.

Lane, Frederic C. *Venetian Ships and Shipbuilders of the Renaissance.* Baltimore, 1934. Review by Lucien Febvre in *Annales d'Histoire Economique et Sociale,* 7 (1935), 80–83.

Lucian. Trans. A. M. Harmon. Loeb Classical Library. 8 vols. Cambridge, Mass., and London, 1961.

Martin Saint-Léon, Etienne. *Histoire des corporations de métiers.* 3d ed. Paris, 1922.

Mélanges d'histoire offerts à Henri Pirenne. 2 vols. Brussels, 1926.

Montesquieu, Charles de Secondat, Baron de. *Cahiers (1716–1755).* Ed. Bernard Grasset. Paris, 1941.

Patin, Gui. *Correspondance de Gui Patin.* Paris, 1901.

Patru, Olivier. *Les Oeuvres diverses.* 4th ed. 2 vols. Paris, 1732.

Pérouse, Gabriel. *Etude sur les usages et le droit privé en Savoie au milieu du XVIᵉ siècle.* Chambéry, 1913.

Renan, Ernest. *Fragments intimes et romanesques.* Paris, 1914.

———— *The Future of Science.* Boston, 1891.

Robert, Ulysse. *Testaments de l'Officialité de Besançon, 1265–1500.* 2 vols. Paris, 1902–1907.

Rousseau, Jean-Jacques. *Emile, or On Education.* Trans. Allan Bloom. New York, 1979.

Sorel, Charles. *Histoire comique de Francion.* Ed. Emile Roy. 4 vols. Paris, 1924–1931.

Tallement des Réaux, Gédéon. *Historiettes.* Ed. Antoine Adam. 2 vols. Paris, 1960–1961.

Vaissière, Pierre de. *Gentilshommes campagnards de l'ancienne France.* Paris, 1903.

Voltaire. *The Works of Voltaire.* 42 vols. Akron, Ohio, 1905.

———— *Philosophical Letters.* Trans. Ernest Dilworth. Indianapolis, Ind., 1961.

Index